New York Native

Two Books by the Publisher of a Newspaper that Changed the History of AIDS and Chronic Fatigue Syndrome

Charles Ortleb

A Note from the Publisher

From 1980-1997, a little newspaper in New York found itself at the center of one of the darkest chapters in the history of science and medicine. In *Rolling Stone*, David Black said *New York Native* deserved a Pulitzer Prize for its pioneering reporting on the AIDS epidemic. The number of important stories *New York Native* broke about AIDS, Chronic Fatigue Syndrome, and AIDS fraud should have guaranteed several Pulitzer Prizes. Even Randy Shilts acknowledged the *New York Native*'s unique coverage of AIDS in *And the Band Played On*. But the uncompromising nature of *New York Native*'s investigative reporting ultimately made it a thorn in the establishment's side. The moral of the *New York Native* story is that no important and independent journalism goes unpunished. Books by Larry Kramer, David France, and others have disparaged and distorted the history and legacy of *New York Native*. It's time to correct the record.

New York Native contains two previously published books by Charles Ortleb, the Publisher and Editor-in-Chief of *New York Native*. The first book, *The Chronic Fatigue Syndrome Epidemic Cover-up*, is a detailed history of *New York Native*'s coverage of AIDS and Chronic Fatigue Syndrome. The second book, *The Chronic Fatigue Syndrome Epidemic Cover-up Volume Two*, is Mr. Ortleb's continuation of *New York Native*'s eye-opening reporting and critical thinking about the connection between AIDS and Chronic Fatigue Syndrome.

In 1989, Katie Leishman wrote in *Rolling Stone*, "It is undeniable that many major stories were Ortleb's months and sometimes years before mainstream journalism took them up." The two books In *New York Native* are dramatic evidence that Mr. Ortleb has not lost his touch or relevance and is still a leading intellectual and journalistic figure in one of the most consequential events of our time.

The Chronic Fatigue Syndrome Epidemic Cover-up

How a Little Newspaper Solved the Biggest
Scientific and Political Mystery of Our Time

Charles Ortleb

For Francis and everyone who worked at
or supported the *New York Native*.

Contents

Book 1

Book 2

Introduction

> The history of epidemics, narrowly studied, does not suggest the risks of the great plague to come that will dominate the planet.
> —Nassim Nicholas Taleb, *The Black Swan*

In *The March of Folly*, Barbara Tuchman uses the word "folly" to describe periods in history of egregious, self-defeating misgovernment, and one of her most dramatic examples of folly is America's catastrophic policies during the Vietnam era. I think that the AIDS and "chronic fatigue syndrome (CFS)" era would have easily fulfilled the requirements of her definition of folly or counterproductive misgovernment, and in terms of the medical and social damage that the foolishness of the AIDS/CFS era has caused and is still causing, Vietnam by comparison starts to look like a minor example of the political vice she describes.

Tuchman identifies periods of government folly as ones in which policies are pursued which run counter to a government's best interests. They are periods of presumptuousness and hubris that practically beg the gods for comeuppance. They are the times in history that prompt one to ask, "What were they thinking?" They involve "woodenheadedness" and massive "self-deception." Governments, frozen in "fixed belief," ignore all "evidence to the contrary" that warns them away from the precipice of disaster. Essentially, during Tuchmanesque periods of "folly," governments stop thinking and forsake common sense and sound judgment.

To qualify for Tuchman's certificate of "folly," a "policy adapted must meet three criteria: it must have been perceived as counterproductive in its own time, not merely by hindsight." The second criterion is, "a feasible alternative course of action must have been available." And the third criterion is, "that the policy should be that of a group, not an individual ruler."

For any jury of historians that tries to determine if the AIDS era truly satisfies Tuchman's criteria for a judgment of folly, I offer *New York Native* as Exhibit A for the prosecution. During the formative years of the AIDS epidemic the critical reporting and editorials of the

New York Native continually pointed out that the AIDS/CFS policies of the government and the AIDS establishment were "wooden-headed" and counterproductive. As the folly of the epidemic proceeded inexorably, *New York Native* made it abundantly clear that there was a feasible alternative to the catastrophically mistaken, bigoted politics, epidemiology and virology of AIDS and "chronic fatigue syndrome" that concealed one shocking multisystemic pandemic. And as the horrific story of the epidemic unfolded in relentless detail in the pages of *New York Native*, it became painfully obvious that there was plenty of blame to pass around and no single individual was the unifying tyrant completely controlling this dystopian period of biomedical totalitarianism and abnormal science. The demise of *New York Native,* which itself came under fire from the gay community (as well as the AIDS and "chronic fatigue syndrome" establishment) for its diligent and inconvenient truth-telling, is just another layer of the epidemic's tragic folly.

*

Ron Rosenbaum devotes a chapter of his fascinating book, *Explaining Hitler: The Search for the Origins of His Evil,* to the *Munich Post,* the fearless newspaper which Hitler's party referred to as "the Poison Kitchen." According to Rosenbaum, the newspaper was Hitler's "nemesis," "the persistent poisoned thorn in his side." Rosenbaum wrote, "The *Munich Post* journalists were the first to focus sustained critical attention on Hitler, from the very first moments this strange specter emerged from the beer-hall backrooms to take to the streets of Munich in the early 1920s. They were the first to tangle with him, the first to ridicule him, the first to investigate him, the first to expose the seamy underside of his party, the murderous criminal behavior masked by its pretensions to being a political movement. They were the first to attempt to alert the world to the nature of the rough slouching toward Berlin." And they kept up their brave journalistic resistance "for a dozen years." Hitler was obsessed with the defiant newspaper because "they knew how to get to him, get under his skin."

The newspaper nicknamed "the Poison Kitchen" might never have stood a chance to prevail, but its writers and editors persisted in the face of the darkening political situation of Hitler's rise to power. Rosenbaum noted, "It was an unfair, unseen struggle. They were a small band of scribblers taking on a well-financed army of murderous thugs. But in ways large and small, they made his life miserable." The newspaper consistently referred to the Nazi party as "the Hitler Party," because "their repeated use of the term was a relentless reminder to their readers that the crimes they reported on by Nazi Party members were the personal responsibility of one man, that the party they reported on was less a serious, ideologically based movement than an instrument of one man's criminal pathology." The heroic reporters, "men such as Martin Gruber, Erhard Auer, Edmund Goldshagg, Julius Zertass, among others—were in the trenches every day, taking on Hitler, facing down his thugs and their threats, testing the power of truth to combat evil, and sharing the Cassandra-like fate of discovering its limits." That "Poison Kitchen" of a newspaper showed the power of great journalism to peer into the future. According to Rosenbaum, the journalists of the *Munich Post* "even glimpsed through a glass darkly, the shadow of the Final Solution. In fact, they picked up the fateful Hitler euphemism for genocide—*endlösung*, the final solution—in the context of the fate of the Jews as early as December 9, 1931, in a chilling and prophetic dispatch called 'the Jews in the Third Reich.' " The *Munich Post* correctly saw the Nazi Party "as a homicidal criminal enterprise beneath the façade of a political party." Rosenbaum writes that, in the end, as their fate and the fate of Germany became clear, they had to accept "the shocking, crushing realization that despite their best efforts, their sacrifices, the years of struggle against Hitler, the ridicule, the exposés, the crimes, the death toll they pinned on him, Hitler had won—and all he'd threatened was about to come horrifically true." According to Rosenbaum, the *Munich Post* fought to the bitter end. Rosenbaum explained that his goal in writing about the *Munich Post* was "to restore the Poison Kitchen vision to historians whose attempts to explore Hitler could not help but benefit from exposure to the kind of investigative intimacy the *Munich Post* achieved in its hand-to-hand, eye-to-eye combat with [Hitler]."

It could be argued that if there was one "Poison Kitchen" during the AIDS and "chronic fatigue syndrome" epidemic, it was the *New York Native*. Although the newspaper was as unsuccessful as the *Munich Post* in preventing a human disaster of unprecedented scope, it at least put up a very determined fight, "hand to hand, eye-to-eye combat" with the political and pseudoscientific forces that gave the world the HIV/AIDS and "chronic fatigue syndrome is not AIDS" paradigms. The *New York Native* stood up week after week to the puppet masters of the catastrophe and, although the journalists of the *New York Native* did not suffer the same consequences as the journalists of the *Munich Post*, at the beginning of 1997, after fifteen years of being the AIDS and CFS establishment's "Poison Kitchen," the *New York Native,* was silenced.

1981-1984: The Fog of Epidemiology

News of what would eventually be called the AIDS epidemic first surfaced formally in the mass media in a shocking story in the *New York Times* on July 3, 1981, which I remember was an extremely hot day in Manhattan. I had left the *New York Native* office on West Fifty-seventh Street late and picked up an early edition of the *New York Times*. When I got home I was very tired but I was shaking by the time I finished reading the story. It would be one of those moments when time stood still, like the Kennedy assassination or the moment decades later when I turned on the TV the morning of 9/11. At the time I was the publisher and editor-in-chief of a struggling gay literary magazine called *Christopher Street* and *New York Native*, a gay paper that had been started the previous December in hopes of saving our struggling little publishing company. After reading the disturbing report about a supposedly mysterious cancer that was striking gay men, I immediately called the editor of both publications, Tom Steele, who had been working with me late at the office. My voice was quavering as I read him parts of the article. I didn't get much sleep that night.

In the ensuing days and weeks, I struggled to get ahold of the emerging amorphous facts about the mysterious new disease while grappling with the state of severe anxiety that the terrifying news had aroused in me. We asked a gay doctor we knew, Dr. Lawrence Mass, to investigate the cases—which were soon called "Gay-Related Immune Deficiency Syndrome"—for the paper. This was totally uncharted territory for me and we initially relied on Mass's medical background to help clarify what was going on for our readers. As I began to calm down and accept the situation we were in I soon chose a determined, pragmatic path for the newspaper. We would devote the paper to methodically getting to the bottom of the epidemic and make the disease the newspaper's signature story. While I was personally terrified of the implications, as a publisher I sensed that this was going to be a huge event. I tried to be optimistic. I told myself that in an age of scientific and technological genius and daily miracles surely a cause would be found and a cure would follow. Wasn't that how science operated?

In those early days, when what was initially labeled "Gay-Related Immune Deficiency" was evolving into "Acquired Immune Deficiency

Syndrome," a significant part of every business day was consumed with just trying to provide myself with the beginnings of a scientific education. English major, meet epidemiology, immunology and virology. Tom Steele had more of a scientific background than I did and he helped me familiarize myself with the workings of the immune system which seemed to be going awry in the gay victims of the epidemic. In that early period of the epidemic scientists noticed first that specific disease fighting cells in the immune system, namely T-cells, were not functioning or were decimated in gay men. Many gay men started going to their doctors to find out whether anything was wrong with their T-cells, and to my chagrin, at the time it seemed like everyone I talked to, who had a T-cell test, found out that they were suffering from a T-cell deficiency. It was hard at the time not to wonder apocalyptically if they all were going to get this disease and die. Unfortunately, it was mostly *gay* American men who were suddenly looking closely and suspiciously at their immune systems. If the whole country had followed suit, history might have turned out differently. Had we known about the so-called chronic fatigue syndrome epidemic at that point, we would have been talking about gay men as having an extreme or acute form of the immune dysfunction that had been seen in the chronic fatigue syndrome patients.

From 1981 to early in 1983, every kind of scientific hypothesis in the world was discussed as the possible cause of AIDS. As a publisher eager to know every possibility and to share them with the readers of *New York Native*, I was willing to listen to anyone who had an idea. I felt that the right answer could come from anywhere. Some people thought that AIDS was caused by recreational drug use. The director of the Centers for Disease Control's AIDS task force made a remark that he *hoped* it was poppers (amyl or butyl nitrite), a drug then heavily used by gay men to enhance sex. The drug causes the constriction of blood vessels and makes the heart beat faster, so that an orgasm is much more intense. But the CDC was unable to find a perfect correlation between the use of poppers and the mysterious disease. The same lack of correlation held true for other drugs that were then being used by gay men. The CDC also could not correlate any specific sexually transmitted disease with the array of symptoms which they had labeled "AIDS."

During those first two years of the epidemic, I was generally trustful of our government and the CDC scientists initially assigned to the problem. They seemed sincere and decent. When I talked to CDC

16

scientists like James Curran, they seemed responsive and respectful. The scientists I had contact with did not strike me as being particularly anti-gay, although disconcerting AIDS jokes were beginning to circulate, even among physicians and scientists. I hoped they were not a sign of things to come.

Alarmingly, the cases began to mount and Lawrence Mass thoroughly covered each disturbing development that basically kept gay men in a permanent state of dread, always waiting for the next shoe to drop. As our reporting on the epidemic took up more and more space in *New York Native*, the circulation started to go down. Many people in the New York gay community wanted me to downplay the epidemic because they felt it was bad for the image of gay people and disastrous for gay businesses. One prominent businessman who spent a great deal of money advertising in the *Native* told me he was considering leaving the paper if we continued to cover the epidemic. I was concerned about the community's business—and the *Native*'s— but I felt it was the paper's responsibility to cover the story and to get to the bottom of it. To borrow a notion from Hannah Arendt, I felt like world history had broken out and *New York Native* was destined to play a part in the thick of it. I even fantasized that *New York Native* might play a significant role in ending the epidemic.

At one business meeting early in the epidemic, two of my advertising salespeople, Derek and Daniel, implored me to cut down on the coverage of the epidemic or at least keep it off the cover of *New York Native*. I told them that was not possible and that they would both have to try harder to sell ads. Within four years they were both dead from AIDS.

Frankly, *New York Native* did not have much of a skeptical or even investigative attitude towards the government during those first two years. A dramatic example of the paper's misplaced trust occurred when the director of the National Gay and Lesbian Task Force, Virginia Apuzzo, expressed some concern about confidentiality with regard to some AIDS research that was going on. I wrote an editorial suggesting that gay men would have to share information about their health to enable scientists in their search for the cause of the epidemic. I was assuming everything was being done in good faith in those days. Patients, doctors, scientists, the gay community, the government, we were all in it together. Supposedly.

In 1982, there was one thing that happened that did start to make me wonder about the government's role and integrity. There was a report that had nothing to do with AIDS directly, but was about two government agencies sharing the names of gay men in a variety of studies. It suggested that the government was playing fast and loose with gay privacy issues. I began to wonder if the CDC might be capable of similar questionable antics.

On March 14, 1983, I published what would turn out to be the most talked about piece—and most consequential—in the *New York Native's* history. At 5,000 words it was also the longest. "1,112 and Counting," by screenwriter and novelist Larry Kramer, appeared prominently on the cover and many now consider it the cri de coeur that launched (for better or worse) the era of AIDS activism.

Looking back three decades later at the piece, what I am most struck by is the way it captured the terror and the panic and the sense of impending catastrophe and doom in the gay community. At the time I was committed to making the pages of the *Native* available to any writer who would make a credible attempt to explain politically or scientifically what was going on or offer ideas on how to deal with the disaster that seemed to be growing exponentially on a daily basis.

Kramer began the article, "If this doesn't scare the shit out of you we're in real trouble. If this article doesn't rouse you to anger, fury, rage and action, gay men may have no future on earth. Our continued existence depends on just how angry you can get."

His call for anger and more anger would turn out over the years to be boilerplate Kramer. One person with chronic fatigue syndrome told me years later that she approached Kramer after one of his public jeremiads and said, "Mr. Kramer, I just want to thank you for your anger." Over the years urging people *to be angry* began to strike me as a very peculiar gospel.

Throughout his piece Kramer portrayed the gay community as being on the brink of extinction. He presented the current numbers of dead and dying and left the impression of a tsunami of a plague that might engulf every gay man in its path. He wrote, "For the first time in the epidemic, leading doctors and researchers are finally admitting they don't know what is going on." His parade of horribles included a doctor who was sorry he ever got involved with the mysterious disease, packed hospitals, patients being treated as "lepers," and gay suicides in the face of the horror. He spoke of an outrageous lack of funding for research, blaming it on anti-gay prejudice. He wrote that the straight medical community which supposedly knew the disease was not going to stay limited to gays could "use us as guinea pigs to discover the cure for AIDS before it hits them, which most medical authorities are still convinced will be happening shortly in increasing numbers." And use "us" they ultimately did.

Kramer took a shot at the man who would become his personal bête noire: New York City's Mayor Ed Koch. He wrote, "Repeated attempts to meet with him have been denied us. Repeated attempts to have him make a very necessary public announcement about this crisis and public health emergency have been refused by his staff." He complained about the mayor's liaison to the gay community, Herb Rickman, basically portraying him as a gay enemy of the gay community, someone who was incompetent and insensitive to the political needs of the hour.

In a litany of things Kramer was "sick of," he listed elected officials "who in no way represent us," "closeted gay doctors," "closeted gays," "guys who moan that giving up careless sex until this blows over is worse than death," "guys who think that all being gay means is sex in the first place," and "every gay man who does not get behind this issue totally and with commitment—to fight for his life." We didn't realize at the time the degree to which that getting behind this issue meant getting behind Kramer and his poorly grounded epidemiological beliefs and rage-driven rhetoric.

Kramer criticized "the *Advocate*, the country's largest gay publication, which has yet to quite acknowledge that there's anything going on . . . . And their own associate editor, Brent Harris, died from AIDS." He wrote, "With the exception of the *Native*, and a few, very few other gay publications, the gay press has been useless."

What he said about the Centers for Disease Control in the piece is quite ironic, given what was to come to light in the next three decades. He wrote, "If there have been—and there may have been—any cases in straight, white non-intravenous drug-using, middle-class Americans, the Centers for Disease Control isn't telling anyone about them. . . . The CDC also tends not to believe white, middle-class male victims when they say they say they're straight, or female victims when they say their husbands are straight and don't take drugs." Regardless of his criticism of the CDC's competence, its funding, or its ability to keep up with the expanding caseload, there really wasn't much daylight between the CDC's epidemiological presumptions about what AIDS was and how it was transmitted—and the "careless sex" notions that were implicit and explicit in Kramer's historic rant. And every other piece he vented in during the next three decades.

19

One red flag about Kramer's addled political judgment that stands out in his piece is this statement: "Southern newspapers and Jerry Falwell's publications are already printing editorials proclaiming AIDS as God's deserved punishment to homosexuals. So what? Nasty words make poor little sissy pansy wilt and die?"

He ended the article with the names of twenty-one people he knew (some with just first names) who had died of the illness and closed with, "If we don't act immediately, then we face our approaching doom."

In the same issue, Larry Bush reported on a development that certainly would give "poor little sissy pansies" pause. Margaret Heckler was about to become the Secretary of Health and Human Services. Bush wrote, "Heckler had served in Congress for 16 years before being defeated by Rep. Barney Frank (D. Mass.) in last fall's general election. Frank received the largest single contribution from the Human Rights Campaign Fund in 1982, partly because he was matched for re-election against a woman who had voted to deny gays access to federal legal services and to retain the ten-year prison term provided for sodomy convictions in Washington, D.C."

Shortly after we published the Kramer piece, I received a phone call from John Berendt, then an editor at *Geo* magazine. He had just read an interesting hypothesis about the cause of AIDS in *New Scientist*, a colorful British scientific journal that is a mixture of serious and "pop" science. The brief article was about a letter that had been published in one of the world's leading medical journals, *The Lancet*. In the letter a young scientist in Boston named Jane Teas proposed for the first time that AIDS might be caused by African swine fever virus. She pointed out that the symptoms of AIDS closely resembled those of African swine fever. She also noted that in Haiti, which also had a growing AIDS epidemic, there was simultaneously an epidemic of African swine fever virus in pigs. She hypothesized that vacationing gay men might have contracted the disease by eating undercooked pork.

I instantly thought the theory was reasonable and should be explored. It had the ring of truth to it. I discussed the hypothesis with James D'Eramo, a man with a Ph.D. in medical ecology and infectious diseases, who had become our new science reporter, and I asked him to call Teas and arrange to interview her in Boston, which he did the following weekend. I was feeling very competitive about the story. I wanted *New York Native* to publish the first lengthy interview with her.

When D'Eramo got back from Boston and filled me in on her ideas,

I was even more convinced that her hypothesis was the most compelling one I had heard in two years. We published his interview with Teas in the May 23, 1983, issue and started it on the cover with the headline, "Is African Swine Fever the Cause?"

The day the article appeared, something weird happened. A gay activist in New York attacked the idea publicly and said he thought the Teas idea was racist. That struck me as very strange and I wondered if we had hit some mysterious political nerve. It wasn't the reaction I was expecting from anyone in the gay community.

At the time that Teas wrote her letter, she was a postgraduate student at the Harvard School of Public Health and she didn't have much money. I was soon talking to her on a regular basis and she told me she wished she could attend a conference in Florida about exotic animal diseases because some sessions of the meeting were going to focus on African swine fever. I offered to pay for the trip to the conference because I was convinced the scientists there might support her idea and help test it.

She called us after the first day of the conference and was elated. She had presented her ideas at one of the African swine fever sessions. When she was done, the man who was leading the session denounced her idea to the audience, but afterwards, a number of scientists approached her and expressed their enthusiasm about the idea that there was a link between African swine fever and AIDS. She began to make arrangements at the conference to test her hypothesis with some of the scientists. At that point I thought the money to send her there had been well spent.

But that all changed later that week. She called to tell us that at a reception near the end of the conference, she had seen the interested scientists talking to government officials who were in attendance. Subsequently, one by one, the scientists who had previously been enthusiastic about her idea approached her to tell her they would not be able to investigate her hypothesis. She felt that they had all been pressured to change their minds.

From the very beginning of the epidemic, government scientists had given the impression that finding out what was the cause of AIDS was their first and only priority. It therefore puzzled me when there was government resistance about testing Teas's very reasonable African swine fever hypothesis. When Jane Teas wrote directly to the CDC in April of 1983 to explain her ASFV idea, she received a cold shoulder. Dr. Michael Gregg, the deputy director of the Epidemiology

Program Office, wrote to Teas that he had shared her thoughts with Dr. James Curran (of the AIDS Task Force) and Dr. John Bennett, Assistant Director for Medical Science at the Center for Infectious Diseases. Gregg wrote back to Teas, "Rest assured that if they and other members of the senior staff here feel that more effort should be directed to uncover any real association between [AIDS and African swine fever], it will be done. As I believe I implied in our telephone conversation, it is relatively difficult for outside scientists such as yourself to impact directly on research programs within a center such as CDC. Quite frankly, perhaps the best you can expect is an acknowledgement with thanks. Nevertheless, I do wish to convey to you my personal thanks for your obvious interest and encouragement. As you state, the power of the pen should not be underestimated." In retrospect, this looks like the elitist don't-bother-us attitude that is typical of the hermetically sealed world of abnormal science that AIDS turned out to be.

On May 14, 1983, the first scientific rebuttal to Teas's hypothesis appeared in *The Lancet*. Five European researchers signed a letter that indicated that they had tested hospital patients with AIDS for antibodies to African swine fever virus. They reported that none of the patients were positive. However, they did leave a door open: "Attempts at ASFV antigen demonstration and at growing the elusive AIDS agent in swine cells supporting ASFV isolation could be made to investigate further the ASFV hypothesis in AIDS patients. Our results, however, make it unlikely that ASFV and the AIDS agent will be found to be related." Teas was dissatisfied with their approach and felt that their negative findings were questionable.

That same month, Gary Noble, the Acting Director of the Division of Viral Diseases at the CDC, sent a memo to his colleagues noting, "Considerable interest in the possible role of African swine fever virus (ASFV) has been generated by Dr. Jane Teas's letter to *The Lancet* . . . . Although no known human infection with ASFV has ever occurred, the presence of ASFV infection among swine in Haiti and the ability of the virus to induce some immunosuppression among pigs has led to the hypothesis proposed by Dr. Teas of the Harvard School of Public Health. . . . We have received calls from Dr. Sheldon Landesman, Director, AIDS Haitian Study Group, Downstate Medical Center, New York, asking if we would test sera from Haitians with and without AIDS. Dr. Fred Siegel, Director of Medicine, Mt. Sinai School of Medicine, has offered to send sera from AIDS patients for testing for ASFV antibodies. We have also been asked by Jane Teas and Lawrence Altman, *New York Times*, if we proposed to do testing for sera from AIDS patients for antibodies to ASFV."

Noble then added that the Department of Agriculture had shipped the CDC materials necessary to test AIDS sera for antibodies to ASFV and he made some suggestions about how the testing should be done.

In June, a very odd letter appeared in *The Lancet* in response to the Teas hypothesis. It was written by Ronald K. St. John of the Epidemiology Unit of the Pan American Health Organization. He wrote that he took issue with her hypothesis of a "possible cycle for the accidental introduction of ASFV into the human population. She speculates that, through an improbable series of events, AIDS originated in Haiti. There is no epidemiological evidence to support the ideas. Allegations, without strong supporting epidemiological evidence, that one country is responsible for introducing an illness are reminiscent of syphilis in the Middle Ages, when the French worried about the 'Italian disease,' and vice versa."

St. John wrote, "Investigation in Haiti by the Haitian Ministry of Health, the Pan American Health Organization (PAHO), and the U.S. Department of Agriculture indicated that African swine fever is not being transmitted from pigs to man, and for these and other reasons it seems unlikely that it could be the cause of AIDS."

Tragically, Teas's hypothesis was being totally distorted. She wasn't blaming Haiti. She was just suggesting that a relatively unsurprising zoonotic event may have occurred there. Pigs have a lot in common with humans and it is hardly shocking to think that a disease other than the flu could come from pigs. If her idea was correct it could have had the effect of saving many lives in Haiti itself.

I began to realize that ASFV was an emotionally loaded and very political issue. Suddenly AIDS had become a matter that involved international relations. I started wondering how, in such a rancorous, hypersensitive environment, the search for truth could proceed in earnest. I didn't realize that the environment would turn into a virtual minefield for anyone with an open mind who dared to get involved in the years that followed.

A month later, on July 9, in *The Lancet*, several scientists attempted to put the matter completely to rest. Curiously, they reported that in December, 1982, before Jane Teas had even sent her idea to *The Lancet*, they "looked for antibody to ASFV in serum from Haitian patients with AIDS. In the serum of eight patients and four normal controls there was no evidence of antibody to ASFV." At the very least they clearly had shared her epidemiological suspicions about ASFV. The letter ended on what was becoming a rather familiar political note: "The hypothesis that AIDS originated in Haiti . . . is damaging to Haiti and to Haitian communities abroad." What they didn't mention is that the hypothesis, if confirmed, was also potentially damaging to the multibillion dollar pork industry in America and all over the world.

From the first day I heard about ASFV, I made an effort to get my hands on every article ever written about the wily and devastating virus. At the time there were over a thousand written about ASFV which had been discovered in 1909 by a Dr. Montgomery. For a while African swine fever was called Montgomery's disease. The more I read about ASFV, the more the porcine disease matched aspects of AIDS that had emerged in the early research. As new data was published on AIDS I kept comparing the findings to what was known about ASFV and the Teas hypothesis became more and more credible. Soon I had a sheet of paper with a list of twenty symptoms or immune problems that AIDS and African swine fever had in common. The cavalier and dismissive way the idea was being treated by AIDS researchers and the government increasingly seemed odd and irrational.

After the first response to her hypothesis was published, Teas wrote to *The Lancet*, noting that the experiment conducted by the European scientists "has not definitively disproved my idea." She pointed out that the scientists had not established which strain of the virus they utilized. She also noted that the antigen used in the test was irradiated (a process through which live virus is subjected to levels of radiation that render it harmless), which could have reduced the sensitivity of the test. She also argued that the clinical status of the patients could have affected the ability of the scientists to detect the presence of antibodies to the virus. She also warned that there is often a decline in circulating antibodies in pigs late in an ASFV infection. She ended her letter by describing the biggest problem in researching the possible link between AIDS and African swine fever: "The near impossibility of obtaining ASFV antigen in the continental United States and the reluctance of the United States Department of Agriculture at Plum Island [New York] to study human pathogens shrouds the question of an ASFV-AIDS link in unnecessary mystery." What Teas didn't know is that she had gotten herself involved in the opposite world of abnormal science which is always shrouded "in unnecessary mystery." Or worse.

24

At the time, all research on African swine fever had to be either performed on Plum Island, a small island off the coast of Long Island, New York, or it had to be conducted using virus that is irradiated in order to prevent accidental outbreak of African swine fever on the mainland of the United States. The USDA lived in mortal fear of an ASFV epidemic which, if it ever spread across the United States, in addition to destroying the pork business overnight, could become a permanent fixture because there is no treatment, no vaccine, and the virus can infect ticks and become endemic. Unfortunately, the dangerousness of the virus gave the government almost absolute power over the act of researching it on the mainland of the United States. There could basically be no research on ASFV without the willing participation—and oversight—of the American government.

Other scientists and lay people were beginning to take an interest in the possible connection. Fred Maurer, a retired veterinarian who had conducted extensive research on African swine fever virus in Africa, wrote to James Curran at the CDC, "Having worked with African swine fever virus (ASFV) for several years in Africa and on the pathology of it here, I fully agree with the possible relationship made by Jane Teas." He suggested that a pig be inoculated with the blood of a febrile AIDS patient, because "the remarkable similarity of the infection relative to the destruction of the immune system and the rapid mutation potential of the ASF virus, surely make such a study worth doing."

The CDC began to test the AIDS-ASFV hypothesis in June. Memos obtained by the *Native* that were written by Gary Noble, the Acting Director of the Division of Viral diseases, indicated that they planned to search for African swine fever virus in AIDS tissue samples using antisera provided by the U.S. Department of Agriculture. A Brooklyn doctor sent the CDC blood from ten Haitians with AIDS and five non-Haitians with AIDS, as well as additional blood from healthy Haitian controls. The CDC also planned to send some of the blood to Spain to be tested by African swine fever experts there.

A memo I obtained about the testing from the CDC, which was signed by "Paul," who was probably Paul Feorino, a lab worker who was involved in the testing, stated, "We must finish off the ASFV issue." His word choice beautifully captured the CDC's attitude toward the hypothesis.

I called the CDC frequently all that summer to try and find out what the results were. Late that summer, I was told by AIDS researcher

Donald Francis that the results were negative. At that point I thought the matter was dead and African swine fever had no involvement in AIDS. Case closed.

But things changed dramatically in the fall.

Earlier that summer, I had been in touch with Susan Steinmetz, a legislative aide to Congressman Ted Weiss of Manhattan. Weiss served on a committee that had, among other things, the responsibility of overseeing the activities of the Centers for Disease Control. As Weiss's assistant, Steinmetz helped audit the activities of the CDC and during a visit to the CDC offices in the autumn, she accidentally happened upon a memo on the results of the African swine fever testing and knowing I was interested, she sent me a copy. The results as reported on the ASFV memo couldn't exactly be described as negative. Out of ninety different blood samples from AIDS patients and controls, five showed some degree of positivity for African swine fever virus. Two of the CDC's ten control samples were positive, as well as three of the sixteen AIDS patients from San Francisco. Around that same time, I learned that the USDA had tested 47 members of its staff at Plum Island for antibodies to ASFV and 6 had tested positive.

What all of this told me was that the matter was not closed at all and that additional research would be appropriate. I called Jane Teas and told her that I felt that Francis had misinformed us. I also called Don Francis and confronted him with what was in the memo. He told me that because some of the controls were positive, he had made a *judgment call* that there was no relationship between AIDS and African swine fever. I had met Francis at one of the first major AIDS conferences in New York City the year before and I had listened to him talk at a reception later at Leonard Bernstein's apartment. Francis has struck me as arrogant and pompous, and unlike most of the assembled (mostly gay) guests, I was decidedly *not* impressed by him. Even though he was slightly older than myself, he seemed young and cocky and the last person whose judgment call should be taken as the final word on something as important as the cause of AIDS. It was chilling to me to think that this character had the power to make such fateful decisions.

In August of 1983, Jane Teas had written a two-page letter to Senator Durenberger of Minnesota, in which she asked for help in pursuing her ASFV hypothesis further. She complained that the negative letters published in *The Lancet* gave "no information . . . on the patients, and in addition, almost no information is given on the source of the antigen, the type of antigen used, or details of the tests employed." She underlined the political issues she feared were impeding thorough research: "Clearly the USDA is worried that the pig farmers may get upset, and the Pan American Health Organization is worried that I and the boat people, as well as the Haitian AIDS patients, are giving Haiti a bad name. However, it remains that at least 160 Haitians in Haiti have AIDS, and that there have been no reported cases from other Caribbean resort areas also frequented by gay American vacationers. To declare that Haiti is blameless seems irrelevant in trying to trace the cause of AIDS. With more than 2,000 AIDS patients, a more complete study of this association between a suddenly low virulent strain of ASFV and a suddenly appearing human disease is warranted."

On August 29, 1983, Durenberger forwarded the Teas letter to the CDC and requested that information on the inquiry be sent to his office. On September 23, Dr. William Foege wrote back to Durenberger's office, "ASFV does not appear to play any role in AIDS. With the help of virologists at Plum Island, the Centers for Disease Control has performed tests on serum from AIDS patients using target cells infected with ASFV. No positive reactions have been observed from AIDS patients' serum. In addition, CDC has used methods similar to those used to grow ASFV from pigs to culture circulating blood cells from over 100 people including patients with AIDS, patients with lymphadenopathy, and healthy contacts of AIDS patients. No cytopathic effect or other signs of ASFV have been detected. Although work continues, there is no laboratory evidence to confirm an etiologic link between ASFV and AIDS, as suggested by Dr. Teas. CDC, the Food and Drug Administration, and others have concluded that such a link is extremely unlikely."

On October 14, 1983, Durenberger forwarded the letter to Teas, and though she was unhappy with the response, she didn't write again to Durenberger until January 24, 1984. She thanked him and told him that she had thought the matter was closed but that "the *New York Native* editor, Chuck Ortleb sent me copies of CDC memos which clearly state that there were at least some positive for ASFV in the samples they tested. Dr. Donald Francis appears to have given incorrect information to Dr. Foege . . . with regard to the results of the CDC test, [and] the tests at Plum Island, where 6/47 workers were positive for ASF. . .."

She also told Durenberger that I had pressured the CDC to do more testing, which I had done through a series of phone calls and editorials in the *Native*. Teas asked for Durenberger's help in getting the Secretary of Agriculture's assistance, because his cooperation was required for the CDC to do additional research on African swine fever. She also outlined her plans to take this matter to scientists outside the United States: "In disgust, and after being told it was necessary to go outside of this country to have my theory tested, I have turned to research institutes outside of this country. However, in both England and South Africa, officials have told me that it is illegal to study African swine fever virus, they have no experience with AIDS and/or no experience with African swine fever virus." She then expressed a concern that if AIDS was indeed caused by African swine fever virus, then it was only a matter of time before all of the American pigs and all the pork products were infected with the virus, thus endangering every American who came in contact with undercooked pork. What she didn't know was that, unbeknownst to AIDS researchers, at that very time an AIDS-like illness *was indeed* spreading throughout the pig population in parts of North America.

By the beginning of 1984, I had become extremely concerned about the games that the CDC and the Department of Agriculture seemed to playing with the Teas ASFV/AIDS hypothesis. I tried something I had done before in *New York Native*. I wrote an editorial in the form of an open letter. This one was addressed to James Mason, Director of the CDC, John Block, the Secretary of Agriculture, Edward Brandt, the Director of the National Institutes of Health, and Lawrence Altman, a medical reporter for the *New York Times* (and ex-CDC employee) who was covering AIDS. I included Altman because of the paltry coverage he had given in the *Times* to the Teas hypothesis. In general, he seemed to just parrot whatever the government said about the AIDS issue. Here is the text of the open letter:

Dear Gentlemen:

As our readers know, this paper has provided more diverse and up-to-date information about AIDS than any other non-medical publication in America. Even at the risk of being labeled "The New York Native Journal of Medicine," we have consistently tried to stay on top of the AIDS story, which we continue to feel is the biggest medical story of the Eighties. We have provided information on the results of all kinds of research. We have given every theory its day in the sun, and we still don't know *what* causes AIDS. From where we sit, we see all kinds of work going on in appropriate areas; most hypotheses have at least some degree of funding and adequate personnel working on them. Still nothing looks terribly promising, although we've been told privately that more encouraging news may soon emerge from the French team who discovered LAV (Lymphadenopathy Associated Virus).

Yet one thing continues to puzzle us: the resistance that has confronted pathobiologist Jane Teas's hypothesis that African swine fever virus is the cause of AIDS. And some recent information with which the *Native* has been presented has us even more puzzled.

Apparently, back in June, the Centers for Disease Control tested some AIDS sera for antibodies to African swine fever virus. Virologist Dr. Donald Francis, who is coordinator of AIDS laboratory activities, told us a few months later that the results were "negative." We were interested in studying exactly how the tests were performed, and we asked Dr. Francis if he intended to write up the methods and results for a medical journal. Dr. Francis told us that the CDC could not get much done if it went about publishing all its negative results. Perhaps, but negative results did not prevent the CDC from publishing the outcome of its analysis of receptive anal intercourse as a risk factor for developing AIDS. (If only African swine fever virus involved some sexual act which would capture the prurient imaginations of the CDC and the NIH, we'd have some thorough testing— pronto.)

When Dr. Francis told us about the African swine fever test results and his intention not to write up the results for publication, we probably should have been a good little gay newspaper and politely withdrawn without asking any further questions. Instead, we tracked down the CDC memorandum that described some of this testing. It turns out that "negative" is not exactly the report given by the memorandum. . . . Out of over 50 sera tested, two of the controls and two of the AIDS sera apparently showed some degree of positivity. The controls were from the CDC staff. (One researcher with whom we discussed the methods remarked that the CDC staff sera might not be the best of controls in such testing.) The fact that two of the controls tested positive contributed to Dr. Francis's judgment that all the positives were false positive. If Dr. Francis had been an experienced African swine fever virus researcher, he probably would have performed 11 further conventional tests just to verify his results. Any positivity should cause enough alarm to generate further testing. To the best of our understanding . . . a plan was subsequently devised to do additional testing with "whole [ASFV] virus from Plum Island." At the same time, Dr. Francis was apparently having the AIDS sera tested to determine whether African swine fever virus had a cytopathic (cell-killing) effect on human lymphocytes. (It is possible that the modified form of African swine fever virus is non-cytopathic and non-hemadsorbing. Sorry if that's too technical; please keep reading.) There was no cytopathic effect found.

Meanwhile, back at Plum Island (which is a USDA testing center off the coast of Long Island), a messy little situation had developed. They were also testing their own staff's blood for antibodies to African swine fever virus, and, lo and behold, six of the staff tested positive. The test they used is called the E.L.I.S.A. test, and it is touted as one of the most sensitive (with no more than a one percent false positive.) Out of the total number of sera tested, 20 percent were positive. Again, because some of those tested had no exposure (so far as they knew) to African swine fever virus, they assumed that these were false positive results, and they did one additional test to make sure. The results, as far as we know, were kept secret from the staff and the rest of the world. When one of the world experts on African swine fever virus who works at Plum Island was told by the *Native* about the results of the tests, he was quite upset that he hadn't been informed by his associates. When he confronted one of his associates about the results, the response was, "How did you find that out?" Well, a gay newspaper told him, of course. The secrecy that surrounds this testing just adds a little more spice to the mystery of the story.

Meanwhile, back at the CDC, plans were being made to send AIDS sera to Madrid for testing for African swine fever virus. They could just as easily have been sent to Plum Island, which is quite capable of doing the testing. That was in June.

When we confronted CDC Drs. James Curran, Fred Murphy, and Don Francis with the memoranda that we had seen, the story of AIDS and African swine fever changed a bit. Now Dr. Curran describes the tests as "inconclusive." Dr. Murphy describes the tests as "incomplete." When we asked Dr. Francis if the CDC had the results from the June tests from Madrid, we were told that they did not. We offered to call Madrid if the CDC was too busy to bother. We were told that "maybe they're having the same problem with their test that we're having." Yes, true positives or false positives would be a problem. Especially true positives.

The point to all of this is that the possibility still remains that African swine fever virus is the cause of AIDS. The CDC may have already given the first indication of that without realizing it. In any case, Dr. Francis should not be giving the scientific community the impression that the results of the CDC testing of this hypothesis are a good reason for them to dismiss it.

The whole matter could be regarded from another perspective. The United States Department of Agriculture has the major responsibility of making sure that African swine fever virus is not present in any animal (human or otherwise) in this country. It is absurd for the USDA to put anyone in the position of begging that agency to do its job. One of their fraternity, Dr. Fred Maurer, a respected Doctor of Veterinary

31

Medicine and a Ph.D. who has worked with African swine fever virus in Africa, has notified the USDA that he thinks there is a strong possibility that AIDS is caused by ASFV. Dr. Jerry Callis, the director of the Plum Island facilities, has a responsibility to take this matter seriously for the sake of all the farmers he is supposed to be protecting from African swine fever virus. Dr. James Mason, the director of the CDC, has a responsibility to take this matter seriously for the sake of all the American he is supposed to be protecting from AIDS.

As a result of the letter, I received a call from Don Berreth, the director of the press office of the CDC. He told me that the director of the CDC was coming to New York in April and that he wanted to meet with me. I became optimistic that we could talk the CDC into doing additional research on the possible African swine fever connection when we met with Mason.

Meanwhile, it appeared that we had made enough noise to force the CDC to give the appearance of taking the ASFV hypothesis seriously. Over and over we had argued that the strongest and most direct way to investigate the hypothesis would be to inoculate healthy pigs with blood from someone with AIDS. The seriousness with which the CDC took this idea was reflected in a memo dated December 1983 from Frederick Murphy, Director of the Division of Viral Diseases at CDC. Sent to Don Francis, the memo outlined their plan: "Per telephone conversation with Dr. J. J. Callis, Director, Plum Island Center (P.I.A.D.C.) on 13 December, it was agreed to proceed with planning toward conducting an experiment at Plum Island (under P-4) conditions wherein swine would be inoculated with materials from AIDS patients. This experiment would provide final resolutions of the premise still being made publicly that AIDS is caused by ASFV virus. Final decision as to the feasibility of doing this experiment will be made by Dr. Callis shortly." (This porcine AIDS experiment, which was supposed to put the matter to rest, *was never done.*)

I had several conversations about African swine fever virus with Callis in which he was consistently contemptuous about the very notion that AIDS was *anything at all* like African swine fever. I had come close to having verbal fisticuffs with him on one occasion. His personal field of expertise was hoof-and-mouth disease. I was disturbed by the fact that he told me things about African swine fever that I knew from my survey of the scientific literature were absolutely false. He insisted that ASFV is not a very changeable virus even though the whole history of this virus, which was discovered in 1909, is characterized by dramatic and insidious changes in virulence. When it was first discovered, it killed over 97 percent of pigs infected, but, by the time it hit Haiti, in 1976, it was killing less than 3 percent of the pigs it infected. Its characteristic symptoms had evolved from severe hemorrhaging to symptoms like pneumonia, arthritis, and motor disturbances. I thought that either Callis was deliberately lying or was surprisingly stupid. He was clearly miffed that he was being forced by lay people to deal with this hypothesis. No doubt the fact that this whole affair was being driven by a gay newspaper made the matter even more unpleasant for him.

Throughout this period, I tried to get other newspapers interested in the story. I didn't want the issue ghettoized in our little newspaper. I didn't want to own the story. That was a formula for credibility disaster. I made contact with a local newspaper on Long Island that served the area near Plum Island and convinced a reporter to do a story about the planned testing. A CDC memo from Don Francis noted that Callis called Francis to tell him that the local press was "breaking a story on Plum Island doing AIDS research." The memo also stated, "Callis is reluctant about having potentially infectious [AIDS] sera at Plum Island and does not want sera to be irradiated and is going to suggest CDC do the testing." Even though Plum Island worked with the most dangerous animal viruses, Callis was concerned about having AIDS sera there. That's how scary AIDS was in those days.

Callis sent a memo to the nearly 300 employees who worked on Plum Island: "A letter by Jane Teas of the Harvard School of Public Health, published in the journal *Lancet*, April 23, 1983, speculated that since AIDS occurred in Haitians and African swine fever also appeared in Haiti, AIDS might be caused by African swine fever (ASF) virus. Most who are knowledgeable of ASF have rejected this supposition, including medical authorities in Haiti. Swine ill from ASF show very little clinical similarity to AIDS in men. Also those who have worked with ASF virus or have lived in areas where the disease has existed for long periods of time have not become ill because of this contact. In spite of the overwhelming evidence that these are different diseases, the hypothesis may require testing. Thus, discussions are continuing with scientists from the Centers for Disease Control (CDC) in Atlanta, and they may request such work be undertaken under controlled conditions in secure animal facilities so that ASF virus may be used in the studies required. It is federal policy that all agencies of the government will assist each other as circumstances dictate as described above."

On March 1, 1984, the CDC's Don Francis wrote a memo describing a conference call with Callis and Dr. Kenneth Cell of the National Institutes of Allergy and Infectious Diseases. He noted, "Although there was strong serologic and virologic evidence against any association between ASFV and AIDS, some further testing was necessary to confirm previous results." The memo outlined plans for additional serological testing that would be more sophisticated than the original testing performed by the CDC. It also noted that Dr. William Hess, a swine fever expert with whom I had been speaking several times each week, would come to the CDC to work with Dr. Paul Feorino in conducting tests. Francis also wrote, "Following the results of these serologic tests, further consideration will be given to injecting pigs with AIDS material at Plum Island." (Again, *that was never done*.)

Teas, D'Eramo, and I were very concerned that the new testing still might not be sophisticated enough to settle the matter. D'Eramo wrote to Mason, giving him suggestions on how to perform the tests so that the results would not likely be challenged. D'Eramo emphasized that it was important that AIDS sera be tested for a wide variety of strains of African swine fever virus. He noted that three different kinds of tests needed to be done just to reach a 90 percent level of confidence. He also urged the CDC to publish the results of the tests with a full description of the testing process. Most importantly, he strongly suggested, "Materials from CDC-defined AIDS cases and materials from ARC [AIDS-Related Complex] patients should be inoculated (with controls) into laboratory swine. This procedure may provide a satisfactory animal model for AIDS."

This all came to a crashing halt in April 1984, when D'Eramo and I met with CDC Director James Mason at the Health Department in Manhattan. Mason was a bland bureaucrat who didn't strike me as being the brightest bulb in the world during the forty-five minutes we spent with him. The CDC's press officer, Don Berreth, sat beside Mason, often qualifying his boss's statements. I implored Mason to contact African swine fever expert William Hess, who had been open-minded about an ASFV-AIDS connection in my discussions with him.

34

It was unfortunate and a bad sign that Mason kept referring to African swine fever as "Swine flu." At the meeting Mason told us that the CDC was about to announce that they knew what the cause of AIDS was: a retrovirus called Lymphadenopathy Associated Virus which had been discovered by the Pasteur Institute in Paris. I have been told by reporters that I should have been flattered that in essence we were being given privileged inside information. Journalists have found it ironic that at the very moment it became clear we were not going to get to first base with the CDC on ASF, we were actually being giving a world-class scoop by the director of the CDC. At the same time our concern about ASFV was being blown off, it simultaneously showed the uncanny power of the *Native*. It was the last moment in history when the *Native* had that kind of importance to the government or the AIDS establishment.

But when the whole world learned that the cause of AIDS had supposedly been found, it wasn't LAV, the virus Mason had told us about, that was celebrated. On April 23, 1984, Margaret Heckler, then Secretary of Health and Human Services, called a press conference in Washington, D.C. to announce, "The probable cause of AIDS has been found—a variant of a known human cancer virus, called HTLV-III." She also told the press that a test to screen the blood supply for the presence of this virus would be available in six months, and that a vaccine would be ready for testing in two years. The people she credited for the discovery included Robert Gallo, Dr. Edward Brandt (Assistant Secretary of Health), Dr. Vincent DeVita (Director of the National Cancer Institute), Drs. James Mason and James Curran of the CDC. She also pointed out the contributions of the French scientists had made—which would turn out to be the understatement of the century. Within a year the French and American scientists would be viciously fighting over the issue of who had actually discovered the so-called cause of AIDS.

The Heckler announcement was electrifying. Suddenly there was a light at the end of the terrifying AIDS tunnel. I had mixed feelings about the announcement because of my distrust of Gallo and his close associate at Harvard, retroviral researcher Dr. Myron Essex. A scientist named Larry Falk had approached Jane Teas after her letter had been published in *The Lancet* in 1983. At the time, Falk was one of Essex's collaborator's on HTLV-related AIDS research. He had suggested to Teas that perhaps the virus that Essex had found in AIDS patients was actually the form that African swine fever virus took in man, an extremely odd suggestion given that ASFV is a large DNA virus and the HTLVs are retroviruses. I was wary of the fact that Essex was a consultant to the USDA's Plum Island facility at the time when the USDA was being very uncooperative in testing the Teas ASFV hypothesis, which was certainly competitive with Essex's retroviral AIDS hypothesis. And then there was the disturbing moment when a leading AIDS researcher at St. Luke's Roosevelt Hospital in New York—one of the few who remained trustworthy over the three decades of the epidemic—said to me during the time that Gallo and Essex were originally trying to prove HTLV-I was the cause of AIDS, "You know, scientists in Europe consider Essex and Gallo to be crooks."

The *Native* was one of the first newspapers to do an extensive interview with Robert Gallo after the Heckler announcement. In the August 24, 1984, issue, James D'Eramo asked Gallo why he thought that "AIDS" had broken out in gay men and he replied, "Well it's not staying in the homosexual community anymore; now the virus has spread. I have the impression that there's too much attention paid to all the details of the sexual practices. There's too much interest in that." Ironically, Gallo may inadvertently have been onto the very issue of biased epidemiology, or what I have coined as "homodemiology," which had completely distorted the picture of "AIDS" with tragic consequences for the whole human race. It was almost as though Gallo, at least subconsciously, could see the real epidemic that lurked below the Potemkin epidemic of HIV (as HTLV-III eventually became known) when he said to D'Eramo, "What about normal healthy people with no disease symptoms at all who aren't sexually active, who are not IV-drug users—are they completely risk free? I don't think so. I think they're at risk of getting infected too. The virus just needs to grow in these populations."

Gallo could also have been unknowingly pointing to the real underlying pandemic when he said, "Rather than focusing per se on the nature of sexual practice, I believe this virus can be transmitted by any form of intimate contact. I don't care what it is." He went beyond the government's official epidemiological line when he said, "I don't think kissing on the cheek is a problem, but if you exchange saliva, you may be at risk."

At that point Gallo had dug his heels in on the issue of AIDS causation: "Clearly HTLV-III causes AIDS. Anybody who doesn't say that doesn't know the facts. There's no question about it. . . . I think there's more evidence that this is the cause of AIDS than there is on the majority of microbiological agents that you and I routinely accept as the cause of other diseases." Gallo might as well have declared that science was about to proudly march into the darkness and total domination of totalitarianism for the next three decades.

D'Eramo asked Gallo, "Do you think other viruses, like CMV or EBV, play a role in the development of AIDS? Dr. Jane Teas told us a long time ago about the idea of African swine fever virus coming from Africa to Haiti and then from Haiti to America." Gallo replied, "It turns out even though she had the wrong virus, she seems to have had the right idea about the origins of the virus."

When D'Eramo asked about HTLV-III fulfilling Koch's postulates (a set of traditional scientific rules for proving causation), Gallo basically pooh-poohed the idea: "We should remember we have progressed in some ways since that time. Some people don't seem to know that. For example, Robert Koch did not have modern microbiology or serology; he didn't have seroepidemiology." (Or, what I might have called sero*homo*demiology.)

Gallo insisted to D'Eramo that HTLV-III was not an opportunistic infection. He didn't think that anyone should look for any other cause.

When D'Eramo asked whether further experiments had been done to determine if Gallo's virus was the same as the Pasteur retrovirus, Gallo, true to character, went ballistic: "This is a question that is asked too much, and people don't even know why they're asking it anymore." He then told D'Eramo something that was later shown by *Chicago Tribune* reporter John Crewdson to be a lie: "I have 86 isolates of HTLV-III and I have shown that those 86 isolates are the same virus. We published 48 isolates at once."

About gay men, Gallo said, "I have heard there are some so seriously driven that they are like alcoholics . . . . Yes, I have that from Dr. Curran. There are some that are so hypersexual that they're like alcoholics or chronic cigarette smokers." Although Gallo often had his differences with the CDC, one could say that, epidemiologically speaking, he was on the same page.

Gallo told D'Eramo, "I would advocate sexual abstinence until this problem is solved. It may be a while, it may be a lifetime. I'm sorry, I'm doing my best." About transmission Gallo said, "I think it's close contact of any kind, like sharing a household, that may expose you to the virus."

At the time, Gallo was clearly the source of the government's public face of optimism about a possible vaccine. He said, "I'm not pessimistic about preventing disease. We will have a vaccine ready in a few years."

D'Eramo told Gallo, "Many gay men are afraid that people like Jerry Falwell and others of right-wing persuasion will use the HTLV-III tests results to recommend quarantine, or job restrictions, or even concentration camps. They're also concerned that all their names and addresses might be kept for a 'big round-up' someday." Gallo told D'Eramo, "If I believed that were going to happen to me, I would still be willing to take the chance, to take the gamble. I don't think Jerry Falwell has that kind of power, and although I would never recommend that somebody be quarantined, it is not irrational. They quarantined people for things in the past. But we're not going to spread HTLV-III through casual contact with people on the streets. That's clear from all the epidemiological data so far. But among our own friends, we need somebody to say that if we're not careful, we may all be dead. And maybe we all have to be super strong and super-sacrificing for a while and support the scientists who are trying to resolve this."

While Gallo was riding high on the credit of discovering the so-called cause of AIDS, throughout the rest of 1984 Teas continued to seek help in testing her ASFV hypothesis. She traveled to Italy, Spain, and England to meet with members of various members of their respective health ministries. Scientists in Italy were afraid to investigate a pig virus with which they had no experience. When she sought the help of the U.N.'s Food and Agriculture Organization, she was told that they would only investigate "unexplained illness among people if it occurred coincidently with an epidemic of ASFV." In an article she wrote for the *Native* she noted, "When I pointed out that this had indeed happened in Zaire, Haiti and the Cameroons, I was told that the Minister of Health [of those countries] would have to make the request for testing." Given the politics of ASFV that we had previously seen, *that* was not likely to happen.

Teas was successful in getting the Spanish Health Ministry to agree on further ASFV testing. Spain had had a problem with African swine fever in its pigs that year. She also visited the Pirbright Animal Research Center in England and was told that scientists would be willing to test her hypothesis if she would provide them with sera from AIDS patients. She returned to the United States and arranged to obtain AIDS sera from Dr. Michael Lange, an AIDS researcher in Manhattan. Early that summer of 1984, James D'Eramo and I nervously took a box containing fifty samples of blood from AIDS patients by taxi to LaGuardia Airport where we met Jane before she flew to London. She left the blood at Pirbright and then flew on to Nepal where she had a temporary job. Several months later she wrote a piece for the *Native* about her Pirbright experience: "In October, somewhat disappointed that I had not heard from anyone about the AIDS testing, I returned to England. They had not done the tests. I delicately indicated that I planned to remain in England until the tests were conducted and [subsequently] was surprised to learn that some of the sera had shown definitely positive results to African swine fever virus."

The scientist who performed the ASFV tests on the AIDS blood was Dr. Robert Downing. Downing had used virus from epidemics that had occurred in three different countries. Teas wrote in the *Native*, "It was particularly interesting that the 50 samples tested against ASFV [strains] from Zaire, the Cameroons, and Haiti were only positive for Haitian ASFV. This series of tests used the whole virus, whereas previous tests by Belgians and Haitians had used only a single viral protein. I was told there was nothing further I could do, and that they would certainly repeat the tests in the near future."

Teas flew back to New York and we were amazed when we saw the results. We looked forward to her writing up the results and submitting them to a scientific journal. But in order to do that she needed the cooperation of Dr. Downing. Unfortunately Downing subsequently refused to take any of Jane Teas's phone calls. And a woman who helped Teas set up the experiments also refused to respond to her inquiries. It was very strange. We were just beginning to get a sense of what we were dealing with.

1985: Throwing Down the Gauntlet

Because the *Native* was having financial problems, I was not able to keep D'Eramo on the payroll and he left the paper at the end of 1984. At the time I thought that a book written by Ann Giudici Fettner, *The Truth About AIDS*, was one of the best books on the subject, so I asked her to write periodically about the epidemic. In early 1985, she penned a piece for us on a disturbing epidemic of Multiple Sclerosis in Key West, Florida.

Fettner wrote, "Multiple Sclerosis (MS) is a mysterious illness which affects about 25,000 Americans. The disease gradually and irreversibly destroys the myelin of nerves, causing paralysis and death. Apparently an autoimmune phenomenon, MS sets the macrophage cells in action to literally eat away at the infected person's nerve tissues. . . . In Key West, at least 30 people are suffering from MS. Eight of them are nurses, who live and work in local hospitals. When the outbreak was first noted, there was speculation that it had some correlation with AIDS, but only one of the 30 is positive for LAV/HTLV-III. . . . Dr. Robert Gallo's group and the National Cancer Institute subsequently became involved, and they, with others, found that 60 percent of the MS patients have antibodies that react with proteins from HTLV. This may well be an artifact of autoimmunity, as the antibody seems to come and go in the patients. Because of the clustering of these unusual cases in Florida, close, prolonged contact—at least in the nurses—appears to be a factor in transmission, if a virus triggers the disease. . . . Researchers are trekking to the island community to try to solve the current mystery and find the cause of the disease."

Based on the fact that southern Florida was a major locus of AIDS and the fact that macrophages, which are a prime target of African swine fever virus, were involved, I wondered if the nurses were infected with ASFV. During that period I spoke with a clinician and researcher named Dr. Mark Whiteside who was working in Belle Glade, Florida. Whiteside felt that the presence of a retrovirus in AIDS patients was opportunistic and he told me that he suspected that government scientists had declared the wrong virus to be the cause of AIDS, that LAV (or HTLV-III) was actually a red herring. Whiteside suspected that AIDS was probably caused by an arbovirus which is usually an RNA virus that is characterized by its ability to be transmitted by insects. Whiteside urged the government to test AIDS patients for all known arboviruses. African swine fever virus, even though it is a DNA virus, is also characterized as an arbovirus.

Throughout the early years of the epidemic, a gay man named James Monroe had been a kind of "Deep Throat" for me both at the New York City Health Department and then at the CDC where he eventually worked in the director's office. The stories he told me about what was going on inside those organizations helped shape my evolving understanding of the questionable politics and pseudo-science of what would turn out to be an epidemic of lies. Monroe told me one day on the phone that while he was working with the CDC in New York City he had observed a peculiar thing about how the CDC determined who was positive for the AIDS virus. He said that when the CDC was trying to decide what HTLV-III antibody level actually constituted a real infection, that is, the dividing line between a positive and a negative reading, if two men, one heterosexual and one gay had the same exact borderline reading, the heterosexual's blood would be marked negative, and the gay's positive. It bothered Monroe and it more than bothered me. When Monroe began to express doubts about HTLV-III, he was transferred out of AIDS research and it was suggested by his superiors that he was suffering from "delusional thinking." He told me that the insinuation was that he was suffering from such thinking because he was gay and might himself be suffering from the effects of the virus which was capable of infecting the brain. (It was a kind of medicalized demonization that came to be a regular feature of dissent-bashing in the epidemic.) Oddly enough, after Monroe was transferred to a position in the CDC director's office, he told me that whenever his boss, James Mason, a devout Mormon, went to Washington, he spent a great deal of time with Orin Hatch, the anti-gay Mormon right-winger. Years later Monroe also informed me that all CDC decisions about AIDS were actually being made in the Reagan White House.

As time went on, I noticed that my phone conversations with the CDC's top AIDS researcher, James Curran, became increasingly strained as I began to ask more and more skeptical questions about the so-called AIDS retrovirus. Curran adopted a somewhat mocking and sarcastic style when talking to me. He once asked in an insulting, snark-inflected tone of voice whether I thought he was being "homo-phobic." One could say I was beginning to peer beneath one of the civil masks of the raw heterosexism that was actually the driving force of the CDC's epidemiology. Eventually he stopped returning my calls. It was now abundantly clear that the little gay newspaper in New York City would no longer be the CDC's stenographer. And we were going to pay a stiff price for that.

In late May of 1985, I attended a gay press awards ceremony and ran into Dr. Joseph Sonnabend, a gay Manhattan clinician who had a large AIDS practice and a great deal of insight into the questionable politics of AIDS research. He had been involved in interferon research and he was an outspoken critic of the idea that only one virus was the cause of AIDS. I was grateful to be able to call him on a regular basis with technical scientific questions about the epidemic, viruses and the immune system. At the press ceremony Sonnabend handed me a little gift that would change my life. It was a book, *Betrayers of the Truth: Fraud and Deceit in the Halls of Science,* which was written by *New York Times* science reporters Nicholas Wade and William Broad.

Sonnabend had grown increasingly indignant about the way Robert Gallo was claiming that he, and not the French scientists, had discovered the so-called cause of AIDS. To Sonnabend it seemed at the time like a double absurdity. HTLV-III wasn't really the cause *and* Gallo hadn't even really discovered it. Sonnabend was also convinced that a couple of Gallo's other discoveries—on which his reputation was based—had also been lifted from the work of other scientists.

I spent the weekend devouring the Wade and Broad book. By the time I finished it, scales had fallen from my eyes and I saw American science in a whole new light. The book made it clear that scientists could easily cover up each other's frauds if they were powerful enough. The book made the case that scientists basically did not like to expose other scientists' misdeeds *and they distrusted any form of outside scrutiny.* It was just as full of old-boy networks and protection rackets as the business world. The scientific world, as depicted by *Betrayers of the Truth*, was one in which scientists could easily get away with theft and fraud. Suddenly the idea that we could depend on the scientific process to expose any wrongdoing, or incorrect conclusions of a Robert Gallo, seemed pathetically naïve. The book, and my growing indignation about stories that had been emerging about Gallo's strange "scientific" behavior, inspired me to take the biggest risk of my publishing career. I decided to cross the Rubicon.

When I arrived at the office on Monday, I told Bruce Eves, the art director of *New York Native,* what I wanted on the cover of the forthcoming issue (June 3, 1985). Under a headline of "AIDSGATE BEGINS," I wanted, in the largest possible type, "SHOULD GALLO AND ESSEX BE IN JAIL?"

I then began working on a full page editorial and started putting together a news page of four stories to back up the cover. One was about a letter by Dr. A. Karpas of the Department of Haemotological Medicine at the University of Cambridge to the British publication *New Scientist*. Karpas's letter essentially challenged Gallo's claims that *he* had discovered HTLV-III. The Karpas letter outlined the chronology of Gallo's work and the Montagnier group's work, concluding that Gallo had conveniently discovered his retrovirus at the exact same time that he had succeeded in growing the retrovirus which the French had supplied to him.

I also wrote a brief story which pointed out that *New York Native* was not the first publication to challenge Gallo: "In the February 7, 1985, issue of . . . *New Scientist*, Omar Sattaur explained how Gallo's misclassification may have resulted in the false claim that he discovered the 'AIDS virus.' " Sattaur had stated, "Evidence is now mounting that Robert C. Gallo has misclassified the virus that causes AIDS. The result of this misclassification is that the world has ignored the true discoverers, Luc Montagnier and colleagues at the Institute Pasteur in Paris, and has given Gallo the credit instead."

Sattaur also wrote, "Gallo, head of the Laboratory of Tumor Cell Biology at the National Cancer Institute in Bethesda, Maryland, was convinced from the outset, and still is convinced, that the AIDS virus belongs to a family of viruses called HTLV, which he discovered in 1980. But there is new scientific evidence to prove he's wrong. HTLV stands for human T-cell leukemia virus. Two members of the group cause a type of cancer. The two viruses make T-cells multiply, in an uncontrolled manner. The AIDS virus, however, actually kills T-cells; yet Gallo calls the AIDS virus HTLV-III. While large sums of research time and money are spent on trying to understand how the AIDS virus fits into the HTLV group, thousands continue to die from AIDS." The same article reported that Montagnier was experiencing a lot of pressure to change the name of his virus from LAV to HTLV-III, but he refused to do so.

We also reported in *New York Native,* that in a speech before a group of medical writers in New York, in February 1985, Montagnier "was trying to tell them that there was something suspicious about the fact that the isolate of HTLV-III which Dr. Gallo 'discovered' was nearly identical to the isolate of LAV Montagnier and his team had identified months earlier at the Pasteur Institute."

I also added a disturbing story about Gallo which I had found in *Betrayers of the Truth*. I sensed that it might be a clue to Gallo's character. It was headlined "Gallo Was Witness to Scandal in 1981." The text follows:

> Robert C. Gallo was a witness to a major scandal involving scientific fraud in 1981, according to a book called *Betrayers of the Truth: Fraud and Deceit in the Halls of Science* by *New York Times* writers William Broad and Nicholas Wade (Touchstone/Simon and Shuster, 1982). Although Gallo was not implicated in the incidence of scientific fraud, the authors use him as an example of how scientists often do not blow the whistle on their colleagues when the inability to replicate their experiments makes them suspicious.
>
> The fraud was uncovered when a number of scientists were unable to replicate the work of Cornell University cancer researcher Mark Spector. According to Broad and Wade, Spector was a brilliant young researcher whom many expected eventually to win a Nobel Prize. Many of the world's leading cancer researchers suspected something was wrong in Spector's experiment with the products of tumor-causing genes, but no one stepped forward to ask if fraudulent procedures were involved. One scientist explained that Spector's work was so "beautiful and convincing" the scientist was "seduced" into working with Spector. When other scientists couldn't repeat Spector's experiments, they merely gave up and didn't publicly challenge his credibility.
>
> Gradually, scientists began to notice that Spector's experiments "only worked when he was around to do them" until one of his colleagues realized there was "forgery" involved. The results of the experiments had appeared in the "prestigious" magazine *Science*. According to Broad and Wade it was eventually discovered that Spector "possessed neither an M.A. nor a B.A. from the University of Cincinnati as he had

claimed."

"Why wasn't the falsity of Spector's result discovered much earlier?" Wade and Broad ask in their book. "Why did none of the many biologists caught up in his theory not try first to replicate some of the basic results? The answer is: they did. Their failure to get the same answers as Spector should have stopped the theory dead in its tracks. It didn't."

And one of the scientists who found that he could not repeat Spector's experiments was Robert Gallo.

One of the main points the authors try to make in their book is that the notion of science as a "strictly logical process . . . rigorously checked by peer scrutiny and the replication of experiments" is largely a myth. A sick joke. According to the authors, scientists who are unable to replicate others' experiments are more likely either to assume they are performing the experiment incorrectly, or to quit the project in which they are involved.

On the news page, we included the response from the National Cancer Institute to our request for an interview with Gallo: "Robert Gallo would not return the *Native*'s phone calls, nor did he issue a statement about the allegations that his work on HTLV-III constitutes scientific fraud. A spokesperson for the National Cancer Institute told the *Native*, 'The charges are preposterous, and we will comment no further.' "

Below is my full page editorial from that issue titled "AIDSGATE":

It's time every scientist in the world with a shred of integrity began asking whether certain members of their community are up to their necks in scientific fraud.

There are at least two allegations that must be resolved immediately before public health guidelines for any treatment or diagnostic test based on the work of Dr. Robert Gallo of the National Cancer Institute, Dr. Max Essex of the Harvard School of Public Health, and their colleagues can be trusted by the American public and their physicians. The fact that these allegations are being whispered privately among scientists is a disgrace to the reputation of American science.

Tragically, cowardice abounds among many who have shown great courage in the past. Major scientific and medical publications have actually published articles which may have contained falsified test results and other scientific fraud.

Allegation #1

That Robert Gallo "discovered" the virus Dr. Luc Montagnier of the Pasteur Institute gave to him—i.e. that Gallo's lab "stole" the discovery from the French, after ignoring the French discovery for over a year, thereby setting treatment and vaccine research back immeasurably.

The issue of "virus lifting" might seem academic and irrelevant to uninformed Americans, but certainly it has implication for the ethics and validity of American AIDS research right now. If Gallo is the kind of man who would ignore others' significant breakthroughs and then falsely claim to have made the same discovery himself—and get away with it—what else would he be willing—and able—to falsify, and for whose convenience? What small, seemingly insignificant matters about the so-called AIDS virus might he also be fudging on—or overlooking completely? Do we have a virus-lifter running AIDS research at the National Cancer Institute?

We've been told that Gallo has had lunch dates at the White House. Who is Gallo's boss, anyway? Is AIDS policy being set in the Reagan Administration by open homophobes such as Patrick Buchanan?

Allegation #2

That the linking of an AIDS associated virus with HTLV-I and HTLV-II was a deliberate attempt to confuse scientists and the public, to enjoy acclaim, and to obtain grants and other benefits, including public monies. Such a deliberate linkage would constitute scientific fraud—and not one word of it can be tolerated during an emergency that many predict will affect every human life on the planet. Are we really supposed to believe that, after all his experience with HTLV-I and HTLV-II, Gallo could innocently have made such a mistake?

Sleaze Factor #1

Why has no one in the medical press decried Gallo's control of "his" virus. You'd think he was the sole possessor of the Coca Cola formula (albeit, in this case possibly stolen), the way other scientists have accepted and sustained his monopoly. The *Native* pointed this out last December.

Perhaps the most circumstantially convincing evidence that the powers that be are "protecting" something are the regulations Dr. Robert Gallo of the National Institutes of Health has imposed on "his" virus, HTLV-III. First, a higher level of security clearance is now required, eliminating many scientists. Secondly, only those people to whom Gallo personally gives the virus may work on it, and they may not give it to anyone else. Third, and most damning, only papers on which Gallo is a co-author may be published from work done on "his" virus. This means that any evidence contrary to the HTLV-III theory would remain unpublished.

Sleaze Factor #2
Gallo's Media Fan Club

Not only has Gallo found a way to control the flow of medical information about "his" virus, he has also bamboozled members of the lay media (we won't name them here; they know who they are) creating a coterie of groupies who have been given the privilege of calling the esteemed scientist "Bob."

We remember all too well the day we discussed AIDS with a *Wall Street Journal* reporter. With more than a hint of satisfaction in her voice, she let drop the fact that she had "talked to Bob Gallo the other day."

The formation of this "Bob Club" among reporters is at least part of the reason the real story about AIDS is not getting out. Too many media "Moonies" are giving "Bob" a free ride.

The "Bob Club" should disband, and these reporters should start doing their job—instead of believing everything "Bob" tells them.

Essex Allegation

Dr. Max Essex of the Harvard School of Public Health has the responsibility of making sure that his students conduct sound scientific research. His own research should also be sound (if only to set a good example), and should be absent of any form of fraud or falsification.

Essex has been a longtime collaborator with Gallo. In good conscience, how has Essex been able to remain silent?

Why this is important

Why are these allegations so important, and why must they be resolved immediately? Because the crucial decisions we make about our own health, and the decisions our doctors make, are life-and-death decisions—they cannot be based on fraudulent science. We cannot tolerate inertia on the part of scientists and public health administrators who feel they can look the other way while other scientists steal viruses and push them into phony categories.

We've been smelling a rat in AIDS research, and the odor is now overpowering. Indeed, AIDS has become AIDSGATE.

After Gallo saw that issue of *New York Native*, I received an unexpected phone call from him. It inspired another intense issue of the paper (June 17, 1985) and another long editorial, titled "Castro and the Two Gallos":

On Friday, May 31, Dr. Robert C. Gallo of the National Cancer Institute was scheduled to appear at a West Coast conference held by the Association for the Advancement of Science. He was also supposed to be interviewed by National Public Radio for their program, *All Things Considered*. The program's producers wanted Gallo to respond to my recent allegations, which include the charge that his "dis-

48

covery" of HTLV-III was in fact nothing more than the rediscovery of another research team's identical virus.

I've followed Gallo's behavior for a couple of years now. He has emerged as the most powerful and influential figure in American AIDS research, partly by dint of his personality. Gallo is famous for his lightning bolt appearances at scientific conferences; intimidating, sweeping performances that are really "press opportunities" for the media and his colleagues to photograph him. Perhaps because of this demeanor, the science of Robert Gallo as applied to AIDS has generally not been the sort other scientists could easily or readily challenge in public. I've also heard that scientific papers which contradict Gallo's "findings" are generally rejected by the leading medical journals. Such is the man's power.

I called Gallo's office on the morning of May 31, to find out whether he'd gone to Los Angeles as scheduled. Not surprisingly, his secretary told me he was in a meeting and asked, "Would he know what this is in reference to?" I replied that I thought he would. Within a half-hour, I was told that someone describing himself as "Mr. Ortleb's star witness" was waiting to speak to me on the phone.

It was Gallo.

I want here to present the salient points of our conversation (during which I did most of the listening), because I think Robert Gallo has had more impact on the course of the AIDS epidemic than anyone in America. I also think he is deeply disturbed.

I began the conversation by asking what must have struck Gallo as an odd question. Had he told Loretta McLaughlin, medical writer for the *Boston Globe*, that he didn't know anything about African swine fever virus (as McLaughlin had reported to me)? He replied that the only thing he knew about the virus was that I was interested in it. He then told me in rapid succession:

1. I had made a tremendous mistake, the mistake of my lifetime (in accusing him of fraud.)

49

2. He "couldn't be mad at me" because I "was sincere."

3. There was something very "big and wrong with my thinking."

4. I was either being "manipulated by a schizophrenic scientist" (he would not tell me the name of the scientist), or I was "irrational."

5. I should "try to be a friend."

6. I could be compared to President Reagan, because I "make statements with no basis in fact."

7. Margaret Heckler "perhaps had not done the right thing" at her historic press conference called to announce Gallo's findings a year ago.

8. He didn't need HTLV-III to be considered a success; he had been warned to stay away from AIDS because "situations like this" (I presume he meant the *Native*'s AIDSGATE allegations) might arise. "I don't *need* AIDS," he said.

9. He didn't know how to do the right thing with the press; he had never called a press conference in his life; he was a nervous wreck at the Heckler press conference; he had told Heckler that he felt he had enough data and that he felt he knew the etiology of the disease. He blamed his erratic performance at another press conference on the fact that his father had just died. He told me that his father had worked his way from welder to businessman. He pointed out that he doesn't like publicity. "I do not want to be noticed," he said.

10. He felt that he had the idea and the methodology that led to the discovery of LAV and that, in science, ideas and methodology are everything. I told him that providing methodology didn't mean he could lay claim to every discovery associated with his methodology. (I didn't say it then, but I'll say it now: By that logic, HTLV-III was discovered by Leeuwenhoek, inventor of the microscope.")

11. He said that Omar Sattaur, who wrote a piece criticizing Gallo in *New Scientist*, "didn't know the difference between a bacterium and a virus."

12. He wouldn't dignify A. Karpas (of Cambridge University) with a response to his letter to *New Scientist* (3/28/85) suggesting that there was something fishy about the fact that Gallo's lab discovered HTLV-III just three months after they had been able to grow LAV, the virus the Pasteur Institute had already associated with AIDS.

13. The nomenclature of HTLV-III was decided in an agreement with Japanese researchers in Cold Spring Harbor.

14. He didn't want the virus he named HTLV-III to be called "the AIDS virus," because it would stigmatize homosexuals. (I love the idea of taxonomy by charity.) He also said, "I don't care what the virus is called."

15. When I told him that I called one of his ex-employees who said Gallo was not really responsible for the work done on HTLV-I and Interleukin-II (other Gallo "discoveries" which might result in a fraudulently gained Nobel Prize), he said that he had two disgruntled ex-lab workers who had gone no-where in science. (When I asked him for their names, he wouldn't tell me.)

16. He said that there were competitive scientists who were out to "cut" his "legs off."

17. I told Gallo a few of the basics about African swine fever virus, and he thanked me. He seemed to know nothing about the virus.

18. I asked him if he would be livid if one of his colleagues thought that AIDS was caused by some agent other than HTLV-III and failed to share their knowledge with Gallo. He said he would be "doubly livid."

19. I reminded Gallo that he had discussed African swine fever virus with James D'Eramo, Ph.D., in the now famous interview the *Native* published last summer. D'Eramo: "Do you think other viruses, like CMV or EBV play a role in development of AIDS? Dr. Jane Teas told us a long time ago about the idea of African swine fever virus coming from Africa to Haiti

and then from Haiti to America." Gallo: "It turns out that even though she had the wrong virus, she seems to have the right idea about the origins of the virus. She didn't have any knowledge of HTLV-III; she didn't know it existed—why should she?—so hers was a good insight. I agree." Gallo called this a "miscommunication" on D'Eramo's part. (The interview was tape recorded in full.)

20. Gallo continually told me, "If you'd only read the science, if you only understood the science." I told him I wouldn't be browbeaten by him or his so-called science, even if most of the AIDS researchers in America are afraid of him. I told him that if he wanted to learn more about swine fever, he should call Dr. William Hess of the U.S. Department of Agriculture's Plum Island facility, or ask his collaborator at the Harvard School of Public health, Dr. Max Essex. He said, "I will look into it."

21. I told him that scientists who didn't believe that HTLV-III is the cause of AIDS can't get funding if they don't write his virus into their grant requests. He said he had nothing to do with funding, and that he agreed it was wrong to censor grant requests on that basis. He alleged that he had not gotten one additional cent of funding as a result of his discovery.

22. At one point in the conversation, Gallo listed his achievements with HTLV-III. He was proud that they had proved that HTLV-III doesn't cause Kaposi's sarcoma, that the virus replicates in the brain, that his lab was the first to sequence the virus, and that they were the first to link it with thrombocytopenia.

23. He told me that the original papers on LAV written by the French researchers would never have been published if he had not intervened. He argued that the French did not link the virus to the disease.

24. I asked if he had been reading the AIDS coverage in the *Native*. He said that he had not. I urged him to read the *Native*. He remarked that this would require some bravery on his part. (It would.)

Our conversation left me with the impression of a

man who is to say the least, emotionally very high strung. His claims of powerlessness are contradicted by the former associate who told me that Gallo had very little to do with the discovery of HTLV-I and Interleukin-II. The associate did not want his name used because, he said, Gallo could destroy his career. He told me that Gallo's ex-employees are "a gold mine of information about Gallo" and that I "would not believe some of the things that go on in his lab."

Earlier that very morning, Gallo had called Ann Giudici Fettner, co-author of *The Truth about AIDS* (which recently won the American Medical Writers Association Award) and a frequent contributor to the *Native*. During the conversation, he told Fettner that, because of her association with us, she would never be able to write about science again, because no one at the National Institutes of Health would talk to her. Fettner remains undaunted. To say the least, she cannot be bullied.

Then, on the morning of June 4, Gallo called Dr. Hess at Plum Island. According to Hess, Gallo asked him "how the whole African Swine disease thing got started," and who Jane Teas was. (Gallo has a slight memory problem.) Hess told me he found it rather difficult to believe that Gallo was so ignorant about swine fever. He described Gallo's speaking manner as "hyper," and said that Gallo was "ranting and raving."

Hess is a rather circumspect, soft-spoken, highly methodical man. He said that Gallo fired questions at him so rapidly, he hardly had time to respond. Gallo asked Hess whether African swine fever virus killed T-cells, and as Hess was about to answer, Gallo snapped, "Well, I guess you don't have the information there." Hess said that Gallo kept going on and on about his "115 isolates of HTLV-III," and eventually offered to send one of them to Hess. (Hess is not interested in Gallo's isolates.)

Gallo began to harangue Hess, insisting that he has nothing to do with funding, even though that's of no interest to Hess, whose work is primarily focused on trying to understand the nature of African swine fever virus, the basis of Hess's reputation and career.

By this point, the call apparently turned from an inquiry about swine fever into another defense brief from the "star witness." Hess told me that he couldn't quite ascertain what the purpose of Gallo's call was, and that he was getting tired of receiving calls from researchers who seemed bent on "finding out how much I know" about the possible connection be-tween AIDS and African swine fever virus.

Hess didn't know where Gallo was calling him from, but it must have been Boston, because on that same day, June 4, Gallo made a presentation to medical researchers at Boston University.

Gallo's presentation, according to a source who wishes to remain anonymous, contained interesting scientific observations as well as a rather bizarre slide projection intended to explain how Gallo's virus, HTLV-III, destroys lymphocytes. Uninfected lymphocytes were illustrated on the slides as little "happy faces." Infected lymphocytes were drawn as bald women trying to seduce the happy faces. Once seduced, the little happy faces died and became angels, who went to lymphocyte heaven. (*Native* readers may be on the floor laughing at this point, but reportedly most scientists present did not say anything, although there were apparently some groans in the audience. One scientist who was present told us, "I found myself trying to deny that he was actually portraying it in that manner.")

After the conference, Gallo went out to eat with some of his colleagues. The anonymous source told us that, at the lunch, Gallo told his companions that he blamed Fidel Castro for sending "diseased homosexuals" to America during the Mariella boat lift, thus bringing AIDS into the U.S. Gallo made extremely negative remarks about Haiti, and referred to homosexuals as "homos." According to our source, "He went into a whole thing about people fucking sheep; he was berserk on the topic."

Gallo had just told the audience at the conference that 65% of the blood donors in Brazil were testing positive for HTLV-III, and expressed surprise that there were so many homosexuals in Brazil. (The way he reportedly put it was that he "didn't realize there were so many of 'them' in Brazil.") Our source said that throughout the conference and the luncheon Gallo gave the impression of being a man who is deeply "erotophobic and homophobic." One of the top medical writers in America, with whom I shared this report, concurred, saying, "It sounds like Gallo is losing his grip on reality."

To borrow some of Gallo's own "scientific language," I think we have discovered two isolates: Gallo-I and Gallo-II (there may be more to come.)

Gallo-I is a reasonable scientist, who knows a great deal about retroviruses (though not a thing about African swine fever virus). Gallo-I is a well-respected scientist, whose name appears on a lot of scientific papers for work he may have, at times, done himself. Gallo-I is a jet-setting, fast-talking retro-virologist who craves the approval of the scientific community, an award-winning scientist awaiting the preordained day he will be called to Stockholm to receive that ultimate honor, the Nobel Prize.

Gallo-II is a fraudulent, vindictive, arrogant, anti-gay little bully. Gallo-II makes sure that anyone who disagrees with him suffers bad consequences professionally. Gallo-II is xenophobic and racist. Gallo-II is obsessed with the idea that AIDS is caused by people sleeping with sheep and green monkeys (hopefully not in threesomes).

Fools like Dr. James Mason, Director of the Centers for Disease Control, who recently told a group of people with AIDS that Gallo "had his problems, but he's a brilliant scientist," may subscribe to the notion that we have to live with Gallo-I and Gallo-II

I don't.

Gallo told me that he thought a schizophrenic scientist was manipulating me. If any schizophrenic scientist has tried to manipulate the entire scientific establishment, it is Dr. Robert C. Gallo himself.

In the same issue of the *Native*, I wrote a short ominous news story (that captured the menacing atmosphere of the epidemic) headlined "Reagan Administration Considering AIDS Quarantine: CDC Director Reveals Discussions to PWAs." It began, "At a May 20 meeting in Washington, between a group representing people with AIDS in America and Dr. James Mason, the director of the Centers for Disease Control revealed that the Reagan Administration is considering a quarantine of people with AIDS. Paul Boneberg who heads the Mobilization Against AIDS, told the *Native* that Mason revealed to the stunned group of 12 people that he had been at an administration meeting that morning at which quarantine for AIDS patients had been discussed. According to Boneberg, Mason says he is personally against quarantine. The group pleaded with Mason to provide more money for public education on AIDS, to which Mason responded, 'Do you really believe gay men can be changed through education?' The head of the CDC is from a Mormon college in Utah which allegedly has used electroshock 'aversion therapy' to 'change' homosexuals. Boneberg told the *Native* that his impression was that Mason is totally unapologetic for the administration's approach to the AIDS crisis. He said he was shocked at how insensitive Mason was to the PWAs in his presence . . . . Boneberg feels that the meeting with Mason was unproductive and that dialogue with the Reagan Administration has reached a dead end."

On June 14, 1985, I visited Albany at the invitation of Mel Rosen, the director of New York State's AIDS Institute. There I met with Andrew Fleck, an advisor to the State Health Commissioner David Axelrod. I had talked with Fleck several times on the phone during the preceding year and he had seemed to be a sophisticated theoretician on matters of epidemiology and public health.

Fleck was an aristocratic-looking registered Republican in a Democratic state administration. I wrote in the *Native*, "His standards of excellence in epidemiology put the Centers for Disease Control to shame, and I had told him on more than one occasion that the AIDS epidemic could use some of his experience and wisdom. But he has maintained that he prefers to work outside of the limelight. I trust that he's part of the reason State Health Commissioner David Axlerod has not become a proponent of the fuzzy CDC epidemiological data or the virological fraud coming out of the National Cancer Institute. Fleck seems to play the role of the avuncular professional wall off of which [Axlerod] can bounce ideas before taking action."

Joining us was Dr. Jean Dodds, a prominent scientist in the New York State Health Department who had been the chief of the state's Hematology Laboratory for two years. I had called her on and off during the previous year-and-a-half, trying to enlist her in Teas's efforts to test the ASFV AIDS hypothesis. But she wouldn't have any of it. I had assumed that she didn't know anything about African swine fever virus; certainly she'd never let on that she did.

When Rosen and I arrived in Albany around lunchtime, we went directly to Fleck's office. Dodds was there. She was a single, rather perky, fortyish woman who talked rapidly and was capable of leaping deftly from issue to issue. I wrote, in the *Native*, that she was "brainy and always seemed to have ideas moving on the forecourt and back-court."

I was quite surprised when, upon our arrival at Fleck's office, she handed me three research papers on African swine fever virus which had been published in the *American Journal of Veterinary Medicine* and in *Veterinary Pathology*. The lead author on these papers, J. F. Edwards, was someone I had actually talked to a year or so before that. I had tracked him down at a university in Texas to question him about the relationship between African swine fever and AIDS. On the phone he had been very hostile about such a suggestion. Edwards angrily insisted that there was absolutely no similarity between AIDS and African swine fever. When I pointed out that pigs with ASFV developed pneumonia just like AIDS patients, he retorted that the pneumonia in pigs was more like tuberculosis than the Pneumocystis carinii pneumonia that was occurring in AIDS. (It became clear, as the AIDS epidemic progressed, that tuberculosis was in fact a major problem in AIDS.) Edwards's research interest at the time was thrombocytopenia in swine fever. (Thrombocytopenia is basically a disorder in which the blood fails to coagulate properly.) From my own research I knew that thrombocytopenia was a problem in AIDS but Edwards seemed annoyed when I pointed out that AIDS and ASFV had that pathology in common. My conversation with him *was* another puzzling moment in the AIDS era when I ran into an uncanny hostility that seemed to be coming out of nowhere. AIDS had the whole country on edge, but I now think it was more than that.

57

That day in Albany, when I told Jean Dodds that I had spoken to Edwards, she said that she had been one of his students which surprised me.

Fleck took us to lunch and when Fleck ordered veal, I followed suit. Dodds glared at us. She pointed out that she was an animal rights activist and she asked if we were really going to order veal. She went on to describe the horrible things that meat companies do to calves. She obviously wanted us to change our orders, but Fleck shrugged her off and stuck to his veal. I felt awkward at first, but I grew annoyed. Dodds then told us that she had been up late the night before because she had to put one of her "hemophiliacs to sleep." She lived with several hemophiliac German Shepherds in a farm-house in Albany.

The conversation at lunch was basically about Gallo and African swine fever virus. Fleck described Gallo as "a burden to science," but tended to speak of him in a kindlier manner than I have. We also discussed a member of the Centers for Disease Control, Richard Rothenberg, who was stationed in the New York State Health Department. I complained to Fleck and Dodds about the CDC's ability to impose its own agendas on state and local governments by providing them with staff and money. The CDC had very long arms.

Over our controversial veal and her pasta, we discussed what the State of New York could do to test the hypothesis that AIDS and African swine fever were related. Fleck said that when Teas had introduced the hypothesis two years earlier, it had made a great deal of sense to him, considering the geographic distribution of the two epidemics. I told them that I was planning on writing an editorial attacking Gallo for placing "T-cell blinders" on the scientific community that recognizing the full scope of what AIDS was. I also told them that Kaposi's sarcoma was probably one of the most visible clues that AIDS was a form of African swine fever. Dodds bristled at the notion that lesions in pigs with ASFV might be at all similar to Kaposi's sarcoma lesions. She made a few arcane remarks about necrosis of the endothelial cells in African swine fever virus infected pig tissue being a totally different phenomenon in KS. I told Dodds that she was talking about the acute cases of ASFV infection as opposed to infection with the chronic strains, which Teas has suspected might behind the AIDS epidemic. She let me know, rather cuttingly, that she knew the difference. I was caught off guard, surprised that Dodds knew so much about ASFV. I had brought along 30 research papers on ASFV and had planned to discuss them with her, but we never got to them.

Dodds didn't see the epidemiological patterns of ASFV as being either convincing or interesting. She said that everything I had told her about swine fever and AIDS could be said about parvovirus and AIDS, an area of research interest for her. I responded by saying that if she thought that AIDS is caused by parvovirus, she was in an excellent position to get *her* idea tested. She agreed that every idea should be tested which made her sound open-minded, but I suspected it was just another way of saying ASFV was another crazy dime-a-dozen idea about the cause of AIDS.

Mel Rosen was getting a little impatient as the lunch ended. He had told me in the weeks before that he didn't like the idea that the testing on African swine fever had been basically stonewalled at every turn for two years. While he insisted that he had no investment in swine fever as the cause, he continually told me, "I just want to do the right thing." He turned to Dodds and Fleck and said, "What can we do for Ortleb?"

Dodds said that she would be overseeing the grants process of New York State's AIDS Institute, and she suggested that I ask Teas to apply for a New York State research grant.

I wasn't pleased. I thought that just meant more delays, more foot-dragging. I told Dodds that the problem wasn't money but rather getting the cooperation of the U.S. Department of Agriculture. The USDA's assistance was required to do any research on African swine fever virus.

Fleck and Dodds assured me that if a researcher got a state grant and then had trouble getting African swine fever virus for testing purposes from the USDA, the state would step in. I replied, "Why don't you step in now, Jean? Why don't you try to test sera from ten people with AIDS for the presence of African swine fever virus?"

She responded, "I can't drop everything and just test your hypothesis."

I said, "I didn't ask you to *drop everything* and test the hypothesis."

It was getting a little unfriendly and Rosen looked exasperated. I felt like Dodds was playing games with me and that I was about to reach another dead end. Dodds got up to leave the table and I wondered why I even had bothered to come up to Albany. Rosen had made the prospects of something happening in Albany seem better than this.

Rosen took me back to his state office, where I was to wait for two hours until we both got the train back to Manhattan. While he attended a meeting, I sat down and started to read the three research papers on African swine fever virus that Dodds had given me. When I looked at the authors of the papers I got quite a shock. On all three of the ASFV papers Jean Dodds was listed as one of the researchers. Why hadn't she told me that she had personal research experience with the virus? Something didn't smell right. In order to do ASFV research she had to have had some kind of contact with the USDA at Plum Island. That she had co-authored one of the papers on thrombocytopenia in ASFV was disturbing to me because that was also a tell-tale sign of AIDS. If she knew so much about ASFV, why did she refuse to acknowledge their obvious similarities? I found it bizarre that she didn't discuss her own ASFV research at lunch. What was really going on?

When Rosen returned from his meeting, he took me to meet Richard Rothenberg, the CDC's man in Albany. Rothenberg was a tiny man who somewhat resembled Woody Allen. I had heard from Rosen that he was not respected by the top people at the state's health department. As I understood it, his job was to convince Albany to faithfully follow the CDC agenda, which I was gradually becoming convinced, was more about politics than real science. I had been told that in meeting after meeting Rothenberg had been trying to convince the skeptical health commissioner that HTLV-III was the real cause of AIDS.

Rosen left me alone in a room with Rothenberg. He asked me what I thought of Fleck. I told him I thought he was a brilliant scientist. He didn't seem to agree. I told Rothenberg that I had heard he was having problems with Axelrod. He told me that the problem was that there were a lot of "advocates" in the New York State Health Department. I gathered that he didn't see himself as any kind of "advocate." He went on to tell me that the problem with his boss was that he "shoots from the hip." We turned to the subject of African swine fever virus, and he asked me why I was an "advocate" of that theory. Although I resented the rather patronizing insinuations implicit in the term "advocate," I began to go over the list of reasons. I borrowed a piece of paper and drew a rough map that included Africa, Haiti, Cuba and Brazil. I drew an arrow point from Zaire to the Caribbean Basin. I said, "Let's see, swine fever seems to have gone from Zaire to the Dominican Republic in . . . ."

"In 1978," he said.

"Oh yes," I said, wondering how he knew. I continued, And then it seems to have shown up in Brazil . . . ."

"In 1978," he interrupted. He then said that he understood why I saw similarities, but that there were two important differences. The first, he said was that in swine fever there is a tremendous release of pyrogen (a substance released by macrophages that causes fever), and that in swine fever the central pathological event is vasculitis. (Unfortunately Rothenberg may have known more about African swine fever than AIDS. His two big differences turned out to be two big similarities.) Interestingly, Rothenberg did say that if African swine fever was the cause, it would eventually come out and said that if it did the role I was playing might make it come out sooner. Most surprisingly, he also told me that Don Francis, the CDC researcher who told us that the CDC's testing for ASFV in AIDS patients had come out negative, was now saying that ASFV might be a cofactor in AIDS. That didn't make any sense to me. I asked Rothenberg if Francis was being facetious and he replied that Francis was serious.

On the train back to Manhattan, I grilled Rosen on Dodds, asking if he thought Dodds was playing some kind of political game with the ASFV issue. "If Jean Dodds is a villain, I'll go nuts," Rosen said. I told him I found it odd that she was intimately involved in both AIDS and ASFV research. It was quite a coincidence.

The more I thought about the Albany meetings, the more annoyed I became. On the following Monday, I sent a Mailgram to State Health Commissioner David Axlerod: "It's amazing that Jean Dodds knows so much about African swine fever virus and has connections to Plum Island, USDA, and yet has done so little to make sure that men, women and children with AIDS are not actually infected with swine fever virus. This is a moral and scientific outrage. We raise this issue in the next "AIDSGATE" section of *New York Native*. Please tell Rich Rothenberg that there is vasculitis in AIDS. Rich should try to keep up with the AIDS literature instead of just trying to hoodwink you. . . . I suggest that we meet for a full discussion without the presence of Dodds as soon as possible."

Several days later, I received the following letter from Dodds:

June 19, 1985, 6:10 a.m.

Dear Chuck,

After we met last Friday, I had intended to drop you a personal note to say how much I enjoyed meeting you and that I liked you a lot and found you very clever and intuitive. By the way, it's a beautiful clear morning as I sit at the dining room table and look through my many windows onto the hills in the distance. Country living is peaceful and comforting.

You can imagine my surprise and hurt feelings when I learned on Monday morning of your telegram to Commissioner Axelrod (whom I admire very much) and your concerns about me and my role in the African swine fever "issue." I had just returned from teaching our alternate site counselors and had proudly told them of our Friday meeting and joint decision to encourage other avenues of research on AIDS—including looking into the cofactor/role of ASF virus and trying to obtain reagents should an appropriately designed study plan be developed.

We invited you to Albany (in fact it was my urging along with Mel [Rosen's] encouragement that developed the invitation) in good faith and with honest intentions—because I feel scientifically and medically that anyone's or any theory has the right to be pursued. In fact, freedom of scientific inquiry is what science is all about. We are now embarrassed and feel somewhat betrayed by what happened. My dear friend (if you'll allow me to call you a friend), how can I or we help you to achieve your goal unless you trust us to stick to our agreement? Surely by being so zealous about the conspiracy you fear exists and then extending it to include the very group that has agreed to help you, you are potentially undermining the effort and creating a situation whereby despite what we do to promote a proper study of the matter, the department may not agree—for fear of being "slapped in the face" again! I'm really sorry about all this. Personally, I'm disappointed that you think ill of me or my intentions, but my conscience is absolutely clear. I've dedicated my life to public service and compassionate concern for all living things. I stand on my loyalty, sincerity, and honesty. I still want to help you and will do so in good faith. I've already contacted Plum Island as promised, and the department has assured access to the reagents needed should a study like the one we suggested be undertaken.

The ball is in your court. Hopefully, you can reach out to us (me) again as I'm doing in this letter.

God bless and care for you.

Shortly after that, the Health Commissioner of New York State ordered that blood from people with AIDS be tested for the presence of African swine fever virus. In the July 15 issue, I wrote an editorial that outlined some of my concerns about the predispositions and trustworthiness of the people who would be doing the blood testing:

> As we went to press with this issue, there were no available details about the nature of the intended state research which might end two years of speculation in this publication about why the government has avoided investigating the obvious connection between AIDS and African swine fever, the virtually identical disease in pigs. Concern about the tremendous economic impact of a swine fever outbreak may explain the Centers for Disease Control's avoidance of a serious investigation.
>
> In the February 22, 1984, issue of the *South Jersey Courier-Post*, Judy Petsonk wrote about Dr. James Curran, head of the CDC's AIDS Task Force, and his feelings about Jane Teas's theory that AIDS is caused by African swine fever virus: "Curran also said he was afraid that Teas's theory might make people afraid to eat pork, thus harming the pork industry in the U.S." If Curran has put the welfare of the pork industry before the welfare of patients, it would not be the first time the Centers for Disease Control put ethics on a back burner while patients suffered or died. James H. Jones's book, *Bad Blood: The Tuskegee Syphilis Experiment, A Tragedy of Race and Medicine* (Free Press, 1981), documents in full a case in which the Centers for Disease Control apparently found nothing wrong with continuing a 1930s experiment in which government doctors studied the effects of untreated syphilis in 400

black Alabama sharecroppers, who did not know they had the disease. The Tuskegee experiment has many interesting parallels with the way AIDS is being handled by the Public Health Service; the current paucity of funding for therapeutic research projects seems to be a deliberate strategy to let AIDS patients die.

Curran's attitude toward the potential victims of AIDS, as described by Robert Gallo of the National Cancer Institute, strongly resembles the attitudes of white doctors toward blacks in the late nineteenth century, also explored by Jones in his book. In our August 27, 1984, issue, Gallo told the *Native*, "I have heard that there are some who are so sexually driven that they are like alcoholics. . . . I have heard that from Dr. Curran. There are some that are so hypersexual that they're like alcoholics or chronic cigarette smokers." From *Bad Blood*: "White physicians of the late nineteenth and early twentieth centuries blamed the decline in black health on self-destructive behavioral traits. . . . Physicians hammered away at the black man's distaste for honest labor, fondness for alcohol, proclivity to crime and sexual vices, disregard for personal hygiene, ignorance of the laws or good nutrition, and total indifference to his own health. [Black people] had only themselves to blame."

Whether such an attitude toward the gay community also pervades the New York State Health Department remains to be seen. Frances Tarlton, spokesperson for the department, seems preoccupied with the sexuality of those who suspect AIDS could be caused by African swine fever. She told *Newsday* (June 27, 1985), "The State Health Department will test a theory that African swine fever virus may be linked to AIDS, a belief held by few scientists but supported by some in the homosexual community."

One non-gay, non-journalist who has suspected a link between AIDS and swine fever is Dr. Frederick Maurer, a retired Lt. Colonel of the U.S. Army [and an experienced ASFV researcher]. On July 3, 1983,

Maurer wrote to the CDC about the connection, but was ignored by Curran.

A swine fever outbreak could cost $25 billion annually. It is reasonable to expect that there are people in the government who would find it more advantageous to cover up any presence of swine fever in the U.S., and to let the disease continue spreading among the pig (and/or human) population, rather than suffer the economic consequences that would follow an admission of swine fever is in the U.S. (One ASFV scientist informs us that Brazil has adopted such a policy.)

In a staff paper from the Institute of Agriculture, Forestry and Home Economics entitled "Potential Economic Consequences of African Swine Fever and Its Control in the United States," E.H. McCauley and W.B. Sundquist wrote, "It is clear that because of the large size of the U.S. swine production industry and the large volume of domestic consumption and export marketing of pork and related products, economic impacts of endemic African swine fever will quickly run into the billions of dollars." The writers argue, "In addition to the loss of exports for pork and related products should ASFV become endemic in the U.S., some countries, particularly those with domestic swine production of their own, are likely to place a partial or complete embargo on the imports of other agricultural products from the U.S. for fear that these products may serve as carriers of ASF to their swine populations. Though it is difficult to isolate and quantify the magnitude of such potential losses, U.S. agricultural exports, among which grains, soybeans, cotton, and animal products predominate, currently total to about $25 billion annually."

That report was published in 1979.

Ironically, the United States Department of Agriculture distributes many pamphlets to American pig farmers warning them to be vigilant and aware of African swine fever's symptoms. According to one such pamphlet, "Plans for a U.S. emergency eradication program against ASFV have already been developed. State and federal animal health authorities will begin eradication immediately upon confirmation of an outbreak." The same pamphlet warns, "If any hogs show signs of African swine fever or Hog Cholera, notify your veterinarian, state or federal animal health official, or your country agricultural agent at once."

There is already some evidence that swine fever is in the country and is being ignored by federal health officials. Dr. Peter Drotman of the Centers for Disease Control told Joe Nicholson of the *New York Post* six months ago, "Federal doctors stopped investigation of the pig disease even though its only study found that 'a few' AIDS patients tested positive for the pig virus."

If it does turn out that "AIDS" is caused by African swine fever virus, Drotman may be sorry that he made such a remark. To say the least, it may leave the CDC open to major multimillion-dollar litigation from swine fever victims and their families.

In the same issue, we reported on a direct mail letter sent out by Jerry Falwell, leader of The Moral Majority, Inc. In it he wrote, "Until recently AIDS was a disease that raged through the male homosexual community, largely because of homosexual promiscuity. But during the last few months, AIDS has begun to infect even larger portions of the general population, heterosexual as well as homosexual. . . . I am going to launch this campaign in Washington and attempt to make strides toward curbing this 'gay plague' as the press calls it." He also wrote, "Over 1 million people are right this minute carrying the AIDS virus, according to medical authorities. You don't have to be gay to get AIDS—anyone can get it."

Falwell went on to bemoan the "innocent" people who had gotten AIDS: "hemophiliacs, unborn children, a transfused nun." He continued, "My friend, if we don't stop this epidemic soon, our entire population could be at risk." After outlining draconian legislative measures that Falwell wanted enacted to stop the epidemic, and asking his readers to send in $15, $25 or $50, he added a P.S.: "I am not persecuting the homosexuals. I pray for their conversion."

Given Jean Dodds's attitude toward me and her rather petulant skepticism about Jane Teas's African swine fever hypothesis, I was dubious about her ability to conduct the necessary research thoroughly and objectively. Where the science of AIDS was concerned, it increasingly struck me that objectivity was in the eye of the beholder.

I must say that the design of the New York State ASFV experiment was quite clever. Instead of testing a large number of AIDS patients for African swine fever virus in a *straightforward* manner, Dodds designed a research project to determine whether HTLV-III and African swine fever were co-factors in AIDS. Instead of testing the Teas hypothesis, they seemed to be disingenuously testing some kind of Dodds's hypothesis. In the *Native* I wrote, "the design of the research project indicates that the hypothesis that AIDS is caused by African swine fever virus may either have been deliberately avoided or at least obfuscated by a faulty research design."

Predictably, the state found no correlation between HTLV-III and African swine fever virus. Out of a total of 160 blood samples tested, only ten were from AIDS patients. That was a ridiculously small number of people to test for a virus which can be difficult to find *even when you know the pigs are infected with it*. Sometimes many different kinds of tests are required to detect ASFV infection. But the state did inadvertently uncover something that was very disturbing.

Out of 110 blood samples from the New York blood supply that were tested, four percent tested positive for African swine fever virus, a virus that the United States Department of Agriculture assured us could not be found anywhere in the continental United States. Actually, the number may have been higher than that because an additional 25 percent of the blood showed some degree of positivity, and if they had been included in the count of positives, the conclusion could have been drawn that 27 percent of the blood in New York's blood banks was infected with African swine fever virus, which could have suggested that there might be a catastrophic epidemic *of some kind* simmering in the general population.

I complained, in a September 30 editorial, that the person who performed the actual testing was not a specialist in the field of African swine fever, and I pointed out that the testing the state did was not thorough. I wrote, "Given that the State Commissioner of Health, David Axelrod, functions under the thumb of the Centers for Disease Control, there may be little that Axelrod will do to pursue the findings. In the past, the head of the AIDS Task Force at the CDC, James

Curran, has expressed a great deal of concern that the pork industry could be affected by the hypothesis that AIDS is caused by African swine fever virus. There is a great deal that the public can do to make sure that their government is protecting them. By demanding that blood banks screen for African swine fever virus, scientists may be forced to face the now very real possibility that the virus is present in the nation's blood supply."

I also expressed my concern that the state did not consult with William Hess as I had recommended to Dodds. Hess had spent much of his life studying African swine fever virus and was working at Plum Island at the time the state was doing its ASFV tests. In a paper on African swine fever in 1981, Hess wrote, "The first diagnosis of ASFV in a country should be based on virus isolated." The state chose to look for antibodies first. Hess also warned in his paper, "No single test can be expected to detect the disease under all conditions." He insisted that only a "comprehensive" battery of tests could be counted on to determine if a pig is infected with ASFV.

I wrote in the *Native*, "If between four and 27 percent of the blood in New York City does indeed contain infectious African swine fever virus, and the public health authorities continue to adhere to the dictates of the pork lobbies and the USDA, the City may be sitting on a time bomb that will make the epidemic to date look quite minor. The governor, the mayor, the city's health commissioner, and the state's health commissioner all have new facts about swine fever's presence in our city's blood supply. Whether they will act in time remains to be seen."

Around the same time that New York State did its testing, Jane Teas and two collaborators, John Beldekas and her husband, James Hebert, had obtained irradiated ASFV from Plum Island so that they themselves could test AIDS blood for the presence of the virus. They had waited months for the USDA to finally comply with their request.

In the course of his ASFV experiments, which were conducted at Boston University, Beldekas also tested the blood from a pig from a local farm. Surprisingly, the pig's blood tested positive for African swine fever virus. When Beldekas notified me, I called the USDA, assuming that alarms would go off, because any discovery of swine fever in pigs in this country would be tantamount to a national agricultural emergency. The day after the USDA was notified, they flew three swine fever experts to Boston to consult with Beldekas. Teas, in a letter to Senator Edward Kennedy about the USDA's visit to

Beldekas, wrote, "During their first visit they indicated to Dr. Beldekas that they have data from slaughterhouses surveys [indicating that] pigs in New York, New Jersey and Texas have been exposed to African swine fever virus. The work of Dr. Beldekas, however, is the first to show the presence of actual virus in a pig from the United States."

Teas wrote to Kennedy because she was afraid that the USDA might prevent Beldekas from continuing the research. She told Kennedy, "Until I began working with Dr. Beldekas, I only wanted to test the idea of whether African swine fever virus causes AIDS. Based on information obtained through a Freedom of Information Act request, and two Congressional inquiries, one conducted by Senator Durenberger and one by Congressman Weiss, I learned that the CDC had done testing on AIDS patients, but had decided that the positives to African swine fever virus must have been mistakes. I do not doubt their right to their opinion, but I strongly object to their decision not to publish their information, along with their methodology and results. I want more from my government than science behind closed doors."

She told Kennedy about her trips to Spain, England, and Uganda in which she attempted to get her hypothesis tested. She wrote about the positive results from England as well as the puzzling problems she encountered in Spain: "I carried duplicate samples of the same AIDS blood to Madrid for testing. Although I had the verbal agreement of the director that the test would be done, when I have called to ask about the results of the tests, the telephone lines have suddenly gone dead when I mention African swine fever virus. Likewise, my letters have gone unanswered."

I figured I had reached the end of the road with the State of New York and after I saw the state commissioner of health saying some bizarre things on television about AIDS, I wrote an angry editorial voicing my frustration in the October 14, 1985, issue of *New York Native*:

> "We continue to find it interesting that the state's Health Commissioner David Axelrod has, as one of his employees, one of the few researchers in the world with swine fever expertise, Jean Dodds, a woman who bragged to us that she was handling the next round of AIDS grants. We also find it interesting that Axelrod is not stopping the transfusion of ASFV-infected blood into unsuspecting New Yorkers.

We had been led to believe that Axelrod is a decent man and a decent scientist. We thought he would be part of the solution of the AIDS epidemic. It turns out he is part of the problem. On a recent telecast of *Inside Albany* (a New York political news show) on October 1, Axelrod talked about AIDS: "This is a behavioral problem," he said. "And I think we have an obligation to help these people and those who become ill as a result of these behavioral activities."

Axelrod clearly had become a hopeless cause and not so different from the gay-behavior-obsessed political epidemiologists who had crafted the AIDS paradigm down at the CDC. Mel Rosen had told me that he and Axelrod used to pray together. Rosen, who was gay (he was a former director of Gay Men's Health Crisis in New York), also told me that Axelrod used to ask him who was gay in Mayor Ed Koch's administration and was very eager to know if Koch himself was gay. Rosen said he liked to tease Axelrod by telling him that he knew who was gay in the administration, and then would refuse to tell him. In many ways Axelrod seemed to be just another public health official pruriently preoccupied with sniffing out gays during the epidemic.

Rosen and I soon stopped speaking and one of the last things he told me was that they had a nickname for me in Albany. They called me "Oink." Rosen himself would eventually die of AIDS. Maybe that wouldn't have happened if the state had done the right thing.

In the October 21 issue, I wrote an editorial about the confusion between CMV, a virus often seen in AIDS, and African swine fever virus: "Here's an open challenge to doctors who read this newspaper. Did you know that CMV (cytomegalovirus) and African swine fever virus, when viewed in thin sections, are morphologically very similar? Did you know that experienced diagnostic laboratories have confused the two in the past? Would you bet your patient's life that you're not confusing the two? Would you bet your own?" When the Centers for Disease Control had first investigated AIDS, they thought the cause might be CMV because it was present in all AIDS patients. They ruled it out because no single strain could be found in all patients. I suspected that they were staring at African swine fever virus and just assuming it was CMV.

In the same issue, I also wrote a story about something very curious

I had learned regarding a possible connection between AIDS and insulin derived from pigs: "A source in the medical community who wishes to remain anonymous has informed the *Native* that there is currently a secret investigation underway to determine whether there is a connection between AIDS and pig insulin." My source had told me that research was being conducted at the Joslin Clinic in Boston, a major diabetes research center, because several people who had received insulin from pigs had gone on to develop AIDS. The director of the clinic denied the story.

Throughout that autumn, I had been trying to get the reporters who helped write Jack Anderson's syndicated column to address the question of whether the government was covering up the connection between AIDS and African swine fever virus. In Anderson's October 7, 1985, column, he reported, "Some medical researchers suspect that the federal government is discouraging tests that might identify a deadly swine virus as a cause of AIDS for fear that such a revelation would wreck the pork industry." Anderson also reported, "Memos reveal that the tests did show a couple of positive reactions, but agricultural researchers dismissed the results as 'false positives.'"

That October, the true political colors of the epidemic started to reveal themselves when Ann Fettner obtained a document on AIDS policy from an influential right-wing think tank called The Free Congress Research and Education Foundation. She described the contents of their document in that same October 21 *Native*:

> AIDS is defined as presenting two types of problems, "behavioral," and "biological." Gay men and drug abusers fall into the first category, and all others with AIDS, "especially the 'unknown' and the blood recipients" into the second, which "poses a health problem of a totally different order; eliminating the biological cause of the problem where the patient's disease was not the result of his own behavior."
>
> A section of the document titled "Gay Rights Dilemma/Agenda Regarding AIDS," includes the following: "At present, homosexuals are faced with two options, either of which is generally unacceptable and therefore unworkable within that political community: 1) give up their sexual practices, a large part of their identity); 2) threaten their newly won civil

71

rights by continuing their society-threatening behavior. Two courses of action may deliver them from
their dilemma: 1) A quick spread of AIDS to the
population at large; 2) a quick development of AIDS
vaccines. Both will lead to a 'status quo ante' situation.
The only way to avoid the homosexual bashing by the
'gay groups' is to frame the whole issue as a public
health problem and by identifying homosexuals as
'high-risk' risk-takers with the public health. This
approach will help to stop the spread of AIDS, and by
that fact, heighten the dilemma."

The document further recommends "education"
and "sanctions" for those with "the human behavior
problem." These sanctions have to have high visibility
and the concurrence of the population, or they will
backfire on the education effort and the social pressure
effects. Sanctions could have the opposite effect (social
protection of the risk-takers) if they are not seen as just
and effective. "Given the civic ramifications of AIDS-
risking behaviors, a trade-off between civil rights and
civic responsibility seems in order here. If this trade-
off is publicly acceptable, the sanctions should be the
mandatory reporting of all intercourse contacts of the
AIDS-riskers."

Among the "sanctions," the document recommends, "for AIDS carriers who are sexually com-
pulsive, make Deprovera optional. Deprovera reduces
sex drive." Deprovera, a female hormone which is no
longer used in this country due to the suspicion that it
causes birth defects, is used in Third-World countries
for birth control. Its long-term effects on males are
completely unknown.

When Fettner first showed me this document, I felt like I was
staring into the abyss. It was like seeing papers from the Wansee
conference in Nazi Germany. If there is ever an honest AIDS museum,
this document deserves a prominent display. As far as I'm concerned,
the document didn't just express the politics of the Reagan White
House and its conservative friends. It also was built on the
epidemiology of the Reagan CDC which, as would become clearer and

clearer, was ignoring the nature of the real epidemic.

Even medical professionals began to sound like the right wing crazies. Scientist John Beldekas wrote an article, for the same issue of the *Native*, about an October 3, 1985 speech by Dr. James O. Mason, the Mormon Director of the Centers for Disease Control: "Dr. Mason of the CDC began his talk with an overview of the epidemic, stressing the idea that behavior is the cause of AIDS. He emphasized male-to-male and female-to-male transmission in both America and Africa, and stated that anal intercourse is the chief mode of transmission. According to Mason the permissive nature of the 1960s and 1970s made the environment ripe for AIDS, and the increase in promiscuity among homosexuals and heterosexuals and increased jet travel introduced the virus into the United States. Mason's idea of behavior as causal . . . was all-pervasive and indicated not only his bias, but attitudes at the highest level of the government. He stressed that casual contact is not a means of transmission, and that the risk of acquiring AIDS in this manner is nonexistent. Mason claimed that 'All people are not at risk for AIDS,' and stated that drastic changes in behavior will be the only way out of the problem. 'High-tech science will not save us from AIDS,' said Mason, 'but changes in behavior will.' "

Beldekas also wrote, "Mason stated that over ten million Africans are infected with the so-called 'AIDS virus,' that AIDS is not a new disease, and that it was introduced into Africa's human population through the eating of green monkey meat or through monkey bites. He claimed that the disease is biologically caused in Africa. This raised the possibility that, if ten million Africans are infected with HTLV-III and if the rate of AIDS is lower there, perhaps HTLV-III is not the cause of AIDS."

Around that time, the serious contradiction in the HTLV-III theory also surfaced in the recommendations about the Elisa test for AIDS which were provided by the American Medical Association. Because the test for HTLV-III was so inaccurate at that point, the AMA had one list of recommendations for "high-risk individuals" with repeated positive results, and a different list of recommendations for "low-risk individuals" with repeated positive test results. A "high-risk" person who tested positive for the virus was to assume that the test result was a true positive, but a "low-risk" [i.e. heterosexual] individual should "be advised about interpretation of these test results. This should include an understanding that the prevalence of false positive results in the low-risk group may be high, and that the patient's particular result may be of questionable significance."

In an October 14 editorial, I wrote, "What all this means is simple. Many positive tests are actually negative and many negative tests are actually positive, and there is no definitive way to discern which tests are true anything. This is a blood test on the basis of which many researchers would like us to make decisions regarding sex, pregnancy, school attendance, marriage, employment, insurance, and other little routine matters of life. The AMA can't tell up from down with this test, yet we are asking Americans to alter the basic social fabric of our culture on the results of the Elisa test."

One of the most articulate and outspoken challengers of the idea that HTLV-III was the cause of AIDS at that time was the previously mentioned Dr. Joseph Sonnabend, who had an eight-year-old practice in Greenwich Village that served gay men. Sonnabend had spent a great many years doing medical research and had assisted the man who discovered interferon. He had extensive experience in cancer research, venereal diseases, and herpes. Sonnabend was critical both of the definition of what AIDS was and of the theory that the single virus, HTLV-III, was the cause of AIDS.

In an interview, in the October 7 issue, Sonnabend had told our reporter Barry Adkins that the CDC "had a very simple-minded way of looking at things." He argued, "The environment in which people with AIDS have been living, or to which they have been exposed, is a complicated microbiological environment in the case of gay men, and that the nature of the exposure is such that you expect multiple diseases, multiple conditions to occur. We know that people with AIDS generally report a much higher frequency of syphilis than people who don't have AIDS. You don't assume that syphilis is a pathway toward AIDS. But to tell you the truth, according to the view that I would have about the development of AIDS, I would say syphilis may indeed contribute to the development of AIDS."

Sonnabend, who was a "multifactorialist," was convinced that AIDS had many causes which interacted "in such a way cumulatively, over a period of time" to produce the syndrome. He complained, "The people researching this disease, the physicians who write in the journals, just see men who have been referred to them. They know nothing about the setting, the overall environment of the patient. They don't look at the disease in the totality."

Sonnabend insisted, "The cause of AIDS is not known—that's the one true thing to say. I have to keep coming back to this. To say that the cause of AIDS is known is cruel. If you say that the cause is known, it means you can go after treatment for the cause and you neglect, unfortunately, not only the other treatments . . . but also research."

Without realizing it at the time, Sonnabend was onto something that linked AIDS to what would ultimately turn out to be the other face of AIDS in the general population—chronic fatigue syndrome. He was convinced that the reactivation of Epstein-Barr virus in AIDS was a major factor in its pathogenesis. In its early days the reactivation of that virus was thought to be the iconic characteristic of chronic fatigue syndrome which initially was called "chronic mono." He told Adkins, "EBV is the virus that causes mononucleosis. The idea is to consider the known factors in the environment of people who got sick. The ones where we know and understand the effects, and to ask how these could interact and combine to produce AIDS. One factor is the reactivation of a good number of such agents—EBV, CMV, HTLV-III. HTLV-III may be no more than another virus reactivated by the true cause of AIDS. There is no evidence that would say differently."

Sonnabend was not afraid to name names (which got him occasionally into political trouble): "Unlike what Dr. Anthony Fauci [the head of the National Institute of Allergy and Infectious Diseases (NIAID)] and Dr. Robert Gallo tell us, we are very far from understanding this disease. Very little is known. The sort of smugness that emanates from the government scientists is offensive, considering what's at stake and what is happening now. The only people who are pleased over this are the ones who've received millions of dollars' worth of support, and these are the government scientists and big medical centers and also people who really, I think, have missed the boat, who have an inordinate influence on media accessibility and are responsible, along with many others, for the panic that's going on now—and the disaster."

Sonnabend was from the school that believed the single virus theory was actually a ploy to take away the onus from the gay lifestyle—a theory that I have argued is also "homodemiological" and an essentially ironic betrayal of the gay community by a gay doctor. He told Adkins, "It's easier to say, bad luck, a virus hit. That's another reason why people might have favored the single virus theory. In the fullness of time, however, the virus did come, and we find the gay men who wanted it so much, now they've got it. And what they've also got is quarantine, and in fact the very thing they were fighting for is not so

75

wonderful." Why Sonnabend thought his own gay lifestyle theory was so helpful to the gay community always somehow escaped me throughout the epidemic. His absurd kind of loose talk (based on even looser reasoning) about what gay men *wanted* to be the cause, was very strange. That gay men, who, at that time, were basically chickens running around with their political heads cut off, could be accused of such a conscious monocausal conspiracy was a real stretch.

What was interesting about the way Sonnabend argued about causation was that it always questioned the motives of the theorizers and the social implications of the theory. One was held responsible for the political consequences of one's ideas about the cause of AIDS. At the time Sonnabend was open-minded about the possible involvement of African swine fever virus in AIDS, but not very enthusiastic because it too was *a single-virus theory* and hence it was—in his mind—politically dangerous. Sonnabend's thinking was typical of an environment in which one could easily be intimidated from telling the truth because the consequences of the inconvenient truth might be too horrible. I was getting very frustrated by this kind of thinking that had a strong whiff of emotional blackmail. I thought the only way out of the epidemic was through discovering and telling the raw factual truth without regard to political consequences. I didn't think politics would save a single patient if there was not a commitment to unvarnished, scientific facts and medical truth. I couldn't even bring up African swine fever virus to Sonnabend without him suggesting it was an idea that would lead to quarantine.

Because Sonnabend did not buy the government's party line on HTLV-III, he was gradually elbowed out of an AIDS organization and an AIDS journal that he had help start. The AIDS Medical Foundation, which he started with millionairess and scientific researcher Mathilde Krim, moved toward an alliance with the HTLV-III establishment at Harvard and the National Cancer Institute. Sonnabend resigned when the organization sent out an alarming press release by Terry Beirn, a man with a public relations background that Sonnabend had hired as the administrative director. The press release said, "Nobody is now safe from AIDS, it's on the loose." Sonnabend was offended that the press release suggested that AIDS was being casually transmitted. It broke Sonnabend's don't-scare-the-horses rule.

After his break from the Krim organization, Sonnabend grew increasingly dissatisfied with what Mathilde Krim was saying publicly about the epidemic and privately mocked her rather uptight and puritanical attitude toward sex. What I didn't like about her organization was that it was a private organization that took money from well-meaning people and then used it to basically back research into the exact same ideas that the government was promoting about AIDS. Over the years it increasingly seemed to me to be a very big part of the problem of the real epidemic rather than a solution. Her organization had essentially privatized the Big Assumption.

In the October 28 issue of *New York Native,* Ann Fettner wrote a piece about Douglas Feldman, a medical anthropologist who taught at New York University. He had visited the small African country of Rwanda in order to investigate its AIDS epidemic. Fettner reported that Feldman told her, "While green monkey skins are used for clothing, the animals aren't eaten (as alleged by the Centers for Disease Control head James O. Mason). About 20 percent of the population, however, eats pork when it's available. In the south around Butari, there is no pork left. All the pigs died about two years ago." He also said, "There was an epizootic in the south central region near Butari which has not been identified as to its cause," and "While I'm sure HTLV-III/LAV is necessary to AIDS, I'm not at all convinced that it is alone sufficient to cause this syndrome. I definitely have questions about differences in the rate of AIDS and antibody positives between the two areas of Rwanda. The death of pigs really has to be looked at now."

Even as it became clearer and clearer that HTLV-III was not the cause of AIDS, the social and biomedical agenda was proceeding throughout 1985 as though it was an incontrovertible fact. A new kind of professional was emerging: "the HTLV-III counselor." Orwell would have loved it. These were paid busybodies who would "educate" (that is "re-educate") people on how to live their lives if they tested positive for a virus that had not been shown to cause AIDS—by a highly unreliable test. Congress was only too willing to pay for this propaganda campaign. Senator Patrick Moynihan announced he wanted to spend 25 million dollars on "public education" about AIDS. "Public education" is one excellent way to keep the conventional wisdom of science carved in stone. "Public education" is one way to discredit and stigmatize doubt and dissidence.

Unfortunately, most so-called gay leaders were on the same page as the government. In the July 29 issue, I wrote an editorial about the director of the National Gay Task Force, titled, "Jeff Levi, the Nightmare":

> Anyone who reads this newspaper knows that there are many researchers who can't get sufficient money to do important research into treatments for AIDS. A conspiracy-minded person might actually see a deliberate attempt to create a medieval situation that will evoke draconian medieval solutions.
>
> We know that "treatment" is a dirty word for God's spokespeople on the New Right, and apparently a matter of indifference to the director of the Centers for Disease Control. We also know that the level of funding for research at the federal and state level, given the enormity of this public health problem, constitutes a sick joke.
>
> So what does Senator Daniel Patrick Moynihan propose to do? Instead of proposing a commitment of 25 million dollars for treatment research, he proposes the commitment of 25 million dollars for public education. How can anyone be against public education? It's as American as Mom and apple pie. And that's exactly our point: public education for a syndrome like AIDS often comes down to throwing mom and apple pie at a problem which should be addressed through vigorous research and by declaring a scientific war on the virus itself. Destabilize the virus, not American sexuality. Public education on AIDS comes down to a war against sex, and guess who always wins that one?
>
> According to Mark Bernstein of Moynihan's office, two of the biggest proponents of the legislation are Dr. James Curran of the CDC, who has botched everything he's touched for four years, and Jeff Levi, the acting director of The National Gay Task Force. Levi thinks that changing the sexual behavior of gay men is what NGTF should be doing to deal with the epidemic. Gay men got the message on that years ago. Levi should be demanding the development of serious, effective treatment for AIDS instead of falling into the New

Right trap of using prevention as a way of keeping America zipped up for Biblical reasons.

Bogus public education may win Jeff Levi a mom and apple pie constituency in D.C., but the rest of us, hopefully, can see though his antics. Levi may become a major New Right hero as the man who destroyed NGTF.

A clear picture of what was really happening was starting to form in my mind. In the August 11 issue, I went even further, in another editorial, titled "The United States of AIDS":

As things stand, the basic public health plan is to create a two-tier system in America of the sero-negative and the seropositive. All will be *counseled*. The seronegatives will be counseled to stay away from the time bombs.

Thus, there will be no freedom from AIDS. Either you will have it, or you will be in danger of getting it. A disease has been found with which to forge the most diabolical program of sexual control yet conceived by the very clever fascistic types in the public health service in collusion with God knows who else.

Life will cease to be life as we know it. It will be lived under the aegis of "protection and control" guidelines. One will not think of oneself as a human being, but as a member of a "risk group," a kind of caste with the biological mark of Cain. If one is gay, one will always be guilty of not "changing one's behavior" or "reducing one's risk" until proven innocent. And no matter how high the percentage of gay people who do buy into the "prevention and control" is, there will always be some auto-homophobic voice on a *Phil Donahue* show to say, "Oh, no, my friends haven't changed at all—they're still promiscuous." And "Tsk, tsk, you just can't change homosexuals through education." Then will come the attempts at treating the behavior itself, Soviet-style.

It's time for gay Americans to think of "counseling programs" as a kind of parole, and AIDS counselors as "parole officers." These people are the vehicles of sexual control. . . . They are the benign face of an evil social strategy that has been devised to put the gay community back in its place.

Only our deepest evolutionary political instincts will get us out of this one. Any heroes out there? Start creating new gay institutions. Don't get suckered into the National Gay Task Force or the Gay Men's Health Crisis approach to things. There are good and bad things about both organizations. But we need many more individually tailored, imaginative approaches to fight the New Right agenda on AIDS. And where are the Goddamned gay intellectuals?

I was to learn over the next quarter of a century that the phrase "gay intellectual" was kind of an oxymoron, at least where the epidemic was concerned. Those who could deconstruct Sondheim were not necessarily also able to decipher the horrific reality of the situation around them that had covertly transformed their community into biomedical dystopia. As Hannah Arendt said about Nazi Germany, "The purely personal problem was not what your enemies were doing but what your friends were doing."

Also in the August 11, 1985 issue, John Lauritsen, a Harvard-educated research analyst, who eventually wrote around 50 articles for *New York Native*, explored the role of poppers in AIDS. He reported, "Poppers are a liquid mixture of isobutyl nitrite and other chemicals, packaged in small bottles under such names as 'Rush,' 'Ram,' 'Thunderbolt,' 'Locker Room,' and 'Crypt Tonight.' . . . When inhaled just before orgasm, poppers seem to enhance and prolong the sensation. With regular use, poppers become a sexual crutch, and many gay men are incapable of having sex, even masturbation, without the aid of poppers. . . . In 1981, the Stanford Medical Laboratories tested different brands of poppers and found them to contain kerosene, hydrochloric acid, and sulfur dioxide, among other impurities."

Lauritsen criticized the FDA for not regulating poppers as a drug. They were allowed to be sold as room odorizers. In 1985, they were declared illegal. Lauritsen argued in the *Native* that scientists had known about the toxic effects of poppers for many years. Lauritsen did his own epidemiological survey: "In Massachusetts, where poppers have been banned for years, only 178 cases of AIDS had been reported as of May 6, 1985. In contrast there had been 3,756 cases in New York State, where poppers were sold legally in sex shops, baths, discos, and even smoke shops until this June." For Lauritsen, there was no question that poppers were involved in AIDS; the question was how much of a factor were they? He argued, "96-100 percent of the gay men with AIDS used poppers, usually quite heavily. These men were also heavy users of other 'recreational' drugs including amphetamines, cocaine, heroin, Quaaludes, LSD, barbituates, and ethyl chloride." He pointed to a study that had concluded that all men who had Kaposi's sarcoma had been poppers users and another study that correlated poppers use with immunological abnormalities. In one study of mice exposed to poppers, all the mice died. Another study showed that the T-4 cells which are depleted in AIDS patients could also be depleted by exposure to poppers. One of the things that poppers are capable of causing was cardiovascular collapse. Lauritsen mocked a local group of gay doctors called Physicians for Human Rights, who urged gay men not to use poppers or other recreational drugs because they could "impair your judgment." Even discussions about drug use had to be framed around the so-called AIDS virus, rather than the damage the drugs could do to the body all by themselves.

1986: A New Virus or a Renamed Old One?

By early 1986, the CDC was beginning to urge people—especially gay people—to be tested for antibodies to HTLV-III. James Curran, the director of the AIDS Task Force, visited New York on January 6 and called for massive HTLV-III testing because it was "the most important infection in the U.S. in adults." In our article on the matter, Barry Adkins reported, "Gay Men's Health Crisis Executive Director Richard Dunne and AIDS researcher Dr. John Beldekas of Boston University both told the *Native* there is no evidence to support Curran's conclusion." In the same *Native* article, Adkins also reported, "Curran said anyone who truly tests positive to LAV/HTLV-III antibody is infected with the virus. He explained that the virus is very difficult to isolate, and one third of those antibody-positive cases in which virus is not isolated are basically a fluke. Curran maintains that these people are actually infected. Dunne and Beldekas later told the *Native* that Curran's statements were inherently homophobic. Disagreeing with Curran's statistics, Dunne said that in 40 percent of antibody-positive cases, the virus is unable to be isolated. Beldekas explained that in order to isolate the virus from lymphocytes, scientists must create an 'artificial in vitro condition,' which is then manipulated by various drugs, creating an unnatural situation. According to Beldekas, there is no clinical data to support Curran's theory, and Curran is making a 'quantum leap from antibody to infection.' " Curran also told Adkins that while he had some problems with contact tracing, he would not necessarily rule it out as an option. At that point the New York City Health Department said there were no plans for HTLV-III contact tracing.

During that same period, the Texas Board of Health was considering measures to quarantine people with AIDS, "if he or she has certain circumstances which create a threat to the public health if not immediately controlled." In an interview with the *Native*'s John Fall, published in the January 20, 1986, issue, the Texas commissioner of Health, Dr. Robert Bernstein, said that a quarantined person with AIDS who was still "having sex with the public would remain in medical isolation until this behavior changes."

Among the media organizations in 1986, the *New York Native* was virtually alone in questioning the orthodox notion that HTLV-III was the cause of AIDS. The lockstep that would characterize the media during the epidemic had begun. Even the *Village Voice*, which most people erroneously think of as anti-establishment and pro-gay, adopted an aggressive policy of trusting and supporting the government's scientific pronouncements about the epidemic. (Most people forget that the *Village Voice* actually had to be dragged kicking and screaming into its support of gay civil rights issues.) Early that year a *Village Voice* writer named Anna Mayo tried to start writing critically about AIDS, but she was discouraged by a gay writer at the *Village Voice* named Richard Goldstein. She called me at the *Native* and told me that she had written an article on AIDS called "The Principle of Uncertainty," which her editor at the *Voice*, Robert Friedman, was refusing to publish. She also told me that Goldstein was trying to manipulate the situation at the paper so that she would never write about AIDS. While I hadn't agreed with many of Mayo's ideas on AIDS, the suppression of her writing concerned me. I agreed to publish the article, and on the March 10 *Native* cover, we showed a bound-and-gagged woman in a *Village Voice* T-shirt with the headline, "The Article the *Village Voice* Suppressed Begins on Page 15."

Mayo's piece was a look at several alternative theories about the cause of AIDS. She examined Dr. Ernest Sternglass's hypothesis that AIDS is caused by "interactive exposure to radiation during the nuclear weapons tests in the 1950s and '60s." She reported on Sternglass's visit to an AIDS conference in Europe at which he presented his ideas to Robert Gallo. Sternglass told Mayo that Gallo had eventually taken him seriously, but Mayo had her doubts: "Gallo come around? I didn't believe it for a minute. Gallo works for the National Cancer Institute, one of the National Institutes of Health (NIH). Any halfway smart government scientist knows enough not to propose an investigation of radiation effects. (If you work for the nuclear state, you sign an unwritten nuclear loyalty oath.) And Gallo could have other motives for not subscribing to Sternglass's theory. It could appear to him as a challenge to the dogma that AIDS is caused by HTLV-III, which Gallo claims to have discovered. . . . Gallo sits on the review committees for grants and makes recommendations for government jobs and contracts to private industry. He's said to hanker after a Nobel Prize for discovering the cause of AIDS. But what if some other virus were shown to be the cause of AIDS and HTLV-III were reduced to the status of a mere marker? Prizes might slip from Gallo's grasp."

Mayo interviewed Gallo, who told her that at first he thought Sternglass was just another "nut." But he said that later in the evening he realized that Sternglass was a serious person, but didn't know anything about AIDS. Predictably, Gallo yelled at Mayo, "HTLV-III is the sole cause of AIDS! There's no question about it. You don't need any cofactors. It gives you AIDS all alone." Then came my favorite part of her article: "His [Gallo's] tone turned ugly. 'This guy Sternglass sounds like Chuck Ortleb, the editor of the *New York Native*. Do you realize Ortleb has actually persuaded the government to spend money on this ridiculous swine flu [sic] idea?' Gallo continued, 'At first I thought Ortleb must be mentally off, but I talked to some gay leaders in New York—no, I can't say who—and they explained to me that he is just out to make money selling newspapers. Now I can understand that mentality, but I don't want to have anything to do with that sort of journalist. You're not one of them, are you?'"

In the same article, Mayo examined the fact that HTLV-III had not fulfilled Koch's postulates, which are generally accepted as necessary to prove that an organism causes a disease. She pointed out that a high percentage of AIDS patients do not have HTLV-III in their blood, and that health care workers who had become infected with the virus had not developed the disease. She also explored the African swine fever virus hypothesis. She quoted Jane Teas as saying, "I think HTLV-III may be an endogenous virus. That is, in a latent state, it has been present in most of us from birth. When swine fever or some other virus weakens the immune system, HTLV-III appears."

Mayo also examined the theory that the use of oral recreational drugs was the original cause of AIDS, as well as the Sonnabend theory that repeated viral infections weakened the immune system. She also brought up the Belle Glade, Florida researcher, Dr. Mark Whiteside's idea that HTLV-III was just a marker for AIDS. He thought the disease was caused by an insect-borne arbovirus. He told Mayo, "In Belle Glade where they have neither homosexuality nor heterosexual promiscuity, the disease is passed by insects that breed in open sewers and at night enter windows that have neither screen nor glass."

When we asked for a comment from the *Village Voice* editor, about the failure to publish Mayo's piece, Robert Friedman told us, "I felt that the end product was too speculative. It didn't convince me. The alternative theories [presented] did not completely undercut the HTLV-III [case], which I'm not particularly wedded to myself. It is well-written and entertaining. I just had qualms about printing it."

One of the jobs of future historians of the epidemic will be to try and track down all the articles critical of the AIDS establishment that were not published because of editorial "qualms."

Three years after she first proposed the hypothesis that AIDS is caused by African swine fever virus, Jane Teas succeeded in testing her hypothesis in an American laboratory. With her husband, epidemiologist James Hebert, and Boston University researcher John Beldekas, she obtained viral testing materials from the U.S. Department of Agriculture. It was only because the press (mostly the *Native*) had taken an interest in the matter that the USDA cooperated. Teas, Beldekas, and Hebert used two kinds of tests to detect African swine fever in AIDS sera: one called hemadsorption technique and one called direct immunofluorescence. They tested the blood of 21 people with AIDS, 12 with lymphadenopathy and 16 controls. Using the direct immunofluorescence test, ten of the 21 AIDS patients, 4 of the people with lymphadenopathy, and one of the 16 controls tested positive. The team submitted their results, in the form of a letter, to the British Medical Journal, *The Lancet*, and the letter was published on March 8, 1986. The authors concluded that they had "found evidence consistent with African swine fever virus (ASFV) infection in the plasma of U.S. patients with Acquired Immunodeficiency Syndrome (AIDS) and lymphadenopathy syndrome." They were cautious about the interpretation of their findings: "The results of these various tests suggest the presence of a hitherto unknown virus in these cell cultures. ASFV has not been thought to be infectious to humans or known to occur in U.S. swine. Therefore, these results point either to an anomaly of the testing procedures by cross-reactivity with some unknown AIDS-associated virus, or they suggest a new variant of ASFV that is infectious to people." The Teas team criticized the prior testing that had been reported on in *The Lancet* because the "sample sizes were very small (seven and eight patients), sera were only examined for antibodies. Since ASFV infects only an estimated 1 percent of macrophages at any one time, large sample sizes, special target assay systems, and several tests may be required to show an effect if a true relationship between ASFV and AIDS exists."

"Is the Reign of Error Over?" was the headline we gave the story about their research on the March 17 cover of the *Native*. In the article I wrote about their findings, I brought up the issue of potential litigation which may have caused some of the hesitation in researching the connection between African swine fever virus and AIDS: "One possible issue of medical liability may involve the recommendation that the USDA makes when a country is exterminating its pigs [because of ASFV]. The recommendations include urging people to consume the infected pigs to speed up the disposal process. A USDA source told us that many Brazilian newspapers told people not to eat pigs infected with African swine fever virus, for fear that human illness would result. The *Native* has also been told by another source in touch with a retired American meat industry executive that there have been three outbreaks of African swine fever in the United States, in the 1940s, the 1950s, and the early 1970s. The retired executive told the *Native* that the outbreaks were described as a different disease at the time. The unnamed USDA official further told the *Native* that one additional problem which is occurring around swine fever is that the Animal Plant Health Inspection Service, the agency responsible for detecting the presence of swine fever, now lacks the competence to detect the disease in the United States."

I also underlined the fact that we had been told that the USDA had data from slaughterhouse surveys of pigs to indicate that pigs in New York, New Jersey, and Texas has been exposed to African swine fever virus. I also wrote that the question before Congress and the media should be "whether the Centers for Disease Control has been aware of the connection between AIDS and African swine fever since the inception of the AIDS epidemic. Because African swine fever resembles cytomegalovirus (CMV) in appearance, it is possible the CDC made an honest error. The CDC has informed the *Native* that their antibody testing for African swine fever virus in 1983 had negative results. But a memo [about the tests] obtained from a CDC file could more accurately be described as inconclusive. Of 16 AIDS patients from San Francisco, three showed some positive reactions for antibody to the virus. A USDA official who asked not to be named has told the *Native* that such results merited additional testing. USDA literature warns that cautious and thorough testing must be done on herds of pigs for African swine fever virus. In pigs, African swine fever virus has sometimes been misdiagnosed as porcine CMV as well as several other diseases. A manual on African swine fever virus contains the following warning: 'Even with good samples, no single test is sufficient. . . . For instance, accurate diagnosis for the acute and chronic phases of African Swine Fever require different tests. In addition, it's now felt that different strains of the virus exist, which are not detected by every test.' "

I again reminded *Native* readers that Judy Petsonk, a reporter for *South Jersey Courier Post*, had interviewed the CDC's James Curran and he had told her "he was afraid that Teas's theory might make people afraid to eat pork, thus harming the pork industry in the United States."

In April, one of our readers sent me a clipping of a column by Ben Stein that appeared in the March 25 issue of the *Los Angeles Herald Examiner*. I suspected that historians would look back on the column as perhaps the first time a journalist inadvertently had picked up on the fact that a chronic form of African swine fever was manifesting itself as an illness in the general population that was eventually called "chronic fatigue syndrome." If it was ASFV, it was spreading throughout the human population in America in exactly the way you would expect it to, manifesting itself in a wide variety of ways as it wrought evolving multisystemic pathologies on its new vulnerable human population. Stein wrote that it seemed to him that everyone in Los Angeles seemed to be sick at the time. People would develop a flu which lasted two weeks and then they would recover. But then a few weeks later they would get sick again. He described "a vague, spaced-out feeling, chronic fatigue just over your shoulder, always breathing down on you, a susceptibility to wild upsets of the bowels all became part of daily life." Stein complained that even though an incurable flu seemed to be spreading throughout Los Angeles, no one was doing anything about it. Public health officials were silent. (That silence would become deafening over the next three decades.)

Stein also wrote, "Already my friends in the East tell me the non-stop flu has hit Washington and New York in a big way. This nation can be genuinely disabled by these incurable diseases. The individuals who have them are severely pained, physically and psychically. Having the flu half your life hurts, take it from me. Can anyone help? Isn't this worthy of national attention? Are we just going to have the stock market go up forever while everyone gets incurable viruses? I'm scared."

In an editorial on Stein's article, in the April 14 issue of *New York Native*, I wrote, "We have warned the Centers for Disease Control, New York State Health Commissioner David Axelrod, the City of New York, gay leaders, Congressmen Ted Weiss and Henry Waxman, and several members of the scientific press about the implications of finding African swine fever in 'AIDS' patients. Any sober expert on swine fever would immediately worry out loud that 'AIDS' is just the tip of the swine fever iceberg and that the virus doesn't select hosts by means of their sexual proclivities, and the disease would be much more widespread in the general population in a matter of time. . . . Swine fever doesn't only cause 'AIDS' in pigs. It can cause chronic respiratory problems for life. And swine fever is not spread only through the kinds of sex that give the geniuses at the Centers for Disease Control hard-ons and hate-ons."

I also reminded our readers about the positive ASFV results that turned up in the New York State testing of blood from blood donors in New York City: "In this population the African swine fever virus antibody is present in 4.5% (5 out of 110) of the population. Moreover, 26 blood samples from that group had what is called 'atypical fluorescence,' which the state did not consider positive. We've said before that they may be playing with fire, because these results suggest to us that African swine fever may be presently infecting the general population of New York City." I concluded my piece by stating, "I certainly wouldn't like to be the one to have to tell the people of Los Angeles that the result of the cover-up of the connection between AIDS and African swine fever is that the entire city of Los Angeles is running around infected with a chronic pig disease. Those people who laugh about our exposé of the swine fever cover-up may soon have to look elsewhere for a chuckle."

"Soon" of course turned out to be another example of my excessive optimism.

It took me a while to track down Ben Stein on the phone. When I finally reached him in Malibu and explained what I thought was going on, he seemed polite enough. But several weeks later he wrote a nasty piece in the right wing publication called *The American Spectator* which, without naming me, mocked me and the things I had told him. He also misrepresented what I had said to him on the phone.

We reported, in the same issue, on a documentary which was filmed by WGBH of Boston as part of its Frontline series. The documentary's filmmakers had followed a man with AIDS who was destitute and dying. The man continued to have sex after he was diagnosed with AIDS. It was a highly inflammatory film which clearly was meant to turn the public against people with AIDS and like most of what was written or said on TV during that period, was meant to equate the AIDS epidemic with the gay citizenry. In a story in the *Native* by Allen Barnett and Barry Adkins, Richard Dunne of Gay Men's Health Crisis said it was "the single worst media representation of gay in recent years." He also said, "You don't frame a discussion of public policy around one aberrant example. People will walk away from this program thinking that this man was spreading AIDS. The program will only lead to discussion of quarantine, for that is the only point of reference in the film."

The film, which was made in gay-friendly Texas, focused on a twenty-year-old man named Fabian Bridge, an African-American man who was warned by gay people in Houston not to have anything to do with the film crew. Sue Lowell, the head of the Gay Political Caucus in Houston, told our reporters, "The film crew left town and left a lapful of problems in a town where gay activists are overworked." She also told *New York Native* that the controversy inspired the Texas Commissioner of Public Health to attempt to gain authority to implement quarantine-like measures in isolated cases. That was the constructive way the media worked with public health authorities during the epidemic. Even the so-called liberal media.

In that same issue of the *Native,* Anne-Christine d'Adesky began a two-part series called "Haiti: The Great AIDS Cover-Up." She reported that, two months after Jean-Claude "Baby Doc" Duvalier was overthrown, doctors began to freely discuss how they had been kept from speaking publicly about the true nature of the AIDS epidemic in that country. She reported that AIDS was actually first diagnosed in Haiti in 1978, *putting it closer to the time that African swine fever broke out in pigs in that country.* For a proper historical reconstruction of the true nature of the AIDS epidemic, it was of great interest that she noted the majority of those with AIDS in Haiti "do not fall into any Centers for Disease Control defined 'high risk' category. Only 40% could have gotten AIDS from bisexual contact (for men) or as blood transfusion (mostly women). Only 10% have Kaposi's sarcoma (KS), while 40% have tuberculosis (mycobacterium TB) or other opportunistic infections. In addition, a higher percentage of women have AIDS in Haiti than in the U.S., and some say that they may pass it on to men."

An organization called GHESKIO, a Haitian study group on Kaposi's sarcoma and opportunistic infections, that had been formed in 1982 in collaboration with doctors at Cornell University in New York, may have inadvertently provided evidence that HTLV-III was not the cause of AIDS. According to d'Adesky, "GHESKIO used the ELISA test to verify presence of HTLV-III antibodies in people's blood. 40% of the patients tested were negative." This should have alerted authorities in our own country that something was seriously wrong with the HTLV-III hypothesis, but unfortunately the etiological train had left the station.

In the following issue of the *Native*, d'Adesky continued her report from Haiti with a story about a former political figure in Haiti who, during the pig eradication program, had been hiding pigs in his home, suggesting that African swine fever may never have been fully eradicated from pigs in that country. It left open the possibility that if ASFV was the actual source of AIDS, that there were still porcine reservoirs of virus that could endanger human health.

On April 21, the *New York Native* published one of its most revealing pieces on the real nature of the fake epidemiology that the CDC was then doing on AIDS and the same kind of epidemiology they would eventually do on chronic fatigue syndrome. "A Place to Die and a Drink of Water," by Ann Fettner, asked, "why the CDC was studying AIDS in Belle Glade when they've already decided to ignore the facts." The CDC investigated the epidemic in the small, poverty-stricken Florida community in order to put to rest the suspicion that AIDS was spread in ways that the CDC had not informed the public about. Fettner described the investigation in a brutal, uncompromising manner: "In lockstep with local health authorities, the CDC is busy predetermining exactly the results it will find in the four-month epidemiological survey currently underway. This is cosmetics, a public relations initiative to rescue the town's reputation while furthering the CDC's control over the shaping of the epidemic. Epidemiology it isn't. They're after sexual and drug use transmission, and any evidence of an unusual cofactor will be sidestepped."

According to Fettner, what the CDC didn't like was "too many non-identifiable risk (NIR) cases" of AIDS which threatened their prevailing paradigm. The CDC wouldn't believe people who said that did not fit into the official gay or drug-taking risk groups. Darlene Lee, the Chief Nursing Officer at a clinic in Belle Glade, made fun of the CDC's sex and drug presumptions to Fettner: " 'There's something about their lifestyles that they're hiding, you keep getting that. They're all closet homosexuals or shooting up,' she says sarcastically. 'We have 25 people right now who're in their 50s and 60s; nowhere else are they seeing these 50- and 60-year-olds, and I'm saying, Sure! They're turning tricks on the side!' "

Fettner reported, "When the CDC surveyed 250 people from the poor southwest neighborhood in Belle Glade, the overall rate was 8% positive. Belle Glade proper was 11% positive in the CDC pilot study, and 60% of all the positives had no risk factors." What a high percentage of the patients did have, according to Fettner, was a significant percentage of insect-borne viruses. Mark Whiteside, a physician who treated patients in Belle Glade told Fettner, "It's incredible that we should still be arguing about NIR [No Identifiable Risk] cases . . . . The disease is not explained by heterosexual transmission in the NIR patients, none of whom have had sex with members of so-called high-risk groups. . . . We're seeing non-characteristic disease and in general it's not explained by heterosexual transmission. For example, I have a 56-year-old woman who has been married for 27 years to her 77-year-old husband. He's healthy, exonerative for HTLV-III. They've had no outside sexual contact—none, zero—and she now has AIDS manifested by disseminated histoplasmosis. Her only chance for a risk is a blood transfusion in 1981." But Fettner reported they tracked all the donors and they were negative for the virus. Interestingly, Whiteside told Fettner "She lives in the same apartment as two other AIDS cases, including one of our original NIR cases, a 30-some-year-old who had fewer than ten lifetime sexual partners and had lived with a woman for seven years—and the woman is still healthy. He's dead."

The health care workers who were seeing inconvenient things the CDC didn't want people to know about were treated in the way most people were when they came in contact with any of the abnormal science of the epidemic. The nurse, Darlene Lee, said, "Everything is fine as long as you don't make waves. You do as you're told and as long as you comply with everything they want, it's okay. But when you're a little bit independent or start asking questions—or God forbid, you do something on your own and try to help these people!" Whiteside and his colleague, according to Fettner, were "perceived by the CDC as an annoyance, objects of ridicule because of their insistence that more is going on in Belle Glade than is explained by the CDC party line. The two physicians had done a door-to-door survey and came up "with 9% positive for HTLV-III, and most did not have an identifiable risk factor."

In her *Native* piece on Belle Glade, Fettner also reported the shocking story of Gus Sermos who had been a CDC surveillance officer for two-and-one-half years in Florida. When Sermos started to raise some serious questions about what was going on in the CDC's

AIDS efforts in Florida, it inspired an investigative series of articles in the *Miami Herald*, and he was punished by being summarily transferred back to a temporary assignment at the CDC's headquarters in Atlanta, in what appeared to be a humiliating demotion. Sermos had suggested that CDC AIDS funds were not being properly used. He told Fettner that while on the job in Florida, he had "uncovered fraud and mismanagement, cavalier attitudes on the part of the CDC, and general lying and cheating." He also told Fettner, "They hired me to do surveillance, but I found out that wasn't what they wanted at all. They didn't want to know anything about what's going on. [CDC AIDS officials] Curran or Jaffe come down and all they want to talk about is fishing, not AIDS. When I started in Florida, I had one supervisor. Then there were two, then three—this raft of people doing nothing but waiting for my reports to come in."

But those Sermos reports were not appreciated. According to Fettner, he said it was like, "I was digging manure and putting it on their plates." He told her, "90% of what they're doing up in Atlanta is public relations. For AIDS there're four people in the field and 40 in Atlanta. If all they're doing with AIDS is lying about it, creating subterfuge, then why not disband them? He described the scientists working on AIDS with Curran and Jaffe in Atlanta as "a bunch of kids right out of medical school, because it's politically so unhealthy to get involved with the CDC AIDS Task Force that older doctors with experience don't want anything to do with it."

One of the epidemiologically embarrassing things that Sermos uncovered in his surveillance was the presence of older people in Florida who had AIDS *without risk factors*, which was clearly a threat to the CDC's AIDS paradigm. Sermos was accused of not asking strong enough questions to prove that the people really did belong in the CDC's politically crafted risk groups. He told Fettner, "I'll tell you the truth, in my wildest dreams I would never have thought they'd get away with what those guys have gotten away with as far as just being, if nothing else, just being bad showmen. And for forgetting that the show has any substance. Basically it's like an old vaudeville show that's been running too long. I can't believe that house of cards in Atlanta can just stand up and take all the wind. But boy, evidently—I've told my wife and I hate admitting it—but they are totally impervious to anything. If you say something disagreeable, you're either unpatriotic or you're a kook. . . . I'm like a citizen who sees a robber running out of the store and calls the cops, and the police arrest you and lock you up for reporting a crime. I wasn't going to be a whore for them; I felt like I was a guard at Auschwitz, a traitor. But they're traitors to their profession and [James] Curran [head of the CDC's Task Force on AIDS] is not a scientist by any definition. He should be selling cars like his father."

What is so uncanny about his story is that his description of the CDC's behavior in the investigation of AIDS would be echoed in everything the CDC eventually did in its fake investigation of chronic fatigue syndrome. The fact that the CDC was able to behave this way for three decades shows that powerful institutional forces were keeping Sermos's so-called house of cards safely in place. It may have seemed like a "vaudeville" act, but we have to remind ourselves that there were those in Germany who didn't think the Nazi leaders would amount to much because they resembled clowns.

What made these Sermos revelations so historically important was that for the first time word was publicly coming from *an insider* that there was something rotten in Denmark. People on the outside with growing doubts about the integrity of the CDC and its story about AIDS were *not crazy*. Everything about what happened to him lends support to the notion that what could be called totalitarian or abnormal science (as well as "homodemiology") had already become the official culture of AIDS. The CDC didn't want to know what was really going on. Or they did know all too well and they didn't want the public to know the truth. To borrow a notion from Hannah Arendt, they had manufactured a false epidemiological image of what was going on and used powerful public relations resources to make it the conventional wisdom for America and the rest of the world. An honest, courageous man warned the world from inside the belly of a authoritarian beast that public health had turned itself into something evil. His reference to "Auschwitz" was downright prophetic.

In the April 28 issue of *New York Native,* Fettner again addressed the quality of the CDC's epidemiology. She wrote, "The days I spent recently in Belle Glade, Florida, have left an even more sour taste in my mouth than usual over the mishandling and manipulation of the AIDS epidemic by the federal Centers for Disease Control in Atlanta. Because there can be little question that the two tenured AIDS experts down there, Drs. James Curran and Harold Jaffe, have insufficient stature to be guiding such important matters, it's obviously been someone like Dr. James Mason (who you may recall served as acting

Assistant Secretary for Health and Human Services while still head of the CDC, and who is back in Atlanta now) who's running the show, with directions from someone near the President or whoever does his AIDS-thinking for him)." Any definitive understanding of the history of the epidemic will ultimately have to take a close forensic look at the chain of command in the White House and the source(s) of that political "AIDS-thinking." She also wrote, "The function of the CDC is to do epidemiology. One wonders if they know what that means. Originally 'epidemiology' meant the study of epidemics, but its definition has grown broader and includes tracking outbreaks of poisonings, keeping track of non-communicable diseases, and developing statistics about the whos, wheres, and hows of such as automobile fatalities, mental illness, cancer, and communicable diseases. Basically, one can sum up the function of epidemiology in three major variables: Person, Place and Time. When it comes to communicable diseases, there are certainties about each that need to be known. The CDC long ago exhausted its imagination by designating the Person category to gays, junkies, hookers, a few hemophiliacs, transfusion recipients, etc. All others—including Africans—are in the 'unknown risk factor' category. The *real* risk factors, as promulgated by the CDC, are gay sex and dirty needles. This has cast AIDS into a category that transcends the category of 'virus' and lays the disease on the doorstep of 'misbehavior,' which is the way it is often perceived worldwide."

Fettner asserted, "Epidemiologists should report what they find. Period. Not as Jaffe recently did in Belle Glade, predict what they will find, which implies they're looking to prove certain presuppositions. And certainly, epidemiology should not define the social aspects of a disease."

Fettner was more than right that this was "social" epidemiology that had been politically engineered by social insiders about social outsiders. And she was only looking at the tip of an iceberg. It had nothing remotely to do with attentiveness to factual reality. It imposed categories on inconvenient reality and just snipped off any unsightly loose ends that threatened to reveal the truth about the real epidemic.

In the May 5 *Native*, Fettner reported on a journalism conference she attended at the Harvard School of Public Health. There she encountered scientists and reporters who expressed a great deal of contempt for the *Native*. Although Fettner had not covered the ASFV story herself, she was attacked for the *Native*'s coverage of the Teas ASFV hypothesis. Larry Kessler, a Boston AIDS activist, angrily held up a copy of the *Native* after Fettner gave a talk on AIDS reporting and he charged that the *Native* was alarming his "clients." According to Fettner, Harvard AIDS researcher, Jerome Groopman, made a point of announcing to the assembled that ASFV was "not the cause of AIDS because the cause of AIDS is known." *Boston Globe* reporter Judy Forman said that her paper has not reported on Jane Teas's findings of ASFV in AIDS patients because "We decided it was a lot of crap."

Fettner summed up her feelings about the AIDS groupthink that was hardening in cement at that point: "In no other area of science of which I am aware does such an absolute lock of the orthodox philosophy prevail as it does in AIDS. A siege mentality holds fast against opposing views and alternative theories, and those proposing such, regardless of their scientific credentials, are viewed as being part of the lunatic fringe. Not only is this in the remarkably tight scientific circles that have conspired to co-opt research, but also in the reporting on the disease. So restrictive and exclusive has been the formulation of these cadres that no influential person outside these walls has come forward to insist on the legitimacy of alternative ideas. Many privately voice concern over the AIDS 'lockstep,' but fear putting themselves in the position of being branded fringe lunatics—scornfully if they are of marginal reputation, by innuendo if they have an affiliation deemed 'respectable' or susceptible to retaliation."

In the May 26 issue, we published news of what I thought was going to be a real game changer. A story I wrote began, "A potentially important clue in the AIDS epidemic has been discovered by researcher Jane Teas in Belle Glade, Florida. Pigs. Sick pigs. . . . In late April, Teas and [her husband James] Hebert visited Belle Glade to gather ticks, which they intended to have tested to determine if they were carrying African swine fever virus. The spread of AIDS in Belle Glade has been attributed to other factors besides sexual practices and drug use there. Even researchers from the Centers for Disease Control have been quoted as saying that there may be other factors involved in Belle Glade."

I reported, "Teas and Hebert discovered a small pig farm just outside Belle Glade, where they saw between 60 and 80 pigs, some of which were extremely thin and sickly. Are the pigs infected with African swine fever virus? While that remains to be determined by the

U.S. Department of Agriculture, the *Native* has received an unconfirmed report that the pigs in Belle Glade are testing positive for antibodies to HTLV-III."

In the June 9 issue of the paper, I reported on new developments in Belle Glade: "After three years and three months of attempting to bring the connection between AIDS and African swine fever to the world's attention, researcher Dr. Jane Teas may finally have outmaneuvered top officials at the United States Department of Agriculture who have stood in the way of her research. . . . What Dr. Teas found in Belle Glade only substantiated her theory that the solution to the AIDS riddle may be found in part of the world's pig population. She discovered a small dirt-poor farm on which there were 150 pigs. Many of the pigs were sickly, scrawny and dying. The owner of the farm, Ed Wilcox, told Teas that a lot of pigs had died a few months before her visit."

I reported that Teas, along with her husband, James Hebert, and local Belle Glade physician, Mark Whiteside, took blood and tissue samples from the pigs which Jane brought back to Boston and they were subsequently examined by Dr. John Beldekas of Boston University. Teas told me, "The internal organs of several of the slaughtered pigs had lesions that are characteristic of African swine fever."

Beldekas was able to test the pig blood for both ASFV and the so-called AIDS retrovirus, HTLV-III. I reported that Beldekas tested 16 blood samples for ASFV and nine blood samples for HTLV-III. Nearly all of the blood showed positivity by western blot for HTLV-III, and one out of the 16 blood samples tested positive in two different antigen tests for ASFV. Because ASFV is extremely infectious but difficult to detect, if one pig tests positive for the virus, the whole herd is assumed to be infected."

I had notified the USDA of the findings and a veterinarian in Belle Glade was asked to collect pig blood to send to the USDA Plum Island testing facility. I was dismayed that only two samples were being sent to the USDA. I also urged the USDA to take some of the swine blood that Beldekas had found to be positive for HTLV-III and ASFV to see if they could replicate his results. I reported, "On Thursday, May 22, samples arrived at Plum Island. On Tuesday, May 27, the Animal and Plant Health Inspection Service (APHIS) announced to the press that one of the samples tested positive for antibodies to ASFV. It was the same blood sample that tested positive for ASFV antigen in Beldekas's lab."

I notified Jon Nordheimer of the *New York Times* Miami bureau and Keith Schneider of the Washington bureau and both subsequently wrote stories on the ASFV development for the *Times*. APHIS was caught playing games when one APHIS official implied that he would have been nervous about ASFV if the Belle Glade pigs had shown signs of diarrhea, and maintained that the pigs *did not*. A Belle Glade veterinarian, however, told the *Times* that the sick pigs *did have diarrhea*. In addition, Teas and Beldekas, as well as Whiteside, had told me that they had observed that some of the pigs had bloody diarrhea when they had visited the Belle Glade farm—often a telltale sign of African swine fever.

In that same issue, we published a document which I think historians may someday call the smoking gun of the ASFV-AIDS hypothesis. Anne-Christine d'Adesky, who had previously written about the AIDS situation in Haiti, was given a three-inch file of documents on Haiti by a political activist. She reported that among the documents she "came across a memo written to officials at the Haitian Ministry of Agriculture in Damien (outside Port-au-Prince), regarding their participation in the national African swine fever eradication program begun in late 1979. . . . In the memo members of the rural Haitian district of Desforges questioned the plan to kill Haitian pigs and stated that a high number of human deaths from a mysterious fever posed a more immediate threat to their communities. The letter confirms earlier press reports that the Duvalier government ignored information regarding a link between African swine fever and AIDS, [which] developed in the region at the same time."

New York Native published a photocopy of the explosive memo which was sent from several Haitian community councils to the Haitian Minister of Agriculture. The memo began, "Desforges is located 10 km east of the township of Bombardopolis. In the area it rains approximately one month a year, rarely two months. From September to the beginning of the month of February, we have buried three (3) persons every day, all victims of a fever which still persists in the community."

The memo complained that the people in that area of Haiti relied on pigs for financial support. The memo also noted that pigs "allow us to send our children to school, to buy food . . . when hunger sets in." The councils were concerned about "a rumor that all our pigs must be killed before the beginning of March." The councils asked that only pigs that appeared to be sick would be exterminated, something that ran counter to the USDA recommendation that all the Haitian pigs had to be presumed infected or susceptible and therefore had to be killed. The most disturbing and perhaps revealing part of the memo said, "From September to date we have been burying people not pigs, we wonder whether there will be a plan to kill the sick people also. We would like to know what we will live off of when all the pigs have been killed?"

While the memo reflected desperation about how they would survive without the pigs, it also might constitute some kind of inadvertent basic epidemiology indicating that ASFV may have crossed the zoonotic threshold and might have become a human infection. Had officials identified ASFV as the cause of the 1979 deaths mentioned in the Haitian memo, Jane Teas might not have had to fight a losing battle with the USDA and the CDC for over half a decade in a battle to show the AIDS-ASFV connection. The question for forensic historians of the epidemic will be whether those Haitian deaths were the real beginning of the AIDS epidemic in the Western Hemisphere.

On June 23, Robert Gallo was back on the cover of *New York Native*. The headline was "Science's Greatest Living Performer" and the piece provided more evidence that Gallo is one of science's most amazing pathological liars. Ann Giudici Fettner interviewed scientists who worked with Gallo but were afraid to be identified. She wrote, "As you read the following, the result of speaking with several scientists involved with AIDS research at the National Institutes of Health (NIH), it will become apparent why going against the power base is professionally and politically dangerous." About the ongoing battle over who had discovered the so-called AIDS virus, Montagnier or Gallo, she wrote, "Behind the scenes the whole business has generated some extremely hard feelings among the researchers and others involved. What appears in the medical journals for instance, would seem to be merely results of research. Research is reported on, of course, but underlying the selection of data is what seems to be a granite-like agenda to distort the realities of the epidemic into a single theory which increasingly does not hold water. It's as if there are two disparate versions of the disease. One is a research version, the other a clinical version, and the two often have little relationship. Much of this started when the virus was misclassified as belonging to the human T-cell leukemia virus family."

Fettner quoted one anonymous source as saying, "The story is clear to anyone who looks at it rationally. Montagnier—as stupid as he is, and he's a petty little man—the only reason he's still alive today is because Gallo kept him alive. Montagnier discovered a unique virus, but he didn't have the guts to characterize it as his own. He wanted Gallo to hold his hand. So he sent the virus to Gallo twice. First of all, Gallo didn't get it. Then the French produced a bill of lading showing that [Gallo's assistant] Popovic in his lab signed for it. So that's lie number one. Lie number two is that he couldn't get it to grow. That lie has been exposed because of the electron micrograph." (An electron micrograph is a picture of an organism taken through a microscope.)

The source also insisted to Fettner that Gallo calling the French virus a form of "HTLV" was just a ploy to get credit for the discovery. The source also told Fettner, "Now the lie is that he got it to grow but [Gallo argued that] it didn't grow very well. The fact that the sequences are unique proves that's also a lie. They were guilty of intellectual arrogance. They thought since [Montagnier's] virus grew the best—though they had 40 others—they'd just use it; the world would never know the difference."

Fettner also documented the corrupt, authoritarian mess that professional scientific publishing was turning into during the epidemic. She wrote, "One of the major complaints heard from numerous scientists not part of the 'old-boy' network between NIH/NCI/Harvard is the impossibility of getting anything that relates to AIDS published by *Science*. Gallo is routinely called upon to review such papers, and a negative response from him evidently dooms the chance of publication. By the same token, papers from coevals, despite pertinent criticism from reviewers, are slid right through. It is unfortunate that examples of this told to me are from those who would put themselves in jeopardy if the specific cases in point were detailed."

Fettner was one of the first journalists to warn the world about the dangerous power of Robert Gallo. Just as importantly, she was also onto the moral culpability of the rest of the apathetic and morally insensitive scientific community that just let Gallo go his merry way. She concluded her piece noting, "Other scientists laugh when asked about Gallo's patent miscategorizing HTLV-III in the wrong family. Is that funny? I don't think so. Many are defensive when the subject of Montagnier's virus comes up . . . . Meanwhile, millions of lives are at stake as Gallo continues to play games." A middle-aged heterosexual woman with children, Ann Giudici Fettner was not particularly sensitive to the dynamics of heterosexism that may have lurked beneath nervous laughter of the scientists, but she deserves a great deal of credit for noticing that something was seriously out of whack in the scientific community as a whole. Fettner didn't live long enough to see just how many lives Gallo's antics would ultimately cost, but her reporting certainly contributed to a growing awareness that we were entering a period of totalitarian and abnormal science.

On July 22, Phil Donahue hosted a panel of guests on his talk show that discussed the topic of AIDS in the workplace. Near the end of the show, inspired by all the stories about AIDS and African swine fever (and showing the impact the *Native* had on the issue), he asked, "What about pork?" Dr. Mathilde Krim, who was one of the panelists, told Donahue that the involvement of pork and African swine fever virus in AIDS was an outlandish theory that was being investigated. I wrote an open letter to Donahue about the show in our August 4 issue: "I wish that Dr. Krim had given you an answer that was more thorough and more honest about her feelings about this theory, with which you are obviously familiar. I sat in a room with Dr. Krim a few months ago while she listened to a presentation of data on African swine fever, given by Drs. Jane Teas and John Beldekas. It is my understanding that Dr. Krim encouraged Beldekas and Teas to make the long presentation to her board, and she also urged them to apply for a grant from her foundation to continue their research. Shortly after the presentation, Dr. Krim sent a letter to Beldekas encouraging him to continue his work. I was under the impression that Dr. Krim had become quite fascinated by the swine fever theory."

I also told Donahue in that letter, "I would like to encourage you to do a show on AIDS and African swine fever virus. You should also invite the woman who has fought the federal government for over three years in her attempts to research the connection between AIDS and African swine fever. You should also invite Dr. John Beldekas, who found evidence of swine fever infection in AIDS patients, and HTLV-III antibodies in sick pigs in Belle Glade. You should also invite Dr. William Hess and Dr. Richard Wardley, two of the experts on African swine fever who have publicly stated that more research needs to be done."

I also wrote, "You should also invite Dr. James Mason, the director of the Centers for Disease Control, and his sidekick, Dr. James Curran, to defend the actions of the CDC. Having encountered both of these characters on several occasions, I can tell you that your show will be quite entertaining. Maybe you could get Jim Curran to say that he didn't want to explore swine fever because he was afraid of hurting the pork industry. I predict that Mason will mistakenly say 'swine flu' several times as he did in an interview with me. . . . Over the last three years, the government has repeatedly tried to sweep questions about African swine fever and AIDS under the carpet. The CDC and the White House are playing games with the lives of all Americans."

In the same issue, Ann Giudici Fettner wrote about an interesting phone call she had received: "Several weeks ago, Dr. Robert C. Gallo of the National Cancer Institute (NCI), called me early on a Saturday morning to ask, in effect, why I was on his case so hard. The Office of Cancer Communication at the National Institutes of Health (NIH) had told him that my article in [New York Native] was 'the worst thing anyone could have written about him.' Gallo claimed that there were 'some facts' in the article, but that some of it was 'just crap.' He complained about my use of anonymous sources."

Not surprisingly, given his modus operandi, Gallo agreed to be interviewed by Fettner and she met him for several hours a week later in his office at NCI. In the interview, he protested to Fettner that he had no power over who gets grants in research. He told her, "I haven't reviewed a single AIDS grant in my life." He also told her that he made no money from the so-called AIDS test beyond "an inventor's prize of $2,000." He argued that he had all the money he needed and was set because he would inherit money from his successful father. Fettner asked him about rumors he was leaving NIH and he said that his future was up in the air, but that he didn't want "to leave in the middle of the vaccine attempt." (We know how that turned out.) He told Fettner that he didn't think any cofactor was necessary for his retrovirus to cause AIDS. He also insisted that the main lesion in AIDS was "definitely the T-4. Anyone who's studied this can dismiss the T-4 lesion. It's fantastically important. . . . Right now, the field accepts the notion that the infections and cancers arise from immune suppression due to the lack of the central cell of the immune system. The T-4 cell." (And that turned out to be a fantastically simpleminded and wrong. The myopic T-4 paradigm was the big mistake or big fib at the very heart of the bogus science and epidemiology of the epidemic).

In the August 18 issue of *New York Native*, Fettner penned a piece calling for a congressional investigation of the CDC. She wrote, "The Centers for Disease Control AIDS reports and activities are increasingly viewed by impartial researchers with disbelief and anger. Some assign various of the CDC's actions and reports to mere incompetence; others express the view that there may be an agenda to deprive the National Institutes of Health (NIH) of its autonomy; yet others see the CDC as an instrument for helping the Reagan administration to cut expenditures for all health-related measures. In other words, both the CDC's motives and the quality of their science are at issue."

Fettner complained that the CDC was out of touch with the real nature of the epidemic, but, it had "successfully positioned itself as the ultimate authority on AIDS." She argued, "Without question, from the first, political influences have been allowed to intrude on the management of this grave, international health crisis. Having positioned itself as the central authority on AIDS and, given the antagonism they continue to engender between themselves and the scientific community, the activities of the CDC demand outside peer review as well as examination by a select Congressional committee." Fettner quoted Dr. Peter Skrabanek of the University of Dublin as saying, "When epidemiologists begin advising governments" they "declare themselves as agents of social control." (Fettner was onto something far more monstrous than even she, with her sensitive political antennae, recognized.) She wrote that when epidemiologists "choose to become such agents, they leave the sanctified halls of science and enter an arena in which performance and influence are open to examination. The CDC is long overdue for just such an examination. It's time the CDC was called to account. We've had enough of their twisting the epidemic into their own design, whether to cover their erroneous assessments or following an agenda from Washington." Fettner, like most of us back then, didn't realize that the CDC was just getting started.

Fettner also noted, "We have been treated to the CDC's determination to hide black Belle Glade's undoing by AIDS, their lies or incompetence about testing African swine fever-positive sera. I don't know who's ultimately responsible for it and may never know, but I do know it's time to take this disease out of their hands, to get them away from the microphones and reporters. It's also time for a panel of clinical scientists—not enumerators—to decide what is and isn't AIDS. . . . Why are the major researchers standing back and letting the CDC adjudicate at what point one can be diagnosed as having AIDS?"

Fettner once again attacked the top AIDS researcher: "James Curran, head of the CDC's AIDS task force, stood in front of a world audience in Paris and made five-year predictions for the spread of AIDS—based on what? After his plenary session performance, those who know how the epidemiology is being done, and who increasingly despise the CDC's manipulations, came away furious. . . . Does the CDC have information they aren't revealing? In the context of their record for large-scale, long-term predictions, the ones for AIDS have been about as accurate as those of the loonies who periodically appear with signs announcing 'the end of the world is today.' Fettner was onto one of the key aspects of what would turn out to be the CDC's shady way of framing the disease: "The CDC's continually shifting gospel-truth currently asserts that hardly anyone—'fewer than 100'—have survived what the epidemiologists have defined as the 39-month 'natural history,' [of AIDS] but there are probably hundreds who have and do survive. Is it fair to assume that many of these survivors stay away from CDC body counting facilities? I think so."

Unfortunately for the gay community, it would become more and more difficult for people to stay away from the incompetent body counting and the tentacles of the CDC's public health agenda.

Fettner's calls for an investigation fell on deaf ears. In retrospect, she was just seeing the first round of the diabolical game when she noted, "The CDC has consistently mischaracterized AIDS." The bottom of the iceberg—chronic fatigue syndrome and other HHV-6-related conditions—were not fully visible yet. Fettner and the gay community were totally unaware that the blind spot of heterosexism was preventing the medical and scientific establishment from seeing the looming catastrophe ahead.

In the September 15 issue, Gallo was back in the news. I reported that I had learned from a source close to Dr. Robert Gallo that his lab had "isolated a new virus from AIDS patients. The new virus is a DNA virus with a strong resemblance to cytomegalovirus. The source speculated that the new virus may actually be African swine fever virus. . . . According to the source close to Gallo, his lab has also isolated the new DNA virus from a new epidemic, described with various names that is occurring around the country. Some have called this epidemic

103

"non-stop flu," while others term it a variant of mononucleosis. One source [even] refers to it as the 'secondary epidemic of AIDS.' " That epidemic, of course, turned out to be so-called chronic fatigue syndrome.

I pointed out that if African swine fever virus "causes both acute AIDS and a chronic flu-like illness in the general population, it would be imitating the same patterns of infection that occur in herds of pigs infected with ASFV."

Curiously, in terms of the case the *Native* had been building in our reporting about the CDC, in the same issue of the paper, we ran a story by Barry Adkins about a Congressional investigation of the CDC: "Senator Lowell Weicker (R-Conn.) dispatched a Congressional staffer to the . . . CDC AIDS unit in Atlanta on September 3 to investigate charges that researchers had been wrongly fired, and that viral studies had been sabotaged. . . ." Weicker had been concerned about a *Miami Herald* report that suggested that researchers at the CDC had been suppressing and sabotaging AIDS experiments.

In the September 29 issue of the *Native*, Adkins reported, "Numerous incidents of purported sabotage directed at viral projects dealing with the causes of AIDS have been discovered by investigators at the Federal Centers for Disease Control (CDC) in Atlanta. Investigators from outside the agency, as well as internal watchdogs, have uncovered several CDC memos which claim that research has been destroyed by an unknown person or persons over the past several months." The article went on to detail numerous incidents in which AIDS experiments were tampered with or sabotaged. Hopefully historians will one day conduct some forensic work to determine what bearing that sabotage might have had on the scientific truths that were concealed by the CDC during the epidemic.

In November, Ann Fettner strayed off the *Native* reservation and wrote a piece about Robert Gallo's discovery of his mysterious new DNA virus for the *Village Voice*. The virus was called "Human B-cell Lymphotropic Virus" or "HBLV." Based on what I had learned from behind-the-scenes conversations, I reported in our November 3 issue, "Gallo has told the *Native* that he could not rule out the possibility that his new virus is African swine fever virus." I also reported, "Discussions with Fettner have indicated that the epidemiology of the new virus suggests that it may be highly contagious and cause ailments such as flu, encephalitis, multiple sclerosis, arthritis, and possibly AIDS." I noted, "In the American population the new virus is behaving the same way that African swine fever behaved in pigs during the last decade. The new virus is the same size as African swine fever virus. The new virus also looks like cytomegalovirus (CMV) a herpesvirus which the Centers for Disease Control at first thought was the cause of AIDS. African swine fever virus has been confused with [porcine] CMV by researchers in the past." I also wrote, "Fettner's report in the *Voice* that HBLV is now widespread in the population is consistent with the behavior of African swine fever virus, which is highly contagious. Fettner reports that 30% of the people around Lake Tahoe are positive for HBLV." Lake Tahoe was the area in which the cluster of what would be called "chronic fatigue syndrome" was first identified.

In the same article, I noted, "If HBLV [which was eventually called HHV-6] is African swine fever virus, then several strains of swine fever may be circulating in the human population. No strain may be strong enough to cause serious disease. But if humans are now infected by African swine fever virus, the multiple exposures to different strains of the virus could result in serious health problems which in pigs include dermatitis, lymphadenitis, hyperplasia of the lymph nodes, enlarged spleen, hemorrhages, tonsillitis, gastroenteritis, pulmonary edema, interstitial pneumonia, pericarditis and meningo-encephalitis." (The list of pathologies was a foreshadowing of the spectrum of multisystemic dysfunction in chronic fatigue syndrome and HHV-6-related illnesses.)

I also noted in the article that ASFV, like AIDS, was sometimes difficult to recognize because the disease manifestations could be confused with many other diseases. I suggested that the emerging epidemic of Epstein-Barr Virus (EBV), which would eventually be called chronic fatigue syndrome, might "actually be a mild form of African swine fever."

Newsweek had reported, in their October 27 issue, that CFS sufferers "are plagued by low-grade fevers, aching joints, and sometimes a sore throat—but they don't have the flu. They're overwhelmingly exhausted, weak and debilitated—but they don't have AIDS. They're often confused and forgetful—but it isn't Alzheimer's. Many patients feel suicidal, but it isn't clinical depression. They shuttle from doctor to doctor with a variety of symptoms—but it isn't clinical hypochondria." I started to see that the emerging politics of chronic fatigue syndrome were building a biomedical wall of apartheid between CFS and AIDS and I pointed out in my article, "Many if not most, AIDS patients also suffer from reactivated EBV. [Gallo's new DNA virus] HBLV may then turn out to be the cause of viral reactivation and autoimmunity in both AIDS and chronic EBV disease."

In the November 3 issue, I also raised the alarming possibilities that health care workers and AIDS scientists and their families might be at special risk for contracting the newly discovered AIDS-related DNA virus. I reported, "One AIDS researcher told the *Native* that everybody in his lab working on AIDS research has started to show elevated antibodies to Epstein-Barr virus" and I also noted, "One lab research staff has even refused to work with Gallo's new virus. Ironically, every AIDS researcher may have inadvertently been working with HBLV/African swine fever virus for years." (According to a reliable source, there is even a possibility that Gallo brought the virus home to his son, who years later would suffer from chronic fatigue syndrome.)

I also suggested in the article that the new virus would seriously complicate the already treacherous and complex politics of AIDS, especially if Gallo admitted that HBLV was a human adaptation of African swine fever virus. The merging of a human health problem with an animal disease involving a staple of the American diet in a brand new epidemiological narrative was potentially an apocalyptic political and biomedical mess.

Curiously, at the same time, officials in New Jersey were considering halting regular testing of pigs for ASFV in that state. *New York Native* had raised questions about the wisdom of that move and on May 7, 1986, a USDA official, Dr. E.C. Sharman, wrote in a memo, "New Jersey was exploring the possibility of discontinuation of sampling about a year ago. We encouraged them to continue participating at that time. The discontinuation of ASFV sampling if it became known to the gay community may provide ammunition for falsely accusing us of 'hiding the existence of the disease in the country.' " It's amusing that the little *New York Native* was basically being perceived as "the gay community." Would that it were so. And even if true, who knew that the gay community could so easily affect the policies of the USDA?

I also reported, in that same piece, that I had spoken to a clinician in Atlanta who had told me that he had seen cases of the new chronic EBV infection [that turned out to be chronic fatigue syndrome] *at the same time he started seeing AIDS cases*. I noted, "Gallo's new virus HBLV

106

may be the cause of both epidemics. If HBLV is African swine fever virus, the linkage would make a great deal of sense. African swine fever is not [strictly speaking] a sexually transmitted disease, but the outcome of the infection may be tied to the number of exposures, amount of exposure, immune status of the host and the orifice in which the virus is contracted." I also reported, "When I talked to Robert Gallo on Wednesday, October 22, I urged him to resolve the matter of whether HBLV is African swine fever virus as soon as possible. I told him that even the safety of his lab workers was at stake. He told me that the materials which he planned to use to test whether his new virus is African swine fever were from the USDA were not of sufficient quality to make a determination, and that the matter is still unresolved. I urged him to contact the USDA's Director of Animal Health and Inspection Service, Burt Hawkins, to obtain the materials necessary to do a DNA probe—a test which Gallo feels is necessary to determine if HBLV is African swine fever virus. I asked Gallo if he would change the name of his new virus from HBLV to African swine fever virus if it turns out that the viruses are identical. He replied, 'You have an absolute promise that if this is African swine fever virus, the name will be changed instantly.' "

In my December 1 editorial, I commented on a *New York Times* November 7, 1986, editorial which asked, "Is AIDS about to become epidemic among the general public in America, too?" The editorial insisted, "The evidence of breakout is far from conclusive." I wrote, "The problem is that the *Times* remains convinced that HTLV-III is the cause of AIDS. The pattern of HTLV-III infection has been reassuring to the *Times*. . . . Imagine how catastrophically wrong the *Times* might be if HTLV-III is not the cause of AIDS. . . . When the *Times* bases scientific conclusions on data from the CDC, they are using public relations data, not science. HTLV-III has not been shown to be the cause of AIDS. HTLV-III has been declared the cause of AIDS. There is a difference." I asked, "What if AIDS is caused by HBLV, the new virus which Robert Gallo is now comparing with African swine fever virus? First of all, we need new epidemiology. Preliminary reports from Lake Tahoe suggest that 30% or more of the general population is infected with HBLV. If HBLV is the cause of AIDS, then we are in the middle of a major pandemic whereby entire American cities and towns could begin the same source of suffering as cities and towns in Africa. No scientist has yet tried to force HBLV into the category of sexually transmitted viruses, because the pattern of infection is too widespread and appears to be too casual. HBLV may escape the control of the VD moralists at the CDC. Is HBLV to be found in 100% of the blood of people with AIDS? Not yet according to Dr. Gallo. His staff has found it in only 30% of AIDS patients but Dr. Gallo notes that these are early findings, and his assay is still imperfect."

In the editorial I suggested that New York City's Health Commissioner, Dr. Stephen Joseph should "put together a task force to study the relationship between HBLV and AIDS. Among the areas that should be investigated are: 1) What percentage of health care workers are now infected with HBLV? 2) What can be done to prevent health care workers from spreading HBLV to patients in their hospitals? 3) What percentage of AIDS researchers are now infected with HBLV? 4) Is HBLV a virus that is present in any animals that are consumed by humans? 5) Should the Blood Center be screening blood for HBLV?"

In the December 8 issue, I raised questions about the judgment of the man who was quickly becoming the country's de facto AIDS Czar: "Tony Fauci, the young (46-year-old) director of the National Institute of Allergy and Infectious Diseases (NIAID) was profiled by Christine Russell in the November 3, 1986, issue of *The Washington Post*. Young Fauci may be one of the most powerful people in AIDS politics in America." I pointed out that his institute then controlled 60% of the total AIDS budget. I noted, "He came across as an insensitive jerk" when he spoke about AIDS publicly earlier that year. I wrote that Fauci's bedside manner is not as worrisome to me as the fact that he's a man with a hypothesis about AIDS that may be dead wrong, and his own honor may be on the line every time any part of NIAID's budget is spent on AIDS research. The question in my mind is this: Is Tony Fauci an American Lysenko?"

In the 1930s, Trofim Denisovich Lysenko was a Russian scientist who had ideas about agriculture that turned out to be dead wrong. According to *Betrayers of the Truth*, the groundbreaking book on scientific fraud by Nicholas Wade and William Broad, the Russian government threw its complete political and financial support behind Lysenko's crackpot agricultural ideas in 1935. Wade and Broad note, "It was an act of willful desperation. The bureaucrats realized they were not making much progress with the agricultural situation; . . . so the bureaucrats chose a bureaucratic solution, which was to put someone in charge and let him cope with the problem. Unfortunately, the person they chose was Lysenko." In my editorial I asked if "AIDS is a similar situation and does Fauci have the power of a Lysenko? Science in America is an expensive proposition and he who controls funding also controls science. In Russell's profile of Fauci, she notes that one scientist described Fauci's "insistence on keeping his laboratory [as] a potential danger . . . because 'it brings all sorts of suspicion,' however unfounded that his loyalties to his lab might interfere with his duties as an impartial institute director." I also noted that Russell reported that one of Fauci's colleagues said, "There is something in him that has to show people he can do it all." Fauci had at least one prescient colleague. One could say that Fauci came closest to being the epidemic's control freak. Or worse.

In that same issue of the *Native*, we reported that William Buckley retracted his "AIDS tattoo" proposal for HIV positive people after a meeting with representatives of the Gay and Lesbian Alliance Against Defamation. (I'd love to see a film reenactment of *that* meeting.) His proposal first appeared on the March 18, 1986, *New York Times* op-ed page and before that in his nationally syndicated column. He also made the proposal on his PBS television program, *Firing Line*. "Everyone," Buckley wrote, "detected with AIDS should be tattooed in the upper forearm to protect common-needle users, and on the buttocks, to prevent the victimization of other homosexuals."

Serendipitously, in the same issue of *New York Native*, we published an interview with Richard Plant by Allen Ellenzweig about Plant's book, *The Pink Triangle: The Nazi War Against Homosexuals*. Plant had been a friend of Hannah Arendt's and a professor at the New School. We also published a brief excerpt from Plant's book with this chilling passage: ". . . Himmler was not optimistic about the prospects of rehabilitating men suffering from the disease of homosexuality. Perhaps a few hustlers might be salvaged, but he was doubtful about the immoral homosexual majority. Not long after, he would come to believe that the final solution was inevitable for gays as for Jews and other 'contragenics.' He dubbed it 'delousing,' a term favored by other Nazi theoreticians as well." One could say that Himmler was an AIDS epidemiologist before his time.

1987: An Epic Epidemiological Battle

In the January 12 issue of *New York Native*, I wrote about a December 27, 1986, interview in *The Washington Post* with Robert Redfield, a top military doctor involved in AIDS research. I suggested that if the interview was any indication, the gay community was in for a wild new round of scapegoating and repression. Redfield was a proponent of universal testing for HTLV-III (HIV) and he was one of the first people to start directing veiled threats at those who stood in the way of the government's AIDS agenda. According to *The Washington Post* interview conducted by Phil Hilts, Redfield said, "Anyone who tries to persuade people not to get tested 'has the blood of more gay men on his hands.' "

According to Hilts, Redfield issued a major warning to the gay community on HTLV-III (HIV) testing. He told Hilts that not testing and not telling " 'is threatening the health of the whole community. And ultimately it's going to threaten [gays'] freedom. They don't understand it, but a lot of people are going to be angry when they learn that public health authorities of our country have been paralyzed because of this concern about confidentiality. . . .' "

Ironically, after making a threat that would become an all too familiar motif of the epidemic, Redfield urged the gay community to trust people like himself. Hilts reported that Redfield "believes people must summon enough trust to begin more widespread testing for AIDS." Redfield then mouthed words to Hilts that are some of the most haunting of the whole AIDS era: " 'Lots of doctors run away when their patients die. I maybe started to do that a little, because I have been through so many deaths in this epidemic. But I try to make a point of not running away; I want to help them die, and to work the family through it.' "

In the same issue, we reported on measures then being taken by police in Germany that might have pleased Redfield. In the city of Munich the police were keeping files on homosexuals. According to John J. Vischansky, the lists included "the names of customers" who patronized "gay bookstores and sex shops," "patrons identified in raids on gay bars and cruising areas," "the names of people passing by and identified in the vicinity of gay bars at night," "anybody whose papers have been checked in a public restroom or close to one, no matter what the reason," and "known or admitted homosexuals, transvestites and call boys." Vischansky reported, "For years, the German police have publicly, flatly, and officially denied the existence of such lists, which in part date back to the years long before homosexuality was decriminalized in Germany. Nevertheless, just a few weeks ago, a commission set up to review compliance with federal legislation on data privacy stumbled over these lists."

Vischansky also reported, "The president of the Munich police department, Gustav Haring . . . justified the failure to erase these files "because of the danger of AIDS, which is especially widespread among this group of persons. Gay groups have called for Haring's resignation, to no avail. Worse yet, Haring's boss at the time, Peter Gurweiller, had the gall to state, 'The purpose of [the] regulation is to prevent the epidemic from being spread to families and from affecting the totally innocent.' "

In the January 19 issue of the *Native*, I published a letter that I had written to Burt Hawkins, the Administrator of the Animal and Plant Health Inspection Service (APHIS). I noted in the letter that he must have been aware that Dr. Gallo had stated for the record that he could not rule out the possibility that the newly discovered DNA virus, Human B-Cell Lymphotrophic Virus (HBLV) is actually African swine fever virus. I told him I had heard that APHIS was preparing a DNA probe to help determine whether HBLV is ASFV. I expressed my surprise that this was taking so long since ASFV is one of the most lethal viruses known to the USDA. I wrote, "Surely you must realize that if a scientist of Gallo's caliber suggests a possible relationship . . . the matter should be taken very seriously. I assumed that the [possible] presence of ASFV in our country was considered a national emergency, and would be dealt with in a matter of hours, not weeks or months. You have the necessary expertise. By letting this take so long, I think you and your department have let the country down in this matter."

Twenty days after I sent my letter, I received a response from J.K. Atwell, the Deputy Administrator of the USDA Veterinary Services. He wrote, "An approved diagnostic DNA probe for ASFV has not been developed. . . . bacterial plasmids containing ASFV DNA segments have been developed by the Agricultural Research Service at their Plum Island Animal Disease Laboratory that may be of assistance in distinguishing between ASFV and Dr. Robert C. Gallo's newly discovered HBLV. This product has been promised to Dr. Gallo. However, since it is presently located in a restricted laboratory, it must be safety tested before it can be removed from Plum Island. When this testing is completed, this research product will be provided to Dr. Gallo."

In the January 25 issue, we published another angry rant by Larry Kramer in the form of an open letter to Richard Dunne, the head of Gay Men's Health Crisis. The letter, like everything Kramer wrote, was premised on the CDC's epidemiology and virology. The letter began, "The doomsday scenario that many have feared for so long comes closer. Next week 274 people will die from AIDS. Next week 374 more will become infected with the killer virus. In four years at least 270,000 people will have AIDS. Of these, 179,000 will have died. Four million people already are infected. As many as 50% of these millions will die. Two out of three AIDS cases are still happening to gay men."

His letter criticized Dunne and GMHC for not being prepared for what was coming. He urged GMHC to "fight for gay men." The paradigm that Kramer promoted in the letter was the one he pushed throughout the epidemic which tragically meant that he generally got everything exactly backwards. He attacked Dunne for not standing up to "a world filled with heterosexual connivance almost bordering on collusion at the least and conspiracy at the most—ignoring us, treating us like so much offal fit to die in agony while tests, trials, delays, ignorance, inhuman uncaring, lying, ass dragging, characterize the daily activities of just about everyone and everything in sight, particularly the 'appropriate medical journals.' " Kramer wanted a kind of whirling dervish political activity to occur on every front except the one that absolutely mattered the most to the gay community: the AIDS establishment's questionable epidemiology and virology which *really were* replete with what he called "heterosexual connivance." If there is anything more heterosexually conniving and apartheid*ish* in human history than the "HIV causes AIDS and CFS isn't AIDS" paradigm, I don't know what it is.

Kramer also wrote, "I do not *care* what the *New England Journal of Medicine* reports about AIDS; or *Science* or *The Lancet* or the *Journal of the American Medical Association*. From the very beginning of this epidemic, they have shown scant concern for us, for our rights, for our continued health survival on this planet."

Not caring what was being reported about AIDS in the world's leading medical journals, was a very strange way of being attentive to what was happening to the gay community. Like it or not, the fate of the gay community and the epidemic was being negotiated in these very journals. The problem wasn't the "scant concern." Au contraire. The problem was that garbage-in-garbage-out epidemiology and its consequential misguided virology were being published on a nonstop basis, and Kramer, because he was blind to the fact that the epidemiological fundamentals were replete with "heterosexual connivance almost bordering on collusion," ended up being a fraud enabler and a hapless cheerleader for the underlying deceit and self-deceit of the epidemic. It is ironic that he screamed at Dunne in his letter, "How dare you be so trusting and naïve—you who are head of Gay Men's Health Crisis?" This is one of the great pot-meets-kettle moments in the Kramer legacy. He was not the first person in history to excel at what could be called the politics of the tantrum which were a poor substitute for well-informed and savvy political judgment—and due diligence. Perhaps young minority communities with no political compass are particularly susceptible to the kind of outrageous narcissistic and delusional performance art posing as canny activism that Kramer offered.

In Kramer's letter, he accused GMHC of becoming fat and rich, a "bastion of conservatism" an organization that would no longer "fight for the living." GMHC had become a "funeral home," "cowardly." One of the more darkly ironic things he said to Dunne in his letter was, "You and your huge assortment of caretakers perform miraculous tasks helping the dying to die." But what he wanted GMHC to do was to "fight" for the living. He wanted them to "use their strength to confront our enemies, to make them help us. This is what political strength is about. It is all." Actually, in the context of the epidemic, real political strength would have been forcing the government to tell the entire inconvenient truth about what was really going on. Or just daring to find out the truth for ourselves.

The point Kramer was missing was the war he didn't even know the gay community really had to fight: an epic epidemiological battle. Like all the woodenheaded collaborators of the epidemic, Kramer called for more "education." Insofar as Kramer was urging GMHC to "fight for the education of everyone," he was basically calling for GMHC to fight for more *HIV propaganda* bearing the CDC's hardwired antigay epidemiology. He was inadvertently calling for more shovels to dig gay graves.

113

Kramer's call for GMHC to fight for more drug trials was of course based on the premise that the CDC had gotten the virology of AIDS *right*. That premise ended up getting a lot of people poisoned thanks to the clueless activists who had been urged to "fight" a battle they couldn't even fully comprehend. AZT was the great hope at that time and not yet perceived to be the iatrogenocidal disaster that it actually was. Kramer wrote in his letter to Dunne, "It is now reported that AZT is going to cost each patient $5,000 a year when it becomes available. What are you doing to confront this abhorrent future, in which few patients will be able to afford the very drug that might save them?" Unfortunately, it would turn out that the cost was not the biggest problem with AZT. Its high cost may actually have *saved* some lives. Complaining about the cost or AZT turned out to be like complaining about the high cost of a train ticket to Auschwitz.

In retrospect, it is amusing to note that at this point in the epidemic, Kramer still admired what we were doing in the pages of *New York Native*. He chided Dunne and GMHC, writing, "Why do you not ride herd on research rather than leaving it to others (such as the *Native*) to cry out in alarm when false trails are championed and legitimate avenues are ignored?" Alas, Kramer followed the *Native* only so far down those avenues.

In more of the Kramer style of irony, he wrote that Dunne and GMHC "continue to deny the political realities of this epidemic. There is nothing in the whole AIDS mess that is not political. How can you continue to deny this fact and assert that your role must remain unpolitical?"

And even more ironically, in terms of Kramer's own petulant intolerance for differing opinions, he wrote, "You have shut out every dissenting voice you have effectively cut yourselves off from much of the gay community. If anyone doesn't agree with you they are ignored."

Near the end of his letter, Kramer inadvertently nailed not only the problem with GMHC but also the problem with Larry Kramer: "We are all exceptionally tired. We are all AIDSed out. In our exhaustion. Let Someone Else Do It. In our exhaustion, we foster our continued ignorance; we don't keep up with what is going on; we don't want to know; we don't read the *Native*; we don't read every article on AIDS. In this ignorance and exhaustion is our destruction." These words belong on the AIDS community's collective tombstone—and Larry Kramer's. Looking back at the Kramer legacy, one always has to ask the question, "Did this guy ever listen to anything he himself was saying?" Kramer would eventually lead the gay community in a formal huffy exodus from the *Native,* unable to face the uncompromising truths that the *Native* kept publishing until its demise at the beginning of 1997.

A story about a magazine survey of doctors, which we ran in the February 2 issue, presented a stark warning to the gay community about the attitudes it could face from the medical community throughout the epidemic. The survey had been published in the January issue of *MD Magazine.* According to the poll, seventy-eight percent of the respondents favored contact tracing of high risk (guess who?) patients followed by tracing and testing all sexual partners. Thirty-five percent favored testing food handlers and most disturbingly, 28 percent favored some form of quarantine. These were the people who would, in their medical practices, activate and promote the public health agenda that followed logically and inexorably from the CDC's us-versus-them epidemiology.

In the February 9 issue, we published several pages of letters from GMHC's workers and supporters in defense of the organization that Larry Kramer had attacked as being run by a bunch of apolitical sissies. In retrospect, my favorite letter, from a person named Gordon Grant, was also the briefest: "Regarding Ms.(sic) Kramer's open letter to GMHC . . . sissies—feh! You old bitchy queen."

We published a long piece on the Tuskegee Syphilis Experiment by Martin Levine in the February 16 issue. The disturbing article began, "They say we have bad blood. Nearly forty years ago they told some black men that they had bad blood." Levine then recounted the details of the forty-year experiment in which public health authorities conducted a study that monitored the effects of untreated syphilis in poor black sharecroppers in the South. Levine discussed James Jones's classic account of the experiment, *Bad Blood.* At the end of the article Levine voiced the concerns he felt about the warnings the Tuskegee Syphilis Experiment had for the gay community: "In both Tuskegee and AIDS the socially franchised studied the socially disenfranchised. White doctors experimented upon illiterate black men. Heterosexual researchers explore a disease which usually strikes gay men, as well as Haitians, intravenous drug users, and hemophiliacs." He pointed out, "While there are a few gays involved in the Centers for Disease

115

Control's work on AIDS, the overwhelming majority of the staff is straight. Consider the composition of the AIDS Activity's Group's full-time personnel. Those working exclusively at headquarters number ten—seven doctors, two public health professionals, and one research sociologist. All of them are straight; one is an orthodox Jew and another is a deacon in his church."

Surprisingly, even after writing a book like *Bad Blood*, James Jones still didn't see much for gays to automatically worry about. Levine wrote, "What do these similarities [between the Tuskegee Syphilis Experiment and AIDS] mean? After listing them for the author of *Bad Blood*, I asked what implications he thought Tuskegee had for us. Dr. Jones replied, "The Centers for Disease Control has done a lot that is wrong, a lot that is heroic. The fact that they were responsible for the Tuskegee experiment does not automatically mean they will exploit a minority group. The information in *Bad Blood* needs to be shared and raised as a note of caution. You have every right to be cautious, but don't fear conspiracy until the hard evidence is in."

Levin reported, "In the last few weeks I have discussed Tuskegee with gay people working on AIDS across the country. All reacted deeply to Tuskegee's unethical nature, racist overtones, and method- ological flaws. All felt it had significant implications for AIDS. Many of the people I spoke to are not in a position to be quoted publicly. Two were most concerned about ethics. They wondered if the researchers were again violating human experimentation regulations. 'The researchers are gathering gay men's names, addresses, and sexual histories. The public disclosure of this information could potentially harm those men. I see no safeguards for protecting the men's anonymity,' said a person working with AIDS victims in San Francisco. This individual further commented upon the failure of some researchers to get informed consent from the men. Another worried about the possible danger in the Centers for Disease Control's case studies. 'They are going around the country collecting names and addresses of gay men. Can we trust them not to use the lists in harmful ways? What are they doing with it?' "

Levin also reported, "Others wondered if the research had homophobic overtones. Racist science prompted the Tuskegee ex- periment. It was thought that the innate characteristics of blacks made them sexually promiscuous. 'This notion has become the foundation for all the Centers for Disease Control's studies. From the onset, they theorized that if AIDS hit gay men, it had to be because they were promiscuous,' said a person closely connected to the [CDC]."

Most presciently, Dr. Stephen Murray, a San Francisco based sociologist, told Levine, " 'If Tuskegee was such poor science, why not AIDS? . . . All they have done is taken a group of sick people and seen what they have. It is nothing more than the correlations based on a sample of the sick, and all while the relationship may be caused by a third factor. And from this they build an infectious agent theory, and panic the public into believing our blood is diseased. It's a medical counterrevolution—from the mental hospitals to the quarantine.' "

On March 9, we published a piece by John Lauritsen in which he reviewed a report on AIDS prepared by a committee sponsored by the National Academy of Sciences and The Institute of Medicine. Lauritsen noted, "This report was intended to inform an appropriate national response to the various problems arising from AIDS . . . . The resultant report—nearly 400 pages of highly condensed and often technical material—reflects an enormous amount of intellectual effort. It is an impressive performance in every respect save one: the logic of its underlying premises."

Lauritsen criticized the report's assumption, from its very first page, that HIV without any qualifications was the cause of AIDS. He noted that at one point in the report "reference is made to 'HIV *and its unambiguous identification as the AIDS virus'* which is rhetorical overkill." He argued, "In fact HIV has consistently failed to fulfill even a single one of Koch's postulates, the series of tests which medical science has traditionally required a microbe to pass before it can be considered the cause of a particular disease." Lauritsen had found his way into the opposite world of abnormal science.

One of the best examples of the lack of scientific standards operating in the field of AIDS research is the fact that, as Lauritsen points out, nowhere in the report "is convincing evidence presented which could establish HIV as the cause of AIDS; at the same time, evidence is occasionally cited which would suggest either HIV is not the cause of AIDS, or that it plays a causal role only in conjunction with other, potent cofactors." He pointed out the epidemiological embarrassment in the report which "acknowledges that it is impossible to isolate HIV from many AIDS patients and that some AIDS patients show no evidence of ever having been infected with the virus. (That is to say, they are negative for HIV itself, as well as for HIV antibodies.)"

Lauritsen criticized the report for suggesting that HIV was

responsible for the depletion of T4-cells when in fact "HIV appears to infect very few T4-cells." And "in AIDS patients, the immunological functioning of all T-cells is severely compromised. The cells are sick regardless of whether or not they are 'infected' (nearly all of them are not) and regardless of what the T-cell ratio may happen to be." Lauritsen wrote, "It is mysterious that the authors do not entertain the possibility that something other than HIV is responsible for weakening all of the T-cells." He was concerned that recreational drugs were responsible and that their role was completely ignored by the report.

Lauritsen took issue with the report's assumption that IV drug users were developing AIDS because they shared needles, noting that it wasn't certain if all those affected had even shared needles, and perhaps more importantly, the fact that health care workers were not getting AIDS from needlestick injuries involving AIDS patients made the whole HIV theory doubtful.

In his piece, Lauritsen asserted, "Before the 'AIDS virus' bandwagon really got under way, AIDS was understood as a condition. . . . Now that HIV ideology has achieved almost total hegemony, AIDS has come to be conceptualized as a disease: 'HIV infection.'" He took issue with "the equation of AIDS with HIV" arguing, "A not-inconsiderable proportion of AIDS patients show no evidence of ever having been infected with HIV" and "hundreds of thousands of people are estimated to be HIV seropositive, and yet the vast majority of them are not sick in any way."

Lauritsen argued that the CDC acted in a Procrustean manner in the way they manipulated their definition of AIDS. If a case of AIDS had no evidence of HIV, it was not considered AIDS, but according to Lauritsen, "At the same time, the CDC is sufficiently flexible that if confronted with an AIDS case with negative tests for both virus and antibodies, it can also declare *on faith* that the patient is infected with HIV, even though there is no evidence that he is." Lauritsen was floored by the crazy logic and asserted, "May it be recorded in the annals of science that the CDC succeeded linguistically in establishing HIV as the cause of AIDS, even though the virus never succeeded in fulfilling even one of Koch's postulates."

Lauritsen was troubled by the predictions the committee made in the report about how many of the seropositive would develop AIDS and how large the epidemic would become in America. He was also alarmed that their recommendations for future spending and research revolved around the assumption that HIV was the true cause.

Lauritsen argued, "We need to know the characteristics of people with AIDS. As it is now, we know almost nothing about the gay men with AIDS other than the 'homosexual/bisexual' label that has been slapped on them." He described the original epidemiology of AIDS done by the CDC as being out of date and incompetent.

Lauritsen was onto the fact that the whole affair was political: "The patient characteristics statistics, which the CDC periodically releases to the media, have been incomplete and misleading. We have no idea, for example, what percentage of the total AIDS cases are Haitians; the CDC described, for political reasons, that Haitians should disappear as a 'risk group,' and disappear they did." Unfortunately gay men did not have the political clout to make themselves disappear from the CDC's skewed epidemiology.

Lauritsen excoriated the report for ignoring the role of cofactors like recreational drugs, the centerpiece of his personal AIDS theory. He was concerned that an educational campaign to stop the transmission of HIV, the questionable official cause of AIDS, ignored the toll that recreational drugs *by themselves* would continue to have in destroying the immune systems of those who would eventually be diagnosed with AIDS.

Ominously, Lauritsen wrote that while the report suggested, "Coercive measures would not be effective in altering the course of the epidemic" they "are by no means ruled out completely. Indeed, having painted the picture of a *killer virus* on the loose, of more than a quarter of a million AIDS cases in the U.S. alone in the next four years, the committee might have been more consistent had they called for draconian measures to control the spread of infection." It was another symptom of the bizarre logic of abnormal science.

Lauritsen came to a Barbara Tuchmanesque conclusion about the whole report, noting that it "illustrates once again that group intelligence is below individual intelligence—that even a committee composed of brilliant individuals, as this one appears to have been, is capable of monumental folly. In sum, this is a well-intentioned book which has a great potential for harm."

In the same issue of *New York Native*, the possibility of coercion got all too real in a story by Bill Bahlman about a resolution that was introduced in the New York City Council by Council member Joseph Lisa. His resolution "would allow forced testing for antibodies, to HIV (the so-called AIDS virus), contact tracing of sexual partners of those who test positive, as well as possible quarantine for those who are

HIV-antibody positive, those with AIDS-related complex, and persons with AIDS (PWAs)." Interestingly, according to Bahlman, "Only one witness testified in favor of the resolutions, Dr. Robert Redfield, former head of Walter Reed Army Medical Center."

Topping everything off in that issue, Mike Salinas reported that the Indian government had begun deporting foreign students who tested positive for antibodies to HIV.

In the March 16 issue, we published a long account, written by Darrell Yates Rist, about a two-day forum held by the CDC on "The Role of AIDS Virus Antibody Testing in the Prevention and Control of AIDS." The more appropriate title would have been "The Role of AIDS Virus Antibody Testing in the Persecution and Control of the Gay Community and Others." Rist reported that the CDC director, the devout Mormon, James O. Mason, opened the conference saying, "In coming together these two days we have one purpose in mind: to define a common enemy. The enemy is not me, it is not public health, it is not the people who have expressed interest in civil liberties." (Well, he got one out of three right.) Mason spoke the language of inexorable public health logic: "In the face of a deadly virus, we are determining now what is best for the health of the nation, not what makes people happy." This is the kind of "health of the nation" rhetoric that would also have wowed the perpetrators of the hybrid of medicine and politics that was the Third Reich.

Rist reported on the categories of testing Mason described that were up for debate which ranged from strictly voluntary to mandatory. Rist questioned the CDC's sudden agnosticism on the testing issue, pointing out, "This was a very different tale from the one that had hit the press in early February when according to the *New York Times* (among a host of other papers), the CDC was urging mandatory tests for hospital admissions, pregnant women, patients at STD clinics, and applicants for marriage licenses."

In retrospect, Rist's sociological description of the CDC meeting is quite revealing: "This is a new community of purpose born of AIDS, public health, and civil liberties, which confounds the sexual orientation lines—the ever-more-easy assimilation that many gays will argue is the goal of fighting for gay rights. And many of the lesbians and gays at the conference in Atlanta, it would seem, find themselves more comfortable here than they ever did among the strict devotees of the 'movement.' " One could say that Rist had taken an inadvertent

Polaroid snapshot of the gay community's incipient collaboration in its own self-destruction. To borrow from Arendt, they were essentially assimilating to the biomedical heterosexism of the fraudulent "HIV is AIDS" and "chronic fatigue syndrome is not AIDS" paradigms.

One of the more memorable images in Rist's article on the CDC forum was provided by a member of a small group (only 5 people) named the Lavender Hill Mob, a so-called radical gay group that basically was there to show rage and to yell that people should be angry and yelling. Rist reported that Lavender Hill Mob member Michael Petrelis, who was dressed in "faux concentration camp garb with a pink triangle and an ID number stitched to the pocket on his shirt," asked Mason if he would "take the test and announce your antibody status to the press?" Petrelis was not onto the real game. That was *exactly* the kind of thing the CDC wanted to happen in every quarter of American society. (Flash forward to the Obama years during which it seems like Obama and his wife turned publicly taking HIV tests into public health agitprop.) Rist wrote that in response, "Mason smiled, as though he'd been confronted not so much by an evil devil as a silly one, and said, 'We're tryin' to find a way to save you guys' lives,' and punched the air towards Petrelis's arm paternally."

Rist noted that all the panels during the forum failed to do one basic thing: question the epidemiology and virology. He wrote, "No one questioned whether or not this virus, HIV, is the cause of AIDS or merely a cofactor or simply a marker. No one questioned whether or not this antibody test for HIV is accurate. . . . No one questioned *testing* (except for the [Lavender Hill] Mob, and then not coherently.) It was, everybody seemed to think, a boon to the public health . . . ."

Rist reported that, "The ACLU [American Civil Liberties Union] acquiesced perfunctorily to the good of the antibody tests." (Generally speaking, the ACLU was good for nothing but acquiescing throughout the epidemic.)

Rist also reported that 19 AIDS advisory and service organizations signed a "consensus statement" (which ultimately helped seal the fate of the gay community). It called for testing that was anonymous "coupled with in-depth counseling." "Counseling" of course became another working euphemism for propaganda during the epidemic.

One of the absurdly self-defeating things the gay community did throughout the epidemic was to constantly—in an insipid, abject manner—call for more "education." Had the call been for "re-education" it would have been on the money. When the professional gays and AIDS activists weren't calling for education, they were calling for the funding of "prevention" which was basically a call for more "education." They turned the gay community into one big AIDS re-education camp.

Rist caught the degree to which gays were politically deprived of a seat at the table at this very political forum. One gay leader complained to him, "Gay groups weren't included in the panels (though individually, openly gay people were) . . ." Bizarrely, Urvashi Vaid, of NGLTF told Rist, "Being visible as the NGLTF or GMHC or whoever is not always the route to take." You could call it the gay politics of self-imposed invisibility, a novel form of closeted politics. Gay leader Tim Sweeney manifested these absurd politics when he told Rist, "The way to kill mandatory testing is to go for the public health angle, not civil liberties. The people who need to be convinced don't want to hear from gay organizations." The politically more astute gay leader, Ben Shatz, saw what was really happening and told Rist, "I think it sets a precedent for further exclusion. . . . When we lose visibility we lose power."

One of the more bizarre political developments in the epidemic was the establishment of the opposite world meme that discrimination against the HIV positive was bad because it discouraged HIV testing—a premise that had several diabolical homophobic layers. Robert Redfield, the Army doctor who attended the forum, represented the craziness of the meme beautifully, when according to Rist, he said, "As long as there's a perception of discrimination, it interferes with routine testing to help control the epidemic. We must support the kind of anti-discrimination measures talked about today." Anti-discrimination was really a Trojan horse for medical testing and the incorporation of gays into a Brave New Epidemiological Paradigm. Right before one's eyes one could see the morphing of the fight against discrimination directed towards gays becoming the fight against discrimination toward the HIV positive, which turned the paradigm of gay liberation upside down and inside out. Invisibly it insidiously supported the fraudulent presumption that HIV was the cause of AIDS, while subsuming the fight for gay civil liberties under the Orwellian logic and stigma of public health measures. Throughout the epidemic, gay rights would be supported as a way of fighting AIDS, creating an unprecedented toxic hybrid of self-defeating politics and fraud-based medicine for the gay community.

In the same issue, we published a story about an historic meeting between the Gay and Lesbian Alliance Against Defamation and the editors of the *New York Times*: "The discussion ranged from the GLAAD claims of *Times* undercoverage of gay events and the political implications of AIDS, to the *Times* refusal to use the word 'gay' except in direct quotation." The world's leading newspaper, the one that would be the first and last word on AIDS, always giving the rest of the media its marching orders, couldn't even call gays "gay." (It was amazing how quickly the supposedly very liberal *New York Times* adopted the pernicious and breathtakingly stupid trend of using the insulting word "queer" less than a decade after that meeting. More on that later.)

In the June 15 issue, Mike Salinas covered an ACT UP demonstration that took place across from the White House. According to Salinas, the protestors were pressing for five initiatives that included a "Manhattan Project" on AIDS, "a guarantee of confidentiality between doctor and patient," and "a national AIDS policy to prohibit discrimination against persons infected with HIV." This was yet another Potemkin protest that in essence supported the government's HIV ideology and propaganda.

Salinas reported, "The Reagan administration was still smarting from what it considered to be the bad manners of the dying and their friends, who had booed the president during his speech, the night before, at a fundraising dinner for the American Foundation for AIDS Research (amfAR). During that speech (his first attempt to explain his position on the epidemic since he assumed the presidency), Reagan pledged his support for what he called 'routine testing.' Although it remains unclear exactly what Reagan meant by that, he did outline his hopes that couples seeking marriage licenses, Federal prisoners, and aliens applying for American residence would be subject to blood tests to determine the possible presence of antibodies to HIV, the so-called 'AIDS virus.'"

Salinas noted, "Those who heard the President's speech were clearly shocked by such an idea—which had already been discussed by health officials and dismissed as unworkable for several reasons—and almost equally dismayed that he had chosen the amfAR dinner as the forum to announce it. A chorus of boos and hisses greeted the President's proposal, leaving him 'visibly shaken,' according to sources. Actress Elizabeth Taylor, chairperson of The American Foundation for AIDS Research, was 'rattled' by the heckling said the *New York Post*, and [Surgeon General] Koop was quoted as saying he was 'embarrassed' by it."

Meanwhile, ACT UP protestors in Washington D.C.'s Lafayette Park were met by police who were wearing yellow latex gloves. Salinas reported that the "offended crowd shouted 'Take off the gloves' furiously to no avail." Salinas added, "Then with a giggle a new chant was born: 'Your gloves don't match your shoes/You'll see it on the news.' "

Salinas reported that a rumor was making the rounds among the activists that Vice President George Bush had made some kind of offensive comment earlier that afternoon: "It was reported that he, too, had been booed while proclaiming his support for mandatory blood tests and that his response—clearly audible—was, 'There must be a gay group in here.' "

Salinas also reported that two of the drivers of the buses that ferried the protesters around D.C. "were allegedly approached by officials from the United States Health Service who, according to two of the drivers, apprised them of the 'danger' of their cargo. The drivers, who asked to remain anonymous, told the *Native* that they were informed that they were in danger of contagion by casual contact with anyone with AIDS, and that 'we should fumigate the buses when we get back to New York.' "

Salinas reported, in the same issue, that the Louisiana House of Representatives had "passed from committee a bill that would allow quarantining of persons who tested positive to HIV. . . . The bill, HB 1041, empowers the state's Department of Health and Human Resources (HHR) to obtain 'a civil arrest warrant' to indefinitely detain any person considered to be an 'imminent menace' to public health."

In his column, in the June 22 issue, Ed Sikov, our media reporter, critiqued disturbing pieces that had been written by two of America's leading public intellectuals, Norman Podhoretz and Nat Hentoff. On October 22, in the *New York Post*, Podhoretz had issued his own epidemiological challenge in a piece titled "AIDS Is Not a Risk For All." He wrote, "Is AIDS a danger to heterosexuals? In all probability the answer is no. Yet almost everything we hear—including a good deal of what is being said at the International Conference on AIDS in Washington this week—seems concentrated to create the impression that heterosexuals will soon be as much at risk as homosexuals already are." About the Podhoretz piece, Sikov wrote, "At great pains to prove that the world's public health experts are mere puppets, Podhoretz claims that most, if not all members of the often-cited 4% group of heterosexual AIDS cases bent on duping their doctors." Podhoretz would not be the only person to declare heterosexual AIDS a myth. In some ways it was a logical response to the politically crafted epidemiology the CDC was using to name and count cases of AIDS while turning a blind eye on the entire mostly-heterosexual chronic fatigue syndrome side of the AIDS equation. Podhoretz had the skeptical eye of an inquisitor when it came to the truthfulness of so-called heterosexual AIDS patients. He insisted, "Denials by AIDS patients of homosexual encounters cannot be taken at face value." It was a little like the CDC's logic which declared that if one had AIDS and one was HIV-negative, in reality, one was really HIV-positive by definition. Podhoretz was promoting one of the most toxic opposite world memes of the epidemic, that the gay community was actively engaged in a political conspiracy to promote politically correct epidemiology that *falsely* presented the epidemic as an equal opportunity plague. Podhoretz railed, "If heterosexual, white, middle-class Americans no longer regard AIDS as an imminent threat to them, the growing effort to contain it may falter."

In the same column, Sikov pointed out that with liberal friends like Nat Hentoff of the *Village Voice*, the gay community needed no enemies. In *The Washington Post*, on May 30, according to Sikov, "The former civil libertarian called for mandatory [HIV] testing." Sikov wrote, "Though his position flies in the face of what almost every public health expert tells us, Hentoff rages against those who fight compulsory testing and contact tracing. . . . Throughout the piece, Hentoff sets up a troubling dialectic between those who should be tested, their rights being sufficiently expendable, and the rest of the country, whose rights are more important. Opposition to mandatory testing [according to Hentoff] "results in violating the civil liberties of the unknowing victims of those who are victims of AIDS. These may well be termed violations caused by withholding crucial information from them.' This position stands solely on the idea that there can be innocent 'victims' of AIDS who acquired the disease in a funda-mentally different manner than those who are somehow more responsible for their fate."

Hentoff attacked the ACLU's position of supporting voluntary testing with strict confidentiality. Sikov argued, "Like many other anti-gay bigots who have jumped on the testing bandwagon, Hentoff labors under the delusion that it's possible to deny other people their civil rights while maintaining his own. For Hentoff, 'mandatory testing' does not mean that he would be subject to governmental intervention in his most private life; that's only for other people. His position will likely change when insurance companies and their friends in Congress, using compulsory 'AIDS testing' as a precedent, begin to agitate for mandatory testing for genetic predispositions to cancer, cystic fibrosis, and other illnesses. By then, however, it will be too late to quibble about who deserves civil rights."

In the July 6 issue of *New York Native,* we introduced the scientist Peter Duesberg to the world, in the form of a long interview by John Lauritsen. Lauritsen wrote, "The hypothesis that Human Immuno-deficiency Virus (HIV) the so-called 'AIDS virus' is the cause of AIDS may have been dealt a death blow by an article that appeared in the 1 March 1987 issue of *Cancer Research*: 'Retroviruses as Carcinogens and Pathogens: Expectations by Peter H. Duesberg.' The article broadly reviews the putative role of retroviruses (such as HTLV-I) in causing leukemia or other forms of cancer, as well as the role of HIV in causing AIDS. Duesberg concludes that it is far from proven that retroviruses play any role whatever in causing cancer, and that the claim that HIV causes AIDS is equally unfounded."

Lauritsen quoted Duesberg's judgment about HIV and AIDS from the *Cancer Research* article: "It seems likely that AIDS virus is just the most common occupational viral infections of AIDS patients and those at risk for AIDS rather than the cause of AIDS. The disease would then be caused by an as yet unidentified agent which may not even be a virus."

In the July 27 issue of *New York Native,* I wrote an article that challenged all of the epidemiological premises upon which conservative and liberal homophobes and heterosexists were basing their political attacks on gays. Titled "The Real Epidemic," I asked "Is AIDS actually an acute form of Chronic Epstein-Barr virus (CEBV) [another predecessor term for chronic fatigue syndrome]? That is bound to be the most urgent question to be settled by scientists in the months ahead. But other questions arise. Do CEBV and AIDS have the same cause, but different outcomes? Does every person who has AIDS have CEBV? And is the cause of CEBV Dr. Gallo's virus HBLV [eventually called HHV-6]?"

I reported, "In the May 30 issue of *Hospital Practice* magazine, Dr. Anthony L. Kamaroff, Director of the Division of General Medicine and Primary Care at Brigham and Women's Hospital, Harvard Medical School, gave one of the most complete descriptions of the syndrome called CEBV to date. Komaroff chooses to call the disorder Chronic Viral Fatigue Syndrome (CVFS). [Kamoroff's] report summarizes research performed on more than three hundred patients from various parts of the country who have chronic mononucleosis. . . . Komaroff concludes that CVFS [CEBV] is a real organic disease because of 'recurrent pharyngitis and other symptoms of upper respiratory infection, recurrent cervical adenopathy, and low grade fevers 99.4 to 100.4).' There are also striking neurological symptoms that occur in the first weeks of the illness. The symptoms improve but do not disappear. According to Komaroff, the patients generally describe the onset of symptoms in the same way. They were fine until one day 'they developed what seemed to be a simple "cold" or "flu" with sore throat, cervical adenopathy, myalgia (sometimes), gastrointestinal symptoms, fever and profound fatigue. But unlike any previous cold or flu, the illness never went away.' "

Regarding his notions about the cause and contagiousness of the syndrome, I reported, "Komaroff concludes that 'common exposure to some external agent, infectious or environmental, seems to be the unavoidable conclusion' because his research team found 'clusters of cases of affected persons who lived with one another and developed the illness at the same time.' " I also reported, "Komaroff admits that until the agent or agents which cause the disease are identified, diagnosis may be difficult." (One of the great understatements of all time.) I then stated what I thought was painfully obvious: "Because the cause of AIDS has not yet been established, the search for the cause of CVFS (CEBV) may also offer clues as to what causes AIDS because AIDS is so closely related to the syndrome. Two graphs which accompany Komaroff's article list the symptoms and clinical findings of people with CVFS (CEBV). People with AIDS show a number of these manifestations."

I also noted, "One scientist I talked to said that AIDS-related complex (ARC) is very much like [the syndrome Komaroff described]. Another referred to the syndrome as 'closet AIDS.' " I also pointed out, "As close readers of this newspaper would expect this writer to note, the question of the cause of CVFS (CEBV) may lead back to the virus which has been suggested as the cause of AIDS by some

127

scientists: African swine fever virus. In pigs ASFV can cause acute disease (AIDS?) or chronic disease (CVFS/CEBV?)."

Had CEBV (chronic fatigue syndrome) been recognized as "closet AIDS" and been nudged out of its disingenuous closet, the pseudoscientific witch-hunt that intellectuals like Podhoretz and Hentoff were on might have been stopped in its tracks.

In that same issue of the paper, we reported again on the antics of New York City Councilman Joseph Lisa who was on that same bandwagon. Lisa had been considered for the leadership of the Council's Health Committee, but his name was withdrawn after he gave an interview to Joe Nicholson of the *New York Post* in which he reportedly said, "There are going to be instances of people who are out of control" that he thought should be quarantined. The *Post* had printed the story with a front page banner saying "AIDS Quarantine Urged." Another memorable moment in the abyss.

In that same issue of *New York Native,* we ran an interview with Gore Vidal by Terry Miller in which Vidal weighed in on AIDS and the state of the country: "You've got to remember, the aim of the government is to achieve total control over its citizens. Any government of any sort. It's instinctual. Drugs as an issue, was a godsend, so now they can have blood tests, and if you're in the government you have lie detector tests too. Have you been taking drugs? Now it's: Do you have AIDS? The idea is to create prohibitions and make *sure* that people break them. The government doesn't give a damn whether you take drugs, or go to bed with one another, or for that matter, whether you have AIDS or not. *They like the idea of control.* They want to have enough prohibitions so that they can, if they wish, put you in jail and *shut you up.* This is the hand our government plays, and not just with sex, but with everything."

In the August 10 issue, Mike Salinas reported on President Reagan's "National Advisory Panel to Address the Issues of the AIDS Epidemic." Salinas noted that many medical experts were stunned "by his appointments of men and women with little or no experience or prior experience with AIDS on any level." One AIDS activist called the commission a "death squad" and "the Inquisition." Salinas reported that the panel included a chairman "who had absolutely no AIDS experience, an Illinois legislator who had called for mandatory AIDS testing, a retired chief of naval operations who had called for mandatory testing and the president of a major corporation who was

128

very active in right wing politics. One of the medical professionals on the panel was a regular guest host of televangelist Pat Robertson's program, *The 700 Club*." The wackiest appointee was probably "a sex therapist who favors abstinence as the best possible solution to the spread of AIDS." And, according to Salinas, "the panel's only ethnic minority member" was "the Health Commissioner for the state of Indiana who has used that position to call for the isolation of [HIV] seropositive individuals." The fact that there was also one openly gay appointee didn't make up for the disturbing fact that the panel also included John Cardinal O'Connor, Roman Catholic Archbishop of New York. Salinas noted that although O'Connor had personally volunteered to empty the bedpans of AIDS patients at St. Clare's Hospital in Manhattan, "He was also active in the fight to defeat Intro 2, the so-called 'gay rights bill' in New York City."

In the September 28 issue of the *Native*, we printed some of the testimony presented at the illustrious panel's first public meeting in Washington, D.C. While all of the testimony from AIDS activists was impassioned and perhaps well-meaning, like most of the thought-free activism of the epidemic, it was blind to the heterosexism that was the concrete foundation of the epidemic's epidemiology and the toxic public health agenda that it engendered.

Amy Ashworth, a well-known figure in Parents and Friends of Lesbians and Gays, told the committee, "On the Weekend of July 4, 1981, I first found out about AIDS. The *New York Times* had just a few lines mentioning a new disease that mostly attacked the gay community. I called my oldest son and told him my fears. I remember telling him that AIDS would become the worst plague, since prejudice against gays would prevent decisive action. Now I feel I have been living in two worlds: the terrible world of AIDS and the other, complacent world of those who ignore it. My fears were justified." (Ashworth's fear would be even more justified in the following years. Her only two sons, both gay, would die of AIDS.)

Bill Bahlman, a member of ACT UP and Lavender Hill Mob told the commission, "The use of placebo control trials in testing treatments for a life-threatening disease such as AIDS is highly immoral. Not only is it immoral, but persons with AIDS will not cooperate with placebo studies." (While this was driven by humanitarian intentions, it was a major threat to doing biomedical science that could be considered objective and trustworthy.

Scientifically speaking, it was sheer madness.) The good news was that he also criticized the government's obsession with AZT at the expense of other promising treatments for AIDS.

Martin Robinson, a member of ACT UP, also attacked the government for letting other drugs wait in line "behind a fleet of AZT studies." He called AZT the "dubious flagship of the NIH and the FDA." He insisted, "Seven years into the epidemic, scientific efforts that would lead to curative medicines are almost at ground zero." Ironically, given the subsequent legacy of the AIDS activists and the HIV establishment, he asked, "Who's to blame for this folly? Who has been complicitous? Are we suicidal? Are we genocidal? Medicine is the ethical response to AIDS, not opinion. There's no time. There's no time here for agendas—private agendas, using AIDS as a weapon." (Unfortunately. there was also no time for serious critical thinking on the part of either the establishment or the activists. And the AIDS activists had their own agenda.)

Henry Yeager, also a member of ACT UP and the Lavender Hill Mob, attacked mandatory HIV testing, arguing, "Since there is no cure for AIDS, no treatment, what does the government envision for people who test positive for HIV antibody? Incarceration? Ware-housing? Quarantine? Attorney General Meese states publicly that HIV infection should be a factor in parole eligibility for incarcerated persons. In effect he is saying that people exposed to HIV belong in jail. At all government levels, there are proposals to legalize discrimination against [people with AIDS], people who test antibody positive, and even people perceived to be at risk for AIDS." While one can't find fault with sentiments like Yeager's, the baggage of epidemiological presumptions that usually came with such seemingly noble concerns were fated to sink the gay community into a hopeless quagmire of scientific mistakes and deceit. Like all AIDS activists, Yeager was a promoter of "education": "Only the radical modification of individual behavior will affect the trajectory of the AIDS epidemic. Such modification will only come, not from mandatory screening, but from a public commitment to the kind of sexual education that will entail an unprecedented willingness to suspend moralism in the name of life." This could be called a major gay "Stepin Fechit" moment (there were many) that most of the AIDS activists who spoke in public eventually performed, totally unaware that education which was based on the CDC's ersatz science. AIDS activism was essentially a great big gay minstrel show.

Larry Kramer, who billed himself as the co-founder of GMHC and the founder of ACT UP, also testified. He told the committee, "The field of AIDS research is a huge mess. It's strangled in bureaucratic red tape, inefficiency, and a lack of cooperation between people, agencies, and countries." Interestingly, Kramer told the commission that Dr. Anthony Fauci was being described "by many experts as 'in way over his head,' " and "the best scientists and researchers seem to be too scared to come anywhere near AIDS at all. Thus we're at the mercy of Drs. [Samuel] Broder and [Robert] Gallo of NIH, who use their positions of power to intimidate. Indeed, Gallo is known at NIH as 'the Godfather.' "

Once again, one thing AIDS Activist Numero Uno did not protest was the basic epidemiology and science that was employed in the construction of the HIV/AIDS paradigm. All the AIDS activists maintained an attitude of unquestioning, servile trust of the government's basic paradigm. Even in their angriest and most defiant moments their heads were bowed to the CDC's "homodemiology." Had the activists dared to accuse the government of not admitting that the emerging cases of CEBV or chronic fatigue syndrome were also part of the AIDS epidemic, it all would have turned out so differently. The gay and black communities might not have had to live with the yellow stars and scarlet letters of an HIV diagnosis.

In the same issue of *New York Native*, Charles Linebarger reported, "Northwest Orient Airlines refused to sell a ticket to the nation's capital to Leonard Matlovich, a Vietnam war hero and person with AIDS (PWA) who wishes to attend the October March on Washington for Lesbian and Gay Rights. Representatives of the local news media watched as ticket clerks and supervisors for the airlines explained to Matlovich that it is the airline's policy not to fly people who are believed to be infected with HIV, the so-called 'AIDS Virus.' "

In the October 19 issue, we ran one of the first hard-hitting exposés of the questionable AIDS treatment, AZT, by John Lauritsen. He analyzed a double-blind study of AZT that was published in the July 23, 1987, *New England Journal of Medicine*. Lauritsen wrote, "The description of methodology is incomplete and dishonest. Not a single table is acceptable according to statistical standards. Indeed not a single table makes sense."

The thing that upset Lauritsen the most was that the highly toxic drug was being given for "symptomatic HIV infection" when HIV hadn't even been proven to be the cause of AIDS. At the time Lauritsen was overly optimistic that the tide was turning against the HIV theory. He wrote, "The HIV edifice appears to have collapsed and the 'AIDS virus' crowd have resorted to stonewalling." Unfortunately that collapsing edifice stood for at least another quarter of a century.

The AZT study, as described by Lauritsen, sounded like a total unscientific mess: "The AZT trial was characterized throughout by sloppiness and lack of control. Recording forms were poorly designed, leading to confusion when doctors were asked to make judgments." Lauritsen argued that the seemingly impressive mortality data of the study did not stand up to scrutiny, pointing to "the inadequate descriptions of causes of death, the lack of verification of death causes, the lack of autopsies, and the refusal to release medical records." He concluded, "There is no doubt that AZT is a highly toxic drug, that it will be harmful to patients, many of whom are already severely debilitated. On the other hand, there is no scientifically credible evidence that AZT has any benefits whatsoever. The 'double blind, placebo-controlled' trial of AZT is unworthy of credence. . . . I submit that it is malpractice for physicians to prescribe AZT, a poison which can only harm the patient. I submit that it was unethical for AZT to be approved on the basis of research which was, to put it as generously as possible, invalid."

In the November 2 issue, we ran a *Bay Area Reporter* story by Jay Newquist who reported from California, "An AIDS scare campaign is being considered by state and national Republicans as a strategy to unseat Democrats who are sympathetic to the health crisis. A San Francisco political consulting firm under contract to the Republican Party has proposed a plan to 'incite public groundswell,' against Democratic candidates who are 'soft' on AIDS issues."

In the November 16 issue, I reported on a rather extraordinary event in the history of *New York Native*: "On November 2, I received a telephone called from Jim Warner, the Senior Policy Analyst in the Office of Policy Development in the White House. He had seen my name in an article in the September issue of the *Atlantic Monthly*. Warner knew that the *Native* has published a number of articles suggesting that HIV may not be the cause of AIDS, and he expressed concern that HIV may not adequately explain the epidemic. I asked

Warner about the President's position on the epidemic, and he told me that the President wants 'the best people to do the best thing,' but that the President doesn't feel that is being accomplished. Warner also told me that the White House could be seen as being divided into two groups on the issue of AIDS. One group, which he said is in the minority, wants to adopt an 'Auschwitz model' by quarantining all those infected with 'the virus.' 'The other group,' he said 'is incompetent.' Several times during our conversation, Warner stressed that there are many incompetent scientists working for the government. He said he was not impressed that a majority of scientists believe that HIV is the cause of AIDS, because throughout history majorities have been wrong. He is very concerned about the haphazard collection of data on HIV, and noted that between a million and a million-and-a-half Americans are 'infected.' If the epidemic is indeed spreading, Warner wonders why the CDC's estimates don't reflect it. Warner also asked me whether Dr. Robert Gallo (the man credited by some with the discovery of HIV, and by others with having stolen it from researchers at the Pasteur Institute in Paris) had ever stated that HIV is the cause of AIDS. I told him that Gallo had on numerous occasions. Warner expressed a desire to establish the real cause of AIDS so that the government resources could be spent on treating those infected. . . . Warner wanted to know how he could get in touch with Peter Duesberg, the retrovirologist who believes that Gallo is wrong about HIV's connection to AIDS. I gave him Duesberg's telephone number."

In the same issue, we published an article by Phil Zwickler about a fundraising letter that was being mailed to Manhattan businesses by a group called The Coalition for Public Health which was sponsored by The American Policy Institute. The letter was another example of the politically dystopian world that AIDS had become. The very nasty and hypocritical political letter accused the gay community of playing politics with the epidemic. The letter, according to Zwickler's report, called "on all New Yorkers to get involved in stopping the spread of AIDS." And it promoted "mandatory AIDS testing." The word "mandatory" had become a menacing rhetorical baseball bat through-out the epidemic.

In the December 7 issue of *New York Native*, we published the text of a speech that was given by Larry Kramer at the Sixth Annual Human Rights Campaign Fund Dinner at the Waldorf Astoria Hotel in

Manhattan. Kramer said, "In reading over my collected diatribes of the past years, I realized I am still unable to resolve this fundamental problem: how to inspire you without punishing you." (Kramer was from the bizarre school of speakers who announce what effect they are going to have on you. ACT UP was cut from the same presumptuous cloth in that the organization often announced what impact their actions were having. It was never left to observers or historians. It really was just another way of telling the gay community what they were supposed to be thinking.) Kramer noted in his talk, "We have managed to turn mourning into some kind of art form," making one wonder just how authentic that kind of mourning really was.

Kramer once again pontificated on a litany of the gay community's failures: "We are woefully unprepared;" "We still have no leaders with national recognition;" "We still have not learned how to broker our power;" "We still have no national publication that is worthy of respect;" "We still have no national organizations that are strong."

One of Kramer's questionable themes was always the lack of cooperation between gay and AIDS groups and the constant pedestrian demand that they "consolidate." In retrospect, during the epidemic, there was *too much* cooperation between gay groups, which turned them into one big unthinking gay blob.

Ironically, considering the salient theme of this book, Kramer said, "In my writing, I make a lot of comparisons between gays now and the Jewish community before the war. The Jews thought of themselves as good Germans first and good Jews second. When the horror started, they couldn't believe what their fellow Germans were doing to them." The irony here is of course that at least the Jews could eventually see what was actually transpiring around them, but the epidemiologically clueless Kramer and his ilk were totally blind to what was really happening to the gay community—with their help. Kramer argued, "The battle is first and foremost for a cure." That sounds good, but that battle was secondary to a far more important one Kramer didn't even know he should have been fighting, a battle for the whole truth about the real epidemic that was concealed by heterosexist epidemiology that created the demonic public health paradigm.

Kramer does deserve some credit for calling Anthony Fauci "Public Enemy Number One" in the speech. He accused Fauci of setting up treatment centers that did not work and of squandering millions of dollars on studies of AZT. Kramer was constantly screaming murder and genocide without himself really understanding what the primary source of the murder and the genocide actually was. In the speech he also said, "Oh, my people, why don't you hear me when I use the word 'murdered?' Why don't you believe me when I tell you that Dr. Fauci and his boss, Dr. Wyngaarden, and our president, Ronald Reagan, and our Mayor Edward I. Koch—all megalomaniacs playing god—are murdering us?" The only thing one can say about this list is that it is a judgment-free collection of apples and oranges. In many ways Ed Koch, who Kramer was oddly obsessed with and often accused of being a closet homosexual, was considered at that time to be a reliable friend of the gay community. As far as Kramer's charge of "megalomaniacs" goes, it was coming from the inside of a glass house.

In the same issue of the *Native*, we published an article by Ed Koch which was sent to us by his office in response to Kramer's speech. In it Koch attacked anti-gay members of Congress for trying to pass an amendment to an AIDS bill that would declare, "None of the federal money that is appropriated to the Centers for Disease Control in Atlanta can be used directly or indirectly for propagating or expanding directly or indirectly the homosexual lifestyle." The amendment was an indirect attack on Gay Men's Health Crisis which, ironically, through its education efforts was itself propagating the government's scapegoating epidemiology and AIDS paradigm. The right-wing Congressmen should have been cheering the propaganda efforts of GMHC.

In the December 28 issue, we published an update on AZT by John Lauritsen. He reported that despite the growing doubts about the safety and efficacy of AZT, "Doctors in New York have become even more aggressive in persuading and even bullying their patients into taking AZT. I have twice had the gut-wrenching experience of talking to young men who are healthy, although they have tested positive for antibodies to HIV and have low T-cell ratios, trying to dissuade them from going on AZT. Both times I failed. They agreed with everything I said, but the bottom line was that they trusted their doctors."

Lauritsen also reported that he was "now investigating a report of a young man, admitted to a New York hospital with his first case of Pneumocystis carinii pneumonia, was immediately put on AZT, despite his strong objections. If this report is true, then fundamental questions of medical ethics are involved. Do doctors have the right to force a patient against his will to take a highly toxic drug whose benefits are entirely speculative?"

1988: The Public Relations of the Epidemic

The new year brought with it the hope that a meeting scheduled by James Warner for a debate about whether HIV was a huge scientific mistake would actually take place in the White House. Warner had invited both Peter Duesberg and Robert Gallo to the meeting. But, on January 8, Joe Nicholson reported in the *New York Post* that the meeting had been canceled.

Ironically, a man who was no friend of the gay community, Gary Bauer, President Reagan's top domestic adviser, was a sponsor of the meeting and was concerned that HIV might not be the cause of AIDS. Nicholson reported that Bauer told him, "I've sort of bristled at the finality with which some have made statements about AIDS and how it is transmitted. When findings run counter to accepted wisdom, there is a tendency to muzzle or ignore rather than have an open debate."

Harvey Bialy, who was a research editor at *Bio/Technology* magazine and was a supporter of Peter Duesberg's criticism of HIV, had been called by the White House to help organize the meeting. Bialy had suggested that the White House invite Gallo and Fauci to the debate. In his book, *Oncogenes, Aneuploidy, and AIDS: A Scientific Life and Times of Peter H. Duesberg*, Bialy wrote, "The day of our 1987 Christmas office party I spoke with Jim Warner for the last time when he called to tell me that sadly the meeting was off. He had been advised that Anthony Fauci, far from reacting as I anticipated, threw a 'snit fit' when he was invited, and demanded to know why the White House was interfering in scientific matters that belonged to NIH and the Office of Scientific and Technology Assessment. . . . I always thought that the short-circuiting of the scientific meeting was a watershed moment in the battle over the etiology of AIDS." In retrospect, had it happened, it might have altered the course of AIDS/CFS history. But for AIDS dissidence, bad luck seemed to rule the day.

In one of the more bizarre chapters in the *Native*'s history, Ann Fettner, who had done such an astounding job of exposing the deceitful nature of the CDC's science (for which I am eternally grateful), suddenly got HIV religion and in a shocking betrayal of everything I thought she stood for, she wrote a piece attacking Duesberg, in the February 2 issue of the *Village Voice*. In my editorial response, I wrote, "On the subject of the epidemic, the *Voice* gets stranger and stranger. Those of us who used to love the *Voice* because it spoke truth to power are in a state of shock that the paper has been turned . . . into a house organ for the government's line of baloney on the epidemic. As far as Fettner is concerned, I have to take the blame for having created a monster. But I do think that most of what she wrote for the *Native* had—and still has—merit. The idea of Fettner treating Duesberg as if he were some kind of crackpot is absurd. Everybody in the field of retrovirology knows that he is a serious scientist, and that his ideas are anything but frivolous. The same cannot be said about Fettner's [new] 'scientific' ideas." In her *Voice* piece, Fettner quoted the ever-petulant Fauci as saying that major AIDS researchers would not take Duesberg seriously because "they're much too busy, they've got too much to do to do that."

Fettner was on a personal mission that was clearly driven by a certain amount of spite towards me for not being able to afford to keep her writing for the *Native*. She now mocked the whole idea of African swine fever being the cause of AIDS, framing it as just a grand conspiracy theory. (She wouldn't be the first to concoct that tactic to try and permanently stigmatize the idea.) According to her, "HIV is fabulous enough to provide all the answers needed to explain the equally fabulous disease it kicks off." Such cogent thinking is why the epidemic turned out to be such a "fabulous" time for all involved. It's tragic to think that if the *Native* had not been hanging by a financial thread and I had enough money to pay her to write for the *Native* she might never have ended up on the HIV bandwagon, attacking virtually the only publication (other than *Spin*, a monthly magazine which published Celia Farber's excellent investigative journalism) that dared to do any critical reporting on the epidemic.

In the February 29 issue, John Lauritsen penned a critical piece about the way the *Voice* and Fettner handled the Duesberg story, starting with the intentionally nasty way the paper photographed Duesberg. He wrote, "The *Voice* sent a team of photographers to shoot Duesberg in Berkeley. They treated him like royalty, shot him in many different poses and left. After an hour, they returned and took still more shots. After all that, the photograph published in the *Voice* shows Duesberg leaning forward, his hand stretching toward the camera, his eyes almost closed, his expression tense. The camera angle is grotesquely lopsided. The lighting is harsh, from the side and below—

the kind of lighting known as 'monster lighting,' because of its use in horror movies. The photo makes Duesberg look sinister and demented—like a 'mad scientist' from a cheaply made science-fiction/horror movie. In fact Duesberg is a very photogenic man. I have photographed him on two occasions and found it almost effortless to obtain excellent portraits. . . . All photographs need not be flattering, but they should at least be truthful. The *Village Voice* published a photograph that does not look anything like Duesberg: a cheap propaganda trick."

Lauritsen reported that when Fettner "interviewed Duesberg, she flattered him in every way, agreed with him again and again, and indicated that she was simply thrilled to be talking to such an important scientist. . . . Out of a long interview she conducted, Fettner quotes only a few sentences of Duesberg's, and these are hopelessly mangled and out of context. . . . From Fettner's article, no one would know what Duesberg's ideas are, or where to find them. Fettner doesn't want the reader to know. . . . After spewing out quite a bit of impertinent and distasteful gossip, Fettner suddenly shifts gears and goes into rather wild speculation on ways in which HIV might cause AIDS. . . . Fettner concludes her piece by accusing Duesberg of holding back the fight against AIDS. With so much new research being generated, and so much that needs to be done, she asks, why are we now forced to stop and deal with Duesberg's passé propositions? Fettner's accusation is despicable. All that is being asked of Gallo, Fauci, Haseltine, Essex and Montagnier, is that they fulfill their obligations as scientists and defend their hypothesis, in an appropriate publication, against Duesberg's critique."

In the March 21 issue, in an editorial, I brought up the matter of the possible relationship between HHV-6 and African swine fever: "As most readers of this newspaper know, I presume that the large DNA virus with which Robert Gallo is currently playing science is African swine fever virus. As data leaks out of his lab, it's clear that his virus is linking itself to both chronic fatigue syndrome and Acquired Immunodeficiency Syndrome. People like Howard Streicher, Gallo's charming Guy Friday, hem and haw about not having a good test for their swine virus, and have therefore come to no conclusions. But discussions with a source close to the heart of their research suggest a necessary cofactor for AIDS has been found. If that's true, Gallo's African swine fever virus could also become a nominee for the "cause"

139

of AIDS. Perhaps African swine fever is the pathogen toward which we should be directing our vaccine and antiviral efforts. And shouldn't we be screening the blood supply for African swine fever virus if it is a cofactor of AIDS and a cause of chronic fatigue syndrome? Gallo's biggest problem with his [recently discovered] virus is that it destroys cells in the immune system more efficiently than his Human Immunodeficiency Virus (HIV). The pathogenic difference between the two viruses is so dramatic that one well-known scientist in New York is reported to have said that if Gallo's DNA virus had been discovered before his RNA virus, it would have been declared the cause of AIDS."

I also wrote, "One of the more amusing developments in swine fever research involves scientist Jane Teas and British researcher Robert G. Downing. Several years ago, Downing helped Teas test blood from AIDS patients for the presence of several strains of African swine fever virus. As we have reported in these pages, the tests [performed in England] were positive for a number of samples. Teas flew back to the U.S. expecting to write up the results with Downing and submit them to a medical journal. But over the ensuing weeks, Downing wouldn't acknowledge her phone calls, and their collaboration fell apart. But Downing suddenly resurfaced in the August 15, 1987, issue of *The Lancet*, where he reported on the isolation of a large, DNA virus from AIDS patients in Uganda. And what does he call it? A 'human herpesvirus.' [It was of course the virus that turned out to be HHV-6.] Based on a conversation I had last year with a senior member of the U.S Department of Agriculture, I've come to think that Gallo and Downing's basic game plan is to exploit the limited similarities between African swine fever virus and cytomegalovirus (CMV), another DNA virus for which ASFV has been mistaken, to keep the public from knowing the truth about AIDS and chronic fatigue syndrome. The last time I talked to Gallo, he was not too happy about Downing. I would be wary of him, too, since he's familiar with the Teas [ASFV] data and could expose the truth about Gallo's virus whenever he wants."

I also noted, "The emergence of a new cause or co-cause of AIDS will add to the credibility of retrovirologist Peter Duesberg's theory. Duesberg has challenged the orthodoxy that HIV is the cause of AIDS. . . . In a related matter, we must all try to educate ourselves about the plight of people affected by chronic fatigue syndrome. Their suffering is enormous. My discussions with students of the chronic fatigue

140

syndrome epidemic suggest that its breadth dwarfs the AIDS epidemic considerably. And although it may not seem as acute, it may be creating a nation of chronically ill men and women. Chronic fatigue syndrome is still in the closet, partly due to the politics of HHV-6 and African swine fever virus, but it is expected to get a media boost from Congressional hearings in the months ahead. Chronic fatigue syndrome should be declared a priority health problem by the National Institutes of Health. Funding for chronic fatigue syndrome research is miniscule and the public knows little about the disease. . . . People with the illness exhibit a wide array of unusual symptoms and clinical problems. Cancer and circulatory problems can occur. Most ominous is the neurological damage that some researchers have encountered. People with the syndrome sometimes have trouble concentrating and make perceptual mistakes."

In the same issue of the *Native*, we ran an article by Phil Zwickler about the reaction to a book by Dr. William H. Masters, his partner Virginia Johnson, and Dr. Robert Kolodny. *Crisis: Heterosexual Behavior in the Age of AIDS*, which was published by Grove Press. The authors concluded, "Authorities are greatly underestimating the number of people infected with the AIDS virus in the population today." The writers had strayed off the AIDS reservation and dared to tell truths which came very close to outing the real epidemic behind the political veil of the HIV epidemic. Zwickler wrote, "While stating that AIDS is 'now running rampant in the heterosexual community,' they maintain that three million Americans, more than twice the number claimed by public health experts, are seropositive." The authors shocked the nation by asserting, "Infection with the AIDS virus does not require intimate sexual contact or sharing of intravenous needles; transmission can, and does, occur as a result of person-to-person contact in which blood or other body fluids from a person who is harboring the virus are splashed onto or rubbed against someone else."

Masters, Johnson, and Kolodny seem to have inadvertently glanced into *something closer to the real epidemic* and were more in touch with what was going on behind the jerry-built paradigm than even they realized. They paid a price for trying to tell it like it is. A series of reactions gathered by Zwickler did a stunning job of catching in real time the vicious political correctness that was forming around the government's paradigm. It also showed how an unholy alliance between AIDS activists, quasi-governmental AIDS organizations and the gay community was forming. Masters, Johnson, and Kolodny had called for something draconian which helped cement an unholy alliance of opposition. According to Zwickler, "The authors call for mandatory HIV antibody testing for couples seeking a marriage license, pregnant women, convicted prostitutes, and all hospital in-patients between the ages of 15 and 60, as a way of stopping the epidemic."

Dr. Stephen Joseph, the New York City Commissioner of Health, told Zwickler that the authors raised "all the old 'bugaboos' about transmission." Interestingly, Joseph inadvertently caught the constantly shifting landscape of information about the epidemic when he said, "The book is damaging in that it takes us off on a swing. In the media, nine months ago, a heterosexual explosion of AIDS was cited. Three months ago *Cosmopolitan* said heterosexuals were not at risk. Now, Masters and Johnson write this book. It does confuse people. Heterosexual transmission is a real problem, but rampant spread, an image of diffuse spread—that's not happening." That was of course very true if you didn't factor chronic fatigue syndrome into the paradigm of AIDS. If the public was confused, it is because of the unsteadiness and lack of consistency at the very heart of the public relations image of the epidemic that the CDC was promoting. Masters, Johnson, and Kolodny were hopelessly trying to make sense out of a paradigm that was half self-deception and half noble epidemiological lie meant to keep everybody pacified.

Mathilde Krim, the founding chair of the American Foundation for AIDS Research, told Zwickler, "I believe it is an insult for Dr. Virginia Johnson to suggest that the time-tested methods of medical investigation have resulted in 'benevolent scientific deceptiveness' concerning AIDS, its modes of transmission and its rate of transmission." Peter Drotman, an epidemiologist with the CDC's AIDS Program told Zwickler, "The book is not helpful. It is not a scientific contribution to our understanding of AIDS. It stresses some farfetched scenarios that seem designed to provoke anxiety rather than to make useful suggestions. . . . AIDS is pretty clearly not running rampant among heterosexuals." He was right of course because the form of acquired immunodeficiency that was running rampant in the heterosexual population was simply renamed chronic fatigue syndrome. Epidemiological rebranding was an instant cure for AIDS in the heterosexual population.

Unfortunately, the gay people Zwickler interviewed performed like a perky backup chorus to the AIDS establishment. Christopher Babick, Acting Director of People With AIDS Coalition, said, "I think their book is a reckless piece of literature. AIDS continues to affect mostly the communities it always has—namely, gay men, IV-drug users and their sexual partners." Maria Maggenti of the Women's Committee, AIDS Coalition to Unleash Power went even further, telling the *Native*, "I'm pretty horrified by the whole thing. Major actions should be taken against the book because it is only fueling the misinformation out there." (The gay community developed a very unfortunate and self-destructive taste for "major action" censorship during the epidemic.) Lori Behrman, the spokesperson for Gay Men's Health Crisis said, "Masters and Johnson have squandered their credibility to exploit a grave public health issue. Every AIDS researcher in the country will tell you that HIV cannot be transmitted casually. Their conclusion that mandatory testing is the answer overlooks the less expensive, more effective tool, which is education. The gay community has proved that safer sex and not testing can provide protection." In truth, the least expensive and most effective tool was actually the CDC's political epidemiology, which used public relations and a biased anti-gay paradigm to keep the disease from *appearing* to spread in the general population. This was just another example of the gay community having to do its abject "education is protection" minstrel show in the face of the draconian, spiteful call for mandatory testing. Every time the word "mandatory" was used it had more than a nasty little soupçon of "Get the gays" to it. The gay community, in such a dire situation, had to make a pact with the AIDS establishment to accept all the elements of its very political epidemiology—or else! Had the gay community called it out for the biased "homodemiology" that it was, everything would have been different.

Masters, Johnson, and Kolodny were threatening to expose what Daniel Goleman (after Ibsen) refered to as a "vital lie" which, Goleman describes as "a family myth that stands in place of a less comfortable truth." In this case it was a "vital lie" about the AIDS epidemic that prevented social anxiety. In Zwickler's survey of the AIDS and gay elite, one could see the social construction of a comforting false reality, a psychological phenomenon explored at length in Goleman's book, *Vital Lies, Simple Truths*. This moment in the epidemic captures Goleman's central thesis: "We are piloted in part by an ingenious capacity to deceive ourselves, whereby we sink into obliviousness rather than face threatening facts. This tendency to self-deception and mutual pretense pervades the structure of psychological life."

143

You could say that a kind of conspiracy of self-deception had begun on a massive scale in America and Masters, Johnson, and Kolodny (like the *Native*) were playing the role of unwelcome truth-tellers who needed to be neutralized by a kind of thuggish mockery. This moment was yet more evidence that, during the epidemic, there was never any such thing as what Goleman refers to as "acceptable dissent."

In the March 28 issue, we published John Lauritsen's most hard-hitting attack on AZT titled "AZT Iatrogenic Genocide." Lauritsen complained that five months after his first exposé of AZT, "the same old lies continue to appear in the mainstream press. It is still claimed that AZT 'extends life.' AZT not only continues to be marketed, but is being promoted more heavily than ever. In New York City, nearly all doctors with an AIDS practice are prescribing AZT, some of them indiscriminately. According to an article by Gina Kolata, in the *New York Times* (December 21, 1987), some doctors " 'have no set guidelines but let the patients decide if they want the drug.' " One wonders what the government would have done if the gay community had decided en masse *not* to take the drug. What if there had been an AZT version of the Boston Tea Party?

The tragedy of the epidemic was captured in technicolor by Lauritsen: "Not all patients have taken AZT voluntarily. Some have been bullied into taking it by their doctors. In Trenton State Prison, prisoners are being forced to take AZT against their will. In St. Vincent's Hospital, a patient's request not to be given AZT was ignored. And in Chicago, a hospitalized AIDS patient was declared insane because of his refusal to take AZT; the doctors said his refusal meant he didn't want to live and he was forced to take AZT."

Lauritsen was shocked at the course of events and his critique of what was going on was devastating: "It isn't supposed to happen like this. In fiction or the movies, once the crime and the criminal have been exposed, the plot is almost over. The malefactors are apprehended and brought to justice. End of story. But in real life, when your opponent is a wealthy, powerful, and unscrupulous drug manufacturer, who is aided and abetted by the stupidity, venality, and authoritarianism of the medical profession, the struggle goes on and on. A reasoned analysis, backed up by plenty of evidence, is countered with a propaganda juggernaut (advertising campaign) that shows total contempt for reason and evidence. And it works. Most people forget about facts if they haven't heard them repeated within the past few weeks (or days)."

Lauritsen summed up the AZT situation at that point: "We know for sure that AZT is a highly toxic drug, so toxic that about half of all AIDS patients cannot tolerate it and have to be taken off the drug. AZT destroys bone marrow and causes anemia so severe as to necessitate frequent transfusions. We know that AZT is cytotoxic—it kills healthy cells. We know that AZT attacks DNA synthesis. . . . In San Francisco, where doctors are more critical of AZT, doctors admit to having seen horrible results from AZT: liver, kidney, and neurological damage as well as the inevitable anemia and trans-fusions."

Lauritsen also noted, "On February 19, 1988, Dr. Anthony Fauci of the National Institutes of Allergy and Infectious Diseases, who is in charge of federal AIDS funding, appeared on the television program *Good Morning, America*. (Prof. Peter Duesberg was also to have appeared on the program, in order to debate Fauci on whether HIV causes AIDS, but he was disinvited at the last moment, for reasons that have yet to be explained.) Fauci was asked why only one drug had been made available. He replied, 'The reason that only one drug has been made available—AZT—is because it's the only drug that has been shown in scientifically controlled trials to be safe and effective.' " Lauritsen noted, "This brief statement contains several falsehoods. (Since I don't know whether Fauci told these untruths deliberately or out of ignorance, I'll simply call them 'falsehoods,' as opposed to 'lies.') First . . . there have been no 'scientifically controlled trials' of AZT. Second, AZT is not 'safe.' It is a highly toxic drug (the FDA analyst who reviewed the toxicology data recommended that AZT should not be approved). Third, AZT is not known objectively to be 'effective' for anything, except perhaps causing anemia, destroying bone marrow, and blocking DNA synthesis."

Lauritsen came to a very dark conclusion: "It is difficult to avoid thinking that we gay men have been targeted for destruction. . . . At this point, we don't know the long term effects of AZT; no one has taken it for more than two years. However, death within a few years would appear to be the consequence of a drug that causes severe anemia, destroys bone marrow, and blocks DNA synthesis."

The unmitigated horror of the epidemic was also caught in Lauritsen's report that Dr. William Haseltine of the Dana Farber Institute in Boston told the Presidential Committee on AIDS on February 19 that AZT should be given to all members of 'high risk' groups." Lauritsen wrote, "His reasoning was as follows: 'HIV infection' is still confined to the present risk groups, gay men and IV-drug users. However, uninfected gay men face an annual risk of becoming infected, and this in turn represents a threat to the general population. Therefore, as a containment measure, HIV-antibody negative gay men should be given AZT in order to prevent their becoming 'infected.' " Lauritsen asserted, "Haseltine's analysis is based on the probably false premise that HIV is the cause of AIDS. It assumes that AZT kills or somehow inhibits HIV, whereas there is no evidence that it does. Everything about Haseltine's suggestion is wrong, unless one believes it is a good thing to kill off gay men and other members of 'risk groups.' "

Lauritsen then let out a clarion call for which he deserves a special place in history: "It's time for us to wake up. Healthy gay men are being targeted for genocide. Why do we let them do this to us? Where is our anger? We have become numb: From mourning, when we couldn't mourn. From held-in-rage and disgust at the lies, the greed, the malice, and the incompetence of those we ought to be able to depend on. From unrelenting fear, from confusion, from not knowing what to do. Our wills have become paralyzed."

He continued, "We must act to prevent our brothers from being poisoned. The time has come to express our anger. The time has come for us to be honest with our friends who have been gulled into taking AZT. We should tell them, tactfully but directly, that they are being poisoned, and that if necessary, they should change directions."

He closed his piece by declaring, "AZT doctors should be sued for engaging in false and misleading advertising. Public Health Service officials should be sued for unethical and illegal conduct. The time has come for lawsuits."

Earlier in 1988, I had hired a woman named Neenyah Ostrom as my assistant. She had been working at Biogen in Boston and, for a while, was the assistant to Walter Gilbert, a Nobel Prize Winner. She had originally pursued a career in medicine but decided during her pre-med courses that it wasn't for her. I was so impressed with her intelligence and editorial talents that soon after I hired her I asked her to begin covering chronic fatigue syndrome on a regular basis for *New York Native*. I also chose to do this as a way of sending a signal to the AIDS establishment that we were absolutely not going to back down on our concern that CFS and AIDS were totally intertwined. We made

146

her work a regular feature and gave her column the title "Chronic Fatigue Report." The *New York Native* thorn in the AIDS establishment's side was about to become more painful.

Ostrom's first article was titled "Movement in Search of a Name." The piece began, "A new disease is ravaging our country. An increasing number of people are no longer able to work, to care for their families or themselves. They suffer from fevers, sore throats, swollen lymph glands, depression, headaches, neurological dysfunction, memory loss, cognitive disorders. Some develop brain lesions; some, B-cell lymphomas. Pervading all these symptoms is an overwhelming exhaustion that leaves patients unable to lift a toothbrush, stand long enough to shower, or even get out of bed. These frightened, exhausted people deplete their savings in search of medical care. In desperation, they go from one physician to another, most of whom are unable to diagnose their illness or—even more devastating—pronounce it to be psychosomatic."

Ostrom then asked a question that would be asked continuously for the next quarter of a century: "In this age of lasers and holography, when it has become routine to rearrange the DNA of living organisms, how is it possible that a debilitating new disease is falling through the cracks of scientific inquiry?"

Ostrom reported, "Chronic Epstein-Barr virus (CEBV) syndrome was the name given to the outbreak that brought the illness to national attention, a mini-epidemic near Lake Tahoe, Nevada, in 1985." She noted that the name was falling into disfavor because it was becoming clear that EBV was not the cause. She then cut to the chase and made a point that would be maintained by the newspaper until its demise in 1997: "But what has most impeded research has been the (recently reversed) refusal of the Federal Centers for Disease Control" to acknowledge the syndrome's existence. Ted Van Zelst, a philanthropist who had created an organization to fund research into the syndrome told her, "The CDC took the position very adamantly until mid-1986 that no such disease existed."

Ostrom wrote that at that point an organization for sufferers of the syndrome had "12,000 paid members and more than 200 local chapters across the U.S." A leader of the San Francisco chapter of that organization, Jan Montgomery, told Ostrom that the "illness does not stand alone, but is part of a group of immunosuppressive syndromes, including, but not limited to, AIDS and AIDS-related complex." (It was, as we shall see, a rare moment of unflinching honesty from a CFS patient and activist.)

At that time, according to Ostrom, "The two names the association is considering for the disease" were "Chronic Fatigue Immune Dysfunction Syndrome and Acquired Chronic Immune Dysfunction." The use of the word "fatigue" was already seen as a serious scientific and political mistake. Ostrom wrote, "The people I discussed it with at several local CEBV Association chapters were unanimous about eradicating 'fatigue' from the description, because of the trivializing effect. Overwhelming fatigue is a symptom, along with flu-like symptoms such as fever, swollen glands, sore throat, headaches, muscle aches and depression. These symptoms don't go away for months, sometimes years. In some cases, there is a progression to extreme mental and neurological deterioration, lesions in the brain, and a rare form of a fatal malignancy, B-lymphotropic cancer."

Ostrom also reported that the CDC's Dr. Gary Holmes had been dismissive of the disease in the *New York Times* and *Hippocrates Magazine* where he blamed the fuss on the media and physicians who got caught up in a kind of mania and started seeing and diagnosing the disease everywhere.

The scope of the epidemic was controversial then in 1988 and remained so for the next 25 years. Ostrom pointed out that in a *JAMA* article in May of 1987, Harvard scientist Anthony Kamaroff "reported major symptoms of chronic fatigue syndrome in 21% of 500 randomly selected hospital patients."

In mid-April, the *New York Times* and *The Washington Post* published stories raising questions about the scientific integrity of David Baltimore, a Nobel Prize winner and someone who was part of the nation's AIDS inner circle. I wrote in the *Native*, "A research paper published by Baltimore and others is not backed by research which they conducted, and Baltimore refused to retract the paper and has done everything he can to hurt the career of a scientist who discovered his phony conclusions. The pattern emulates the behavior of Harvard School of Publish Health researcher Myron Essex when scientists began to find that an antigen called F.O.C.M.A., which Essex 'discovered,' does not really exist. Soon their careers did not exist."

I took the opportunity to raise a larger issue: "The possibility that Baltimore is a con artist doesn't help the case of HIV, which he has been backing for some time. Fraud seems to be a way of life among scientists who are in charge of AIDS research in this country. One of the key questions Congress needs to ask is whether the domination of American AIDS research by scientific crooks such as Essex, Baltimore, and Robert Gallo, and incompetents such as Samuel Broder, Anthony Fauci, and Harold Jaffe, has discouraged scientists with brains and integrity from getting involved. Who would want to work in a scientific cesspool in which you get fired or lose grants because you tell the truth?"

I then laid out the case for HHV-6 being the new politically correct name for African swine fever virus: "As the papers about a virus called human herpesvirus-6 (HHV-6) slowly appear (and there is some speculation that the White House has ordered HHV-6 papers to emerge slowly), it looks like the cause of AIDS will turn out to be that virus (or a related DNA virus), and *not* HIV. The trail of epidemiology and lab research also leads to this conclusion: HHV-6 will turn out to be African swine fever virus. Jane Teas will turn out to have been correct when she hypothesized that African swine fever virus causes AIDS, and Gallo and Luc Montagnier will turn out to be wrong. (Teas has not publicly posited the theory that African swine fever virus is the cause of chronic fatigue syndrome, but the *Native* has.) Teas has found it difficult to find a job in science as a result of the promulgation of her ideas. If she turns out to be correct, she deserves every scientific award imaginable, and a major position at the scientific institution of her choice. It is worth pointing out that the person who noted the errors in Baltimore's research paper was a woman, too. Women who tell the truth don't fare well in American science."

I also let Mathilde Krim have it in the editorial: "In *Omni* magazine's November 1987 issue, Mathilde Krim said, 'In today's system of science, I think at the top there is less difference between men and women because those of both sexes who are different have already been eliminated. At the top all have learned to play the same game. And it's a bit of a con game.' My question to Krim is: Which con game are you and the American Foundation for AIDS Research playing this week? How difficult would it be for amfAR to admit that AIDS research has revolved around the wrong virus for five years, and that we have a lot of work to do with African swine fever virus? The best course of action at this point would be not to continue throwing good money after bad. Krim has an opportunity to lead our nation out of this huge scientific mistake. Americans can live with mistakes, but will face total catastrophe if the lies about African swine fever virus continue much longer."

I asserted, "Gallo's scam of trying to sell African swine fever virus as HHV-6 is yet another example of his crookedness. He doesn't want Teas to get credit for figuring out the cause of AIDS from both her epidemiology and the lab work she did with researchers John Beldekas and James Hebert. Gallo's lies are dangerous to himself, his staff, and the nation. A source close to Gallo's staff has told the *Native* that the wife of one of Gallo's associates is sick with the chronic disease (CFS) that may be caused by African swine fever virus. Is Gallo telling the poor woman that she's infected with HHV-6, when in reality she's suffering from a chronic infection with swine fever virus—which is absolutely *not* a herpesvirus. (Even Dr. Pearson of George Washington University told me that they're not certain [HHV-6 is] a herpesvirus.)"

Again the eternal optimist who thought change was right around the corner, I wrote, "There are at a least dozen scientists in America who have done extensive research on African swine fever virus. They should be summoned to the National Institutes of Health to help the nation figure out what to do about the virus Gallo tried to con the nation into believing was a herpesvirus."

In her "Chronic Fatigue Report" in the same issue, Neenyah Ostrom introduced the *Native* readers to Stephen E. Straus of the National Institute of Allergy and Infectious Diseases (NIAID), the man who would become public enemy number one to CFS patients and activists. Straus was in charge of what NIAID called its CFS research for the formative years of the CFS epidemic or cover-up, depending on your point of view. Ostrom reported, "Straus remains a vocal proponent of the psychoneurotic theory of CFS. In his [*JAMA*] March 1988 article he states, 'It is impossible to completely dispel the notion that the chronic fatigue syndrome represents a psychoneurotic condition. On the contrary, there are observations that support the hypothesis.' Straus cites an outbreak of 'mass hysteria' at the Royal Free Hospital in London in 1955. He also references the unpublished observations of Dr. Markus Kruesi at the National Institutes of Health that psychiatric evaluations of patients with CFS reveal that a 'very high proportion' have a history of depression, phobias or anxiety disorders. His article concludes: 'Ultimately, any hypothesis regarding the cause of the chronic fatigue syndrome must incorporate the psycho-pathology that accompanies and, in some cases, precedes it.'"

In the same report, Ostrom noted that early testing of CFS patients for HHV-6 was not producing any clear-cut results. (Testing would turn out to be a persistent political and scientific problem for the virus.)

She noted, "Because four of the six patients from whom HHV-6 initially was isolated had B cell cancers similar to those seen in CFS, a number of investigators suggested that HHV-6 might be the cause of CFS. Reports have appeared in the press that one of the Incline Village physicians, [Paul] Cheney, sent blood samples to Gallo's lab to be assayed for HHV-6." Cheney wasn't specific but told Ostrom the results were disappointing. Ostrom also reported, "In a March 1988 article in *Journal of Experimental Medicine*, Stephen Straus of NIAID quotes unpublished observations about HHV-6 from Gallo's laboratory. According to Straus, antibodies to HHV-6 are found in 10%-40% of 'normal American adults,' and in 6-80% of patients with AIDS, B cell lymphomas, and CFS. Despite the high prevalence, and 'relatively insensitive' serological methods, Straus concludes that HHV-6 remains an orphan virus in search of a disease.' "

"Relatively insensitive" serological methods turned out to be an understatement. The HHV-6 story was just begining and one could almost say that when HHV-6 finally found its disease, it was the most catastrophic multisystemic pandemic in history.

In the May 9 issue, I wrote an editorial note about something that foreshadowed the *Native*'s rocky relationship with the gay community: "One of our writers showed me a letter he'd received from a friend suggesting that he was bored with the *Native*'s AZT stories. Enough already, the writer implied. This is precisely the kind of attitude the *Native* has had to struggle with since the beginning of the epidemic. Some readers complained when we suggested that there was an epidemic under way seven years ago. Once we won on that point, we were faced with disgruntled readers who felt that our skepticism about the government's claims to have found the cause of the epidemic were out of line. The idea that gay people would trust government scientists working for the current administration is one that historians will ponder for decades to come. It probably will take a mind like Hannah Arendt's to sort through the reasons that so many gay people chose to believe so many lies. If one is a student of the Holocaust, however, one can find many instances in which people collaborated in their own demise. What we need are community leaders who can inspire people to question every statement that government scientists utter about the cause and treatment of so-called 'AIDS.' "

In the May 16 "Chronic Fatigue Report," Neenyah Ostrom interviewed Dr. Paul Cheney: "I recently asked him to describe the neurological symptoms displayed by his 200 CFS patients. Cheney told me that 90% of his patients exhibit 'soft' neurological symptoms, which he defined as symptoms in which the physician is 'struck more by the description than by the exam.' " Ostrom reported, "Hard neurological dysfunction affected 5-10% of his patients." And she noted, "Hard neurological symptoms include seizures, encephalitis, loss of muscular coordination, and weakness on one side of the body."

The amazing thing about Cheney's work, was that it always seemed to be a direct challenge to the "chronic fatigue syndrome is not AIDS" paradigm that was quickly becoming the epidemiological law of the land. But Cheney never played the role—at least not directly or loudly—of the boy in "The Emperor's New Clothes." The neurological symptoms in chronic fatigue syndrome, which Cheney thought were caused by "the elevated levels of gamma interferon, an immune system regulator" should have been a red flag about the connection between AIDS and chronic fatigue syndrome but it was just the beginning of the stubborn and catastrophic denial that would engender unimaginable suffering and cost countless lives.

Despite the *Native*'s reporting, the toxic drug AZT, thanks to AIDS activism and the dearth of critical thinking, looked like it had a very bright future. In the May 30 issue Phil Zwickler reported, "The City of New York plans a wider distribution of the highly toxic and controversial drug AZT, or Retrovir, to prisoners who suffer from AIDS. . . ." Zwickler wrote that New York planned "to identify all inmates who qualify for AZT treatment and insure that they receive AZT." Zwickler wrote, "Many AIDS specialists, including noted researcher Dr. Joseph Sonnabend, maintain that 'AZT is incompatible with life,' and that it is a 'poison' whose adverse effects far outweigh evidence that it prolongs the life of some AIDS patients who take it. Others point out that since quality health care in prison is extremely limited, giving AZT to inmates amounts to cruel and unusual punishment.' " Community activist Philip Reed told Zwickler that coercing the inmates "sounds like institutional genocide to me. In their shortsighted rush to find a solution, they have not looked hard enough."

In the same issue, I once again raised questions about HHV-6, suggesting that Gallo was "trying to sell African swine fever virus as a human herpesvirus, when in fact African swine fever virus is *not* a herpesvirus. It's in a class all by itself. I've talked to three scientists who are growing the DNA virus and none of them is willing to bet their lives that it is a herpesvirus."

I also wrote, "In the May 11 issue of the *Miami Herald*, Rosemary Goudreau reported the following: 'A newly discovered highly contagious herpesvirus might play a role in causing several types of cancer and could be a cofactor in wiping out the immune systems of AIDS patients, one of the nation's premier virologists [Robert Gallo] said Tuesday.' She also wrote, 'Since the AIDS virus kills only a small percentage of T-4 cells at a time. Gallo said the new herpesvirus [HHV-6], if proven to be the cofactor, could explain the total annihilation of T-4 cells in AIDS patients. 'The virus kills cells after using them to replicate, he said.' Goudreau quotes Gallo as saying, 'So if a cofactor is involved in the development of AIDS, and I'm not convinced it's absolutely needed . . . then we want to consider this one strongly.' "

This struck me as being backwards and I wrote, "Wait a minute. If this DNA virus explains the 'total annihilation' of T-4 cells, it seems to me that if a cofactor is involved it would be HIV, not 'HHV-6.' I wish Gallo would stop playing name games with viruses. If this virus is not really a herpesvirus, and clinicians try to treat it with anti-herpes medications, the results could be treatment failure or worse. If the DNA virus is African swine fever virus, then pigs could be used for experiments, rather than AIDS patients. And that way controlled experiments could really be controlled."

I also wrote, "From my discussions with scientists at the Department of Agriculture, I've been able to surmise that in all probability, there is an epidemic of chronic African swine fever in pigs in various parts of the country. As part of a cover-up of this epidemic, the department is stopping most of the research on African swine fever. . . . The department is also retiring a swine fever expert named William Hess, who has complained in the past about the way the USDA has handled testing for African swine fever virus. He was reprimanded for taking his ideas to the press. He has also been the primary source of my information about African swine fever virus for the past five years. I assume that he is being retired because he is something of a whistleblower and because of the information he has given the *Native*. If our nation is now in the middle of a swine fever epidemic in people and pigs, one way to deal with it is to fire everyone who tells the truth. I'm an optimist. It won't work."

Well, it kinda did.

In the May 23 issue, I reported on some shocking information I had found in a recently published textbook on African swine fever virus: ". . . it looks as if we were right about the similarities between 'AIDS' itself and African swine fever. Several officials at the U.S. Department of Agriculture ridiculed our assertions that the two diseases are similar in their clinical courses. In 1984, J. J. Callis, Director of the USDA facility at Plum Island, wrote in a memo, 'Swine ill from ASF show very little clinical similarity to AIDS in man.' A book called *African Swine Fever* by Yechiel Becker, published last year by Martinus Nijoff Publishing, presents the following sea change: 'The ability of ASF virus to infect and destroy cells of the reticuloendothelial system leaves a defenseless host that succumbs to an infection which may be described as an *acquired immune deficiency disease* of domestic pigs [italics mine].' After five years of trying to convince the USDA that this was true, at least it's nice to see that the *Native* was right all along. Wouldn't it have been nicer still if pigs instead of people with 'AIDS,' had been used to test the effectiveness of AZT . . . and other toxic antivirals?"

The in-your-face outrageousness of the Callis lie about AIDS and ASF, was a shocking warning to me about just how far the government was willing to go in deceiving the public about the epidemic. It was starting to appear that the government would do or say *anything* to maintain the epidemic's prevailing AIDS paradigm for the epidemic.

In the June 6 issue, John Lauritsen took the *New York Times* to task for its uncritical report on an AZT trial reviewed by the Food and Drug Administration. Gina Kolata had reported, "Drug company researchers say AZT prolongs life for patients." When Lauritsen looked closely at the study, the news story was based on he found no supporting evidence. Lauritsen found all kinds of anomalies in the study, especially in the way that patients who took AZT and those that didn't were compared. Lauritsen was troubled by the fact that patients on AZT still alive 11 months after they had begun treatment was considered some great kind of victory. The FDA study seemed very disingenuous because, as Lauritsen wrote, "According to an AIDS researcher who was involved in the AZT trials, only a handful of the AZT patients are still alive, and even these frequently had to be taken off the drug and/or given reduced doses."

Lauritsen sent out another warning to the gay community: "It's not easy to keep a clear head in the midst of the current 'health crisis.' The performance of the medical establishment and the media has been abysmal. On all sides we are assaulted by contradictory information. An AIDS mythology, a self-perpetuating delusional system, has developed, and irrationality of all kinds is flourishing."

In the June 20 issue, we published the text of a letter that was being sent out by Ira Glasser, the director of the American Civil Liberties Union. It was another of those "with friends like these" moments in the labyrinth of the epidemic. On the surface it seemed "right on": the letter began, "Will it come to this? Will AIDS sufferers be compelled to wear identifying badges like the Jews in Nazi Germany? Everyone knows that during World War II, Jews were made to wear yellow stars of David. What is not as well known is that homosexuals were made to wear pink triangles. Today in America, some have suggested similar methods to identify and stigmatize people with AIDS. There have even been proposals to tattoo people with AIDS. While such proposals have not been taken seriously, hysteria and fear are already producing astounding examples of inhumanity."

One can't argue with such liberal sentiments, but it is in the well-intentioned details of what the ACLU proposed that one can find the devil. All the ACLU's calls for the protection of civil liberties came wrapped in the almost Orwellian notion that the really bad thing about discrimination was that it prevented patients from getting "the education and medical services they need." The ACLU's calls for confidentiality in AIDS testing completely sidestepped the more fundamental issue of the epidemiological violation of human rights implicit in the HIV test and the anti-gay paradigm it maintained.

As soon as the ACLU joined in the charade of calling for "public education," the organization was unknowingly becoming an enabler of the "chronic fatigue syndrome is not AIDS" paradigm, which, by defrauding the gay community of the uninflected facts of the epidemic, turned the ACLU's crocodile tears about civil liberties into cold comfort. Ira Glasser closed his misguided letter with a statement that perfectly captured the unholy alliance that the civil liberties group was making in the name of helping the gay community: "We don't have to give up our freedoms to successfully fight AIDS. The twin goals of sound public health policy and a healthy respect for civil liberties are not incompatible." What Glasser didn't grasp was that everything about the AIDS paradigm violated what I would call the fundamental *epidemiological rights* of the gay community—the right not to be scapegoated for an epidemic by totalitarian, abnormal science as well as the right to epidemiological truth, something every AIDS patient and every member of the gay community was deprived of (along with the CFS sufferers and other victims of HHV-6).

John Lauritsen summed up the state of AIDS epidemiology in the August 1 issue: "Psychological warfare is being waged against gay men in the United States. For the past month or so, the media has been disseminating hostile propaganda, with the message that we will all die, that we must die. The death threats do not issue from the usual bigots—not from Roman Catholic agitators or menopausal beauty queens or fundamentalist TV hustlers or quack psychiatrists or Hasidic zealots. We are not being drummed to death by voodoo witch doctors or anathematized by prurient priests. We are being cursed in the name of science, and the imprecations directed against us have the imprimatur of the Public Health Service. The prognosis of doom is emanating from that peculiar form of medical survey research known as 'epidemiology.' "

Lauritsen was horrified by the paradigm that was forming, the one that held that all HIV-positives would die. He quoted from an article by Michael Specter that was published in *The Washington Post* on June 3: "The AIDS virus [sic] will almost certainly kill everyone it infects unless effective drugs are developed to treat it, federal researchers have predicted for the first time."

Lauritsen was alarmed that epidemiology-based research would condemn the HIV-positives to be treated with AZT and indeed, Specter confirmed it, reporting, "Public health service officials . . . hope the new study will encourage those at highest risk to be tested so that they will seek medical attention if needed. . . . Many physicians are prescribing AZT for their patients who are infected but have not developed AIDS, although the drug has not yet been proven effective for those patients. Public health officials say that this study is likely to encourage other doctors to prescribe it to patients infected with HIV."

Lauritsen argued that the study Specter reported on did not support the draconian conclusion that was being echoed in the mainstream press. The study of patients in San Francisco, which was published in *Science*, just didn't seem right in the context of what was known then about the mortality of AIDS patients. Lauritsen argued, "A basic principle of analysis is that data must make sense. This may seem too obvious to mention, but novice analysts often are slaves to the numbers they see in front of them, and will concoct bizarre explanations rather than come to grips with contradictions in the data. In actual practice, when data don't make sense, it is almost always because they are wrong." Lauritsen noted that it didn't make sense that at the time in New York City only 1% of HIV positive individuals were coming down with AIDS and, according to the questionable study, 25% of positives in San Francisco were developing AIDS. He asserted, "If HIV is the sole cause of AIDS, it is not possible for both sets of data to be correct."

Lauritsen was sensitive to the way terror of the epidemic was being used to manipulate the gay community. It was daring of him at the time to even say, "I sometimes think that too much attention and sympathy have been given to those who are sick and dying, and not enough to those of us who have healthy minds and healthy bodies. We, after all, are also targets of psychological warfare. We also are increasingly being portrayed as sources of pollution, as threats to the 'innocent' heterosexual population. . . . Our survival depends on not accepting the role of victim. If people direct death wishes at us, we should direct death wishes right back again at them. No one should be allowed to attack us with impunity. At the same time, we need to retain a sense of cool, an appropriate balance of self-preservation, anger, and a sense of humor. Aside from the fact that our lives are at stake, current events are pretty ridiculous, aren't they?"

Michael Dukakis was running for president against Ronald Reagan that autumn, so I was concerned about the person who might become his Secretary of Health and Human Services if he prevailed. In an editorial titled "An Open Letter to Mathilde Krim," I wrote, "There has been a rumor around for some time that you want to become Secretary of Health and Human Services under President Dukakis. In fact, a few weeks ago, a source in the White House told me that he thought it was your obvious objective. I've had many arguments about your motives over the last few years. When I first met you, I found you to be intelligent and charming and witty. Over the last seven years you have come to be celebrated as a great humanitarian. I may be the only person in the world to stand up and say this: I don't trust you or your organization. Nonetheless, I would like to make the following suggestion to you: Let's stop the fraud of HIV once and for all. Your organization has turned out not to be an independent critical force in the epidemic, but rather the handmaiden of the government's lying. Now amfAR has been able to extend its web of lies into Senator Edward Kennedy's office by sharing your Director of Programs and Special Projects, Terry Beirn, with Kennedy's staff, in the capacity of Legislative Aide. I assume that Beirn is there to keep Kennedy from asking the hard critical questions about the real cause of AIDS and Chronic Fatigue and Immune Dysfunction Syndrome [CFIDS]. I believe that Beirn did everything he could to discourage research into the link between AIDS and African swine fever virus. . . . Let's face it, Mathilde, science and life are full of surprises. Who would have thought that after all the pronouncements about HIV, and all the testing, and all the research, and all the conferences, and all the celebrations of the discoverers, that it would turn out that HIV is not the cause of AIDS? While it is a tragedy for the human race, it is kind of a reminder to scientists that they should always keep an open mind and know that experiments—not powerful individuals like Gallo and Myron Essex—are what determine the truth in science. The cost of the HIV mistake and the African swine fever virus cover-up is the Chronic Fatigue Immune Dysfunction Syndrome epidemic. Now that scientists have spent years lying about the cause of AIDS, they are being forced to lie about the cause of Chronic Fatigue Immune Dysfunction."

In the October 31 issue, Neenyah Ostrom wrote a piece about a man in Boston whose plight captured the craziness of the emerging "chronic fatigue syndrome is not AIDS" paradigm. Steven Rose told her, "I've been sick for ten years with what I think is chronic fatigue syndrome, and if I do have AIDS—which I don't think I do—I want the quality of my life to improve *now*. I've spent my entire adult life ill and basically unable to function. I'm one of those 'loose cannons' who never really bought HIV, who never trusted AZT, and who got into this mess by insisting that I be treated for CEBV [Chronic Epstein-Barr Virus Syndrome]. I wound up in a maze of bureaucracy and sheer terror so bizarre that I wouldn't know how to make the movie without Alfred Hitchcock."

Ostrom reported, "Rose was diagnosed with 'AIDS dementia' at Massachusetts General Hospital in Boston. For a time, he participated in the National Institutes of Health Protocol 005 under the direction of Dr. Martin Hirsch of Harvard University, an 'AIDS dementia' study in which participants were given AZT."

Ostrom noted, "Rose doesn't think he has 'AIDS dementia'; he has been ill for ten years with what he believes to be chronic fatigue syndrome (CFS). The symptoms of 'AIDS dementia' are virtually identical to the neurological symptoms seen in CFS patients: forgetfulness, short-term memory loss, difficulty concentrating, impaired judgment, and mood changes (March 1988 *Psychology Today*.) Rose believes that he has been misdiagnosed because physicians are unwilling to admit that CFS exists."

Ostrom also reported, "In the spring of 1987, Rose collapsed while visiting friends in Rhode Island, after a period of time during which he had been working long hours in a stressful job. His friends rushed him to a hospital where he remained for four days." He told Ostrom, "As a gay man I knew the first thing they were going to say was 'HIV.' I didn't think that HIV was the problem, and I didn't want to get stuck in the HIV ghetto, with all my other problems being ignored."

Ostrom reported that Rose was positive for HIV as well as Hepatitis B and that he had high titers to CMV and EBV, telltale signs of chronic fatigue syndrome. He told Ostrom, "Trying to get treatment for chronic fatigue is infuriating and futile. In Boston, Harvard says no to even talking about it—especially with an HIV-positive patient— because they are afraid that you [the *New York Native*] are right . . . I have asked to be tested for HHV-6. . . . But even the 'Gay' clinic won't touch it."

Rose recounted to Ostrom that, eventually, he was told by his psychiatrist that he was not displaying signs of "AIDS dementia," and that he never had it, but, "as a gay man it was the most convenient label for the medical establishment to put on him."

Rose told Ostrom, "If I have AIDS I should be a star patient—a survivor of ten years! In fact, I would go so far to say that I was misdiagnosed—hustled into the HIV-AZT machine—and am perhaps the biggest walking, talking threat to [major AIDS researcher] Marty Hirsh and his cronies around. I never got as sick as they had obviously planned on, and I think I irritate them by being alive at this point."

Rose had found his way into the opposite world created by the bogus totalitarian science that was the foundation of the epidemic. His case was a scientific anomaly that might have awakened the scientific community to the error of their ways, had we been living in a world of normal science.

In the November 14 issue, we published Neenyah Ostrom's report on a CFS symposium that was held in Rhode Island and was attended by more than 300 physicians, scientists, and journalists.

Ostrom reported that pioneering chronic fatigue syndrome researcher, Dr. Anthony Kamoroff of Harvard, told the audience, "Fever is a common symptom; five to ten percent of Komaroff's patients have daily fever, and 40 to 90 percent experience recurrent fever. Twenty percent of his patients experience severe night sweats, and Komaroff emphasized that there is a new finding that physicians should note. In contrast to the fever findings, a number of patients have low body temperatures. A body temperature of less than 98.6 was found in 13 percent, less than 97 degrees in 16 percent, and less than 96 degrees in seven percent" of his patients.

The pathological findings in CFS patients were all over the place, which was one of the reasons that the confusing epidemic would remain hidden in plain sight. It played all too easily into the hands of a medical establishment that seemed determined to sweep the complicated "AIDSish" epidemic under the rug of psychoneurosis.

Ostrom reported that, according to Komaroff, "Like the temperature data, white blood cell counts are both above and below the normal range. Twenty percent of patients have elevated, and twenty percent have decreased, white blood cell counts. In addition, 36 to 41% of Kamaroff's CIDS patients have extremely low sedimentation rates (a test which shows the presence of viral infection) of less than 5; the normal sedimentation rate is around 25. This is a result that is found in people with sickle cell anemia, and led Kamaroff to raise the possibility that a red blood cell membrane abnormality exists in people with CIDS."

Ostrom also wrote that, according to Komaroff, there is often liver pathology in CIDS and "Twenty-five percent of patients have elevated liver enzymes, and develop a non-A, non-B hepatitis at some point in their illness."

Ostrom also reported that there were striking neurological symptoms in Kamaroff's patients: "Disorientation is seen in 15 to 20 percent; each of the following symptoms was reported by approximately five percent of Komaroff's patients: primary seizure, acute profound ataxia (failure of muscular coordination), localized weakness, and transient blindness. Sensitivity to light, blurred or double vision, forgetfulness, distractibility, and peresthesia (an abnormal sensation, such as burning or prickling) also are reported."

That the government refused to acknowledge what was going on, became more and more unbelievable. Government scientists were flatly refusing to legitimize or accept the research findings that were pointing to a picture of an AIDS-like, or AIDS-intertwined, or AIDS-related epidemic in a non-gay population.

In a November 28 article, Ostrom took up the question of how common the syndrome was. She reported, "A number of researchers have expressed concern that the epidemic of CIDS is reaching worldwide proportions, and may dwarf that of 'AIDS.' " Dr. Paul Cheney, the pioneering researcher had written in a CFS journal, "CFS [CIDS] . . . now appears to be . . . epidemic, and generalized across national boundaries. . . . An apparent rise in cases probably from the 1970s in this country and overseas suggests a pandemic." He also wrote, "Despite the increasing weight of evidence that this syndrome is a real disease with measurable immunology, serologic, and neurologic abnormalities, many institutions and prominent physicians continue to scoff at this problem and the patients who have it. . . . Quite apart from the professional divisions over this syndrome, this could be a very serious and widespread health problem."

1989: A Strategy Emerges

In the January 2 issue of *New York Native,* in an article titled "Murmurs of the Heart," Neenyah Ostrom discussed some of the more serious pathologies associated with chronic fatigue syndrome: "Spontaneous abortions, heart murmurs and arrhythmias, chest pain, thrush—all of these symptoms of chronic fatigue syndrome (CFS) that appeared in early descriptions of the illness, but have received little emphasis or have faded entirely from the recent literature. All are symptoms that are not included in the Centers for Disease Control 'working case' definition of the disease."

She reported on a study of 189 CFS patients conducted by Dr. Anthony Kamoroff which found that 'atypical pneumonia' developed in five percent of the patients, and that 34 percent exhibited a chronic cough."

She also reported, "In a recent telephone interview, [Dr. Paul] Cheney said that thrush was 'reasonably common' among his CFS patients." Also according to Ostrom, "Chest pain, several types of arrhythmias (a variation in the normal rhythm of the heart beat), heart murmurs and tachycardia (an abnormally rapid beating of the heart) occur in Cheney's CFS patients. He has seen a few patients with 'focal myocarditis,' an inflammation of a section of heart muscle. Mitral valve prolapse is not infrequent in 10-20 percent of his patients. This is a type of heart murmur caused by the prolapse (displacement or partial collapse) of the mitral valve on the left side of the heart."

In the same issue, John Lauritsen brought our readers up to date on the dark progress of AZT and its acolytes: "It's now more than a year since the *New York Native* published my exposé on the Phase III AZT trials which were the basis of the drug's hasty approval by the Food and Drug Administration (FDA). In that article . . . I demonstrated that the FDA-conducted trials of AZT were not merely sloppy, but fraudulent. In the meantime, a lot of water has gone under the bridge. On the one hand, Burroughs Wellcome, the manufacturer of AZT (now known as Retrovir) has launched a worldwide propaganda juggernaut, with great success: the majority of physicians treating AIDS now prescribe and even proselytize for AZT, and thousands of gay men (including those with AIDS, with ARC, and merely with antibodies to HIV) are being dosed with the drug. On the other hand, there is now a groundswell of opposition to AZT."

Lauritsen wrote about a conference that was held at Columbia

University to discuss the state of AIDS treatments. At the panel on AZT, a prominent AIDS activist who had been an "important opponent of AZT" did a complete about face and played down the frightening toxicity of the drug. But AIDS doctor Joseph Sonnabend told the audience "that the toxicities of AZT should not be dismissed lightly." He pointed out, "Never before has a drug as toxic as AZT been prescribed for long term use. The long-term effects of AZT, the cumulative toxicities, are unknown. Sonnabend emphasized the ethical responsibilities of the physician to be sure that there was a sound scientific basis for the benefits of the drug, considering that its toxicities were firmly established."

When Lauritsen tried to ask a question from the audience, Laura Pinsky, the moderator, "screamed that there would be 'no discussion from the floor.' The panel was over." (It was the kind of discourse that characterized the whole epidemic.)

When Lauritsen attempted to question one of the speakers on the panel, a gay doctor named Ron Grossman who had defended AZT turned his back on Lauritsen and when Lauritsen returned to his seat he was approached by a security guard who said he had been asked to "escort" Lauritsen from the building. Lauritsen wrote, "I don't like being silenced, and I don't like having security guards called on me because someone is afraid of my presence: that I might say something out of place or write an article for the *New York Native*. I don't like showcase conferences devoted to creating delusions so fragile that they would be shattered by free and open discussion. This is totalitarianism."

The game the government was about to play for three decades became clearer in a report titled "The Straus Strategy Emerges," by Neenyah Ostrom that we ran on January 23. She wrote about research published by Stephen Straus (Anthony Fauci's CFS puppet at NIAID) and several colleagues that had appeared in the December 29, 1988, *New England Journal of Medicine*. She began her piece with the money quote from the researchers: "Our findings are reminiscent of data showing that psychological factors contribute to one's vulnerability to delayed recovery from acute infections and are in accord with recent findings that a history of affective disorders is frequent among patients with chronic fatigue syndrome."

The researchers showed the government's cards when they asserted, "Although we could not identify a reliable laboratory marker of disease severity, we did find an association between the results of psychological tests and patients' sense of well-being. Significant improvement in levels of anger, depression, and other mood states correlated with overall clinical improvement. These results indicate that affect plays an important part in the perception of illness severity in the chronic fatigue syndrome." Thus did the "CFS is not AIDS" paradigm begin morphing into what would turn out to be three decades of treacherous psychological jabberwocky.

Ostrom noticed the anomalies in the study: "Straus's continued assertions that CIDS 'represents a psychoneurotic condition' and that 'a history of affective disorders is frequent among patients with chronic fatigue syndrome' are rather inexplicable, particularly in light of some of the results that he and his colleagues report. Study participants had 'higher geometric mean titers of antibodies to cytomegalovirus than age-and-sex-matched controls'; three patients displayed antinuclear antibodies (indicative of possible autoimmune disease) and one exhibited a 'low-positive tier of rheumatoid factor' (indicative of possible rheumatoid arthritis). Ten of the 63 blood samples from study patients showed elevated levels of circulating immune complexes (compared to one of 27 from controls); ten of 73 patient serum samples showed elevated levels of the immune system modulator interferon; and levels of an interferon-induced enzyme, 'reflecting the activation of some immune pathways,' were 'higher in patients than in controls' in this study."

Not only *didn't* the data cry out "AIDS" or "AIDS-like" to the researchers, but they wouldn't even admit that what they were seeing was a real disease. Ostrom wrote, "Indeed, Straus appears to have an adversarial relationship with those very people whose illness he is trying to elucidate and ameliorate. He has written that, 'It is difficult and at times unpleasant to address the demands of such [CIDS] patients or to test hypotheses as to the etiology of their woes.' " Ostrom asserted, "Straus demonstrates a healthy disrespect for the information provided by CIDS patients. . . . The language of this report is contemptuous, incorporating such comments as, 'we could not confirm the relentless clinical deterioration reported by some pa-tients.' "

Ostrom captured the disconnect between the science of chronic fatigue syndrome that was going on inside and outside the government: "Straus and his co-workers are correct in stating that there is currently no 'reliable laboratory marker of disease severity.' [But] while it may indeed be difficult to correlate abnormal laboratory findings with subjective reports of health and well-being, other investigators have experienced no difficulties identifying a myriad of serious clinical abnormalities in CIDS patients, very few of which were identified by Straus et al."

Ostrom reported, "A partial list of such laboratory findings includes: lowered populations of natural killer cells; perturbations in T4/T8 lymphocyte ratios; elevated levels of the immune system modulator interleukin-2, development of brain lesions; elevated liver enzymes, elevated immunoglobulin G, presence of autoantibodies; and decreased cell-mediated immunity." (In other words, like AIDS patients, they were an immunological mess.)

Ostrom pointed out, "In stressing the psychological components of CIDS (which every disease certainly possesses), Straus and colleagues ignore the well-established fact that numerous viruses infect the central nervous system, thereby causing perturbations in mood, cognition, memory, and a host of neurological symptoms."

Ostrom reminded our readers that a "virus which has been isolated from people with CIDS and considered as a possible causative agent, is human herpesvirus-6 (HHV-6 or Human B-Lymphotropic Virus, HBLV)." She also noted that, in a different research project, "Dr. Howard Z. Streicher and collaborators (a group that included Straus) report finding antibodies to HHV-6 in 70 percent of CIDS patients."

The political problem with HHV-6, of course, was that HHV-6 was also found in AIDS patients. That made the virus much too much of an epidemiological hot potato. It threatened the comfort zone of both the AIDS and CFS paradigms which were being maintained by the government's very peculiar "science."

One of the great tragedies of the balkanization of one unified epidemic into a biomedical state of apartheid with a political firewall of bias between so-called "AIDS" and "chronic fatigue syndrome," was that any real scientific progress in one arbitrarily separated part of the epidemic could not benefit its sister epidemic(s). In the February 6 issue of *New York Native* I wrote a piece that tried to capture the tragedy of that epidemiological balkanization: "In 1987, three researchers from the Department of Internal Medicine at Shirnrakuen Hospital in Niigita, Japan, along with one researcher from Pittsburgh, Pennsylvania, published a paper which may have inadvertently resolved the chronic fatigue syndrome/AIDS epidemic, without any of the authors fully realizing what they had accomplished. The paper was published in a journal called *Natural Immunity and Cell Growth Regulation* (1987;6(3):116-28). Anyone who thinks that our crooked, incompetent scientific establishment at the National Institutes of Health has completely screwed up our understanding of the CFIDS/AIDS epidemic should track down this study. The paper reports on 23 patients who were suffering from symptoms that we in American would suspect are part of the Chronic Fatigue Immune Dysfunction and Acquired Immune Deficiency epidemics. The patients had remittent fever and uncomfortable fatigue which had persisted for more than six months. Because the symptoms the patients experienced reminded the physicians of AIDS, the researchers performed tests to determine the status of the patients' immune systems. What they consistently found in the patients was that their natural killer cell activity was lower than that of the general population. They decided that the finding was a definite laboratory abnormality and they immediately sought to correct it." The researchers gave the patients, whom they labeled Low Natural Killer Syndrome (LNKS) patients, 'an immunopotentiator called lentinan, a glucon extracted from the Japanese mushroom *Lentinus edodes'* otherwise known as shiitake mushrooms. According to the researchers, the 'LNKS patients responded well to the administration.' The lentinan was 'administered every other day. Or twice a week intravenously by drip infusion for one hour or injected intramuscularly.' Initially the natural killer cell activity decreased even further, but after continuous administration of the lentinan for six months, the activity returned to the normal range. The researchers also reported 'the return of a feeling of well-being and a disappearance of fever was seen after 2-4 weeks of treatment.' " The researchers noticed that when treatment was discontinued, the symptoms returned.

I also noted, "It seems that the Japanese are way ahead of us in understanding the chronic fatigue syndrome and immune dysfunction (CFIDS) epidemic. Researchers here are still debating whether it exists in reality, or only in the patient's mind. These Japanese researchers may have performed a great service by framing the diagnosis of the disease around an immunological test in combination with several clinical symptoms in a relatively straightforward manner. Indeed, they assert boldly that 'the syndrome is readily detectable by NK assays, and may be treatable with lentinan.' What is the cause of LNKS? The researchers suggest that 'one possibility is that the patients were infected with some unknown virus.' The researchers report that the 23 patients generally have normal T4/T8 ratios, but in some cases they noted a low T4/T8 ratio. When I looked at the T4/T8 ratios of the 23 patients, I noticed that most of the patients had ratios on the low side of normal. Indeed, three or four of the patients had ratios that would have American physicians immediately diagnosing 'ARC' [AIDS Related Complex]."

I also pointed out, "It's my understanding that most AIDS patients have lower NK activity than seen in the general population. It seems reasonable to suspect that in addition to whatever else they're suffering from, they have LNKS, which may be caused by the same agent that is causing LNKS in Japan."

Once again—and it would happen over and over—epidemiologically speaking, AIDS and CFS were two ships passing in the night. Had they been seen then in 1989 as one connected but variable epidemic manifesting a spectrum of illness, both AIDS patients and CFS patients might have had their lives saved or improved by lentinan and the research community would have had a better understanding of the role of NK cells in what was really a pandemic threatening everyone, not just the unpopular risk groups. But once again, tragically, it was not to be.

The chronic fatigue syndrome patients were outraged by the ridiculous Straus research that had been published the previous December. On April 3 we published "The Patients Revolt," an article by Neenyah Ostrom. She reported, "A blistering attack upon 'CFS expert' Dr. Stephen Straus at the National Institute of Allergy and Infectious Disease (NIAID), the National Institute of Health (NIH), and its director, Dr. Anthony Fauci, is delivered in the January/February issue of *The CFIDS Chronicle* [a patient advocate publication]. An editorial and two articles detail the inadequacies and meanspiritedness that characterize Straus and the NIH's lame efforts to address Chronic Fatigue and Immune Dysfunction Syndrome. . . . The charges leveled at Straus and the NIH appear to lay the groundwork for a class action suit on behalf of people with CIDS."

Unfortunately, such a suit never materialized.

Ostrom also reported that the editor of *The CFIDS Chronicle* recommended pressuring "Congress to remove Stephen Straus from his position as 'CFS expert' at NIAID. The two editors wrote, 'Rather than being intrigued and challenged by the complexities of CFIDS, Dr.

Stephen Straus seems to be bothered and disgruntled with its patients and determined to characterize it as a psychological disease. . . . We do not know whether Dr. Straus's failure to illuminate the real nature of this illness is attributable to misguided methods or motives (or both). But we do know that the results of his campaign to 'psychologize' CFIDS are enormously damaging to those who have the disease. . . . Patients are viewed as being morally deficient and somehow responsible for their own illness (as has been the case with AIDS.)' "

The irony of chronic fatigue syndrome patients comparing themselves to AIDS patients would become exponential throughout the next three decades.

The *Native* used the Freedom of Information Act to request all documents concerning chronic fatigue syndrome from the Centers for Disease Control and, as a result, on May 18, we published most of the text of a letter sent to Surgeon General C. Everett Koop by a physician who had been diagnosed as having Chronic Epstein-Barr Syndrome (CEBV), as chronic fatigue syndrome was originally known. The physician wrote, "This letter concerns chronic mononucleosis and the possibility that the contagious but unidentified-as-yet virus causing it is also the trigger for full blown AIDS. I *personally* know many (about 40) health care workers who have contracted CEBV since 1981, all of whom were personally healthy, and all of whom worked with AIDS or lymphoma patients, usually through working in intensive care units, direct patient care, or as oncology nurses or as ear-nose-throat doctors at the time they became ill. I am writing about a highly contagious, rapidly spreading new epidemic in America now occurring that is a more serious threat to our society than AIDS."

The suggestion in the letter that people working with AIDS patients were getting CFS underlines the epidemiological message of this book. But of course it was an epidemiological epiphany that nobody really wanted to seriously think about for the next three decades.

The doctor wrote that he was "a middle-aged board certified physician [who] had the misfortune of contracting 'Chronic Epstein-Barr virus reactivation syndrome' . . . four years ago. I had a productive, satisfying medical practice, prior to that time and had been in excellent health, but awoke with a severe sore throat and flu-like illness one day and have been totally disabled since, solely due to 'CEBV.' There are many thousands of other patients totally disabled by this disease, almost all of whom have caught it since 1980. Like AIDS, the rate of new cases seems to be accelerating."

The physician also speculated, "The cause is a very contagious virus spread like the common cold." He also noted, "The immune system damage and other abnormalities produced by this virus resemble in some ways those found in AIDS patients. The reason that this is a more serious threat to our society than AIDS is that it is spread by much more casual contact, is much more highly contagious, and rapidly spreading. Rather than killing the victims, it renders them permanently disabled. Many are on Social Security Disability. The dollar cost to our society of CEBV is already comparable to that of AIDS and may soon exceed it."

The physician warned, "The CEBV epidemic could have a disastrous effect on our armed services, much more dangerous than AIDS, due to its ability to *rapidly spread like the common cold*. Since it can spread as quickly as it recently did in Lake Tahoe, where over 500 people contracted it within several months, it can quickly disable entire bases, as well as leave a large number of personnel permanently disabled at great expense." (Hello, Gulf War Syndrome.)

In the letter, the physician listed all the immune abnormalities then associated with the disease and named several possible viral causes, including HBLV (or HHV-6) and even African swine fever virus. He also warned Koop, "There is reason to believe that the same virus that causes CEBV causes many lymphomas."

The physician presented his own game plan: "There should be the appointment of an accomplished *senior* investigator, who has a track record of success in identifying new pathogens, to spend *full time* heading the NIH's CEBV program. Another accomplished investigator should be appointed to head the CDC's CEBV program. Power similar to that of a general in war time should be given to these senior officials. This would help ensure full and rapid cooperation of competing labs and scientists working on these problems."

Well, that didn't happen.

Other documents we received, from our F.O.I.A. request, captured the exasperating games the CDC was going to play with chronic fatigue syndrome for three decades. On May 22 we published an exchange of letters between the CDC's Gary Holmes, and Dan Peterson, one of the two Incline Village (Lake Tahoe) physicians who discovered and characterized the CFS epidemic in their area. Peterson wrote to Holmes, "I would like to update you on the current conditions at Lake Tahoe. We now have nine patients who have developed B-cell lymphoma from the original study group that had evidence of reactivated herpes diseases in the form of elevated early antigens for Epstein-Barr virus and tissue culture positivity for human herpesvirus-6." Holmes wrote back to Peterson, "The case histories of the patients you presented in the letter are quite interesting. However, I believe most of the researchers in the field agree that CFS is a diagnosis of exclusion, and that the identification of other diseases, such as lymphomas that occurred in your patients, or of MRI abnormalities that are suggestive of multiple sclerosis (MS), moves such patients out of the CFS category. CFS is little more than a collection of symptoms at the present time, and it remains highly likely that many patients' CFS symptoms are actually caused by occult lymphoma, multiple sclerosis, or any of multiple other chronic diseases that may not be diagnosed in the initial evaluation. Continued grouping of patients who have such definitive diagnoses as lymphoma or MS under the title of CFS may artificially imply that such patients have a single cause for their varied illnesses."

That is how the game of CFS Three-Card Monte would be played for the next three decades. One couldn't even begin to point out that CFS was part of the AIDS epidemic if serious complications of CFS were constantly and disingenuously used to undermine the very diagnosis of CFS itself. By CDC fiat, no CFS patient would ever be seen as suffering from AIDS-like secondary infections and of serious CFS complications. Neenyah Ostrom summed up the diagnosis problem: "The circular reasoning applied in this instance appears to be a classic case of throwing the baby out with the bathwater: if the diagnosis of CIDS is one of exclusion, and the subsequent development of a known illness (such as cancer) removes the patient from the subset of people with CIDS, not only will the possibly progressive nature of the illness never be investigated—a specific diagnosis will not be developed. At least not by the CDC."

The transformation of the gay community into the HIV Pink Triangle Community made a great deal of progress that summer. According to the *New York Post*, the New York City Health Commissioner, Stephen Joseph was planning to call for the collection of the names of everyone who tested positive for HIV. The Health Department denied that any plan was in the works and released the complete text of Joseph's speech that was given at the annual AIDS conference in Montreal. The ideas in the speech were chilling enough. In his speech Joseph said, "It is only a matter of time before reliable published studies demonstrate the effectiveness of treatment for the asymptomatic HIV-infected person, or for preventing infection in an exposed person, or for reducing infectiousness of the person with HIV infection. These changes in our capacity to prevent and treat infection will usher in a new era in which policies will shift towards a disease control approach to HIV infection along the lines of classic tuberculosis practices. Medically confidential counseling and testing both become more aggressive and routine in high prevalence areas of all clinical settings. Within a confidential public health framework, reporting of seropositives, follow-up to assure adequate treatment, and more aggressive contact tracing will become standard public health application for controlling HIV infection and illness."

Anyone who knew what a massive political fraud the HIV paradigm was felt like they were staring into the depths of hell when they realized what Joseph was calling for. To politically force AIDS into a TB paradigm was frightening because TB patients could be arrested and quarantined in prisonlike conditions if they did not cooperate and take the state's prescribed treatment. It was one thing for the AIDS establishment to say what it thought the cause of AIDS was and what treatments might be the most helpful. This was different. The state was about to turn its theories or mistakes, depending on your viewpoint, into law. It was diabolically brilliant.

The AIDS activists were worse than useless in the face of the approaching totalitarian darkness that Joseph's agenda represented. Their opposite world activism was driving the growth of this horrifying AIDS empire. A couple of letters we published, in the June 19 issue, captured the degree to which the AIDS activist community was turning the gay community upside down. At the beginning of June there had been a ceremony in Manhattan's Sheridan Square to celebrate Gay/Lesbian Pride and History Month. The ceremony, which was attended by the mayor of New York, was disrupted by ACT UP. Jim Puzio of San Francisco wrote, "Instead of a ceremony honoring the Lesbian/Gay community for the achievements over the past twenty-five years, I saw a demonstration by ACT UP in which the mayor and other speakers were shouted down. Instead of feeling proud, I was embarrassed. In my view, and that of others I spoke with that day, what was ruined was one of the accomplishments of the Lesbian/Gay

171

Rights movement—to be recognized by the city government and have our voices heard. I wouldn't blame the mayor if he never did another thing for the Gay/Lesbian community. . . . At the ceremony I was handed a flyer urging me to join another demonstration at the Pride Rally. If ACT UP is going to screw up that also, I think I'll stay home."

Another reader, Walter J. Phillips, wrote, "ACT UP's action at the unveiling of Stonewall Place in commemoration of the Stonewall riots was a disgrace. AIDS, while very tragic, has only been with us a few years, while gay oppression has existed for hundreds of years. When the highest elected official chooses to speak about that oppression in a manner to give hope and courage to all gay people, the chanting of ACT UP and prevention of those who wanted to hear from doing so was misguided to say the least. While both AIDS activism and gay activism are necessary and desirable, actions must be constructive and beneficial to the gay community."

We published another letter in that issue on a different matter that provided more evidence that not everyone in the gay community was being bamboozled by ACT UP's deceptive activism. Don C. Olson had dared to point out at an ACT UP meeting "that they have lost their focus since challenging the HIV theory is a major issue in fighting AIDS. Well, all hell broke loose, since my sentiments were too controversial for them, because they are fixated on the HIV/AZT/let's find a vaccine rot. To put it mildly, I caused a big stir. Several members accused me of disrupting the meeting. I said I thought this was ACT UP (had I come to the wrong place?). They tried to sweep me under the carpet by suggesting I talk with their HIV-Treatment Committee. Well, I did approach their HIV-Treatment Committee and (pathetically) all they wanted to discuss was HIV treatment. . . . I am furious with S.F. ACT UP'S dangerously narrow perspective, and with N.Y. ACT UP's boycott of the *Native*. They are sadly misinformed, because they choose to ignore (and in this case, resist) new findings published by such responsible papers as the *New York Native*. . . . And in so doing, ACT UP members perpetuate right-wing style censorship at the cost of continued suffering of their gay brothers and sisters. (I guess ACT UP has moved so far to the Left, it has become part of the New Right.)"

In the June 26 issue, Neenyah Ostrom covered CFS research pioneer Dr. Paul Cheney's testimony to Congress concerning the CFS epidemic. Cheney told Congress that CFIDS might have a relationship with the AIDS epidemic. He also said that one informal "survey of patients in CFIDS groups from 35 states shows an exponential rise in cases produced each year since the 1970s. This curious temporal and case production relationship with the AIDS epidemic has prompted some researchers to project CFIDS as an AIDS epiphenomenon. Indeed, the new human herpesvirus HHV-6 may be about the most important cofactor shared by both AIDS and CFIDS."

A report by John Hammond, in the July 3 issue, once again captured the cockamamie nature of AIDS activism. At a breakfast meeting which took place in New York City's Gracie Mansion with Mayor Koch in June, a prominent group of "health care professionals and other experts involved with the City's response to the 'AIDS' crisis firmly rejected Health Commissioner Steven Joseph's suggestions, originally aired in a speech before the Fifth International AIDS Conference on June 4, to give serious consideration to the possible use of coercive measures in responding to HIV infection."

Hammond reported, "These measures included adopting 'confidential' (as opposed to the current 'anonymous') procedures for recording HIV-antibody tests, mandatory reporting of positive test results, and involuntary contact tracing and notification for all persons who tested positive for HIV antibodies. Most health care advocates and professionals agree that such methods are unlikely to be productive in this epidemic, where many people at risk fear discrimination, and there is evidence that where such measures have been tried, as in the state of South Carolina, they have discouraged many from seeking diagnosis or treatment."

In the same issue, we ran a fascinating interview with Dennis King conducted by Neenyah Ostrom. King is the author of *Lyndon LaRouche and the New American Fascism*. The interview is a reminder of how easily the CDC's biased epidemiology could be used for all kinds of vicious right-wing agendas. King told Ostrom, "You've got to understand that, two years ago there was an enormous scare in our society about AIDS. Now it's like everything else—it hits television, and people become somewhat inured to it. People are still worried about it, but the hysteria two years ago was a media event. And LaRouche knew this was a golden opportunity for some demagoguery. So he called his followers together, and gave them a slogan—and if you ask me for a *classic* slogan of demagoguery, I couldn't come up with a better one. LaRouche said, 'Spread panic, not AIDS.' I think that the panic was there, especially

173

with people believing that AIDS was going to spread very rapidly into the heterosexual community, which it didn't, but at the time people were worried that it would do so. The hysteria was out there in the land and LaRouche had no difficulty getting 700,000 people to sign a petition to put that referendum [Proposition 64] on the ballot. What happened next is even more interesting. The people who were opposed to Proposition 64 formed a committee called Stop LaRouche. They publicized all over the state the fact that Lyndon LaRouche, the dangerous extremist, was behind this measure. And that anti-LaRouche agitation apparently had very little effect on people's voting patterns. People didn't care. They were worried about AIDS, and they couldn't care less that it was a Nazi behind it. When the election took place, the *New York Times* reported—without giving any statistics—that the referendum had been overwhelmingly defeated and that it was a great victory over LaRouche. Bullshit. LaRouche got over two million people in California to vote in favor of quarantining a minority. It was a great victory for him and for the forces of neofascism in America. For the first time, they had inserted into the public mind the idea of rounding up a minority, and inserted it in such a way that people could feel it was legitimate, by disguising it as a public health measure. And LaRouche learned how to do that from *Mein Kampf*. If you look at what was going on in our society at that time, the AMA [American Medical Association] poll [that found that 50 percent of Americans thought it was okay to deprive people with AIDS of their civil liberties] was really minor compared to the enormous violence that was erupting against gays all over the United States. And the violence is continuing today. And that is something that is not being looked at closely enough by people who should be concerned, like the government, civil liberties groups, Jews—who after all, are the next target, because it's skinheads doing it. They may beat up on gays now, and they may beat up on blacks, but the ultimate target is the Jews. It always is in these situations. . . . LaRouche has praised skinhead attacks on gays, openly, and he has called the skinheads the 'vanguard of the nationalist revolution.' "

In the July 24 issue of the *Native*, Ostrom raised the question of whether Gilda Radner, the *Saturday Night Live* comedienne, was a victim of chronic fatigue syndrome: "Gilda Radner died on May 20 at the age of 42, following a long illness that culminated in ovarian cancer. But three years before her death, and, approximately a year before the diagnosis of cancer was made, Radner was told she had . . . 'Epstein-Barr virus' disease" as chronic fatigue syndrome was then known.

Ostrom asked, "Did Radner develop ovarian cancer from the chronic immune dysfunction caused by 'chronic fatigue syndrome?' " Radner had written a book about her illness called *It's Always Something* and her description of a cold that would never go away, as well as the fog that filled her brain, low-grade fevers, and a panoply of other symptoms matched the pattern that was seen in CFS patients all over the country. Radner, like many or most of the patients in those days, was told she was suffering from depression or neurosis. Ostrom sarcastically wrote, "In October 1987, Radner's 'neurosis' resulted in abnormal liver function tests. That same month, the ovarian malignancy was discovered—almost a year-and-a-half, by her chronology, after Radner experienced the cold that wouldn't go away." Ostrom concluded her piece by asking, "How long will it be before serious research on this debilitating illness is begun by U.S. health authorities? How many lives must be destroyed—and perhaps lost—while desperate patients go from doctor to doctor, like Radner did, being told that their symptoms are psychological?"

In that same issue, Ostrom noted that *The Washington Post's* Michael Specter had reported on a rather troubling alliance that was forming between the government and the AIDS activists. In the July 9 report, on a meeting in D.C., Specter wrote that federal officials "had gathered here today with community activists from around the country to discuss ways to dramatically speed the distribution of experimental new AIDS drugs." While it was a huge victory for the activists, it opened up AIDS to all kinds of scientific confusion in which adverse side effects might not be recognized in an orderly way. Drugs would not be tested as rigorously as they had been in the past. That was what was considered progress in the new opposite world the AIDS activists were helping to create. Specter never wrote more truthful words in his entire career than these: "Fauci and some other AIDS researchers have begun to sound almost as if they were shadow spokesman for groups like ACT UP." (A vice versa version of that statement is also painfully true.)

Meanwhile, in the same issue, we reported on the tragic story of a drug that AIDS patients had been experimenting with in the process of doing their own clinical trials on themselves. John Hammond reported that a number of deaths had been caused by "Compound Q or GLQ233, a chemical extract made from the root of a particular

175

variety of Chinese cucumber." Hammond wrote, "Compound Q, long used for other medical purposes in China, became a matter of near-hysteria among some 'AIDS' patients when, on April 13, Dr. Michael McGrath of the University of California in San Francisco (UCSF) published his finding that, in a test tube, the drug completely destroys human macrophages previously infected with so-called Human Immunodeficiency Virus (HIV) and, apparently, only those cells. The drug is also highly toxic and this spring two people with 'AIDS' nearly died after eating homemade cucumber root preparations."

Hammond reported that, "In the case of Compound Q, Project Inform, a San Francisco-based 'AIDS' information organization headed by Martin Delaney, decided to sponsor its own trials of the drug, in an effort to make the drug more readily available to patients willing to participate in trials and in order to speed up the overall approval process. Instead of minimal test dosages, the Project Inform trials combined Phase I and Phase II testing and began with larger, therapeutic dosages of Compound Q, tested on 42 patients. One patient in the Project Inform trial committed suicide and a second lapsed into a coma and choked to death on his own vomit. In New York, a third patient who was not part of the Project Inform trial but who had obtained the drug on his own, died after taking his second dose under a doctor's supervision." Such stories were emblematic of the tragic desperation that characterized those dark times.

In the July 31 issue, Neenyah Ostrom reported on a fascinating experiment conducted by Japanese researchers that may have re-flected the best understanding to date of chronic fatigue syndrome. As previously noted, the Japanese had, instead of using the goofy moniker of chronic fatigue syndrome, focused on a measurable biomedical marker and called the malady "Low Natural Killer Cell Syndrome." Ostrom reported, "A group of researchers led by Tadao Aoki at Shinrakuen Hospital (Niigata, Japan), together with Dr. Ronald B. Herberman at the Pittsburgh Cancer Institute, defined 'Low Natural Killer Cell Syndrome' (LNKS) in 1986 (before the U.S. Centers for Disease Control even published its case definition of chronic fatigue syndrome). They defined LNKS as 'a newly proposed category of immune disorders, being characteristically diagnosed by lowered NK cell activity . . . in association with general clinical symptoms of remittent fever and uncomfortable fatigue, persisting without explanation for more than six months.' " The scientists speculated that

176

the cause might be "a new, unknown virus or an unknown substrain of known viruses."

Once again, the tragedy was that AIDS also was obviously a form of Low Natural Killer Cell Syndrome. The overlapping nature of these politically separated epidemics was met by radio silence. It is especially tragic because the Japanese researchers also discovered that intravenous lentinan (derived from shiitake mushrooms) could turn the condition around. The games the CDC was playing with CFS prevented it from being recognized as treatable LNKS. The American government's scientific establishment seemed determined not to let doctors or the public see CFS as an epidemic of immune compromised people, let alone AIDS. God only knows how many people would still be alive today if the American government had adopted an LNKS paradigm for both CFS and AIDS, and attempted to control the real epidemic with lentinan.

In that same issue, Ostrom reported that Fauci's department (NIAID) was "sponsoring a new clinical trial to evaluate the safety of AZT in pregnant women who are infected with the human immunodeficiency virus (HIV)." Ostrom noted, "The stated aim of the study is to determine 'whether AZT given during pregnancy can prevent the transmission of HIV from mothers to their newborn babies.' " She pointed out, "At a time when most responsible physicians urge pregnant women not to take so much as an aspirin if it can be avoided, how can NIAID possibly justify giving a drug as toxic as AZT to pregnant women? Poisoning black babies after birth apparently isn't good enough. . . . The government will now poison black babies *in utero*."

Ostrom also noted, "According to the *New York Times*, 52 percent of women and 76 percent of children with 'AIDS' are black even though blacks compose only 12% of the general population." ("Black Doctors Urge Study of Factors in Risk of AIDS," by Felicia R. Lee, *N.Y. Times,* July 21, 1989.)

One of the more horrific passages from the Fauci press release about the AZT experiment on pregnant black women stated, "During labor, they will again receive intravenous AZT until the infant is born."

As I studied the issues of the *Native*, in the process of writing this book, it was surprising how much of a treasure trove the letters to the editor will be for future historians of the epidemic. We published two that were stunning in the August 7 issue. A German writer named

Kawi Schneider had just become familiar with the *Native* and wrote, "Unfortunately, I got to know your brilliant newspaper criticism of 'AIDS' not before yesterday. In a future article, I will describe your brilliant resistance against AIDSzism. My grandfather was in a social democrat anti-Nazi resistance group. When I see how victims of the 'AIDS' misdiagnosis are killed today with poisons (like AZT) that even the healthiest people wouldn't have a chance to survive long-term, I more and more come to believe that we have a U.S.-based reincarnation of Nazism in only slightly different disguise. And again, good and naïve people are being abused to do the holocaust job. Again, resistance is too weak. Again, dissenters are being ridiculed. Again, there is a Fűhrer cultism (if you doubt this, just join the next Gallo-worship AIDS conference). . . . AIDSzism is not just a concealed renaissance of Nazism, but it is also a strategy to annihilate modern medicine and modern science."

In the same issue, we published a letter from Stephen F. Temmer, another person who was not hoodwinked by what was happening in the gay community. Temmer wrote, "In arranging for the meaningful distribution of my charitable funds, I was struck by the incongruity of Gay Men's Health Crisis donating funds to ACT UP, a strictly political, and I dare say, counterproductive group. I wrote a letter to Richard Dunne, GMHC's Executive Director and he responded with a thoughtful, two-page letter indicating that GMHC as a tax exempt organization is permitted by law to funnel up to 5 percent of its contributed income to organizations it supports, even though such organizations may not themselves be eligible for tax-free status, as is the case with ACT UP. I feel very strongly that organizations involved with the care of people suffering with AIDS should stay strictly out of the political arena and leave such work to those not primarily involved with the community's suffering. I am sure it cuts deeply into their ability to raise the needed funds for their urgent work and on that basis alone it should preclude their supporting controversial groups." While Temmer may have made a very practical point, the money flowing into ACT UP from GMHC was evidence that ACT UP was getting its political claws (the ones that were also basically bolstering the government's epidemiological agenda) into every aspect of gay life.

In the same issue of the *Native*, I wrote an editorial expressing my concern about a new toxic drug, DDI, that had been touted by the *New York Times*: "Gina Kolata's *New York Times* report on Friday, July 28, on DDI will be hailed by many with the same enthusiasm that greeted the early stories on AZT. While doctors' phones will start ringing off the hook, let us at least note that the DDI story acknowledges what a toxic disaster its predecessor AZT was. Without qualification, that is something to celebrate. At the same time, the ghost of AZT (and we do hope it will become a ghost) should offer a cautionary tale about DDI and other chemotherapies that may take center stage. The people who have voted to boycott the *Native* are the same ones who have demonstrated to lower the cost of AZT or to make the drug available for free."

I also pointed out, "The *Native*, thanks to the persistent analytical work of John Lauritsen, has been a lone voice in calling attention to the dangers of AZT. Even though we faced a boycott by ACT UP, we continued to tell the truth about AZT. Two months ago, when NYC Health Commissioner Stephen Joseph announced his plans for contact tracing and the adoption of a tuberculosis model for the containment of 'AIDS,' I asked an official in the Health Department if that meant that people would be contacted and encouraged to take the appropriate treatment. The official said yes, and that he assured me that the treatment would be AZT because it has been shown to extend life.' "

Kolata had written in the *Times*, "In a study of 26 patients, being reported in the journal *Science*, the 23 patients who received the highest doses of the drug [DDI] showed increases in their immune system cells, decreases in AIDS viral proteins in their blood, as well as weight gain. Three even had a reversal of their dementia."

But she also reported that Sam Broder, the Director of the National Cancer Institute, "warned that the drug could still have dangerous side effects. At very high doses, higher than those in the new study, researchers have found that DDI may damage the pancreas or aggravate nerve problems in the hands and feet that can lead to difficulty in coordination."

I was very alarmed by what seemed to be the appalling logic that was emerging and wrote in the editorial, "One issue of concern to us is that DDI is being compared with AZT to make sure it is a better treatment. What a standard to hold DDI up to! The fact that DDI is less toxic than AZT should not come as much of a surprise to anyone familiar with the awesome toxicity of AZT."

The chronic fatigue syndrome patients, who were in essence sitting in the front of the government's fraudulent epidemiological AIDS/CFS bus, while lucky not be turned into clueless toxic dumps like the folks in the back of the bus, had their own problems to contend

179

with. In the same issue of the paper, Neenyah Ostrom wrote a piece about their inability to obtain insurance benefits: "The Centers for Disease Control's definition of chronic fatigue syndrome . . . as an illness with a 'diagnosis of exclusion' has created a myriad of difficulties for physicians, patients and health insurance providers. One of the potentially most explosive—and expensive, in terms of the public health, as well as money—is that insurance companies have begun to deny reimbursement to some, if not all, expenses related to [chronic fatigue syndrome]."

John Lauritsen was back on the AZT case, in the August 21 issue of the *Native*. He noted, "The AIDS industry has not given up on the drug. There is apparently a huge stockpile of AZT, and billions of dollars of sales depend upon a continued, and expanding, market for the commodity."

Lauritsen was outraged that Tony Fauci's National Institutes of Allergy and Infectious Diseases (NIAID), which had sponsored the AZT study (that was terminated early), had issued a press release, "in which Anthony Fauci called the results 'exciting' and urged that AZT be given to all of the estimated 100,000 to 200,000 Americans who, like the study participants, are somewhat sick and have HIV antibodies. Another study is currently in progress, testing the effects of AZT on *perfectly healthy* people who have HIV antibodies. If equally 'exciting' results can be obtained from this study, the AZT market may explode to as many as 1,500,000 hapless Americans."

Lauritsen noted, "After a little investigation I found out that the much touted AZT study has not been published in any form, very little is known about it, and much of what was said in the media reports is not true. . . . NIAID's press release was reprehensible in many ways." Lauritsen argued, "With regard to AIDS coverage, the media are exquisitely cognizant of an 'elite consensus'—the consensus of the AIDS establishment. The consensus consists of a paradigm, an elaborate mythological system, which though its tenets sometimes change, is so well internalized by most AIDS writers that they could recite the basic catechism in their sleep: AIDS is a deadly new disease, which is invariably fatal, which is caused by HIV. Intravenous drug users got AIDS by 'sharing needles.' Gay men got AIDS by being 'promiscuous.' AZT 'extends life' and is the 'best hope.' All or nearly all of those who are 'infected with HIV' (have HIV antibodies) will get AIDS. Africa is a continent ravaged by the AIDS epidemic, with millions of people sick and dying. And so on. Facts that don't fit into the official paradigm transmute into unfacts [and go down the] memory hole. The propaganda model suggests that mainstream AIDS coverage might best be understood as collusion between the media and parts of the Medical Industrial Complex. It suggests that we always keep in mind the economic underpinnings of the epidemic."

The gay community's unfortunate cooperation with its own epidemiological persecution and humiliation was starkly captured in a piece written by James D'Eramo, in the September 11 issue. He wrote, "Joining with long standing federal recommendations and the recent barrage of media coverage urging widespread HIV antibody testing and AZT use, Gay Men's Health Crisis (GMHC)—in a break from its cautious stance on these issues—has endorsed what can be seen as essentially the government's often stated and most recently emphasized position. In his swan song press conference at GMHC office, on Tuesday, August 15, Executive Director Richard Dunne (he has since resigned) read a statement saying, 'There are compelling reasons to get tested and to know your HIV status.' Dunne cited a New York State law that protects confidentiality, and the availability of 'drugs which can prolong life by slowing the development of AIDS' as the 'compelling reasons' for testing. In GMHC's concurrent testing campaign print ad, 'Think about it,' only AZT is mentioned by name as one of the drugs that can slow AIDS onset."

D'Eramo noted, "Over the past months, there has been a highly orchestrated national campaign urging that all those at risk of being exposed to AIDS be tested for the presence of antibodies. The federal government health agencies, and local public health officials, including New York City's Health Commissioner, Stephen Joseph, have recommended that the names of persons who test positive be reported—and kept on a 'confidential' list—and that their contacts be tracked down, tested and listed as well."

D'Eramo also noted, "For years now, many psychosocial professionals, physicians, scientists, civil rights activists, and AIDS organizations—including GMHC—have pointed out that the HIV antibody test could actually cause an individual more harm than good." Perhaps most disturbingly, D'Eramo reported that when Dunne was asked at the press conference if GMHC had received a grant from Burroughs Wellcome, "Dunne said he did not know the exact amount, but it was used exclusively for client services rather than for salaries or operating expenses. For some, the fact that the not-for-profit organization first accepted money from the AZT manufacturer, then later recommended extensive use of the drug, has created an impression of impropriety."

GMHC was making the trains run on time.

Before I discuss another piece by Neenyah Ostrom that was in the same issue, I must quote the uncanny first two paragraphs of Randy Shilts's *And the Band Played On*. They inadvertently reveal how epidemiologically intertwined AIDS and CFS were at ground zero:

> Tall sails scraped the deep purple night as rockets burst, flared, and flourished red, white, and blue over the stoic Statue of Liberty. The whole world was watching, it seemed; the whole world was there. Ships from fifty-five nations had poured sailors into Manhattan to join the throngs, counted in the millions, who watched the greatest pyrotechnic extravaganza ever mounted, all for America's two-hundredth birthday party. Deep into the morning, bars all over the city were crammed with sailors. New York City had hosted the greatest party ever known, everybody agreed later. The guests had come from all over the world.
>
> This was the part the epidemiologists would later note, when they stayed up late at night and the conversation drifted toward where it all started and when. They would remember that glorious night in New York Harbor, all those sailors, and recall: From all over the world they came to New York.

It's a shame the attention of those same AIDS epidemiologists didn't also focus on the September 11 issue of the *Native*, in which the article by Neenyah Ostrom, on a gay man with chronic fatigue syndrome, began, "The long downward spiral of illness for Rich Jones began on the night of the Fourth of July, 1976. It was the culmination of the nation's Bicentennial celebration and 24-year-old Jones was excited by New York City's festivities. 'That Fourth had a Disney-like quality,' he remembers. He and a friend sat on the dunes, watching the fireworks over the Hudson River; they built a small fire, and stayed up all night, drinking and talking and celebrating the country's two-hundredth birthday. Walking home in the early morning, Jones suddenly felt quite ill. 'Something is wrong,' he said to his friend. 'I feel very sick.' 'Of course you feel sick,' Jones's friend replied. 'You've just stayed up drinking all night.' 'No, that isn't it.' Jones insisted. As it turns out, it wasn't. That night was the turning point in Jones's life, a change in his health that was, he now says, 'very, very, very dramatic.' Jones has chronic fatigue syndrome. That morning, a 13-year odyssey through illness began."

The rest of Ostrom's piece describes Jones's struggle and the details of his illness were not all that different from the other patients that Ostrom would interview and profile during her eight years of reporting on CFS. But it was an amazing coincidence in the opening of his story that one gay man's chronic fatigue syndrome also began at the precise moment in time that epidemiologists suspected AIDS had begun in America. It was an epidemiological Tweedledum-Tweedledee moment for AIDS and chronic fatigue syndrome, a moment that supported the notion that the two epidemics had been politically separated at birth.

As I have argued, if the real epidemic had not been sexually, socially and racially divided epidemiologically into a kind of medical apartheid, the tragedy of genocidal AZT might have been averted. At the very least, the Cassandras who were concerned about AZT might have been listened to with more respect. Ostrom interviewed one of those Cassandras, in the September 18 issue of the *Native*.

Dr. Bernard Bihari, a member of the Community Research Initiative, was a pioneer of research into relatively nontoxic treatments for AIDS like naltrexone and lentinan. While he believed that AZT could help patients who had AIDS dementia, he was concerned about giving AIDS patients AZT in the early phase of their illness. In addition to HIV resistance, he was concerned about "some long-term cumulative toxicity. . . . We may be doing more harm than good. . . ." He was mindful of the fact that one could not project long term effects of AZT on studies that had only lasted a year. Interestingly, he noted that the early studies "showed reduction in opportunistic infections." In the next two decades many critics would argue that the anti-AIDS drugs were not helping because they targeted HIV, but because they had broad spectrum effects against the dozens of infections that AIDS patients (and CFS patients, by the way) suffered from.

In the October 2 issue, Ostrom wrote a piece titled "The

Andromeda Strain" which looked at the reasonableness of the possibility that chronic fatigue syndrome was actually caused by African swine fever virus, a virus (we later learned) that may have been circulating undetected in America's pigs with immune system problems for a number of years—under the disingenuous diagnosis of "swine mystery disease" and eventually porcine respiratory and reproductive syndrome (PRRS). Ostrom noted, "One of the more compelling arguments for a multifactorial explanation of chronic fatigue syndrome . . . is the improbability of a single pathogen being capable of causing the wide range and variable severity of symptoms seen in the illness. Numerous systems of the body are affected by CFS—the immune, nervous, muscular, circulatory, and endocrine systems all experience some form of dysfunction. Even the reproductive system may be affected."

Ostrom asserted, "The multifactoral explanation of the cause of [chronic fatigue syndrome] may, in fact, be simply a reflection of how little is known about the illness. But the central question remains: is it possible that a pathogen exists that could cause the wide-ranging symptoms and variance in severity that is seen in [chronic fatigue syndrome]?"

Ostrom looked at the possibility that African swine fever virus, which had been proposed by Jane Teas as the cause of AIDS, was also the cause of chronic fatigue syndrome. She pointed out that African swine fever "is an example of an illness that affects many biological systems: the immune, circulatory, nervous, gastric, reproductive, and pulmonary systems are affected in both acute and chronic forms of the disease." While she didn't say it in the piece, behind the scenes we were wondering if AIDS was acute ASFV and chronic fatigue syndrome was a chronic form of the disease.

Ostrom wrote, "It may seem silly to look at a pig illness when searching for a paradigm for CFS, but human and porcine immune systems are extremely similar. In fact, pigs are a major repository for human influenza viruses, and passage from humans to pigs and back to humans accounts for the wide variety of strains of influenza from year to year." She also noted, "African swine fever, despite the identification of its causative agent and several well-defined clinical courses, remains a truly mysterious illness. It renders the infected animals' immune system unable to respond by mechanisms that are still unexplained; it can cause fever, arthritis, nervous, and immune system dysfunction, skin lesions, pneumonia, susceptibility to bac-

184

terial infections, miscarriage, and can lead to death through cardiac insufficiency or coma. Or it can evolve in an infected population into a chronic form, in which relapsing fever, malaise, and other symptoms continue over months or years."

In her summary of the ASF-CFS hypothesis, she noted, "There is no data linking ASF virus to [chronic fatigue syndrome]. But as a model system, ASF would seem to be appropriate. As a model system, it proves that a single agent could in fact be responsible for the myriad of symptoms exhibited by people with [chronic fatigue syndrome]."

Neenyah Ostrom summed up where we were, in terms of the relationship between AIDS and chronic fatigue syndrome, in the November 27 issue. She wrote, "The continuing furor over the Centers for Disease Control's name, 'chronic fatigue syndrome,' for what has been called, at various times, chronic mononucleosis, Chronic Epstein-Barr virus Syndrome, post-viral syndrome and a host of other names, is a good example of how a name can be chosen to dramatize, trivialize, or clinically describe an illness. The number of patient support groups that refuse to use the name chronic fatigue syndrome—many of them substitute 'Chronic Fatigue and Immune Dysfunction Syndrome'— also is testament to the power of a name."

Ostrom also noted that a disturbing game was also being played with AIDS at the same time: "There is an ongoing movement to have Acquired Immune Dysfunction Syndrome, 'AIDS,' renamed 'HIV disease.' " She suggested that the two diseases of immune dysfunction "be renamed to recognize what is probably the most serious infectious agent they have in common: Human B-lymphotropic Virus (HBLV, also called human herpesvirus-6 (HHV-6)." She pointed out, "HBLV [HHV-6] infection may constitute the initial attack on the immune system, weakening it and allowing opportunistic—usually bacterial— infections and transformed (cancer-causing) cells to grow out of control. . . . HBLV is clearly more lethal to immune system cells than is HIV and infects a large number of types of cells—T- and B-cells, macrophages, monocytes, megakaryocytic, glioblastoma cells (cells of the nervous system), and muscle cells. In fact Gallo and co-workers claim that the primary target for HBLV is T-cells, the cell depleted in 'AIDS' and other immunodeficiencies."

In that same issue, we published the first roundtable discussion by the editors of the *Native* about issues related to the epidemic. The topic was a survey then being conducted among gay men in Minnesota about their sexual activities and drug use. Some AIDS activists in Minnesota were concerned that it was a continuation of the state's "unrelenting prying into the sex lives of gay men." John Hammond started the discussion off saying, "I recall a friend, about 15 years ago, blowing up and saying, I'm sick of being studied, and sick of being counted, and sick of being analyzed, and why doesn't someone start treating me like a human being? And this whole thing has the potential for resulting in the kind of sex surveys that Magnus Hirshfield ran in the twenties and thirties [in Germany] that got people to answer exactly such questions, and then after 1934, Hitler used those surveys to round people up."

In the course of the roundtable, I said, "There's the deeper question of sex and the epidemic of chronic fatigue syndrome. They're not interviewing Gene Wilder, for instance—we believe that Gilda Radner died of [chronic fatigue syndrome]. Should Gene Wilder be questioned about his sexual behavior with Gilda Radner? Or, for example, Cher has chronic fatigue syndrome—should all her sexual partners be tracked down? No, it wouldn't happen. Because the paradigm involves basically scapegoating gay people for an epidemic that's widespread, and still mired in fraud and bad science."

In the December 18 issue, John Lauritsen wrote one of his most alarming reports on AZT: "AZT causes cancer in animals. This finding was divulged by Burroughs Wellcome, manufacturer of AZT . . . in an advisory sent on December 5 to thousands of physicians who treat AIDS patients. Widespread consternation ensued. Confused and contradictory statements were issued to the press by physicians, Public Health Service officials and 'AIDS activists.' " Lauritsen reported that the conclusion of the study which involved "60 male and female rats and mice" was pretty clear: "No tumors were found in any of the control rodents," but a significant percentage of the rodents given AZT developed cancer.

If the AIDS establishment was shaken by the finding, they kept it to themselves because, according to Lauritsen, "Immediately promoters of AZT rushed in to downplay the significance of the findings. In an Associated Press story, Dr. James Mason, Assistant Secretary of the Department of Health and Human Services, said the results 'do not establish that the drug has a carcinogenic effect in humans.' Along the same lines, Burroughs Wellcome stated in its letter that 'results from rodent carcinogenicity studies are of limited predictive value for humans.' These are strange things to say. If rodent

186

carcinogenicity studies have little 'predictive value for humans,' why do them in the first place? If rodent studies are meaningless, why are they a standard part of the toxicity screening of new drugs?"

Lauritsen was troubled by some of the the reactions to the study: "In responding to news about the rodent carcinogenicity studies, a number of AZT apologists sounded a peculiar theme: The risks of AZT must be weighed against its benefits." Lauritsen noted that one activist had been quoted in the mainstream press as saying he was more afraid of AIDS than cancer. Lauritsen wasn't having any of it and wrote, "There is a large and growing body of information on the risks of AZT. In addition to the risk of cancer, AZT . . . destroys the bone marrow and causes severe anemia; it damages the kidneys, liver, and nerves; it causes severe muscular pain and atrophy (wasting away). What then are the 'benefits' of AZT that could offset such terrible toxicities? I have maintained, and continue to maintain, that there is no scientifically credible evidence that AZT has benefits of any kind."

In that same issue, we took up the subject of AZT in another editorial roundtable titled "Concentration Camp without Walls." I opened the discussion saying, "Let's discuss whether prescribing AZT is a form of genocide or not."

Ron Gans was critical of the gay groups that were cooperating with the authorities who were promoting AZT: "It's an amazing circumstance when you have groups that are born in opposition to the established order deferring to the established order. The whole purpose of groups like Lambda, all the gay groups, all of them, is an opposition to challenging the established order. . . . It boggles the mind. The only conclusion I can draw from this is that people have always trusted the government, deep down they always have." I made this remark about ACT UP's involvement with AZT: "Why would anybody want to take a drug that has been approved because people sat in somebody's office and wouldn't leave until they okayed that drug? That's what scares me about AZT." John Hammond suggested, "Maybe there's an area . . . that the entire movement has never thought through and that nobody has talked about very much and that is, is there a way to get leverage and apply pressure and get results in which you're not making research decisions or forcing research decisions in a way that warps them and makes the scientific evidence illegitimate?" Neenyah Ostrom pointed out, "People keep saying, 'I'm not a scientist. I can't question HIV or Robert Gallo's work.' But those very same people feel capable of saying, 'Give me this drug, make this drug available now.' They didn't say 'I'm not a scientist, I can't decide whether this drug is good for me or not.'"

I said, "You know it's interesting, the risk that some activist organizations are taking with AZT. The odds really are against them, the odds are that all these people that are pushing [and taking] AZT are going to be dead. . . . You'd have to be hoping for a miracle for that not to happen. . . . People with AIDS—many of whom probably haven't had much access to medical care—are now in the medical system for the rest of their lives. They're in a concentration camp without walls. . . . If only they were giving AZT to dogs we'd have the animal rights groups on our side. They wouldn't allow it."

1990: Creepier Events

In the January 15 issue, we ran a story which—without saying it explicitly—may have actually been a sighting of the AIDS/ASFV epidemic in pigs all across America. I wrote a piece titled "Purdue University Looking into Possible Link between Epidemic in Swine and the AIDS Epidemic." I reported, "Scientists at Purdue University have isolated an organism from pigs suffering from a mysterious swine disease which has been called mystery swine disease, or swine reproductive syndrome (and eventually porcine respiratory and reproductive syndrome). The organism is called a mycoplasma, and it is one of several organisms which have been hypothetically linked to the swine epidemic."

I noted that a mycoplasma had also emerged as a serious factor in AIDS: "Recently, scientists at the Armed Forces Institute of Pathology reported that they had isolated a new mycoplasma from AIDS patients as well as six people who did not have AIDS but who died of multiple organ failure. They named the organism *mycoplasma incognitus*. The team, which is headed by Dr. Shyh-Ching Lo, also has reported that they have infected four silver leaf monkeys with their newly discovered mycoplasma. The monkeys subsequently died."

The Des Moines Register had reported on May 11, 1989, "Purdue University has been studying a mysterious outbreak among pigs in Wabash County, Indiana, where 60 to 70 baby pigs are reported to have died on a dozen farms."

I pointed out, "If it turns out that the affected swine are infected with the same mycoplasma that the Armed Forces has found in AIDS patients, it will not be the first time that AIDS has been linked to a swine disease. Several years ago, a team of scientists headed by Dr. Jane Teas reported that they were able to find evidence that suggested that AIDS might be caused by a virus called African swine fever virus. Mycoplasma infection is sometimes a sign of underlying African swine fever virus infection."

In the January 22 issue, John Hammond reported on a troubling development in New York City. The mayor, David Dinkins, was considering appointing a man named Woodrow A. Myers as New York City Health Commissioner. Myers had been the head of the Indiana's

Board of Health. Hammond noted, "Despite having acquired a national reputation for liberal progressivism, in his home state Myers has been involved in enforcing some of the worst AIDS legislation in the country." Hammond reported that Myers had originally been recommended for consideration by Mathilde Krim of amfAR.

Hammond wrote, "As reported by Michael Tomasky in the *New York Observer* this week, the Indiana Health Commissioner ran afoul of the gay community and civil libertarians in 1985 when, ostensibly to protect public health, he sought to have regular health department inspections, not only of gay bathhouses, but also of gay bars and bookstores."

Hammond also reported, "In 1987 Myers supported legislation that allows draconian quarantine measures to prevent the spread of infectious disease, including 'AIDS.' The law, according to Marla Stevens, of the Indiana Civil Liberties Union's Gay and Lesbian Task Force, allows officials to warn, then place in counseling and ultimately in forced, involuntary quarantine—either in a hospital or in jail— anyone who engages in behavior that could contribute to the spread of disease. . . . The standards of evidence under which a person could be quarantined are considerably less stringent than would be required for conviction in a criminal case: by direct confession, by accusation from two corroborating sources, by being arrested for a crime that could spread disease, or accusation from a single person who has the disease and says it could only have been contracted from the accused person. Evidence from any of those four sources would be enough to permit the Indiana Board of Health to act."

In the same issue, Neenyah Ostrom wrote a piece about a book that was getting a lot of attention at the time, Michael Fumento's *The Myth of Heterosexual AIDS*. The premise of the book was that AIDS, in reality, was never ever going to become a major epidemic among heterosexuals. Ostrom questioned whether there was already a major AIDS epidemic in the heterosexual population that was being masked politically by having been euphemistically called chronic fatigue syndrome. She pointed to the fact that both AIDS and CFS had HBLV [HHV-6] in common, noting that the virus attacks T-lymphocytes and "a decreased number of T-cells is seen in both 'AIDS' and [chronic fatigue syndrome], as are decreased natural killer (NK) cell population sizes and activity levels."

Ostrom asked, "Has 'AIDS' broken out in the general population? That is a question that must be investigated immediately, taking into account all available evidence—not just those data that fit an already-established paradigm."

John Hammond revisited the Myers appointment controversy in the January 29 issue. Hammond reported that ACT UP had sent protesters to Gracie Mansion to protest the Myers appointment. Myers had defended the right to isolate AIDS patients in a *New York Post* interview. The *New York Post* had also reported that Myers said he would keep a citywide list of HIV positives. The controversy had given the new mayor pause and he held a press conference to announce that he wanted to give the appointment more thought.

In the same issue, Ronald Gans reported on one of the Indiana victims of the kind of AIDS public health policies that Myers supported. Gans wrote, "Louis Van Slyke, a 27-year-old native of Indiana, is the first PWA there to stand up to that state's 'AIDS' and HIV antibody reporting and quarantine program. Mr. Van Slyke was the recipient of a 'Health Directive' under Indiana's HIV reporting and quarantine law. The directive, which charges that he has been engaging in unsafe sexual practices, ordered him to avoid unsafe sexual practices under penalty of confinement. In an interview with the *Native*, Mr. Van Slyke categorically denied the changes implied in the Health Directive . . . the Department issued to him on December 11, 1989. Mr. Van Slyke told the *Native* that as far as he has been able to ascertain, no one from the Health Department checked with his family, his friends, or the person from whom he rents a room, Jane Damron. Van Slyke has been unsuccessful in discovering who it was that denounced him to the Health Department, but both he and Damron suspect the anonymous accuser was one of two people, both of whom they characterized as vindictive."

Gans noted that, in a *New York Post* interview, published on Thursday, January 18, 1990, "in response to a question about accepting tips from anonymous sources, Dr. Myers said, 'That doesn't sound very familiar to me at all.' But he later amended that to say, 'Certainly an anonymous person can give information.' On the subject of whether accused persons have the right to confront their accusers, Myers said, 'Well, yes. The accuser, however is the state. There is no right for the individual to know the individual from whom the state received its information.' "

Gans also reported, "Mr. Van Slyke's troubles began on November 11, 1989, when he received a call from Karl Milhan of the Health

Department requesting a meeting. Van Slyke agreed to meet Mr. Milhan at the Damien Center where Van Slyke was attending counseling meetings. When they met at 1:30 in the afternoon, Milhan gave Van Slyke a verbal warning from the Health Department. The warning mentioned that there would be a follow-up written within 72 hours, but nothing transpired until December 11, when Milhan showed up unannounced at 8:30 a.m. to present Van Slyke with the Health Directive. The Health Directive . . . states unequivocally that 'it has been determined that your behavior is a serious and present danger to the health of others.' The directive further prohibits Van Slyke from 'engaging in any unprotected intimate sexual act with anyone.' The penalty for failure to comply with the directive may be a court order for 'restrictions upon you in order to protect the public health.' Besides Van Slyke, health directives have been given to nine other persons, one of whom is under 'restrictions,' that is, incarcerated in a state mental hospital."

Showing the kind of contempt in which the gay community was held, even by its so-called liberal friends, Mayor David Dinkins went ahead with the appointment of Woodrow Myers to the position of New York City Health Commissioner after Myers caved and said he had no intention of instituting mandatory HIV reporting *at that point.*

In the February 5 issue, I took Mathilde Krim to task after we learned that Myers was on amfAR's board of directors: "Mathilde Krim has been generally treated by the press and 'AIDS' activists as someone for whom canonization would not be enough. This paper has never quite bought into the halo however, and the recent discovery that our next health commissioner, Woodrow Myers, was on her board of directors only increases our distrust of her motives and her agenda. The names on amfAR's 'scientific' advisory board read like a *Who's Who* of the HIV/AZT establishment. The illustrious list includes one of the biggest scientific crooks in America, Dr. Robert "I-didn't-steal-it" Gallo, and the incompetent Margaret "Let-them-eat-AZT" Fischl. And with Bill Haseltine and Jim Curran also on board, Gallo and Fischl are not alone in their sleaziness. We predict that while Krim and her cronies may be fooling some members of the gay community and some in the health activist community, history will sort out amfAR's real agenda from its public persona. Back in the early part of the epidemic, *Harper's* publisher Lewis Lapham got a whiff of the agenda. On May 10, 1985, he wrote about Krim (without naming her) in *The Washington*

Post: 'AIDS so conveniently fits the political and theological specifications of the Reagan administration that a prophet of the ascended right might be pardoned for welcoming it as the long-awaited scourge of God. On a television program, I heard a doctor say with more than a hint of comfortable righteousness in her voice, that the affliction was impervious to medical science. 'No,' she said, 'we know of nothing that can cure it except a change of behavior. I'm sorry, but people will just have to learn to mend their ways.' It is possible that I do the doctor an injustice, which is why I refrain from mentioning her name. I know nothing of her motives, her religion, or her politics, but her pious manner reminded me of the way in which the Reagan administration has elected to deal with the outbreak of AIDS. Several government spokesmen have managed to convey the unfortunate impression that the victims of the disease deserve what they get. . . . Here is a secular authority preaching a sermon of sexual Armageddon, and as I listened to her foretelling of doom it occurred to me that AIDS was a disease uniquely suited to the American temperament."

Well, at least uniquely suited to Mathilde Krim's temperament. And agenda.

In the February 12 issue, we published more alarming news about AZT. John Lauritsen reported, "An advisory committee of the Food and Drug Administration (FDA) recommended on Tuesday, 30 January 1990, that the use of AZT (or Retrovir) be greatly expanded. At present AZT is officially recommended only for patients who have T-4 cell counts below 200, or who have been diagnosed as having 'AIDS.' The committee's recommendation was that AZT be approved for treatment of the estimated one-half million or more people in the United States who have slightly subnormal T-4 cell counts (below 500) and who have antibodies to the immuno-deficiency virus (HIV-1)—a retrovirus that is officially, though probably erroneously, considered to be the cause of 'AIDS.' It is always the policy of the FDA to follow the recommendations of its advisory committees."

Lauritsen pointed out, "The new recommendation, if adopted by the FDA, will greatly expand the market for AZT in two ways. First, it would overcome the reluctance many physicians have had about prescribing a highly toxic drug for any but the desperately sick patients. Second, it would facilitate payment for AZT treatment, currently estimated at $4,000 per year, from Medicaid and from private health insurance plans."

Lauritsen warned, "The committee seems to have taken a light-minded approach to the extreme toxicity of AZT. The drug can cause life threatening anemia, severe muscular pain and atrophy, and damage to the liver, kidneys and nerves. In addition, our best information indicates that long-term use of AZT will result in cancer. . . . Considering that nothing is known about the long-term effects of AZT therapy, the committee's recommendation is frivolous. No human being has taken AZT for more than three-and-a-half years. Virtually no patients have been able to take what was originally the full dose of AZT, 1200 mg. per day, for more than a few months without requiring transfusions and for discontinuance of the drug. The acute or short-term toxicities of AZT are horrible enough. The chronic or long-term toxicities have yet to be discovered, and there is no reason to be optimistic."

In the same issue, Neenyah Ostrom reported on a new development that should have given pause to anyone married to the HIV/AIDS paradigm. She wrote, "In a striking reversal of 'AIDS' dogma, two recent scientific reports presented data demonstrating that the Human Immunodeficiency virus (HIV) is not the cause of Kaposi's sarcoma (KS). These reports, in the British medical journal *The Lancet*, suggest that the KS seen in gay men (and others) with 'AIDS' may be caused by an 'as yet unidentified' infectious, sexually transmitted agent."

In another ill-considered judgment, the AIDS establishment, rather than recognizing this development as an epidemiological warning from nature that HIV-negative KS meant that HIV could not be the cause of AIDS (since KS was considered one of the dramatic hallmarks of AIDS), decided to split HIV/AIDS and KS into separate epidemics rather than lose face with the public by admitting that they had gotten the basics of the epidemic dead wrong.

Ostrom pointed out that neither of the new *Lancet* reports "takes into account research performed in 1985 by researchers at the University of Miami School of Medicine in which KS was found in greater than 94 percent of autopsied patients with 'AIDS,' leading those investigators to postulate that 'this autopsy series suggests that Kaposi's sarcoma may be present in all patients with AIDS.' (L.B. Moskovitz et al., *Human Pathology*, May, 1985)."

In their study, the University of Miami scientists stated that their "findings indicated that Kaposi's sarcoma is more common and has a wider morphological spectrum in AIDS than is generally appreciated."

Ostrom also reported, "More than 90 percent of the patients studied by the group displayed 'microscopic evidence of Kaposi's sarcoma in one or more organs.' In fact, these investigators found that 'in only one of the patients was Kaposi's sarcoma limited to the skin'; only 26 percent of the group had cutaneous (on the surface of the skin) KS. The most common sites of identification of KS were lymph nodes and spleen."

For anyone with half a brain, what the University of Miami research suggested was that *KS was the fundamental pathological event in AIDS*, not a secondary one, and the presence of it in people without HIV indicated that HIV could possibly be ruled out as the real cause of AIDS. One of the reasons this did not register with the scientific community was that rampant fear among doctors had resulted in a limited number of autopsies being performed on AIDS patients. More autopsies might have resulted in a shift in the whole HIV/AIDS paradigm.

The University of Miami scientists stated, "The [94.2%] prevalence of Kaposi's sarcoma in patients with AIDS that was observed in this series had not been reported previously; there are a number of possible explanations for this disparity." Ostrom reported that one of the reasons for the discrepancies was "that the autopsies examined many organs not just skin and occasional lymph nodes. They note, however, that autopsy 'is not an infallible method' for identifying KS. For example, tissues can be altered beyond recognition by other infectious agents; inadequate sampling (of lymph node tissue, primarily) can lead to a missed identification; and in some instances, autolysis, the spontaneous disintegration of tissues after death, can occur."

The most chilling conclusion of their study, was one that should have been another dramatic beginning of the end of the HIV theory of AIDS: "It is possible that, as we suspect, all of the patients in this series had Kaposi's sarcoma, although we could recognize it in only 94 percent. . . . The remarkable occurrence of Kaposi's sarcoma in T-cell domains in virtually all of our cases suggests it may play a more important role in the pathogenesis of AIDS than is generally appreciated. We believe that Kaposi's sarcoma contributes to the deterioration of cellular immunity seen in patients with AIDS by invasive destruction of T-cell domains, as in lymphoma or Hodgkin's disease."

Katie Leishman also reported on the story, in the January 28 issue of the *Los Angeles Times,* and Ostrom covered her piece: "The CDC explains these results, Leishman states, by postulating that a second epidemic must have started at the same time and in the same populations as the 'AIDS' epidemic. According to the CDC, HIV is still responsible for 'everything except Kaposi's sarcoma.' "

Leishman wrote, in the *L.A. Times,* "One is driven to wonder whether the researchers might have been correct on the point they have abandoned—that Kaposi's sarcoma and all the other dismaying symptoms of AIDS do indeed have the same cause—but are wrong in the one that they still cling to: that HIV is the cause of AIDS. To question this has been denounced as heresy. But it was also once heresy to question HIV's role in Kaposi's sarcoma."

Even Randy Shilts, one of the fiercest acolytes of the HIV paradigm, was shaken by the findings. According to Leishman's report he said, "It is the strangest twist in terms of medical news in the epidemic in years. It calls into question everything—the existing paradigm for the epidemic, the direction of research treatment modalities, and even the integrity of the blood supply."

What this major development made us wonder about, at the *Native,* was whether there was an epidemic of unrecognized Kaposi's sarcoma spreading throughout America and the rest of the world, an epidemic of a form of KS that was perhaps slower and different in its manifestations, perhaps mostly internal and not obvious on the skin. Was variable, chronic KS the real AIDS epidemic? We immediately wondered if chronic fatigue syndrome patients (who officially were HIV-negative) had a form of KS in their internal organs that nobody would even think to look for. Or dare to.

Because we were overly optimistic that common sense would kick in and the political wall between AIDS and chronic fatigue syndrome would soon come crashing down, we went so far as to express our concern that children with chronic fatigue syndrome might end up getting the same kind of treatment—AZT—as children diagnosed with AIDS. In the February 19 issue Neenyah Ostrom wrote that rumors circulating at the time about possible "retroviral activity" in CFS patients meant, "the line between [chronic fatigue syndrome] is becoming more indistinct. As that line blurs, people with [chronic fatigue syndrome] should be prepared to have increasingly toxic drugs, such as AZT, proposed as treatments for their syndrome. (In fact, other rumors are circulating that some physicians have already began giving patients with [chronic fatigue syndrome] 'small doses' of AZT)."

Ostrom noted, "[chronic fatigue syndrome] like 'AIDS' is a somewhat different disease in children than in adults, and children with [CFS] also experience a more subtle form of discrimination: parents and teachers often don't believe the child is ill. Ironically, as Ostrom pointed out, they were lucky to be treated that way rather than to be given the toxic AZT the way that children with AIDS were.

Ostrom captured the emerging racial politics of the "CFS is not AIDS" paradigm, when she pointed out, "According to a report in the *New York Times*, 72 percent of children with AIDS are black ('Black Doctors Urge Study of Factors in Risk of AIDS,' June 21, 1989). To date, most people diagnosed with [chronic fatigue syndrome] are white; economic factors probably account for these differential diagnoses." Ostrom warned, "It is easy to conduct experimental drug research on black infants with 'AIDS.' What advocacy groups do black infants and children with 'AIDS' have? A July 10, 1989 NIAID (National Institute of Allergy and Infectious Diseases) press release announced that such a study was beginning under the auspices at the University of Miami and the UCLA School of Medicine. The mothers of the children in this study are former I.V. drug users 'infected with HIV' and probably do not possess the political clout and sophistication to argue with government scientists."

In the following issue (February 26), Ostrom spilled some more beans about the retroviral findings in CFS patients; "The *Native* has learned that three separate research teams are preparing to announce that they find evidence of 'retroviral activity' in the blood of people with [chronic fatigue syndrome]. The *Native* has also been informed that one of these teams is about to publish a research report identifying a retrovirus in a majority of [CFS] patients studied—and it is not HTLV-1. Such findings are certain to cause a setback to the proponents of a psychiatric cause of [chronic fatigue syndrome]."

In the same issue, I noted that Stephen Joseph had not become a public health slacker subsequent to his departure from his position as Health Commissioner of New York City. In the February 10, 1990, issue of the *New York Times,* Joseph had written a piece titled "Quarantine: Sometimes a Duty," about "When to employ a quarantine, the isolation or detention of individuals determined to be an infectious danger to others. . . ." In his familiar menacing style he wrote, "It is probable that we may have, perhaps sooner than many expect, a treatment that renders infected individuals less infectious. Would there not then be a clear obligation to take all reasonable measures to insure that the infected take their medication, thus protecting others?"

I wrote, "On the surface that sounds rational and well intentioned." But when one also considers the fact that the medication may actually kill the patients and render them permanently noninfectious to others, one has to worry. Those who know the history of the 'AIDS' epidemic know that Joseph's policies are neither rational nor well-intentioned. Like many other public health types, Joseph continues to base his diatribes about 'AIDS' on the work of the totally discredited Robert Gallo, while at the same time touting, albeit indirectly, the therapeutic wonders of AZT. . . . Joseph writes as though these matters are not open to debate. God-like objective scientists have spoken and now public health authorities must act. Unfortunately, the truth about 'AIDS' has been established by propaganda and fiat rather than by well-researched and well-reasoned science. The power to define what 'AIDS' is and what to do about it has been left in the hands of a few unscrupulous 'scientists.' Given the consequences of their actions and words, that is an awesome amount of power."

Having met with him in the past, I wrote, "Joseph is the kind of man who likes power. He is a strong man whose face reddens when he is angry. One senses in his regal presence that any challenge to his brilliant, earth-shaking ideas is a challenge to his masculinity and the future of Western Civilization. . . . Joseph's career and his op-ed piece are grim reminders that the world does not seem to remember that the Holocaust in Germany was aided, abetted, indeed organized by salty, strong, masculine, tough-talking, no-nonsense doctors. Yes, doctors. The kind of public health polemics that Joseph employs, especially when he begins to divide the public into the dangerously infected and the endangered innocent, often leads to final solutions like the concentration camps, or, in this case, to the camps in the form of a pill that one takes every four hours."

In that same piece, I noted that Larry Kramer had reached a new low point in his toadying to the worst members of the AIDS establishment. In *Outweek* magazine (the *Native*'s competitor) Kramer addressed rumors that Gallo was on his way out of the National Cancer Institute. Kramer wrote, "For all his craziness, for all the scientific chicanery that probably went on in his lab, Gallo still knows more about AIDS than almost anyone around. He may even be essential.

But he's been rendered useless. In a way we killed him. A lot of us went off after him, including Randy [Shilts], the *Native*, Charles Ortleb, Katie Leishman, *Spin* Magazine; I've gone after him myself." I thought "Oy Vey" when I read those words for the first time, and still do.

In the March 5 issue, I wrote about a recent series of articles by Nicholas Regush in the *Montreal Gazette*, on the chronic fatigue syndrome epidemic in Canada. Regush wrote, "A mysterious infectious illness causing severe fatigue and other crippling symptoms is sweeping across Canada, an Ottawa doctor says." A doctor named Byron Hyde told Regush that he was getting referrals from all over Canada.

I wrote, "Regush interviewed a Toronto physician, Dr. Anne Mildon, who told him that she has seen 1300 cases of the syndrome and she is currently diagnosing 15 to 20 new cases a week. The physician told Regush that she is seeing people with the syndrome who are losing their eyesight, while others are so weak they can't move." Ken Rozee, the head of the microbiology lab at the Laboratory Center for Disease Control in Ottawa told Regush, "There is no question that immune mechanisms are substantially perturbed." He insisted, "This is the hallmark of the disease."

Regush also reported, "International medical studies reveal that CFIDS patients have depleted numbers of both T-cells known as the generals in the immune system, and natural killer cells, a major line of defense against infection." In his article Regush noted, "Testifying recently on CFIDS before a U.S. Senate Committee, Dr. Paul Cheney of Charlotte N.C. said there are signs the illness is on the increase and that its 'relationship to the AIDS epidemic will need to be investigated with great urgency.' " Well, that didn't happen.

I also wrote, "If 'AIDS' and CFIDS (CIDS) turn out to be manifestations of the same basic disease, there is a good chance that much of what we know now about 'AIDS,' and much of what 'AIDS educators' are telling the public is inaccurate. The bad news is that it could turn into a public health disaster."

I suggested, "If 'AIDS' and CFIDS (CIDS) are both caused by herpesvirus-6 (a virus the *Native* has suggested might actually be African swine fever virus in its new Galloesque form), then there is good news coming out of Lake Tahoe where [chronic fatigue syndrome] patients are being treated with the immune stimulant and antiviral drug Ampligen. The recent issue of *The CFIDS Chronicle* reported on a trial in which ten patients who were seriously ill with CFIDS were treated with Ampligen. According to the report, the doctor conducting the study, Dan Peterson, 'described dramatic improvement that occurred in a majority of the Ampligen trial patients. Most experienced substantial gains in tests of neurological integrity. The drug, which must be administered intravenously, also reversed high levels of HHV-6 proliferation in most patients. . . . Peterson said he and his collaborators had observed 'identical patterns' of improvement in eight out of ten patients. The two who failed to respond to the drug did not improve on tests of intellectual integrity, did not improve on exercise tolerance tests and remained HHV-6 positive."

Peterson's Ampligen results should have been a miraculous turning point for the HHV-6 and CFS epidemic(s). Unfortunately, HHV-6 would be the CFS road not taken because it would have to be shared with the political victims of the misbegotten HIV/AIDS paradigm. I was basically wasting my time when I wrote, in response to this development, "If it turns out that 'AIDS' is actually caused by HHV-6, a virus that most, if not all 'AIDS' patients test positive for, it could mean that Ampligen will prove to be a much more beneficial drug than the highly toxic AZT. It may also turn out that levels of HHV-6 may correlate better with the stages of 'AIDS' than the virus HIV which most of the scientific establishment has assumed is the cause of 'AIDS.'. . . It will be interesting to observe the behavior of scientists who have helped shape the nation's understanding of the 'AIDS' epidemic. . . . One wonders how the federal government will explain how such a big mistake in defining the paradigm of AIDS/CIDS could have been made."

I need not have wondered. No such admission would be forthcoming in the following decades.

In the same issue, Neenyah Ostrom wrote a piece about the way the growing epidemic of chronic fatigue syndrome could even threaten the public safety. A pilot who had CFS had written about his illness in the December, 1989, *Aviation, Space, and Environmental Medicine*. William T. Harvey recalled how he had been in a plane in the air when he suddenly had difficulty remembering a flight plan "and recalling common radio phrases" that had been familiar to him for 26 years. Harvey, like many CFS patients, had trouble even getting a CFS diagnosis. Harvey wrote, "The numbers of us getting the illness seem to be increasing" and he expressed concern that the emerging epidemic

200

could have a serious impact on airline safety. One important point that he also made was that the notion that CFS was mainly a woman's disease was the result of men being less willing to admit that they are impaired.

As the story of so-called chronic fatigue syndrome unfolded in the pages of the *Native*, an unfortunate pattern emerged in which today's research heroes often became tomorrow's backsliders. Neenyah Ostrom wrote about one of the first depressing developments in the March 12 issue, the transformation of Anthony Komaroff. Ostrom asked, "What is happening to one of the country's premiere chronic fatigue syndrome (CIDS) researchers, Dr. Anthony Komaroff? Komaroff, who is affiliated with Harvard Medical School and the prestigious Brigham and Women's Hospital in Boston, has accomplished what the Centers for Disease Control have still been unable to do: estimate the incidence of CIDS. Komaroff and co-workers did a landmark study published in 1987 that estimated that as much as 21 percent of the general population displays symptoms of CIDS. Komaroff also has vigorously opposed the 'psychoneurotic' theory of CIDS that is perpetrated by such researchers as Stephen Straus at the National Institute of Allergy and Infectious Diseases."

Ostrom worried that Komaroff seemed to be backtracking, insofar as his patients were being given handouts (as of September, 1989) about CFS that stated, "There is no evidence that CFS seriously damages the immune system." Ostrom noted, "In fact, there is a great deal of evidence that [chronic fatigue syndrome] damages the immune system, either by over stimulation (resulting in production of allergies and other sensitivities) or suppression (such as the development of anergy, or complete lack of response to antigens). Komaroff, himself, along with his co-workers, has dismissed some of that evidence." He was part of a very disturbing trend in which CFS researchers (most likely because the empirical research always seemed to inconveniently point CFS in the direction of AIDS) talked out of both sides of their mouths. Ostrom wrote, "Now, however, Komaroff seems to be leaning towards accepting the theory that CIDS is not a communicable illness, but a syndrome that is produced by an idiosyncratic response to stress or certain environmental agents. He cannot entirely get around the fact that there is immune system involvement in [chronic fatigue syndrome], however, and he mentions that 'new viruses that affect the immune system' might someday be implicated in causing

201

[chronic fatigue syndrome]. But he rushes to reiterate that the immune system is 'not severely weakened.' Reading the new Komaroff discussing possible causes of [chronic fatigue syndrome] is rather like watching a man play a game of ping pong by himself." One could say the epidemic of AIDS/CFS consisted of the whole biomedical establishment of America playing the same game with itself.

Ostrom speculated that the reason for the shift in Kamaroff's perspective may have come from his desire to "allay the fears of his patients. In his handout he wrote, 'You may have heard that there are some immunological problems with CFS. Many people have been frightened by this. We have been studying this question with immunological colleagues. There is no evidence that CFS seriously damages the immune system, or prevents the body from being able to fight off serious infections.'"

In essence, he was saying, "Don't worry your pretty little heads about CFS possibly being a form of AIDS. Move along, there's nothing alarming to see here." Unfortunately, several of the other pioneers of CFS research would soon join his disheartening revisionism in one way or another.

In her piece, Ostrom asked a question that could have been asked every day for the next three decades: "Wouldn't [chronic fatigue syndrome] patients—many of whom read the scientific literature on the illness assiduously—be better served by being told the truth? Sugar pills and phony psychologizing have not yet 'cured' people with [chronic fatigue syndrome]; perhaps recognition that their damaged immune systems need to be bolstered would lead to improved health." Ostrom even went out on a limb and asked, "Is there in fact an active cover-up of the breadth and severity of CIDS being conducted by the United States health authorities? And is participating in that cover-up the price individual research teams must pay to be recipients of federally funded research grants?"

One of the creepier events of 1990, was a conference sponsored by the National Institute of Allergy and Infectious Diseases (NIAID) which was held in Washington in early March. In the March 19 issue of the *Native*, John Lauritsen covered the conference which was called "State of the Art of AZT Therapy for Early HIV Infection."

Lauritsen reported, "The timing of the conference coincided fortuitously with the decision of the Food and Drug Administration the day before . . . to approve the use of AZT for healthy people having antibodies to the tendentiously named human immuno-deficiency virus (HIV), also known as the 'AIDS virus.' With the new recommendation, physicians will be encouraged to have their 'high risk' patients (like gay men) tested for HIV antibodies, and then to prescribe AZT for those patients who test positive and whose T-4 cells drop below a count of 500 cells per cubic millimeter of blood (a count which is slightly below normal)."

Lauritsen argued, "The conclusions of the conference were obviously determined well in advance. . . . The panel was stacked, inasmuch as it contained no critics, but many advocates of AZT. The panel members fell into two main segments. The first segment, comprising the majority of panelists, were independents, who were willing to be persuaded one way or another. The other segment consisted of hardcore AZT partisans, players on the Burroughs Wellcome team (and, presumably, payroll). The struggle was unequal—as Lenin forcefully demonstrated, both in theory and practice, a disciplined and surreptitious minority can powerfully prevail against a fragmented and unorganized majority. The independents were concerned with the truth, as well as the welfare of the human beings to whom AZT might be prescribed, and so they were properly hesitant or cautious at times. The AZT partisans had no such inhibitions: they acted in concert and in line with a clear and predetermined goal."

Lauritsen noted that his own "presence was regarded as a threat by the organizers of the conference, and with good reason. I have now written far more on AZT than any other writer in the world. . . and I am one of the very few writers (including Joseph Sonnabend, Peter Duesberg, Celia Farber, Ian Young, Brian Deer, Katie Leishman, and Gary Null) who have dared to expose the lies supporting this deadly panacea."

The bombshell presentation, at the conference, was a Veterans Administration study evaluating AZT treatment which, according to Lauritsen, concluded, "There was no evidence that AZT had benefits of any kind." Lauritsen noted, "This was the last thing the Burroughs Wellcome Mob wanted to hear. Why should a physician prescribe a toxic drug for long-term use if the drug has no benefits at all?" The negative study did little to stop the juggernaut that AZT had become.

In the same issue, in an editorial, I took the *Times* to task for its pathetic lack of due diligence and skepticism in its AIDS reporting. I wrote, "On Saturday, March 3, the lead editorial in the *Times* aimed a rather jaundiced eye at the government's latest pronouncement on the American diet: 'The federal government felt moved this Lenten week to get up in the pulpit and urge its flock to discipline their diets. It admonished every citizen above two years of age to east less fat and more spinach. This sermon is probably salubrious but the sanctimony can be taken with a modicum of salt.' "

Pained by the irony of the *Times*'s concern, I wrote, "Anyone who has watched the *Times* swallow the federal government's pronouncements on 'AIDS' and its perpetual willingness to . . . recycle every [AIDS] press release, may be startled by the skepticism of the editorial. We were amused by the following passage: 'Dr. Richard Carleton, the chairman of the cholesterol panel argues that 38 different professional organizations endorse his panel's conclusions. Their message he says, is "Let's not confuse. Let's speak with the same voice." . . . But that's not how science works. Eminent authorities can err en masse, especially when they coalesce and suppress confusion. The premature release of the Salk polio vaccine is just one example close to home. The cholesterol panel may be right, but its methods are those of puffery, not science.' "

I pointed out, "On the same day, the federal government announced that it had approved the use of AZT for some people who are infected with HIV, a virus that has been declared en masse to be the cause of AIDS. . . . Thousands of Americans will now be subjected to one of the most toxic substances ever given to human beings on a long-term basis. And as this newspaper has repeatedly documented, it will *not* be done with the blessings of *all* scientists and thinking human beings. It will be done for reasons that have to do with political power and a group of 'authorities' who have coalesced and suppressed 'confusion.' "

I also wrote, "When an individual decides not to resist the government's AZT agenda, we hope they pause a moment to think about Peter Duesberg, a man who is a distinguished microbiologist at the University of California at Berkeley. . . . He has spoken extensively about AZT. Most people who take AZT will not have the extensive education in retroviruses that Duesberg has. People who choose AZT should consider what Duesberg said about people who take AZT to Celia Farber in *Spin* magazine: 'These people are running into the gas chambers. Himmler would have been so happy if only the Jews were this cooperative.' "

I noted, "These are very disturbing words from a very intelligent man. What do gay leaders say to themselves about Duesberg? Just another Ph.D. nut? The government would never do anything deliberately to hurt gay people? The government would never make a mistake like that? It is unfortunate that the *New York Times* science writers aren't as sensitive to HIV/AZT dissidents as they are to people who doubt the government's wisdom in the area of fat and spinach. It is lamentable that readers of the *New York Times* don't know that several well-respected scientists along with this ACT UP-boycotted newspaper, think that AZT is one of the biggest crimes the scientific establishment has ever committed. The *Times* allows for many voices in the area of cholesterol, but seems to prefer to hear one voice on the subject of 'AIDS' causality and treatment."

A fascinating story by Neenyah Ostrom, in the same issue, should have raised a red flag about the nature of the real epidemic being concealed behind the government's peculiar AIDS and CFS epidemiology. Ostrom interviewed a woman named "Ruth" (a pseudonym to protect her identity) who had been diagnosed [with CFS] several years before. The woman had a pet, a small white Maltese dog that became sick and was subsequently put to sleep. Ostrom reported that the woman "has an elevated level of antibodies to the human herpesvirus type 6 (HHV-6, also called Human B-Lymphotropic Virus, HBLV); and Murphy [her dog] did too."

Like CFS patients, the dog developed multiple medical problems and blood test abnormalities were very similar to its owner. Ostrom reported, "The *Native* has learned of a number of other [CFS] patients whose dogs 'mysteriously' have become ill. Is HHV-6 the culprit? Is this virus capable of infecting more than one species? . . . And if it can infect more than one species, is it not necessary to pose the question— as the *Native* repeatedly has done—of whether this virus has been misidentified. Is it not possible that HHV-6 is, in fact, a variant of another large DNA virus to which it appears to be quite similar, African swine fever virus?"

We were quite excited to see our critical, often scathing, coverage of Robert Gallo finally being vindicated in the form of a front page story by John Crewdson in the March 18, 1990, issue of the *Chicago Tribune*. His report indicated that an investigation conducted by the National Institutes of Health in 1985 to determine whether Robert Gallo actually discovered HIV presented a false picture of what really happened in Gallo's laboratory. Crewdson wrote, "A secret government inquiry four years ago into the AIDS research of Dr. Robert C. Gallo uncovered evidence that he was not the discoverer of the AIDS virus and that Gallo's principal virus was probably the same one isolated nearly a year before at the Pasteur Institute in Paris."

In my coverage of the very detailed Crewdson report, I wrote, "One disturbing fact revealed in the Crewdson investigation is how easy it is for powerful scientists inside the federal government to commit fraud. Most scientific reporters (like Gina Kolata of the *New York Times* and Michael Specter of *The Washington Post*) usually cover government scientists with reverence and treat government press releases like new chapters from the Bible. The public has generally been brainwashed into thinking that scientists are honest and the scientific process is self-correcting. Given the pattern of dishonesty and fraud that has emerged in 'AIDS' research, it would probably be safer for most reporters to presume that most 'AIDS' science is fraudulent until it can be replicated by scientists who are not connected in any way with the government funding process and scientists who do not live in fear of discovering facts that powerful government scientists might find unpleasant."

At that time, I was hopeful that Crewdson's mind would be opened up to the possibility that Gallo's credibility problem extended all the way to his HIV theory itself, but that would turn out to be a bridge too far.

In the same issue of the *Native*, I reminded our readers about another journalistic investigation that touched on something potentially far more important than the theft of credit for the discovery of HIV. In the July 10, 1989, issue of the *Washington Business Journal,* Bonar Menninger had written a piece about one of Gallo's top lieutenants who was under investigation by the Inspector General of the Department of Health and Human Services. Menninger reported that the investigation involved "alleged ties between Syed Zaki Salahuddin and the Pan Data Systems Inc., a biotechnology firm involved in AIDS research that Salahuddin's wife helped form in 1984. . . . Sources at the National Cancer Institute and elsewhere have alleged that Salahuddin has maintained a close relationship with the management of Pan Data for a number of years and regularly made key decisions involving marketing, hiring, and procurement opportunities for the company in violation of federal conflict of interest laws."

The investigation, according to Menninger's story, included looking at allegations that "Pan Data commercially sold viruses that had been removed without authorization from NIH laboratories." Amusingly, Menninger also noted that Salahuddin "uses the title 'doctor' although he acknowledged he does not have a doctorate or M.D. degree." Menninger also reported that Salahuddin, the faux doctor, "recommended Pan Data for a subcontract from Rockville-based Microbiological Associates, Inc. to develop testing methods to detect antibodies to the HHV-6 virus." According to Menninger, Salahuddin "said Pan Data was the only laboratory he knew of that was qualified to do the work."

It was the involvement of the politically charged HHV-6, in the Salahuddin financial shenanigans, that particularly alarmed me. I wrote about my concern that in the middle of this ethical mess involving the so-called co-discoverer of HHV-6, "Dr. Gallo has attempted to steal credit from Dr. Jane Teas, the scientist who authored the hypothesis that African swine fever virus as the cause of 'AIDS.' The *Native* has encouraged a full scale investigation of whether Gallo's team has changed the name of ASFV to HHV-6 in order to claim credit for a bogus 'discovery' and to reap the financial rewards for various diagnostic tests which will be required to screen patients and the blood supply for the immune-system-destroying virus. The only lab that has compared HHV-6 to ASFV is Gallo's lab. Jane Teas, who reviewed a paper co-authored by the Gallo team (including Salahuddin) which is titled 'HBLV is not ASFV,' described the work done on the comparison of ASFV to HBLV as unsatisfactory at best and 'a cut-and-paste job' at worst. If Salahuddin is perceived as a crook or a scientific fraud, all of his work may have to be examined for traces of fraud. Salahuddin also performed a great deal of the research on HIV for Gallo." And, of course, that never happened.

In the April 9 issue, Neenyah Ostrom reported on a study of an orchestra in which a number of people had developed chronic fatigue syndrome: "The most compelling evidence to date linking chronic fatigue syndrome to the development of cancer was presented by Dr. Ronald Herberman (a professor at the Cancer Institute at the University of Pittsburgh) at the First International Conference on Chronic Fatigue Syndrome and Fibromyalgia (Los Angeles February 16-18). Herberman presented data from an outbreak of 'epidemic chronic fatigue syndrome' among members of a [South Carolina] symphony orchestra. Members—and their spouses—developed cancers 27 times

207

more frequently than would be expected in a similar population, and, perhaps even more disturbingly, quite a few asymptomatic people who were either in the symphony orchestra or spouses of orchestra members displayed the same immune system aberrations—low natural killer cell activity and disturbed T4/T8 cell ratios—as did those diagnosed as having chronic fatigue syndrome, cancer, or both."

The orchestra was a stunning microcosmic image of the HHV-6 spectrum disaster that was occurring behind the veil of AIDS/CFS apartheid. Under normal circumstances one would have expected the CDC and the public health establishment to go into a crisis mode in response to this study. But it was not the era of normal circumstances.

The pandemic nature of what was really going on, was dramatically revealed when Herberman and his associates attempted to use another orchestra in a different part of the country as a control group. Ostrom reported, "The orchestra chosen was the Pittsburgh Symphony. However, they then discovered that one individual came to the Pittsburgh Symphony from the South Carolina orchestra in which the cancer-chronic fatigue syndrome outbreak had occurred. This person had low NK activity, as well as a high T4/T8 ratio, similar to the South Carolina Symphony Orchestra members. Several other members of the Pittsburgh Symphony were found to have low NK activity. However, because of the movement between the two groups (Herberman seems to be assuming that an infectious agent is involved), the Pittsburgh Symphony was deemed 'not a good control group.' "

Herberman's group also reported on an outbreak with ominous implications involving the possible spread of the complex, variable disease throughout America's educational system. Ostrom reported, "An outbreak of 'epidemic chronic fatigue syndrome' in an elementary school in Ohio was also described. Seven teachers developed chronic fatigue syndrome over a one-year period. Similar immunologic studies were performed on this population twice, five months apart. 'About half' of these cases showed low NK activity."

Herberman could clearly see CFS as an iceberg with only the apparent cases at the tip, and Ostrom concluded her piece with a pointed rhetorical question: "When will government health agencies—like the Centers for Disease Control and the National Institutes of Health—heed Herberman's warnings not to be 'too exclusionary' in studying chronic fatigue syndrome and recognize the threat to the public health of the nation?"

208

We ran an interesting first person piece, by a man using a pseudonym of "Martin," in the April 23 issue. He described what it was like to test positive for HIV. He wrote, "I began to ask questions. A lot of questions. I turned to a number of gay, 'AIDS,' and HIV organizations. Members of every organization I visited or called suggested that I should immediately 'consider taking AZT.' GMHC was the most AZT-insistent. I even visited a prominent psychiatrist, who told me that I was at great risk for something he called 'HIV dementia'—I still do not know what that means. Do you? . . . . One thing is for certain: AZT—at full or low dosage—will kill any living cell at random. That's what it's designed to do. The damage AZT causes to liver, pancreas, and bone marrow functions—alone—has been shown to be permanent. Whenever the cure—and cause—of 'AIDS' are found, AZT's irreversible damage will be done."

In the April 30 issue, John Lauritsen wrote a round-up report on the state of AZT research that included an interview with Peter Duesberg. When Lauritsen asked what he thought the prognosis would be for people on AZT, Duesberg said, "I do not see how they could possibly survive in the long run. So the prognosis is clear—either a fast or a slow death of the immune system, or death altogether, because all growing cells will be killed by incorporation of AZT. AZT is a DNA chain terminator. That's what it was designed for. So I don't think anybody could sustain that for a very long time."

The tragedy of the political bifurcation of AIDS and CFS, into two supposedly different epidemics, was underlined by another article in that issue by Neenyah Ostrom. It focused on Ampligen. She interviewed a woman named "Shirley" who had been incredibly sick and incapacitated by CFS. The woman was able to obtain Ampligen with the help of Senator Pete Domenici who, according to Ostrom, "lobbied the Food and Drug Administration (FDA) to release Ampligen" to treat the woman under a compassionate care plea.

The woman told Ostrom, "By the time I was treated, I was close to being the first documented fatality from CFS." Ostrom reported, "By the time the Ampligen was made available she was having 12-15 seizures a day, She couldn't walk."

The woman also told Ostrom, "Three months after the first treatment I could go home to my husband. . . . I have had no infections at all since I started getting Ampligen. I have never had any serious side effects—just slight chills and occasional nausea while getting the

209

drug."

Her improvement inspired an Ampligen trial of 15 patients which was conducted by Dr. Daniel Peterson. David Strayer, a scientist involved in the study who worked at the Department of Neoplastic Disease at Hahnemann University Hospital in Philadelphia told the *San Francisco Examiner* that he considered HHV-6 to be a marker for chronic fatigue syndrome and that at the beginning of the study, the patients showed high levels of HHV-6 replication which plummeted after treatment with Ampligen.

One looks back, in horror, at the lost opportunity of treating both CFS and AIDS patients with anti-HHV-6 drugs if the HHV-6 pandemic hadn't been divided into artificial disease categories.

The similar neurological dysfunction, in CFS and AIDS, was emphasized in a number of pieces that Neenyah Ostrom wrote for the *Native*. In the May 14 issue, she wrote about a scientist whose research supported the notion that there is such a thing as "CFS dementia." Dr. Carl Sandman, who was Professor-in-Residence in the Department of Psychiatry and Human Behavior at the University of California at Irvine, found in a study of 39 CFS patients that there is serious memory disturbance. He discovered that there is a problem with "memory speed" in CFS patients. His study concluded, "CFS patients don't make memories as efficiently as other patients: they have a memory consolidation deficit. They do not lay down as strong a memory trace: the memory trace they do lay down is easily interfered with. And they have inefficient mental scanning speed."

In the following issue of the *Native* (May 21), Ostrom wrote a disturbing article about chronic fatigue syndrome in children. She covered a study by Dr. David Bell on a cluster outbreak of CFS in upstate New York that involved a number of children. Ostrom wrote that Bell (who was a clinical instructor in the Department of Pediatrics at the University of Rochester), in a presentation given at a CFS conference, "gave an overview of the children's immune system abnormalities—including a nearly total lack of cell-mediated immunity and lowered natural killer cell activity—and discussed the 'family clusters' he has observed as a result of the 'cluster outbreak' in upstate New York. He stated that 50 percent of the children who meet the Centers for Disease Control (CDC) criteria for chronic fatigue syndrome . . . have at least one other immediate family member who exhibits 'exactly the same complex of symptoms.' "

Ostrom also wrote, "The symptoms seen in children are quite similar to those seen in adults, Bell pointed out. During the outbreak in upstate New York, 200 people, both children and adults became ill. Bell performed a retrospective study of 107 of these patients who fulfill the CDC criteria for CFS and concluded that the illness seen in children and in adults is the same disease, even though it may present slightly differently in childhood."

Interestingly, Bell reported that children had slightly more symptoms than adults. According to Ostrom, he also found, "that children tend to have 'more diffuse' symptoms which are 'more equal in severity.' Bell commented that, in children, the symptom that was most severe each day would be different; in adults, however, one symptom tends to predominate during a period of time."

We watched in horror and disbelief as what looked to us like a form of "AIDS" *with different presentations* was spreading in families while being deliberately ignored by trusted public health authorities. Now it is all too clear that it was handled that way because CFS was just too much like AIDS for them to deal with it honestly. Nobody wanted to scare the horses.

The CDC's intentions became clearer, in a pamphlet it put out on CFS, that year, which Ostrom reported on, in the May 28 issue: "The Centers for Disease Control (CDC) issued their latest bit of disinformation on chronic fatigue syndrome . . . in January 1990. Entitled 'The Chronic Fatigue Syndrome: An Information Pamphlet Produced by the Centers for Disease Control,' it is almost completely devoid of useful information, is based on outdated information, and trivializes the syndrome almost to the point of nonexistence."

Ostrom noted, "They are ignorant of studies on the trans-missibility and progression of [chronic fatigue syndrome] as well as the decrease in natural killer cell activity" in people with the syndrome. A line in the pamphlet certainly qualifies as one of the big lies of the epidemic: "Although there are situations in which two or more members of a household are thought to have CFS, there is no convincing evidence that the illness can be transmitted from person to person. Until a specific marker for the illness is identified it will be very difficult to address the question of transmissibility. . . ."

One of the reasons that the HHV-6 spectrum pandemic was able to hide (or be hidden) in plain sight, was due to something that has come to be called "the HHV-6 paradox," which simply comes down to the fact HHV-6 is supposedly ubiquitous and therefore thought to be basically latent and harmless—except when it isn't. And, when it isn't, it can be destructive to just about every system in the body.

In the June 4 issue, Neenyah Ostrom wrote about a researcher's work which helped keep the epidemic of HHV-6 paradoxical. She reported on AIDS researcher, Jay Levy, and his colleagues, who had a study published in the May 5, 1990 issue of *The Lancet*, in which "they attempted to determine the prevalence of HHV-6 in the world population."

Ostrom noted, "Levy and colleagues can't quite maneuver around (or explain) the paradox that, although HHV-6 is both widespread and casually transmitted, it is capable of devastating the immune system. While they report that 'seroconversion occurred between one and three years of age, seroprevalence ranged from 80 to 100 percent among adults under 40 and decreased to 35 percent between ages 62 and 88,' they also found that 'Immune cell dysfunction in patients was associated with high geometric mean HHV-6 antibody titers.' "

Ostrom wrote, "This research is constructed carefully to establish HHV-6 as an essentially harmless virus, similar to EBV, which causes disease in a very small number of infected individuals."

Ostrom also reported that Levy and his group had found an isolate of HHV-6 that was different from the ones reported by previous investigators and "They believed that strain was associated with cenotaphic effects, or cell-killing that they observed in peripheral blood mononuclear cells."

In retrospect, Levy's group may have been onto the fact that there were different strains of HHV-6—*more than we even know of now*. While Levy could not find a direct correlation of their new form of HHV-6 with any specific disease state, they did notice a correlation of antibodies to HHV-6 and T-cell dysfunction." (Another finding that should have shaken up the HIV paradigm, but didn't.)

Ostrom underlined the confusing nature of the findings: "So, according to Levy and co-workers, HHV-6 is a harmless virus that infects 90 percent of the world population—harmless except that it kills the cells of the immune system, and antibodies to it are higher in people with immune disorders."

Ostrom asked, "If HHV-6 has been infecting humans for decades (or longer) why wasn't the T-cell dysfunction it is correlated with identified before the 'AIDS' epidemic? . . . Is it possible that those people [who are infected with HHV-6] that Levy characterizes as 'healthy' may also have undetected dysfunctional immune systems?"

In the same issue, we published a piece, by Ronald Gans, about the word "queer," which some AIDS activists had been trying to get the gay community to adopt. A New York City gay publication called *Outweek*, which had basically been started to give the *Native* some competition and to push the AIDS activist HIV paradigm, had spitefully adopted the word and was trying to make "queer" the word gay people would regularly use to describe themselves and the gay community without even giving it a second thought. The utterly bizarre tactic struck most of us at the *Native* as insane and self-destructive. It was more evidence we were living in a new kind of gay opposite world.

In an open letter to the Gay and Lesbian Alliance Against Defamation, Gans wrote, "This weekly [*Outweek*] has tried to make it *de rigueur* to refer to gay people generally by insulting terms. Readers of its pages are called names they've only heard before the rocks land on their heads or the beatings begin. If you find that odd, as I think you should, there is something stranger still: apart from a few letters recently published in *Outweek*, I know of no outcry over this, even, or especially, from the organized guardians of our pride and position."

Gans was horrified by what happened when he brought the issue up to a representative of the Gay and Lesbian Alliance Against Defamation. He wrote, "In fact, I was informed by GLAAD that the use of these terms [like 'queer'] is entirely appropriate. It is part of the 'reclamation of language,' a silly and offensive project by which the oppressed supposedly take charge of another facet of their meager lives by 'reclaiming' hurting terms as their own. Frankly, when I hear arguments like this, I look for my shovel: This is just a pile of shit. I don't know what it is, if anything, that *Outweek* has on GLAAD, but they are clearly immune from its consideration. . . . It is *Outweek*'s constant use of these terms that cause me to wonder what they are really up to. Do they have some secret agenda to popularize, under the guise of gay reportage, anti-gay bigotry, to make it a common and accepted feature of our lives? . . . Just remember: It is only on the front cover of *Outweek* that you can read at the newsstands headlines like 'Queer Fashions.' If a Jewish paper published 'Kike Fashions' it would be roundly, and rightly, rejected by its Jewish readership. Are gay people different? Has our community already become so inured to the evil message of self-hate in this speech that no one finds it ugly, demeaning, and worthy of rejection? This is truly a very sad state of affairs and one, I might add, that doubtless brings joy to the hearts of our enemies, the Jesse Helms . . . and the Pat Buchanans of the world. You will not find this kind of thing tolerated in Jewish or African-American publications. What is going on here?"

I addressed the same matter, in an editorial in our June 25 issue, after seeing a letter sent out by ACT UP: "At this point in the struggles of gay people to survive the epidemic of AIDS/CFS and homophobia, it strikes us as absurd for anyone to begin playing name games with the gay movement. A recent letter from ACT UP to lesbians and gays began with the salutation 'Dear Esteemed Queers' and called for a 'Queer-in' in Central Park. In addition, a new activist organization called 'Queer Nation' has surfaced in the City. We think we speak for the majority of self-respecting lesbians and gay men when we say that this 'queer' banner is one we will not march behind. We are beleaguered but we are not stupid. We don't know *who* exactly has decided to play these name games with our community. But we *do* know we would not feed them after midnight!"

If ACT UP's real main agenda was to turn the gay community into circular firing squad, they couldn't have found a better tactic than trying to hoodwink the members of the gay community into referring to each other as "queer." It was almost a test of the degree of abjection of the gay community to see how easily it could be manipulated into uncritically using epithets of self-hate based on a kind of logic that seemed to emanate from some strange agenda. In a way, "queer" was the perfect cultural condiment at the buffet of pseudoscience that had been served up to the gay community.

Such fifth column antics were the last thing the gay community needed at a time when violence against gays was on an upswing. A story in the same issue by Hank Robinson noted that a recent study by the National Gay and Lesbian Task Force reported, "7,031 incidents ranging from harassment to homicide against gay men and lesbians" occurred in 1989. According to Robinson, the report concluded, "Violence, harassment, and attacks against gay men and lesbians are 'widespread' and continue to 'plague the nation.' "

While the gay community seemed to be thrown under the bus by ACT UP and its "queer" siblings, in the same issue, Neenyah Ostrom made an attempt to provide it with a wakeup call. She wrote a piece titled "An Open Letter to the Gay and Lesbian Community: You've

Been Had!" It began, "You've been snookered. You've been scapegoated. You've been the pawns in one of the most intensive cover-ups that has ever taken place. And you are going to have to take an active role in redressing this situation. There is an epidemic of immune dysfunction sweeping the nation, and possibly the whole world. At one end of the spectrum is 'AIDS'; at the other end of the spectrum are the constant colds, increasing allergies, and general ill health that much of the population is experiencing. . . . These are simply points on a continuum of immune dysfunction which are most likely caused by the same primary infectious agent which attacks the immune system. And health officials—and some patient advocates—are doing everything in their power to keep the public from figuring this out."

Ostrom reported that when *Spin* magazine published a piece by Nicholas Regush, about the relationship between AIDS and CFS, the staff received a complaint about the linkage from a CFS support group leader. Ostrom argued, "Acknowledgement that these two new illnesses are initiated by the same agent might be the best thing that could happen to people with [chronic fatigue syndrome]: more attention—and more of the billions of dollars spent on 'AIDS' research each year—might be devoted to the disease. Patients would no longer be told they had a psychiatric illness. Effective treatment for the illnesses might be developed—but only if the cover-up is stopped."

Ostrom's bottom line was uncompromising: "Why would people who are supposedly 'patient advocates' cooperate with such a cover-up? To avoid the stigma associated with 'AIDS' is the logical answer—a stigma that is based on homophobia. . . . Why has the CDC procrastinated? Perhaps they understand the magnitude of the combined 'AIDS'/CFS epidemic all too well."

In closing, she wrote, "Gay men and lesbians have been scapegoated by a medical bureaucracy that is deliberately refusing to acknowledge a possible health calamity in the entire population of the United States. And gay men and lesbians will have to be instrumental in ending both the cover-up and the scapegoating. Because as long as a compliant, cooperative scapegoat is available, the truth will be concealed."

That year, at the Gay Pride Parade, AIDS activists performed a "die-in" during the parade, a stunt in which a large number of people wearing black ACT UP t-shirts suddenly stopped marching and laid down in the street as if they had all "died." In our July 9 issue, Bob Satuloff, who normally covered the arts for us, described his feelings about the action in a piece called "Mixed Messages." He wrote, "Standing there on the sidelines, watching large masses of gay people falling down in the street, acting out death on a grand scale, like children playing *Guernica* . . . that's street theater. It's supposed to make me feel sick, and it does. The grim faces, the tight body language, the vocal fury: There's a level on which I can understand it, but I can't take it on as my own. Is all that anger going to turn government policies around or alter the consciousness of those who misunderstand us or refuse to understand us? I don't think people hear what the voices are saying. The message is overwhelmed by the tone with which it's delivered. What you wind up with is a dark wave of primordial emotion that closes minds rather than opens them. And I'm not even sure how much of it is about AIDS and how much involves a working out of something else, something personal. The level of sheer righteousness that I felt so palpably in the air is something I learned to mistrust in the protest days of the early 70s, when most of them I suspect, were little kids. I don't pretend to know how to respond to everything that's going on. In such surreal times, even the strongest sense of purpose gets vague and confused when trying to figure out how to channel itself. Yet, if the activists I saw on Sunday expressing their rage are the biggest political game in town, I can't help but feel that there's a more reasoned, more strategic, better balanced way of going about it."

One of the more bizarre Larry Kramer moments, occurred that summer, and was covered in our July 16 media column. In San Francisco, at the Sixth International Conference on AIDS, Kramer had urged that there be actual riots. When they didn't occur, John Leo of *U.S. News and World Report* wrote on July 9 that he had called up Kramer "to see how he was coping with the bad news" that the riots he wanted had never materialized.

Leo was not fond of ACT UP, which he described previously as "a bunch of gangsters" and "Greenwich Village's answer to the Red Guard." He sympathetically quoted one of ACT UP's political victims as saying about the organization, "If you get on their wrong side, they're hell bent on silencing you. They're a youth cult, a bunch of spoiled, angry children with no understanding of politics or the mechanisms of American democracy."

In his phone conversation, Kramer told Leo, "There should have been violence in San Francisco," and "Just picture what it's like if just about every one of your friends is dead of AIDS." In an iconic moment Kramer said to Leo, "There's a positive piece on me coming out in the next week's *People*. It will balance out your column." And if that didn't show his freak flag enough, Kramer told Leo, "I just want to be loved." Baffled by that bit of self-analysis, Leo wrote, "Good grief. What a comment from a philosopher of riot and intimidation."

The July 9 *People* article was written by Ken Gross, who described Kramer watching the Gay Pride Parade from his balcony: "There he looked on with his supporters, sick and dying friends. As the marchers approached and proudly saluted him, Kramer raised his clenched fists in response. On his left wrist is a silver bracelet, made of metallic plus signs, signifying a bleak solidarity—that he too has tested positive for the HIV virus. . . . 'I have no more tears,' says Kramer. 'I know 500 people who have died in the past ten years. Five hundred. I counted. I wrote them down, and I counted the names.' " (Exactly 500?)

The piece was accompanied by a full page photo of Kramer, with the caption: " 'I was unloved,' says Kramer, reflecting on his child-hood. 'I was unhappy, too, and I knew it.' "

In the same issue of the *Native*, John Lauritsen covered the annual AIDS conference. The mainstream media has referred to the conference as a "no news conference" but, according to Lauritsen, "There were a number of important developments—but they mostly took place off stage, like acts of violence in a Greek tragedy." What should have been the most important development at the conference, as usual, was not. Lauritsen reported that in an event "outside the official conference, Luc Montagnier, the discoverer of LAV/HIV (the so-called 'AIDS virus') admitted that HIV was not sufficient to cause AIDS, and perhaps not even necessary."

Lauritsen reported that Montagnier now believed "the retrovirus HIV becomes lethal only in the presence of a mycoplasma, a super-tiny bacterium-like organism. When one such mycoplasma was added to a laboratory dish containing an HIV culture, the retrovirus grew faster. And when an antibiotic which killed the mycoplasma was added to the dish, HIV again became quiescent. Montagnier showed a slide entitled 'HIV, Mycoplasma & AIDS: a Pathogenic Model,' which indicated that HIV left to itself remains completely inactive and benign, but the addition of the mycoplasma transformed the Sleeping Beauty into a ravening werewolf." Lauritsen also reported, "Montagnier further disconcerted his listeners by affirming some of the ideas that have been formulated and popularized by Peter Duesberg: Retroviruses are the most harmless and benign of all microbes; it is not in their nature to cause lethal illness. Montagnier said it was puzzling that HIV could cause death, since almost immeasurably small quantities of the virus were ever found in PWAs, and since HIV is a retrovirus, a class of viruses which normally coexist with the host, 'reproducing slowly without killing.' 'It is not in the philosophy of retroviruses to kill all the cells of the host,' stated Montagnier."

A study titled "Human Herpesvirus-6 Associated with Fatal Haemophagocytic Syndrome," that indirectly showed us how much HHV-6's behavior resembled that of African swine fever virus, was published in the July 7 issue of *The Lancet*. Reporting on the study in the July 23 issue of the *Native*, Neenyah Ostrom wrote, "A team of Taiwainese researchers lead by Dr. Li-Min Huang reported the death of an eight-month-old infant from internal bleeding and 'active human herpesvirus-6 (HHV-6) infection.' . . . The infant's illness began with an upper respiratory infection and rash, followed by fever, 'diffuse petechiae' (round, raised, purplish bumps caused by bleeding under the skin), and an enlarged liver. She was diagnosed as having 'haemophagocytic syndrome' in which scavenger cells of the immune system attack and destroy blood cells, resulting in internal bleeding. Despite aggressive antibiotic and antiviral treatments and blood transfusions, 'She died of diffuse internal bleeding and multiple organ failure 13 days after admission.' HHV-6 was cultured from the infant's blood cells, and tissue culture cells incubated with the child's blood serum 'showed a typical HHV-6 cytopathic effect.' "

In the same issue, Ostrom wrote a piece challenging some of the thinking of Peter Duesberg, "the godfather of AIDS dissidence." The title of the article was "Peter Duesberg's Big Mistake" and the subtitle was "Peter Duesberg probably deserves every major award for his critique of HIV, but he could still be wrong about 'AIDS.' " A piece by Duesberg and Bryan J. Ellison had just been published, in the Summer 1990 issue of *Policy Review*, in which the two had argued that AIDS was not a transmissible illness. Ostrom countered, "While Duesberg and Ellison's arguments against 'AIDS' being caused by HIV for the most part make a great deal of sense, the idea that 'AIDS' is not a transmissible illness is completely undermined by its co-epidemic, an illness not recognized by Duesberg in his continuing

218

argument against HIV: the epidemic of chronic fatigue syndrome. . . . In fact, many of the [critical] points Duesberg makes about HIV can be explained in the context of the wider epidemic of immune dysfunction that embraces both 'AIDS' and [chronic fatigue syndrome] and the infectious agent that is the leading candidate as the cause of the immune dysfunction seen in both syndromes—Human B-Lymphotrophic Virus (HBLV or human herpesvirus-6, HHV-6)."

Ostrom made the case that HHV-6 was capable of doing many of the things to cells that Duesberg *insisted HIV could not do* in AIDS patients. She quotes Duesberg as saying in his article, "HIV must therefore be credited with doing far more than simply depleting the immune system; it would have to destroy neurons and make cancerous other cells, while simultaneously killing or preventing the growth of immune cells. . . . Indeed, any AIDS microbe would face the same difficulties."

Ostrom argued, "Duesberg ignores the data showing that [HHV-6]—not HIV—can be associated directly with numerous cancers and lymphomas, destruction of T-cells, and can infect not only immune system cells but also various body tissues, including the brain. [HHV-6] would seem to be a logical candidate for the cause of neurological dysfunction and 'dementia' seen in both people with 'AIDS' and [chronic fatigue syndrome]."

If HHV-6 was a multisystemic virus looking for a multisystemic epidemic, it had found it in AIDS and CFS. For starters.

It became painfully clear, as our coverage of chronic fatigue syndrome continued, that the CFS community was *not* necessarily going to be a strong ally in any attempt to expose the links between CFS and AIDS. In the July 30 issue, Neenyah Ostrom wrote about one of the local CFS associations in Kansas City that was quite upset about discussions of the connection between the two epidemics. Ostrom reported that Nicholas Regush's previously mentioned article on CFS in *Spin* magazine had inspired a letter writing campaign: "Janet Bohanon of the National Chronic Fatigue Syndrome Association in Kansas City . . . doesn't think any evidence exists to link the two illnesses. So she wrote a form letter and sent it to some [CFS] support group leaders for them to send to various researchers and government health officials if they agreed with her that the [Regush] article was damaging to people with [CFS]. The letter asks these officials and researchers to disavow speculation that there is any connection between 'AIDS' and [chronic fatigue syndrome]." The letter included an angry complaint: "Sufferers of Chronic Fatigue have enough problems coping with their illness without a hysteria-producing article of this nature. . . . First of all there is no scientific evidence that a link does exist. Furthermore, the article has caused [CFS] sufferers and their families numerous problems. Discrimination can exist in the areas of friends, relatives, employers, and in school environments which makes coping with a debilitating illness such as this more unbearable."

Not all the CFS leaders agreed with her. Marc Iverson, a cofounder of the CFIDS Association in Charlotte, North Carolina had told Regush in *Spin*, "You have to be blind not to make the connection" between AIDS and CFS. Honest statements like Iverson's would soon become a political liability for activists in the CFS community.

As far as the contention that the link between AIDS and CFS would cause discrimination, Ostrom wrote, "To argue that establishing a link between the two illnesses—even if it exists—should be avoided because [chronic fatigue syndrome] patients might suffer discrimination is disingenuous at the very least: Do people with 'AIDS' *deserve*, by this reasoning to be victims of discrimination? If a link between 'AIDS' and [chronic fatigue syndrome] does exist, campaigns to cover it up could result in destroying the lives and health of people with [chronic fatigue syndrome] by denying them diagnoses and treatment."

Which is exactly what happened.

In the August 6 issue, we reported on the indictment of Syed Zaki Salahuddin, one of Robert Gallo's top lieutenants in his NCI laboratory. We reported that he was charged "with one count of Conflict of Interest and one count of Accepting an Illegal Gratuity arising out of his relationship with Pan-Data Systems, a biomedical research firm. . . . The criminal charges allege that Salahddin's wife, Firorza, was one of the founders and initial stockholders of Pan-Data, and that she worked there from October 1985 until July 1986. During that same time period, the National Institutes of Health had a procurement agreement with Pan-Data, which enabled Mr. Sala-huddin to order goods and services from Pan-Data as part of his government position." And order them he did, to the tune of $65,000.

We reported, "Each of the two counts filed are felonies, and each carries a maximum penalty of two years' imprisonment and a $250,000 fine.

There were rumors at the time that Gallo might also be indicted, but that never happened.

What really concerned us was that Salahuddin's credibility and integrity were also potentially intertwined with an issue regarding the virus HHV-6 that he supposedly co-discovered. In my piece on the Salahuddin matter I noted, "The *Native* has urged the Acting Director of the National Institutes of Health to investigate whether Salahuddin and Gallo have renamed African swine fever as HHV-6. African swine fever virus is a large virus which could be mistaken for a herpesvirus. ASFV has been found by researchers in some patients with AIDS."

It concerned me that Salahuddin's financial shenanigans with Pan-Data heavily involved HHV-6. Clark B. Hall, a staff member of the House of Representatives Subcommittee on Oversight and Investigations of the House Subcommittee on Energy and Commerce testified in Congress on April 30, 1990, about Salahuddin's involvement with Pan-Data. In that testimony he stated, "In October 1986, Syed Zaki Salahudin, Dharam Ablashi and others isolated Human B Lymphotrophic Virus (HBLV) (human herpesvirus 6— HHV-6). A Pan-Data System employee told us that in late 1986, Dharam Ablashi, NIH researcher [and another Gallo employee] trained this Pan-Data Systems employee in Salahuddin's lab to conduct assays to detect the presence of HHV-6. . . . Following the discovery of this virus, Pan-Data Systems sold Gallo's laboratory more than a quarter of a million dollars in HHV-6-related products and service, starting in November 1986. Records indicate that Pan-Data systems HHV-6-related sales to Gallo's laboratory were $14,400 in 1986, $58,505 in 1987, $96,241 in 1988 and $93,918 for 1989."

It was a financial crime involving HHV-6 that was successfully exposed, but the potential scientific crime concerning the real nature of the virus itself (and its related multisystemic pandemic) was significantly more important.

In June, a scientific paper had been published by CFS researcher Nancy Klimas, one that we thought would immediately alter the whole CFS/AIDS landscape. Neenyah Ostrom reported, in the same August 6 *Native*, that Dr. Nancy Klimas and colleagues at the University of Miami had come to the conclusion from their study of 30 CFS patients that, "CFS is a form of acquired immunodeficiency." Those historic words deserved a prominent place on the front page of every newspaper in the world, but instead dropped into the memory hole of the epidemic.

221

The Klimas study, which was published with the title "Immunological Abnormalities in Chronic Fatigue Syndrome," in the June issue of the *Journal of Clinical Microbiology*, had found that in CFS "the ability of the cellular immune system to deal normally with latent herpesviruses is impaired." Ostrom noted that the most dramatic finding in the study "was the reduction in activity of natural killer cells—even though the number of natural killer cells in these patients was elevated."

In the middle of the AIDS epidemic, for scientists to conclude that another group of patients who were not members of the so-called AIDS risk groups were also suffering from "acquired immunodeficiency" should have set off all the public health alarm bells. If it did, it all happened behind closed doors.

Adding fuel to that fire, was the work of Jay Levy in San Francisco which Elaine Hersher had reported on in the July 23 issue of the *San Francisco Chronicle*. Hersher wrote, "Researchers at the University of California at San Francisco say they are within months of developing a blood test that will help identify victims of chronic fatigue syndrome, a major step in the fight against the mysterious illness." She also reported that they are convinced that, like people with AIDS, "victims of chronic fatigue syndrome suffer from an immune system disorder." The Levy blood test to identify CFS seems to have drifted off into outer space.

John Lauritsen may have arrived at the epidemic's political heart of darkness, in his August 13 article, "Lesbian and Gay Health Providers: Friends or Foes?" He asked, "Does the gay movement really belong to us? The hundreds of thousands of gay groups in the United States, the gay magazines and newspapers, the gay radio and television programs—is it possible they may be nothing but Potemkin Villages? Or even worse, could ostensibly gay groups be collaborating, consciously or otherwise, in their own destruction? Those and even more horrible thoughts were going through my mind as I attended a conference, or rather conferences, of gay health care professionals. Meeting in Washington, D.C., at the Washington Hilton and Towers, were the Twelfth National and Third International Lesbian and Gay Health Conference and the Eighth National AIDS Forum. . . ."

Among other things, Lauritsen was disturbed by "a sort of New Age irrationalism" and "spirituality" that pervaded the conferences. But that was nothing compared to the attempt to silence any criticism of the prevailing wisdom about AIDS and its treatment which he witnessed there. At a panel on AZT Lauritsen was shouted down when he tried to make points that were critical of the drug. His microphone was cut off. Subsequently there were attempts to silence him when he tried to speak at three other panels at the conference.

One of the most disturbing events that Lauritsen attended at the conference, was a workshop entitled "Nursing Based AZT Clinic." Lauritsen reported, "The workshop described a clinic being set up at the gay Whitman Walker Clinic in Washington, D.C. The clinic has only one purpose: to facilitate AZT therapy by filling prescriptions, counseling patients, evaluating side effects, and so on."

When Lauritsen attempted to speak up about the dangers of AZT, at the sparsely attended workshop, he reported, "The presenters were horrified, and asked me to leave, saying that I should find another forum for my ideas, and that the workshop was only for those who wanted to learn how to set up nursing-based AZT clinics. I replied that a conference organizer had announced that all events were open to everybody, and that the official conference program specifically stated that all events were open to the press."

Lauritsen noted that the presenters at the workshop "appeared to be terrified of my presence, especially when they saw me writing in my notebook. To me this indicates that at some level of consciousness they know that the consequences of their AZT therapy will be the deaths of their patients. There is no need to mince words on this matter. The patients will die." He pointed out, "The nursing-based AZT clinics appear to be an answer to a marketing problem faced by Burroughs Wellcome, the manufacturer of AZT."

A psychiatrist, named Basil Vareldzis, attended the workshop. Lauritsen wrote, "Suppose that a patient should begin to have doubts about AZT. That's what psychiatrist Vareldzis is there for. The patient is given [an] opportunity to talk it over, to deal with his anger, pain, or whatever. Vareldzis will counsel him. He will stay on AZT."

In the conclusion to his coverage of the conferences, Lauritsen wrote, "At present, the principle of free enquiry has been violated time and again where AIDS is concerned. In the media, a degree of censorship obtains, on matters of AIDS, that would be found only in a totalitarian country in the midst of a war. . . . In the present crisis, we need all the free speech we can get. There is no place for savagery or totalitarianism in the gay movement."

In the August 27 issue, Neenyah Ostrom again covered the evolving activist politics of chronic fatigue syndrome and the issue of the disease's relationship to AIDS. She noted that an editorial in the Spring/Summer 1990 issue of *The CFIDS Chronicle* which was published by the CFIDS Association in Charlotte, North Carolina, "took the courageous step of examining the possible relationship between AIDS and [chronic fatigue syndrome]." Ostrom reported, "The editorial, 'CFIDS and AIDS: Facing Facts,' was written by Editors Marc M. Iverson and Caryn H. Freese, and begins with the statement, 'CFIDS is not AIDS.' But after pointing out what they consider to be the two major differences between CFIDS and 'AIDS,' the editorial continues—for two pages—to describe everything that the syndromes have in common."

Accepting the conventional and official wisdom, the writers tried to make the case that AIDS was terminal and CFS was chronic and also that AIDS was sexually transmitted while chronic fatigue syndrome showed "a broader pattern of transmission." Having said that, the two writers noted, "Much can be learned from the 'AIDS experience.' . . . To suggest otherwise one must be either uninformed or disingenuous."

Ostrom noted that Iverson and Freese had asserted that they were "appalled and dismayed" by the "national patient leaders and government officials who deny the existence of *any* relationship between CFIDS and AIDS and oppose any dialogue or cooperative efforts among CFIDS and AIDS organizations."

Iverson and Freese also wrote, "CFIDS and AIDS *are* running on parallel tracks," and they argued that CFIDS patients could learn from AIDS activists how to cope with the "growing stigma of CFIDS." They insisted, "To get well, we must aggressively pursue *the truth*. . . . Much discussion of the similarities and differences between these two disorders has been carried on informally throughout the CFIDS movement *for years*, yet rarely are addressed directly (or publicly) because of the enormous stigma associated with AIDS and because many questions about the origin and nature of CFIDS have been unresolved. . . . We believe it is time to consider the relationship between these two epidemics in an open forum, and to explore the facts and our thoughts and feelings about them."

Even though Iverson and Freese wrote, "There are stark similarities between AIDS and CFIDS which make their relationship unique and intriguing," the CFS patients were not about to line up behind these two intrepid leaders and in the same issue of *New York Native*, Neenyah Ostrom captured the essence of CFS patients' resistance in the story of a mother of a child who had chronic fatigue syndrome. The woman was furious at a recently published article [in *SPIN* magazine] discussing a possible link between AIDS and CFS. Her story had been included in a letter that had been circulated by the National CFS Association in Kansas City.

Ostrom reported, "In the letter, signed only 'Kathi' [the mother] states that she is 'shocked and appalled that any CFIDS patient would want to be connected in any way to AIDS.' Kathi states that friends of her sick son no longer visited him. 'Now that this article [about CFIDS and AIDS] is circulating everyone has abandoned him,' Kathi writes. 'He now refuses to go to school on his good days due to this horrible connection to AIDS. . . . Some of his good friends now think he might be gay and that he really has AIDS.' Kathi writes that the family is relocating and will keep her son's illness a secret in their new hometown."

Kathi's letter captured the tragic manner in which CFS patients were sucked into a black hole of disinformation and militant denial.

I criticized the *New York Times* for their lack of coverage of chronic fatigue syndrome, in our September 3 issue, in the form of an open letter addressed to reporter Natalie Angier: "You wrote an excellent and extremely important article on August 24 [titled] 'Cancer Rates Are Rising Steeply for those 55 or Older, Study Says.' However, due to the editorial policies of the *New York Times*, you may be unaware that this worldwide increase in cancer rates among older people may be just the tip of the iceberg. The *New York Times* has chosen to ignore the epidemic of Chronic Immune Dysfunction Syndrome (CIDS), also called Chronic Fatigue and Immune Dysfunction Syndrome (CFIDS). It is an epidemic that some researchers estimate may affect millions of people in the United States alone. Outbreaks of the illness have been reported in Japan, Germany, Canada, Britain, Australia, and New Zealand. . . . The *New York Times* has not reported on this global epidemic of chronic immune dysfunction. The 'dramatic and rapid' increases in the worldwide incidence of some cancers, including brain cancer and multiple myeloma, that you have reported, may signal a new phase in this epidemic."

In the same issue, we ran this curious item in our media column: "The *Native* hears that Burroughs Wellcome, manufacturer of AZT, has been paying for the dinner meetings of a group of gay physicians who meet regularly to protect our health. Is there an investigative reporter out there? Hopefully, if Burroughs Wellcome is paying, they dine at La Côte Basque on the profits from poisoning their patients."

In the September 10 issue, I reported on a finding that brought chronic fatigue syndrome one step closer to AIDS: the supposed discovery of a retrovirus in CFS patients. According to a press release from the Wistar Institute in Philadelphia, "A possible link has been found between the illness known as chronic fatigue syndrome (CFS) and a member of the human T-cell lymphotropic virus (HTLV) family of viruses—viruses that use RNA to make DNA. The HTLV family is linked with certain human T-cell malignancies such as leukemia and lymphomas and with chronic diseases of the central nervous system. The virus that might be implicated in CFS is similar, but not identical, to HTLV-II, a retrovirus discovered by Dr. Robert C. Gallo; its association with known disease entities is only being defined now."

The study, which was conducted by Dr. Elaine DeFreitas of Wistar, as well as veteran CFS researchers, Dr. Paul Cheney and Dr. David Bell, "showed that 82 percent of 11 adult patients and 74 percent of 19 pediatric patients had blood cells containing a viral sequence similar to the HTLV-II virus. Many of these patients had antibodies in their blood reacting with HTLV. None of the ten newborn babies of healthy mothers showed presence of such virus-positive cells in their blood."

Even though DeFreitas noted that the patients did not test positive for HIV, we wondered if the truth really was that she was actually staring at a phenomena (through a retroviral glass darkly) that, in essence, was the same kind of questionable finding as HIV. Was an irrelevant distinction actually being made into a major diagnostic difference in order to keep the apartheidish wall between AIDS and CFS? If the finding actually panned out it might have supported the contention that CFS and AIDS were separate epidemics. This agenda—which had its heterosexist and ultimately racist aspects—was fated not to pan out. The very corruptible and relatively young field of human retrovirology was not a totally reliable partner to the culture's sexual and racial biases. So-called hard science which was abnormal could not completely be counted on to work society's values conveniently into a neat and clean retroviral paradigm that would keep the insiders medically separated from the outsiders. Political epidemiology and public health propaganda would have to do that.

It was hard to completely fault the CFS's community desire to keep the "CFS is not AIDS" paradigm unchallenged when one saw the horrific Associated Press story from Buffalo, N.Y. which we ran in the same issue titled "Red Stickers Identify Prisoner Who Tests Positive to HIV Antibodies."

> In "The Scarlet Letter," Hester Prynne had to wear a scarlet "A" because she is was an adultress.
>
> Louise Nolley says she is being tagged with a red sticker because has the "AIDS virus."
>
> Mrs. Nolley has taken Erie County to court because sheriff's deputies in the county jail used a red sticker on her handcuffs, cell door, legal papers and a bag containing her clothing to identify her medical status.
>
> In testimony Tuesday and Wednesday before a federal judge, Mrs. Nolley, 37, said she has been in and out of jail since 1971. But the red-sticker treatment only began in June 1988, after she tested positive for antibodies to HIV.
>
> The next time she was arrested, she said, she was sent directly to the Erie County Holding Center's medical isolation unit. Deputies told her, "That would be the part I would be returning to anytime I came back to the holding center."
>
> In the medical unit, she said, she was kept in isolation and forbidden to attend religious services or use the jail's law library. She is seeking $500,000 in damages and an end to what she claims is discrimination against people with acquired immune deficiency syndrome.

Another AP story (out of Albany), "NY Health Department Doctors Must Encourage More HIV Testing," that we ran in the same issue assured that there would be no shortage of folks eligible for red stickers.

> The AIDS epidemic requires doctors to get over their reluctance to talk to their patients about sex, says the New York State Health Department.
>
> Officials said Tuesday the failure by doctors to do

this is at least partly to blame for the disappointing number of New Yorkers who've come forward to get testing for the "AIDS virus" (meaning, testing for presence of antibodies to HIV).

Health Commissioner Dr. David Axelrod renewed his call for all state residents who have used intravenous drugs or had sex with multiple partners during the last 10 years to be tested for HIV.

"We want doctors to routinely raise the issue, to routinely talk to patients about it just like they would talk to you about not smoking or not eating fatty food," said Frances Tarlton, department spokeswoman.

The word "routinely" was routinely served to the gay and black communities on a silver platter.

In the September 17 issue, Neenyah Ostrom took Anthony Fauci to task, for talking out of both sides of his mouth, on the issue of chronic fatigue syndrome. She noted, "While Fauci testified supportively about [chronic fatigue syndrome] in 1988 Congressional hearings, stating that 'CFS results from a complex interplay between viral agents and immunological effector systems,' his chief investigator of CFS at the NIAID, Dr. Stephen Straus, continues in 1990 to maintain that [chronic fatigue syndrome] is a psychoneurotic illness. Fauci has apparently done nothing to correct public perception of the illness as a psychoneurotic disease, and has taken no perceptible steps to redirect Straus's research . . . . Fauci does not seem to be aware that the information distributed by the NIAID Office of Communications does not agree with his assessment of CIDS as an illness which [he told Congress] "is triggered by an infectious agent, probably a virus, which grows in lymphoid tissue and results in immune dysfunction."

Ostrom noted that, in a *New York Times* piece on Fauci, Phil Hilts had reported that an unidentified colleague of Fauci had said that the NIAID Director's "ability to lead comes from his almost obsessive desire to please people," and he "is very good at telling you what you want to hear, that he will take care of problems, and through it he develops a sort of intimacy. He makes people feel connected to him. That allows him to be seen as being on different sides of the same issue."

The sociological and epidemiological problem, that helped catalyze the real epidemic and all its collateral damage, may have been the tragic fact that its de facto AIDS and CFS Czar was a politically savvy and narcissistic little man who told the American people exactly what they wanted to hear about AIDS and CFS—depending on the group he was talking to.

In the September 24 issue, Neenyah Ostrom reported that Gallo's associate, Syed Saki Salahuddin, had pled "guilty in September to two felony indictments. . . . The two counts to which Salahuddin, 49, pleaded guilty were charges of interest and accepting an illegal gratuity."

Anyone aware of what was going on in Gallo's lab knew that the apple had not fallen far from the tree.

In the October 1 issue, John Hammond reported on the draconian direction that the CDC wanted to take the epidemic: "Gay and Lesbian community leaders and people concerned with 'AIDS' caregiving reacted angrily to reports that Dr. James Curran . . . had once again publicly expressed his support for mandatory reporting of names of those who test positive for HIV."

In the October 8 issue, I discussed the first mainstream media article that was critical of AZT.

> University of California retrovirologist Peter Duesberg has compared scientists who promote the use of AZT to treat "AIDS" to Joseph Mengele, the Nazi doctor. For the last few years writer John Lauritsen has reported in the *Native* that the research which has been conducted on AZT is fraudulent, and that doctors who prescribe AZT are purveyors of genocide.
>
> But the "mainstream media" has generally avoided asking the difficult and embarrassing questions about the legitimacy of the claims that AZT should be prescribed for all people who test positive for antibodies for one or more members of Robert Gallo's "family" of retroviruses. Currently, 100,000 people have been put on AZT, and eight million people

worldwide have been targeted for the deployment of the substance which causes DNA to stop replicating.

But that situation could be about to change, if a recent article published in the September 23 edition of the *Miami Herald* is any indication.

In a long article titled "The Queen of AZT," *Miami Herald* reporter Elinor Burkett raises serious questions about the competence and honesty of Dr. Margaret Fischl, one of the most powerful "AIDS" researchers in America. Much of what Burkett has uncovered has appeared in [John] Lauritsen's reports on AZT in the *Native*, but for the first time this material will be reaching over a million readers. The report has caused a major flap in Florida, where activists have called for a Congressional investigation of Fischl.

The portrait that Burkett paints [of Fischl] is of a person who basically had no major accomplishments in the scientific field, but rose to great prominence as the front-woman for a drug that does not work and may be causing cancer in hundreds of thousands of people across America. (Duesberg has argued that AZT can be considered a cause of "AIDS"—that it would cause immune deficiency and death even in someone who is perfectly healthy.)

Burkett explores the legitimacy of claims made by a 1987 study of AZT which was published in the *New England Journal of Medicine*. The lead author was Fischl. When Burkett tried to find out why an unaccomplished newcomer to serious scientific research would have been made the principal author of such an important study, she was told by Fischl to ask Burroughs Wellcome, the company that manufactures AZT. Burroughs Wellcome told Burkett that local investigators were "picked based on their reputations with antiviral work." But according to Burkett, Fischl had not done any antiviral work. "Since then," Burkett reports, "Fischl has been either the lead or second author on virtually every important story on AZT. She is one of only ten members of the executive committee of the AIDS Clinical Trials Group, which directs the

$100-million-a-year government research effort. She is the sole U.S. representative to the International AIDS Society, which coordinates the global effort against the disease. At the University of Miami, she is a franchise player: Fischl's research brings in more than $10 million a year in federal and private grant money, half of which goes directly into the university general fund."

Burkett asks whether Fischl, who "owes her dazzling rise to prominence to the same corporation whose drug she is testing, can possibly be objective about her findings."

One of the leading AIDS activists at the time, Michael Callen, described Fischl to Burkett as "a middle-level, third string scientist who the big boys shoved out front. But I think that my people have paid a hellish price for AZT. To the extent that Margaret is a part of that, despite her best of intentions, she is complicit in the deaths of thousands." According to Burkett, Callen writes in his forthcoming book, "If I saw a friend about to drink a cup of Drano, I would without hesitation knock it from his hand. I consider AZT to be Drano in pill form."

In the October 15 issue, Neenyah Ostrom reported on the visual pathologies associated with chronic fatigue syndrome: "An eye condition sometimes seen in people with CFS is 'uveitis,' defined by the Merck Manual as inflammation of various parts of the eye, including the iris, ciliary body, choroid, and retina; it is a condition that can occur by itself, or as part of a 'systemic disease.' " Ostrom noted, "Dr. Anthony Komaroff (Harvard Medical School) and co-workers reported that in a group of 189 CFS patients, 51 percent experienced blurred vision. These researchers also report 'transient blindness' in three percent of that patient population."

The opposite world nature of the AIDS era was underlined by the sentence received by Gallo's colleague, Syed Zaki Salahuddin, who pled guilty to two felony charges that involved accepting an illegal gratuity and criminal conflict of interest. In the November 5 *Native*, Neenyah Ostrom reported, "The maximum penalty for each of the two felonies is two years imprisonment and a $250,000 fine." The court took the loony tact of sentencing Salahuddin to "continue his work in AIDS-related viruses" (like HHV-6) rather than to be imprisoned. It was a WTF moment if there ever was one.

Ostrom was appalled that Salahuddin would be allowed to have anything to do with HHV-6: "What is the value of research conducted as a punishment for crimes committed? How should it be evaluated? Should it be accepted as valid? And doesn't this situation raise the question: What is HHV-6, Salahuddin's most important discovery? Shouldn't all his research undergo the same rigorous review that his boss, Gallo's work is now undergoing? And it raises the more ominous question: What if Salahuddin was as dishonest in his scientific investigations as he was in his financial dealing?"

In the November 19 *Native*, Ostrom reported on the biggest media breakthroughs to date regarding the chronic fatigue syndrome story: "Chronic fatigue syndrome finally broke into the mainstream media in a major way—an extensive cover story in the November 12 issue of *Newsweek*. And an article appeared in another national magazine almost simultaneously: *Spin* magazine's November 'AIDS' column also discussed chronic fatigue syndrome . . . ."

Ostrom noted, "While both articles point out disturbing similarities between the signs and symptoms of [CFS] and those of 'AIDS,' *Newsweek* stops short of concluding that the syndromes are related. However, the *Spin* article emphasizes that CFIDS researcher Paul Cheney believes that 'CFIDS and AIDS are closely related: He [Cheney] even refers to CFIDS as AIDS minor.' "

We ran one of the most bizarre stories we ever published, in the November 26 issue. Neenyah Ostrom reported, "A new study in the [September 1, 1990 issue of the] scientific journal *Cancer Research* found in a sample of 144 healthy and unhealthy dogs at a veterinary teaching hospital, that 50 percent of them tested positive for antibodies to the Human Immunodeficiency Virus, HIV."

Ostrom also reported, "One Boston scientist who reviewed the paper told the *Native*, 'Maybe HIV is a joke. Maybe HIV is just a reactivated, endogenous retrovirus. The results of the tests argue for the presence of HIV in the dogs. He also said that if these results are confirmed, they argue for a reinterpretation of HIV: It may be a ubiquitous secondary infection that can be found in a broad variety of species. This scientist noted that, several years ago, antibodies to HIV had been found in pigs in Belle Glade, Florida (a city with a heavy 'AIDS' caseload). The Centers for Disease Control disputed the Belle Glade findings. The Boston scientist complained that other scientists simply joked about the findings rather than recognizing that it may be time to re-examine the HIV theory of 'AIDS.' "

In the December 10 issue, Ostrom again addressed the possibility that a virus was being transmitted between CFS patients and their pets: "Karen Garloch reports in the November 18 *Charlotte Observer* that 'Fourteen of 28 patients surveyed by Charlotte's Dr. Paul Cheney reported that 15 of their pets came down with severe and unusual illnesses before, after, or at the same time the owners got sick.' Seven of the sick pets died, Garloch reports. And most of the sick animals—seven cats and eight dogs—developed neurological problems like weakness and lack of coordination. According to the *Observer*, those CIDS patients whose pets became sick shared food with their animals. 'The animals are getting sick from the humans,' Cheney told Garloch."

In the December 17 issue, Neenyah Ostrom penned an editorial focused on the hypocrisy of testing health care workers for AIDS but not for chronic fatigue syndrome: "There is a burgeoning movement to require surgeons and other health professionals to take 'the test' to determine whether they have developed antibodies against the virus generally assumed to cause 'AIDS,' the Human Immunodeficiency Virus (HIV). Some advocates of such mandatory testing further suggest restricting the professional activities of health care providers who test positive for HIV antibodies. . . . While federal health officials dither over mandatory testing for exposure to a virus that, by their own dogma, is extraordinarily difficult to contract or disseminate, absolutely no attention is being paid to an illness of immune dysfunction that mounting scientific evidence indicates is casually transmissible: Chronic Fatigue Immune Dysfunction Syndrome (CFIDS). . . . Should health care professionals with an illness of immune dysfunction that appears to be transmitted far more easily than even tuberculosis be allowed to expose their unsuspecting patients to it? But doesn't it all come down to politics? Politically, it is far easier to suggest restricting the professional activities of health care providers who are HIV-positive—most of whom are suspected of being homosexuals or drug users—than it is to consider the same kind of plan for health professionals who have CFIDS. 'AIDS,' no matter what anyone says, still carries the taint of sin, while CFIDS does not. To date, not one article has been written about the 'innocent victims' of CFIDS. Restricting the activities of—in effect, punishing—those who have contracted an illness by engaging in socially unacceptable behaviors is an easily rationalized step for public health officials to take. But it's becoming clear that CFIDS is the far greater health threat of the two illnesses. Already it is estimated that three to six million Americans may have CFIDS. What will be the cost over the next few years of caring for *millions* of disabled Americans? Perhaps the CDC should leave the titillating arena of illicit sex and drug use and 'AIDS' and concentrate on finding a solution to the epidemic that poses a far greater threat to the public health."

Ostrom wrote a column on the burgeoning tragedy of chronic fatigue syndrome and its impact on children and adolescents, in the December 24 *Native*: "There are many—unfortunately, no one knows how many—cases in which CFIDS has affected entire families. One such tragic case was recently reported to the *Native*. It is the case of a family in which one family member became ill; within a few months, the rest of the family—the mother, two teenage girls and a teenage boy—all developed symptoms of CFIDS. The severity of their illnesses ranges from completely bedridden to being able to function fairly normally. Perhaps the saddest case is that of the family member who is in the best health. One of the teenagers is able to conduct an almost 'normal' life; however, three of the people that teenager has dated over the last year have now developed symptoms of CFIDS. Should this teenager be counseled that even kissing can constitute 'risk behavior?' "

Ostrom noted that while the government was doing everything it could to prevent the spread of the so-called AIDS virus, nothing was being done to stop the spread of so-called chronic fatigue syndrome.

1991: Conspiracy of Dunces

The lead news story, in the first issue (January 7) of 1991, once again inspired misplaced optimism that AIDS was finally going to have a dramatic etiological and epidemiological course correction. I wrote a piece about a major *Miami Herald* article by Elinor Burkett which asked "whether government scientists have made a terrible mistake by labeling 'HIV' the cause of 'AIDS.' "

I noted that Burkett was "the first writer on a major newspaper to ask the questions the *New York Native* has been asking for several years. The five-page article was featured on the cover of the December 23, 1990 issue of *Tropic*, the newspaper's magazine section."

Burkett pointed to four major problems with the HIV theory:

> 1) Two healthy people can have sex with the same HIV-infected person, and one of them will come down with the infection after a single encounter, while the other one will still not have it after 500 encounters. Why? No one knows.
> 2) The vast majority of those known to be HIV-infected remain healthy for years—and there is no proof that they will not live a normal life span. Why? No one knows.
> 3) Diseases presumed to signal AIDS are cropping up in individuals without any trace of HIV. Why? No one knows.
> 4) How could a virus found to be active in only minute quantities in the bodies of even the sickest AIDS patients devastate the immune system as HIV purportedly does? No one knows.

Burkett reported that Luc Montagnier, the real discoverer of HIV, was one of the chief challengers of the HIV-only theory of AIDS. She noted that he now thought that there were "too many short-comings in the theory that HIV causes all signs of AIDS." Montagnier theorized that HIV only became lethal when it combined with a mycoplasma that he had claimed to have discovered.

It still amazes me that Montagnier's rethinking of HIV was almost totally neglected by the scientific and media establishment. At the 1990 AIDS Conference, when Montagnier presented his new data challenging the HIV-only theory, a mere 200 attendees out of 12,000 came to hear him speak. Burkett reported that one attendee, Peter Duesberg, said, "There was Montagnier, the Jesus of HIV, and they threw him out of the temple." Harry Rubin, considered to be the dean of American retrovirology, told Burkett that Montagnier "became an outlaw as soon as he started saying HIV might not be the only cause of AIDS."

Burkett explored some of the psychological factors that prevented scientists from considering the possibility that HIV was a big mistake: "If HIV is not the sole cause of AIDS, then the effort to fight the disease is in chaos. In fact we wouldn't even know what disease we are fighting. HIV is the glue that holds together an amorphous syndrome of usually common and non-lethal ailments that are hitting uncommon groups of people or becoming strangely lethal. . . . If there is fear about questioning this established line of thought, it is not because there is any conspiracy against skeptics: It is the intuitive understanding that the last thing anybody wants to hear is what the skeptics are saying. It is just too scary."

One AIDS activist asked Burkett, "What epidemiologist or federal official wants to admit that the entire thrust of research and education might be misguided?"

In the same issue of the *Native*, John Lauritsen had a piece that was extremely critical of Burroughs Wellcome's AZT marketing campaign. He wrote, "Those who have eyes to see are witnessing genocide—the genocide of gay men. Millions of dollars are now being spent on an international advertising campaign, 'Living with HIV,' in which gay men and other members of 'risk groups' are being told: Get tested for antibodies to HIV [the alleged 'AIDS virus']—if you 'test positive' you need 'medical intervention' which could 'put time on your side.' The 'medical intervention' is AZT (also known as Retrovir and zidovudine), and the campaign is paid for, directly and indirectly, by Burroughs Wellcome, the manufacturer of AZT."

Lauritsen summed up the disturbing agenda, asserting, "The campaign consists of a phony diagnosis followed by a lethal treatment. Already tens of thousands of objectively healthy gay men have been scared and bullied and bamboozled into taking AZT, allegedly in order to 'slow the progression' to 'AIDS.'"

For Lauritsen, it was painfully obvious: "Death is the expected biochemical consequence of taking AZT, for the fundamental action of the drug is to terminate DNA synthesis, the very life process itself."

Lauritsen knew that people would blanch at his judgment: "A British journalist once told me that no one would ever believe what I wrote if I persisted in using words like 'genocide.' My response is that, while I want my argument to be convincing, I write what I consider to be true, not necessarily what people find believable. Genocide has occurred at other times and in other places, and it is happening here and now, whether or not anyone wishes to believe it."

Lauritsen noted that the AZT agenda was aided and abetted by the government: "Concomitant with the Burroughs Wellcome ads, the New York City Dept. of Health put up posters with the theme, 'Living Longer, Staying Strong,' conveying essentially the same message, that 'people with HIV' are sick, and doomed, but might 'stay healthy longer' with the help of 'early health care and new medicines.'"

Lauritsen was especially chagrined by the cooperation of the gay media with the promotion of AZT: "Gay publications all over the world, from local bar rags to those with international circulations, are now carrying the 'Living with HIV' ads. . . . Some of the ads in the gay press were sponsored by branches of the Public Health Service, paid for with our tax money."

Lauritsen also reported on how Burroughs Wellcome was marketing AZT to doctors: "A few months ago doctors who treat AIDS patients received a video cassette from Burroughs Wellcome, 'The Psychology of Treating Patients with HIV Disease.' The basic premises of this video are the same as those of the 'Living with HIV' campaign that, 'HIV infection' and 'AIDS' are more or less equivalent, and that early medical intervention with AZT/Retrovir is called for. Beyond this, doctors are told to 'ally with the treatment.' By knocking down any hesitations or objections their 'HIV-infected' patients might have to going on and staying on AZT therapy."

Lauritsen closed his piece with a declaration of war: "All of us who know the truth about AZT have to do what we can. Friends who are on AZT must be told directly and forcefully that they must get off the drug if they want to live. Public health officials, representatives of AIDS organizations, and various and sundry other 'AIDS experts' must be confronted with their lies. Above all, doctors must be told that they have no right to prescribe a drug that can only lead to the deaths of their patients. The buck stops with the AZT-pushing doctors. They are responsible."

In the January 14 issue, we ran an excerpt from a book by Neenyah

Ostrom, *What Really Killed Gilda Radner? Frontline Reports on the Chronic Fatigue Syndrome Epidemic*, which we were about to publish as a trade paperback.

Her introduction to the book began, "After two-and-one-half years of investigating and reporting on the chronic fatigue syndrome epidemic, I became convinced that government health agencies have done everything in their power to ignore, suppress, and even actively cover up the fact that there is a new epidemic sweeping the United States—an epidemic of immune deficiency similar to AIDS—that claimed Gilda Radner as one of its first fatalities. The illness is chronic fatigue syndrome; a considerable body of evidence suggests that it is a highly contagious disease that produces profound damage to the immune system's ability to function. It can result in cancer and death."

Ostrom concluded her introduction without mincing words: "For whatever reasons—reluctance to admit the presence of another AIDS-like epidemic sweeping the nation in the shadow of (and linked to) the official AIDS epidemic, simple incompetence, or more sinister reasons—health authorities have tried to deny the very existence of the chronic fatigue syndrome epidemic in the United States, have tried to prove that an illness of immune dysfunction is caused by 'psychoneurosis' . . . . The personal tragedies of people with chronic fatigue syndrome are staggering—marriages dissolve, careers and livelihoods are wrecked, insurance coverage discontinued, and disability benefits almost impossible to obtain. Many [CFS] patients to whom I have spoken have attempted suicide; many others have at least contemplated it. . . . Such personal terror and tragedy will only end when the mysteries of chronic fatigue syndrome are understood. This crippling illness must be socially recognized, scientifically dissected, and effectively treated—before it cripples the nation."

In the same issue, we ran an Associated Press story about a Utah health director, who basically wanted to set up a mandatory AIDS treatment facility "to quarantine uncooperative patients with infectious diseases. 'With the increasing number of cases of tuberculosis associated with AIDS, it will be necessary to again open a facility for confining patients with infectious diseases, especially those with tuberculosis and perhaps noncompliant AIDS patients,' Dr. Harry Gibbons, City-County Health Director, said."

In the January 24 issue, we ran an interview with Dr. Ronald Hoffman, conducted by Neenyah Ostrom. Hoffman was one of the few Manhattan doctors at the time treating people with chronic fatigue syndrome. In addition to asking him about his thoughts on the nature of CFS, Ostrom quizzed him on a CFS conference that had recently been held by the CFIDS Association in Charlotte, North Carolina. Hoffman informed Ostrom that the president of the CFS organization told the audience, "I've never known a single person with full-blown CFIDS who's not considered taking their own life. From an experiential perspective, CFIDS lives in the brain. It cripples the spirit and the mind."

Hoffman told Ostrom, "One of the things I learned at the conference is just to do a regular neurological examination, like you might do for a patient who is senile. Now I have a patient who's a former mathematics major, and she has CFIDS. I asked her to count backwards from 100 by seven—but she was completely bollixed up by that. That's called a serial seven subtraction, and it's a standard test for evaluating people for premature senility. Clinically it's a pearl, because many patients with CFIDS just can't do it readily—they can't even balance a checkbook."

Hoffman also told Ostrom that, at the conference, he learned "that there are a lot of domestic animal illnesses associated with CFS: Now 58 percent of Paul Cheney's series reported a domestic pet with serious illness or death—neurological impairments, seizures, the kinds of health problems that your pet doesn't ordinarily have. That was quite impressive."

Hoffman was also taken with what he learned about the higher incidence of cancer in the first-order relatives of people with CFIDS. He told Ostrom, "In one study, thirty-five patients reported 38 cancers in 205 first-order relatives. There's a lot of cancer in the country, but 38 cancers in 205 relatives?"

Hoffman told Ostrom that chronic fatigue syndrome "clearly, is an immune dysregulation: There's no predicting how that's going to be manifest, it seems to me."

In the February 18 *Native*, I wrote a piece about a letter published in the February 7, 1991, issue of *Nature*, about HHV-6 that was written by Robert Gallo. Gallo was attempting to find a place for HHV-6 in AIDS, but not one in which he etiologically supplanted HIV with the DNA virus. Gallo presented the HHV-6 as a virus which could expand "the range of HIV-1 susceptible cells."

I noted, "Ever since Gallo claimed to have discovered HHV-6 in

1986, he has been suggesting that the virus could explain the total destruction of T-cells in AIDS patients. Indeed, because of the ability of HHV-6 to destroy cells in the immune system, one AIDS researcher told the *Native* that he's convinced Gallo would have called HHV-6 the 'AIDS virus' if he had 'discovered' it before HIV."

I reminded our readers, "Gallo claimed the discovery of HHV-6 several months after a scientist, Dr. John Beldekas, visited Gallo's lab and showed him evidence that African swine fever virus (a large DNA virus which has been confused with herpesviruses) is involved in 'AIDS.' Under pressure from the *Native*, Gallo's associates 'compared' HHV-6 to a piece of African swine fever virus and concluded that the two viruses were not related. The problem with that research is that Gallo's credibility, as well as the credibility of some of his associates, has been undermined by ongoing investigations of Gallo's published scientific work, as well as financial matters. Gallo's claims that HHV-6 may be the 'AIDS' cofactor comes at a time when Luc Montagnier, the French researcher who discovered LAV before Gallo discovered HTLV-III, is now claiming that a form of bacteria called a mycoplasma is the main cofactor in 'AIDS.' "

I reported, "Dr. John Beldekas, now the Director of Clinical Laboratories at Boston University, and one of the proponents of the theory that African swine fever virus may be the cause of 'AIDS,' told the *Native*, "Well, it's about time. He's coming around to the possibility that a DNA virus may be causing 'AIDS.' A few years ago I tried to tell him that when I presented my research at a formal seminar at his laboratory at the National Cancer Institute. At that time, my colleague Jane Teas and I were convinced that African swine fever virus was the critical virus for the development of 'AIDS.' It's very curious that two or three months after I gave him some of our materials to work on, he published a paper on his new DNA virus."

Beldekas also told me, "No matter what HHV-6 is, if these new findings are true, then you'd better stop HHV-6 from replicating [in 'AIDS' patients]. He's saying that HHV-6 allows more than just T-4 cells to be infected. It extends the range of infection."

I also interviewed Peter Duesberg to ascertain his reaction to Gallo's HHV-6 cofactor. He said, "If you postulate a cofactor, is it possible that the cofactor can do the damage itself. Is there any evidence that HHV-6 even needs HIV?"

In a February 23 front page article, *New York Times* journalist, Gina

Kolata, reported that a new federal study raised questions about who would be helped by the AIDS drug AZT. Kolata wrote, "The study, conducted by the Department of Veterans Affairs, found that AZT, or azidothymidine, slows the development of symptoms in some people infected with the AIDS virus, yet people who took the drug before they had symptoms lived no longer than those who took it after they had symptoms."

The most disturbing part of the study involved black and Hispanic patients. According to Kolata, "Eleven of the 63 who took AZT immediately developed AIDS symptoms, and 12 of 56 who waited developed the disease." She also noted the results provoked speculation that "people of different races react differently to AZT" as well as criticism that most participants in AIDS research have been white men.

Kolata asked three physicians to evaluate the study: "Dr. Paul Meier, a committee member who is a statistician at the University of Chicago, said he found it 'discouraging' that AZT taken early in the course of the disease did not prolong life." He also told Kolata that, given the potential side effects of the drug, it would be difficult to deduce whether it was worth taking. He said to Kolata, "We're fussing and fuming with a therapy that's not very good."

In keeping with the insane opposite world positions that most gay organizations seemed to be taking on anything concerning AIDS, the National Gay and Lesbian Task Force issued a press release saying that the organization "seriously questioned the conclusion of a government antiviral study that suggests people of color are significantly less likely than others to be affected by AZT, the only government-licensed treatment for fighting AIDS." NGLTF's Lesbian and Gay Health Lobbyist, Belinda Rochelle, "cautioned people of color with HIV from 'misinterpreting' the study." Lobbyist Rochelle said, "This may send a dangerous message of hopelessness to communities that are just beginning to focus on prevention and early intervention. We believe the data in this study is inconclusive and points out the need for more detailed reports on AIDS and minorities."

I was shocked by their take on the matter and wrote in an editorial, "Here we have a study which only confirms the dangers of AZT, so what does NGLTF want? More studies on the effects of AZT on blacks and Hispanics. NGLTF wants larger studies. NGLTF wants different dosages. At what point did the gay community—or anybody, for that matter, targeted as an 'HIV risk group'—become the prisoner of AZT? You'd think from the sacred way in which AZT is approached, even by people who profess to be gay, that the Great American Mission is to find some use for this weed killer. AZT is a clear violation of human rights, and it's absolutely disgusting that our so-called gay rights organization is now doing the equivalent work of those evil Burroughs Wellcome 'Living with HIV' posters all over town. There have been many stories in the press making fun of the high percentage of black citizens who think that 'AIDS' is a conspiracy. We don't subscribe to that theory, but we respect the profound distrust that many people feel toward the sleazy, self-serving people who are running the 'AIDS' show. Pumping AZT into blacks will only increase their distrust—and ours. . . . Seeing the National Gay and Lesbian Task Force take part in the poisoning of Americans is heartbreaking."

In the same issue, Neenyah Ostrom wrote about the bizarre development in which one of the scientists in Gallo's lab who worked on HHV-6, Zaki Salahuddin, was sentenced to community service—doing scientific research—for two financial crimes. Ostrom reported, "Salahuddin pleaded guilty on September 7, 1990, to two felony indictments: accepting an illegal gratuity and conflict-of-interest charges arising from his involvement with a Maryland biotechnology firm, Pan-Data Systems Inc., during the time he was employed at the National Cancer Institute. The maximum penalty for each of these felony indictments was two years imprisonment and a $250,000 fine. According to the United States Attorney's Office in the District of Maryland, Salahuddin received an exceptionally lenient sentence at the hands of U.S. District Judge John R. Hargrove. On October 21, Salahuddin was sentenced by Hargrove to pay a fine of $12,000 (approximately the amount he received from Pan-Data Systems in illegal gratuities) and to perform 1,750 hours of unpaid research. Paul W. Valentine reported in the October 22 *Washington Post* that Salahuddin's defense attorney, Seymour Glanzer, 'said Salahuddin has already begun voluntary research on chronic fatigue syndrome, known as CFS, a disorder caused by a virus similar to those found in AIDS and herpes.' "

Given the integrity and credibility of America's AIDS and chronic fatigue syndrome research, it was the perfect place for Salahuddin to do time.

In the March 4 *Native*, John Lauritsen reported on a February 14 meeting of the Antiviral Drug Advisory Committee of the Food and

Drug Administration (FDA). The meeting was called to discuss the aforementioned Veterans Administration study of AZT therapy for AIDS which, Lauritsen noted, "indicated that early AZT therapy conferred no benefits in terms of overall survival, and might be harmful to black and Hispanic patients."

Lauritsen wrote that, in the wake of the study, "Widespread panic and consternation ensued—in the 'AIDS establishment,' among 'AIDS activists,' and in the stock market." (Burroughs Wellcome's stock went down.) Lauritsen asserted, "A well-orchestrated campaign of flak began."

We published a transcript of Lauritsen's remarks at the hearing and these are some of the highlights:

> I'm John Lauritsen. I'm here as a working journalist, also as an AIDS dissident, so my comments will be against the grain. In the United States, AIDS dissidents are not sent to Siberia, the way that dissidents were in the Soviet Union when they argued with the tenets of Lysenkoism. However, we are punished. Two physicians who questioned the HIV-AIDS hypothesis had their practices destroyed and were driven to the edge of bankruptcy. Molecular biologist Peter Duesberg, an outstanding scientist, had a grant canceled. And I've taken my share of abuse. All this was for questioning what was probably a false hypothesis.
>
> For two decades I've made my living analyzing statistical data. Before analyzing data, there are two things one needs to know. Number one, are the data good? And number two, are the premises correct—is the study design good? I maintain with regards to AZT that much of the data are bad, and in some cases manifestly fraudulent. And secondly, that most of the AZT research is based on a false hypothesis—the hypothesis that a retrovirus, tendentiously named the Human Immunodeficiency Virus (HIV), is the cause of AIDS. . . .
>
> There have been many other drug scandals. Take Thalidomide. I submit to you that the Thalidomide scandal was utterly trivial—it didn't amount to a hill of

beans—compared to the AZT scandal that is happening now.

I know some of the people on AZT. You know, it's not real to think of 125,000 people. But I know three, or four of the nicest people I could describe. Young, intelligent people who ought to live for a long time.

Please do your job. Find out the real facts. Don't believe everything you hear at these meetings or that you read in the medical journals, about the alleged benefits of AZT. . . . It is your duty to learn the truth and to speak out—to stop the tragedy that is now taking place.

In the March 18 issue, Neenyah Ostrom once again wrote a critical piece about Peter Duesberg: "Berkeley's Dr. Peter Duesberg, the most prominent critic of the 'virus-AIDS hypothesis,' has published an article [in the February 1991 issue of the *Proceedings of The National Academy of Sciences*] criticizing both that hypothesis and the putative pathogenicity of the human immunodeficiency virus, HIV. Using the epidemiological evidence generally presented to prove that infection with HIV results in the development of 'AIDS,' Duesberg argues convincingly that HIV has not been demonstrated to be a disease-causing entity. But in pursuing his theory that the acquired immunodeficiency defined as 'AIDS' is caused by 'risk behaviors,' Duesberg ignores two crucial bits of evidence: That there exists a large population of people with an 'acquired immunedeficiency'—i.e. chronic fatigue syndrome (CFS) or Chronic Immune Dysfunction Syndrome (CIDS)—that may be linked to the 'AIDS' epidemic; and, perhaps more importantly, Duesberg ignores the pathogenic capabilities of a virus that infects a large percentage of both populations, human herpesvirus 6 (HHV-6)."

Ostrom noted that, "Since 1986, when HHV-6's isolation from 'AIDS' and cancer patients was first described, it has been suggested repeatedly that the virus may play a role in causing illnesses of immunodeficiency. HHV-6 has been found to infect monocytes and macrophages, two of the immune system cells infected by HIV. It infects—and kills—T-cells far more effectively than HIV. Disturbingly high percentages of patients with various types of cancers, conditions of immunodeficiency, and autoimmune illnesses are found to have high antibodies to HHV-6. . . ."

244

Ostrom took Duesberg to task, writing, "Curiously, while attempting to prove that 'AIDS' is not caused by an infectious agent but by 'risk behaviors,' Duesberg presents a long list of the infectious agents found in people with 'AIDS'—leaving out only HHV-6."

Ostrom asked, "Are the data on HHV-6 so compelling that to present them would nullify Duesberg's 'risk behavior' hypothesis? Duesberg's arguments about the validity of the hypothesis that 'AIDS' is caused by HIV are lucid, elegant and probably correct. But there *is* an agent that infects the same cells as HIV, kills them effectively, and with which high levels of antibodies are associated in illnesses of immunodeficiency: HHV-6. A serious examination of HHV-6 might make Duesberg revise his 'AIDS risk' hypothesis."

In the March 25 issue, we ran a long piece by Neenyah Ostrom that took up the relationship between HHV-6 and African swine fever virus. She asked, "Is it possible that HHV-6 is not a newly identified human herpesvirus but is actually African swine fever virus (ASFV) that has become capable of infecting humans? Has the National Cancer Institute laboratory of Dr. Robert Gallo misidentified HHV-6? (This is the laboratory from which two researchers have been suspended for proven and alleged misconduct, and whose research was halted by the U.S. government because regulations protecting study participants were ignored.)"

Ostrom reminded our readers that "Using reagents supplied by the U.S. Department of Agriculture (USDA), investigators [Teas, Beldekas and Hebert] found 'evidence consistent with African swine fever virus (ASFV) infection in the plasma of U.S. patients with AIDS or Lymphadenopathy Syndrome (LAS).' Teas and co-workers concluded that their results 'point either to cross-reactivity with some AIDS-associated virus other than HTLV-III or to the existence of a new variant of ASFV.' "

Ostrom noted, "When the Centers for Disease Control was unable to confirm these findings, a meeting of seven scientists convened at the Cold Spring Harbor Laboratory on September 11, 1986, to discuss the controversial ASFV findings. The group of scientists [which included Gallo's buddy, Harvard's Myron Essex], concluded that the avenue of research should *not* be pursued and sent one of the most bizarre memos in the history of science to the USDA on September 12, 1986 recommending that no further action be taken in the investigation of ASFV's potential involvement in causing 'AIDS.' "

Ostrom also noted that Malcolm Gladwell had written a piece about HHV-6 in the March 12 *Washington Post*. Interestingly, he reported that HHV-6 is "as malevolent as HIV" and Phil Pellet, the head of the herpesvirus laboratory at the CDC told him, "The reality is: It's its own critter."

Ostrom wrote, "The number of symptoms common to ASF, 'AIDS,' and chronic fatigue syndrome is startling, especially when the whole range of clinical illness is considered."

Ostrom also noted, "Pigs who survive the subacute form of ASF develop chronic ASF, the symptoms of which include 'irregular and undulating fever, somnolence, capricious appetite, loss of weight and delayed growth. . . . Lungs, skin and joints are involved in the illness, difficulty breathing and pneumonia . . . are common in chronic ASF.' All of which sounds like chronic fatigue syndrome in pigs."

Ostrom described what Gallo's staff did after the *Native* constantly raised the question of whether HHV-6 was really African swine fever virus: "After a great deal of pressure from this newspaper, former NCI researcher Syed Zaki Salahuddin (who was suspended from his job in late 1990 after pleading guilty to two felony indictments, conflict of interest and accepting an illegal gratuity), along with five colleagues from the Gallo laboratory, wrote a letter to the editor of *AIDS Research and Human Retroviruses* in 1988 titled 'HBLV Is Not ASFV.' Interestingly, Gallo himself was not a co-author of the letter. . . . The two-paragraph report was accompanied by an illustration of the Southern blot results that one scientist familiar with the controversy told Jane Teas looked like a 'cut-and-paste-job.' This scientist also pointed out that such observations would be highly strain-specific, and that Gallo's lab members did not specify the strain of ASFV used."

At the end of her piece, Ostrom asked, "Shouldn't all the HHV-6 research be reevaluated? Should the public believe anything that comes out of Gallo's lab?"

Robert Gallo wrote a very defensive book, *Virus Hunting*, about his career and the so-called discovery of HIV, and we published a review of it by Peter Duesberg in the April 29 *Native*. Duesberg wrote, "In *Virus Hunting*, Robert Gallo offers a highly personal view of his triumphs and agonies with the human retroviruses he believes cause leukemia and AIDS. Gallo's greatest triumph was the notorious press conference in April 1984 when he and the Secretary Of Health and Human Services Margaret Heckler jointly announced that Human

Immunodeficiency Virus (HIV) is the cause of AIDS and that Gallo had discovered HIV. It set the unique precedent, that a scientific hypothesis of immense clinical consequence would be nationally accepted prior to a single publication on the subject by Gallo or any other American scientist. Moreover, Gallo managed at the same time to file together with his employer, the National Institutes of Health, for a lucrative AIDS test patent. However, subsequent nucleic acid sequence analysis proved Gallo's virus from 1984 to be the same virus discovered by Luc Montagnier in 1983. Since Montagnier had sent his virus to Gallo in 1983, it appeared that Gallo had rediscovered Montagnier's virus. In addition, a legal investigation proved that the photograph of HIV in Gallo's first AIDS papers was that of Montagnier's virus 'inadvertently' used 'largely for illustrative purposes' (p. 210-211). That would have been the end of all claims to immortality by ordinary, academic scientists now working for a government that had committed itself to Gallo's hypothesis."

Duesberg mocked much of the book's arguments in great detail and he pointed out, "Gallo is uneasy about cofactors [in AIDS], in particular if they come from others: 'Nonetheless I am surprised that Montagnier has suggested a mycoplasma [not even co-discovered by Gallo] as a possible or probable prerequisite for AIDS development with HIV' (p. 279). Gallo realizes that cofactors have been the beginning of the end of many once spectacular hypotheses. Gallo expresses his concern with a quote from Lewis Thomas: 'Multi-factorial is multi-ignorance. Most of the factors [and quite possibly even HIV] go away when we learn the real cause of disease' (p. 148). Adopting cofactors has in fact become the admission of failure in the new era of big science. In view of the large personal and commercial investments in big science, like AIDS and cancer research, it has become virtually impossible to admit a fundamental mistake. Big science can respond to errors no better than the Titanic to icebergs."

Duesberg ends his review with a grim assessment: "All this 'Virus Hunting' would be just another, albeit expensive, scientific comedy if it weren't the only basis for the chronic treatment of currently 125,000 symptomatic and even healthy HIV-carriers with AZT (Duesberg, *PNAS* 88, 1575-1579, 1991). AZT is an inevitably cytotoxic terminator of DNA synthesis—and DNA is the central molecule of life. It is administered to HIV carriers to inhibit HIV DNA, but unfortunately it inhibits human cell DNA just as well. Since according to Gallo, '. . . fewer than one in 10,000 cells express virus [and fewer would make

247

HIV DNA] at most times' (p. 248), 9,999 uninfected human T-cells will be killed by AZT for every T-cell infected by HIV—the hypothetical cause of AIDS! This is called a high toxicity index in pharmacology. Obviously the M.D. Gallo is not unaware of these 'side effects' . . . chiefly [on] cells . . . of the bone marrow [that] are dividing and, therefore, making DNA. So AZT might cause a decline in the number of certain blood cells' (p. 305)—the very cells AIDS patients are deficient in to begin with! It would appear that AZT is the most tragic consequence of 'Virus Hunting'—inevitably fatal to those who receive it and possibly fatal to the future reputations of those who have prescribed it."

In the same issue, we ran a long interview, conducted by Neenyah Ostrom, with a very honest and outspoken doctor named Paul Lavinger. He was an internist who developed chronic fatigue syndrome in December 1989. His wife had contracted it in 1987. Ostrom reported, "In his extended household, five people now have been diagnosed with or are starting to develop symptoms of CFS. The Lavingers also have a five-year-old dog that 'collapses for three hours' after being taken for a walk."

Lavinger told Ostrom, "From 25 years' experience of practicing medicine and seeing how government agencies deal with outbreaks of illnesses, [he] believes that a 'conspiracy of dunces' is keeping the truth about chronic fatigue syndrome from the American public. . . . It's absolutely ironic that the patients who have this illness, who are often turned away by physicians, are sicker than most patients in any doctor's practice." He also said, "The government doesn't want to let the public know that they might be at risk, because if the public knew that they were at risk, then the public would demand certain things of the government. . . . But the government doesn't want a public outcry. I think the government really wants to keep this quiet."

He also believed, "The insurance companies are glad that the government doesn't want to admit that this thing is real, because the insurance companies don't want to have to pay."

He also told Ostrom, "Families are in this conspiracy because they don't want to feel guilty for not taking care of the sick family member—it's easier to say that it's your own damn fault. Can you imagine walking up to someone in an iron lung and saying 'It's your own damn fault you're in this iron lung?' So families absolve themselves of guilt. I know this story of a young girl with this illness: She had a typical story, there were lots of things she couldn't do. So the family put her in a mental institution. I mean, they do this in Russia, but . . . the family doesn't want to admit that the CFS patient is so sick that they might have to care for him or her. It's easier to get rid of the sick person."

Lavinger had an apocalyptic view of CFS and warned, "If you think the infrastructure of this country is the bridges, tunnels, and highways, you're wrong—it's the people. And I'm telling you that everybody could get sick—well, not everybody because there are people who are naturally immune to different kinds of illnesses. But it's possible that half this country could get sick and that would be a disaster."

In the May 6 issue, we ran the second installment of the interview with Dr. Lavinger. When Ostrom asked him about the transmissibility of CFS, he said, "First of all, this disease is probably caused by a virus. Why do I say that? You know the story about the duck: If it walks like a duck, if it quacks like a duck, it's a duck? Well if this disease isn't a virus, it's a duck. . . . The sheer number of people who are estimated to have CFS, as much as two to five percent of the population—maybe five to twelve million people—speaks to the issue of transmissibility. Too many people are getting the illness."

Lavinger told her, "Practically all the people who got this disease, chronic fatigue syndrome, got it after 1980. . . . I spoke to a doctor who has been sick with CFS for six years but continues to work. In addition to his regular gastroenterology practice, out of the kindness of his heart, he takes care of 100 CFS patients. He told me that, among these 100 patients, he has 10 families. Eight of the ten families have two family members who had CFS; two of the ten families have three sick family members."

Even though most of the evidence pointed to CFS being transmissible, he told Ostrom, "If you call the hotline at the CDC and press the right buttons on your touch-tone phone, they'll tell you that CFS cannot be transmitted from person to person, period. And in the CDC pamphlet to doctors about this disease, it says exactly the same thing."

In the July 1 *Native*, Neenyah Ostrom once again explored the issue of pets as carriers and victims of whatever was causing chronic fatigue syndrome. Ostrom reported, "In a research paper to be published later this month, Dr. Paul Cheney reported that 15 of 21 [CFS] patients studied had cats or dogs that developed dramatic illnesses such as seizures. . . . What is becoming increasingly clear is that an illness of immune dysfunction is being spread by a transmissible agent—assumed to be a virus—that can infect more than one species."

In the July 15 issue, Ostrom took up the intertwined relationship between AIDS and chronic fatigue syndrome. She wrote about " . . . a study [in the May, 1991 *Journal of Infectious Diseases*] of men who have tested positive for HIV antibodies for nine years, but who have not developed any symptoms of 'AIDS.' The case demonstrates that those men have increased suppressor T (T8 or CD8) cell counts and decreased natural killer (NK) cell activity—which is part of the pattern of immune dysfunction that recent studies have identified in people with [CFS]."

Ostrom interviewed a CFS doctor in the July 22 issue: "Perry A. Orens, M.D. is a Long Island physician who has practiced medicine for more than 30 years. Orens currently has a patient population of approximately 1,000 people who suffer from chronic fatigue."

Doctor Orens's daughter had fallen ill with chronic fatigue syndrome five years before, so the matter had become very personal to him. He told Ostrom, "I've found that the vast majority of patients who develop CFIDS are the shakers and movers of our society. They are people who were able to work all day and go out all night and who really burned the candle at both ends. They were the people who were extremely active in every phase of life, social and professional, and they have been much maligned. Suddenly, they lose their enormous energy, and they become depressed, they become withdrawn, they go to a doctor and he examines them and says, there's nothing wrong with you, it's all in your head. And for the last 5-7 years, people have been hearing that over and over. I have patients who have seen as many as 22 doctors and who have been told the same thing: There's nothing wrong with you, it's all in your head, go and exercise. Probably the worst thing you can do to a patient with CFIDS is to tell him or her to exercise. This will make all patients worse—as a matter of fact, one of the criteria that you must apply when you take a history to make a diagnosis is, 'What happens when you push it?' And with CFIDS patients, the answer invariably will be, 'Exercise makes me worse.' So all of these doctors . . . who are saying that people with CFIDS just have depression or some other psychiatric illness, are doing a terrible injustice to these patients, and may actually be harming their health."

In the July 29 issue, I wrote about the "proposal by North Carolina Senator Jesse Helms that would mandate ten-year prison terms and fines up to $10,000 for health care workers who knew that they had 'AIDS,' but had failed to notify patients on whom they had operated."

Tim McFeeley of the Human Rights Campaign Fund called the Helms amendment "a tragedy for our country and everyone who is struggling to live with HIV and AIDS." David Hansell, the Deputy Executive Director for Policy of Gay Men's Health Crisis said "making non-disclosure of HIV status a criminal offence does absolutely nothing to protect patients from HIV transmission." A press release from Lambda Legal Defense Fund insisted, "Patients are more likely to be killed by an asteroid than to contract HIV from an HIV+ health care provider."

In my coverage of the matter, I wrote, "The criminalization of doctors who are HIV positive comes at a time when more questions are being raised about whether HIV is really the cause of 'AIDS,' and whether 'AIDS' is actually part of a larger epidemic called Chronic Fatigue and Immune Dysfunction Syndrome (CFIDS). HHV-6, a large DNA virus, is believed by some to be the cause of both 'AIDS' and CFIDS. If doctors who are HHV-6 positive, or who have high titres of HHV-6, were not allowed to practice medicine, thousands of doctors—including many chronic fatigue syndrome researchers who suffer from the syndrome themselves—would find themselves unemployed or possibly in jail for practicing medicine. While some have argued that 'AIDS' and CFIDS are different, more and more research suggest that they are outcomes of the same infection. Even Robert Gallo has suggested that HHV-6, the virus that seems to cause most of the immune damage in CFIDS, is a major part of 'AIDS.' "

I also pointed out, "According to a newsletter of the CFIDS Action Campaign for the U.S., on June 12, a CFS activist, Megan Shannon, 'a former respiratory therapist at Children's Hospital, told a Congressional panel that CFIDS should be renamed 'Acquired Immune Deficiency Syndrome, Non-HIV.' Shannon complained that the nation is doing nothing to protect health care workers from the CFIDS form of 'AIDS.' Shannon is not alone in her assessment that CFIDS is related to 'AIDS.' One of the leading CFIDS researchers in the country, Dr. Paul Cheney, has referred to CFS as 'AIDS minor.' One of the reasons that many CFIDS activists have tried to separate their disease from 'AIDS' is that they don't want to suffer the same stigmatization that gays and blacks have suffered."

In the same issue, we published a piece by Phillip Bockman, which grappled with what we at the *Native* continued to feel was the insane, self-destructive tactic of some in the gay community who insisted on calling themselves "queer" or other self-denigrating terms. Bockman wrote, "On the moonlit night of Saturday June 22, I joined a crowd of several thousand angry demonstrators who were surging through my West Village neighborhood, filling the narrow streets with torrents of curses and ripples of laughter, clenching their fists and holding up their joined hands, alternately chanting 'What a difference a gay makes!' and 'Queers, take back the night!' It was an exciting action, and filled me with such an overwhelming sense of exhilaration that I had to disengage myself—from the arm of a lesbian with a drum on one side, and a young man with the word 'queer' scrawled in lipstick across his bare chest on the other—to calm myself down for a moment and wonder at the powerful emotions I was feeling."

Bockman, who was a generation older than most of the people in the march, thought something different from the gay actions and marches in his past was happening. He wrote, "It seemed to me a flashback to the spirit of Stonewall—fresh, exuberant, boisterous, direct, angry and celebratory at the same time."

But his feelings turned ambivalent when the gay crowd suddenly "poured across Sixth Avenue into Eighth Street, converging on a few struggling tourists who had not seen us coming in time to escape." Bockman wrote, "As I stepped onto the sidewalk, the crowd in front of me circled around a pale young man and woman who dropped their packages and backed up with their arms against the wall of Dalton's bookstore, wishing I'm sure that they could crawl up it, their eyes glazed in terror. 'Go home, heteros!' one group began chanting, and everyone took it up. 'We're queer, we're here!' they screamed, shaking their hundreds of fists in unison at the quaking pair. 'Fuck you, get used to it!'"

Bockman felt "for a quick unthinking instant, a twinge of instinctive pleasure at the vengeful scene, versions of which I've often imagined when some bonehead calls out 'Faggot!' or 'Queer!' from a passing car. But there's a difference—a very big difference. These tourists had done nothing. They were being scapegoated and terrorized, by people who have been scapegoated and terrorized so often that their anger can be blindly instinctive—I had felt it myself—like trapped cats that will bite and claw at whoever comes by. But we must be above that, I thought, or is it too late? Have we come to the point where we're reduced to clawing and biting?"

Bockman then noted, "It startled me to see my friend with the chestful of lipstick lurch up beside me, flashing the word 'queer' from tit to tit. (What a chest he would have to possess, I thought, to write 'homosexual' instead!) 'We're queer!' he shouted, raising his fist at the heterosexuals, who were now edging their way toward the corner of Dalton's and freedom."

When Bockman asked the man with the lipstick "queer" written on his chest about the treatment of the heterosexuals who were cornered by the angry gay crowd, he said, "Fuck them."

The next morning, the march received this headline on one of the New York papers: "Perverts riot under the full moon in Greenwich Village." That inspired Bockman to write "Perverts. Fags. Faggots. Queers. 'What's in a name?' a great gay poet once wrote. . . . I knew that to my bare-chested friend the word "queer" was merely a term he would claim he had appropriated, smeared on his chest, and made his own. Somehow its connotations were supposed to have changed. But I could not see beyond the fact that it called attention to his rather interesting chest, that it was anything but what its long history has made it: a term of contempt and disgust, lobbed at gay people by ignorant hoodlums, with the support and approval of a society of similarly dubious sophistication. Looking at it, or hearing it on his lips, only makes me cringe." When Bockman told the man with the lipstick "queer" that he didn't like the word and the man asked why, he said, "I'm not queer. I'm not what that word means. I'm not what *they* like to think I am. Queer is *their* word. When they see it, it brings up their connotations. I will not admit to it. I will not label myself with it. Gay is a word of defiance—my word, our word. They can damn well get used to using my word, seeing me as I am, respecting me, whether they like it or not."

In the August 19 *Native*, we revisited the African swine fever story, in an interview with John Beldekas, which was conducted by Neenyah Ostrom. In her introduction, Ostrom wrote, "John Beldekas Ph.D., is one of the scientists—along with Jane Teas—who developed and tested the theory that 'AIDS' might actually be caused by a large DNA virus called African swine fever virus (ASFV). Their investigations began in 1983 and continued actively until 1986 when the United States Department of Agriculture, in an unprecedented move, established by

253

decree (a memo written by USDA officials) that no more government resources would be devoted to investigating the possibility that ASFV was involved in causing 'AIDS.' "

Beldekas told Ostrom that he thought that HIV is an endogenous retrovirus and that the primary infection in AIDS was African swine fever virus which was "suppressing people's immune systems to the point that one of the ancient retroviruses is being reactivated and you're finding HIV as a marker for the really bad infection, which is ASFV in the macrophages."

Beldekas discussed his trip to Gallo's lab in 1986, which was arranged for him by journalist Ann Fettner. He told Ostrom that he and Jane Teas had gone to Florida where they "found a whole bunch of feral pigs that the Haitians had brought from Haiti. So we went down and bled them and started our African swine fever study. I came back from Florida with sera from some infected pigs, and I did Western blots. And I looked at the serum from the pigs that we suspected were infected with African swine fever virus, to see if they would cross-react with HIV. Because I was thinking, well maybe this whole HIV thing was just a sham, and what we were really looking at was ASFV. So I did these Western blots, and sure enough, I got some protein bands that were very reminiscent of HIV."

Beldekas told Ostrom that after he called Robert Gallo about the finding he was invited to visit Gallo's lab "and gave his entire laboratory staff a two-hour lecture on African swine fever, complete with slides, and explained what we had found. And he looked at the blots—everybody looked at the blots—and finally, somebody said 'Well, we can't ignore this. We have to explore it.' "

Beldekas also told Ostrom, "They were all very attentive—they were really listening—and very polite. After we went through the epidemiology and the spread of swine fever from Africa to Haiti to Florida, Gallo said, 'Now I understand this. Now I understand why people think ASFV could cause this.' So I was playing this political game and saying, 'Well, you know, maybe ASFV is suppressing people and it's allowing HIV to come on board, or the other way around.' I didn't want to say, 'I think your HIV theory is ludicrous.' I wanted to let him know that I was willing to include his virus in my theory, too."

When Beldekas got back to Boston, the Gallo lab pulled the rug out from under him, saying that the HIV virus prep they had given him—the one he had used in the pig tests—was contaminated. Beldekas was very annoyed that they were sending out the same contaminated HIV preps to other scientists. Beldekas told Ostrom, "I was thinking, people are using these virus preparations to perpetuate this [HIV] theory, and you're telling me that the blots are no good—that they're contaminated with all kinds of crap? Which makes no sense. So they determined that there was nothing of value in our ASF work, and that was that. And it was dropped like a hot potato."

Beldekas was chagrined by what happened next: "It wasn't more than two or three months later that Gallo came out with his HBLV [Human B-Lymphotropic Virus, now human herpesvirus-6 or HHV-6] paper. And I swear that there was a lot of stuff going on behind my back. And that was when they latched on to African swine fever virus and renamed it HBLV, now HHV-6. I gave him the pig sera—and at one point, Gallo actually got ASFV DNA clones from the government. They actually had this big research project to prove that ASFV was not HBLV. Gallo got the stuff from the government when no one else could. Jane Teas and I were told that, because of legal technicalities, we couldn't go to Plum Island [where the nation's ASFV research takes place], we couldn't get clones—and all of a sudden, Gallo gets them. And they publish a paper saying the two viruses [ASFV and HBLV/HHV-6] were not the same. So I really think I was set up to go down there—this has never been told publicly, you know. It was an amazing time. But it was just peculiar that I went down there and gave this big talk and then lo and behold, three months later, he comes out with his new HHV-6 theory."

Beldekas speculated about the relationship of HIV and African swine fever virus: "And now he's saying that HIV lives in the macrophages, that it's actually a macrophage virus—and *now* he finds pieces of DNA. It's my feeling that no one knows how to characterize this virus [ASFV]—it's in its own class and nobody quite knows what the hell to do with it. So who's to say? Maybe HIV is an immature particle shed in the maturation process of HHV-6, a.k.a. African swine fever virus."

When Ostrom asked Beldekas if he told Gallo that he thought HHV-6 is African swine fever virus, Beldekas replied, "Well no, but when I was down there, I told him that I thought that ASFV was in the macrophages, and that was what was cutting down the regulation and that's why the T-4 cells dropped. And that was all you really needed—you didn't need a fancy T4 tropic virus. He knows that I'm a DNA-virus-macrophage-that's-why-people-get-AIDS person. I've never actually called him and said, 'You know I think your HHV-6 is

African swine fever virus.' I probably should, but after so many years, it's sort of pointless."

Ostrom asked him if he thought that chronic fatigue syndrome is a form of AIDS and he said, "Oh, yes, I think they're linked. Absolutely. There's no question that there are very profound problems with the immune systems in people with chronic fatigue syndrome. It's the same epidemic, the people at the CDC are just doing their pigeon-hole epidemiology, like they've been doing for years. And they don't want to link the two illnesses, because they desperately want to find treatment for both. But if they link them, people are going to react badly."

Ostrom asked him about the memo signed by the U.S. Department of Agriculture Cold Springs Harbor meeting in 1986 saying that no more research should be conducted by the government on the relationship between ASFV and AIDS—a memo signed by a group of scientists that included Dr. Myron Essex of Harvard. Beldekas replied, "What can I say? I've never known science to be done that way before. I always thought that the way that the scientific process worked was that the theory was exhaustively studied, and only when the theory was studied exhaustively would conclusions be made. But the triumvirate doesn't meet before the science is complete. And never once were we ever given the option to present our data to them. So even at Cold Spring Harbor, where the meeting took place, we weren't allowed to present our data. We tried to get in touch with the committee members, we wanted to work with them. That's not how you do science in a free country. I don't know if they do science that way in the Soviet Union. But clearly, in a democracy, science isn't supposed to be done that way."

Beldekas's take on his interaction with Gallo wasn't that different from legions of other people who crossed paths or swords with him. Beldekas thought Gallo had invited him to give a seminar at his lab because he was afraid the DNA virus his people were working on was actually ASFV. Beldekas had been asked to send Gallo antibodies to ASFV, but Gallo said they didn't cross-react with his lab's (supposedly just discovered) DNA virus. Beldekas had his doubts about the veracity of that. Beldekas told Ostrom, "I must say though, on the surface it was all very gracious, and all very nice, and all very flattering. . . . Gallo kept inviting me to go to work for him. I couldn't believe it—here's this person who's trashing our [ASFV] theory, telling people that our theory is wrong. I was not exactly on his best friend list, but he was trying to win me over or just trying to shut me up. How can I be his mortal enemy on the one hand, and on the other hand, he wants me to go down there and work with him? . . . I think Gallo always has desperately wanted to be accepted by the gay community. He has always thought that if we accept him, and we give him credibility, then the world won't turn against him, like we'll back him up. He knows the power that the community has. I mean, when we went out to dinner with him—Terry Beirn [of amfAR], and myself, the man who was in charge of the National Gay Task Force, the man from the National Association of People with AIDS—I mean, we are talking about the big guns, at that time, in gay politics. And he was having dinner with all these gay men, and he kept saying, 'Let's be friends. Let's work together.' I kept thinking that he just wants us to embrace him so he will get our support. When he asked me to come to work for him. I thought it was nothing more than a ploy, to get him on my good side, so I'd go back to all these people and say, 'No, he's really a good person, don't trash him.' And also to defuse the swine fever thing. He wanted me in his lab like he wanted poison."

One wonders what would have happened if Beldkas had said yes.

In the September 2 *Native*, I covered reports about an outbreak of a mysterious AIDS-like illness in Canadian pigs: "The possible link between 'AIDS' in people and 'AIDS' in pigs may have to be reexamined in light of new information coming out of Canada. According to a report presented to a veterinarian conference in May, 'A new respiratory disease has been recognized recently in several Quebec swine herds.' The report was presented by Michel Morin, Christine Girard, and Youseef El Ashardy of the Department of Pathology and Microbiology at the University of Montreal in Quebec. The researchers reported, 'The so-called Mystery Swine Disease is characterized by a severe proliferative pneumonia in young pigs often complicated by Pneumocystis carinii and/or secondary bacterial invaders, and by reproductive failures in sows having fever and anorexia. The capacity of affected pigs to fight common infectious agents appears to be impaired.' "

I noted, "The Mystery Swine Disease has broken out all over the world. It is a serious problem in the Midwest of the United States and it is an even more serious problem in Europe, where it can cause herds to lose as many as ten percent of their offspring—really impairing the swine industry's profits."

I reminded our readers, "The emerging research on the epidemic will be watched closely by two scientists who have argued that 'AIDS' in people is caused by a swine virus called African swine fever virus. Jane Teas and John Beldekas, who have conducted research into the connection between ASFV and 'AIDS,' have had their careers nearly destroyed for suggesting such a link. When Teas first suggested that 'AIDS' is caused by African swine fever virus in 1983, the government and the pork industry seemed to do everything they could to discredit her idea."

I pointed out, "Some scientists at the U.S. Department of Agriculture suggested that if 'AIDS' were caused by African swine fever virus, then pigs in this country would themselves be sick with the disease. The subsequent emergence of Swine Mystery Disease in this country, and the fact that the disease seems to leave pigs immune-compromised, at least as described by the Canadian researchers, would seem to strengthen the Teas-Beldekas argument. In light of the fact that ASFV causes hemorrhagic changes in pigs, it is interesting to note that the Canadian Swine Mystery Disease pigs show signs of hemorrhagic lymph nodes."

I also pointed out again that the USDA officials had basically been lying when they said that AIDS and ASFV were two dramatically different diseases: "A textbook on swine fever virus, which was published in 1987, says just the opposite. According to the preface, which was written by Yechiel Becker, a molecular biologist from the Hebrew University of Jerusalem, 'The ability of African swine fever virus (ASFV) to infect and destroy cells of the reticuloendothelial system leaves a defenseless host that succumbs to an infection which may be described as an acquired immune deficiency disease of domestic pigs.'"

I argued, "If both 'AIDS' and chronic fatigue syndrome are caused by African swine fever virus, that would explain why there could be two clinical forms of the same disease. Two scientists, A. Ordas Alvarez and M.A. Marcotegui, write in the Becker ASFV textbook that, 'African swine fever is a disease which evolves under different clinical forms.... When ASFV is present for long periods of time in a country, the initial clinical forms of rapid evolution revert to slower clinical courses and even new clinical forms appear.' (We should note here that some observers of chronic fatigue syndrome have called it 'Slow-AIDS' or 'AIDS-minor.') The scientists also note that, 'In a complex disease, as ASF is, with its variable clinical forms determining the

258

duration of the incubation period is very difficult, since it may very largely depend on a series of factors, including amount of virus, virulence, route of penetration, resistance to the pig, natural or experimental infection, etc.' "

I closed my piece with a warning: "The politics of African swine fever are very volatile. A country where the virus is found can often be blocked from exporting agricultural products because of fear of contamination. Countries often find it easier to lie about the presence of the virus rather than to go to the expense of trying to eradicate it. Brazil, for instance, is supposed to be free of the virus, but one agricultural expert the *Native* talked to said that he thinks it still is a problem. Because the new forms of swine fever tend to be chronic in nature, some countries may be tempted to try and live with the virus. But . . . such a strategy is very dangerous because the disease can always revert or evolve quickly into a more lethal form."

In the same issue, Neenyah Ostrom wrote a piece about a woman who was a doctor suffering from chronic fatigue syndrome: "The debilitating disease, worsened by the abusive treatment she received from some fellow physicians throughout the years of struggling with her illness, has not only destroyed the life she was trying to build, but also destroyed her faith in medicine, in society—in fact in human kindness itself."

Dr. Smith (not her real name) "first became ill between her second and third years of medical school. She developed night sweats, diarrhea, and severe fatigue—and lost 40 pounds in two months." She was diagnosed (and eventually undiagnosed) with MS and she developed "terrible memory problems and generalized cognitive problems." And, of course, she was also diagnosed with psychiatric problems.

She was sick during her residency and received little sympathy from her bosses. She told Ostrom that during the second portion of her residency she was "in great pain and suffered severe cognitive difficulty. 'It was pure torture,' Dr. Smith recalls. 'I was terribly out of it.' . . . Because she was suffering from a poorly understood illness, Smith was 'ignored, made fun of, and abused,' she says."

She told Ostrom, "Even if I recover from this illness, I will never recover from the way I was treated. . . . I was very idealistic before this whole experience. I spent a lot of time with patients, and people trusted me because I listened to them. I was taught to listen to patients—you know, they told us, 'Listen to the patient, he's telling you the diagnosis.'

No one listened to me. I was taught that physicians take care of people, but no one cared for me."

Ostrom reported, "One of the things that astonished Smith most is that her colleagues at several prestigious universities didn't notice what she calls her 'dementia.' " She recounted to Ostrom, "I couldn't remember the names of my patients or the names of their diseases. I could remember how to treat them, but I couldn't remember where to find them. I was criticized by my superiors for being disorganized when, in fact, I was extremely organized. When you have no memory, you have to be well organized. My colleagues didn't seem to recognize that I had neurological problems. They blamed the patient—me. I think it's worse for a patient who is a physician, especially if you're seeing a doctor in the institution where you're working. I really don't trust physicians anymore."

In the September 9 issue, Ostrom wrote about a report from the College Board that SAT math and verbal scores had fallen dramatically. Ostrom wondered whether the drop in SAT scores might be "due to an increasing prevalence of chronic fatigue syndrome among teenagers. Is the crisis in education which the low scores have helped to underline really just a reflection of the nationwide epidemic which affects the ability of children and teenagers to think clearly? . . . Has CFS become so widespread that its cognitive symptoms are affecting college entrance exam scores? With estimates of CFS's incidence ranging from three to five million in the U.S. population—and nobody knows how many children are already sick—isn't it a possibility that should be considered?"

John Lauritsen covered a forum, which had been sponsored by an AIDS organization called Positive Action of New York, in the October 7 Native. Lauritsen wrote that it "turned into a shouting match and near brawl over the personality and conduct of one of the evening's speakers, Larry Kramer, a prominent playwright and 'AIDS spokesman.' " The forum was titled "The Treatment of HIV Infection in 1992" and was attended by people who were expecting to hear Robert Gallo speak—who failed to show up. It turned out that Gallo's scientific misconduct issues had led to his bosses forbidding him to make any public appearances.

Kramer had made himself controversial by outing the positive HIV status of an openly gay New York City politician, Tom Duane. A small group handed out a flyer accusing Kramer of "violating the right of HIV positive people to make their own decisions about divulging their own HIV status." (To the gay community's detriment, being HIV positive was being conflated more and more with being openly gay and coming out.)

When Kramer got up to speak at the forum, an activist and lawyer named Bill Dobbs stood up and attacked Kramer for what he had done to Duane. After some hostile back and forth between the forum's moderator and Dobbs, Kramer began his talk:: "I spoke to Dr. Gallo several times last week and I found the experience exceptionally sad. In a strange way I had grown rather fond of him over the last six months or so. I don't know if we will ever know the answer to the charges made against him. But they certainly, I believe, are not so black-and-white as so many would believe."

Dobbs interrupted Kramer's defense of Gallo saying, "Why would we rely on your judgment that Gallo is right? You're going to stand up there and defend Gallo? Horseshit! How many times have we been forced to depend on your judgment? And you sell out AIDS for a cheap political tactic!"

After more screaming back and forth between Dobbs and the moderator, Kramer continued with his speech. He bemoaned the lack of an effective treatment for AIDS and said, "What does it take? Nobody knows. I don't know anymore. I helped start the two biggest organizations. They've turned to shit! Both of them. GMHC is a bureaucracy that's so ludicrous—it's a joke. They can't get together. Nobody agrees with anything . . . I deserve a little respect for what I've done—in this room, These people like to write me love letters [saying] the essence of Larry should be bottled, and we should all drink it . . . . And suddenly I do one thing that they don't agree with. Then I'm Hitler. What kind of extremism is this?"

Among the curious points he made in the long rant, he called Anthony Fauci a "damned bungler." He complained that President George Bush was "closed off" from the AIDS activists. He once again complained, "Nobody has a master plan." (Actually, the pseudo-epidemiology of AIDS which he foolishly believed in was itself a brilliant kind of master plan.) He closed his speech saying, "I don't know what to do anymore, and I never said that before. I think ACT-UP doesn't work anymore. I think the tactics it represents don't work anymore. I think the anger that is in us has fallen on deaf ears. And I don't know what to do next. I don't know what kind of organization

261

to start. I don't know how to fight. I don't know how to lead anyone, should they want to follow. I don't know what to write anymore. I don't know how to write any part of this, because I have said what I have said to you tonight, in one form or another, for ten fucking years. And I say to you in year ten, as we face the figure of 40 million infected people, the same thing I said in 1981, when there were 41 cases. Until we get our act together, all of you, until we learn to plug in with each other, and fight and make this President listen, we are are as good as dead." (Kramer's audiences were buried, dug up, and re-buried throughout his histrionic activist career.)

And finally, he thanked Bill Dobbs, the activist who had confronted him "for stirring me up, because I didn't think I would have made such a potent speech otherwise." Kramer was his own most generous critic. That's what passed for gay leadership in the epidemic.

About Kramer, Lauritsen wrote, "Most people I've spoken to now regard Larry Kramer as an embarrassment to the movement, although some of them expressed admiration for his courage in the past. The problem is that vehemence alone isn't worth very much. If one examines his diatribe from the Thursday evening forum (which Kramer himself described as a 'potent speech'), or for that matter any of his recent talks, one finds that, aside from obscenities, tidbits of gossip, and personal asides, there is very little content. His entire talk could almost be summarized as follows: 'THINGS ARE A MESS!!! WHY DOESN'T SOMEBODY DO SOMETHING?!?!?' "

Lauritsen asserted, "On questions on 'AIDS,' I think that Kramer has been wrong as often as not. For a decade, his main contribution to 'AIDS' discourse has been hysteria, when calm, honest, and analytical minds were needed. He has never supported those of us who are calling for a free and open investigation of the HIV-'AIDS' hypothesis. Nor has he done anything to stop the pharmacogenic manslaughter of gay men which is happening through AZT and DDI therapy. Nor has he supported free speech for those he disagrees with. On at least two occasions Kramer attempted to silence me at ACT UP meetings, when I challenged the HIV hypothesis or criticized nucleoside analog therapy. In my book, no one can claim to have intellectual courage if he is afraid to hear what his opponents have to say. I am sorry to say so, but at this point I don't think Larry Kramer has anything positive to contribute to the fight against 'AIDS.' "

In the same issue, in our publishing column, we reported, "None other than the publisher himself, Harold Evans, has announced that

Random House has signed Michelangelo Signorile, of outing and *Outweek* notoriety, to write a book about the gay, lesbian and 'AIDS' movement over the past five years. According to Random House's press release, 'It will demonstrate the presence of lesbians and gays throughout contemporary society—including their presence in the power structures of New York, Washington, and Hollywood—and it will explain the pros and cons of outing and its relationship to the right of privacy. The press release also points out that Signorile 'has been described' by author Larry Kramer as 'one of the greater contemporary gay heroes.' Signorile's book is due in November 1992. The title? *Queer in America.*" A perfect title for the Orwellian and Kafkaesque world we were living in.

In the October 14 issue, Neenyah Ostrom wrote about two extraordinary research findings that seemed to support the critics of the HIV theory of AIDS: "There was a stunning development in the world of 'AIDS' research, September 26, when the prestigious British scientific journal *Nature* published an editorial that Berkeley Professor Peter Duesberg may be correct that HIV alone is not sufficient to cause 'AIDS.' Written by *Nature* editor John Maddox, 'AIDS Research Turned Upside Down' cites two new research findings that may support Duesberg's argument and lead to an entirely new paradigm to explain 'AIDS.' These findings involve experiments in which it was discovered, to the experimenters' surprise, that mice not exposed to HIV created antibodies against the virus after injection with foreign lymphocytes and that monkeys *not* immunized against the simian immunodeficiency virus nevertheless were protected from infection with that virus by merely injecting them with foreign T-cells. The conclusion drawn from these two pieces of evidence: 'AIDS' is, in fact, an autoimmune disease in which T-cells lose their ability to differentiate between 'self' and 'non-self' and indis-criminately kill each other."

Maddox wrote, "Professor Peter Duesberg from the University of California at Berkeley is probably sleeping more easily at night now than for five years, since he first took up the cudgels against the doctrine that AIDS is caused by the retrovirus HIV. . . . Duesberg has been pilloried for his heterodox views . . . and faced with the threat that his research funds would be snatched away. Now there is some evidence to support his long fight against the establishment (among which, sadly, he counts this journal)."

Ostrom noted, "Just over a year ago, *Nature* published a particularly vicious attack on Duesberg (complete with an offensive caricature of him—scarcely standard operating procedure for a scholarly journal) written by Robin A. Weiss and Harold W. Jaffe. 'Duesberg, HIV, and AIDS' contends that Duesberg's proposition that HIV does not cause 'AIDS' to be 'equally absurd' as suggestions that HIV 'originates from outer space, or as a genetically engineered virus for germ warfare which was tested in prisoners and spread from them.' (*Nature*, June 21, 1990)."

In the October 20 *Native*, Ostrom reported on a study by a Canadian group of researchers which concluded, "Human herpesvirus-6 is a likely candidate for the cause of CFS." Ostrom wrote, "The research team (from Montreal General Hospital and McGill University) presented their findings at the 31st Interscience Conference on Antimicrobial Agents and Chemotherapy (ICAAC), held in Chicago September 30 . . . . Led by Dr. D. Eymard, the group compared 17 patients who met the major criteria for CFS with a group of eight patients who [did not] . . . Eymard and colleagues found only three parameters by which the patients who met the CDC criteria differed from those that did not: They had more frequent sore throats, a 'recurrent type of fatigue,' and elevated levels of antibodies against HHV-6."

The researchers concluded, "Elevated titers against HHV-6 could suggest an etiological [causative] role of the virus in this syndrome."

The cover story of the October 28 *Native*, written by Chris McManus, captured one of the kinds of dark episodes that were occurring in the nooks and crannies of the epidemic—most of which we'll probably never know about.

McManus wrote about Steve O'Banion, who received a jaywalking citation in Cincinnati on September 3, an event that "escalated to a three-and-half-day incarceration and charges of attempted murder. O'Banion was indicted before a grand jury Friday, October 10, on four counts of attempted murder and four counts of felonious assault for allegedly spitting and throwing blood on three corrections officers and one nurse at the Hamilton County Justice Center."

McManus reported, "O'Banion has denied all charges and plans to file a civil suit against the Hamilton County Police Force." McManus wrote that O'Banion and a friend, "David Johnson, were crossing

Walnut Street in downtown Cincinnati around midnight when two city police officers stopped them midway, within crosswalk borders, the light at that point blinking 'Don't Walk,' to give them a jaywalking citation, according to O'Banion. A second city police car arrived and one of the officers yelled, 'Hey you've got two faggots there,' to which O'Banion responded, 'Cowabunga, dude.' Two officers then grabbed his arms from behind while the officer from the second car pushed O'Banion's head forward, forcing him to the ground, causing two abrasions (left eye and left arm), and breaking his sunglasses and jewelry, said O'Banion. . . . He was then handcuffed on the ground, hands behind his back, and put in the backseat" of a police vehicle.

O'Banion was taken to the Hamilton County Justice Center. McManus wrote, "Inside the Justice Center, the entire staff yelled homophobic and blatantly 'AIDS'-phobic remarks at him." A nurse was brought in who called him "girlie." O'Banion told McManus that when he asked to be taken to the hospital one of the policemen "began to choke him, holding his neck and pressing his jawline. O'Banion started gagging and vomited." The nurse ran out of the room and according to O'Banion, the policeman punched him "three or four times in the face and slapped him with the back of his hand, causing a laceration above his left eye, he said. He sat up and blood was coming from his eye, nose and mouth. 'I [was] choking, literally on my own blood.' The officers fled the cell, returning an hour later with a sheet, which they placed over his head, asking if he was done spitting on them."

McManus reported that one of the officers insisted that O'Banion screamed, "I am HIV positive and I have hepatitis, and you are all going to go with me." The nurse said, "O'Banion sprayed blood from his nose 'like a whale blows off.' " McManus also wrote, "According to O'Banion's story, she fled the cell before officers hit him, therefore she would not have been present after O'Banion began to bleed. O'Banion maintains, 'At no time did I physically or verbally abuse or harass anyone,' stating that he merely informed officers and the nurse of his medical history and asked repeatedly to be taken to Christ Hospital."

McManus reported, "On the morning of September 5, O'Banion was given a first hearing before Judge Albert Mestemaker, who said, upon O'Banion's entrance to the courtroom, 'You're not going to spit on anyone are you?' Judge Mestemaker insisted on a $100,000 bond covering felonious assault charges pending the result of O'Banion's

HIV test. After his HIV status was confirmed by a phone call by O'Banion to Christ Hospital, he was not released, but returned to a cell and held until 1:30 p.m. the next day. The following morning (September 6) O'Banion was once again brought before Judge Mestemaker, who announced that three counts of attempted murder had been brought against him."

Just another ordinary day during the epidemic.

In the November 11 *Native*, Neenyah Ostrom reported on a list (issued by the Centers for Disease Control) of illnesses and conditions that should alert a physician to the possibility that a woman has "AIDS." Ostrom noted, "There is considerable overlap between that list and symptoms seen in women with chronic fatigue syndrome, which gives rise to the question: Are women with 'AIDS' and women with chronic fatigue syndrome suffering from a similar type of immune dysfunction? The Centers for Disease Control (CDC) list contains 19 items, ten of them overlap with indicators seen in chronic fatigue syndrome.... The CDC list of conditions that 'should alert a physician to a possible risk of HIV infection' was published in the October 31 *Medical Tribune*."

Ostrom reported, "The ten indicators seen in both the CDC's 'AIDS' profile and in CFS are: low T-cell count, positive test for any sexually transmitted disease, evidence of oral thrush (candiadiasis); recurrent or severe vaginal candiadiasis; vaginitis that doesn't respond to treatment; lymphadenopathy (lymph node pain); chronic fatigue; night sweats; positive Pap smear; and chronic, severe gastrointestinal illness and/or diarrhea."

In the same article, Ostrom discussed the finding of Dr. Denis Wakefield who discovered "that both the number and function of T-cells was decreased in" 100 CFS patients he studied. Ostrom reported, "Wakefield found that 50 percent of the 100 CFS patients were completely 'anergic.' Another one-third of the patients had a reduced response to skin testing, or 'hypoanergy.' Ostrom pointed out, "Anergy is seen in 'AIDS' patients, and is a sign that the immune system—particularly T-cell functioning—is seriously compromised."

In the November 25 issue, I wrote about documents we had obtained from the USDA under the Freedom of Information Act. They provided what looked like a smoking gun that suggested there was an epidemic of African swine fever in America—and Canada. The documents indicated that three pigs from Iowa and Kansas had tested positive for African swine fever virus. I reported that the pigs tested positive by the ELISA test, which is the preliminary test used to screen pigs for the disease in this country. Only one of the three pigs was tested by an additional method, and that test proved negative. The other two, according to the documents the *Native* obtained, were not tested because there was not a sufficient amount of sera from the pigs available. There was no indication that any kind of emergency was declared at that point, or that any kind of emergency testing program was instituted.

The pigs that were tested for ASFV were suffering from "Swine Mystery Disease." I argued, "Given that the pigs that were being tested were suffering from a disease that bears so many similarities to African swine fever, it is difficult to understand why the Department of Agriculture did not take the positive test results more seriously."

I pointed out, "Normally when even one pig tests positive for African swine fever virus, the USDA launches an exhaustive series of tests to try to isolate the virus. African swine fever virus, which causes the collapse of the pig's immune system, is considered the most serious threat to pork production because it is so contagious and so difficult to eradicate."

One of the most shocking bits of new data about the epidemic of "Swine Mystery Disease," once again, was the discovery that young pigs with the disease suffered from the same kind of pneumonia (Pneumocystis carinii pneumonia) that was associated with AIDS.

I wrote, "The descriptions of the damage done to the organs of pigs with 'Swine Mystery Disease' in America dramatically underline the similarities of the disease to African swine fever. When I read the descriptions to a retired African swine fever virus expert (who has spoken anonymously to the *Native* in the past), the scientist said he could not rule out African swine fever virus as the cause of 'Swine Mystery Disease.' Although African swine fever virus can cause a whole range of disease manifestations, from acute to subclinical, one of the telltale signs of the disease is the presence of hemorrhages throughout the affected pig's body. Reports obtained by the *Native* from the Department of Agriculture indicate that hemorrhages could often be found throughout the bodies of the pigs affected by 'Swine Mystery Disease.' "

I also noted, "Pigs that are affected by African swine fever virus often die of secondary bacterial complications. One field researcher said in his report [on 'Swine Mystery Disease'] that there seemed to be a problem with the immune system of pigs that were diagnosed as having 'Swine Mystery Disease' because they have several bacterial infections."

In a world where science was allowed to proceed without political interference, all of this startling information would have made it into the newspapers with larger circulations than *New York Native*.

In our eleventh anniversary issue, on December 16, I wrote about a recent article by Larry Kramer that had appeared in the *Village Voice*: "Kramer seems to have come slowly but surely to many of the conclusions that this newspaper came to many years ago. About 'AIDS,' Kramer wrote, 'I don't believe anymore that education works, and we're putting too much trust in it.' Actually we agree, because the content of the education is built on scientific fraud. What has been called education is actually propaganda, and the kind of education that Chinese students get if they support democracy in Beijing. People who disagree with what the government says about the epidemic are generally deemed 'ignorant' and in need of 'AIDS education.' That would mean that people like HIV-dissenter Peter Duesberg, the distinguished retrovirologist who does not believe that 'HIV' is the cause of 'AIDS,' need to be educated. It would be quite amusing to see one of these bozos who call themselves 'AIDS educators' arriving at Duesberg's office to correct his thinking and give him an 'AIDS education.' . . . Mr. Kramer writes, 'I believe it's easier to get this disease than we think. I don't believe much of what my government tells us: about AIDS, statistics, safe sex, saliva, the blood supply, anything.' This of course sounds like ad copy for the *New York Native*, the newspaper boycotted by ACT UP for saying exactly that."

I also noted, "Mr. Kramer writes, 'If you'd spent as much time as I have dealing with these bureaucrats, you'd know how second-rate so many of them are, how mentally, intellectually, morally, and spiritually bankrupt, how immature, inexperienced, naïve, and badly educated in their fields.' Mr. Kramer didn't have to attend those meetings or telephone those bureaucrats to find that out. He could have just read the *Native*."

In his *Voice* piece, Kramer also wrote, "How could anyone possibly trust a government that puts out a definition of AIDS which denies that women get it?" That inspired me to write, "Well, Mr. Kramer, if you had been reading your *Native* closely, you would understand. The problem is that 'AIDS' and chronic fatigue syndrome are so similar that recognizing the immune dysfunction in women might blow the whole cover that the government has created for the chronic fatigue syndrome epidemic."

Kramer had also written, "We are in the midst of a huge war and there is no general." Which moved me to write, "Mr. Kramer, couldn't we forgo our search for father figures and get down to more pragmatic problem-solving? If Mr. Kramer doesn't trust the government—and we don't—then why would we trust it more if there were a Czar or Czarina of AIDS?"

Kramer also wrote, in his *Voice* piece, "It would make not one bit of difference to the progress of the plague if GMHC weren't here, if amfAR weren't here, and yes if my beloved ACT UP (which has turned into a disorganized and uncontrollable bunch using tactics that no longer work) weren't here." In my editorial I wrote, "Ironically, we disagree with that assessment. If Mr. Kramer were to use his own prominence and media power, and were to hold a press conference with his "beloved" ACT UP, and GMHC, and amfAR, and tell the American public that 'AIDS' and so-called Yuppie Flu (CFIDS or CFS) are the same disease and that HIV is a big lie, the whole house of cards that has been built up by the AIDS establishment would come tumbling down. ACT UP, amfAR, GMHC, and even Mr. Kramer himself have played a role in disseminating the 'facts' about the epidemic that Mr. Kramer now tells us he doesn't believe. An about-face would be a form of redemption. We're not holding our breath."

In the December 30 issue, we ran an Associated Press story that captured the dreadful new world the epidemic had given birth to: "The tiny 'AIDS' stickers that are popping up in restrooms, telephone booths and parking garages around the country are a company's effort to give people who don't have 'AIDS' a chance to boast about it. The neat-and-colorful stickers ask 'AIDS or HIV Negative?' and give a toll-free telephone number to call to participate in a voluntary certification program. . . . The stickers are being spread in New York, Los Angeles, Chicago, St. Louis, and cities in Florida and Utah. 'HIV Negative' certification costs $29.95. It does not include the costs of testing. Eric Janssen, chairman of the newly formed Partnership for AIDS-Free America (PAFA), said he hopes to register millions of Americans and eventually spread the program around the world. . . . Here's how the program works. People send in $29.95 to get an application kit they

269

give to their local health clinic or doctor. If they test negative for HIV, the clinic or doctor mails the form back to Janssen's company. A phone call is made to ensure the results are authentic and then a laminated card with the date, the person's name and a photo, along with a sticker for a driver's license, are mailed to the person. The front of the card says 'International Certification for HIV Negative.' "

1992: HIV-negative AIDS

"It may take a fascist to solve the AIDS crisis."
—Larry Kramer

The slovenliness and disingenuousness that characterized AIDS research was on full display in the March 30 *New York Native*, when John Lauritsen wrote about documents he obtained from the Food and Drug Administration "which describes in detail many acts of fraud committed in the conduct of Phase II AZT Trials. It was on the basis of the Phase II Trials that AZT was approved for marketing by the FDA in 1987."

After "an arduous three-month battle" with the FDA to get the documents, he concluded, "Anyone who requests government documents under the Freedom of Information Act should be aware that he or she's in for a hard time. If the requested documents are completely innocuous, then the government will probably lose them through incompetence. If the documents are not innocuous, then dilatory tactics of every kind will be employed, on top of the usual incompetence. If the documents should eventually be found and released, they will be heavily censored."

Lauritsen wrote, "A bit of background is in order. In the approval process for a new drug, the most important tests are the Phase II trials, which are supposed to determine whether the new drug is safe and effective. (The Phase I trials are concerned solely with toxicity— whether it is possible to administer the drug to human beings, and if so, to estimate what a proper dose might be.) The Phase II AZT trials were conducted in 1986, in 12 centers around the country. They were designed as 'double-blind, placebo-controlled' studies though in practice they were nothing of the kind."

One of the medical centers, located in Boston, had violated protocols so much that, according to Lauritsen, an FDA investigator recommended that the data it generated be excluded from the multicenter trial. Lauritsen noted, "A series of FDA meetings were held in order to decide what to do about the numerous violations of protocol, and in particular, about the delinquent Boston center. The decision was made to exclude nothing, to throw in all of the garbage along with the good data. The rationale for this appalling decision was two-fold: *One*, if all the patients with protocol violations were excluded, there would be almost nobody left in the study; and *two*, including the bad data didn't really change the results very much. Needless to say, these are the excuses of crooks and idiots. No ethical scientist would knowingly use bad data."

So Lauritsen was very eager to see the FDA's inspection report on the Boston center—which he got from his Freedom of Information request. His reaction was intense: "After nine years of research and writing on 'AIDS,' from a critical standpoint, I'm not easily shocked anymore. But this report succeeded in making my mind reel, from time to time, as it described innumerable, brazen acts of fraud committed by the investigators in the conduct of the trial. Even more shocking is the fact that the FDA, at the very highest level, chose to excuse and cover up these acts of fraud."

Lauritsen reported, "In October and November 1986, FDA Inspector Patricia Spitzig made a 'For Cause Inspection' of the Massachusetts General Hospital Clinical Center, which was used in the Phase II multicenter AZT trials. Her findings are contained in her 76-page 'Establishment Inspection Report' (EIR). The principal investigator at this center was Robert Schooley, MD, who was assisted by co-investigator Martin Hirsch, MD."

Lauritsen noted that the report indicated, "The record-keeping at the Boston center was incredibly sloppy. Often there were no indications of when, by whom, or why entries had been made, erased, or changed." And, according to the Spitzig report, deaths and adverse reactions had not been reported, raw records had been discarded, changes were made on case reports "with no explanation, date or initials," and "Accountability of the study medication is inadequate; 87 bottles/containers shipped cannot be accounted for; Pharmacy kept the inventory and it does not correlate with shipping records; study medication returned by subjects was not counted, stored properly, or signed off by the clinical investigator."

Lauritsen reported, "In addition, Spitzig found that Schooley and his accomplices frequently indicated in Case Report Forms that patients were in the study much longer than they really were." Lauritsen also pointed out that there were serious discrepancies between the patients' medical records and the information in the "Case Report Forms" which were "the official recording forms of the study."

According to Lauritsen, "The rules of the study indicated clearly that all adverse reactions were to be recorded in the Case Report Forms and reported immediately. Schooley et al. often failed to do so, especially if the patient was on AZT. . . . From the standpoint of the study's 'data,' many serious adverse reactions were concealed by not recording them in the Case Report Forms, even though they were mentioned in the patient's medical records. And this appeared to be tendentious—that is favoring AZT—as all except one of the eight cases where serious adverse reactions were concealed involved patients on AZT."

Lauritsen concludes his very detailed analysis of the document, once again, in a state of horror: "In England, Welcome PLC, the parent company of Burroughs Welcome, recently made the claim that 4000 studies demonstrated the benefits of AZT. Of course this is pure bluff. If one devoted a mere ten minutes to studying each of the 4000 alleged studies, it would take him 667 hours to do so, or assuming he worked for 12 hours a day, a total of 56 days. In fact, the Phase II trials remain the most single important test of AZT: they were the main basis for the drug's approval by the FDA; they are still cited as proving that AZT 'extends life'; they were one of the 'historical controls' upon which [the toxic AIDS drug] DDI was based—and they were fraudulent. . . . If there were justice in the world, the crooks in the FDA, NIAID, Burroughs Welcome, and their accomplices in the medical profession would pay for their crimes. But it is more important now to save lives. Right now, well over 150,000 people are being poisoned by the nucleoside analogues, AZT, DDI, and DDC. Most of these are gay men. We must all sound the tocsin. We must stop the genocide."

In the April 6 issue, I wrote an open letter to Jerry Brown, who was running for president and often appeared in public with the iconic AIDS red ribbon.

Dear Governor Brown:

You are in a unique position now to raise the nation's consciousness in any way you choose. Every time you appear wearing that red ribbon, you raise the nation's consciousness about AIDS. We would like to ask you to expand the meaning of that red ribbon. If that red ribbon means giving more money to the liars and crooks who are the nation's AIDS establishment, then your efforts will only worsen the AIDS disaster. We have been telling our readers that the government

273

is covering up the fact that AIDS and the so-called "Yuppie Flu"/chronic fatigue syndrome are the same disease. . . . Millions of people are seriously ill with chronic fatigue syndrome (far more than the government's big lie of one million HIV-infected). The only reason that it is not called "AIDS" is because of official lying. If the lying continues, and if it's funded by additional money which your red ribbon encourages, the epidemic will only get worse. You should be aware that anyone who challenges the official lies about AIDS faces serious censure. This newspaper has been boycotted by an AIDS activist organization called ACT UP because we have been informing our readers about the government's lies. Hundreds of thousands of people are being poisoned every day by the government's official treatment for AIDS: AZT. You could save millions of lives by wearing a button that says "AZT=Death." AZT is a prime example of profits being put before people. The science that went into the approval process for AZT is riddled with fraud. . . . When your campaign reaches California, we urge you to convene a major meeting on AIDS with all of the voices that have been censored throughout the epidemic. We urge you to meet with Peter Duesberg and a group of thirty scientists who have joined him in urging a re-examination of the government's paradigm for AIDS. . . . We also urge you to meet with patients and activists in the chronic fatigue syndrome movement. As long as the government refuses to level about the connection between AIDS and chronic fatigue syndrome, the problem will not begin to be solved.

In the same issue, we seem to have introduced the term "HIV-negative AIDS," for the first time, to describe chronic fatigue syndrome—in a column on anergy in AIDS and CFS by Neenyah Ostrom. She wrote, "Americans have been told repeatedly that so long as they do not have a positive result on an HIV-antibody test, they are unlikely to have 'AIDS.' But there may, in fact, be as many as ten million Americans whose immune systems have lost a vital component: cell-mediated immunity. People who have lost cell-mediated immunity are said to be anergic, and anergy occurs not only in 'AIDS' and cancer, but also in chronic fatigue syndrome. . . . It might be said that people with CFS who have no cell-mediated immunity have HIV-negative 'AIDS.' "

In the April 13 issue, Neenyah Ostrom walked our readers through the scenario of mistaken identity that may have explained the total confusion that the virus HHV-6 was causing in AIDS and chronic fatigue syndrome research.

Looking back over the prior decade, it now appeared that in the very beginning when the CDC was investigating AIDS the scientists who thought they were looking at CMV in the early patients—and most patients had serious CMV infections—they were actually staring directly at the then-undiscovered HHV-6, which it turned out, according to Ostrom's piece, "is far more similar to CMV than to any other herpesvirus." Adding another dimension of potential mistaken identity to this virological and epidemiological mystery was the fact that *CMV and African swine fever virus could also visually be mistaken for each other.* Ostrom wrote, "William Hess, a long time ASFV researcher (now retired) at the USDA Plum Island Disease Laboratory, the only facility in the U.S. at which the virus is studied, noted the possible confusion of ASFV and CMV in a 1971 [article] on ASFV: 'Herpes simplex virus and . . . human cytomegalovirus have morphological appearances similar to ASF virus when seen in thin sections.' "

So at the center of perhaps the biggest medical disaster in history was simply the mistake of scientists not knowing what they were really looking at when they were looking at CMV in the early days of AIDS—when research was about to go tragically in the wrong direction for three decades.

In the April 20 issue, I wrote another editorial about Larry Kramer, after he had written a piece in the April 13, 1992, issue of *Newsweek*, which echoed the one he had written for the *Village Voice*. Again it was full of the kind of skeptical questions about the epidemic that sounded like they could have come directly out of the *New York Native*. He again raised the issue of whether we really knew how AIDS was spread, whether one agent was really the cause and whether the blood supply was safe. He asked, "How can we completely avoid contracting something we can't accurately test for and that might not be the sole cause of the plague even if we could?" He concluded, "The world must face the unfortunate fact that after some 11 years of government apathy, precious little is known about AIDS, about the various causes of AIDS, and about how this plague is being spread."

In response, I wrote, "Now wait a minute, Mr. Kramer. If you don't recognize that these thoughts have been aired in a variety of ways in the *New York Native* during the past several years, you are intellectually dishonest and should not be trusted any more than the scoundrels who are running the AIDS circus. . . . One continuing disappointment is that you refuse even to acknowledge the epidemic which has been referred to as 'AIDS minor.' I'm referring, of course, to Chronic Fatigue and Immune Dysfunction Syndrome. Calling CFIDS 'AIDS minor' is a little like calling AIDS pregnancy and CFIDS pregnancy minor. . . . It's time, Mr. Kramer, for you to set aside your ego and petty vindictiveness. The media loves you. Use the most potent weapon available. At least use [the media] to support a national debate on the connection between AIDS and CFIDS. Where that connection is concerned, Mr. Kramer, Silence equals Death."

In the April 27 issue, Neenyah Ostrom raised the question of whether the increasing incidence of asthma was associated with the chronic fatigue syndrome epidemic. She reported, "Asthma has increased so precipitously among inner-city children that an eight-city, five-year, $2.5 million study was initiated in March 1991 by the U.S. Department of Health and Human Services."

Was this another example of the government acknowledging one of the pathological by-products of so-called chronic fatigue syndrome without being willing to admit the existence of the underlying one-virus-one-paradigm epidemic? Ostrom pointed out that Karen Bell and her CFS research colleagues had reported in a 1991 publication "the results of a comparison of 21 CFS cases (all were students attending schools in Lyndonville, New York Central School District) with 42 control subjects. They found that 15 of the 21 CFS patients reported allergies/asthma (71 percent) as compared to 7 of 42 controls (17 percent)."

AIDS and chronic fatigue syndrome were again two ships passing in the night. In an article on Ampligen, by Neenyah Ostrom, in the May 4 *New York Native*. she wrote, "A major development to emerge from the recently concluded clinical trial of Ampligen as a treatment for chronic fatigue syndrome is one of the 'missing links' in current research: a consistent, reproducible physiological marker for the disease. According to information presented at an international scientific meeting, a natural antiviral immune pathway is consistently impaired in CFS patients. The same antiviral pathway [called the 2-5A Synthetase/RNAse L antiviral pathway] is also impaired in 'AIDS' patients, and in both patient populations it appears to be corrected by administration of Ampligen."

That Ampligen could help both AIDS and CFS patients should have raised some eyebrows and serious questions about the relationship of the two epidemics, but once again, no cigar.

The coinventor of Ampligen, Dr. William Carter, had some interesting things to say about Ampligen's effect on CFS and HHV-6: "It [HHV-6] is found in a very high percentage of people with AIDS, and it is found in more than 85 percent of people with chronic fatigue syndrome." Ostrom wrote that Carter "noted that NIH scientists have reported . . . that Ampligen is a strong inhibitor of HHV-6 in laboratory studies."

Carter said, "We do not yet know whether this virus is the cause or critical cofactor of CFIDS" or whether it is irrelevant. Ostrom noted, "He pointed out that amounts of HHV-6 seen in CFS patients gradually decreases with Ampligen administration."

Ampligen could have been a turning point for both AIDS and CFS, but for the next two decades a number of CFS patients would improve on it during clinical trials, but then find themselves back in the same boat when the trials were over, at which point their health again declined and they no longer had access to the expensive drug. And for AIDS patients Ampligen never really had a chance to be vetted during the AZT boondoggle.

In an editorial, in the May 25 issue, I used a recent interview with Noam Chomsky to make a point about the *New York Times*: "In the [May 28, 1992] issue of *Rolling Stone*, there is a fascinating interview with Noam Chomsky by Charles M. Young. Young wrote that Chomsky 'has been unrelenting in his attacks on the American hierarchy and the nation-state in general.' Chomsky has some pretty choice things to say about the *New York Times*. . . . According to Young, 'He has left the *New York Times* in an especially vulnerable spot: How to explain that one of the smartest people on earth thinks the newspaper of record is a reeking pile of lies about U.S. war crimes.' "

I wrote, "What we really lack is someone of Chomsky's stature to take a critical public stand on the issue of AIDS. Five years ago, I tried to convince Susan Sontag to do that but her writings on 'AIDS' have since echoed the government's propaganda. Gore Vidal has missed an opportunity to stir things up. No Frances Fitzgerald of 'AIDS.' No Seymour Hersh. Here we have an epidemic that threatens to dismantle the entire Constitution, as well as the health of every American, and the intellectuals are either looking the other way, or they just can't grasp the nature of the Big Lie."

I noted, "Chomsky argues that reality and freedom are essentially defined in a 'democracy' by what Big Business says they are. If Chomsky were to start looking at 'AIDS' probably the first thing he would focus on would be corporate involvement. Where that is concerned, all roads seem to lead to the bottom line of Burroughs Wellcome, and to keep that bottom line healthy, more people need to be dosed with AZT. The scientists who suggest that AZT actually causes 'AIDS' are a major threat to that bottom line. Writers who document the fraud that backs up the claims about AZT also threaten that bottom line. Those people are not honored in most gay publications, let alone the *New York Times*."

I noted that Chomsky had said, in *Rolling Stone*, "We honor Soviet dissidents who condemn Soviet crimes. Except we don't apply the same logic at home. That would be inconceivable. That would be rational. And honest. And if you're rational and honest, you're pretty much excluded from the educated classes, the privileged classes. These are properties that are pretty dangerous."

I wrote that I wondered "what Chomsky would make of the *Times* editorial last week that warned the black community that AIDS and AZT are not a plot against them. . . . Nicholas Wade used to write editorial propaganda like this about the epidemic. Now the job has fallen mostly to Phil Boffey. 'Bizarre as it may seem to most people, many black Americans believe that AIDS and the health measures used against it are part of a conspiracy to wipe out the black race,' writes Boffey and his editorial gang. There go those bizarre blacks again. And that's just a week after the Rodney King verdict. And that's just twenty years after the Tuskegee Syphilis experiment was brought to a close. And what do those bizarre blacks think of AZT? 'Worse yet,' Boffey and company write, 'the treatments and preventive against AIDS have become suspect. Some blacks believe that AZT, the harsh drug used to combat the disease, is a plot to poison them.' "

I shot back, "The *Times* has failed to report that this newspaper, the gay newspaper of record of New York City, has built part of its reputation on John Lauritsen's amazing reporting on AZT. . . . The *Times* has also failed to report on all the bizarre scientists who have suggested that HIV is not or may not be the cause of 'AIDS.' They've failed to report that the bizarre discoverer of HIV, Luc Montagnier, is now having serious second thoughts about whether his baby is the AIDS monster. They've failed to report that bizarre retrovirologist Peter Duesberg now argues that AZT causes 'AIDS.' *The Times* has also failed to report on the bizarre links between 'AIDS' and chronic fatigue syndrome. . . . It could be said that essentially when [white] heterosexuals get 'AIDS,' it is usually called 'chronic fatigue syndrome.' How about a full-scale debate about that? We're not holding our breath for such a debate. Not from a 'reeking pile of lies.' "

One of the blood sports that the epidemic gave birth to was the picketing by a small group of religious fanatics at the funerals of people (usually gay), who were reported to have died of AIDS. In the June 1 issue of the *New York Native* we ran an Associated Press story that the Attorney General of Kansas, Bob Stephan "said in a legal opinion May 19 that a bill passed by the Legislature prohibiting picketing at funerals is constitutional. Stephan said the prohibition is a valid, limited restriction on a citizen's right to freedom of speech. The bill is in response to funeral picketing by anti-gay activists who believed the funeral was being held for a person who died from AIDS complications. . . . 'Any picketing focused on funeral attendees is the evil sought to be prevented, regardless of the content or subject of the picketing,' Stephan said. He also said preserving the sanctity and integrity of funerals is a legitimate government interest. . . . 'It is disgusting and reprehensible that anyone would want to increase the suffering and anguish of family members who are mourning the loss of a loved one,' Stephan said in comments beyond his opinion."

In the June 8 issue, we published a compelling letter that had been sent to the *New York Times*, by a man named Henry Chinn, Jr., about the *Times*'s recent editorial, the one I myself had previously addressed. He wrote, " 'The AIDS Plot against Blacks' (*New York Times* editorial, May 12) only makes it more evident to me why the chasm between the majority population and black people in this country will continue to grow. Your labeling it as 'bizarre' that many blacks believe that AIDS and the health measures used against it are part of the conspiracy to wipe out the black race in and of itself reeks of an insensitivity to the history of blacks in this country and why they would have good reason to feel conspired against. Again the onus is being placed on the victim to correct and 'discredit the pernicious and dispiriting rumors' that AIDS is genocide. Obviously your newspaper has accepted not only the government definition of AIDS, but it has also accepted the toxic drug treatments they recommended. Everyone does not. This group includes many doctors, microbiologists, and scientists who don't agree that HIV is the main cause of AIDS and they do not recommend using the treatments that have the Food and Drug Administration's approval."

He also wrote, "Blacks in this country have every reason to be skeptical about how they should go about dealing with this situation. Our history in this country gives us no reason to accept your word or the government's word about how we should proceed in this matter. The Tuskegee Experiment is a prime example. . . . You do a disservice when you portray the black community as if it is the only group in this society that has suspicions about the nature and source of this illness. There are many who have such suspicions as well as a distrust of the government's health recommendations, especially the use of AZT. . . . The distrust comes from a long history of abuse, harassment, lies and deceit. . . ."

In the same issue, Neenyah Ostrom reported, "A study published in the May 28 *New England Journal of Medicine* found that human herpesvirus-6 (HHV-6) a virus found to be active in 'AIDS' and chronic fatigue syndrome patients, is an important cause of febrile (feverish) illnesses in children under the age of two. 'Primary Human herpesvirus 6 Infection in Young Children' was co-signed by pediatrician Prasong Pruksananonda and colleagues from the University of Rochester School of Medicine, as well as investigators from the Centers for Disease Control and DuPont Merck Pharmaceuticals. The study suggested, according to the researchers, that 'HHV-6 is an important cause of acute illness in young children in the United States.' Based on the finding that 14 percent of infants admitted to emergency rooms with acute fevers had HHV-6 infection, the researchers concluded that 'although the full spectrum of initial infection with HHV-6 needs further delineation, our findings suggest that this newly discovered virus causes an appreciable proportion of the emergency room visits for children with acute illness in the first two years of life and that the clinical manifestations are varied and often worrisome. . . . This study further emphasizes the need for a means of diagnosis of primary HHV-6 infection that is rapid and feasible in out-patient settings.' "

In the same issue, Neenyah Ostrom wrote about another symptom that suggested that AIDS and chronic fatigue syndrome belonged in one paradigm rather than two: "Another cat's out of the bag—and it's not a kitty cat, either, but a full-grown mountain lion. A study, published in the April *American Journal of Medicine*, concludes that 'fibromyalgia is a common cause of musculoskeletal symptoms' in a subset of 'AIDS' patients, and thought to occur in 11 percent of all 'AIDS' patients. Fibromyalgia syndrome is characterized by muscle and joint pain—identified by localized 'tender points'—as well as fatigue, recurrent headaches, anxiety, poor sleep, and irritable bowel symptoms. The similarities between chronic fatigue syndrome . . . and fibromyalgia are so striking that some CFS researchers believe them to be the same illness. . . . If fibromyalgia syndrome is a 'symptom' of 'AIDS,' as well as being a 'symptom' of CFS, what does that mean? It means that, in addition to isolated symptoms and immune system abnormalities, CFS and 'AIDS' patients now share a syndrome, an entire constellation of signs and symptoms, in common. And it makes the argument that CFS and 'AIDS' are actually part of the same illness even more difficult to ignore or refute."

The absolute intolerance of the AIDS establishment for any criticism or skepticism towards its etiological sacred cow, HIV, was manifest in a report John Lauritsen wrote in the July 15 issue about an international symposium, "AIDS: A Different View" which took place in Amsterdam in May. Lauritsen reported, "The goal of the conference was to provide an exchange of ideas, as the first steps toward developing a multicausal approach to 'AIDS.' Conference participants were asked to have respect for ideas different from their own, and to adopt a spirit of questioning."

While the conference was set up to give the AIDS critics a chance to speak and exchange ideas, members of the AIDS establishment showed up to essentially sabotage the spirit and the substance of the conference. Lauritsen reported, "Although Peter Duesberg was undeniably the star of the conference; he was put into situations which made it difficult for him to make his points effectively." Because the conference caught the attention of a few of the mainstream papers in

Europe, members of the AIDS establishment were determined not to let the critical views of the HIV theory of AIDS be treated with any respect. Lauritsen wrote, "What might have been a small conference, where 'AIDS' critics exchanged views with each other, became instead a prime-time controversy. As a result, the 'AIDS' establishment, which might otherwise have been content to merely observe, intervened by engaging in various forms of disruption, disinformation, and dirty tricks. In radio communication, this sort of thing is known as 'jamming.' It soon became apparent that the 'AIDS' establishment was out, covertly as well as openly, to 'get Duesberg.' . . . An evening panel on 'Virology and Epidemiology' turned out to be a setup against Duesberg. . . . All kinds of insults and abuse were hurled upon Duesberg, who, when he tried to reply, would be interrupted in mid-sentence and told to let others speak."

One of the other big disappointments of the conference was the unhelpful presence of a major AIDS celebrity. Lauritsen reported, "Much interest was aroused by the appearance of Luc Montagnier, the man who discovered HIV. Two years earlier, at the international 'AIDS' Conference in San Francisco, Montagnier had stated that the 'AIDS virus' by itself couldn't do much of anything, and required cofactors. He believed that the necessary accomplice might be a mycoplasma, but he also admitted in questioning that the necessary cofactor might be a toxin. More recently Montagnier has spoken of 'AIDS' cases without HIV. There was speculation that Montagnier might finally have the guts to admit he'd been wrong—that HIV was not the cause of 'AIDS.' This did not happen. Montagnier backpedalled and dithered around aimlessly. Although he asserted that HIV was necessary for 'AIDS,' he did not address a single one of Duesberg's criticisms of the HIV-'AIDS' hypothesis. He asserted that AZT is beneficial—a possible consequence of his having recently taken a trip paid by [AZT manufacturer] Burroughs Wellcome. Montagnier has become a millionaire thanks to HIV; he receives $100,000 a year from royalties on the HIV-antibody test. Perhaps honor and honesty are too much to expect of him."

In the June 29 issue, I wrote a piece about a suspicious outbreak of disease at the facility (the only one in the United States) where African swine fever virus is researched: "On June 16, John McDonald reported in *Newsday* that an employee who used to work at the U.S. Department of Agriculture Plum Island Disease Center just off Long Island, is

282

suffering from a 'mysterious flu-like illness.' The story may reopen questions about the link between chronic human illness and one of the viruses that are researched there, African swine fever virus (ASFV). In 1983, a scientist named Jane Teas suggested that ASFV might be the cause of 'AIDS.' It is also the virus that another researcher has suggested was renamed HHV-6 by Dr. Robert Gallo, the National Cancer Institute scientist who is under investigation for scientific misconduct. The *Native* has produced numerous reports since 1983 suggesting that there is a major cover-up being conducted by the Centers for Disease Control and the U.S. Department of Agriculture regarding the relationship of African swine fever virus to the epidemic of 'AIDS' and chronic fatigue syndrome. *Newsday*'s McDonald reported that 'Lab officials said there is no record of a Plum Island employee becoming ill from a disease under study at the facility. But they also confirmed that the ill former employee, Phillip Piegari, was one of three workers inside laboratory building 257 late in August when Hurricane Bob knocked out power to the building and disabled its 'negative-air' system, the lab's primary device for preventing the spread of bacteria and viruses. That system directs air flow toward areas in the lab where the diseases are kept.' According to McDonald, the sick employee 'said in an interview that during the 24 hours he was inside the building, he was responsible for monitoring viruses that were thawing in inoperative freezers and working to control the escape of raw sewage from pens containing diseased animals. Without power, the sewage could not be decontaminated. He was laid off at the lab in October, and in February developed the chronic flu-like symptoms. As recently as this week he had a fever of 100 degrees.' "

I reported, "The *Native* has been told by a source familiar with the case that six other people who work at the Plum Island facility now have symptoms similar to Piegari's. According to McDonald, 'Since February, Piegari has been repeatedly tested for Lyme Disease and been examined by a battery of specialists in infectious diseases. None of the physicians has been able to identify his ailment.' Piegari's treating physician, Dr. Vishnudat Seodat, told *Newsday*, 'It is important for us to see if this could be something he picked up over there on Plum Island.' "

I pointed out, "If Piegari's symptoms are indicative of chronic fatigue syndrome, which is believed by some researchers either to be caused or exacerbated by human herpesvirus-6, there is the possibility that his illness was caused by a pig virus which is researched at Plum

Island. African swine fever virus, according to a brochure from the U.S. Department of Agriculture, 'is a contagious, usually fatal viral disease of swine. It can be the most deadly of all foreign diseases of hogs. The acute form kills almost all hogs that become infected. . . . Since the 1960s, a mild form of ASF has been increasingly reported. Because this chronic strain has a lower death rate than the acute form, it is more difficult to diagnose and thus harder to eradicate."

In the July 6 issue, I wrote a very long editorial titled, "Gallo's Epidemic of Lies."

> As readers of this publication know only too well, we believe that the central lie about the AIDS epidemic involves both the chronic fatigue syndrome epidemic and the virus called "HHV-6." We believe that the evidence that AIDS and chronic fatigue (and immune dysfunction) syndrome are variations of the same immune system disorder is so overwhelming that we would say there was less evidence that the proverbial Emperor was wearing no clothes. The evidence that HHV-6 (and its many strains) is the leading contender for the title of sine qua non of AIDS and chronic fatigue syndrome also strikes us as compelling. In addition, the charges by Boston scientist, John Beldekas that National Cancer Institute scientist Robert Gallo appropriated Beldekas's research on African swine fever virus (the way he appropriated Montagnier's research) and gave ASFV the new name of HHV-6 is very credible.
>
> Which brings us to the events of last week.
>
> On Wednesday, June 24, Paul Recer of the Associated Press reported, "A meeting to allow Robert C. Gallo to publicly discuss his co-discovery of the AIDS virus was canceled Wednesday after a Nobel laureate got what was called a 'threatening letter from a federal lawyer.' "
>
> Recer reported that Howard Temin, "the scientist who had organized the meeting so that Robert Gallo could defend himself against charges of fraud and scientific misconduct, had received a letter from

284

Health and Human Services General Counsel ordering him not to hold the meeting."

Temin told Recer that he found the letter from Health and Human Services threatening because it suggested that Temin and others would be exposed to various types of liability.

Temin is the chairman of the National Cancer Advisory Board on AIDS, which meets four times a year.

Temin was also told by Health and Human Services, according to Recer, "that as chairman of the committee on AIDS he would no longer be permitted to select the topics that the advisory committee will discuss" at the meetings.

This is all very curious.

It only reinforces our contention that most of what the government has produced in the way of statements about "AIDS" is essentially politics rather than science. And very sinister politics to boot.

We contend that the reason there has been a coordinated cover-up of Gallo's scientific crimes is not that a lot of money is involved, but that the crimes Gallo has committed may lead to the exposure of the biggest crime of all: the cover-up of the relationship of AIDS and chronic fatigue syndrome, as well as the ASFV/HHV-6 connection. The government doesn't do this kind of cover-up just to save fifty or a hundred million dollars. Let's face it: If the American public ever learns that the government has lied to them about the definition and cause of "AIDS," heads will—and should—roll. All of Gallo's bosses are implicated. The political and financial liability involved here would dwarf the Savings and Loan catastrophe.

One thing that continues to puzzle us is that the media has not seen fit to go back and examine the impact of Gallo's lying on our understanding of "AIDS" itself. We now know that Gallo was more than willing to change scientific papers to suit himself. Why believe anything the man says?

Perhaps Peter Duesberg has articulated best the

285

absurdity of Gallo's LAV theft. He told Celia Farber in the June issue of *Spin* magazine, "To me that whole affair is just a story of who stole whose fake diamonds. The point that everybody is missing is that all of those original papers Gallo wrote on HIV have been found fraudulent. Well, then, that throws into question the entire HIV hypothesis, doesn't it? The HIV hypothesis was based on those papers."

Unfortunately, Duesberg himself hasn't radically questioned the basic definition of "AIDS" as much as he thinks he has. Duesberg's whole modus operandi has been to point out the logical inconsistencies of the CDC's "AIDS" definition. He comes to the conclusion that there really is no infectious epidemic that could be called "AIDS." He argues that several different groups of people whose lifestyles or risk factors have resulted in illnesses have been illogically pooled into one epidemic. There is a great deal of merit to Duesberg's critique, but it rests on one falsehood and an uncritical look at the birth of the definition of "AIDS." The falsehood occurs every time he says that there is no known disease like AIDS. We have told him over and over again that African swine fever is a perfect model for a disease with a definition like "AIDS." Frankly, it is such a perfect fit that ASF is now called the "acquired immunodeficiency" of pigs.

And Duesberg really should go back and analyze how the definition of "AIDS" was formed. Back in 1981, when nothing about "AIDS" was carved in stone, it was defined provisionally, and scientists were afraid that any agent they identified as the cause might turn out to be a red herring or only a marker for the disease. An incredible intellectual tragedy occurred in those days which will come back and haunt public health authorities for years to come. "AIDS" was defined too narrowly, and that narrow definition, we believe, resulted in the identification of the wrong agent as the "cause" of the epidemic.

In the August 1982 issue of *Science*, Jean L. Marx, while acknowledging the T-cell abnormality in "AIDS" patients, wrote, almost presciently, "Precisely which immune cells might be important here is uncertain." She also pointed out, "In addition to the T-cell abnormality, AIDS patients may have a reduced population of another type of immune cell, the natural killer, which has been implicated in cancer surveillance."

Imagine if that sentence had been written in the following manner: "In addition to the natural killer cell abnormality, AIDS patients may have a reduced population of another type of immune cell, the T-cell." In other words, what if they had instead called "AIDS" "Low Natural Killer Cell Syndrome?" Given the immunological data, and the importance of natural killer cells, they very well could have.

But had "AIDS" been called "Low Natural Killer Cell Syndrome," and had scientists begun testing more than just the so-called risk groups, here's what they would have found: the chronic fatigue syndrome epidemic. And they would have found millions of people affected by it.

It now seems incredibly ironic that Jean Marx wrote in *Science* magazine on June 21, 1983, that there was ". . . the possibility that many individuals who do not have full-blown AIDS may have a milder form or be asymptomatic carriers of an infectious agent." We now know that [chronic fatigue syndrome] was breaking out simultaneously with the "AIDS" epidemic. While there was a concerted effort to say that only certain risk groups were at the bottom of the "AIDS" iceberg, it now seems that the entire nation is down there too. Curiously, the chief investigator of [chronic fatigue syndrome] at the National Institute of Allergy and Infectious Diseases, Stephen Straus, whose primary mission is to cover up the chronic fatigue syndrome epidemic, and to keep it a very safe distance from "AIDS," began his [chronic fatigue syndrome] research around the same time that the Centers for Disease Control was discovering, or pretending to discover, the "AIDS" epidemic. Had "AIDS" been

287

described as a syndrome involving the natural killer cells, there would have been a good chance that, if they'd checked the immune systems of the chronic fatigue syndrome patients that were coming to the National Institutes of Health, they would have seen that they had the natural killer cell defect in common. That defect would have motivated any scientist with half a brain to ask what virus or bacteria the two groups had in common. It might have led them to HHV-6. It might have led them to consider more seriously Jane Teas's hypothesis that African swine fever virus is the cause of "AIDS." At least one paper on ASFV has established that the natural killer cells are affected in the course of ASFV infection.

Five years ago, when Japanese researchers encountered chronic fatigue syndrome patients in their own country, their research went right to the heart of the matter: They identified the main defect as being the natural killer cell depletion, and defined the disease as "Low Natural Killer Cell Syndrome." (They also developed a promising treatment.) Had the definition of "AIDS" not left its provisional status, or at least kept the natural killer cell defect as a major part of it, the connection between the two epidemics would have been obvious.

Lymphadenopathy is one of the symptoms of both AIDS and chronic fatigue syndrome. In the August 13, 1982, issue of *Science*, the CDC's Tom Spira told Jean Marx that, "We don't know if the lymphadenopathy is a prodrome [premonitory symptom] or milder manifestation of more severe disease." Why didn't they see the connection to the emerging cases of chronic fatigue syndrome? We think it's at least partly because Gallo and his crooked cronies moved in for the kill. The discussions of HIV and AIDS over the years have become increasingly circular. At first, because the definition of AIDS focused on the T-4 cell defects, the investigators went after a virus that was specific for T-4 cells. Enter LAV, HTLV-III, ARV, HIV. "AIDS" was defined ad nauseum as a syndrome that involved the destruction of the T-4 cells by the T-4 cell-infecting-and-killing HTLV-III. The breakdown of the rest of the immune system and the rest of the body resulted from this primary insult. End of story. If any agent was not specific for T-4 cells, it was ruled out of the story.

Only after several years, when HIV came under attack because it seemed to infect so few T-4 cells, and because Peter Duesberg was tireless in his critique of HIV "science," researchers began to show that HIV could infect many different kinds of cells. But keep in mind that it was the specificity of HIV's tropism for T-4 cells that Gallo used to try to lock up the etiology argument. And that specific piece of proof was simplistic. There were other agents infecting and killing cells in the complexly dysfunctional immune systems of AIDS (and chronic fatigue syndrome) patients: most specifically, the virus which looked like CMV to the Centers for Disease Control, but which in all probability was ASFV, the virus which John Beldekas has suggested was renamed HHV-6 by Robert Gallo, an experienced re-namer.

The provisional nature of the initial multisystemic definition of AIDS was quickly altered by Gallo and his crowd to fit their own retroviral work. And it wasn't just the natural killer cells that were elbowed out of the definition of "AIDS." In a paper in the May 20, 1983 issue of *Science*, a team led by Gallo noted, "The T-cell dysfunction is often marked by an absence of delayed hypersensitivity." If researchers had kept an open mind, and had they looked around in the general population for people with "the absence of delayed hypersensitivity," they would have bumped into the chronic fatigue syndrome epidemic. Studies have shown that over eighty percent of the patients with that syndrome also suffer from "the absence of delayed hypersensivity." Because Gallo was driven to vindicate his own HTLV work, and because HTLV was associated with T-cells, he used his power to nail the definition of "AIDS" to the Procrustean bed of retrovirology. Even without Gallo the tragedy we have faced and the even greater—almost apocalyptic— tragedy we still face, would exist. (He once told the *Native* not to blame him, that he didn't start the epidemic.) But what that man did to control the direction of "AIDS" research, and the fraud-riddled research that he helped produce, still pollute the "AIDS" paradigm.

If the paradigm hadn't been hijacked by Gallo and his lying cronies, and if the connection between AIDS and chronic fatigue syndrome had been seen, there is a good chance that we would be further along in terms of effective treatment for both manifestations of the same syndrome. For one thing, the focus might be on the natural killer cells or on the whole issue of anergy. The autoimmune aspects of AIDS/CFS might also have been addressed therapeutically.

Once Gallo had narrowed the definition of the disease to fit his retrovirus, the stage was set for the tragedies of the "AIDS test" and the administration of AZT. People killed themselves because of Gallo's paradigm. Burroughs Wellcome swept in like a toxic cloud, and, with the cheering and assistance of "AIDS activists," began the genocidal orgy that continues to this day. People who need whatever immune system they have left are given a poison bound to destroy the natural killer cells they have, not to mention red blood cells, and God only knows what else. And as readers of the *Native* know only too well, the research into AZT turned out to be as riddled with fraud as Gallo's HIV papers in *Science* magazine. And "AIDS activists" like Martin Delaney egged the community on to swallow their poison while taking money from Burroughs Wellcome. And this is only the tragedy that affects the erroneously labeled "AIDS community."

There is also a group called "the CFS community." This is where the tragedy, and the impact of Gallo's lying, becomes exponential.

Gallo, by narrowing the definition of AIDS through a combination of stupidity, arrogance, and thuggishness, and having gotten HIV declared the "cause" of "AIDS," contributed to the growth of the *real* epidemic, which involved anergy, natural killer cells, monocytes, macrophages, B-cells, brain lesions and you name it. As a result, *that* epidemic continues to spread unabated. Millions of CFS patients are now sitting ducks for cancer and TB—because the wrong definition of the disease led to the wrong agent being identified as the cause, which led to over 11 billion dollars being pointed in the wrong direction.

There are now estimates that up to 13 million Americans are suffering from the immune dysfunction that has erroneously been called chronic fatigue syndrome. And as anyone who has read Neenyah Ostrom's groundbreaking reporting knows, the syndrome is very contagious. Most people who suffer from CFS have another family member who is also suffering from it. If there are 13 million, there could soon be 26 million. If there are 26 million . . . and so on, and so on. The Centers for Disease Control seems transparently uninterested in telling the American public how many people really have this clearly AIDS-related syndrome. Their main goal seems to be to foot-drag, perhaps until enough legislation is put through to give the medical powers-that-be enough extra-Constitutional powers to deal with the disaster without the messy complications of people's civil liberties. Or perhaps they just hope it will work itself out. There are so many religious nuts in the Bush Administration working at the CDC that they may even think this is a sign of the Second Coming and that if we just wait eight years You-Know-Who will arrive on earth and heal all the good ones. Who knows?

But for those of us who still savor our secular sense of reality, there is a disaster here, one which has been aided and abetted by Gallo and Company and one which must be addressed rationally by people who are not pathological liars.

For the sake of the human immune system, Dr. Pinocchio has got to go.

In the July 13 issue, Neenyah Ostrom wrote another disturbing story about AZT: "A document supplied to the *Native* reports that babies of mothers on AZT are being born with extra fingers and/or toes. The document, part of the ACT UP monthly newsletter . . . reports that the deformed babies are being born to women enrolled in a clinical trial testing whether administration of AZT (Retrovir) prevents transmission of HIV to their infants. AZT is known to be a carcinogen; this new information suggests that it is also a teratogen, a substance capable of causing birth defects when administered to pregnant women."

Ironically, in the same issue, we ran an Associated Press article about the cozy relationship between Burroughs Wellcome and ACT UP: "Burroughs Wellcome Co., the pharmaceutical giant that makes AZT, said it would donate $1 million to fund 'AIDS' research aimed at providing experimental treatment to a broad array of people. The announcement Tuesday was made jointly with the 'AIDS' activist group ACT UP, whose members once invaded Burroughs Welcome's headquarters and chained themselves to office furniture to protest the high cost of AZT, the first drug approved to fight the disease. Burroughs Wellcome is the first drug maker to respond to a recent ACT UP request for money to fund 'AIDS' research. ACT UP has contacted 50 drug companies—many described as mom-and-pop operations that have yet to market a product—in an effort to raise $5 million, said ACT UP member Peter Staley. ACT UP applauded the grant, which Burroughs Wellcome officials said might be renewed next year. But observers noted that it pales in comparison with the annual sales of Retrovir, the company's name for AZT."

Neenyah Ostrom began one of my favorite series of articles in the same issue. Titled "The Color Purple," Ostrom reported, "Burke Cunha, M.D. who is chief of infectious disease at Winthrop-University Hospital (Mineola, Long Island), has described what he calls 'crimson crescents' that appear in the throats of more than 80 percent of chronic fatigue syndrome (CFS) patients. Cunha describes the crescents not only as 'crimson,' but 'purplish.' The reddish-purplish regions found in CFS patients' throats sounded quite similar to KS (Kaposi's sarcoma) in the throat, commented an 'AIDS' doctor [who wished to remain anonymous] to whom they were described. Is it possible that the crimson crescents observed in the throats of CFS patients are actually a type of KS?"

292

Ostrom raised the possibility that the lesions in the throats of CFS patients connected them to the theory that Florida researchers held about KS being the unrecognized but unifying central pathological event AIDS. As I previously reported, the Florida team, headed by Dr. George Hensley, had turned the AIDS paradigm upside down, by finding KS in nearly 100% of AIDS patients, when they explored the internal organs closely during autopsies of AIDS patients. Their fascinating work suggested that KS preceded AIDS and caused more of the immune problem in AIDS than previously thought.

Basically, Ostrom was asking if the KS-like lesions, in the tonsils of [CFS]patients, were an indication that some kind of unrecognized indolent KS was present internally, something that physicians would not even be thinking about because of the conceptual wall that socially hostile epidemiology had built between AIDS and chronic fatigue syndrome. And the CFS patients were not particularly interested in finding out if they shared KS with AIDS patients.

Ostrom went even further, in the July 20 issue, and speculated that the dramatic digestive problems in chronic fatigue syndrome were actually the result of the unrecognized chronic or slowly progressive KS in the CFS patients' digestive tracts. Ostrom noted that Dr. Carol Jessop, who was talking to a group of patients at a chronic fatigue syndrome conference, said, "Almost all patients would say to me, 'I was totally well until I got this [chronic fatigue syndrome],' and yet, when I took their past medical histories, I found it wasn't quite true. Now these aren't disastrous problems. In fact, if they had gone to their physicians for any of these problems such as irritable bowel, diarrhea and constipation, abdominal cramping, bloating, flatulence, chronic constipation, heartburn, etc., their physician would probably just say, 'Oh, take this' and that would be it. So we as physicians didn't relate to our patients that this was a problem, so they considered themselves to be totally healthy. Yet, if you look at the numbers, 89 percent of the [chronic fatigue syndrome] patients had irritable bowel syndrome, diarrhea alternating with constipation, and abdominal cramping pain episodically. Another 80 percent complained of constant gas, bloating and flatulence. It's amazing that we can all meet in this room together."

Ostrom wondered if "Jessop may have uncovered a fallacy in the prevailing wisdom of chronic fatigue syndrome: that it begins as a respiratory, flu-like illness. Instead, as she points out, it may be a digestive tract disturbance. Jessop's statistic—that more than 80 percent of CFS patients complain of irritable bowel syndrome, abdominal pain, gas, bloating, etc.—corresponds to the more than 80 percent of CFS patients who exhibit a red-to-purplish crescent-shaped lesion in their throats. (Helot, Paul, in the *New York Times* Long Island edition, January 14, 1992) . . . What if the digestive problems described by the CFS patients are actually caused by KS in the gastrointestinal tract? According to the *AIDS Treatment News*, 'The most common HIV-related causes of gastric symptoms include KS, lymphoma, and CMV [cytomegalovirus].' And while KS is unusual in the esophagus, it 'may occasionally be found there.' KS also can cause colitis and diarrhea . . . in people with AIDS." Ostrom noted, "Gastrointestinal symptoms, it is realized in retrospect, were among the first signs of the 'AIDS' epidemic; and, it now seems, were also among the first symptoms seen in the CFS epidemic. That observation raises what should be a relatively simple question to answer: Are the gastrointestinal symptoms in both patient populations caused, in part, by undetected KS?"

We covered the hell that had broken loose during the Eighth International AIDS Conference held in Amsterdam that summer, in our August 3 issue. Neenyah Ostrom wrote, "Nobody really expected that any big news would be coming out" of the conference, "so major shock waves went around the globe when CNN announced on July 18 that Monday's *Newsweek* contained a major scoop: More than a dozen cases of people with symptoms of 'AIDS,' but no sign of the 'AIDS virus,' were to be announced at the Amsterdam conference."

Ostrom reported, "The controversy about the HIV-negative 'AIDS' cases grew even more heated on July 22, when a research team from the University of Southern California School of Medicine announced that they had identified a new retroviral particle associated with non-HIV immunodeficiency. Their research paper, scheduled to be published in the *Proceedings of the National Academy of Sciences USA* August 15, was released early by the journal because of its possible public health implications. . . . 'Detection of an Additional Human Intracisternal Retroviral Particle Associated with CD4-Positive T-cell Deficiency' is the title of the Gupta et al. report in the *Proceedings*. It describes the isolation of a new retroviral particle, named HICRV, for 'human intracisternal (a cisterna is a closed space inside a cell containing fluid) retroviral particle.' The HICRV particles were isolated from a 66-year-old woman with severe immunodeficiency and from her daughter. Both women tested negative for HIV-1, HIV-2, HTLV-1, and HTLV-2. Gupta and colleagues noted that several cases of Pneumocystis carinii pneumonia (PCP) have been detected in HIV-negative individuals. Their 66-year-old patient, in addition to having a deficiency of CD4 cells, had PCP and 'no risk factors for HIV infection.' Her daughter, also infected with HICRV, was found to have diminished cell-mediated immunity."

Regardless of what HICRV was, the big story now was that HIV was not alone in the game. Ostrom reported, "*Newsweek*'s Geoffrey Cowley . . . wrote, 'Is a New AIDS Virus Emerging?' in the magazine's July 27 issue. He describes the patients seen by Dr. Frederick Siegel at New York's Long Island Jewish Medical Center: 'most' of them have 'HIV risk factors'; their T-4 cell counts plummet; and they develop opportunistic infections. 'The trouble is, their blood contains not a trace of HIV,' Cowley notes. Even the most sensitive tests, like polymerase chain reaction (PCR), have not detected the 'AIDS virus' in these 'AIDS' patients. . . . 'No one knows just what to make of the phenomenon, but health officials fear it could signal the emergence of a new AIDS virus—an agent that acts like HIV but is different enough to escape detection by any available blood test,' Cowley reports, adding: 'That's not a happy prospect.' "

Ostrom took issue with Cowley who suggested in his piece that the AIDS cases without HIV were 'rare': "In fact, the new disease may not be so rare, if the researchers surging out of the woodwork at the Amsterdam conference to announce how many cases of [HIV-negative immunodeficiency] they've seen is any indication of how widespread the phenomena is. And if this new, mysterious, non-HIV disease of immune deficiency is chronic fatigue syndrome, it may already affect millions of people worldwide."

The Centers for Disease Control, very obviously terrified about the prospect of their paradigm and public health agenda turning to dust, issued a reassuring press release titled, "CD4 counts and AIDS-like illness who are not infected with either HIV-1 or HIV-2," which asserted, "The cause of these illnesses is not known at this time. CDC is aware that several laboratories are investigating the possibility that a previously unidentified virus may be causing this condition. However, this information has not yet been confirmed, and other possible causes are being explored. If a new virus is discovered to be the cause of the AIDS-like illnesses, it should be possible to quickly develop a blood test for this virus. CDC is reviewing AIDS case report forms to determine if any cases such as these were reported as cases of AIDS. To date, none have been found. This occurrence appears to be real. CDC continues to recommend that persons who believe they may have been exposed to HIV should seek counseling and testing."

Ostrom reported, "At the time that the CDC press release was written, they could not have anticipated that researcher after researcher would approach the audience mike at the Amsterdam conference and announce that he or she had seen cases of non-HIV 'AIDS.' As we go to press, the number reported at the conference is 30."

In an editorial titled "Honey I Blew Up the HIV Paradigm," in the same issue, I wrote the following:

> Last week was one for the record books.
>
> As Neenyah Ostrom details in this issue, it was not a good week for HIV or the pseudoscientists who call themselves "AIDS" experts.
>
> They all looked like mice caught in glue traps.
>
> And the journalists who covered the stories coming out of the Eighth International Conference in Amsterdam—the same ones who pump out the propaganda that is called "AIDS reporting"—didn't look much better.
>
> The attendees at the conference smelled blood.
>
> The Centers for Disease Control, which should really be called the Centers for Epidemic Cover-Ups, was suddenly caught in the role of hiding information from the public.
>
> What's the CDC afraid of?
>
> Well, for starters, they have played an aggressive role in promoting the religious belief that HIV is the cause of AIDS, a belief concocted of equal parts homophobia, racism, conservative politics, fraudulent science, and flaming stupidity. There's a huge paper trail. This publication vows to track down every statement promoting the HIV paradigm by every member of the AIDS mafia at the CDC and hold them up for public scrutiny.
>
> The CDC has also played an active role in covering up the obvious evidence that AIDS and chronic fatigue syndrome are variants of the same disease. The 66-

year-old woman that Ostrom writes about this week, the woman who is HIV-antibody negative, has a daughter who shows no classic "AIDS" symptoms. But the daughter, like most of the millions of chronic fatigue syndrome patients, is anergic.

The scientific literature on chronic fatigue syndrome is incredibly clear on one matter: CFS is an immunological disorder. CFS is a form of acquired immune deficiency. With no HIV. This couldn't be simpler or more direct.

If the CDC wants to know about all cases of HIV-negative AIDS, we hereby report to them 13 million cases: the estimate of the number of people in the U.S. with chronic fatigue syndrome.

Anthony Fauci, the Director of the National Institute of Allergy and Infectious Diseases, the little man with the compensatory ego, the Ross Perot of AIDS, looked like he was going to have a nervous breakdown in Amsterdam. We kept waiting to see him curled up in a fetal position, naked and crying hysterically—desperate for forgiveness, desperate to create a smokescreen to make everyone forget how he has elbowed every critical question about HIV out of the way. Fauci was trying to sell himself as an open-minded scientist. "Don't panic, don't panic," said the snake. Of course, as long as Fauci has any power, any modicum of respect in this emergency, there is every reason to stay in the panic mode.

As these incompetent, dishonest scientists begin to grapple with the so-called mysteries of an "AIDS-like illness," and so-called "HIV-negative AIDS," may we suggest that what is really needed is Curran-negative "AIDS" and Fauci-negative "AIDS."

We are reminded of something Hannah Arendt said about our government during the Vietnam War: They told so many lies that they began to believe their own lies.

You are reading virtually the only newspaper in America that has consistently reported to you that what the government has told you about AIDS is a tissue of lies. Those of you who have watched the story of the epidemic unfold in this newspaper should get out your score cards.

Even in the face of the boycott by ACT UP, I made the decision that we would report this story exactly as we see it. We will continue to do that.

And you know what? We're just getting started.

In the August 10 issue, Neenyah Ostrom took on an issue that was in the media spotlight: the so-called "Gulf War Syndrome." Ostrom wrote that an army report "about the mysterious illness, 'Investigation of a Suspected Outbreak of an Unknown Disease Among Veterans of Operation Desert Shield/Storm' which describes an outbreak of what sounds suspiciously like chronic fatigue syndrome. Although the Army investigators entertained a diagnosis of chronic fatigue syndrome, it was rejected in favor of stress. Yes, stress. . . . The problem first surfaced in spring 1992, when 125 Operation Desert Shield/Storm veterans who had participated in various capacities, 'reported a variety of nonspecific symptoms including fatigue, joint pains, skin rashes, headaches, loss of memory, mood changes, diarrhea, bleeding and painful gums, and loss of hair.' According to the report, all were assigned to the 123d Army Reserve Command in Indiana; the symptoms appeared, in most cases, after the soldiers had returned to the U.S. from Saudi Arabia and the points referred to in the report as 'southwest (SW) Asia.' "

Ostrom asked, "Did the Army miss making a diagnosis of chronic fatigue syndrome in the sick Gulf War veterans? Only time—or another study—will be able to answer that question. But one thing is certain: If these sick soldiers have developed chronic fatigue syndrome, the 'mysterious illness' will continue to be seen in an increasing number of Army personnel."

In the August 17 issue, I wrote an editorial that was critical of the *New York Times*, and I also took issue with Irving Kristol who had written a disturbing op-ed in the *Wall Street Journal:* "I continue to think that Nazi medicine is the best model for understanding how our government is handling the 'AIDS' epidemic and that if we are not successful in exposing the truth about 'AIDS,' the government will attempt to construct something so horrific that, for lack of a better term it could be called an AIDS Reich."

I noted, "It was refreshing to hear that, two weeks ago, the news-room at the *Times* was filled with dissatisfaction about [Lawrence] Altman's coverage of the HIV-negative AIDS revelations at the Amsterdam AIDS conference. Hopefully, the reporters at the *Times* who have any interest in the truth will realize that the problem isn't just Altman. It's his boss, Nick Wade, who once told me that HIV is the cause of AIDS because the conventional wisdom is usually right. Perhaps the *Times* should change its slogan to 'All the Conventional Wisdom That's Fit to Print.'"

I criticized Altman for going out of his way to find experts who would downplay the shocking HIV-negative AIDS news that had exploded in Amsterdam. One of these experts who questioned the significance of the HIV-negative findings was Luc Montagnier, not exactly a paragon of objectivity—one would think—in matters that threatened the paradigm that made him rich and famous. I complained, "Science reporters regularly like to remind their readers—except where HIV is concerned—that any new findings may turn out to be nothing. But here it is utterly transparent that Altman wants HIV-negative AIDS to turn out to be nothing in order to save his own reputation."

To show how Altman's boss, Nick Wade, was even better at placing a finger on the journalistic scale, I quoted a passage about John Beldekas from Jad Adams's book, *The HIV Myth*, which was published in 1989 by St. Martin's Press:

> John Beldekas tested ten Belle Glade [Florida] pigs and found one positive for African swine fever virus. The Department of Agriculture first confirmed the results, then re-ran the tests and was able to proclaim it was "satisfied that African swine fever does not exist in Belle Glade."
>
> These events had reached the mainstream press and a reporter from the *New York Times* wrote a story which had severe implications for John Beldekas's career. The reporter asked John if it were possible that his test result was a false positive: that the test had shown positive for African swine fever virus which was not in fact there. The reporter wrote: "Presumably, Mr. Beldekas's diagnosis was a false positive test serum with his sample." John Beldekas insists that he only remarked in response to a direct question that an event

was possible, he did not present it as a realistic history.

Unfortunately, when a subject is in print, it assumes a status often quite out of proportion to its true importance. John Beldekas's senior colleagues did not like to see him admitting in public that his research could have been sloppy. He had been trying their patience with his African swine fever story anyway. He did not remain in his job.

I noted in my editorial that the "reporter" referred to by Adams was none other than Nick Wade "who was not a reporter at the time. The action was notable on several counts. First of all, it is curious that Wade introduced this new information in the editorial column of the *Times* rather than the news. Secondly, he had asked Beldekas a loaded [hypothetical] question, which Mr. Wade has admitted to me, but he has never retracted in the *Times*, even though it may have cost Beldekas his job. Actually, it may have cost most Americans their immune systems, if it turns out that HHV-6, the virus found in AIDS and Chronic Fatigue and Immune Dysfunction Syndrome patients, is actually African swine fever virus."

In the same editorial, I wrote, "Irving Kristol's op-ed piece in the August 6 *Wall Street Journal* had to be read to be believed. In 'AIDS and False Innocence,' Mr. Kristol writes: 'Why is Magic Johnson regarded as some kind of moral hero, even a role model for the young? Mr. Johnson, a basketball player of extraordinary talent, has tested HIV positive, as a result—he tells us—of having been sexually promiscuous with over 200 women.' Here we go again. Mr. Kristol tells us that 'Magic Johnson cannot claim the status of an innocent victim. He knew, or should have known, the risk he was running.' And Kristol asks: 'Why are all victims of AIDS treated as innocent victims when so many are responsible for their condition by their own actions? It is the idea of innocence, associated with AIDS, that legitimates all those celebrity fundraising parties to help the victims of the disease.' So even raising money to help 'AIDS' victims is not 'legitimate.' Is it morally reprehensible? Here's the Kristol clinker: 'AIDS is a venereal disease that seems to have been born out of homosexual anal intercourse.' This was in a newspaper that most of our business leaders read. . . . This is essentially what the Republicans would like to say about the epidemic, but often don't because it would backfire. It's what George Bush would like to say. And this hate is all based on science which we

300

think is patently wrong and for the most part, fraudulent."

In the same issue, Neenyah Ostrom reported on Anthony Fauci's August 6 appearance on *Larry King Live*: "King began by asking Fauci to describe what he thought was happening in the 'mysterious AIDS' cases in which patients develop severe immunodeficiency and types of infections suffered by 'AIDS' patients—but are not infected with HIV. Fauci said that between 20 and 30 such cases had been identified and because such a small number of people were affected, it really was nothing to worry about. Fauci said it wasn't clear that these cases represented a new type of 'AIDS'; these patients' immunodeficiency could, he stressed, be caused by something other than an infectious agent. Fauci speculated that the cases might not even represent a new illness, but that increasingly sophisticated testing of people's immune systems was turning up what could be 'background' immunodeficiencies (whatever that is)."

Ostrom reported that one caller to the show asked whether the new mystery cases had "anything to do with chronic fatigue syndrome. . . . People who have chronic fatigue syndrome, Fauci said, do not have the profound immunosuppression seen in the new non-HIV 'AIDS' cases. For instance, he pointed out, they do not have T-cell counts that fall below 300. Fauci was clearly uncomfortable talking about chronic fatigue syndrome, and couldn't quite figure out where to look, so his eyes darted everywhere. . . . The show ended with an angry call from a physician in the Midwest who treats AIDS patients. He demanded to know why Fauci and other health officials had not informed physicians about the cases of non-HIV 'AIDS' before the information appeared in *Newsweek*. Shouldn't the doctors know about this before the mass media, the doctor asked sarcastically. Fauci became very defensive, asserting that it had only become clear in the last couple of weeks that the non-HIV 'AIDS' cases constituted a real phenomenon and, therefore, there had previously been nothing to inform the physicians of. He did not look happy at the show's end. Fauci's good on television, as long as he's being touted as President George Bush's hero or patted on the back for rushing toxic drugs through the approval process without adequate safety testing. But when reporters start acting like reporters, as they have since the non-HIV cases came to light, Fauci's thin skin gets him into trouble; he becomes defensive, condescending and sarcastic."

Ostrom also reported, in her piece, that according "to Celia Farber at *Spin* magazine, Berkeley Professor Peter Duesberg, who had argued for several years that HIV is not the cause of 'AIDS,' was originally scheduled to appear [on the same *Larry King Live* show] addressing the phenomenon of non-HIV 'AIDS.' Duesberg's appearance was, according to Farber, canceled abruptly, with no explanation, at the last minute."

In the September 21 issue, Neenyah Ostrom wrote a piece titled "Has The Gay Press Missed the Boat on 'AIDS' by Not Seeing the Connection to Chronic Fatigue Syndrome?" She noted, "The *Advocate* is reportedly the gay publication with the largest circulation in America. For years, readers of the *Advocate* have been told over and over that HIV is the only cause of 'AIDS.' Now that cases of an 'AIDS'-like illness without HIV have surfaced, it is interesting to observe how a gay publication that has insisted that HIV is the only cause of 'AIDS' is dealing with the crumbling HIV paradigm. . . . Sue Rochman wrote 'Tracking the Mystery Virus' as a media story in the current *Advocate* (issue #162); Rochman blames the media for causing 'a new AIDS hysteria.' "

Rochman reported in the *Advocate*, "Federal health officials were accused of recklessly sitting silent for three years while a new AIDS virus, impossible to detect through blood tests, swept through the population with no apparent pattern."

Ostrom wrote, "Further investigation, according to Rochman, revealed that the story of the non-HIV 'AIDS' cases reported in Amsterdam was 'based on the shakiest and slightest of evidence,' and was essentially dismissed by 'AIDS experts' at a follow-up meeting August 14 at the Centers for Disease Control (CDC). Rochman got some reporters to defend (or apologize for) their initial stories about the non-HIV 'AIDS' cases, now called ICL cases. (ICL is short for 'idiopathic CD4-positive lymphocytopenia,' which means simply an unexplained depletion of CD4-positive cells.)"

Ostrom also noted, "*The Washington Post's* Malcolm Gladwell told Rochman that, during the two weeks following the Amsterdam 'AIDS' conference at which the new cases were initially revealed, the press started to see that 'there really wasn't a lot of evidence' to support the possibility of a new 'AIDS virus' initially reported. But 'even while doubts grew about the existence of a mystery virus, reporters continued to portray the alleged virus as an impending public health disaster,' according to Rochman."

A very exasperated Ostrom wrote that, "For absolute proof that the non-HIV 'AIDS' cases are meaningless, Rochman turned to her 'AIDS experts,' like CDC acting deputy director James Curran. At the August 14 meeting convened at CDC to review the data describing the ICL cases, Curran 'told researchers that the cases reported in the media may not be related to each other and said that if they are, they may have a cause, such as drugs or genetics, that is completely unrelated to HIV.'"

Ostrom complained, "By swallowing the pronouncement from Curran, Rochman fell into the same trap as many other reporters who have tried to debunk the non-HIV 'AIDS' story: She assumes that all 'AIDS' roads lead inevitably to HIV. Other reporters have pointed out that the ICL patients have no 'risk factors' for contracting HIV— which the ICL patients also don't have. So, too, does Rochman fail to point out that it is a less-than-brilliant deduction on Curran's part that the cause of the ICL cases may be 'completely unrelated to HIV,' since these patients are not infected with that virus."

In the October 5 issue, I wrote an editorial, "In Praise of the Leader of the Opposition to HIV Apartheid," which this time defended Peter Duesberg:

> Peter Duesberg is the Nelson Mandela of AIDS.
>
> Peter Duesberg has single-handedly opened up the question of what AIDS is and what causes it.
>
> He has also raised serious questions about the wisdom of giving people with "AIDS" AZT. He has even suggested that AZT can itself cause the condition that has been classified as "AIDS."
>
> Even if Peter Duesberg did nothing else in his lifetime, these are great contributions to humankind. They will assure him a place in history.
>
> His fight against the lies that have been told about "AIDS" could have enormous implications. Think of the potential effects of his fight on the Haitians who are being held in a concentration camp in Guantanamo, just because they are "HIV" positive. That camp could be just the first of many to come.
>
> While we see Duesberg as one of the great men of the twentieth century, apparently others have different notions about him. They would like to mark his place

in history with a little crucifixion.

"AIDS" has transformed life around the world, and Peter Duesburg has helped transform the way we think about "AIDS." The pharmaceutical parasites, the right-wing zealots, the pseudo-activists don't like that one bit.

Thanks to Duesberg we know that "AIDS" is heavily polluted with bad science. He has enabled us to see that many of our so-called "AIDS" experts are actually fools or liars or both.

Duesberg has been repaid by his efforts to save the gay community (and the world in general) from the lies and distortions of the HIV paradigm, by being branded, McCarthy style, as a homophobe.

Why? Because he points to drugs and repeated antibiotic treatment for venereal infections as one possible cause of "AIDS"? New data linking poppers to T-cell fluctuations further supports him as a man of humanitarian vision. Duesburg's attempt to raise serious questions about drugs in the epidemic is a third major contribution.

Even though we think he is wrong about AIDS being *caused* by drugs, he is entitled to his opinion about this. It certainly doesn't hurt to have someone warning people about the dangers of drugs. We were told that at a recent AIDS benefit party on Fire Island attended by thousands, more than a majority of the people were taking a variety of drugs. And from a recent article by Andrew Sullivan, the editor of *The New Republic*, one gets the impression that Ecstasy is consumed like Perrier in Provincetown.

But some would call Duesberg "murderously wrong" for daring to suggest that drugs might take enough of a toll to seriously damage or destroy the immune system, or that repeated infections and treatment for infections might do the same. That's homophobia. The man is just trying to identify factors that people can control to protect themselves. We just don't get it.

One gay person told us that he thought Duesberg

was "drugophobic." Is drug use a liberation movement? Is the gay movement a drug liberation movement, and therefore, any attacks on drugs are homophobic? Huh? Hello!

Most of the pseudoscientists who have given us HIV [dogma] and AZT are now "AIDS" millionaires. Many doctors who poison their patients are now Burroughs Welcome fat cats. Peter Duesberg, who is not himself gay, has sacrificed his funding and his career in order to set the record straight on an issue which, so far, seems to affect gays and other minorities disproportionately. We don't find *black* leaders trying to shut him up, however. [PBS talk show host] Tony Brown has had Duesburg and people who agree with him on his television show several times. The trumped-up charges against Duesberg have originated in the *gay* community, and charges have been concocted to stigmatize him as a "murderously wrong" homophobe. This must please Burroughs Welcome, and the various real homophobes who would love it if every gay person sailed quietly off into the sunset on AZT and its toxic analogues.

Then there is another group of people which has tried to tar and feather Duesburg as some kind of "nut." This character assassination is done with the usual techniques of the Big Lie. Allegations are repeated over and over to make the public think that the notions are widely accepted. Duesberg is a nut like Galileo was a nut. Duesberg is a nut like Hannah Arendt was a nut.

Peter Duesberg has been pilloried in the scientific press. He has been attacked without being given an opportunity to defend himself in the *New York Times*. Powerful (and truly homophobic) psychopath Robert Gallo has run out of expletives to damn Duesberg. And yet Duesberg has persevered. He should be an inspiration to anyone who has to tell the truth. He has been an inspiration to this writer and this newspaper.

We've watched closely to see who in our community is concocting charges of homophobia against Duesberg, a truly Orwellian charge. They seem to be the same kind of "activists" who went into St. Patrick's Cathedral and spat out the Eucharist. (We do hope that everyone realizes that this act has cost the gay community—by design, we assume—tremendous support.) These same pseudo-activists are the ones who would now try to cut down a man whose message is meant only to spread the truth and save lives. These are the same people who have tried to destroy the gay community by introducing the word "queer" to replace "gay."

We have had many conversations with Duesberg, and we still hold out hope of convincing him that "AIDS" and chronic fatigue syndrome are the same disease. Duesberg has at least admitted that if they are one epidemic, and if both are caused by HHV-6 (which might be African swine fever virus), it would make better sense than the story we are being told about "AIDS." We assume that if more data comes out linking chronic fatigue syndrome and "AIDS" that Duesberg will modify his analysis of the situation.

One of Duesberg's biggest problems is that his ideas are generally based on peer-reviewed, published science. That would be okay if so much "AIDS research" didn't turn out to be based on fraud. Duesberg has made his case by seeing the inconsistencies in the published data on the epidemic. But often that just amounts to comparing lies to lies.

That said, we still can't see any way that anyone can take his major achievement away from him. We hope that our readers and all supporters of intellectual freedom and truth, will rally around Duesberg, and tell him that the majority of the gay community appreciates what he is trying to do for the rest of the human race. It is time for all of us to stand up to the liars who call themselves the "AIDS establishment" and the thugs who call themselves "AIDS activists" and say that Duesberg in the great humanitarian that none of them will ever be.

After our competitor, *Outweek*, hit the financial skids and folded, the "queer" and "AIDS" activist community did not have a publication that reflected and supported their agenda—until a man named Bill Chafin put up the money to start another anti-*Native* publication appropriately called *QW* which was essentially a clone of *Outweek*. In the October 26 issue of *New York Native* we noted Chafin's passing in an obituary that began, "Bill Chafin, the publisher of *QW*, died last Friday of AIDS. . . . Chafin told *Newsday* in January that he had financed *QW* (which was then called *NYQ*) with money from his trust fund. Chafin had been a minor investor in *Outweek*, which failed in the summer of 1991. Chafin told *Newsday* that, 'What happened at *Outweek* was a shame, maybe even criminal. The gay community was let down in a big, big way. My job is to make sure this gay magazine survives.' According to the January 21, 1992 *Newsday* article written by David Friedman, QW was started out of 'a frustration born of two factors, say those in the know. First, disenchantment with the city's oldest gay newsweekly, the *New York Native*, because of that publication's bizarre AIDS policy—putting the word AIDS in quotes, believing it to be chronic fatigue syndrome or African swine fever rather than a disease caused by HIV, and shrieking that AZT is a medical plot to kill homosexuals.' "

In the November 30 issue, Neenyah Ostrom lambasted Larry Kramer for a piece he had recently written in the *Times*: "Playwright Larry Kramer reached into his bag of tricks and pulled out every villain associated with the AIDS epidemic and recommended them to President-elect Bill Clinton in an op-ed piece in the *New York Times* on Sunday, November 15. 'Name an AIDS High Command,' Kramer's *pièce de résistance* was called, and just about the only statement in it that most sensible people would agree with was 'It is clear how little we know about AIDS. . . .' "

Ostrom wrote, "One of the most disturbing aspects of Kramer's call to arms for the new administration was his insistence that a 'joint chiefs of staff for AIDS' must have powers that place it above not only the rest of the medical establishment, but also, apparently, above the law. 'As a war must have generals, so must the plague,' Kramer argues, with no regard for medical or historical precedent."

In his *Times* piece, Kramer also wrote that, "An AIDS czar is no longer enough. These joint chiefs would comprise the AIDS czar and the chiefs of AIDS research, drug development, and drug approvals and clinical trials."

Ostrom pointed out, "The only historical instance in recent memory when doctors and public health officials behaved as generals was in Nazi Germany during the epidemic."

In his op-ed, Kramer also wrote, "Dr. Gallo, who probably knows more about HIV than any other person in the world, has been hauled through the mud by critics who have accused him of everything from scientific fraud to cooking the books. We would do well to remember that the U.S. invited a Nazi, Werner von Braun, to come here and build our space program. The transgressions of Dr. Gallo and Dr. Baltimore [who had to resign as President of Rockefeller University because of allegations of scientific fraud], if indeed there were any, are tiny compared to von Braun's. It is a sorry state of affairs when we must render useless our finest brains just when they are needed the most."

In response to that nonsense, Ostrom wrote, "Pity that Dr. Mengele isn't still around, Larry; he'd be offered a real heroic chance to rehabilitate *his* reputation on AIDS."

Continuing to question his judgment, Ostrom asserted, "Kramer also demonstrates that he has no idea of how scientific research proceeds: 'All AIDS research must be consolidated. . . . There is no sensible reason why the Centers for Disease Control and the Defense Department and the numerous institutes that comprise NIH should all be researching AIDS. Such duplication is shamefully wasteful.' " (That statement is a great starting point for any historian who wants to examine the possibility that at the command control center of AIDS activism stood a prehensile moron.)

And last but not least, Kramer also held Fauci up for adulation, calling him "a brilliant scientist but a less than brilliant administrator." Ostrom countered, "As usual, Kramer has it exactly backwards: Fauci is a brilliant administrator and PR person, and a wretched scientist. Fauci may singlehandedly have been responsible for retarding research into both the disease process of and treatments for, AIDS, because he has stubbornly refused to consider the possibility that HIV is not a maniacal, lone killer. Because he has ruled out the possibility that other organisms are making people sick, he has precluded research into treating those other bugs. If Kramer knows any of this, it doesn't appear to bother him."

Historians attempting to grasp the fifth column developments in the gay community, during the AIDS and "queer" era, may find a great deal of grist for the mill in a piece written by Larry Bush which was published in the December 7 *New York Native*. Titled "San Francisco's Nightmare: Anti-Gay Gays Take Charge," Bush gave a disturbing overview of what was going on in a place some have considered the gayest city in America.

It was long after dark when four men stole their way along a hilly San Francisco street. Their target was the home of San Francisco Supervisor Roberta Achtenberg, one of the nation's most prominent elected lesbians, and her partner, San Francisco court judge Mary Morgan. [Achtenberg had recently enraged some in the radical gay San Francisco community because of her support of policies that were deemed a little too heterosexual-friendly.]

Achtenberg and Morgan were hosting a small birthday party for their four-year-old son, and couldn't know they were about to be the target of a Ku Klux Klan like raid.

The four thugs stopped along the way, plastering sidewalks and walls with stickered messages threatening Achtenberg. When they came to the Achtenberg-Morgan household, they found a locked gate that couldn't easily be forced open. They contented themselves with vandalizing the area with more attack sheets and then fled off into the night.

It was the kind of harassment that highly public lesbians and gay men might face in the suburbs or conservative small towns, where homophobic attacks mimic the style of sheet-covered racists.

In San Francisco in 1991, however, there was a difference.

These four bullies were gay men, copying the terror tactics of racists and anti-gay bigots.

In 1991, all four were associated with San Francisco's then-active Queer Nation.

Today, Kurt Barrie, one of the thugs that night, serves as a gay liaison in the anti-gay and right-wing administration of Mayor Frank Jordan. Another thug, Jonathan Katz (not the historian) heads one of the nation's first gay studies programs at a community college.

The cowardly attack, according to reliable sources, was planned in the office of Supervisor Harry Britt, the man appointed to fill Harvey Milk's seat after Milk's assassination by a former colleague and former cop. Barrie was a Britt staffer and Katz a volunteer.

As San Francisco entered the 1990s, the old adage that eventually the political left will meet up with the political right has become a case study of gay politics.

Today's most prominent gay man is a political consultant who helped to elect Mayor Frank Jordan, the former police chief. Among the gay consultant's tactics: a brochure bragging that Jordan would "stand up to special—*all* special interests," accompanied by a photograph of a gay demonstration. The emphasis on "all" is in the original.

While Bush parses San Francisco's political and economic interests with a keen eye for the negative impact that the city's real estate developers had on "progressive" politics, the way he describes gay politicos joining forces with a kind of right-wing urban re-trenchment there reminds one of the unholy alliance of the AIDS establishment with New York's "queer" AIDS activists in New York who also posed as angry "progressives."

Bush argues, "Two forces combined in San Francisco to open the door for Jordan [the right-wingish mayor] and his anti-gay antics. One force consists of the long-entrenched political interests whose silent hand guides many City Hall administrations: the police, fire and construction trade unions, realtors and developers, and the minority of Republicans who remain in America's big cities. By themselves, they cannot win elections, but they remain a strong force against change no matter who holds City Hall. The second force that played a role in Jordan's takeover was a cadre of highly vocal self-proclaimed Queer and AIDS activists who had arrived in the city only a short time before and who sought control by any means necessary."

Bush pointed out, "Those means included the terror tactics practiced against Achtenberg, character assassination of other gay leaders, the open infiltration of gay political clubs by homophobic non-gay squads, the creation of phony front groups pretending to be

310

established gay organization, and finally, forming an open alliance with some of the most homophobic groups remaining in the city. During these years, self-proclaimed gay leaders began a war against other minorities, claiming that to include their concerns in reforms such as family policy was an attempt to 'straight wash' the political agenda. It was a far remove from the politics of Harvey Milk, who preached coalition building and justice for all, not just a few. . . . In these times . . . San Francisco may well be a warning of what can happen when the gay community itself becomes victimized by those who claim to speak for it."

One thing that will be debated for a long time to come is the impact that the *Native*'s determined and uncompromising coverage of the epidemic had on the players and events of the epidemic. In a way one could say that in the small tight-knit world of powerful AIDS researchers and the even smaller world of not-so-powerful CFS researchers, the *Native* became a chip on the scientists' shoulders. Neenyah Ostrom and I had a running joke about "blowback" which was our way of describing the uncanny feeling we had sometimes that we were covering stories that really had only been generated by a spiteful and contemptuous response to something we had published or some editorial stand (usually CFS = AIDS) that we had taken, often with a blazing headline on the front page of our newspaper. Ostrom covered one of those zany "blowback" moments in the December 14 issue: "On Thanksgiving Eve, November 25, the *MacNeill/Lehrer Newshour* on the Public Broadcasting (PBS), aired a focus segment on chronic fatigue syndrome (CFS) titled, 'Too Tired.' In the midst of what was generally a well-informed and sympathetic look at the problems encountered, one of the better-known CFS researchers (at Boston's Brigham and Women's Hospital), asserted, apparently out of the blue and contradicting a large body of research, 'There is no connection between AIDS and the illness.' "

As 1992 drew to a close, the ladies still protested too much.

1993: The AIDS Thought Police

In the February 8 issue, I wrote an editorial about Nat Hentoff's recent attack on a leading black filmmaker:

> Nat Hentoff is one of the best defenders of the Constitution writing today. That's the good news.
>
> The bad news is that, in [a January 22, 1993] *Village Voice* column, he attacked Spike Lee for his "AIDS" conspiracy theory. . . . One of the trendiest ways to question another person's sanity and credibility these days is to suggest that he or she is a conspiracy theorist.
>
> According to Hentoff, Spike Lee said, "AIDS is a government-engineered disease."
>
> We think Spike Lee is probably wrong about this, but we think he is entitled to say whatever he wants to say.
>
> While it is clear that there is major lying going on in the "AIDS" epidemic, we think that the theory that "AIDS" is caused by a carefully engineered virus that could only affect certain groups is disproven by the rather clear evidence that "AIDS" and chronic fatigue syndrome are the same basic disease. When white heterosexuals get "AIDS," it is called chronic fatigue syndrome. They are not stigmatized or criminalized like non-whites (or gays) who, when they get chronic fatigue syndrome are told they have "AIDS," are a danger to society, and should take AZT.
>
> There are many people who wish we would stop saying this. So we are very sensitive to the issue of free speech and the epidemic.
>
> Hentoff writes, "To many young blacks, and not a few whites, Lee, especially since his film on Malcolm X, has become a teacher. But when he teaches that some evil government scientists created AIDS, he is hooking [sic] youngsters—and others—into seeing the world through a grotesquely distorted lens. One fake conspiracy theory leads to another. Plumbing the unreal becomes an addiction [sic]."
>
> "Hooking youngsters?" This word choice is both a

little revealing and very disturbing. And I think one would have to be morally obtuse not to notice the distinctly racist overtones. In case you didn't get the notion that Mr. Hentoff is linking Spike Lee to the world of drug pushing, albeit with a literary sleight-of-hand, he adds the bit about addiction.

If Mr. Lee is "hooking," it seems to us that Mr. Hentoff is "lynching."

Spike Lee is entitled to his opinions and ideas about "AIDS." In fact, in the long run, they may turn out to be politically closer to the mark than Mr. Hentoff's government-approved opinions about the epidemic.

Mr. Hentoff would have us all trust what the government is telling us about the epidemic. From what the *Native* has reported over the last several years, it is clear that what the government is telling the public about the epidemic is a tissue of lies. To believe the government is to collaborate with the liars. Not to believe the government is the first step of true resistance to one of the greatest evil cover-ups of this century.

Hentoff writes supportively of Jason De Parle's *New York Times* article, in which he said that conspiracy theories about "AIDS" can "pose practical impediments, particularly for public health workers trying to stop the spread of AIDS. Such workers say many blacks view them suspiciously, and have disregarded their recommendations, including the admonition to use condoms, as being part of a genocidal plot."

While no one can really argue that condoms aren't a sane protective measure in an era of venereal diseases. . . . It really trivializes the kind of charge that Spike Lee is making by connecting it to condoms. Lee is suggesting that a huge, biologically-engineered crime has been committed. It would be the kind of crime that Nuremberg-type trials would be needed to punish. If a sufficient number of black people believe this, there should be a high-level, independent investigation of the charges. Anyone who knows the history of the

313

Tuskegee syphilis experiment has to be sensitive to charges like this.

Essentially, Mr. Lee has committed an "AIDS" thought crime. It is truly ironic that Hentoff is now setting himself up to be the politically correct commissar of "AIDS" speech. Mr. Lee is endangering the world because people who believe him don't wear condoms. Mr. Hentoff implies that he is a murderer, a pusher. . . . Mr. Lee is not only thrown in the brig with drug pushers. Hentoff also [seems to put him in the same category as] Steve Cokely, a Chicago "activist" who is a bona fide anti-Semite who has concocted a nasty, scapegoating line about Jewish doctors infecting black babies with the "AIDS" virus. There is to be no distinguishing between Mr. Lee, who appears to have suggested that government scientists have created "AIDS," and the views of Mr. Cokely. But then, if Mr. Lee is out there "hooking kids" into this "addiction" of conspiracy theories, why not compare him to every devil on earth?"

Mr. Hentoff feels that Spike Lee needs to be talked to. Mr. Hentoff writes: "So who should speak to Spike Lee, et al.? Some years ago when Louis Farrakhan first began to preach his Jewish conspiracy theories to a national audience, a number of Jewish leaders urgently asked black leaders to publicly chastise Farrakhan for his anti-Semitism. Many black leaders answered that they did not consider it necessary to keep on reaffirming their own lack of anti-Semitism every time somebody black said something that exacerbated Jews."

Again, we have to point out that Mr. Lee attacked the government, not Jewish scientists. And Mr. Lee is not the ringleader of some organized "et al." Why does he have to be educated the way anti-Semites have to be educated? Since he is "hooking" people [and causing] an "addiction" to conspiracy theories, perhaps he needs to be put into some kind of intellectual rehab— perhaps a little Pol Pot type of program.

Would Mr. Hentoff like Mr. Lee to be spoken to by

the 100 scientists who have challenged what the government has told the public about the "AIDS" epidemic, i.e. that it is caused by HIV? These scientists, too, have been told that they are a public health threat to condom-wearing.

Should Mr. Lee be lectured to by John Lauritsen, the *Native* journalist who has made the case that AZT is genocide? Does Mr. Hentoff know how many blacks—including pregnant women and children—are being given AZT?

Maybe Mr. Lee should be forced to wear little red ribbons all over his body. Maybe he should be forced to do an "AIDS" commercial with Madonna and Whoopi and Magic. Maybe he should do some promotion for Burroughs Wellcome so that more people will take their "early intervention" treatment, AZT.

Mr. Hentoff continues: "So again, who's going to publicly speak the truth to Spike Lee? If the conspiracy theory to which he has now lent his name is not going to keep on spreading [sic], light has to be put on it. Bill Cosby once seemed to have some rather inchoate sympathy with the concept that AIDS has been deliberately created, but if he has recovered [sic] from that illusion, he could be an effective teacher—through debate and through television and videos in the schools—about the actual nature of AIDS. Other black figures, respected by blacks, could come forward from the academy, from films, from music, from sports, from the law. They would be of great help in ridding minds, young and old, black and white, of those malignant [sic] conspiracy tales."

So Mr. Lee's ideas are "spreading" and they are "malignant." Eureka! We're talking about cancer, right? Mr. Hentoff may want to consult Susan Sontag on this one. Robert J. Lifton points out in his book, *The Nazi Doctors*, that 'Susan Sontag has written that 'the concept of disease is never innocent,' and that 'to describe a phenomenon as a cancer is an incitement to violence.' " So, in one column, Mr. Lee has been linked to drug

315

pushing and cancer. He is truly a biomedical monster. This looks like a job for AZT.

Mr. Hentoff continues: "But what's really the harm of it all? As Jason De Parle noted, if someone who might need counseling about AIDS believes it's all a government plot, he or she may well walk away. This kind of conspiracy talk can shorten lives."

Actually, "this kind conspiracy talk"—the Lee variety—could be saving lives, if, in fact, it keeps people from taking AZT, the wonderful "AIDS" treatment that scientists like Peter Duesberg have identified as a potential cause of "AIDS."

Mr. Hentoff had really better do a little reading before he starts lecturing Mr. Lee. He might start by reading *Poison by Prescription: The AZT Story* by John Lauritsen. Then I suggest that he start reading all of the articles and scientific literature that have challenged what the government has told the public about HIV.

In the same issue, Neenyah Ostrom reported on a new development in the political effort of AZT dissidents: "Project A.I.D.S. International in making a major presentation to the United Nations' Committee on Human Rights during its February 1 to March 10, 1993, meeting in Geneva, Switzerland. According to Mark Alampi of Project A.I.D.S. International, the presentation includes two years' worth of studies and research, much of which provides 'less than favorable' information about AZT use. . . . The UN presentation will concentrate on the effects of AZT on infants who are 'assumed or presumed,' according to the U.S. Centers for Disease Control's protocol for AZT Administration, to be HIV-positive because they are born to HIV-positive women. Alampi asserts that studies demonstrate that infant mortality is much higher among infants who are given AZT."

Ostrom reported, "The recent announcement by the U.S. CDC that cases of AIDS that have no identifiable HIV exist forms the basis for Project A.I.D.S. International's argument that HIV is not necessary for the development of AIDS. A press release issued by the group January 25 states that, because of the identification of the current HIV-negative AIDS cases, 'the current HIV-equals-AIDS hypothesis is dogmatic and is, itself, life-threatening by precluding research into other potentially viable areas of both the cause and appropriate treatment(s) of the condition termed AIDS.'"

Ostrom noted, "Alampi is extremely optimistic about the outcome of the group's presentation to the UN Commission on Human Rights. At the very least, he says, scientists worldwide will be alerted to the possible dangers of embracing the HIV hypothesis to the exclusion of all others, as well as the toxicity of AZT. The use of AZT will be called into question not only by infant mortality data but also by challenging the HIV hypothesis: If AZT attacks HIV but HIV is not the cause of AIDS, then 'It's like treating a heroin habit with methadone when no heroin habit exists,' Alampi says."

In the same issue, we published another installment of Larry Bush's take on the bizarre "gay" politics in San Francisco, titled "Formula for Defeat: San Francisco's Queer Sanctuary." Bush's article began, "San Francisco should have lavender billboards on highways leading into the city declaring Baghdad-by-the-Bay to be a 'Queer Sanctuary,' Kurt Barrie, then an aide to former gay Supervisor Harry Britt, told the press in February 1991. The billboard proposal would be one way to implement a new resolution urged by the city's Queer Nation chapter, now defunct, formally declaring the city to be a Queer Sanctuary. Unremarkably, the idea drew immediate fire from the Chamber of Commerce and others, who saw the proposal as yet another example of a San Francisco City Hall less concerned with running the city then in making national and foreign policy statements. In reality, however, the effect of the proposed Queer Sanctuary resolution would have been to overturn the existing strong protections provided lesbians and gay refugees in the city of San Francisco, and to undo the protections for those with AIDS."

Bush noted, "there were some who believed that the entire intent of the so-called Queer Sanctuary measure was to drive a wedge between 'gays' and 'queers'—and to more particularly use a phony issue in the effort to discredit pro-gay elected leaders, which ultimately led to the present anti-gay regime that now controls San Francisco politics. Barrie himself, the Queer Nation activist who proposed the lavender billboards, now is an aide to Mayor Frank Jordan—who campaigned that he would veto future 'sanctuary' resolutions. The entire episode involving 'Queer Sanctuary' is a case study in how seemingly pro-gay rhetoric can be used by some outspoken individuals in ways that would both deprive lesbians and gays of hard-won rights already in place, and also divide the lesbian and gay community with only opponents of gay rights benefitting. A telling fact, for example, is that the so-called Queer Sanctuary resolution, allegedly intended to protect foreign lesbians and gay men residing in San Francisco from the anti-gay provisions of U.S. immigration law, was introduced three months after the anti-gay law was repealed by Congress and two months after then President Bush had signed the repeal."

The fifth column nature of what the Queer activists were doing in San Francisco was underlined by the fact that, according to Bush, "The Queer Sanctuary proponents deliberately omitted the protections for people with HIV or AIDS who are still banned under U.S. law. By omitting such people, the effect would have been to withdraw entirely, the existing protections the city offered."

Across America—or at least in the big cities—gays didn't have a clue about what "Queer" activists were doing in the name of the gay community.

In the February 22 issue, we ran a piece that failed to open the etiological can of worms that it should have. Neenyah Ostrom reported, "A new, experimental treatment for 'AIDS,' which consists of porcine (pig-derived) hyperimmune immunoglobulin (i.e. anti-bodies), yielded astonishing results in a Phase I safety trial published in December 1992. The treatment, called 'PASSHIV-1,' is manufactured in a Hopkinton, Massachusetts firm, Verigen Inc., and was tested in a Phase I safety trial. All—100 percent—of the patients who participated in the trial showed significant improvement in clinical symptoms, including: fatigue, fever, weight loss, polyneuropathy (pain), bronchitis, candidiasis (oral and vaginal yeast infections), diarrhea, and dermatitis (rash). Additionally, a transient improvement in one patient's Kaposi's sarcoma (KS) was observed."

Ostrom noted, "PASSHIV-1 is the second pig-derived treatment that appears to be promising in treating immune system disorders such as 'AIDS' and chronic fatigue syndrome. The first such treatment tested was Kutapressin, an extract of pig liver. Originally used to control inflammatory reactions, Kutapressin (which is a byproduct of the production of vitamin B-12) has been found to interact with immune system compounds called cytokines, some of which are produced in increased amounts in both 'AIDS' and chronic fatigue syndrome."

In an editorial, in the same issue, I wrote, "The good news this week is that pigs, the animals that the *Native* has linked to the 'AIDS' epidemic over and over, may be the key to a dramatic new treatment. If there are any open-minded 'AIDS' activists out there who are not on the government's or the pharmaceutical industry's payrolls, we hope they will push to have this new treatment explored as thoroughly and as quickly as possible. And we'd like some help from the rest of the press in determining if this new development lends credibility to the idea that African swine fever virus is the cause of 'AIDS' and CFS. Were the pigs that were inoculated for the creation of hyperimmune immunoglobulin only given HIV? Is it possible that the cells that were used for the lysate the pigs were given were also infected with HHV-6, the virus which John Beldekas suspects is actually African swine fever virus? Remember, Gallo told Laurie Garrett [in the February 2, 1992 issue of *Newsday*], "It seems wherever HHV-6 is going, you're bound to bump into HIV." And here's one more thought, an unthinkable one. If Jane Teas had been listened to ten years ago, would everyone who has died of 'AIDS' in the last ten years still be alive?"

Unfortunately, once again I was engaged in wishful thinking. No minds would be opened up in the AIDS establishment by a promising pig-derived treatment for AIDS. Pigs continued to be the skunks at the HIV picnic.

In the same issue, I celebrated a milestone and bemoaned another betrayal (which was also a self-betrayal) in the CFS community: "Ostrom is celebrating her fifth anniversary of covering the CFS story this week. We nominated her for a Pulitzer Prize for the third time this year, which we assume she will not get because the national media still has not addressed the connection between 'AIDS' and chronic fatigue syndrome. This is a Pandora's Box that everyone is afraid of. Even the director of the Chronic Fatigue Syndrome Association in Charlotte, Marc Iverson, does not want the public to see the link between 'AIDS' and chronic fatigue syndrome. His organization wants the government to take CFS seriously, but not *that* seriously. Iverson has had a hard time raising money, and while he thinks it is a major achievement, the two million dollars that his organization has raised for research is petty cash. All he would have to do is to hold a press conference with several members of Congress, and call for a full investigation into the possibility that chronic fatigue syndrome is actually a form of 'AIDS,' and blank checks would be thrown his way. . . . But 'AIDS' has been so stigmatized that he [now] desperately wants to keep a wide bio-medical divide between the two syndromes. I think the evidence shows all too clearly that in reality there is no divide between those

319

syndromes. Iverson also thinks that the idea that CFS is caused by African swine fever virus (now called human herpesvirus 6) is our gay obsession. His group wants to find its own, special, not-too-much-like-AIDS retrovirus which it can claim as its cause. Iverson argues that HHV-6 . . . cannot be the cause of CFS because most people are infected with it. That's a curious idea from a logical point of view, because Iverson and his associates know all-too-well that the evidence which suggests CFS is very contagious is overwhelming. And the CFS epidemic is 15 or more years old. If HHV-6 (ASFV) is the causative agent, it would be ubiquitous by now. It would be very sad. It would be very tragic. It would be very unbelievable. It would be as widespread as a pathogen in an apocalyptic sci-fi novel."

In the March 8 issue, I reported on "a disturbing but revealing story making the rounds on the West Coast. Apparently, a gay man tried an experiment. He went to one clinic and identified himself as a gay man and took an HIV test. The test was positive. Then he went to another clinic and identified himself as a heterosexual and took an HIV test. The test was negative. . . . A few years ago, we published a story about the experience of a gay man in New York who went to have his blood tested for HIV. He was quite upset because information about his sexual orientation was sent with his blood. . . . Whenever we tell people that we think it is clear that 'AIDS' and chronic fatigue syndrome are the same disease, we are told that can't be true because CFS patients don't test positive for HIV. Well, perhaps if they told their physicians they are gay when they are tested, the result might be different."

In the March 15 issue, I wrote an editorial about Peter Duesberg's take on the HIV-negative AIDS cases that had come out of the closet at the Amsterdam AIDS conference: "Peter Duesberg, the University of California retrovirologist who has, along with dozens of scientists, challenged the notion that HIV is the cause of 'AIDS,' has told the *Native* that he believes that the government scientists who have called HIV-negative 'AIDS' cases 'ICL cases' are conducting a cover-up. Duesberg argues that these cases are the strongest challenge to the HIV hypothesis. . . . Peter Duesberg told the *Native* that he does not like to use the word 'conspiracy,' but that the attempts to cover up, cases of HIV-negative 'AIDS' by giving them a name like 'idiopathic CD4-positive T-lymphocytopenia' could be considered a euphemistic 'conspiracy' to keep the public from knowing the truth."

In the March 22 *New York Native*, in an editorial titled "AIDS and the Flameless Book Burning at *Publishers Weekly*," I took on the issue of censorship which was a very supportive pillar of the totalitarian culture of the epidemic.

In the March 1993 issue of *The Washington Monthly*, Leslie Kaufman described what can happen to someone who challenges the conventional wisdom (of the moment) about 'AIDS.' She describes the plight of Michael Fumento, the author of *The Myth of Heterosexual AIDS*, which was published in 1990. Fumento, whose ideas, I think, are fundamentally wrong, ran afoul of the "AIDS" thought police when he tried to argue that "AIDS," apart from certain risk behaviors, was not becoming a heterosexual S.T.D.

Kaufman, incorrectly, suggests that Fumento is "perhaps the most politically incorrect AIDS writer in America." I'll name *my* nominee later in this column. Kaufman portrays Fumento as a modern-day Galileo who has suffered serious career setbacks because of his beliefs. Anyone who is concerned about free speech, and the open exchange of ideas about "AIDS," should be appalled at Fumento's fate.

According to Kaufman, "Soon after *Newsday* published a book review by Michael Fumento, the newspaper's book editor, Jack Schwartz, began receiving anonymous phone calls late at night. Nasty calls. 'They made a lot of threats,' Schwartz recalls, 'not the least of which was death.' " Kaufman writes that, "Even before Fumento published his book, he had become the target of AIDS activists. They have repeatedly attempted to silence him, often by resorting to violent intimidation, demanding that they refuse the book."

Fumento made appearances on three national television talk shows, which should have guaranteed the book sales of 20,000 to 50,000. But the book sold only 12,000. Kaufman reports that Fumento and his editor "believe it was sabotaged from the top of the line on down. The huge Waldenbooks chain didn't order any copies of *Myth*. Mike Ferrari, Walden's buyer, is reputed to have told representatives selling the book that he didn't want it for political reasons. (Fumento concedes that Waldenbooks did eventually place an order for the book—but only after he singled them out during an appearance on C-SPAN."

According to Kaufman, Fumento's book is impossible to find today. It was never brought out in paperback, and his publisher allowed it to go out of print even when there continued to be a demand for it. A representative who sells for Fumento's publisher told Kaufman, "Look, it was going against everything we know about AIDS, against anything anybody who was reputable was telling us. Why buy a book like that?"

In other words, the publishing and bookselling community only wants "AIDS" books which tell them what they already know. They're happy with the paradigm and the conventional wisdom as it is.

In other words, Fumento was screwed.

It is interesting to note that this publishing story was told in *The Washington Monthly*, not in *Publishers Weekly*, which in addition to being a book trade publication tries to be the conscience of the publishing industry. I don't know what kind of review Fumento got from *PW*, but I assume they reviewed his book.

What is of ongoing concern to me, however, is that *PW* generally gives good reviews to books that promote the government's lies about the epidemic.

Last year when we published Neenyah Ostrom's book, *50 Things You Should Know About the Chronic Fatigue Syndrome Epidemic*, I sent PW galleys of the book in plenty of time for a review to appear. As readers of this publication know, Ostrom has uncovered many links between "AIDS" and chronic fatigue syndrome epidemics, links that even independent Michael Fumento would not want to hear about. When it became clear that *PW* was not going to review the book, I wrote an angry letter and sent it to every person on the *PW* masthead. I accused *PW* of "AIDS" political correctness, and of suppressing dissenting opinions about "AIDS." I didn't expect any reaction, but was pleasantly surprised when they reversed themselves and did publish a late review. Of course, the review was mixed and attacked the central thesis of the book, which is the connection between "AIDS" and chronic fatigue syndrome. The review was a polite fuck-you.

For readers who wonder why *PW* matters: It is an important part of the publishing process to get a review in *PW*. A good review can guarantee significant orders from stores.

I also had to deal with the buyer from Waldenbooks. He refused to stock the book, but said he would put it in their computers in case anyone should ask for it. Thanks a lot. I sensed there was more than commercial judgment at work when Waldenbooks refused to order the book, so I am very sympathetic to Fumento and his publisher. Anyone who tries to tell me that a book which links chronic fatigue syndrome to "AIDS" does not deserve national exposure and a vigorous national debate is, in my judgment, a total fool.

I have no trouble believing that gay bookstores would try to create a bookstore boycott of Fumento's book. I've been in publishing for 18 years, and while there are many open-minded people working in gay bookstores, I've seen my fill of Stalinist Cultural Czars who think they can shape the gay *zeitgeist* by what they allow on the shelves. (Oldest trick in the world: Hide the fact that you're really not stocking a book by keeping one copy buried on the shelf at all times.) And, from my experience, the "AIDS" activist thought police seem to be drawn to working in gay bookstores like bees are drawn to honey.

Which brings us to the newest opportunity for censorship by the "AIDS" thought police. This week, The Free Press is publishing *Rethinking AIDS* by

Robert Root-Bernstein. Root-Bernstein is an associate professor of physiology at Michigan State University. He is also the recipient of a MacArthur Foundation fellowship, otherwise known as the "genius grant." Root-Bernstein is also the recipient of a political cold shoulder from *Publishers Weekly*.

Yes, *Publishers Weekly* has struck again. A major book is published questioning the conventional wisdom about "AIDS." It costs $27.95. It is 512 pages long. It has a hundred pages of footnotes. This is what is known in publishing as a serious publishing event.

I called the editor in charge of non-fiction reviews at *PW*, Genevieve Stuttaford, and she told me to call an assistant, who checked their log; indeed, the galleys had been received in time for a review, but a decision was made somewhere in the Bermuda Triangle where decisions are made at *PW* not to review the book. Could I get an answer as to why? No. Sorry, PW can't review all the books it receives. I called the editor of *PW*, Nora Rowlinson, who politely returned my phone call and at least seemed sensitive to the complaint that the reviews of "AIDS" books that appear in *PW* bespeak a political agenda. I'm not saying that she agreed with me. She just basically thanked me for sharing and said she always likes to have her thinking challenged. She offered some hope that Root-Bernstein's book, which may soon be discussed on a national TV news show, could be reported in their news section.

I think that anyone who knows publishing knows that there is no excuse for not reviewing Root-Bernstein's book. It is a big book. It tackles a hot topic and, frankly, its level of controversy is reflected, I think, in the fact that *PW* wouldn't touch it.

PW loves to review books that capture the poignancy of gay men dying of "AIDS" and reconsidering their lives, and being red-ribbon brave in the face of the Grim Reaper. They love "AIDS" books that reinforce the tissue of HIV lies that the government is telling the public about "AIDS." If you don't believe me, go to the library and look at all of their "AIDS" book reviews. "AIDS" political correctness has had a virtual orgy at the *PW* offices. Just about everything I've read in *PW* on "AIDS" smells like AZT.

I think *PW* should change its name to PC. When the real history of the epidemic is written (and not reviewed in *PW*), all the editorial decision makers should be held accountable for keeping the public in the dark about the real epidemic.

Now for a couple of clarifications. Who is more politically incorrect than Michael Fumento? Well, Neenyah Ostrom, of course. No major talk show will touch the topic of the connection between "AIDS" and chronic fatigue syndrome.

I think that both Fumento and Root-Bernstein are in serious denial. They cannot allow themselves to see that "AIDS" and chronic fatigue syndrome are the same disease, and that heterosexuals are suffering the same kinds of immune dysfunction as "AIDS" patients, and calling it chronic fatigue syndrome. . . . But even though I totally disagree with both Fumento and Root-Bernstein . . . I still think we have to fight to make sure that they can speak freely and get their books into the stores. There but for the grace of God goes You-Know-Who."

In the March 29 issue, Neenyah Ostrom wrote about the emerging data that suggested that there were two forms of HHV-6 (HHV-6A and HHV-6B) and that they behave differently. She wrote, "A paradox has confronted researchers studying human herpesvirus-6 (HHV-6). Although the virus appears, at this time, to infect more than 90 percent of the human population worldwide, it is a chillingly efficient killer of immune system (and other) cells in the laboratory. If the laboratory results are not artificial, how can humans harbor such a lethal virus and remain healthy?"

Ostrom reported, "A newly published study of HHV-6 infection of infants—which shows that 97 percent are infected with a different form of the virus than the one infecting immune compromised adults—may provide the key to understanding the seeming paradox."

Ostrom noted, "A group of researchers at the University of Rochester Medical Center studied 76 infants less than two years old who were brought to their emergency room with an acute fever and found to be infected with HHV-6. They found that they were able to isolate the 'B' variant of HHV-6 from 73 of 75 infants tested—97 percent. The 'A' variant of HHV-6—the one found in sick adults—was isolated from only one infant." Ostrom also reported, "these researchers suspect that HHV-6's variant A makes adults a whole lot sicker than variant B makes babies."

Ostrom explained the reasons for the confusion about HHV-6: "A review of the HHV-6 literature reveals that scientists at the National Institutes of Health (including those in the National Cancer Institute laboratory of Dr. Robert Gallo, where HHV-6 was first isolated) have been studying the strain classified as variant A; researchers at the Centers for Disease Control have been studying a strain classified as variant B. Therefore, one source of disagreement over what the virus is capable of doing to humans is that the two major U.S. health agencies *have been studying different variants that appear to cause very different illnesses.*"

Most importantly, in terms of the possibility that HHV-6 was a form of ASFV, and would therefore be acting in the bizarre—even paradoxical—way that ASFV does when it infects pigs (in terms of constantly changing and causing new and very different kinds of epidemics) was the fact that according to Ostrom's piece, "Numerous strains of HHV-6 (besides the CDC and NIH 'index strains') have now been isolated, and seem to have somewhat different disease-causing capabilities."

Ostrom also reported that the scientific studies stated, "Not only do the different strains of HHV-6 seem capable of infecting different types of cells, the type of cell any one strain [is able to] infect can change *after it has been grown in tissue culture for a length of time.*" HHV-6 was certainly doing a wonderful impression of the very versatile African swine fever virus in the lab.

It looked like the spectrum of problems that variable HHV-6 could cause might be incredibly diverse. The real epidemic that this virus caused—behind the HIV and "CFS is not AIDS" smokescreen—was almost too broad, deep, and mercurial for the human mind to grasp.

In the same issue, I wrote a brief piece about a man who was trapped in the interstices of the epidemic: "A couple of weeks ago, *Day One*, the new ABC news magazine hosted by Forest Sawyer, did a story about Roberto Gonzales, the man who is accused of knowingly infecting women with HIV. Putting aside the issue of HIV not being the cause of 'AIDS' for a moment, I want to focus on the rage of the mother of one of the women who supposedly was infected. She wanted to kill Gonzales. She actually went to his apartment with a gun. As I watched her, I thought, what are people like her going to do when they learn that the Centers for Disease Control, the National Institutes of Health, and even a whole array of activist organizations have been promulgating one of the biggest lies ever told in American history?"

The bold headline on our April 12 issue was "Even Gallo may have to admit that HHV-6 is the Cause of 'AIDS' and Chronic Fatigue Syndrome." Inside, Neenyah Ostrom wrote that, "For several years, this newspaper has argued that the evidence that human herpesvirus 6 and not HIV, is the cause of 'AIDS' and chronic fatigue syndrome is overwhelming. Robert C. Gallo, the man who stole credit for discovering HIV, 'the virus that causes AIDS'—which has become the 'AIDS' establishment manta—has continued to insist that the stolen virus is the cause of 'AIDS.' Last week, without fully admitting it, he may have begun to eat his own words. Startling new evidence that HHV-6 helps to cause the immune deficiencies seen in both 'AIDS' and chronic fatigue syndrome has just been published by Gallo and colleagues in an April 1 letter to the British medical journal *Nature*. Gallo and co-workers report that HHV-6 not only infects and kills natural killer (NK) cells—which are the immune system's frontline defense against viruses and some cancers—but also that it is the *only virus known to do so*."

Ostrom noted, "Gallo and co-workers not only establish that HHV-6 can infect and kill NK cells, but they also acknowledge that an NK cell functional deficiency is seen in both 'AIDS' and CFS. Furthermore, they suggest that HHV-6 may contribute to the immune deficiencies seen in both syndromes. 'Contribute to' may be an understatement. Gallo and his associates are probably afraid to admit it, but some other implications that arise from their assertion that HHV-6 causes the initial damage in the immune system in both 'AIDS' and CFS are: 1) That CFS and 'AIDS' are characterized by the same immunodeficiency—loss of NK cell function—and are therefore related, if not identical, diseases; 2) that HHV-6, not HIV, should probably be known as the 'AIDS virus'; and 3) that HIV should be considered to be one of the 'opportunistic infections that HHV-6

327

paves the way for."

In the same issue, Ostrom reported on a study which indicated that "early intervention" with AZT was useless; "A long term study of the effects of AZT in treating more than 1700 HIV-positive, symptom-free individuals in Europe has shown that such treatment neither delays progression to 'AIDS' nor extends life, according to a preliminary analysis published in the April 3 issue of the British medical journal *The Lancet*. Additionally, the study casts doubt on the usefulness of CD4 (T4) cell counts as predictors of disease progression. Despite the European findings, U.S. government health officials have not changed their recommendation that people in 'high risk' groups should be tested for HIV antibodies and treated almost immediately with a toxic, ineffective, but very expensive, drug." With AZT it seemed like the fix was always in.

In the same issue, I penned an editorial about what seemed to be a rare moment of critical thinking about the epidemic in the mainstream media:

> Something on the order of 20 million people saw the ABC *Day One* program titled "State of Emergency." Forest Sawyer began the program by saying, "Tonight we begin an argument that has deadly consequences—how to fight what could be the most serious health threat facing the world today. Nine years ago, the cause of AIDS was identified as a virus known as HIV, the human immunodeficiency virus, and since then we've been living in a medical state of emergency with the disease rapidly spreading around the world and billions of dollars spent to stop it. But now some scientists are saying all that time and money may have been wasted, that HIV alone may not be the cause of AIDS, and that's the argument. "What is the real cause of AIDS? At stake are the lives of millions of people."
>
> Correspondent John Hockenbery then proceeded to interview Anthony Fauci, Luc Montagnier, Nobel Prize winner Walter Gilbert, Joseph Sonnabend, Robert Root-Bernstein, Peter Duesberg, Larry Kramer, and Shyh-Ching Lo.
>
> I think viewers were left with the distinct impression that something scandalous is going on in

'AIDS' research. Root-Bernstein, the author of *Re-thinking AIDS*, and Duesberg made it clear that there is little or no funding being made available for research into alternative hypotheses about "AIDS." Root-Bernstein, who does not believe that HIV is necessarily the cause or the sole cause of "AIDS," told Hockenbery, "I've had people tell me bluntly that, "I agree totally with your viewpoint that there are probably other things involved, that HIV can't cause AIDS by itself, that maybe you can get AIDS in the absence of HIV, but I'm not going to risk my million dollars of funding by saying that."

The man who did lose his million dollars of funding for saying that, University of California retrovirologist Peter Duesberg, provided the show with its most dramatic moment. Hockenbery asked Duesberg, "If I were to dump HIV virus in your cup there and you were to drink it, are you saying that there's no . . ."— to which Duesberg replied, "No problem. To your health." He then sipped from the cup, and said, "There would be no risk. I would drink it all afternoon."

Hockenbery said to Luc Montagnier, the scientist who discovered HIV, "It seems as though, in the United States, especially, that the bet is on HIV." Montagnier replied, "The bet is everywhere, not only in the United States. In Europe, we have the same problem, but I think people should really think and perhaps try to have new concepts. I mean, we have to be very creative on AIDS, because AIDS is a very complex disease."

Harvard Nobel Prize winning molecular biologist Walter Gilbert told Hockenbery, "The major thing that concerns me, like calling HIV the cause of AIDS, is that we do not have a proof of causation. That's our major reason for being concerned." Gilbert also said the problem with the HIV theory is the argument that "all cases of AIDS are associated with the virus and there is an inference made that all people with the virus will ultimately come down with AIDS. That's of course, not known to be a fact."

Dr. Joseph Sonnabend chimed in: "The harm in the whole notion of the speculation being presented as fact is that if the speculation proved to be true, that means that research on whatever is truly going on has been neglected and this, of course, with a disease like AIDS, can be translated into the loss of tens of thousands of lives."

Tony Fauci, the government's scientific "general" in the fight against "AIDS," came across as the quintessential little jerk that we've all come to know and love. When he was confronted with the fact that Larry Kramer has supposedly been HIV-positive since 1978, Fauci said to Hockenbery, "My answer to Larry, as I've told him personally, is that there is a long process that it takes for the immune system to go down, and people are very, very different. Some people have a response to the virus that they get sick. Some people take a longer period of time."

Maybe if Kramer had taken AZT, he wouldn't be such a theoretical embarrassment to Fauci. One almost detected a note of disappointment (amid the condescension) in Fauci's voice that Kramer is still alive.

The Maria Callas Moment in *Day One* came when Robert Gallo stormed out of the ABC interview. Before he got up and walked away from the woman who was questioning him, he said, "Duesberg does his thing—that's a disservice to the country, what you're doing. This I will fight, and I will expose. And I'll call it a deception of the worst order, and you'll be doing a disservice to the country. Yeah. So that's—I don't want to talk to you anymore."

And with that Gallo was gone.

When the truth is finally told, Fauci and Gallo should spend the rest of their lives in jail. In a cell together. They deserve each other.

In the meantime, it wouldn't hurt if people called up *Day One* at ABC and praised the work of producers Paul Slavin and Nicholas Regush. Hopefully, *Day One* will stay on this story until all the facts are on the table.

If one felt that the separation of AIDS and CFS into two separate fields of research was a big mistake, a piece on "The Asthma-CFS Connection" by Neenyah Ostrom in the April 19 issue was of great interest. Ostrom reported, "Asthma has been linked to both 'AIDS' and chronic fatigue syndrome (CFS) both anecdotally and in published reports. One study of CFS in children found that 50 percent had asthma that worsened after the onset of CFS."

Ostrom noted, "Severe inflammatory processes, like those seen in asthma and certain kinds of allergies (as well as in 'AIDS' and CFS), are generally stimulated by an overproduction of histamine. Histamine, in fact, is found at its highest levels in the lungs, the sign of asthma's damage. Overproduction of histamine may be a trigger of numerous symptoms in both 'AIDS' and CFS. In addition to regulating inflammation (as well as the release of acid), histamine is believed to have another action: the suppression of immune functioning. Two anti-ulcer drugs that block histamine's actions have been found to have a second, antihistamine action: They stimulate natural killer (NK) cell activity, thereby boosting immune functioning. In other words: Too much histamine can result in an inflammatory response (such as asthma or allergies), as well as in decreased immune functioning. Drugs that block histamine not only stop inflammation, but also boost immunity by increasing NK cell activity."

Ostrom reported on a revealing bit of AIDS research that explored the effect of histamine-suppressing anti-ulcer drugs on the NK cell activity of HIV-positive men who had a severe impairment of their NK cell activity. The drugs increased the NK cell activity in a significant number of men, suggesting a new way to treat NK problems in so-called AIDS patients. But once again, the political bifurcation of AIDS and CFS would keep the CFS community from being able to take advantage of the findings in dealing with *their* NK cell issues. What was good for the gay goose was never good for the heterosexual gander.

The Tower of Babel that the CFS community was ultimately choosing to occupy, in order to avoid getting sucked into the AIDS paradigm, was reflected in a piece Neenyah Ostrom wrote in the April 26 issue, titled "Diagnostic Chaos: Half of Those Diagnosed with Lyme Disease May Really Have Chronic Fatigue Syndrome."

Ostrom reported, "Lyme Disease, a tick-borne bacterial illness once limited to a narrow ribbon along the Northeastern U.S., is now spreading throughout the country—or is it? A new report in the April 14, 1993, issue of the *Journal of the American Medical Association* (JAMA) states that many people *misdiagnosed* with Lyme disease—in this particular study, one-half of misdiagnosed people—actually have chronic fatigue syndrome (CFS)."

Ostrom asked, "Why is CFS, a putatively viral illness, being confused with Lyme disease, which is caused by a bacterium? According to Paul Lavinger, M.D. who was a practicing physician for 26 years before being disabled with CFS, the misdiagnosis is occurring not because doctors are stupid, but 'because they are blind to the possibility of diagnosing CFS as a 'real' illness. 'A positive Lyme test legitimizes the patient's disease,' Lavinger says, 'and it legitimizes a medical disgrace'—the government's neglect of CFS research. The overdiagnosis of lyme is, according to Lavinger, 'a direct result of [NIAID Director Anthony] Fauci and [NIAID CFS researcher Stephen] Straus and the CDC derogating CFS in their communications to physicians,' Lavinger argues. 'The end result is a failure of physicians to entertain CFS as a diagnostic possibility. Doctors are unable to make a diagnosis of CFS, so patients are forced to get *other* diagnoses to have any credibility.' The 'denial of the CFS epidemic by the CDC has so affected physicians that 'they will diagnose Lyme in people who don't have it before they diagnose CFS in people who do,' Lavinger maintains. And, he points out, a diagnosis of Lyme disease results in heavy-duty drug treatment with often costly antibiotics, some of which can cost as much as $1,000/week. In addition to the personal health problems developed by people who are misdiagnosed with Lyme disease and possibly treated with an expensive and unnecessary antibiotic regimen, Lavinger points out, 'the end result is contaminated research.' In other words, statistics for both Lyme disease and for CFS are terribly inaccurate if CFS cases are being counted as Lyme disease cases. And misdiagnosis can also result in inaccurate measures of the effectiveness of drug therapies as well: A person with a viral illness (such as CFS) presumably will not respond to antibiotic treatment aimed at knocking out a bacterial illness like Lyme disease; therefore, the cure rate of antibiotics used in such tests will appear to be lower than they might actually be. All of which leads to another question: Is the misdiagnosis of CFS as Lyme disease partly responsible for the government not recognizing the seriousness and scope of the CFS epidemic?"

In the May 3 issue, John Hammond reported on the remarks of Congressman Gerry Studds, on the occasion of the formal dedication of the United States Holocaust Museum: "In the decades before Adolf Hitler's rise to power, Germany was home to the modern world's first homosexual rights movement. The Nazis responded with a campaign against 'homosexual degeneracy' during the 1930s. Holocaust Museum historians estimate that 63,000 men were convicted of homosexual offenses in Nazi courts from 1933 to 1944, that as many as 12,000 were incarcerated in the concentration camps and at least 5,000 of them died there. Other historians have estimated that as many as 300,000 homosexuals were incarcerated because of their sexual orientation, while many more closeted gay people were imprisoned because they were Jews, or gypsies, or for other reasons, and never counted among the gay population of the camps. Once in the camps, known gays were often singled out for the harshest treatment, and more than half of them died. The insignia that marked gay prisoners, a pink triangle, has been adopted as a symbol by many in the modern gay rights movement. According to materials compiled by the Holocaust Memorial, gay survivors of the camps faced continued persecution even after the collapse of the Nazi regime. The Allied Miliary Government of Germany refused to release those who had been imprisoned for homosexuality and the law under which they had been arrested remained in effect until 1969."

Hammond also reported, "Studds, who joined in a Congressional tour of the museum on April 19, praised museum officials for including in the displays artifacts and materials documenting the prosecution of homosexuals, as well as other groups. 'For too long, the Nazi victimization of gay people has remained a secret little known and seldom mentioned. The opening of this memorial museum is an important step in redressing that neglect,' Studds remarked. The museum employs various techniques to personalize the tour, including issuing an 'identity card' to each visitor that tells the story of a person with a similar age and gender who lived during the Holocaust. During his visit, Studds was astonished when he was issued a computer-generated card describing the life of Willem Arondeus, a gay artist from the Netherlands who was a member of the resistance. Arondeus falsified papers for Dutch Jews, then set fire to a building that housed records against which the false papers could be checked. He was arrested by the Nazis in April 1943—exactly 50 years ago—and was executed three months later. Before his execution, Willem asked his lawyer to testify after the war that 'homosexuals are not cowards.' In 1945, he was posthumously awarded a medal by the Dutch government."

In the same issue, Neenyah Ostrom covered new research on HHV-6, in a piece titled "Is HHV-6 Interfering with Cancer Chemotherapy?" She reported, "New research suggests that HHV-6 produces a substance that blocks the action of growth factors—proteins that cause cells to mature—in the bone marrow (where most new blood cells are formed and mature), and may even interfere with the normal growth and maturation of another very important immune system cell, the macrophage. Macrophages are instrumental in initiating immune system response, because they 'present' foreign antigens to T-and B-cells; T- and B-cells are then able to recognize the invader and mount an immune response against it."

HHV-6's involvement with macrophages was yet another bit of evidence that supported the notion that it might be a human form of African swine fever virus, and Ostrom asked at the end of her piece, "If [HHV-6] looks like ASFV, infects the same cells as ASFV, and causes the same kind of tissue damage as ASFV isn't it time to determine once and for all if HHV-6 is, in fact, ASFV?"

A John Hammond piece, in the May 10 issue, perfectly captured the gestalt of the epidemic: "Organizers of the 1993 March on Washington, for Lesbian, Gay and Bi Equal Rights and Liberation obtained an internal document, a 'Flight Operations Irregularities' report from American Airlines, indicating that Flight 701 was delayed 13 minutes on the evening of April 25 so that the blankets and pillows on a plane could be replaced, at the request of the flight crew, immediately after the plane had been filled with gay marchers returning home from Washington to Dallas. The incident came just a few days after American Airlines had reminded employees that its rules forbid the wearing of red 'AIDS' awareness ribbons with company uniforms."

Given that the red ribbons had become the sacred cow of so-called AIDS activism, it is not surprising that Gregory Adams, the communications director of the Washington march, said, "I am a man who lives with and will probably die from HIV. The red ribbon campaign is not only symbolic, it is a very visible means of educating people and raising awareness of the devastating effects of the AIDS epidemic in all sectors of our society. American Airlines is being socially irresponsible by denying its employees the opportunity to help educate the millions of people with whom they have direct contact every day."

In other words, the emotional blackmail of the red ribbon wasn't confined to the ground. In the air, at 30,000 feet the thing you needed most from the crew was AIDS education.

In the May 17 issue, Neenyah Ostrom wrote about researcher Paul Cheney's testimony to the FDA on the subject of chronic fatigue syndrome: "On February 18, Dr. Paul Cheney (who, along with Dr. Dan Peterson, recognized the first outbreak of chronic fatigue syndrome in the U.S. in 1984) presented testimony before the Food and Drug Administration's Scientific Advisory Committee."

Ostrom noted, "Although Cheney once referred to CFS as 'AIDS minor,' his interpretation of what is happening to patients in the course of the disease has changed as he has observed the disease itself appear to change over time. And, although Cheney told me in a telephone interview in October 1992 that he believed CFS and 'AIDS' to be completely separate illnesses, he presents, in his FDA testimony, compelling evidence linking the two epidemics of immune dysfunction. . . . In his February 1993 FDA testimony . . . Cheney described CFS as an illness with 'AIDS-like components.' He also reported having seen CFS patients with 'AIDS defining opportunistic infections as well as reporting a number of deaths *not* caused by suicide.' "

In the May 24 issue, I covered a fascinating development in the debate about removing the ban on gays in the military:

> It was one of the most electrifying moments in the debate about the ban on gays in the military. A Marine colonel announced to a Senate panel last week that if the military ends the ban, he will tell his son to stay out of the military. And his son is gay.
>
> Associated Press reported that Colonel Fred Peck, who was a spokesman for the U.S. forces in Somalia, "described his son, Scott, as the military's ideal—a strapping 6-foot-1, blond, blue-eyed senior at the University of Maryland. But he is homosexual, the

colonel said."

Associated Press also reported that Colonel Peck told the Senators, "I love him. I love him as much as I do any of my sons, but I don't think he should serve in the military. I know what it would be like for him. It would be hell. If we went into combat . . . he'd be at great risk if he were to follow my footsteps as an infantry platoon leader or a company commander. I would be very fearful that his life would be in jeopardy from his own troops. I'm not saying that's right or wrong. I am saying that's the way it is. You get into war, the first casualty is truth, the second is the value of human life."

His son Scott, 24, was suddenly in the middle of a national media spotlight.

On Thursday, May 13, Scott Peck appeared on *Larry King Live*, during which he explained the circumstances of his coming out. He told King that his father had learned that he was gay just five days before that. His stepmother informed his father.

Peck told King, "It became clear that he was, indeed, going to be testifying. And I'm out as a gay man in the Baltimore area. I write for the University of Maryland *Student Media*, and I have a longstanding feud going with 'Queer Nation,' a leftist gay rights group. And they made it known to me that they would out me to the media if my father did indeed testify. So we were trying to beat them to the punch."

Peck said that he had been afraid to tell his father. He told King, "I was afraid of his reaction. And it turns out that I underestimated him. . . . I expected a very negative reaction. I always complained about the stereotypes people have towards gay men and lesbians, and it turns out that I had some stereotypes of my own about colonels in the Marine Corps. I expected a hard-nosed, definite 'No' to my lifestyle, my sexual orientation. Instead, he was unbelievably positive."

Peck came across as an incredibly engaging person. He made coming out look all-American, which probably upset the self-defeating arm of the gay movement that thinks we're supposed to put on some kind of diversified freak show in order to secure our civil rights.

Peck told King that he disagrees with his father's opinion about gays being admitted into the military. He said that his father is "living proof that a Marine can be 110 percent dedicated to the success of a mission and dedicated to the Marine Corps, and still have room for a large amount of tolerance toward people—diversity. I wish he could have enough faith in fellow Marines to believe that they could follow his example."

King asked him what he doesn't like about "Queer Nation." He said, "My problem with 'Queer Nation' is that they have the presumption to speak for the entire gay community, and the portrait they paint of us, I feel, are very unfair."

King asked Peck what he thought of "outing." Peck said, "I'm completely opposed to it. For some people—for many people—the closet right now may be preferable to coming out in the type of environment that groups like 'Queer Nation' have helped to create."

King seemed genuinely moved by the way that Peck presented himself. Peck came off not only as a "recruiter's dream," as his father described him, but as a political dream for the gay movement. Any parents of gays who watched it must have felt a jolt of moral support as they heard the father express his love for his gay son, and the son say that their relationship was stronger than ever. Peck told King, "I've received calls from almost everyone in the family, including people I haven't seen for years, and they're all offering their love and support."

Peck told King that he would like to pursue a career as a writer.

We have a suggestion for Scott Peck.

Since "Queer Nation" made such a big difference in his life, why not write a book about the group?

We'd be glad to supply him with the literature we've collected over the last few years. Many people haven't seen the writings that gave birth to the movement. We don't have the space to publish as much as we'd like, but here are a few choice bits:

From a Canadian "Queer Manifesto" published in a publication called *Bimbox*: "We will not tolerate any form of lesbian and gay philosophy. We will not tolerate their voluntary obsolete thought processes. We will not tolerate their voluntary assimilation into heterosexual culture. . . . We will not tolerate their trivialization of racism. We will not tolerate their warped, shallow, twisted concept of feminism. . . . Furthermore, if we see lesbians and gays being assaulted on the streets, we will not intervene, we will join in. . . . Effective immediately, [we are] at war with lesbians and gays."

From a broadside by "Three Anonymous Queers' (these outers are always anonymous) read at Vito Russo's funeral a few years ago: "But to speak of violence initiated by us, by our beloved community, is to speak of necessary violence. The acts of violence we may commit will be acts of self-defense, entirely thought through, taken on with complete responsibility and commitment."

From a broadside called "Wake Up Queers" which was handed out in New York City in June 1992: "I hate gay men. I feel more and more hopeless about our community. Turn any corner in the ghetto and you can grab sex, but you have to search high and low to find real love. I hate how narcissistic we fags are, how easily distracted from the hard tasks, how absurdly trivial in the face of death."

From an article in the *Washington Blade* on September 6, 1991, written by Sidney Brinkley about Jon Katz, a San Francisco member of "Queer Nation": "The words 'Gay' and 'Lesbian' have all but vanished from his vocabulary, except when he used them to describe what he thinks is a lower level of political consciousness. He says the difference between 'Queer' politics and 'Gay and Lesbian' politics is precisely the difference between San Francisco and D.C. 'There is no Queer politics in D.C.,' he says. 'A politics which sees itself as Queer is a politics that does not use the traditional means of dominant culture to effect change in dominant culture. We don't dress up in suits. We don't lobby. We don't raise money for candidates. Because that makes dominant culture stronger. Queer politics says we will use our own culture, our own means, our own approach, to fight the dominant culture. We are not going to play the game, because we don't like the game.' "

Those are just a few of the appetizers from the kind of people who threatened to "out" Scott Peck.

One of the most inspiring things about this noble young man, Scott Peck, is that he is not afraid of them.

In the same issue, Neenyah Ostrom wrote a piece about the manner in which chronic fatigue syndrome is transmitted. She wrote, "There is an increasing amount of evidence that it is casually transmissible between people; outbreaks have been documented among people who have less-than-intimate contact, such as teammates or co-workers. But there is also mounting evidence that CFS can be transmitted between sexual partners as well."

Ostrom reported, "Canadian CFS researchers Dr. Byron Hyde and co-authors discuss the putative sexual transmission of CFS in an introductory chapter of a book published [in 1992] by Canada's Nightingale Foundation," a CFS research organization.

Dr. Hyde and his colleagues wrote in their chapter, "Although the Lake Tahoe epidemic in 1984 appears to have been first documented in a girls' high school basketball team, there is also an anecdotal story from the Lake Tahoe epidemic, that five unrelated men all fell ill with M.E./CFS after having slept with the same prostitute. The prostitute was visiting from Africa. There is no mention of sexual transmission of M.E./CFS in the literature. We have countless cases documented in our files where one spouse with M.E./CFS has had long-term repeated sexual contact with an existing or new spouse without transmission of the illness. We have had a few cases of apparent rapid transmission to a new sexual partner."

In the May 31 *Native*, Neenyah Ostrom wrote a piece about the link between HHV-6 and the cancer known as Kaposi's sarcoma: "This newspaper has argued for several years that human herpesvirus-6 (HHV-6) should be considered to be the primary immunosuppressive agent in both 'AIDS' and chronic fatigue syndrome; that 'AIDS' and chronic fatigue syndrome are different expressions of the same disease process caused by HHV-6; and that Kaposi's sarcoma (KS) is not only a universal feature of 'AIDS,' but is also present in CFS in the form of 'crimson crescents' seen in the throat. Now, a group of Italian researchers has found HHV-6 in more than one-third of the KS lesions they examine, and suggest that the virus may play some role in causing the puzzling cancer. The Italian research report authored by Pasqualina Bovenzi and co-workers appeared in the May 15 issue of *The Lancet* in a short communication titled 'Human Herpesvirus 6 (Variant A) in Kaposi's sarcoma.' "

A rather remarkable scientific paper, that could have brought HIV to justice, was reported on by, Neenyah Ostrom, in the July 12 issue: "A positive result on an HIV antibody test can deal a devastating blow to a person's physical and mental health; such news has resulted in murder, suicide, incarceration, and poisoning with toxic drugs. A positive result on an HIV antibody test has been widely publicized as a virtual death sentence, an irreversible prediction that the person receiving it will develop 'AIDS' and subsequently die. Now, an Australian research team has published a stunning review article that questions not only the accuracy and reproducibility of the HIV antibody test, but also calls into question exactly what the antibody test is measuring—and even the very nature of HIV itself. In the process, the causal link between HIV and 'AIDS' is also shown to be far weaker than most U.S. researchers have admitted."

Ostrom wrote, "The Australian researchers, Eleni Papadopulos-Eleopulos, Valender F. Turner, and John M. Papadimitrious, go so far as to state, 'We conclude that the use of antibody tests as a diagnostic and epidemiological tool for HIV infection needs to be reappraised.' Their article is titled, 'Is a Positive Western Blot Proof of HIV Infection?' and appears in the June 11 issue of *Bio/Technology* (Vol 11:696). Papadopulos-Eleopulos and colleagues examine the standard HIV antibody test, the enzyme-linked immunosorbent assay (ELISA), and the antibody test that is used to 'verify' the elisa antibody test, the Western blot (WB) test. Both of these tests are based on the same premise, they point out: 'In both the ELISA and WB, the patient's serum is added to the antigen preparation [in the test]. It is assumed that if HIV antibodies are present, they will react with the HIV proteins' present in the test to create a positive result. The Western blot (WB) test is 'believed to be highly sensitive and specific, and a positive test result is regarded as synonymous with HIV infection,' they note."

Papadopulos-Eleopulos and co-authors elucidated the problems in *Bio/Technology*: "(1) the antibody tests are not standardized; (2) the antibody tests are not reproducible; (3) the WB proteins (bands) which are considered to be encoded by the HIV genome and may represent normal cellular proteins; (4) even if the proteins are specific to HIV, because no gold standard has been used to determine specificity, a positive WB may represent nothing more than a cross-reactivity with non-HIV antibodies present in AIDS patients and those at risk."

Ostrom reported, "In the course of their examination, Papadopulos-Eleopulos and co-workers come to a number of extremely disturbing conclusions about not only the HIV antibody test but about HIV itself: HIV cannot be found in all 'AIDS' patients, but can be found in non-'AIDS' patients who have other diseases; there is no correlation between a positive HIV antibody test result and the isolation of HIV itself; no two HIVs are the same, even those isolated from the same person; uninfected cells grown in the tissue culture can produce antibodies that create a positive result on an HIV antibody test; and some scientists believe that retroviruses are the result, not the *causes* of disease."

In the same issue, I wrote an editorial about the Papadopulos-Eleopulos paper titled "A Piltdown Test for a Piltdown Virus":

> A research review published in the June 11 issue of *Bio/Technology* and reported on in the *Native* by Neenyah Ostrom debunks any notion that the HIV test is reliable or accurate. And it does a lot more than that. It raises the question of whether HIV is even the cause of "AIDS" in a manner that rivals the work of Peter Duesberg. . . . If there is any justice or intelligence left in the world, the article should have the same impact on "AIDS" that the Pentagon Papers had on the Vietnam War. Hopefully, our lazy—and I do mean lazy—writers and "intellectuals" who have swallowed the government line on HIV and "AIDS" will finally wake up and do the necessary work of helping to

illuminate what our nation's basic "AIDS" policy is: lying to the public. Unfortunately, we live in a time when people seem to think that wearing a red ribbon is a bold intellectual and political act.

What this epidemic really needs is a Hannah Arendt or a Noam Chomsky. (Larry Kramer thinks he is that, but he's really the Professor Irwin Corey of "AIDS.") Someone needs to illuminate "AIDS" the way that Hannah Arendt illuminated the thinking of government officials during the Vietnam War. In a way, Professor Papadopulos-Eleopulos and her colleagues have done in scientific terms something akin to what Hannah Arendt did in her essay, "Lying in Politics." Using closely argued technical analysis, their piece on the inadequacy of the HIV test politely implies that the whole field is mired in pseudoscience, fraud, and propaganda.

They do a beautiful job of undermining the credibility of the HIV test. Their work could be the basis for a class action suit against the government like no other class action lawsuit. I think that the relatives of people who have killed themselves as a result of HIV tests would have an excellent case—as would people foolish enough to take AZT, or any other toxic drug, based on the test.

The implications of the article are not just that the test doesn't work. The test itself was used to establish beyond a reasonable doubt that HIV is the cause of "AIDS." The test is bogus, so the conclusion is also bogus. In that respect, the Australians have done a much more potent job of undermining the HIV paradigm than retrovirologist Peter Duesberg who continually muddies the water with his own silly theory that drugs are the *cause* of "AIDS."

From a practical point of view, the Australian researchers argue that the only way for someone to know for sure if they are infected is to have the virus itself isolated from them. But even if they did, it would not mean that they had or were going to get "AIDS," because many people with the virus don't, and many people get "AIDS" who don't have the virus. (Like the 15 million people who have the euphemistic form of the disease "chronic fatigue syndrome.")

One thing seems clear from a recent discussion with Peter Duesberg. The helm of American science has been taken over by a small group of dishonest retrovirologists. Duesberg argues that these retrovirologists are imposing a Big Lie on America, namely that retroviruses are more important and more lethal than they really are. Of course the celebrity retrovirus is HIV, and Duesberg has argued that it is the biggest con job of all.

We all know who the victims of that lie are and will be. But Duesberg argues that it goes beyond that virus. The whole field is corrupt, and power hungry. Duesberg argues that, as soon as retroviruses are seen as being unimportant, or less important than they have presented as being, the retrovirologists who have become the little kings of American science will lose their power and credibility. In other words, the only way for them to avoid losing power is to control the game completely.

Anybody who thinks that HIV has not been kept alive by power politics just doesn't understand how science works these days. It is still totally an old boys' network. The fact that Clinton has appointed a scientist associated with retrovirology to head the NIH is ominous, even if the man, Harold Varmus, does have a Nobel Prize. David Baltimore has a Nobel Prize, and he is everything that is wrong with science these days.

If you disagree with the HIV propaganda, you are dead in terms of the rewards and sustenance of science. The interlocking between corporate science, academic science, and government science is so tight that the sphere of influence of powerful scientists like Gallo or Fauci is awesome. You fuck with them, and they'll get you. And they can. You don't have to be an Einstein or Oliver Stone to see how this system works. Talk to any scientist off the record, and he or she will confirm this. Any honest scientist.

343

Vietnam has come home. This time it is the HIV agenda. A terrified public that is vulnerable to the smoke and mirrors of pseudoscience can be made to believe anything if good men and women do not stand up and say, "Enough."

In the August 9 issue, I wrote an editorial celebrating some surprising support we got from a scientist: "The *Native* has reported extensively on the role of HHV-6 in 'AIDS' and chronic fatigue syndrome. Our reporting has led us to what we think is a fairly obvious and commonsensical notion, namely that HHV-6 is more likely to be the cause of both these syndromes than HIV, an agent which we now know cannot be found in many 'AIDS' cases not to mention the estimated 15 million cases of chronic fatigue 'AIDS minor' syndrome. We are delighted to report that this idea has at last surfaced in the scientific press. After reading a report on HHV-6 in *Science Times* that ran in the April 3 issue . . . Gordon Edlin sent what we think is an historic letter and it was published in the July 24 issue. Under a headline of "Herpesvirus-6 as AIDS Cause?" Professor Edlin writes, 'The possible role of the ubiquitous herpesvirus-6 in heart disease and immune dysfunction is interesting for several reasons. . . . As everyone knows by now, AIDS is an acquired syndrome. The new evidence raises the possibility that herpesvirus-6 actually causes AIDS by activating normally quiescent HIV infection. Although HIV is universally accepted as the cause of AIDS, the evidence still is not all that compelling. In fact HIV infection is not even required for a diagnosis of AIDS, according to the Centers for Disease Conrol and Prevention. The current definition of AIDS is any one of 27 different diseases accompanied by low numbers of CD4 cells in the immune system. Thus the causal agent (HIV) of the disease (AIDS) is not required to cause the disease. Is it a bit of scientific legerdemain or what?' Gordon Edlin is a Professor of Biochemistry and Biophysics at the University of Hawaii at Manoa in Honolulu. Edlin is in Europe until mid-August, and we were not able to thank him for being the first scientist to speak up in the scientific press."

That summer, there were a number of pieces in the mainstream press that seemed to express the not-so-veiled schadenfreude about Cuba's policy of dealing with so-called AIDS patients. In the August 23 *Native*, Neenyah Ostrom wrote, "Cuba has a unique system for dealing with 'AIDS' patients: They are quarantined. Cuban health officials claim the quarantine policy has sharply limited the spread of 'AIDS' in Cuba, which claims fewer than 1,000 HIV-positive individuals."

Ostrom also noted, "The U.S. press seems to be finding Cuba's solution to the 'AIDS' problem more and more attractive, with positive commentaries appearing in front page articles in the *Washington Post*, *New York Newsday's* 'Discovery' section and Letters to the Editor column of the *New York Times*."

I continued to have a sense of foreboding about the rise of the word "queer" and, in the September 20 issue, I wrote an editorial about a nightmare that seemed to be coming true:

> We have warned the gay community about the dangers of looking the other way while a minority with its own destructive agenda tries to impose the word "queer" on our community.
>
> Most people think the word could never make it into the *Times* to describe gay people.
>
> Last week, the *New York Times* did such a thing. Here's how advertising columnist Stuart Elliott ended a column on the gay and lesbian marketing: "After catalogues what? Several gay and lesbian entrepreneurs are considering home-shopping programs on local cable television stations. That could bring a whole new meaning to the 'Q' in QVC."
>
> Bruce Bawer, who has a hot little book called *A Place at the Table* coming out in November, explains it best in the introduction of his book: "I've chosen not to use the word 'queer,' which is favored by some gay activists and academics but turns off almost everybody else, gay and straight."
>
> A poll done by several gay newspapers shows that his statement is correct: Most gay people are horrified by the word. And certainly every rational gay person would be horrified to see the word "queer" used on a regular basis in the *New York Times*.
>
> In case you want to know where the idea for pushing the word "queer" on the gay community came

from, try to get a copy of *The Homosexual Network* by Enrique Rueda. The book was published by Devin Adair in 1982 and is an attempt to portray the gay community as a giant conspiracy against family values in America. Rueda writes that if the gay movement were to succeed, "the nation we have known would cease to exist."

Rueda urges that the right-wing attempt to get gay people to use language that is demeaning to themselves, as a way of subverting the positive feelings of the movement. Like the "queer" pushers, he hates the word gay and sees the adoption as a victory that must be rolled back.

Rueda writes, "Should the homosexual language and ideology prevail, society would have no way of speaking—or thinking—in traditional terms." In other words, if people adopt positive terms like "gay," America will disintegrate.

Rueda writes: "There is yet another way in which the homosexual subculture utilizes language. As is common with other political movements, the homosexual movement 'frames issues' in its own favor when articulating its understanding of society. The very use of 'gay' and 'homophobia' are examples of such a valuing process. Since 'gay' is by definition a word of celebration and affirmation, while 'homophobia' implies a negative quality (i.e., 'irrational fear'), their use makes it difficult (if not impossible for the user—unless he has a basic value system formed by traditional principles—to reject the values implied by gay (=good) and homophobia (=bad). Even in very specific instances, and the homosexual literature is full of examples, the use of language by the homosexual movement inevitably involves this framing of issues."

Rueda tells his readers that, "The importance of using the word 'gay' as opposed to such better suited words as 'homosexual' or 'queer' is universally acknowledged throughout the homosexual community."

Why does Rueda think that the word "queer" is so

appropriate? Because "Queer, which has as its first meaning 'deviating from the expected or normal; strange' corresponds with the facts that homosexuals are a small minority of the population and that their practices are considered by most people to be in disharmony with the natural order."

Every time a gay person refuses to use the word "queer," he or she is performing an act of resistance and liberation.

Rueda thinks that by destroying the way we talk to each other about ourselves, the first steps of destroying our community are being taken. He may be right.

Let us pray that enough smart, courageous gay people will wake up to what's really going on and fight Rueda's queer agenda.

Of course, what I should have also pointed out in that editorial is that anything words like "queer" didn't do could be accomplished by either "HIV-positive" or "HIV risk group." Epidemiology had far greater power to destroy the gay community by insidiously framing "issues" than any right-wing language police.

In the November 1 issue, we published a cautionary message about the dangers gay people faced on Halloween: "On the eve of this year's Village Halloween Parade, the New York City Gay and Lesbian Anti-Violence Project (AVP) has issued a warning to gay men and lesbians to avoid the parade, citing numerous instances of violent anti-gay assaults and harassments that occur at the crowded event. Last year AVP documented eight serious anti-gay assaults and in most cases police were unable or unwilling to intervene. 'The Village parade used to be a gay and lesbian celebration,' says Bea Hanson, AVP Director of Client Services, 'but that tradition has been stolen from us over the last five to ten years.' AVP recommends that, instead of joining the parade, gay men and lesbians celebrate Halloween at private parties in bars, discos, and clubs. If you go to the parade, they recommend going with a group of friends, and wearing a costume that will not prevent you from running away or protecting yourself, in the event of attack. The AVP also warns that alcohol and drugs can impair your judgment and make you a vulnerable target for attack. 'It's sickening that we have to issue this warning,' said AVP Executive Director Matt Foreman, 'but the level of anti-gay/lesbian violence that now accompanies the parade forces us to do so.' "

In the same issue I wrote an editorial about a magazine piece on ABC that was groundbreaking:

ABC's *Day One* did it again. The show covered a story that the rest of the media is afraid of: AZT.

Close readers of this newspaper were already familiar with many of the facts presented, but some new ones were uncovered, and the whole piece was very effective. Most viewers should have been left with the impression that AZT should never have been foisted upon the public in the first place.

The piece began with an interview with the Nagels, a Minneapolis couple who adopted a Romanian orphan who tested positive by the (totally unreliable) HIV antibody test when they got the child back to the States.

Assuming that the experts know best, the Nagels obtained AZT and gave it to the child for two years. Seeing this child being spoon-fed the stuff was like seeing parents giving their kids Drano in their baby food.

According to the Nagels, the child started shrieking every night. They'd find their daughter pressing her thighs in excruciating pain. The Nagels began to research this so-called treatment. According to *Day One* correspondent John Hockenberry, "The Nagels came to believe that AZT is at best an uncertain therapy and at worst a dangerous poison, and that the government was steamrolled into approving it." The Nagels took their daughter off of AZT.

Hockenberry interviewed Dr. John Hamilton, the chief of infectious diseases at the V.A. Hospital in Durham, North Carolina. Hamilton headed a study that discovered that early treatment with AZT caused a faster progression to death among patients with "AIDS" than the progression in patients who did not take it.

348

Needless to say, Burroughs Wellcome, the manufacturer of AZT—which brings in over $400 million a
year—did not like this study. Hamilton told
Hockenberry that he had received a call from Burroughs Wellcome telling him not to continue the study.
Hockenberry interviewed Dave Barry, the man who
headed Burroughs Wellcome's AZT project and who
was promoted to vice president for his efforts. Barry
denied making the call himself.

Hockenberry asked Barry why the results of the
V.A. study are not included with the literature that is
sent out with AZT. Barry said that it was "because we
disagreed with the statistical analysis."

Hockenberry then pointed out that European researchers, in the largest study on AZT of its kind, had
come to the same conclusion that Hamilton's group
had.

Barry then shot back, "If you want to focus on two
studies, that's your privilege, but it is incumbent on you
to present all the data."

Apparently, it is incumbent on ABC to present all
the data, but not incumbent on Burroughs Wellcome
to present all of the data to doctors and patients who
are the chief victims of AZT.

Hockenberry then asked the question, "How did
AZT get approved, anyway?" He pointed out that it
was approved at one of the bleakest moments of the
epidemic, seven years ago. He notes that, "One flawed,
rushed, never repeated study got AZT approved."

Hockenberry then interviewed Dr. Itzhak Brook,
who headed the eleven-person committee of the FDA
which approved the drug. Brook disagreed with the
approval, then and now. He said that the committee
really had not had a way of scrutinizing the data, that
the whole thing was rushed to capture the market
quickly. He said, "I felt we compromised science and
we compromised safety."

One of the biggest contributions the *Day One* piece
made is to show what a bureaucratic clown David
Kessler, the head of the Food and Drug Admin-

istration, is. While admitting that the study of AZT was flawed, he defended the decision to okay the drug and made his usual lame comment that the riskiest thing is to be unwilling to take any risks.

The person who really spoke truth to power in the piece was scientist Charles Thomas, who said that AZT was "approved under very shady circumstances." Noting that a tremendous amount of money is riding on AZT, Thomas said, "These people are drinking their own whiskey, as we used to say. The human mind is a very inventive organ, especially when it is lubricated by money. There's no argument that a bunch of smart guys can't support." About those involved in the disaster, he said, "They should be penalized for their misrepresentation."

Hockenberry then interviewed a New York doctor who has treated 300 HIV patients, presumably with AZT, for many years. The doctor admitted that he didn't know whether AZT is effective or not, but he thought he had seen some improvement, showing that anyone can graduate from medical school these days. It also shows that so-called HIV patients are having their well-being treated frivolously, as though they were little Ken dolls who were going to die anyway, so doctors can do anything they want with them. The same psychology applied in the Nazi concentration camps.

In a rather haunting moment, the oldest surviving "AIDS" patient, Michael Callen pointed out that until 1991, 80 percent of all government treatment research money went to the study of AZT, which kept other promising solutions from getting a fair test. Callen said, "We dilly-dallied with a class of drugs that was patently useless."

The piece ended with Nagels. Hockenbery said, "The parents came to believe they were involved in some kind of flawed experiment no one told them about." Since they stopped giving the child AZT, her leg cramps ceased, she stopped screaming, started eating, and gained five pounds in two months. She looked like a healthy child. To survive two years of AZT is pretty amazing.

Unfortunately for 300,000 people still being poisoned by AZT, there are no Nagels to protect them from "AIDS" advocates who continue to urge people to take AZT. Since so much "AIDS" advocacy is funded by Burroughs Wellcome, one shouldn't be surprised.

In the November 15 issue, Neenyah Ostrom wrote a piece titled "Anatomy of a Cover-up" which outlined the latest round of the Centers for Disease Control's deceptive (and self-deceptive) attempts to keep the relationship of CFS and AIDS confused and balkanized: "The CFS cover-up is alive and well, as the recent meeting of the Public Health Service Chronic Fatigue Syndrome Interagency Coordinating Committee demonstrated. Distributed at the meeting was a draft version of the new pamphlet, 'The Facts about Chronic Fatigue Syndrome,' which is one of the most remarkable pieces of creative writing ever to be issued by the Centers for Disease Control (CDC). Although the pamphlet is meant for distribution to physicians as well as patients who inquire about the illness, no basis is supplied for the 'facts' presented, no studies are cited, no references in the medical literature are provided. It appears that, in writing the pamphlet, the authors (who are unidentified; Dr. William Reeves, temporary head of CFS research at CDC, is in charge of the project, according to CDC press officer Kay Golan) have assiduously avoided familiarity with any published studies that document immune dysfunction, communicability, or measurable defects of any sort—immunological, serological, neurological, whatever—among CFS patients."

Ostrom also noted, "The CDC pamphlet also engages in major league fudging of the answer to the question, 'Is CFS contagious?' 'There are no published data indicating that CFS is communicable through either casual or intimate contact,' the pamphlet reads. 'Studies of groups of CFS patients and their contacts have shown no evidence of person-to-person transmission of the disease. Furthermore, reports that pets are involved in the transmission of CFS, or that they can contact the disorder, are unsubstantiated.' "

Well, that settled that.

In the November 29 issue, Ostrom reported on a new study from

351

the Gallo group (published in the November 13, 1993, issue of *The Lancet*) which should have resulted in the scientific community's total skepticism of the HIV/AIDS paradigm. She reported, "New data from research teams at the U.S. National Cancer Institute and in Italy show that terminally-ill 'AIDS' patients have widespread, presumably active human herpesvirus-6 (HHV-6) infection in numerous—more than 20—tissues. This new information led Dr. Gallo and his colleagues to suggest that HHV-6 may play a role in 'the pathogenesis of the immune deficits associated with AIDS.' "

Ostrom asked, "Are Gallo and collaborators attempting to sidle cautiously to the conclusion that HHV-6 is necessary for the development of 'AIDS'?"

The Gallo study resulted in these striking findings: "In patients with AIDS, HHV-6 infection was documented in the vast majority of the tissues analyzed (85.2 percent, range 77-100), including cerebral cortex, brain stem, cerebellum, spinal cord, paravertebral, ganglia, tonsil, lymph nodes above and below the diaphragm, spleen, bone marrow, salivary glands, esophagus, bronchial tree, lung, skeletal muscle, myocardium, aorta, liver, kidney, adrenal glands, pancreas, and thyroid."

The Gallo group concluded that, "Our preliminary results show that in terminally ill AIDS patients, HHV-6 infection is widely disseminated and therefore, likely to be active."

The December 13 issue was our thirteenth anniversary, for which I wrote an editorial titled "Happy Anniversary from Barnes and Noble":

> While I had intended to use this space to reminisce about the *Native*'s first 13 years, something a little more urgent and disturbing has come to the fore.
>
> As many of you know, we recently published a book called *America's Biggest Cover-Up* by Neenyah Ostrom. The book argues that chronic fatigue syndrome and "AIDS" are part of the same epidemic and that the government is concealing the fact from the public.
>
> If you know of a more disturbing story with more frightening implications for everyone in this country or on the planet, for that matter, please let me know.
>
> One of the reasons we published the book was so that we could reach an audience beyond this news-

paper. There are approximately 25,000 bookstores in America, and we had hoped to get the book into many of them in order to bring the "AIDS"-chronic fatigue syndrome connection to the public's attention.

Well, in order to bring one of the biggest cover-ups in American history to the public's attention, one has to get the book into stores, and in order to do that, one must get through a gate known as the book buyer. If every buyer in America decides that a book should not be made available to their customers, it can die an early death. Something of this nature happened initially to the hardcover version of Michael Fumento's *The Myth of Heterosexual AIDS* (a book we disagree with but that should, nevertheless, *not* be censored.) Fumento has argued in print that his book ran afoul of the "AIDS" thought police in publishing, and a number of stores and chains initially refused to carry it. The way that you cover something like that is to tell the publisher that you don't think the book will sell. Book buyers pretend generally not to have an ideological bone in their bodies. Their minds are composed of pure, objective, market research protoplasm. Not a single emotion or prejudice enters into their decisions on what book should be allowed a place on their shelves.

Several weeks before we published *America's Biggest Cover-Up*, I contacted Marcella Smith, a very important book buyer who handles small press purchases for Barnes & Noble, one of the nation's leading, if not *the* leading, bookstore chains. I told her about the book and sent her the galleys. When the book came back from the printer, I sent her the copies so she could see what the finished product looked like. I called her and asked whether she would be ordering it. She said that she didn't think the book would sell. I told her that we were spending a great deal of money on advertising the book, hoping to appeal to her commercial sense. She said that advertising didn't make any difference to her. From the rather nasty, condescending tone of her voice, I was convinced there was a little more going on here.

The more I thought about it that day, the angrier I got, and the next day, I called Len Riggio, the President of Barnes & Noble, to complain about the rude, possibly homophobic treatment I got from Marcella Smith.

I didn't expect to hear from Riggio, but I was damned if I was gonna let Smith keep Ostrom's book from reaching a substantial portion of the reading public.

Riggio actually returned my call, and I explained to him the importance of the book and my annoyance at the way Smith had treated me. Riggio said he would look at the book and talk to Smith.

A while later, Smith called back and our second conversation turned into a bit of a screaming match. She said that they would order more books, whatever that meant, but that she resented the suggestion that her condescension was in any way seen as homophobia because, among other things, two of her best friends had died of "AIDS." It was then that I realized what I was dealing with.

I asked her if she had looked at the book. She said she had, but that it wasn't the kind of writing or reporting that she liked. I asked if that meant she wasn't interested in the subject matter. She said no, she was very interested in the subject matter.

Then I told her I thought it was clear that she was imposing her own judgment on the matter, and making a political decision rather than a commercial one. She, of course, disagreed, saying that she often approved books she didn't like and that the chain wanted books to succeed as much as their publishers, no matter what the content.

I tried to end things on a positive note, given her incredible power, and said I was hopeful that the book would do well for them. I, of course, was wary of what she meant when she said they would buy more books.

A few weeks passed, and no major order had come in, so I called her up and asked how many books she had ordered for the chain of 1,200-plus stores. She said, "Thirty-four."

Thirty-four? This is known in some circles as saying, "Fuck you and the horse you rode in on."

Maybe we should have a contest with a $100 prize for the person who can find the 34 books in the 1,200-plus stores. It could be the biggest craze since *Where is Waldo?"*

I think this is incredibly insulting and clearly censorship. Ms. Smith has decided to play God with a book that breaks what is surely the biggest story of her lifetime. I'm sure she is very frightened and upset by what the book says. Anyone would be. But the book is solidly grounded in research, and it deserves to reach the widest possible audience. Ms. Smith is shooting the messenger.

We're sorry that Ms. Smith has lost two friends to the epidemic, but that does not entitle her to set up shop as Barnes & Noble's "AIDS Czar." She'll bury a lot more friends if the cover-up continues. By effectively killing this book, she is helping to maintain the deadly silence about the connection between "AIDS" and chronic fatigue syndrome.

Neenyah Ostrom joined us six years ago. I believe that her reporting (along with John Lauritsen's AZT exposes) will secure the *Native*'s place in history. I have watched the amount of effort and personal sacrifice Neenyah Ostrom has put into getting the truth into print. She has written over two hundred articles on the connection between "AIDS" and chronic fatigue syndrome. If Marcella doesn't recognize its value, she has some serious problems.

On this, our thirteenth anniversary, I consider this issue so important that I am going to make this request of readers who believe as I do. Please write or call Len Riggio and Marcella Smith at Barnes & Noble in Manhattan and tell them why Ostrom's book and her reporting are so important to the nation. Be as polite as possible, but make it clear that as a reader of the *Native*, and as a customer of Barnes & Noble, you would like them to make Ostrom's book more widely available.

And I don't mean 34 more books.

In the December 20 issue, we ran the response I received from Leonard Riggio, Barnes & Noble's chief executive officer, as well as my response:

Dear Mr. Ortleb:

You have gone completely over the line in your editorial; unfairly and brutally disparaging a very fine individual in the process. To intimate that Marcella Smith is homophobic is indecent and demagogic. Neither she, nor the 25,000 other booksellers, who chose not to carry this publication need apologize for their decision.

There is a huge distinction between censorship and selection. So, too, is there a major difference between persuasion and intimidation. Your supreme egoism apparently has given you the moral authority to rationalize these distinctions to suit your own purposes, regardless of the harm you have caused.

We have ordered 37 copies of your book. It sold eight copies, so it didn't exactly jump off the shelves. To suggest that we should place it in our store fronts in 1,200 stores is an exercise in fantasy.

There's nothing like a censorship scare to strike the old fires of demand, is there, Mr. Ortleb?

Sincerely,

Leonard Riggio

Chief Executive Officer

Barnes & Noble Inc.

Dear Mr. Riggio:

First of all, let me say that you have an absolute right to censor *America's Biggest Cover-Up*.

I would be the first to defend your right to censor books. You have the right to sell whatever books you want to sell and to refuse to sell books that you don't like.

But let's not pretend that you're not censoring this

book. Even various secretaries I spoke to at your company were shocked that your hostile buyer Marcella Smith had only ordered 34 books (now you say 37) for your chain of 1,200 stores. I think it is clear that the only reason she ordered any at all was that I called you to complain and she needed to avoid the charge of censorship. An order for 34 books is supposed to turn censorship into selection.

It was clear from my discussion with Ms. Smith that she did not like the book. She said she had a great deal of interest in the subject of "AIDS" and that two of her best friends had died of "AIDS." If you think her prejudice against the book didn't enter into her *de facto* censorship, you're just fooling yourself. The way buyers all over the country cover themselves on this issue usually is to buy one copy of a book and then to make sure it is placed somewhere in the store where the sun don't shine, if you get my idea.

I'm a little surprised that the chief executive officer of a $1.3 billion company would take valuable corporate time to involve himself with the censorship of one book. I think deep down, beneath your-not-so-supreme egoism (and Marcella's for that matter), you both know that this book is a bombshell. It is not a cookbook. It is not a first novel. It is not a collection of poetry. It is a wake-up call to the nation about an impending disaster. The government has tried to suppress the information in this book for at least a decade. And now, so have you.

It's June 1941, Len, and we have published a book warning about a Japanese attack on Pearl Harbor coming in December, and you have refused to carry the book. That's the analogy, if you get the idea.

I think that you both also know that your order was as good as no order at all. Most publishers, out of fear of your supreme bookselling power, would have slunk away and lived with what they knew was clearly *de facto* censorship.

But this book is too important, at this moment in time, in terms of the "AIDS" epidemic, for me to let your act of censorship occur in silence. I'm sure that Ms. Smith, who seems to consider herself to be some sort of "AIDS" aficionado, would be the first one to say, "Silence=Death."

You should know, by the way, that this is not the first time we have been censored by people who considered themselves experts on "AIDS." ACT UP voted several years ago to boycott the *Native* because it didn't like our reporting on AZT. We survived that boycott, and I believe that this book will survive your censorship.
Sincerely,
Charles L. Ortleb
Publisher and Editor-in-Chief
New York Native

In the same issue, Neenyah Ostrom wrote a piece about research that had appeared in the December 10 issue of *Science*, which once again inadvertently linked AIDS and chronic fatigue syndrome. A research team from the National Cancer Institute had reported on a study of the effect of Interleukin-12 on cells from AIDS patients that were cultured in the laboratory.

Ostrom reported, "Earlier research performed at the National Institute of Allergy and Infectious Diseases [reported in a June 30, 1993 NIAID press release] demonstrated that the way IL-12 repairs the immune system is by restoring natural (NK) cell activity. A June 30, 1993, press release from NIAID noted that IL-12 may be able to restore the crucial part of the immune response independent of the T-cells, which are also severely damaged and depleted in 'AIDS.' "

Ostrom also pointed out that, "Although loss of NK cell activity was one of the first immune abnormalities documented in 'AIDS' (and is the most consistently identified immune malfunction found in chronic fatigue syndrome), little research into restoring that activity has been conducted; U.S. researchers have concluded that the T-cell malfunctions are more important in unraveling 'AIDS.' But the importance of the NK cell malfunction could have been recognized, and greater strides toward correcting it could have been made, more than ten years ago when Dr. Jane Teas reported the similarities between 'AIDS' and African swine fever in *The Lancet* (April 23, 1983). Not only does African swine fever virus destroy T-cells, macrophages, and monocytes, but one of the most prominent features of ASFV infection is loss of NK cell activity."

1994: Is HHV-6 the Real Virus?

In the January 31 issue of *New York Native*, Neenyah Ostrom reported, "A British woman has enlisted the support of the Legal Aid Board of England in order to sue the pharmaceutical giant Wellcome, the British manufacturer of AZT, over the death of her husband. Susan Threakall of Birmingham, England, claims that AZT (Retrovir) caused her hemophiliac husband Bob's death, not his HIV-positive condition. . . . Bob Threakall died on February 20, 1991, leaving a wife and three children. He had been a civil servant in the Department of Social Services and had worked full time until he became ill following his treatment with AZT."

Ostrom reported that Graham Ross, the lawyer representing Susan Threakall, said, "This case will involve a significant issue of public importance centering on the marketing decisions of one of the largest pharmaceutical companies in the world. If Bob Threakall's immune system was indeed irrevocably damaged by AZT, then the health of many thousands of other HIV-positive people worldwide is under threat, not by their condition but by their treatment. Questions need to be asked as to why such toxic treatment was recommended for otherwise healthy people when it has now been proven to be of no benefit. It is the classic issue of medical ethics."

In the February 7 issue, I wrote an editorial that was critical of the nation's leading chronic fatigue syndrome organization.

> One of the more interesting facets of the cover-up of the link between "AIDS" and chronic fatigue syndrome has been the behavior of the organizations that are attempting to solve the problem of chronic fatigue syndrome. There are supposedly millions of Americans with the syndrome, which this newspaper, through an enormous amount of reporting, has linked to "AIDS." Putting aside the issue of the "AIDS"-CFS connection for a moment, I think that nobody would argue with our contention that the CFS activists have not been very successful in alleviating the plight of the patients they represent.
>
> Biomedical research is very expensive, and even though breakthroughs can occur by luck at very little

cost, real progress seems to require megabucks, the kind of money that organizations like the Chronic Fatigue and Immune Dysfunction Syndrome Association of America are not really capable of raising. They have valiantly raised several millions of dollars—dollars they have spent pursuing their own pet theories about the cause of the syndrome.

We were initially enthusiastic about the organization and its leader, Marc Iverson. But at some point in the last six years, something quite disastrous happened: When Iverson and his organization stared the truth in the face, they blinked. As they promoted more and more research into the nature of what chronic fatigue syndrome really is, the findings began to upset them and to modify their commitment to finding the truth. Every study pointed to one undeniable conclusion: chronic fatigue syndrome is not only like "AIDS," it could very well be called a form of "AIDS." The doctor who is the hero of their movement, Dr. Paul Cheney, was the first person to refer to chronic fatigue syndrome as "AIDS minor" in an interview in *Spin* magazine by Nick Regush. From where we sit, that's a little like the expression "pregnancy minor." We have a feeling Cheney regrets he ever said it.

The closer they got to the truth of the connection to "AIDS," the more they recoiled. It was only human. And we understand they started getting complaints from people in their movement. One CFS activist in the Midwest has made a career out of trying to publicize the disinformation that chronic fatigue syndrome is not related to "AIDS." She has succeeded in getting articles obscuring the truth about chronic fatigue syndrome planted in national publications.

Iverson's group decided what they wanted to be the cause, and they invested money trying to get their theory proven: They decided they wanted the cause of CFS to be a retrovirus, but they didn't want it to be HIV. So they funded Elaine DeFreitas, formerly of the Wistar Institute, to find them a "not-AIDS" retrovirus.

When DeFreitas started discovering evidence of retroviral activity, they all got excited. Their disease would be taken seriously because they had a trendy cause, a retrovirus, but one that wouldn't point their members to the concentration camps, one that wasn't HIV. And it is not out of the realm of possibility that what DeFreitas had found was a subspecies of HIV. Whoops.

Unfortunately for them, the CDC couldn't confirm work done by DeFreitas. She hasn't published anything about the CFS retrovirus since 1990.

I should point out that along the way they did give some attention to HHV-6, but decided that it couldn't be the cause because it was widespread in the population. What they didn't consider is that the virus that is causing chronic fatigue syndrome *is widespread* in the population; it's just that its manifestations are different in people who are diagnosed with chronic fatigue syndrome and those who are not. Can a virus be the cause of something if it is also present in people who are not clearly sick? Of course. It could be subtly altering their immune systems, and it could manifest itself later in life. Or it could remain latent, or be only marginally damaging. We, of course, know of one virus that acts that way: African swine fever virus, which we suspect is the pre-disinformation name of HHV-6. It was the CDC that played a major role in propagating the line that HHV-6 couldn't be the cause of CFS, or "AIDS" for that matter, because it is widespread. Since it seems to us that the CDC's main task now in America is not ending epidemics, but lying about them, we are not surprised. (Hopefully the new CDC director, Dr. David Satcher, will clean up an institution that has become a scientific and political cesspool.)

And that brings me to another point, the relationship between Iverson's group and the government. It is a fascinating study in naiveté and servility. For several years now, Iverson's group has been on its knees before the CDC and the NIH, believing that through the gentle powers of persuasion, it will be able to get the government to do the right thing. Iverson's organization sends out chronicles patting itself on the back for all the progress it's made in kissing the asses of some of the most corrupt officials in the history of this country. Iverson still doesn't get it. The government does not want to admit that CFS and "AIDS" are joined at the hip by HHV-6. Period. So Iverson and his supporters keep trudging to government meetings that are held for the purpose of obfuscating the truth, and they keep sending out newsletters praising themselves for doing so. Some of their newsletters, which are paid for with funds donated by their very sick members, are hilariously deferential: Here's a paragraph from the December 1993 *CFIDS Chronicle* which discusses a recent meeting with Dr. Phil Lee, the Assistant Secretary for Health. It was penned by the Executive Director of the Chronic Fatigue and Immune Dysfunction Syndrome Association of America, Kim Kenney:

> A few minutes past two o'clock, Dr. Lee dashed into the room through a back door adjoining his administrative offices. He looked like a college professor late for a lecture with his disheveled white hair and black suede sports coat and a stack of loose papers tucked under his arm. Despite his casual appearance, he commanded the respect of every person in the room and all conversation stopped instantly.

It is not really that hard to command the respect of these naïfs. They gave their total respect to the last government bureaucrat who was in charge of keeping the lid on the truth. That was a CDC character—a psychologist—named Walter Gunn. He was treated as their Messiah while he fed them one baloney sandwich after another. He retired in 1991, and they went looking for another government Messiah who would save them.

Iverson and his crew are nice, middle-and-upper-middle-class folk with basically good intentions. Their problem is that they can't face the truth about the disease they are raising money to cure. They also can't make themselves grasp that their government would lie to nice people like them. There is an even darker side to this, too: They don't want to be linked to people from the other side of the cultural track. (Not surprisingly, they refuse to make Neenyah Ostrom's most recent book [on CFS and AIDS] available to their members. The book is fast becoming the most censored book in the history of this country.)

Iverson is in a unique position. He could call a press conference in Washington and charge that the government is concealing the link between "AIDS" and chronic fatigue syndrome. He has the money and he represents thousands of members. (We've heard they have a mailing list of 200,000 names.) He could demand a Congressional investigation into allegations that both "AIDS" and chronic fatigue syndrome are caused by HHV-6. Iverson is the son of one of the nation's top business people. He has the clout to make waves. He would be an international hero.

But we suspect he won't do it. He wants his own retrovirus and he wants CFS to be anything but "AIDS."

In the same issue, Neenyah Ostrom reported, "More than two years have passed since veterans of the Persian Gulf War came home with symptoms of a 'mysterious illness.' For many of them that mysterious illness turned out to be diagnosed as chronic fatigue syndrome. Scattered news reports over those years, moreover, have noted that some spouses of Gulf War veterans were also developing symptoms of 'Gulf War Syndrome.' However, it wasn't until these couples began having babies—in some cases, very sick babies—that the syndrome received intensive attention from the Department of Veterans' Affairs, the Centers for Disease Control and Prevention, Congress, and the media. The babies born to members of four National Guard units near Meridian, Mississippi, are the subjects of a new investigation being conducted by the VA, the CDC, and the Mississippi State Department of Health. That's because 37 of the 55 babies born to Gulf War Veterans in these Guard units—67 percent—are reported to have either birth defects or serious inexplicable illnesses."

The intertwined nature, of the Gulf War syndrome and chronic fatigue syndrome, should have been an opportunity for CFS to come out of the closet. Ostrom wrote, "Unfortunately, much of what is not yet understood about the Gulf War veterans' health problems encompass areas of chronic fatigue syndrome that also remain unexplained (or are being covered up)."

She also pointed out, "If the majority of these veterans have CFS, that means they also have active infections of human herpesvirus-6, the virus that has been linked to 'AIDS.'"

In the February 28 issue, Neenyah Ostrom wrote an editorial titled "The Canonization of Anthony Fauci":

> Anthony Fauci, the man who has so mangled and misdirected U.S. "AIDS" research that 13 years into the epidemic there is no clear idea of its pathogenesis and no effective treatment, was recently raised to near sainthood once again by the *New York Times*.
>
> The task fell this time to Natalie Angier, who opened her February 16 profile with the sentence, "If everyone in the world were like Dr. Anthony S. Fauci, there would be no need for Prozac."
>
> Fauci works too hard to need mind-altering drugs, Angier continues, pointing out that his colleague's remark "on how astonishing it is that he manages to work 16 hours a day, day after day, year after year."
>
> The word used to describe Fauci (the head of "AIDS" research at the National Institute of Allergy and Infectious Disease) in almost every profile written is "obsessive," and Angier is no exception.
>
> "He is religiously organized. . . . He runs seven miles every lunch hour, regardless of the brutality of the weather. He sets aside every Saturday evening and all day Sunday for his family, a commitment that is essential if he is to see his three young daughters while they are awake. And perhaps his is the attitude that

365

must prevail in the plague years: not robotic, because robots break down, but calmly obsessive and matter-of-fact. . . ."

Fauci has, Angier admits in the only slightly negative passage in her full page profile, "a tendency to take things personally."

"When told that Harold Varmus, the new head of NIH, had described him as 'running his institute with an iron fist,' Dr. Fauci made a point of asking every subordinate he encountered that evening whether the description was accurate," Angier reports approvingly. "Most giggled nervously and said variations of, well, yes, but you're always fair."

Angier quotes no one who criticizes Fauci or challenges her appraisal of his "sensitivity"; for balance, she went to Larry Kramer.

"I call him a murderer or hero, depending on the week," Kramer said . . . .

In 1990 the *New York Times* canonization of Fauci was Phil Hilts's responsibility, and he provided as impartial a look at the man and his work as Angier. Hilts's prose was actually more florid than Angier's: "Dr. Fauci gives the impression of an electric wire: crackling with rapid-fire talk, short and thin enough that colleagues joke about anorexia, energetic enough to run up to ten miles at the beginning of each 14-hour workday," Hilts wrote.

The balance provided by Hilts consisted of an unnamed source, who told Hilts, "Dr. Fauci's ability to lead comes from his almost obsessive desire to please people."

"He is very good at telling you what you want to hear, that he will take care of problems, and through it he develops a sort of intimacy. He makes people feel connected to him. That allows him to be seen as being on different sides of the same issue," said the "colleague at the allergies institute, who would speak only if not identified," in September 1990.

"That's really the bone of it. And the meat on top of the bone is that he is one of the top medical scientists in the world," the unnamed source said to Fauci, [according to Hilts].

In the same piece, Ostrom wrote about Fauci's relationship with Peter Duesberg and the critics of the HIV orthodoxy.

> Having staked his career on the HIV theory of "AIDS," Fauci has also invested tremendous effort in silencing (if he can't discredit) critics of that theory. One object of Fauci's attention in this regard has been Berkeley microbiologist Peter Duesberg.
>
> Duesberg has argued for several years that he has not seen any evidence strong enough to convince him that HIV could possibly cause "AIDS."
>
> By early January 1988, Duesberg had received enough media attention that he was asked to speak at a scientific meeting sponsored by amfAR that "was billed as a scientific forum on the cause of AIDS, but was really an attempt to put Duesberg's theories to rest," as Michael Specter characterized it in the January 12, 1988, *Washington Post*.
>
> And Fauci tried to do just that. "The data overwhelmingly suggest that HIV is the cause of AIDS," Fauci told Specter for his report of the meeting.
>
> Then Fauci's strategy shifted to a refusal to debate the subject of HIV with Duesberg or anyone else who questioned that theory.
>
> In the January 12, 1988, *New York Times* report on the amfAR meeting, Fauci told Philip M. Boffey, "The evidence that HIV causes AIDS is so overwhelming that it almost doesn't deserve discussion anymore."
>
> In writing about the meeting for the *Wall Street Journal* February 26, 1988, Katie Leishman pointed out that Fauci's continued response to Duesberg's questions about HIV was to refuse to respond to them: "Anthony Fauci, coordinator of AIDS research at the National Institutes of Health, recently explained on National Public Radio, 'Critiquing a dubious theory would take away from more productive efforts.' "

And then Fauci proceeded to the next level of criticism of Dueberg's very straightforward, simple argument: "He's confusing people," Fauci told Jeff Miller for the June 1988 *Discover*: "The public has no way of judging that Duesberg's claims are totally unfounded."

In the March 21 issue, Ostrom covered a major development in HHV-6 research: "Human herpesvirus-6 (HHV-6) has finally been acknowledged as an extremely important—if not crucial—pathogen in 'AIDS.' In a new study published in the March 5 issue of *The Lancet*, Medical College of Wisconsin researchers Konstance Kehl Knox and Donald R. Carrigan found HHV-6 infection in 'all lung, lymph node, spleen, liver, and kidney tissues obtained at necropsy from an unselected series of nine patients with AIDS.' HHV-6 infection of the lung, in one case, was the cause of death, and Knox and Carrigan concluded that 'HHV-6 is an important pathogen in patients with AIDS.' "

Ostrom also reported, "An accompanying editorial by National Cancer Institute researchers Paolo Lusso and Robert Gallo emphasizes the importance of HHV-6's ability to damage the immune system in 'AIDS.' 'HHV-6's unique biological properties,' according to Lusso and Gallo, suggest that 'it may have detrimental effects on the immune system and expedite progression of the disease.' Gallo and Lusso (and co-workers), it must be noted, have previously suggested that HHV-6's 'detrimental effect on the immune system' occurs in chronic fatigue syndrome as well as causing the virus to act as a cofactor in 'AIDS.' "

I wrote an editorial in the same issue about the development:

> Neenyah Ostrom reports on an extremely important development in the HHV-6 story this week in the *Native*.
>
> As readers of this newspaper will recall, HHV-6 is the virus which Robert Gallo claims to have discovered in 1986 in both "AIDS" and chronic fatigue syndrome patients.
>
> Prior to "discovering" HHV-6, Gallo had received information suggesting that a large DNA virus called African swine fever virus could be found in "AIDS" patients. We believe that Gallo just appropriated that

information when he found a large DNA virus in "AIDS" patients and renamed that virus HBLV, which subsequently was called human herpesvirus-6.

Putting aside the question of Gallo's theft, it is now clear that HHV-6 plays an important role in "AIDS" and may, in fact, be the real cause.

Gallo himself has published several papers suggesting that HHV-6 plays a major role in "AIDS." Of course, he tries to tie it to HIV so that HIV will not be seen as the major scientific error that Peter Duesberg, two Nobel Prize winners, and hundreds of other scientists say it is.

Everything that Gallo says that HHV-6 can do in concert with HIV, HHV-6 is quite capable of doing all by itself. In an editorial, in the March 5 issue of *The Lancet*, Gallo writes with Paolo Lusso, "There is little doubt that HHV-6, like cytomegalovirus, can be reactivated in immunosuppressed people and may behave in some instances as a bone fide opportunistic pathogen. For example it was recently linked to pneumonitis in patients who had undergone bone marrow transplantation. However, the unique biological properties of HHV-6, especially its 'immunotropic' nature and its positive interactions with HIV, strongly suggest that, once reactivated in the course of HIV infection, it may have detrimental effects on the immune system and expedite progression of the disease."

As readers know, we do not believe that HHV-6 is reactivated, but that it is a relatively new infection of people that only now is universal. Twenty years ago, there may have been no HHV-6 in people in this country. But now it is widespread and making some people very sick, and others kind of sick, while still others, even though they are also infected, don't show any external signs of disease whatsoever. (That is typical, by the way, of how an established ASFV infection manifests itself in pig populations.)

HHV-6 doesn't seem to require any interactions with HIV to cause the "AIDS"-like immune dysfunction that is being seen in millions of chronic fatigue syndrome patients. Indeed, some people have called chronic fatigue syndrome "HIV-negative AIDS." But then, as our readers know, there are also cases of "AIDS" itself that are HIV-negative— "AIDS" cases that the HIV establishment has tried to hide from the public. The real tragedy here is that HHV-6 is susceptible to treatment by Ampligen and at least two other medications.

What that may mean is that people may have died unnecessarily over the last several years because HHV-6 was not treated.

And why was that?

Well, one reason is that the HIV establishment has been trying desperately to pump as much killer AZT as possible into people who test positive for HIV (by a bogus test). That establishment has also done everything it can to stifle other avenues of inquiry. Thank you, Tony Fauci. Thank you, "AIDS activists." Someday there might be a movie like *Schindler's List* about you. But you won't be Schindler.

Anyone who has suggested that HIV is not the cause of "AIDS" has been labeled a nut or a murderer. Any scientist who has spoken up has had his or her career threatened.

HIV has become the shrine of some weird quasi-cult. Perhaps people are so terrified by the unknown, by all the questions that would arise if HIV is not the cause of "AIDS," that it is more comfortable to support an agreed-upon untruth than to deal with the messy nature of reality. We are probably in a transition period during which HHV-6 will be called "The Cofactor," until it can safely be called "The Cause." (Like those guys on Broadway with the shell games, watch Gallo's hands very, very closely.) The main reason HHV-6 can't be called "The Cause" is that it doesn't affect only the risk groups that the CDC has propagandized about for the last 13 years. The whole "AIDS" scenario, as presented by the government is a tissue of lies.

Keep in mind that the blood supply *is not* screened for HHV-6. Many new problems of a financial and legal nature may now arise. Just for starters, consider all the doctors and nurses who have HHV-6 disease in the form of chronic fatigue syndrome. There are many thousands of them all over the country. Think of what a lawyer could do for them when they learn that HHV-6 is not only destroying the immune systems of "AIDS" patients but is also the prime culprit in chronic fatigue syndrome.

They have been lied to.

They are not going to be happy campers.

For those of you who are more pragmatic about this issue, here is what needs to be done.

The premise that if one can cure HHV-6, one can cure "AIDS" needs to be explored as quickly as possible. This means that Ampligen must be made available for widespread testing as soon as possible. For the rationale behind that, just check the articles that Neenyah Ostrom has written about Ampligen in the past.

Lawsuits may be the only way to move this issue along. If HHV-6 is the primary cause of "AIDS," any doctor who does not use the safest, most effective treatment to halt the infection should be sued for malpractice. That will get their attention.

One other thing. This newspaper has taken all kinds of grief from some in this community for reporting the story as we see it. Right now our score card looks pretty good.

Just remember: The *Native* was the first paper to suggest that HHV-6 is the cause of "AIDS" and chronic fatigue syndrome. We are also the newspaper that suggested that Gallo stole credit for its discovery by renaming African swine fever virus.

Stay tuned.

In the March 28 issue, Neenyah Ostrom reported on research that raised new questions about HIV: "Just how unreliable is the HIV antibody test? A report from Australian scientists in mid-1993 was the first to demonstrate that it is plagued by potentially fatal flaws, such as the test's lack of specificity for the virus, as well as its lack of reproducibility (among other technical problems). Now Zairian researchers, working with renowned U.S. HIV expert and Harvard professor, Max Essex, have shown that certain bacterial illnesses may cause as much as a 70 percent rate of false positive results in both of the commonly-used HIV antibody tests."

Ostrom once again noted, "The Australian team, led by Eleni Papadopulos-Eleopulos, published a comprehensive review article that questioned not only the accuracy and reproducibility of the HIV antibody test, but also questioned what it measures, the very nature of HIV itself. In the process, Papadopulos-Eleopulos and co-workers showed the causal link between HIV and 'AIDS' to be far weaker than most U.S. researchers have recognized and/or acknowledged. The Australian researchers even suggested that using HIV antibody tests could be counterproductive, stating, 'We conclude that the use of antibody tests as a diagnostic and epidemiological tool for HIV infection needs to be reappraised.' "

About the new development, Ostrom reported, "Essex and his colleagues in Zaire raise slightly different, but equally troubling, questions about the reliability of the HIV antibody test. They found such high levels of false positive HIV antibody tests—that is, a positive result on an antibody test when the virus itself, HIV, is not present—in people with certain bacterial infections that they conclude the test is detecting not only HIV, but also a portion of various types of bacteria. In other words, it's not just that the HIV antibody test is not specific for a viral infection. It can also, apparently, signal the presence of a completely different type of life form, bacteria."

In the April 4 issue, I wrote an editorial about Ross Perot's appearance on *Larry King Live*, during which he expressed concern about the mysterious illness that was afflicting veterans of the Persian Gulf War. Perot announced that he was putting together a plan to research the illness. I noted, "Mr. Perot doesn't know it, but the path he has chosen will lead him deep into the heart of the 'AIDS' epidemic and the cover-up of what HHV-6 really is and what it is doing in the bodies of 'AIDS' patients, CFS patients, and, more than likely, the victims of the Gulf War Syndrome."

In the same issue Neenyah Ostrom reported on new evidence that HHV-6 is capable of causing a wide variety of illnesses:

372

Evidence continues to accumulate that human herpesvirus-6 (HHV-6) is capable of causing a wide variety of illnesses: Graft-versus-host disease and a type of pneumonia (pneumonitis) following organ transplantation are two of the more serious conditions recently shown to be caused by HHV-6. New research now demonstrates that the virus can cause an "HHV-6-associated immunodeficiency" not only in immunocompromised patients—like bone marrow recipients and "AIDS" patients—but also in immunologically competent people.

A research report, in the March 19 issue of *The Lancet*, demonstrates that HHV-6 can cause chronic bone marrow suppression in previously healthy individuals. The authors warn that defining this HHV-6-induced immunodeficiency could have extremely important clinical implications, particularly for "AIDS" and cancer patients. The study was performed by U.S. researchers Konstance Knox and Donald R. Carrigan (who recently demonstrated that disseminated, fatal HHV-6 infection occurs in "AIDS" patients), along with University of London researchers Ursula Gompels and Jenny Luxton.

Knox and colleagues point out that, while HHV-6 has been shown to be able to suppress the bone marrow in "immunocompromised adults," their current paper shows "evidence of HHV-6 associated bone marrow suppression in an immunologically normal healthy 37-year-old male who had recovered from life-threatening pneumonitis [pneumonia] from simultaneous lung infection with HHV-6 and legionella" (the bacterium that cause Legionnaire's Disease). They present evidence showing "an extended chronic HHV-6 infection (lasting at least three months) of his bone marrow."

In other words, HHV-6 doesn't just kill T-cells, B-cells, and natural killer cells in the blood as well as infecting monocytes and macrophages and nervous system cells; it also seems to be able to kill blood cells, or at least stop their germination, before their release from the bone marrow into the blood.

Knox and co-workers report that this patient developed evidence of "severely depressed bone marrow function": numbers of white blood cells, red blood cells, and platelets were all very low.

On day 16 of his respiratory illness, the man developed a rash and a high fever; he remained anemic (because of decreased numbers of red blood cells) and continued to have a low white blood cell count. HHV-6 was isolated from his blood at this time.

Isolation of the virus, along with the spiked fever, rash, and the presence of HHV-6 antibodies, "indicated a systemic HHV-6 infection," Knox and colleagues report. The man's health continued to deteriorate, and both HHV-6 and legionella . . . were isolated from his lungs as well as his blood. The man finally responded to treatment, and was released from the hospital.

"Although recovered from pneumonitis, the patient continued to show evidence of suppressed bone marrow function," Knox and co-workers report. White blood cell levels remained low, as did both CD4 (T4) and CD8 (T8) cell counts, and the man was still anemic a month after being released from the hospital.

The "chronic marrow suppression" exhibited by this patient was due to HHV-6 infection, as a bone marrow biopsy showed.

Knox and colleagues then went a step further, and investigated which subcategory (Variant A or Variant B) the HHV-6 infecting this patient belonged to. An earlier report, they noted, had found that fatal infection could occur when one variant of HHV-6 overtook the other; that is, when a patient becomes infected with more than one type of HHV-6.

They found that this patient's blood and bone marrow cells were infected with a Variant B strain of HHV-6.

"This result supports the interpretation that a persistent HHV-6 infection, rather than infection with

374

a new strain, was associated with the chronic bone marrow suppression," these investigators concluded.

In the media column of the April 25 issue, we reported on a piece that Larry Kramer had written in the April 19 edition of *The Advocate*, a national gay newsmagazine. Kramer wrote, "Why are we our own murderers? Why are the very organizations that we fund with millions of our dollars incapable of demanding and extracting what others receive by right?"

The organizations that Kramer was referring to, primarily, were GMHC and AIDS Project Los Angeles (APLA). Those organizations, Kramer asserted, "are indeed our enemies." He wrote, "They're our exterminators. GMHC is our Dachau, and APLA is our Auschwitz— the places we send all our 'Jews' so that they can be put to death quietly, so that no one can hear our agonizing screams in the dead of night. These AIDS organizations are our censors, our thought police, our SS. They stomp out any disruptive explosions. They tranquilized the infected lest the rest of the world hear or see anything too uncomfortable or embarrassing. . . . The endless stream of volunteers are their storm troopers. . . . Our money is siphoned by their free legal-service providers, who see that our wills are in order so we can leave them our money to build even grander gas chambers to burn us up in."

In a moment of incandescent Kramer irony, he was attacking the very system he had helped create.

In the May 2 issue, I wrote another editorial that was critical of Peter Duesberg.

> Seven years ago, this newspaper first brought Peter Duesberg to our readers' attention. We felt then, and still feel, that his arguments that HIV is not the cause of "AIDS" are cogent and convincing.
>
> Peter Duesberg has also bravely suggested that AZT is a probable cofactor or cause of "AIDS" rather than a credible treatment. He has turned out to be correct about that and certainly deserves every bit of praise that can be mustered by the gay community for his attempt to stop what appears to this newspaper to be a medical agenda that is tantamount to genocide. The fact that the gay community has not risen up en

masse against this atrocity will not stand it in good stead when the history of the epidemic is written. But that is another story.

Peter Duesberg's third idea, or contribution to the understanding of the epidemic, is one which we believe to be dead wrong. Instead of challenging the definition of "AIDS" as provided by the CDC, as well as the CDC's epidemiology, Duesberg chooses to find an explanation for "AIDS" that fits both the bogus definition of the disease and its bogus epidemiology. He asserts that drug use is the cause of "AIDS."

Peter Duesberg tries to have it both ways. He says that no syndrome can have twenty-nine manifestations and be caused by one agent. But then Peter Duesberg tries to say that drugs can cause a syndrome with twenty-nine manifestations and be predominantly represented by one gender and one behavioral risk group. It would only require identifying one person who did not take drugs and who got "AIDS" to show that Duesberg is wrong about drugs being the syndrome's cause.

In the Duesbergian universe, "AIDS" does not really exist. There is only what the CDC *calls* "AIDS," and whatever that is, it must be caused by drugs. So what he takes away with one hand—namely, the reality of the epidemic—he hands back with the other, namely a drug-induced immunodeficiency syndrome. It doesn't matter whether the victim is 23 or 43. Drugs killed the person who doesn't really have AIDS—but does by the CDC's definition. The person with CDC-defined AIDS didn't do drugs? Not possible, according to the Duesberg theory. The person said he or she didn't do drugs? They're lying, according to Duesberg. Hemophiliacs? They don't have the same disease. Africans? There is no "AIDS" [in Africa], just diseases that are fatal and HIV tests that are sometimes positive.

If Peter Duesberg had stuck to his challenge of HIV and AZT, he would be shaping up as a celebrated hero of science right now. When cases of "AIDS" materialized without HIV it appeared that Peter

Duesberg had won the war. But then, of course, by fiat, the CDC, and the nation's number-one official scientific liar, Tony Fauci, declared that those cases were not really "AIDS" because, essentially, they said so.

And then the Concorde study showed how right Duesberg was about AZT.

If "AIDS" were not the complicated cover-up that it is, Duesberg would probably be on the covers of *Newsweek* and *Time* as the Galileo of the twentieth century.

But unfortunately, Duesberg is playing the trifecta, and the drug hypothesis threatens to diminish his contribution, at least in the near term. And his notion that "AIDS" is not contagious is downright foolish.

Peter Duesberg foolish? The man who for so long singlehandedly undermined the HIV hypothesis until reinforcements came from the scientific community? The man who saved thousands of lives by teaching the uninformed that AZT is as dangerous to consume as Drano. How dare anyone call him foolish!

Well, the problem is that this epidemic, this holocaust, this cover-up, is long and complicated. At thirteen years, it has lasted longer than two world wars. Anyone active in dealing with it may be called upon to pass many intellectual tests. This is a unique period in history. Most people don't even grasp the kinds of evil that are involved in the epidemic. Self-appointed "AIDS" prophet Larry Kramer rants about it, but in many ways, Kramer hasn't even begun to understand the truth about the epidemic. (Kramer doesn't understand that it's not a matter of spending more money on "AIDS," it's a matter of getting the government to stop lying about HHV-6.)

Our point about Duesberg is that he has made a couple of world-class contributions to the understanding of HIV and AZT, but he does not understand "AIDS" because he does not grasp how deep the lying at the CDC goes. Duesberg looks at the CDC's definition of "AIDS" and says, well, boys, this can't be an infectious disease because no agent makes people sick in the patterns that you guys have described, i.e. no virus infects only homosexual men and IV drug users and fails to infect the rest of the population in an exponential manner. Furthermore, that agent you guys have fingered, that retrovirus, can in no way damage the immune system in the manner that you say it does.

Duesberg cannot seem to grasp the fact that all of the information being released by the CDC may be cooked, not to create an epidemic, but to cover one up. Duesberg fails to ask whether the CDC has defined its disease too narrowly, and as a consequence has not revealed the exponential spread of a putative agent. We of course believe that if "AIDS" had been defined as a syndrome involving several kinds of immune dysfunction, rather than one central immune defect (the T4 cells) in 1981, the CDC would have begun to try and figure out what was causing what are now considered to be two separate epidemics, "AIDS" and chronic fatigue syndrome. Had the CDC looked for a virus that was linked to both (artificially separated) syndromes, they would probably have blamed HHV-6, the very pathological (depending upon the strain) virus which has been found in both. Duesberg would have had a far harder time debunking HHV-6, which is more capable of destroying the immune system than HIV.

In the May 9 issue, Neenyah Ostrom discussed another problem that linked AIDS and CFS: "Reports of deaths from 'AIDS'-associated heart attacks seem to be appearing in the media more frequently. A new report in *The Lancet* suggests that a cytokine that is increased in 'AIDS' patients, interleukin 6 (IL-6), may also be elevated in patients who've suffered heart attacks. Increased levels of IL-6 have not only been identified in 'AIDS' and heart attack patients, but have also been implicated as being necessary for the development of Kaposi's sarcoma. And IL-6 levels are also elevated in chronic fatigue syndrome patients—who can develop a type of lesion that is suspiciously similar to KS, but also can experience cardiac symptoms and irregularities."

In the May 16 issue, Ostrom looked at another abnormality that linked AIDS and CFS: "How does chronic fatigue syndrome affect the brain? While more than one research team has identified organic changes in the brain, controlled studies comparing the brains of CFS patients to other patients and healthy people had not been performed. In newly published studies, however, it is suggested that the brain damage identified in CFS patients is probably caused by 'viral encephalitis,' and is, in fact, similar to what is seen in 'AIDS dementia' or encephalopathy."

In the May 23 issue, Neenyah Ostrom wrote a piece titled "Is HHV-6 the 'AIDS' Virus?"

> It was quite recently disclosed that chronic fatigue syndrome patients develop organic brain damage, visible on brain scans, that is similar to that seen in 'AIDS' patients. The culprit may now have been identified: Human Herpesvirus-6 has just been shown to be the cause of a fatal infection of the brain. HHV-6 infection of neurons not only caused death of the brain tissue, but was convincingly linked to clinical nervous system collapse.
>
> A new study from the Medical College of Wisconsin not only shows HHV-6 to be capable of causing fatal encephalitis, but also raises a still-unanswered question: Is HHV-6 the true cause of both "AIDS" and CFS?
>
> The evidence suggesting that HHV-6 may be the actual "AIDS" virus—in fact, the cause of the immune system collapse in both "AIDS" and CFS—continues to accumulate, and includes:
>
> HHV-6 has been shown to grow actively in both CFS and "AIDS" patients.
>
> HHV-6 infection has been closely correlated with Kaposi's sarcoma lesions in "AIDS" patients and with the "crimson crescents" seen in CFS patients.
>
> HHV-6 infects and kills natural killer cells, which are dysfunctional in both "AIDS" and CFS.
>
> HHV-6 infects and kills T4 cells, which are decreased in number in both "AIDS" and CFS

patients.

Furthermore, "AIDS dementia" and "CFS dementia" share a number of characteristics: short-term memory loss, disorientation to time and place, lack of coordination drop in IQ, and mood swings, among others.

"AIDS" and CFS patients show similar organic brain damage on SPECT brain scans, leading researchers to suggest that this damage, in both diseases, might be caused by a similar or shared "viral encephalopathy."

Now, HHV-6 has been shown to be capable of causing a fatal viral encephalitis in a non-"AIDS" patient.

The lead author of the new HHV-6 study, Dr. William R. Drobyski, commented that it "directly implicates HHV-6 as an infectious agent in encephalitis."

Medical College of Wisconsin researchers Drobyski, Konstance K. Knox, David Majewski, and Donald R. Carrigan's latest HHV-6 study is published in the May 12, 1994, *New England Journal of Medicine.*

In the May 30 issue, I wrote a long editorial about the former Health Commissioner of New York City, who had moved on to an even more powerful position in the government:

On May 12, 1994, the *New York Times* reported that Dr. Stephen C. Joseph, the Assistant Secretary of Defense for Health Affairs, said in an interview that doctors at American military medical centers around the world would give veterans of the Persian Gulf War 20 to 30 medical tests to try and diagnose their ailment.

As readers of this newspaper know from Neenyah Ostrom's reporting, the ailing veterans have many symptoms and immune problems in common with chronic fatigue syndrome, and therefore "AIDS" patients. Whatever they have seems to be transmitted to their spouses and children who, in many cases, are sick with a similar illness. . . . Dr. B. Milner of the V.A.

hospital in Allen Park, Michigan, has told the *New York Native* that he would like to call the syndrome Gulf War Acquired Immunodeficiency Syndrome (Gulf-AIDS) because of the numerous immunological problems that the 400 veterans he studied seem to have. He expressed concern that there would be some attempt to stop him from using that term because of political considerations.

From what we know about Stephen Joseph, it will be interesting to see whether he tries to conceal the real nature of the Gulf War Syndrome from the public. Stephen Joseph may be staring the real nature of "AIDS" in the face when he looks at the Gulf War vets, but he is hidebound by his own political notions of what "AIDS" is and what must be done about it. It will be surprising if he tells the nation the truth about the veterans.

Throughout his regime as Health Commissioner of the City of New York, we attempted to wake him up to what was wrong with the "AIDS" paradigm, namely the narrowing of its definition to "HIV disease." We even had a personal meeting with him during which his behavior was what we can only describe as thug-like. One of his assistants asked him to leave the room during our meeting. We later found out that Joseph was taken from the room to be lectured on the unprofessional nature of his demeanor.

So now he is, arguably, in one of the most powerful positions in public health. Theoretically, if the President of the United States ever declared something akin to a Medical State of Emergency in the United States (and people like Larry Kramer have urged him in one way or another, to do so), then one can only surmise that the involvement of the military in such a situation would put Stephen Joseph in what could be called the catbird seat.

To refresh our memory about his work in New York City and his nature, we took a look at Joseph's account in *Dragon Within the Gates* (published by Carroll & Graf) of his experience with "AIDS" during his tenure as health commissioner.

In terms of Joseph's character and sense of his own mission, the book is as scary as a Stephen King novel. In terms of Joseph's understanding of science and epidemiology of "AIDS," the book is kind of hilarious. The man is an object lesson in the dangers of stupid people having a great deal of power in the area of public health.

In one paragraph in his book, he dismisses the notion that HIV is not the cause of "AIDS," as well he should, considering that his entire book is about testing and identification of carriers of the virus that he just assumes is the cause of "AIDS." He reports some rather remarkable information about the prevalence of "AIDS" that would boggle anyone else's mind, but not, unfortunately, his own:

> . . . More disturbing was a study at a clinic in the Bronx in 1989, in which the Department of Health selected a group of men with a variety of venereal complaints but with no traditional risk factors for HIV infection. They had no history of sex with other men, or of intravenous drug use. They were, however, all heavy crack smokers. Among these men the rate of infection was 30 percent.
>
> A few rapidly carried out studies showed that HIV prevalence among the 10,000 M.E. (Medical Examiner) autopsies annually was even higher than expected, as high as 40 percent of all autopsies in one series.
>
> . . . In an area of the Bronx hardest hit by both AIDS and drugs . . . men coming to the emergency room for whatever medical or surgical complaints showed a silent HIV infection rate of 27 percent!

It was bizarre, unbelievable numbers like these that gave Joseph his sense of emergency. He wanted to use any public health measures that were available to identify the infected and keep them from infecting the uninfected. Did the unreliable nature of the HIV test bother him in the least? Well, here is Stephen Joseph on the HIV test: "In practice, when used under standard conditions, the HIV antibody test proved to be among the most accurate and useful diagnostic entities we possess." Like so much in the book, the opposite is true.

But given Joseph's rabid belief in the remarkable accuracy of the test, and the wild out-of-control numbers that some of the HIV surveys suggested, he wanted traditional public health (read: draconian) measures put in place. There was just one problem in his mind: "the gay community." Joseph is perhaps one of the greatest "gay conspiracy" theorists of all time. There was a big gay conspiracy preventing him from putting his professional public health agenda into place throughout his reign as Health Commissioner.

But the "gay community was not the only community to define the epidemic socially and politically rather than medically." The gay bad attitude spread to blacks and Hispanics. And here we have the very essence of the gay conspiracy: "The politics of AIDS defined AIDS well before any detailed medical definition took hold. AIDS is the first major public health issue in this century for which political values rather than health requirements set the agenda. The political definition of the epidemic—defined first by gay men and later modified by a stream of civil libertarians and political spokesmen—drove and determined the medical and public health response until well after the epidemic was in full flower."

Not true. The government politically defined and legislated the epidemic. And Stephen Joseph is just as political as anybody else. Who appointed him to his job as Health Commissioner, by the way? The last time I checked, it was a politician (Ed Koch) and not God. In fact, *Dragon Within the Gates* is nothing if not a primer on how Stephen Joseph played his own brand of politics with "AIDS" while calling it public health. "AIDS" turned out to be Stephen Joseph's way of accusing the "gay community" (whatever that is) of endangering the greater society. More evidence of great gay "AIDS" conspiracy: "In particular, the homosexual community asserted its primacy both in defining the epidemic and establishing the yardsticks by which responses to the epidemic were judged—yardsticks of gay identity, autonomy, and expressions of sexuality." (That last "queer" sentence should make him an honorary member of the Gay Academic Union.")

Throughout the book, Joseph defines American "AIDS" as a gay, black, and Hispanic disease. He quotes Robert (he must mean Rodger) McFarlane as saying, "A virus does not discriminate. A virus does not know the difference between black and white or straight and gay or male and female. Why doesn't anyone believe that?" To which Dr. Stephen C. Joseph says, "Answer: Because it's not true."

Joseph writes, "Epidemiologic accuracy . . . requires understanding in accurate detail both the people affected by the condition and the entire population at risk of the condition. An error in defining or counting either group will produce a faulty analysis." That statement is more on the money than he realizes.

As readers of this newspaper know, we believe that the evidence shows that a fatal epidemiological mistake was made by bifurcating "AIDS" and CFIDS (or CFAIDS) into two epidemics when, in reality, they are one. It doesn't take an Einstein to see that these two epidemics are probably both caused by HHV-6. It also doesn't take an Einstein to see the political motivation in trying to sell the public on the idea that the real epidemic was a gay, black, and Hispanic one.

Joseph is downright hysterical on the notion of "AIDS" breaking out in the white, heterosexual middle class. While Masters and Johnson are not experts on the "AIDS"-chronic fatigue syndrome connection, they intuitively may have blown the whistle in 1988 when they wrote with Robert Kolodny their book, *CRISIS: Heterosexual Behavior in the Age of AIDS*. Here's what Joseph said about them: "Alarmist and shrill, the book claimed that 'AIDS' is now running rampant in the general heterosexual population, estimated that over three million Americans were infected, and resuscitated old canards about casual contact and transmission."

More than a few Americans are beginning to see the covered-up link between "AIDS" and chronic fatigue syndrome. The cover-up will not go on forever. But the mythologies fostered by people like Joseph will make the future dicey for gay men. Consider this little gem from Joseph: "Significant numbers of gay men will flee the most heavily affected cities especially as the death toll mounts. This trend has already been documented, especially from San Francisco to the rural Western states. Many of these men are already infected." Perhaps the appropriate public health approach would be to pass laws against gay migration within the country.

Is it really possible that Joseph doesn't know that chronic fatigue syndrome has swept through the white, middle-class American population, leaving millions of people with "AIDS"-like immune dysregulation? In some ways, HIV has become a little like the story about the man who loses his keys and looks for them only under the lamppost because that's where he can see. HIV has created a self-fulfilling hypothesis. If you don't see HIV, you don't see "AIDS." If you see HIV, you poison the person. The person dies. Therefore "AIDS" is universally fatal. If a white, middle-class person has the same basic immune problems, you tell them they are tired and you don't poison them, you actually refuse to give them any medical care. Which may, in fact, save their lives.

Ironically, Joseph writes this about "AIDS": "Eventually we came to recognize that infection with the human immunodeficiency virus (HIV) leads progressively to an entire spectrum of illness, ranging from 'mere' laboratory test abnormalities in an otherwise well appearing person to a wide range of minor and major symptoms. . . ." Curiously, had public health officials gone whole hog with their traditional methods, they might have asked that the entire population be tested for "laboratory test abnormalities." If they had done that, we now know they would have discovered the chronic fatigue syndrome epidemic. But that would have shown the population that the HIV paradigm and the blame-the-gay-conspiracy-agenda, were not founded in reality.

Now that Stephen Joseph is in charge of figuring out whether Gulf War Syndrome is a real thing (which it obviously is), it will be interesting whether, in the face of its similarities to "AIDS," he will put his traditional public health methods into operation. Since what they have is obviously transmissible, will he quarantine the soldiers? Will he quarantine their wives? Their neighborhoods? Will he ask them to carry identification cards? Will they be forced to take AZT, or some toxic substance that will make them "noninfectious?" Will he criminalize their behavior in any way? If they don't cooperate, will he accuse them of obstructing public health?

Somehow we don't think he will practice the same kind of public health on them that he has tried to practice on the gay, black, and Hispanic "communities."

In the June 27 issue, Neenyah Ostrom conducted an interview with Philip E. Johnson, who was a law professor at the University of California, Berkeley, and a founding member of The Group for the Scientific Reappraisal of the HIV/AIDS Hypothesis, which had a membership of approximately 400 scientists and concerned citizens.

Johnson explained how he got interested in AIDS: "At first, I simply had the viewpoint that Duesberg's was an important dissenting voice that was getting punished for raising a very rational argument on the subject. This seemed to me to be very wrong. So I wanted to help him get a hearing. Over the next couple of years, as I became more and more familiar with all the scientific papers, I gradually became convinced that there really is a fundamental error in the paradigm and that the logic of the entire HIV paradigm is unsupportable."

Ostrom asked Johnson how the law could be used to resolve critical questions about the shaky relationship between HIV and AIDS. He told her, "First, you have to find a person who was injured by the product. That wouldn't be difficult, because you would identify someone who was diagnosed as being HIV-positive but wasn't. Now, of course, in a larger sense, even somebody who is HIV positive is being damaged by bad science. That wouldn't be attributable to the test, if the test is measuring what it is supposed to be measuring; the fact that the underlying science is wrong would be somebody else's fault."

Johnson also told Ostrom, "There are two kinds of theories on which a liability lawsuit could be based. One is negligence. That is, that the test makers did something wrong when they should have known better. The other theory is that it is a defective product. In most jurisdictions, there is strict liability for the sale of a defective product, so that you wouldn't even have to show that they should have known better—if the product is defective. Now that would be a very hard-fought issue, as to whether these tests are defective. Because, the manufacturers would say, well, there's a range of inaccuracy and of subjective judgment, but that's inherent in the problem, it's not a defect in our product. So that would be a litigated issue. But another way a product can be defective is it's falsely labeled. That is to say, if it's advertised to do something that it really doesn't do. And I think there may be some real prospects for an attorney to show that these tests have been sold as being accurate in a way that they are, in fact, not."

Johnson also pointed out to Ostrom, "There is no doubt that people are being accused of crimes—one of the more serious crimes—because of the HIV theory. For instance, a sexual assault will turn into attempted murder because of the HIV factor. To my mind, this is just one example of many in which the HIV diagnosis does great damage to the person who is diagnosed. In Thailand, employers are now routinely requiring HIV antibody tests for employment, I have heard. So if you test HIV-positive, you become unemployable. That's another example of how harm is done. Of course, people's marriages break up and lives are changed and ruined in all sorts of ways. So there's no question that this diagnosis of HIV positivity does immense damage to a person. And if the underlying science is ever called into question, as I think it is being called into question right now, then the possibility that a huge, massive harm has been done by bad science is going to create a great reaction from the public."

In the July 18 issue, we ran one of the longest pieces we ever published, a report by John Lauritsen on a day-long symposium sponsored by the Pacific Division of the American Association for the Advancement of Science (AAAS). The title of the symposium was, "The Role of HIV in AIDS: Why There Is Still a Controversy."

Lauritsen reported, "The AIDS establishment did not want the event to take place. Beginning in mid-May, a campaign was whipped up in the pages of California newspapers and the British science magazine, *Nature*, to have the program canceled or at least altered beyond recognition. Up to the last moment it was not known whether the symposium would happen at all, or exactly what form it would take. But it did take place, and was a triumph for the side questioning the HIV-AIDS hypothesis and other AIDS orthodoxies. The AIDS skeptics achieved a critical mass, and spoke with confidence and authority. Those who attempted to defend the official dogmas were apologetic and defensive; they failed to rebut or even acknowledge the points made by the skeptics; and in short, they put on a very poor show. It is now clearer than ever that the official AIDS experts cannot compete in a free and open debate, which is undoubtedly the reason for the intense censorship that has impeded AIDS discourse for the past decade."

Lauritsen noted, "The symposium included 12 main speakers, plus another half-dozen or so in the panels." After a detailed report on the speakers and panels, Lauritsen concluded, "If the HIV skeptics were in high spirits at the end of the symposium, it came from the awareness that they had carried the day. The other side utterly failed to rebut any of their major points. In contrast, the HIV defenders wore tense, defensive, hang-dog expressions, as though they were on trial for something. Although they could still parrot the old, and a few new AIDS myths, none of them was able to put together a reasoned argument. . . . The HIV-AIDS hypothesis is dead. Only in a genuine spirit of free inquiry can we discover exactly what 'AIDS' is and what its causes are."

Unfortunately, Lauritsen's obituary for HIV was premature.

In the August 15 issue, Neenyah Ostrom interviewed Peter Duesberg about his latest thoughts on AZT. Ostrom reported, "Duesberg was rather speechless at the recommendation by the FDA committee to give so toxic a drug to pregnant women." He told Ostrom, "Remember, AZT was made available 30 years ago for one purpose only: to kill human cells, to terminate DNA synthesis in growing human cells, including cancer cells. To put that into babies? That is beyond me. I do not see how one could possibly recommend that, under any circumstances—unless that baby has a wild leukemia or something. Maybe then. But just to put it in there when there is just antibody to a virus? For which, as [PCR inventor and Nobel Prize Winner] Kary Mullis points out so eloquently, nobody can name any paper anywhere in the AIDS literature that proves that HIV is causing AIDS. And on that basis, you put AZT into a baby. I am speechless. I can't say any more than that it is extremely risky. I would even say it is irresponsible. That is truly irresponsible, in my opinion. Even if you had a paper that showed that HIV causes AIDS, where are the data that show that AZT is not hurting the rest of the baby? Where are those studies? Where are the animal studies that show that AZT is compatible with the development of a human or animal baby?"

In the September 12 issue, Neenyah Ostrom covered new research that once again raised the profile of HHV-6:

> It looks like HIV is once again getting some help causing "AIDS" from human herpesvirus-6 (HHV-6). One of the latest theories about HIV is that it is never inactive but is concentrated in the lymph nodes all during the "latent" phase of "AIDS"; only after it has destroyed the lymph nodes, according to this new theory, does HIV cause CD4 cell destruction in cells circulating in the blood.
>
> Now, however, it has been reported that HIV is not the only virus "hiding" in the lymph nodes of "AIDS" patients: HHV-6 is there, too.
>
> The Italian research team that reported these findings in the August 20, 1994 issue of *The Lancet* also suggested that the two subtypes of HHV-6, Variant A and Variant B, are quite different from each other. The

HHV-6 found in the diseased lymph nodes was primarily Variant B. These researchers suggest that this finding, along with the fact of Variant A's "frequent occurrence" in Kaposi's sarcoma tissue, point to the two variants preferentially infecting very different types of tissues.

The Italian research team, led by Ricardo Dolcetti, begins by noting that it is still not completely understood what diseases HHV-6 is associated with, but, "Particular interest has focused on the possibility that HHV-6 may constitute an important cofactor in the progression of HIV infection." Then they outline the evidence that HHV-6 plays a role in causing "AIDS": "This hypothesis is based on several lines of evidence, including the isolation of HHV-6 from AIDS patients and the demonstration that this virus shares with HIV a primary tropism for CD4 T-cells, is able to transactivate HIV regulatory elements [i.e. 'turns on' HIV], can increase HIV replication, and synergizes with HIV in the induction of cytopathic [cell-killing] effects in co-infected cells. The detection of HHV-6 genomes and virus-encoded antigens in various tissues taken at necropsy from AIDS patients suggested that, at least in the late phases of HIV infection, HHV-6 may contribute to the clinical evolution of the disease."

In the same issue, John Hammond covered an ominous development in Russia: "Proposed legislation to control the spread of 'AIDS' in the Russian Federation would mandate forced HIV-antibody testing of anybody suspected of belonging to a 'risk group.' The law would also provide for deportation of any foreigner found to be infected with HIV, according to a report by the International Gay and Lesbian Rights Commission (IGLHRC) in its newsletter, *Emergency Response Network*. . . . The law is directed at 'citizens who according to epidemiological indications threaten massive spreading of HIV infection.'"

The CDC's "epidemiology" had truly conquered the world.

In the September 26 issue, Neenyah Ostrom reported on another development in HHV-6 research: "HHV-6 has been suggested as the cause for a potentially serious kind of disease in a child who had just undergone bone marrow transplantation. HHV-6 has previously been suggested as the possible cause of a childhood skin disease called 'Exanthem Subitum' (also called 'Roseola'). It is characterized by a high fever, which can induce convulsions, as well as lymph node swelling and pain (lymphadenopathy). Swollen spleen and reduced white blood cell count (leukopenia) can also occur. The high fever and other symptoms are followed by the appearance of a flat, red rash (the 'exanthema'). The report in the September 24, 1994, issue of *The Lancet* raises new questions about HHV-6: For instance, is HHV-6 responsible for causing not only life-threatening pneumonitis and GVHD in immunosuppressed bone marrow transplant recipients, but also for the skin diseases that can develop? Is HHV-6 causing some of the rashes and skin disorders described in other immunosuppressed patients, such as those diagnosed with "AIDS" and chronic fatigue syndrome? Most importantly—because it is potentially treatable—is HHV-6 the cause of 'acute Exanthem of HIV disease' in 'AIDS' patients? . . . More and more, it looks like the question in 'AIDS' and CFS research is not 'What does HHV-6 do?' but rather: 'What happens in AIDS or CFS that HHV-6 *isn't* capable of doing?' "

In the October 10 issue, Neenyah Ostrom wrote a piece about the link between HHV-6 and a blood clotting disorder: "Japanese researchers have suggested in a new report in the September 17 issue of *The Lancet*, that human herpesvirus-6 (HHV-6) is able to cause a bleeding disorder called thrombocytopenia. A specific type of this blood clotting disorder, called ITP, is common among 'AIDS' patients. HHV-6 has been associated with other types of bleeding disorders, and this new research raises the question: Is HHV-6 primarily a hemorrhagic virus? 'AIDS' researcher Robert C. Gallo has, for the last several years, documented the other alarming characteristic of HHV-6: that it is capable of destroying cells of the immune system—with or without HIV. It is puzzling that this relatively new virus, capable of causing both immune dysfunction and blood clotting disorders in 'AIDS' patients, has not been given the highest priority for research by the 'AIDS' establishment."

In the October 24 issue, Neenyah Ostrom took on the issue of the size of the CFS epidemic: "How many people in the United States have chronic fatigue syndrome? Apparently the answer provided to that question depends on who you are and what you're trying to prove. According to the Centers for Disease Control, the number of CFS patients in the U.S. is about 20,000. According to private sector researchers, the number is more like half a million—or, possibly, even several times more than that."

Ostrom reported, "New data on the prevalence of CFS were presented at the American Association for Chronic Fatigue Syndrome Research Conference held October 7-10 in Fort Lauderdale, Florida. According to a study performed by Dr. Leonard Jason, professor of psychology at DePaul University in Chicago, as many as 500,000 Americans may already have CFS. How can there be a more than ten-fold difference between Jason's epidemiological data and those collected by the CDC?"

Ostrom noted, "One unacknowledged problem with all of the CDC's research on CFS is that the agency still does not admit that CFS is a communicable disease. The 1994 CDC pamphlet 'The Facts about Chronic Fatigue Syndrome' states: 'There are no published data indicating that CFS is communicable through either casual or intimate contact. Studies of groups of CFS patients and their contacts have shown no evidence of person-to-person transmission of the illness. Several cluster outbreaks of unexplained fatigue reported to CDC in recent years are being investigated. Furthermore, reports that pets are involved in the transmission of CFS, or that they can contract the disorder, are unsubstantiated.' "

Ostrom pointed out, "Most private sector researchers—certainly those studying the 'cluster outbreaks' of CFS—acknowledge that CFS is indeed communicable. Why would nurses for instance, or other medical personnel be at increased risks of developing CFS if they weren't catching a communicable illness from the public? No other explanation makes any sense. Is the CDC operating like the Keystone Kops because the agency is embroiled in covering up 'The Facts about CFS': that CFS is not only contagious but is part of the 'AIDS' epidemic? What would happen if the CDC admitted that there is a fairly casually-transmitted epidemic of immune dysfunction in the country? In other words, that there is an epidemic of immune dysfunction that is spread not through sexual contact, but most likely through saliva—how would the CDC handle that? And how would the agency inform the public that, according to low estimates, half a million Americans might already have this casually-transmitted immune dysfunction syndrome? Is it a sign of the extreme seriousness of the threat that CFS poses to the public health of the U.S. that the CDC isn't even trying very hard to figure out how many cases already exist?"

In the October 31 issue, Neenyah Ostrom reported on very disturbing research that suggested that HHV-6 was in the blood supply: "For a number of years, this newspaper has argued that human herpesvirus 6 (HHV-6) is a threat to the blood supply. To date, no regulatory authority in the U.S. screens transfusion products for the presence of this virus, which has been associated with 'AIDS,' chronic fatigue syndrome, multiple sclerosis, a mononucleosis-like illness, lymph node disease, hepatitis, meningitis, and other neurological illnesses. Now a German research team has published a study suggesting that *transfusions are a vehicle for the transmission of HHV-6 and may be causing unidentified disease.* Although no advisories have been issued about people with active HHV-6 infections not donating blood, privately, Centers for Disease Control officials caution people with HHV-6-related illnesses such as chronic fatigue syndrome—not to donate blood. One possible reason for this unofficial warning was explored, unintentionally, by the new report from German scientists: They documented the fact that there are silent carriers of HHV-6— people with active infections who do not make antibodies to the virus."

Ostrom reported, "The German research team was led by Freimut Wilburn from Frie Universitat in Berlin. Its report, 'Detection of Herpesvirus Type 6 by Polymerase Chain Reaction in Blood Donors: Random tests and Prospective Longitudinal Studies,' was just published in the *British Journal of Hematology.* . . . Wilburn and colleagues begin by noting that transmission of viruses is always a risk in blood transfusion and, 'To be able to judge the danger from newly discovered viruses, we need to study their epidemiology and the disease they cause.' . . . Their conclusion should be viewed with some alarm: 'If we assume that HHV-6 DNA as demonstrated by PCR is DNA originating from infectious virus, we must conclude that blood from a proportion of healthy donors is potentially infectious.' Wilborn and colleagues also caution that people with HHV-6 infection do not always produce antibodies against the virus, and that a negative test is not sufficient to identify the HHV-6 carrier status.' These investigators also consider the possible 'superinfection' of an individual by more than one variant (there are two, A and B), and with more than one strain (nobody knows how many strains there are), and negative health

393

consequences thereof . . . ."

In the November 7 issue, Neenyah Ostrom wrote about the oral pathologies that linked AIDS and chronic fatigue syndrome: "As I opened the new [Fall, 1994] *CFIDS Chronicle*, a word leapt out at me: 'violaceous,' which means just what it sounds like, violet or purple. It was used to describe the 'crimson crescents' that have been found in as many as 80 percent of chronic fatigue syndrome patients, and which the *Native* has suggested are a type of Kaposi's sarcoma. Mouth tissue, which is technically part of the gastrointestinal system, is one of the first places that Kaposi's sarcoma can appear in 'AIDS' patients, and when it does, it's often described as either red or violaceous. Other oral infections and symptoms described for CFS patients in the *Chronicle* are also reminiscent of oral infections, seen in 'AIDS,' like the crimson crescents' extreme similarity to Kaposi's sarcoma. Will the signs and symptoms observed in the oral tissues of CFS patients be the ones that finally link CFS irrevocably to 'AIDS?' Nearly every 'AIDS' or Kaposi's sarcoma expert that the *Native* has consulted about the relationship between 'AIDS' and CFS has conceded that, if the crimson crescents are found to be a form of Kaposi's sarcoma, the diseases would be incontrovertibly linked. If 80 percent of CFS patients have the 'crimson crescents,' why hasn't someone biopsied them to prove they aren't Kaposi's sarcoma? Is everyone afraid of learning the truth?"

In the November 14 issue, Ostrom covered the similarities of brain pathologies in AIDS and CFS. She reported, "Research was published in the *American Journal of Radiology* comparing the SPECT brain scans of CFS patients with those of patients with 'AIDS dementia complex' that found them virtually indistinguishable. These investigators also concluded that their findings 'are consistent with the hypothesis that chronic fatigue syndrome may be due to a chronic viral encephalitis.' The similarities between the SPECT scans of CFS and 'AIDS' patients, according to these researchers, suggest a similar origin for the neurotropic dysfunction in these conditions."

In the December 12 issue, which celebrated our fourteenth anniversary, I wrote an editorial titled "Vindication for the *Native*'s 'Wacky Theories.'"

There has been no shortage of little gremlins around town who are fond of dismissing the *New York Native* by repeating the fifth column mantra—or big lie—that the *Native* is filled with "wacky theories." The hope is that if this is repeated enough times, people will believe it.

I'm sure many of our readers have encountered such remarks. They usually come from someone who is on AZT, or someone who has played a role in the activism that has led to the foisting of incredibly toxic substances upon people who haven't got a clue about what's being done to them.

Well, we survived the "wacky theory" campaign.

Our survival and success has relied on the excellent work of John Lauritsen on AZT and Neenyah Ostrom on HHV-6 and the CFIDS-AIDS cover-up. Their work will stand out as some of the most important journalism of this century.

Last week, the *Native* received a bit more vindication in the form of an editorial in [a November issue of] *AIDS Weekly*, a newsletter that goes to many of the top "AIDS researchers" in the country.

Penned by Daniel J. DeNoon, the editorial asserts that "Human herpesvirus type 6 (HHV-6) is no longer a virus in search of a disease. The time has come to dispense with both alarmist propaganda and hopeful reassurances in order to develop appropriate infection control and treatment guidelines."

While the crack about "alarmist propaganda" is clearly directed at the *Native*, the editorial at the same time is an inadvertent admission that the *Native* has successfully brought HHV-6 to the public's attention, which is no mean feat in an era of massive propaganda about HIV.

Mr. DeNoon writes, "In immunocompromised patients, reactivation of latent HHV-6 can be a major problem. A recent series of autopsies demonstrated that HHV-6 is widely disseminated in late-stage AIDS; indeed, one patient was shown to have died of HHV-6 pneumonitis similar to that seen in a bone-marrow-transplant patient."

Mr. DeNoon, whose career at *AIDS Weekly* seems to involve a loyalty oath to HIV, indicates the following salient points about HHV-6 from studies at the recent Tenth International Conference on AIDS: "1) HHV-6 is reactivated in people with HIV infection; 2) that the degree of reactivation increases with HIV disease progression; 3) that HHV-6 makes a major contribution to AIDS by activating latent HIV and contributing to lymphadenopathy; and 4) that HHV-6 may contribute to AIDS retinitis."

Not bad for a virus that the AIDS establishment would generally not like to talk about, is it?

Mr. DeNoon ignores Neenyah Ostrom's reporting on HHV-6, which has shown how the virus is a lot more destructive than his impressive little list. (And his arm wouldn't have fallen off if he'd written that there have been allegations that HHV-6 is really an animal virus.)

But to be fair to Mr. DeNoon, he is ahead of the major media on this one. He notes, "HHV-6 also has been associated with atypical lymphoproliferation, unclassified collagen vascular disease, chronic fatigue syndrome, rheumatoid arthritis, and systemic lupus erythmatosus."

And it needs HIV to do serious damage to someone? DeNoon writes: "It is unclear whether HHV-6 is involved in the etiology or pathogenesis of these conditions, or whether it is reactivated by an underlying immunodeficiency."

Mr. DeNoon should explore the literature. The matter is *politically* unclear. Scientifically, it is another matter. The wide range of cells HHV-6 is capable of infecting and harming is all too clear.

Mr. DeNoon asserts, "All of these findings cry out for further research." The *New York Native*, the journal of "alarmist propaganda," has been urging such a move for almost seven years.

Mr. DeNoon calls for the screening of the blood supply for HHV-6. The *Native* called for that first.

Mr. DeNoon, like the *Native* for the last seven years, brings up the matter of treatment. He writes: "Treatment options should be considered. HHV-6 is sensitive to ganciclovir and foscarnet, two drugs frequently used to prevent AIDS-related opportunistic infections. Determining whether these or other antiherpes drugs can influence HIV pathogenesis should be a priority. How about influencing HHV-6 pathogenesis? And what about Ampligen? Its effect on HHV-6 is rather clear-cut."

Then comes DeNoon's amusing bombshell: "Despite the importance of HHV-6 as a major cofactor in AIDS pathogenesis, it would be a mistake to focus on the virus to the exclusion of HIV."

Hello?

If any of our readers is aware of any movement to focus on HHV-6 to the exclusion of HIV, please get in touch with us immediately.

Is David Ho now working at the Aaron Diamond HHV-6 Research Center?

Are Whoopi Goldberg and Madonna filming HHV-6 public service announcements?

Mr. DeNoon is being a tad disingenuous, but we forgive him for that because his editorial, which is printed in *Blood Weekly*, will reach some of the most important scientists and public health officials in the nation. *Now they cannot say they were not warned about the seriousness of HHV-6.*

It would have been nice if Mr. DeNoon had given Neenyah Ostrom and the *Native* a little credit for bringing HHV-6 to the public's attention. We had to survive ACT UP's boycott to publish that story.

Nevertheless, we applaud Daniel DeNoon and *AIDS Weekly* for giving this incredibly important virus the attention it deserves.

In the same issue, Neenyah Ostrom wrote another piece about the incidence of chronic fatigue syndrome: "How fast is the chronic fatigue syndrome epidemic growing? While the Centers for Disease Control fumbles around, apparently to minimize as much as possible their estimate of how many people have CFS—and by extension, how contagious it is—the November 28, 1994, issue of the *New York Times* has just reported that CFS is one of the top two causes of new claims made on disability insurance policies. The rapid growth of the CFS epidemic, according to the *Times*, is also contributing to enormous losses for disability insurance providers. This is a development that may, at least, insure that CFS receives more regular coverage from the *New York Times*: While the science section covers the rapidly-growing epidemic with a story every now and then, it may become a regular feature covered by the newspaper's business writers as the economic impact of the illness becomes increasingly apparent." That certainly didn't happen.

In the December 26 issue, Neenyah Ostrom reported on the discovery of the supposed cause of Kaposi's sarcoma: "Kaposi's sarcoma was one of the first conditions that defined 'AIDS,' and it continues to be one of the most disfiguring, frustrating, and ultimately deadly conditions associated with the epidemic. Efforts to control KS have been thwarted by the fact that its cause has been unknown. Now a research team from Columbia-Presbyterian Medical Center in New York City has identified sequences from a putative new herpesvirus that they have found in a greater that 90 percent of KS tissues. Is this virus the cause of KS? Is it in fact, a new virus—or is it simply another variant of human herpesvirus-6, which has also been associated with KS? . . . The Columbia-Presbyterian medical research team held a press conference December 15 to announce their finding of what they believe to be a new human herpesvirus that may cause Kaposi's sarcoma in AIDS patients."

The virus was eventually called human herpesvirus-8 (HHV-8). At the end of her piece on the discovery, Ostrom wrote, "It will be interesting to see if HHV-8 does all the 'AIDS'-like things that HHV-6 does. The differences between HHV-6 and HHV-8 may be politically, economically, and Nobel Prize-driven. Given that Dr. Robert Gallo at the National Cancer Institute claims to have discovered HHV-6, it would be unusual for him not to stake his own claim on this new discovery."

In the same issue, I wrote an editorial about the new finding.

> For almost a decade this newspaper has been reporting that autopsies performed at the University of

398

Miami in 1985 indicated that almost all—not *some*—AIDS patients have Kaposi's sarcoma by the time of death.

The significance then, and now, is that there is a very real possibility that KS = AIDS and AIDS = KS. (We're not speaking here of classical KS). The thinking of the University of Miami team at the time was that if one could find the cause of KS one might find the cause of AIDS. It is not out of the realm of possibility that had those researchers received more attention, the epidemic might now be under control, and the disease might no longer be fatal.

As readers of this newspaper know, AIDS is an all-too-political event that has been driven by a dictatorial HIV (and AZT) establishment. And our readers know all too well who the main victims of this establishment have been.

The new findings described by Neenyah Ostrom in this issue could be the beginning of scientific paradigm-busting of the highest order.

When Ostrom and I attended the press conference for what could turn out to be the discovery of HHV-8 (or HHV-6 variant C?), we were alarmed to find that the youngish researchers were totally unaware of the 1985 research which suggests that all AIDS patients have internal and/or external Kaposi's sarcoma.

We fear that the findings of Drs. Moore and Chang may be mired in the politics of the CDC, where Moore has spent time working in an area called "public health," an area that often could be better characterized as "political health." The Chang-Moore line on KS: "Today, approximately 25 percent to 50 percent of all homosexual males with HIV disease present with or will eventually develop KS during the course of their illness." Of course, this is very different from saying that all AIDS patients, regardless of sexual orientation, present with KS upon autopsy.

Once again, a disease is being characterized as an essentially gay disease, even though it crosses all risk groups. In his front-page *New York Times* story on the virus, Lawrence Altman wrote: "Kaposi's sarcoma is 20,000 times more common in people with AIDS than in those who do not have it. And among those with AIDS, it is far more prevalent among gay and bisexual men. Women with AIDS are more likely to have Kaposi's sarcoma if they were infected by a bisexual man than by an intravenous drug user."

That sounds very interesting, but there is just one problem: It may not be true.

1995: Self-fulfilling Political Prophecies

In the January 16 issue, Neenyah Ostrom covered a promising new treatment for CFS that was reported in *Medical Tribune* on October 20, 1994: "An extract of pig liver has apparently been found by researchers in Texas to be effective in treating chronic fatigue syndrome. The extract, called Kutapressin, is an injectable drug that has been safely used in the United States to treat herpesvirus infections (like shingles) since the 1940s."

Ostrom noted, "This newspaper has reported on considerable evidence over the last ten years that a pig virus, African swine fever virus, has become capable of infecting humans and may be the actual cause of the immune dysfunction seen in both 'AIDS' and chronic fatigue syndrome. We have also reported on allegations that African swine fever virus was renamed in the National Cancer Institute laboratories of Dr. Robert C. Gallo—either by accident or design—and is now called human herpesvirus-6 (HHV-6). The extract of pig liver, Kutapressin, restores a very particular type of T-cell dysfunction in CFS patients: a significant decrease in natural killer (NK) cell function. An identical decrease in NK cell function is seen in 'AIDS' patients. HHV-6 has recently been shown to be able to infect and kill natural killer cells from both 'AIDS' and CFS patients. It has also been suggested that HHV-6 is a major contributor to the (nearly identical) immune dysfunction observed in both syndromes. . . . Like lentinan (a shiitake mushroom extract that also seems to be able to restore natural killer cell function), Kutapressin must be administered for about six months in order to be efficacious. . . . If a treatment corrects an immune system defect observed in both 'AIDS' and CFS, and appears to do so by affecting the course of infection with a virus found to be active in both 'AIDS' and CFS, wouldn't that be pretty strong evidence that the two syndromes are part of the same disease process? Kutapressin can now be added to the list of promising treatments for both 'AIDS' and CFS that are not being pursued. (Lentinan and Ampligen are also on that list.) . . . . Is it because it is identifying a treatment that connects an immune defect in both syndromes too definitely to each other?"

In the January 23 issue, Neenyah Ostrom reported on the peculiar story of Dr. David Ho: "A 'breakthrough in 'AIDS' research, claiming to prove once-and-for-all that HIV is the primary pathogen in the

401

syndrome has been announced by researchers at New York City's Aaron Diamond Research Center and the University of Alabama. Using unpublished (i.e. unproven) technologies and incorporating unpublished clinical trials of unapproved antiviral drugs, the two research reports and an accompanying editorial in the British scientific journal *Nature* recommend vastly expanding the number of people receiving (generally toxic) antiretroviral drugs."

The Ho paper, which turned out to be a triumph of public relations, presented a model of AIDS which in essence was a rather simplistic but dramatically compelling image of what was going on in the bodies of AIDS patients: each day a billion HIV particles were killing a billion CD4 cells in what the Ho paper referred to as a 'titanic struggle.' Ostrom noted, "This is a model that was abandoned some years ago when researchers were unable to show how HIV caused the cells' death."

Ostrom reported that Ho's group "used new, unpublished technologies to assert that there are so many billions of previously-undetected HIV virions in every 'AIDS' patient from the day he or she is infected that the CD4 cells finally become overwhelmed in the struggle between the virus and the immune system. And using unapproved drugs on which there aren't even published experimental data, these scientists report they have stopped HIV in its track and observed high rates of increase in numbers of CD4 cells following treatment. Furthermore, based on these unreplicated observations, these researchers urge that all individuals who test positive on the notoriously unreliable HIV antibody test be treated with toxic antiretroviral drugs immediately and throughout the rest of their lives."

Ostrom noted that, curiously, Ho "was one of the scientists who first discovered 'non-HIV AIDS' cases reported at the 1992 'AIDS' conference in Amsterdam. Furthermore, Ho has known since 1992 that these non-HIV 'AIDS' cases were emerging from another patient population with immune deficiencies: chronic fatigue syndrome."

In the same issue, I wrote an editorial about the Ho development:

> Last week's front page AIDS news in the *New York Times* was the "breakthrough," that occurred in the laboratories of Dr. David Ho and his associates at the Aaron Diamond AIDS Research Center.
>
> Ironically, readers of the *Times* had only been warned two days previously by science writer Larry

402

Altman that scientific discoveries are often hyped and do not receive the appropriate amount of skepticism.

Dr. Ho seems to have sufficient standing to be immune from skepticism at the *New York Times*, *Newsday*, and the *Washington Post*.

While the Ho research has been presented as a revolutionary "new view" of AIDS, it may turn out to be yet another example of special pleading for an untenable hypothesis. Dr. Ho has helped undermine the HIV theory with his discovery of cases of AIDS that occurred without HIV. This matter has never been resolved. It has only been swept under the rug. In a high-handed manner, the AIDS establishment said their epidemiology did not support it. As practiced by the AIDS establishment, epidemiology has turned out to be an agenda-ridden exercise in self-fulfilling political prophecies.

Ho's subsequent silence about HIV-negative AIDS is a red flag to this newspaper.

One story about Ho had him being called to Washington, where he was told that if he continued pursuing the "HIV-negative AIDS" line of thinking, he just might find himself unfunded. Whatever the truth of that story, Ho has certainly come through again for HIV and the AIDS establishment. If the AIDS establishment ever needed Potemkin Village-like reasoning for pumping "AIDS minorities" with toxic treatments, they now have one in Ho's new research.

The first question that scientists now need to resolve is whether Ho's work is competent or incompetent, honest or fraudulent. So much of basic AIDS research has turned out to be riddled with fraud that Ho should not be surprised if one's first instinct is to make sure that he is not pulling a fast one. Don't trust and do verify.

Ho has not helped matters by adopting the demeanor of a sort of smart-alecky AIDS activist himself. Last year, he was threatening to make buttons that said, "It's the virus, stupid!" to counter the scientific critiques of the HIV theory that originated with Peter

Duesberg and have been supported by a number of scientists, including two Nobel Prize winners. Perhaps Ho could be the first stand-up AIDS researcher on Comedy Central.

We are extremely concerned about the first critiques we have heard of Dr. Ho's work. (Neenyah Ostrom reports on Ho on page 14 of this issue.) The research is far too technical for most people to understand. Most science reporters think they are doing their job if they can make some sense of the research like this for themselves and then translate it for their readers. Because they think that their main job is to translate, they often fail to ask hard questions or report opposing viewpoints. When science writers like the work they are reporting on, they conveniently fail to report that the work has not been replicated, and when they don't like the work, they go out of their way to suggest that the work has not been replicated and that the reader should take the findings with a grain of salt. By that standard, the *Washington Post, New York Times*, and *Newsday* like Ho's work. Not a word of caution can be found in any of their reports.

A cry of "foul" comes from some in the group challenging the HIV theory. They charge that there are "internal contradictions, methodological problems, and erroneous interpretations." (Editor Harvey Bialy describing a forthcoming critique in *Bio/Technology*.) This would be acceptable if we were discussing interpretations of Shakespeare's sonnets, but lives hang in the balance here. Before any lives are bombarded with multiple experimental treatments, the matter of the competence and integrity of Ho's research had better be fully resolved. There is no crime in being stupid, but if one scintilla of fraud is to be found in Ho's work, every sanction in the book should be thrown at him.

Dr. Ho is the protégé of Nobel Prize winner David Baltimore, who, it has turned out during the last few years, has a rather unpleasant tolerance for scientific fraud. We hope that is not something that Dr. Ho learned from Dr. Baltimore.

In the February 6 issue, Neenyah Ostrom wrote about the increase of fungal infections which seemed to be the tip of the AIDS/CFS iceberg: "Although government health agencies such as the Centers for Disease Control and Prevention and the National Institutes of Health have attempted to cover up the fact that an epidemic of immune dysfunction called chronic fatigue syndrome is spreading throughout the general population, its numerous manifestations continue to reveal its presence. The latest indication of this epidemic of immune dysfunction appears to be an explosion in fungal infections like *Candida Albicans*. The newly-detected but explosive growth in disease and death due to fungal infections was reported by *Science* magazine's Steve Sternberg. Nearly 40 percent of all deaths from hospital acquired ('nosocomial') infections are currently caused by fungi, not by bacteria or viruses, as had been previously believed, according to Sternberg. And, generally, the fungus implicated was *Candida*, the organism responsible for causing thrush (among other problems) in both 'AIDS' and chronic fatigue syndrome patients (as well as other immune compromised individuals)."

Ostrom noted, "Clinicians and researchers have long debated the amount of morbidity caused by *Candida*. Although it is admitted to be a sometimes very serious opportunistic infection in 'AIDS' patients, *Candida* is not acknowledged as a major problem in CFS by the government researchers who guide the country's research effort (what there is of it). In contrast, private researchers have long argued that *Candida* infections could be playing a major role in causing some symptoms associated with CFS."

Ostrom asserted, "By not admitting that fungal infections are part of the massive, widespread epidemic of Chronic Fatigue and Immune Dysfunction Syndrome—or what looks more and more like human herpesvirus-6 (HHV-6) disease—government scientists are, it appears, further compromising the public health."

In the February 20 issue, we ran an A.P. article on a bill in the New Hampshire legislature: "Anyone injured in an accident could be forced to take an HIV test under a bill in the House. It would require the state to test anyone who could have infected an emergency worker, public safety worker, or volunteer trying to help the person."

In the same issue, Neenyah Ostrom wrote an article titled "Criminalizing the Epidemic: Not Since Nazi Germany Have Politics and Medicine Become So Intimate."

She also wrote, "Are there any circumstances under which illness should be criminalized? Without any real public debate—often, without the public being aware that it is occurring—criminalization of disease is proceeding all over the United States. People with tuberculosis were among the first to face criminal penalties in certain situations, but there is a new and rapidly-expanding population at risk for being criminally prosecuted for being sick: people who test positive for HIV antibodies—on a test that can produce up to 70 percent *false positive* results. Moreover, the pace at which criminal law is proceeding may be outstripping the growth of scientific knowledge, *because the science on which these laws are based is faulty.*"

Ostrom also pointed out, "When Americans discover that 'AIDS' is not confined to the 'risk groups,' as they've been told, but is actually widespread among the general population as 'chronic fatigue syndrome,' they may not be eager to throw people with the illness in jail. When scientists and clinicians are finally forced to admit that the chronic fatigue syndrome epidemic is part of the 'AIDS' epidemic, the 'risk groups' will no longer be limited to gay men, intravenous drug users, blacks and Hispanics. The 'risk groups' will suddenly include a lot of white, upper-middle-class people like health care workers (dentists, doctors, nurses), airline pilots and attendants, and others like teachers who are in contact with a large number of people." She concluded, "If it is admitted that HIV is not the sole cause of 'AIDS,' all of these laws must be invalidated."

In the same issue, I wrote, in an editorial about a very rare recognition of our work: "The *Native* has been notified that it has won an important journalistic honor from Project Censored. One of the stories we have covered, the unreliability of the HIV antibody tests, has been named one of the top 25 censored stories of the year. The story will appear in the forthcoming book: *Censored, The News That Didn't Make the News and Why: The 1995 Project Censored Yearbook.* The stories being honored were compiled from reporting by Neenyah Ostrom and the Associated Press."

In the February 27 issue, Neenyah Ostrom reported on a paper by Gallo that should have stopped the presses: "What causes the clinical conditions observed in 'AIDS' patients? Two prominent researchers at the National Cancer Institute have just published a scientific paper arguing that many manifestations of 'AIDS' are caused not by HIV, but by a putative 'AIDS cofactor,' human herpesvirus-6 (HHV-6). Paolo Lusso and Robert C. Gallo's newly published theory of how HHV-6 assists HIV in causing both the clinical symptoms and primary immunodeficiency of 'AIDS' further complicates the already Byzantine official explanation of how HIV uses various indirect mechanisms."

Ostrom noted, "Ironically, Lusso and Gallo's HHV-6 studies may have provided evidence that will destroy the HIV hypothesis: Without any indirect mechanisms, without complicated interaction with hormones or genes or other pathogens, HHV-6 appears to be able to cause most of the primary signs and symptoms that are associated with 'AIDS.' "

Ostrom also pointed out, "These scientists then tackle a central paradox of HHV-6: If HHV-6 is widespread in the population, how can it possibly be an 'AIDS' cofactor? At the same time, they note a true oddity in HHV-6 research (and one that raises questions about the claims made about the virus's prevalence): There is no test that can be routinely used to detect the virus's prevalence."

Ostrom reported that despite the serious problems in testing, Lusso and Gallo asserted that HHV-6 " 'is emerging as a potentially life-threatening opportunistic agent in immunocompromised hosts.' " She also noted, "They provide a long list of the symptoms and diseases thought to be caused by HHV-6 in such hosts, including: fever, hepatitis, failure of bone marrow grafts, encephalitis, and interstitial pneumonitis. HHV-6 appears to be hardly less damaging in 'immunocompetent adults,' as Lusso and Gallo report, since it has been linked to 'a variety of disorders, including EBV-negative infectious mononucleosis, autoimmune disorders, chronic fatigue syndrome, fulminant hepatitis, non-Hodgkin's lymphomas, and Hodgkin's disease.' "

In a piece published in the April 3 issue, Neenyah Ostrom asked, "What would have happened if human herpesvirus-6 (HHV-6) had been discovered before HIV? Might HHV-6 now be designated the 'AIDS virus?' As more and more is learned about HHV-6, it is clear that the virus can, by itself, cause immense damage to the immune system, as well as to other organ systems. It can cause a number of sometimes-fatal conditions, such as liver disease, cancer, and pneumonia, in addition to infecting and killing various types of immune system cells, including T4 (CD4) cells, T8 (CD8) cells, monocytes/macrophages, and natural killer cells. HHV-6 disseminated—i.e., widespread infection, can, by itself, prove fatal. HHV-6 kills cells directly, unlike HIV, for which numerous indirect mechanisms have been proposed as explanations of how the retrovirus wreaks havoc on the immune system. The damage inflicted by HHV-6 is so direct and overwhelming that, when the evidence is examined, it seems probable that only the chance discovery of one virus before the other has prevented HHV-6 from being identified as the 'AIDS virus.' "

In the May 1 issue, Neenyah Ostrom wrote about an interesting political development: "*Science* magazine's Richard Stone reported, in the April 14 issue, that Minnesota freshman Representative Gil Gutknecht has written a letter to National Institute of Allergy and Infectious Diseases Director Anthony Fauci questioning the role played by HIV in 'AIDS.' The letter was addressed to Fauci, but was copied to seven other government scientists and science administrators."

Ostrom reported, "In a ScienceScope item titled 'Congressman Uncovers the HIV Conspiracy,' Stone points out that the recent election 'ushered in a slew of politicians eager to reinvent government—and at least one who appears earnest about reinventing medical dogma on the cause of AIDS.' Stone notes that many of Gutknecht's questions echo arguments put forth by University of California, Berkeley, Professor Peter Duesberg, 'who insists HIV is harmless.' In his March 24 letter to Fauci, Gutknecht asked the NIAID director to explain, among other things, the large number of 'HIV negative AIDS' cases that have been made public. . . . 'Gutknecht's staffers think they're onto something,' Stone adds. 'The federal AIDS effort—based on the conclusion that HIV causes AIDS—will be seen as the greatest scandal in American history and will make Watergate look like a no-fault divorce,' croons Gutnecht's senior legislative assistant, Brian Hante, who claims to be the "impetus" for his boss's drumbeating.' "

In the May 15 issue, Neenyah Ostrom reported on new HHV-6 research that again challenged the HIV hegemony: "Dementia, with its accompanying loss of memory, cognitive ability, and personal identity, is one of the most frightening of human conditions. When dementia is associated with a communicable condition such and 'AIDS' and is essentially untreatable, it is even more distressing. Now, two researchers from the University of Wisconsin Medical College have not only identified the possible cause of most, if not all, 'AIDS'-associated dementia, but have also disclosed that is treatable infection: human herpesvirus-6."

Ostrom noted, "Human herpesvirus-6 has been shown to inflict considerable damage on humans. It can cause cancer, it can cause brain infection (encephalitis); it attacks the immune system as viciously as any known pathogen; it can simply overwhelm the human body with a disseminated infection that results in death. Konstance Kehl Knox and Donald R. Carrigan, studying HHV-6 at the University of Wisconsin Medical College, report in the April, 1995 issue of *Journal of Acquired Immune Deficiency Syndromes and Human Retrovirology*, that the virus directly attacks and destroys the myelin sheath surrounding nervous system tissues like the brain and is the cause of 'AIDS'-related dementia. 'We have caught this virus at the scene of the crime and believe that HHV-6 is responsible for some cases of AIDS Dementia Complex,' said Dr. Konstance Kehl Knox upon publication of the new results."

Ostrom reported, "Knox and her colleague, Dr. Donald R. Carrigan, found active HHV-6 infection that correlated with demyelination in the brain. This demyelination in 'AIDS' patients creates a condition called 'AIDS leukoencephalopathy,' according to Knox. Its physiological characteristics include demyelination (loss of myelin sheaths), a loss of axons (brain cells), and 'a paucity of inflammatory cells,' according to Knox and Carrigan. Its clinical characteristics can be referred to as 'AIDS Dementia Complex' and include symptoms such as forgetfulness, disorientation, and social withdrawal."

In the May 22 issue, I wrote an editorial about the response I got from Norman Mailer after I sent a letter urging him to look into our allegations about the nature of the real epidemic:

> Since the inception of the "AIDS" epidemic in 1981, the *Native* has been praised and condemned for bringing the story in exhaustive detail to its readers. At the beginning of the epidemic, the *Native* was attacked for covering the epidemic at all, mostly by a nervous gay community that just didn't want to hear the bad news.

Then after a couple of years of relaying information from the government's medical establishment, and trying to translate the technical aspects of the immune system for our readers, we ran afoul of several quarters when our reporting started to take a more independent and skeptical direction. The problem was that once we began to grasp the complex facts of the epidemic, we began to smell and see a rat.

Randy Shilts liked the *Native*'s early, government-approved report on the epidemic, but he didn't care for the *Native*'s investigative forays. What, after all, can a little gay publication do in the way of uncovering anything the mainstream press hasn't uncovered? Shilts tried to portray ex-CDC scientist Don Francis as the great moral hero of "AIDS." We have explained to our readers why Francis could be held responsible for the major wrong turns the research on "AIDS" has taken. A slight difference of opinion.

Larry Kramer helped establish himself as the spokes-messiah of "AIDS" by publishing his first manifesto about the "AIDS" epidemic in the *Native*. He mentioned the *Native* in his plays. But now when he is not accusing us of being "murderers," he is telling people (see the recent *Poz* interview) that no one (that means you) reads the *Native*. Some years ago, he told us in an article in the *Village Voice* just to shut up. Since we had already learned from Larry that silence equals death, we dared to keep publishing and keep investigating.

The *Native* began to be such a threat to the "AIDS activist" establishment that we were subjected to a boycott by ACT UP. We survived our excommunication. To borrow a line from the activists themselves, the *New York Native* means fight back.

We also survived the challenge of two peculiar "gay" publications that seemed bent, basically, on countering our reporting on "AIDS. If we reported A, they seemed to report non-A. The fact that we survived their commercial and journalistic challenges in the marketplace certainly gives the lie to Kramer's notion that no one reads the *Native*.

The *Native*'s coverage of Peter Duesberg's doubts about HIV and the toxic disaster known as AZT, mostly penned by John Lauritsen, really got under people's skin. Lauritsen's incisive reporting makes him one of the few heroes of the epidemic. The fact that he has not been honored by his own community is testimony to the intellectual disarray of what we loosely call our best and brightest.

While the price John paid for truth-telling was generally a lack of recognition, the price Peter Duesberg has paid for challenging the HIV orthodoxy has been his ability to do science. Once a well-funded (by the NIH) contender for the Nobel Prize, he now watches his funds running out to the point where he may lose his lab. The HIV establishment has enough power to cut the supply of funds to any scientist who challenges the party line. The word is out: rock the boat and you go overboard.

Starting in 1988, the *Native* really got into hot water. After reading several articles on chronic fatigue syndrome, including two by Hillary Johnson in *Rolling Stone*, I asked Neenyah Ostrom to begin to explore the possibility that CFS and "AIDS" are related. Since 1988, Ostrom has written three books based on her reporting.

I dare anyone to read all of her work and not conclude that she has broken one of the biggest stories of the century. She has followed every development in CFS research, and she has become the country's leading reporter on the subject. Her reporting raises serious doubts about everything that the public has been told about "AIDS" and chronic fatigue syndrome. No rational person can read her work and not sense that there is an unprecedented cover-up taking place—one that is causing countless deaths and enormous misery.

At the very hub of the cover-up, she has investigated is the virus HHV-6. This is the virus Robert Gallo "discovered" shortly after he was presented with evidence that "AIDS" patients are possibly afflicted with African swine fever virus. Over the past few years, it seems that HHV-6 has become the dominant object of research in Gallo's lab. It has gone from being an opportunistic infection, to being a possible cofactor, to being the probable cofactor. The next step would be to call it the probable cause. But that would be a very big political, emotional, and financial step. The whole house of cards that is the HIV Empire could come crashing to the ground. The citizens of this country would not be happy campers.

Gallo did not just find HHV-6 in "AIDS" patients. Although he has downplayed it, he also found it in victims of chronic fatigue syndrome. HHV-6 doesn't behave one way in the bodies of "AIDS" patients, and then behave another way in CFS patients. It is the most likely explanation for the fact that just about everything that goes wrong in "AIDS" patients' bodies, to one degree or another, also goes wrong in the bodies of some or all of CFS patients. Dr. Paul Cheney let the cat out of the bag a couple of years ago when he told reporter Nicholas Regush, in an article published in *Spin* magazine, that CFS could be called "AIDS minor." We, of course, then asked whether that was a little like "pregnancy minor."

Despite all of this reporting in the *Native*, it seems as though the HIV orthodoxy and AZT still dominate "AIDS" research and treatment. The reason that the lies prevail, we believe, is the wholesale failure of the American media and the intelligentsia to ask the hard questions, to do the investigative digging and the brave reporting that is required to pierce the veil of the Official Story of "AIDS."

And we have not in any way tried to own the story. We have urged dozens of reporters and intellectuals, from Susan Sontag to Noam Chomsky, from Frank Rich to Gary Trudeau, from Seymour Hersh to Bob Woodward, to investigate our allegations. After all, is not "AIDS" one of the defining events of our time? Has it not changed human relations profoundly? Is it not perhaps the future nucleus of an entirely different, and politically dreadful, society? If the government either has the whole thing wrong, or is lying about everything, does it not rank way up there in importance? For whatever reasons, our pleas for coverage of this matter have generally fallen on deaf ears. But, like the Energizer Bunny, we have persisted in our attempts to wake up the intellectual leaders of our country.

Last summer, *Esquire* magazine sent me a copy of the issue featuring Norman Mailer's interview with Madonna. Madonna, of course, is no dummy, except for the fact that she has generally volunteered her celebrity to help get out the government's message on "AIDS," i.e. the basic propaganda. Mailer mentioned "AIDS" a few times in the interview. The way he talked about "AIDS" indicated that he is totally unaware that the facts about "AIDS" are about as reliable as the facts that the government provided to the public during the Vietnam War.

On a whim, I wrote Mailer a letter and asked a very nice publicist at *Esquire*, Peter Vertes, to fax it to Mailer. I told Mailer about Ostrom's reporting and asked him to consider the possibility that the government is not being truthful about the epidemic.

In September, I received this letter.

Dear Mr. Ortleb,

If Neenyah Ostrom really has a case, I'd be interested to read about it. Could you send me the most cogent and/or concentrated of her pieces? As you can imagine, I, like 200 million other Americans, receive a ton of stuff to read in the mail and it's discouraging when you see 50 closely-faxed pages, so the briefer the better within the limitations of explaining what may be a difficult argument. In any event, I think it's damn interesting and if true, more than interesting.
Sincerely,
Norman Mailer

We then sent Mr. Mailer some of Ostrom's reporting, as well as her book, *America's Biggest Cover-Up*.

Even though that was a number of months ago, we still hope to see Mailer look into this scandal. If ever there were a story tailor-made for Norman Mailer's talents, it is the sinister mess that should be called AIDSGATE.

An article about the FBI, in our May 29 issue, will hopefully one day inspire investigative historians to look more closely at the politics of AIDS. Neenyah Ostrom wrote, "According to documents released under the Freedom of Information Act to the Constitutional Law Center in New York City, the Federal Bureau of Investigation (FBI) has, for a number of years, not only monitored but infiltrated numerous gay and AIDS groups. The groups include Gay Men's Health Crisis, the Coalition for Lesbian and Gay Rights, ACT UP, and SAGE (Senior Action in a Gay Environment, an organization for senior citizens). . . . The revelation that FBI agents had infiltrated ACT UP in particular, raises the question of whether some of the policies advocated by the group—like giving the toxic AZT to perfectly healthy people, for instance—were actually formulated by the FBI."

Ostrom reported, "On the same day as the information was made public in the [May 15, 1995] *Daily News* article, New York Representative Jerrald Nadler (Eighth District) wrote a letter of protest to U.S. attorney Janet Reno. "What is particularly disturbing is that, if the allegations in the article are correct, the FBI has carried out surveillance which was initiated without any clear-cut evidence that the groups targeted for surveillance were involved in any sort of domestic violence," Nadler wrote to Reno. He also noted that the FBI's surveillance continued for years "despite the fact that its investigation appears to have produced no evidence that these groups had the intent, or were preparing to, engage in violent or illegal conduct."

In the June 19 issue, Neenyah Ostrom reported on an admission of error by the CDC: "The Centers for Disease Control and Prevention has revised its assessment of how many Americans have chronic fatigue syndrome by up to as much as 50 times its previous estimate. CDC's Dr. William Reeves acknowledged during Congressional testimony May 12 the limitations of the earlier CDC study that produced the low estimate that many researchers in the private sector consider wildly inaccurate. New information compiled by the CDC also appears to correct other mistaken ideas about chronic fatigue syndrome that had been promulgated by the CDC's earlier research. Based on a previously-reported study attempting to determine the prevalence of the syndrome, the CDC estimated that 4-9 individuals per 100,000 Americans have chronic fatigue syndrome (CFS, or chronic fatigue immune dysfunction syndrome, CFIDS). However, information presented by Reeves at the Congressional briefing May 12 revealed that the new CDC study estimates as many as 76-220 individuals per 100,000 have CFS. Even the new, higher estimate from the CDC is starkly lower than some private-sector researchers' estimates of CFS's prevalence, particularly in certain risk groups like health care workers."

In the same issue, I wrote an editorial about the CDC's new statistics.

> This week's lead news story by Neenyah Ostrom is a hopeful sign that the government may have decided that the best policy to adopt on "AIDS" and chronic fatigue syndrome is to tell the public the truth. We're hopeful but not exactly holding our breath.
>
> In the past eight years, this publication has been alone in it investigative pursuit of chronic fatigue syndrome and its relationship to "AIDS." Government scientists have for over a decade been minimizing the significance of the [CFS] epidemic. For years, they pretended that it didn't exist. Then when they admitted that it existed, they tried to downplay both the seriousness of the illness and the extent of the epidemic.
>
> They're still playing games, but by admitting that the prevalence of the epidemic may be 50 times what they originally said it was, they may be on the brink of letting the entire cat out of the bag.
>
> All Americans should be concerned about chronic fatigue syndrome because:
>
> 1. The CDC has added it to the list of Priority-1 New and Reemerging Infectious Disease. It joins potentially lethal diseases like *E. coli* and tuberculosis.

2. Even though the new CDC figures could indicate that half-a-million Americans have the syndrome, it is a contagious syndrome—many or most of the people with CFS report that one or more members of their families have it.

3. It clearly has a virus in common with "AIDS": human herpesvirus-6 (HHV-6).

4. HHV-6 is capable of doing everything that HIV has been blamed for. It may even be the real "AIDS virus."

5. CFS may be a major source of miscarriage and birth defects.

6. CFS may be what is causing the rise of asthma across America.

7. Because HHV-6 can cause dementia, it may be the viral source of a great deal of bizarre or violent behavior. CFS patients have observable brain lesions and other organic brain damage that is visible on a number of types of brain scans.

8. The blood supply is not being screened for HHV-6.

As loyal readers of this publication know too well, this list goes on and on.

I hope it is becoming crystal clear to the members of the gay community that the *Native*'s investment in Neenyah Ostrom's investigative reporting is paying off. Because her reporting has been based on the facts as they have become available about CFS, we have assumed that the world at large would catch up with us sooner or later. Any reporter who really wants to know the whole truth about "AIDS" and CFS will eventually have to read all of the back issues of the *Native*. And we'll be more than happy to accommodate them.

Where was the rest of the media on this story? One of our theories about that concerns denial. We suspect that no one in the media wants to have to tell the public that for over a decade while they have been pretending to do serious reporting on the "AIDS" epidemic, the government was essentially handing them baloney, and they in turn were, in effect, feeding their readers baloney sandwiches. When the truth comes out about "AIDS" and CFS, it could cause a revolution in the way science is covered in this country. Reporters must stop toadying up to dishonest scientists.

Why would the CDC choose to tell the truth about CFS now? One reason is that they are terrified of a book that is coming out early next year. Crown will publish *Osler's Web* by Hillary Johnson in January or February. We hear that the book is a devastating exposé of what the government has and has not done on CFS. Hundreds of galleys of the book are going out to the press in August. The editor of the book is Michael Denneny, who was the editor of *And the Band Played On*. The media attention the book will get should guarantee that it becomes an instant bestseller.

Government scientists may also be getting a little nervous about another exposé due out in October. Houghton Mifflin will publish *The Gravest Show on Earth* by Elinor Burkett. Also a potential bestseller, Burkett's book is being compared to some of best books about Vietnam. The book reportedly turns everything the public thinks it knows about "AIDS" upside down. The book could result in major Congressional investigations of the "AIDS" effort. Could it really be that the times they are a-changin'? Stay tuned.

Well, once again, not exactly.

In the July 10 issue, Neenyah Ostrom criticized a recent piece in one of America's leading intellectual journals: "*The New Republic* is a magazine that targets intellectuals and public policy makers, as well as thoughtful people of all political stripes in government and academia and the arts. . . . To date no serious investigative report on the epidemic has been published in a magazine that probably has one of the most influential readerships in the country. In fact, for a news journal that seems to revel in piquing government goof-ups, nothing *TNR* has published on 'AIDS' challenges any of the government's assumptions about the epidemic. Even more disturbingly, *The New Republic*'s characterization of African-Americans' doubts about the government's 'AIDS' agenda, as outlined in its June 5 issue, approaches racism. *TNR* does not patronize only blacks; it treats all of its readers as if they were children who require information about the epidemic to be overly-simplified and spoon-fed to them within a politically correct framework. This attitude results in the magazine delivering a level of information that is somewhere below that provided by television celebrity public service announcements urging 'AIDS' awareness."

Ostrom wrote, "The June cover of *TNR* screamed the words, 'SEX RACE DENIAL AIDS.' Inside it got worse. In 'Homecoming,' Hanna Rosin examined 'paranoia and plague in black America.' She started out with some statistics to impress upon her readers how serious the problem is: 'Blacks, twelve percent of the population, account for one-third of all AIDS cases. Three out of five new AIDS victims are now black, up from one in five in 1986. Black women are now fifteen times more likely to have AIDS than white women.' "

Ostrom pointed out, "Rosin didn't question any of the government's statistics breaking down the incidence of 'AIDS' by race, however; instead she used them to castigate blacks for the way they are responding to the government's 'AIDS' propaganda and programs. The black community's 'suspicion and mistrust of mainstream medical institutions make it harder to mount an effective communal response to AIDS,' Rosin wrote."

Ostrom also noted, "Rosin wrote, in fact, that 'So widespread are fears of government institutions and white doctors among African-Americans, that they will take any alternative over conventional medical treatments.' This sweeping statement raises some important questions: Is such distrust truly as widespread as Rosin argues? And if it is, might there not be a good reason for such distrust? According to *The New Republic*, black Americans do not believe what their government is telling them about 'AIDS.' Rosin quoted several interviewees from a New York State Health Department training video to make that point."

Ostrom asked, "How many white Americans don't believe what their government is telling them about the epidemic?"

Ostrom also wrote, "Two subjects of black American 'paranoia' are examined by her. . . . The first is the origins of 'AIDS.' African-Americans quoted by Rosin said they believed the government was somehow involved in creating 'AIDS' either as a biological/chemical warfare agent, or as an undefined 'experiment' gone awry. The second 'paranoid' opinion is the apparently widely-held one, supported, one might add, by the conclusions of the international Concorde study,

418

published last year, that the government's main 'AIDS' treatment AZT, is poison."

Ostrom pointed out, "It is curious that *TNR*, which seems to pride itself on its feistiness and challenges to political powerhouses of every party, accepts so totally the government's propaganda about the 'AIDS' epidemic."

In the same issue, I wrote an editorial about HHV-6.

> We have now heard from a couple of sources that a rather amazing scientific paper will soon appear, linking the virus HHV-6 to multiple sclerosis. If such a paper does materialize, we suspect that it will be front-page news for the mainstream media not because it involves HHV-6, but because it involves MS.
>
> As longtime readers of this publication know, HHV-6 has been linked to AIDS and chronic fatigue syndrome by the most famous AIDS researcher in the world, Robert Gallo. He calls it a significant cofactor. We have challenged him to look more closely at the data and consider whether HHV-6 is really the main cause.
>
> We would not be surprised to see data linking HHV-6 to Multiple Sclerosis because there are certainly aspects of both AIDS and chronic fatigue syndrome which mimic MS. Recent papers, reported here by Neenyah Ostrom, have detailed the neurological complications of HHV-6 infection.
>
> The *Native* has for the last nine years shone a bright, continuous light upon HHV-6. We've informed our readers of every new scientific finding about this large DNA virus because the evidence that it is of incredible importance in the pathology of AIDS only increases as time passes.
>
> We think that HHV-6 will turn out to be a more important factor in AIDS than HIV, but from the patient's point of view that is beside the point. The virus is being ignored, and data indicate that it is destroying patients in multiple ways—and not just AIDS patients. Millions of people with chronic fatigue

syndrome may also be suffering the immunological consequences of HHV-6. And unnecessarily.

Something must be done about HHV-6. We fear that politics and threatened egos are blocking work that must be done to understand fully and treat this brain-and-immune-system-destroying virus. A few weeks ago, we reported that one of the leading researchers of HHV-6 thinks that if one can control the virus, one can stop the immune decline in an AIDS patient. Currently, we see no medical treatment that can make that claim about HIV.

Isn't it time to start down at least one bold new pathway in AIDS research and treatment. Billions have already been spent on HIV, with only cemeteries to show for it. Maybe in the long run it will pay off. But the warning signs of a bad investment are already far too apparent.

When Drs. Knox and Carrigan of the University of Wisconsin looked at autopsies of AIDS patients they seemed to find HHV-6 throughout the damaged organs of the victims. If the relatively nontoxic Ampligen would stop the virus from doing its damage, the syndrome might be controllable, like diabetes. What a tragedy if Knox and Carrigan are right about HHV-6 and everybody is mindlessly pursuing toxic therapies for HIV.

In the September 4 issue, Neenyah Ostrom wrote an article on AZT that once again undermined the CDC's credibility: "Zidovudine, or AZT, has had a rough year. Recent studies that have shown the drug to be ineffective at best and, in some instances, actually harmful. The worst news for AZT and its manufacturer Burroughs Wellcome, however, is probably yet to come, when the birth defects found in babies born to women treated with AZT while pregnant become common knowledge among patients, clinicians, and researchers—and the press."

She reported, "The U.S. government has recently begun a new campaign urging all pregnant women to be tested for HIV antibodies and, if testing positive, to take AZT to stop transmission of the virus to their fetuses. Federal health officials insist that there is no threat of deformed babies being born to women who take AZT during pregnancy. In a published report of the Centers for Disease Control study of AZT in pregnant women (ACT 076), it wasn't revealed what types of birth defects occurred; they were simply described as 'minor.' In contrast, a study performed in Asia reports some shocking deformities in babies born to women who took AZT while pregnant."

Ostrom asked, "Why are government scientists continuing to insist that AZT is a safe drug to give to pregnant women? This is especially perplexing in light of recent studies performed in non-pregnant subjects that have shown the drug to be ineffectual, in addition to being extremely toxic. . . . CDC scientists insist that their study of AZT in pregnant women noted only the 'normal' rate of birth defects, i.e. no more than two to three percent of babies were born with deformities. A study performed in Asia however, found that birth defects in infants born to women treated with AZT while pregnant occurred at up to five times this 'normal' frequency. The 'minor' birth defects noted in the CDC-sponsored, prematurely ended study were also observed in the Asian study. An example of such a minor defect is a child born with extra fingers when there is no family history of polydactyle, or extra digits (which is generally a genetic condition; since AZT interferes with DNA synthesis, it is not an unexpected 'minor abnormality'). However, the Asian study documented very serious birth defects in the children born to women who took AZT while pregnant: holes in the chest, abnormally small brains, lowered ears, neurological abnormalities, and heart defects, among others. In a full 25 percent of the 104 women followed in the Asian study, the child either died (from spontaneous or induced abortion, due to abnormalities), or was born with a birth defect."

After the explosion of asthma among children in the South Bronx made the front page of the *New York Times* (on September 5), Neenyah Ostrom raised the question, in our September 18 issue, about its possible connection to HHV-6. Adam Nossiter had reported in the *Times* on the possible link of the asthma cases to environmental factors. Ostrom noted, "Human herpesvirus-6 (HHV-6) has been implicated in causing a fatal lung disease called 'pneumonitis.' Active HHV-6 infections have been documented not only in cases of fatal pneumonitis, but also in patients with chronic fatigue syndrome (CFS) and have been recognized as the transmissible agent involved in CFS. Among children with CFS—80 percent of whom have been shown to have active HHV-6 infections—more than 70 percent are diagnosed with asthma and other allergies."

In our September 25 issue, I wrote a rather indignant editorial about HHV-6 titled "Do No Harm, Dr. Ho."

The purpose of the health care system's approach to the AIDS epidemic sometimes seems not to cure patients, but to find a commercial use for AZT. In the face of studies that show the drug to be useless at best and AIDS-causing at worst, the fight goes on to find some rationale to use the drug.

The new ploy, coming from Dr. David Ho's corner, is to push for AZT treatment as soon as a person seroconverts to being HIV-positive (whatever that means). Based on a dubious, small, short-term study conducted in Europe, Dr. Ho wants to identify newly infected patients and zap them with several potentially devastating antivirals.

It seems only fair and ethical for Ho and others who want to continue experimenting with AZT to inform their patients that the long term survivors of AIDS seem to be people who assiduously avoided taking AZT.

In the interest of fully informing his patients about existing treatment options, we urge Ho to tell his patients about the other more important AIDS virus that may well be affecting them: HHV-6. Surely Ho is aware of what happened at Dr. Gallo's lab meeting last year. Evidence was presented indicating that HHV-6 "is a full-fledged cofactor in HIV disease, not a mere opportunistic infection." This was reported [by Mark Mascolini] in the [December, 1994 issue of] *Journal of the Physicians Association for AIDS Care*.

At Gallo's meeting, researchers Konstance Kehl Knox and Donald R. Carrigan of the Medical College of Wisconsin were reported to have pointed out that, "Because HHV-6 can infect and destroy all major types of lymphocytes, it may substantially contribute to the progressive destruction of lymph nodes and other

lymphoid tissues observed in HIV-infected individuals."

According to *JPAAC*, "Early in 1994, Carrigan and
Knox, a doctoral candidate working in Carrigan's
laboratory, found actively replicating HHV-6 in
autopsy samples from lung, lymph node, spleen, liver,
and kidney of nine people who had died of AIDS."

Knox and Carrigan found that HHV-6 can be
found early on in AIDS cases, suggesting that it is more
than an opportunistic infection. Knox told *JPAAC*
that "AIDS could prove to be a combination of HIV
disease and HHV-6 disease."

Perhaps Ho would be better advised to treat the
HHV-6 part of the syndrome. Knox and Carrigan
believe that AIDS can be controlled by treating HHV-
6. Foscarnet and Ampligen are two promising
treatments. Who knows what kind of damage Ho may
be doing to the cellular immunity of his naïve experimental subjects when he aims toxic treatments at HIV?

A few weeks ago, Neenyah Ostrom reported on the
thinking of Dr. Gene Shearer on AIDS research at the
National Institutes of Health. His research shows that
"the cellular arm of the immune system provides
protection against AIDS."

Perhaps there should be a new motto in AIDS: *Do
no harm to the cellular arm of the immune system.*

Ostrom wrote in our August 14 issue: "If cellular
immunity is crucial to maintaining the health of people
'at risk' for developing 'AIDS,' there will be no
defensible rationale for advocating the use of anti-HIV
drugs like AZT that destroy cellular immunity."

What a tragedy if Ho could be saving lives by
treating patients for their HHV-6 infections rather than
destroying their cellular immunity in the name of the
HIV paradigm.

In the October 2 issue, Neenyah Ostrom reported on new research
on HHV-6 that once again had the potential to turn "AIDS" research
upside down: "A research report that may change the course of 'AIDS'
research is rumored to be in the publication pipeline. This report will

present data suggesting that human herpesvirus-6 is present in the lymph nodes in people with 'AIDS' *from the very beginning of the syndrome*. In other words, the report will raise a very important question: Is HHV-6 the primary infectious agent responsible for igniting the events that lead to the destruction of the immune system in 'AIDS'? That destruction is now generally acknowledged to begin with lymphadenopathy, or lymph node disease. Lymphadenopathy is part of the 'flu-like' syndrome believed by most clinicians and researchers to be indicative of early HIV infection. Recent research has shown, in fact, that lymph node destruction is an important signpost of advancing disease. In people who become very sick very fast, the lymph nodes are destroyed almost immediately. In long-term non-progressors, the lymph nodes remain healthy. The soon-to-be-published paper will reportedly show that HHV-6 is present when the lymphadenopathy seen in early 'HIV disease' first appears."

In the October 9 issue, our media column reported on a story on AIDS in prison that appeared in the September 1995 issue of *Newsline*, the newsletter of the New York People with AIDS Coalition: "While the situations of prisoners with AIDS in northern states like New York may be dreadful, *Newsline* made it clear that, in the South, things can even be worse. Jackie Walker described the situations of several women with 'AIDS' housed in the Medical Isolation Unit (MIV) at the Julia Tutwiler Prison for Women in Alabama. Walker is the AIDS Information Coordinator of the American Civil Liberties Union/National Prison Project. One of the women she profiled was 'M.W.,' who in 1986 was the first prisoner to be isolated at the Tutwiler Prison. 'HIV-positive prisoners during this period were housed on death row with a quarantine sticker, required to disinfect telephone receivers after use, and given meals served on paper plates,' Walker reported. 'M.W. recalls waking up covered with maggots because correctional staff refused to empty her garbage.' "

In the October 16 issue, we ran a piece by Neenyah Ostrom that was critical of research at Johns Hopkins University: "The cover-up of the connection between chronic fatigue syndrome and 'AIDS' has entered a new and possibly even more dangerous phase with the second publication in eight months purporting to show that CFS is nothing more than a easily-cured form of low blood pressure. Although this theory was first advanced in March, 1995 in *The Lancet*, it was just republished by the same group in the more prestigious *Journal of the American Medical Association*. Publication in *JAMA* resulted in this explanation for CFS receiving major attention, from interviews on CNN with government scientist Stephen Straus, who's been trying unsuccessfully for more than a decade to show that CFS is a psychiatric condition, to a half-page article in the [September 27, 1995] *New York Times* by senior science writer Lawrence K. Altman, M.D."

Ostrom also reported, "Perhaps most inexplicably and rather shockingly, the CFIDS Association of America in Charlotte, North Carolina, issued a press release promoting the finding that 96 percent of CFS patients suffer from low blood pressure and can be cured with a simple combination of well-known drugs."

Ostrom criticized the researchers for using a simplistic approach to CFS that seemed to ignore a myriad of symptoms in CFS that went way beyond low blood pressure. She noted, "No other research group has replicated the findings reported by the Johns Hopkins research team." As could have been predicted, many of the CFS symptoms that the research team ignored were ones that would have linked CFS to AIDS.

In the October 30 issue, Neenyah Ostrom reported on new research that linked HHV-6 to the loss of vision seen in some AIDS patients: "Powerful evidence has just been published suggesting that human herpesvirus-6 (HHV-6) may be a frequent cause of the vision loss suffered by more than half of all 'AIDS' patients. Although most eye disease in 'AIDS' has been attributed to cytomegalovirus (CMV) infection, it now appears that, along with the identification of HHV-6 as the most common infection found in 'AIDS' patients (not CMV, as was formerly believed), HHV-6 may in addition be causing a significant percentage of the 'AIDS' retinitis formerly blamed on CMV. In other words, yet another manifestation of 'AIDS' previously attributed to a different virus has been found to be associated with active HHV-6 infection. The new research paper reports finding both HIV-1 and HHV-6 *without* CMV in the retinas (the portion of the back of the eye connected directly to the optic nerve, controlling vision) of patients with 'AIDS' retinitis (which is an inflammation of the retina). The senior author of the paper is Dharam V. Ablashi, one of the co-discoverers of HHV-6 a decade ago in the laboratory of former National Cancer Institute researcher Robert C. Gallo."

In the November 20 issue, Neenyah Ostrom wrote a piece about the link between AIDS, CFS, and Gulf War Syndrome: "In the mid-1800s, English surgeon Joseph Lister created a revolution in the way doctors conceptualized the practice of medicine. Lister insisted that, if his peers washed their hands between operations, they wouldn't spread the infectious agents, later known as bacteria, from patient to patient, as his colleague Louis Pasteur had postulated; as a result, fewer of his patients would die. Lister's insight was resisted for some time for a variety of reasons, but, in the end, doctors came to view the practice of medicine in a whole new light because of it. A century-and-a-half later, it appears that a similar kind of intellectual and psychological breakthrough is going to be required for physicians and researchers to see the 'AIDS' epidemic in its true—larger—context."

Ostrom noted, " 'AIDS' is currently understood by the conventional wisdom to be a life-threatening illness confined to well-defined 'risk group' members and no one else in society (except for the occasional, exceptionally unlucky individual). It is becoming clear, however, that this particular manifestation is simply the most extreme in a continuum of immune system malfunction that certainly includes chronic fatigue syndrome and possibly Gulf War Syndrome. . . . That Gulf War Syndrome (GWS) and chronic fatigue syndrome (CFS) could be similar, if not related, conditions, does not seem difficult for at least some researchers to accept, as a recent conference at which the two were compared illustrates. Centers for Disease Control investigators Dr. Keiji Fukuda and William Reeves discussed the connection between GWS and CFS at the October 31 American Public Health Association Annual Meeting in San Diego. According to the CFIDS Association of America, Reeves and Fukuda reported the research of a CDC study of sick Gulf War veterans. They found that 'ill veterans most frequently reported chronic, persistent fatigue, cognitive problems (such as poor concentration and short-term memory) and joint and muscle pain and weakness.' "

In the November 27 issue, Neenyah Ostrom again wrote about Lindsey Nagel, "a healthy, happy five-year-old who goes to pre-school and takes ballet lessons. When she was less than three months old, however, she was diagnosed as being HIV-positive. Lindsey was then put on AZT for the next 22 months of her barely-begun life—until its side effects became so deleterious, her parents, acting against strenuous medical advice, discontinued the drug. Lindsey's parents, Cheryl and Steve Nagel, adopted her in Romania in October 1998."

Ostrom reported, "Lindsey's problems with AZT did not stop with her weight loss and failure to grow normally, however. In autumn 1992, the child developed a side effect of AZT that is common in adults: peripheral neuropathy, or pain in the limbs, usually the legs. . . . 'Around Lindsey's second birthday in 1992, she experienced leg cramps, and her body was getting smaller and smaller,' Cheryl recalls, adding, 'She was already pretty small.' The child seemed to be tortured by the pain she was experiencing, to hear her mother describe it. 'For about 40 days, we woke up every single night, and Lindsey would be screaming in pain,' Cheryl says. 'I mean, shrieks—this wasn't just a little crying. I'd run into her room, and she'd be sitting up, clutching her knees and her calves.' "

When the Nagels learned about Peter Duesberg's challenge to the HIV theory, according to Ostrom, "Cheryl wrote to Duesberg in November 1992, and almost immediately received a letter back from him. 'Duesberg's letter said, take your daughter off the AZT, or it will kill her,' Cheryl now says. 'So we didn't give her any more AZT, and she didn't sleep too peacefully for the next couple of nights,' Cheryl recalls. 'But on the fourth night, she slept for the first time in about six weeks. It was really a godsend.' The Nagels determined not to give any more AZT to Lindsey and not to continue to see the doctor who was prescribing it."

The cover story of our December 18 issue, by Neenyah Ostrom, was devoted to what we thought was a major mainstream media breakthrough: "Human herpesvirus-6 was finally exposed as a major killer in 'AIDS' (and other conditions) by ABC's *World News Tonight with Peter Jennings* on December 6. On the day of the White House meeting on 'HIV/AIDS,' Jennings broke the news to the American public that there is a second virus involved in the development of 'AIDS.' 'The conventional wisdom has been that AIDS, at its worst, is the consequence of one virus, and one virus alone: HIV,' Peter Jennings said. He continued, however, to reveal that ABC News had obtained an unpublished study that 'points to a second virus, a virus that almost everybody has. It is harmless, sleeping in the body, until HIV wakes it up.' "

Ostrom noted, "Reporter John McKenzie then profiled an HIV-positive patient in Wisconsin, Patrick Prudlow, who McKenzie

427

pointed out, is a 'prime candidate to develop AIDS, the collapse of the body's immune system. There is no telling how long he has to live.' McKenzie added, 'There is not even a clear understanding of how AIDS develops.' Not far away from where Prudlow is being treated, scientists at the Medical College of Wisconsin 'have long maintained that HIV is just part of the puzzle,' McKenzie reported, 'Now those scientists appear to be right.' Virologist Konstance Knox and her colleagues will publish what McKenzie described as 'an extraordinary study' this spring in the *Journal of Acquired Immune Deficiency Syndromes and Human Retrovirology*. Knox and her co-workers studied tissues from AIDS patients and found them to be infected not only with HIV, but also with HHV-6, which McKenzie described as a 'common and usually harmless' virus. 'But this HHV-6 was now attacking key immune cells,' McKenzie warned. Knox described the efforts of HHV-6 infection to McKenzie: 'It can kill people. It can cause fatal brain disease. It can cause fatal bone marrow destruction. It can cause fatal lung infection.' "

Ostrom also reported, "McKenzie explained that researchers now believe HHV-6 'works together with HIV. That HIV, by attacking the immune system, unleashes the HHV-6 to ravage the body. When you compare the two viruses in a laboratory experiment, the more destructive by far is HHV-6. As destructive as HHV-6 is, it can also be the source of new hope for AIDS patients. There are drugs already on the market, anti-herpes drugs that can fight the virus. Knox and others have controlled HHV-6 in bone marrow transplants. Now they need to test the drugs on patients who are also infected with HIV.' "

Ostrom noted, "Knox told McKenzie, 'I have no doubt that there are many patients with AIDS who are dying of HHV-6 disease that could be treated, and that those patients who have improved would have improved health and longer lives.' McKenzie asked her, 'So you're saying that you can stop AIDS cold in its tracks if you can control HHV-6?' Knox replied, 'I think that's a distinct possibility.' "

Ostrom also reported, "McKenzie then consulted 'AIDS pioneer' Robert Gallo, described by ABC News as one of the discoverers of HIV. Gallo, McKenzie emphasized 'agrees that human herpesvirus-6 is an important factor in how AIDS develops.' 'If we can inhibit Herpes 6, specifically and safely, for a long period of time,' Gallo said, 'it is my hypothesis we would help HIV-infected people.' "

According to Ostrom, "McKenzie ended his report by pointing out that for Patrick Prudlow and 'tens of thousands of HIV patients, what's needed is a rapid acceleration of HHV-6 research, so they can find out how much damage it might be causing, how best to treat it, and what it might mean to defeat it.' "

In the December 25 issue, Neenyah Ostrom interviewed Dr. Dharam V. Ablashi, "a member of the National Cancer Institute team that in 1986, first isolated and characterized a virus that may turn out to be crucial in understanding not only AIDS, but chronic fatigue syndrome and other diseases as well: human herpesvirus-6 (HHV-6). Ablashi was then a member of the Laboratory of Cellular and Molecular Biology at the National Cancer Institute, working on the new virus in collaboration with Syed Zaki Salahuddin and other members of Robert C. Gallo's Laboratory of Tumor Cell Biology during 1985-1986 when HHV-6 was first detected. Ablashi is now continuing his HHV-6 research (as well as other virological studies and diagnostic test development work) at a private biomedical company, Advanced Biotechnologies Inc., in Columbia, Maryland, which specializes in viral and immunological reagents."

When Ostrom asked him who actually discovered HHV-6, he responded, "It was jointly discovered by S. Zaki Salahuddin, when he was working in Robert Gallo's National Cancer Institute laboratory (he's now a professor at the University of Southern California), and me. Actually, he'd had the virus in his freezer for some time. When electron microscopy was performed on it, he was told it was a herpesvirus. Since it was in the lymphocytes, he thought it was an Epstein-Barr virus, so he never bothered to do anything with it."

Ablashi told Ostrom that his "interest was in lymphoma in AIDS patients. I was basically looking for EBV virus there. At that time, Zaki told me, well I have another EBV isolate in the freezer, if you are interested in characterizing it. I said sure. So I started working on it and, after about four to six months, I did not find that this was an EBV virus. I told him, 'Zaki, this is not an EBV virus.' He thought that was strange, so I showed him all the data. He then said, 'Let's go see Bob,' that is, Dr. Gallo. So we showed Dr. Gallo all the data, and he looked at it, and he said, 'Are you guys sure this is not contamination?' I said, 'It doesn't look like it.' He suggested we check it again, and I did. I repeated some tests, and I talked to a few of my friends who are herpes virologists—in secret, not telling anybody anything—and they said to me, 'What you have looks different from the herpesviruses we know about.' So we went back to Dr. Gallo again, and he said, 'Well, look, since I am not a herpes virologist, let's talk to someone who is a good herpes virologist. Give me a name' So I told him to talk to Dr. Bernard Roizman at the University of Chicago, who is called the father of herpes virology in the United States."

Ablashi continued, "We told him everything on the phone, and he said, 'Well, it looks like you have something.' He said that one of his postdoctoral fellows, Dr. Elliot Kieff . . . was the leading EBV virologist in the world, and was coming to Washington, and we should show him the data. After Dr. Kieff looked at the data and examined some viral DNA, he said, 'You guys are clear to publish. What you have is something new.' We submitted the paper to *Science*, and then got a lot of criticism from *Science*—because under electron microscopy, this virus looked very similar to cytomegalovirus, another herpesvirus. The criticism that we got from the paper's reviewer was that this might be a variant of cytomegalovirus. We satisfied that criticism by showing all the other data and then the paper was published."

Ablashi told Ostrom, "Once the paper describing the new virus was published, we got a lot of calls—Dr. Gallo did, particularly—saying, 'The cells you guys have shown in the paper—we have seen those cells in our AIDS cultures quite often.' "

One of the most disturbing things that Ablashi told Ostrom was that AZT enhances the growth of HHV-6. He told Ostrom, "We have some evidence, in vitro, that if you take AZT and put it onto HHV-6 infected cells, it will enhance their growth, and their cytopathic [cell-killing] effects become faster, rather than becoming blocked."

1996: Enormous Public Health Consequences

In the January 1 issue, Neenyah Ostrom once again wrote about the use of Ampligen in the treatment of HHV-6: "In 1995, a study was published that showed long-term improvement in patients with chronic fatigue syndrome who were treated with Ampligen. [Dr. Dharam] Ablashi was an investigator in this study, as were Ampligen co-inventor William Carter, CFS researchers Daniel Peterson, David R. Strayer, Robert J. Suhadolnick, Sheila Bastien, HHV-6 researchers Berch Henry and others. The answer to the question of whether Ampligen improved the health of CFS patients, who are known to have active HHV-6 infections, was yes."

Ostrom reported, "Improvement was noted in patients' Karnofsky Performance Scale (KPS), a measure of ability to perform daily activities like taking care of oneself; memory and IQ improved; exercise tolerance was increased; and there was a measurable reduction of HHV-6 activity."

Ostrom noted that Ampligen "reduced the presence of giant cells indicative of HHV-6 infection." 4 of the 14 patients studied "actually became culture-negative for HHV-6 during Ampligen treatment" suggesting, "Ampligen stops HHV-6."

Ostrom asked, "Why has this seemingly safe, effective drug not been approved by the FDA? Is it because a treatment that proves effective for both CFS and 'AIDS' would highlight the connection between the two syndromes?"

In the January 15 issue, Neenyah Ostrom wrote another piece that seemed to bring AIDS and pigs together again: "A drug [an extract of pig liver] that has been in use for 50 years appears to have considerable efficacy against a newly discovered human herpesvirus, human herpesvirus-6 (HHV-6). Kutapressin has few side effects and in the laboratory it virtually stops the growth of HHV-6. So why isn't Kutapressin being used to treat the increasing number of conditions—childhood illnesses such as exanthem subitum and febrile illness, mononucleosis, 'AIDS,' Hodgkin's disease, autoimmune disorders such as lupus, post-transplantation disorders (such as host-versus-graft disease), and chronic fatigue syndrome—associated with HHV-6 infection? That question remains unanswered, but in a recent research report, scientists from the National Cancer Institute and other prestigious research institutions—such as a Harvard Medical School-affiliated hospital—examined the effect of Kutapressin the growth of HHV-6. These researchers, who included Dharam V. Ablashi (then at NCI) and distinguished chronic fatigue syndrome researcher Anthony Kamoroff (from Brigham and Women's Hospital in Boston), found that Kutapressin inhibited the growth of HHV-6 by as much as 90 percent in the laboratory."

Ostrom noted, "These researchers also point out that, 'like Human Immunodeficiency Virus-1 (HIV-1), HHV-6 is tropic for CD4-positive T-cells; dual infection of CD4-positive cells with both HIV-1 and HHV-6 greatly increases the rate of CD4-positive cell death. In other words HHV-6 preferentially infects and very efficiently kills the cells that are decimated in 'AIDS,' the CD4 (or T4) cells."

Ostrom also reported, "In order to show Kutapressin was not contaminated with the virus, the researchers grew cell cultures without artificially infecting them with HHV-6, but in the presence of Kutapressin. No HHV-6 was found in these cultures. These cells were also unharmed by the presence of Kutapressin showing that it is a very non-toxic drug."

Ostrom also wrote, "The other major study of the effect of Kutapressin on CFS patients was performed by Dr. William Hermann at the Memorial Hospital in Houston. He described his findings to Maude Campbell in the October 20, 1994 issue of the *Medical Tribune,* a publication targeted to educating physicians about new clinical findings and treatments. . . . 'In an uncontrolled study of 400 CFIDS patients with documented T-cell dysfunction, Kutapressin treatment resulted in 40 percent having no symptoms, 35 percent having some symptoms that did not interfere with daily activities, 6 percent who still had difficulty functioning, and 10 percent who had no change,' Campbell reported. Six months of treatment is generally required to return natural killer cell activity to normal, Herman said."

Ostrom concluded her piece by asserting, "Clearly, this drug corrects two defects seen in both AIDS and chronic fatigue syndrome patients: Natural killer cell destruction and cell destruction caused by HHV-6. And it does it without toxicity. It has been available to physicians for fifty years. Shouldn't Kutapressin be viewed as an alternative to highly toxic treatments like AZT?"

In the February 5 issue, Neenyah Ostrom wrote a piece that was critical of a young writer's essay that had appeared in *The New York Times*: "It has become quite clear over the last few years that the 'AIDS' epidemic has been used, by numerous forces, to restructure society, to reprogram individuals' attitudes toward others, and, above all, to modify behavior—particularly sexual behavior. It is also becoming clear that, as a result of the 'AIDS' propaganda to which they've been subjected, an entire generation of Americans has been terrorized— about sex, 'AIDS,' and how emotional intimacy can lead directly to death—so effectively that fear has permeated every relationship they might ever have during the rest of their lives. An essay by Meghan Daum in the *New York Times Sunday Magazine* January 21, titled 'Safe Sex Lies,' crystallizes the emotional damage that the epidemic and the epidemic's propaganda have inflicted on a generation."

Ostrom noted, "Daum is angry, for a lot of good reasons. But when she and her fellow Generation X-ers—for starters—find out the lies they've really been told about the 'AIDS' epidemic, they're going to be a lot angrier. Daum writes that she has been tested for antibodies to HIV three times, even though she's not a member of a 'high-risk group' and doesn't really even know anyone who is. She grew up in the middle class and went to an 'elite' college. And despite the fact she knows no one with 'AIDS,' she writes, 'I am terrified of this disease.' Then Daum, who was born in 1970, explains a little bit why she's so frightened of an illness she's never even personally witnessed: 'I went to a college where condoms and dental dams lay in baskets in dormitory lobbies, where it seemed incumbent on health service counselors to give us the straight talk, to tell us never, ever to have sex without condoms unless we wanted to die; that's right, *die*, shrivel overnight, vomit up our futures, pose a threat to others. (And they'd seen it happen, oh yes they had.) They gave us pamphlets, didn't quite explain how to use dental dams, told us where we could get tested, threw us more fistfuls of condoms (even some glow-in-the dark brands, just for variety).' "

Ostrom wrote, "Daum says that she and her friends believed these counselors and swore they would 'protect' themselves by always using condoms. But they didn't. So they'd be terrified. So they'd get tested. The test would be negative. They'd swear again, always to 'protect' themselves. Until the next time, when they didn't. Daum says this is the pattern of her own sexual behavior, which is, she writes, 'a shocking admission'; she adds, however, that 'my hunch is that I'm not the only one doing it.' In fact, she suspects 'that very few of us—"us" being the demographic profile frequently charged with thinking we're immortal, the population accused of being cynical and lazy and weak—

have really responded to the AIDS crisis the way the Federal Government and educators would like us to believe. My guess is that we're all but ignoring it and that anyone who claims otherwise is lying.' "

Ostrom pointed out, "My experience, as I have reported about 'AIDS' over the last eight years, is that many, many people—of all ages, all income statuses, all political convictions—*just don't believe what the government has told them about 'AIDS.'* Like Daum, some doubt the widespread propaganda that *everyone* is 'at risk.' 'Obviously, there are still too many cases of HIV; there is a deadly risk in certain kinds of sexual behavior and therefore reason to take precautions,' Daum writes. 'But until more people appear on television, look into the camera and tell us that they contracted HIV through heterosexual sex with someone who had no risk factors, I will continue to disregard the message.' "

Ostrom pointed out, "Daum, like many others who doubt they need to pay attention to the government's 'safe sex' message because of who they are and what they do, buys into the Big Lie: that HIV is the single cause of the epidemic. Having bought into the Big Lie, they also believe its corollaries: that 'AIDS' is solely a sexually transmitted disease, and that avoiding 'high risk' behaviors will protect them from the plague. An Orwellian truth, meanwhile, lurks beneath the conventional wisdom: While government propaganda that everyone is at risk of contracting HIV (and thereby 'AIDS') is demonstrably untrue, everyone is at risk of contracting the real plague of immune deficiency disease that is sweeping the world."

Ostrom asserted, "The immune systems of uncounted millions of people all over the world have been compromised and, in some cases completely destroyed. Some of these people have developed the most acute form of this immunodeficiency, and some of them are diagnosed—often presumptively, without even being tested for HIV antibodies—as having 'AIDS.' But while HIV is the official focus of all government-sponsored 'AIDS' research, another virus capable of destroying every component of the immune system is spreading, unchecked, throughout the population. That virus, for which there is virtually no government research available, is human herpesvirus-6 (HHV-6). Increasingly, research is showing that HHV-6 alone— without HIV or any other 'cofactor'—can cause enough immune system destruction to result in the clinical condition called 'AIDS.' "

Ostrom wrote, in conclusion, "If people of all ages feel as angry, anxious, and betrayed as Daum by the way they've been 'AIDS'-propagandized and lied to *now*, what will happen when the entire edifice of the epidemic comes tumbling down? How are people going to react when they find out they've been terrorized for years by lies about an epidemic that is not what it's been made out to be? When Daum and others in her generation realize the epidemic is far, far larger than they've been led to believe—and that the lies they've been told are far larger even than they suspect—their anger might be the fuel that explodes all the 'AIDS' myths that have ruled their lives, allowing the truth about the epidemic to be finally revealed."

In the March 25 issue, we published an interview with journalist Hillary Johnson, which was conducted by Neenyah Ostrom. Ostrom wrote, "In 1987, Hillary Johnson wrote a two-part series for *Rolling Stone* about a disease called "Chronic Epstein-Barr Virus Syndrome," with which she's recently been diagnosed. It was the first in-depth examination of the pandemic illness that would eventually be called 'chronic fatigue syndrome' by the U.S. Centers for Disease Control, and Johnson's 1987 article is still considered a classic examination not only of the syndrome but of the government's pathetically inadequate response to it. Nine years later, Johnson has published *Osler's Web: Inside the Labyrinth of the Chronic Fatigue Syndrome Epidemic* (Crown, 700 pages $30). It is an epic history on the unfolding of the epidemic that *Kirkus Reviews* described as a "relentless, meticulous, and highly persuasive exposé by a journalist who spent [ten] years investigating the medical research establishment's failure to take seriously, chronic fatigue syndrome (CFS).' "

Johnson told Ostrom, "*Osler's Web* is the result of ten years of investigation into the way the federal health agencies—the National Institutes of Health and the Centers for Disease Control—have responded to the chronic fatigue syndrome epidemic. I documented the government's crucial, early investigation into this disease, which was undertaken in 1985 in Incline Village, Nevada, one year after an outbreak of CFS occurred there, and the resulting activity around this disease inside the federal health agencies over the ensuing decade. My sources were scientists, doctors, patients, government officials, as well as written documents obtained from the government health agencies *via* the Freedom of Information Act. Over the course of the book, I show how the administrators of these health agencies have systematically misled Congress about the level of commitment to this disease within their agencies; how some government scientists appear to have misappropriated money designated by Congress to research this disease; how clinicians, who over the course of years gained considerable expertise in this disease, were not only shunned by government researchers, but in some cases were destroyed professionally as a result of their advocacy on behalf of patients suffering from the disease."

Johnson told Ostrom, "Beginning in 1986, I interviewed more than five hundred doctors and biomedical researchers in depth on the topic. Most of them indicated to me that CFS was an entirely new and rapidly growing phenomenon in their clinical practices or their research laboratories."

Ostrom asked Johnson if she thought that CFS is contagious and she replied, "There is ample evidence to suggest that it is, the most obvious being the fact that hardly anyone had CFS before the middle 1980s, and one of the most conservative estimates today places the prevalence at two million people in this country alone."

Johnson told Ostrom, "Anecdotal reports from doctors who have specialized in the care of people with CFS provide suggestive evidence that CFS is infectious. Most doctors I interviewed who see hundreds, even thousands, of CFS sufferers, expect that some proportion of their patients have come down with the disease after receiving blood transfusions. . . . CFS can be spread from spouse to spouse, and within families—from parent to child and vice versa. I am aware of families in which every member is ill with the disease. Unfortunately, precise epidemiological data on this issue is lacking because the government has not explored these issues, nor has it supported independent researchers seeking to pursue this research. My book offers evidence of some kind for the contagiousness of CFS on virtually every page."

When Ostrom asked why the government would mislead citizens about the threat of a contagious disease, Johnson replied, "There are those who feel highly-placed government science officials orchestrated a cover-up on this issue essentially for the purpose of avoiding mass panic. I agree heartily that the government has left much unsaid because it wants to avoid panic over CFS. Yet I don't believe that such an explanation fully addresses the questions. . . . Those who read my book will doubtless be surprised at how very influential a handful of people inside the federal health agencies have been in controlling the fate of CFS research and, consequently, the fate of CFS researchers. Much of the blame for the shallowness of the government's research agenda can be placed on a very few people whose influences over an epidemic disease that was raging out of control vastly exceeded their own importance within the federal system."

Johnson pointed out, "The CDC is an extremely clannish agency whose employees are unwilling at almost any cost to criticize one another. In 1991, however, Walter Gunn, the principal investigator into the disease, reluctantly broke ranks and turned whistleblower on his colleagues, confirming for me my suspicions about the misappropriation of CFS dedicated research funds, the agency-wide derision of CFS and its victims, and the extraordinary bias against the disease held throughout the division charged with performing national surveillance on the disease, the Division of Viral Diseases. Gunn took early retirement from the agency in 1993, so convinced was he that a fair and competent research program could never be run within that division at the agency. I would like to point out that the same scientists who were running the CFS research program at the agency then are running it today."

Johnson told Ostrom, "At the National Institutes of Health, a different dynamic has been in place for more than a decade: A single researcher, who has long promoted CFS as a psychiatric affliction of women, has reigned supreme in the field at the National Institute of Allergy and Infectious Disease. With the vast majority of his colleagues focused on AIDS, Stephen Straus has contrived to make CFS his private research fiefdom, burning up along the way an average of $800,000 taxpayer dollars every year for the last decade. Using his position at the prestigious Bethesda agency as his bully pulpit, Straus has wielded vast influence throughout clinical medicine. By failing to critically assess his research, the lay press has been complicit in spreading Straus's propaganda that CFS is primarily an emotional rather than a medical condition. . . . I consider these developments inside the NIH and CDC to be among the most tragic of all to befall CFS sufferers: ten years ago, there was an open playing field. Patients and doctors alike had high expectations that the federal agencies charged with protecting public health would pursue this disease aggressively and fairly. Ten years into the epidemic, thanks to the very people who were invested with the hopes of hundreds of thousands of CFS sufferers, it is today considered axiomatic that if you have CFS you've got a mental, not a physical problem. The fearsome nature of the disease itself has been utterly camouflaged."

When Ostrom asked Johnson if there could be a connection

between AIDS and CFS, she replied, "Given that the two epidemics arose concurrently, and that so many of the laboratory and clinical findings are the same or similar in both patient populations, it almost defies credibility to insist that there cannot possibly be any connection. However, this matter is probably one of the most controversial aspects of CFS, and federal scientists are probably more vehemently opposed to such speculation than they are to any other matter pertaining to CFS. The question seems incredible to most people for one reason: 'chronic fatigue syndrome' sounds so benign that to align the disease with a fatal one seems bizarre indeed. One only need examine the medical literature about these two diseases to see the parallels, however."

Johnson also noted, "CFS and AIDS patients frequently suffer from several of the same recurrent herpesvirus infections, including a newly discovered herpesvirus—human herpesvirus-6—which AIDS researcher Robert Gallo has repeatedly suggested is the cofactor, along with HIV, that causes what we call AIDS. The two diseases share a number of immunological abnormalities as well. CFS and AIDS patients also have similar intellectual processing problems, and the brain damage in the brains of CFS and AIDS sufferers is virtually indistinguishable when viewed by brain imaging techniques. One final linkage between the two diseases comes from the discovery of evidence for retroviral infection in CFS patients. These findings have been made in several laboratories, but so far none of the researchers have been able to pursue their work with any great fervor due to a longstanding shortage of research funds for the disease."

Johnson's description of how she was treated by the CDC in the process of doing research for her book is particularly disturbing: "Only after signing a contract to write a book on the subject did I begin to get an idea of how intractable and cavalier the government's view of CFS really was. In March 1988, I made my first trip to the CDC. On the bulletin board along the corridor where those charged with investigating this disease worked, a letter lampooning CFS patients and their disease was prominently placed for all to enjoy. Jokes about the disease were rife throughout the agency. Gary Holmes, who had been to Tahoe and who had been named principle CFS investigator, refused my interview requests for several days: I finally saw him in the cafeteria one day, where I pleaded with him for a few minutes of his time. Later, speaking to him in his office, I discovered the walls were decorated with visual jokes and verbal barbs about the disease. I stayed in Atlanta for two weeks that March. It was unnerving to discover that most people there knew far less about CFS than I did by then. I was equally unnerved when, on occasion, I sensed a few of them didn't even believe I was a journalist—that I was instead just another 'crazy' with CFS who was posing as a reporter. Actually, reporters by necessity spend some portion of their time interviewing reluctant and even hostile interview subjects, but I have never been treated with disdain equivalent to that shown me by those in Atlanta, whose thoughts and words I sought on this subject."

In the April 15 issue, Neenyah Ostrom interviewed HHV-6 researcher Konstance Knox, Ph.D., who had "just published a study with extraordinary implications for AIDS research and treatment strategies. Along with her colleague Donald R. Carrigan, Ph.D., Knox demonstrated that 100 percent of HIV-infected patients studied (ten out of ten) had active human herpesvirus-6 Variant A infections in their lymph nodes early in the course of their disease. Seventy-five percent of these patients, in fact, had CD4 cell counts higher than 200 (the cut-off for receiving a diagnosis of 'AIDS'), up to as high a CD4 count of 700. This finding led Knox and Carrigan to conclude that 'active HHV-6 infections appear relatively early in the course of HIV disease and in vitro studies suggest that the A variant of HHV-6 is capable of breaking HIV latency with the potential for helping to catalyze the progression of HIV infection to AIDS.' The new study, in other words, presents data further implicating HHV-6, particularly Variant A (HHV-6A) as a cofactor (at the very least) in the development of AIDS."

When Ostrom asked Knox what the bottom line of the new findings was, she replied, "HHV-6 is present from very early in HIV infection. So we're not talking about waiting until people have opportunistic infections, and CD4 counts between 100 and 200. We're finding HHV-6 in the lymph nodes early—active infection: this virus is replicating. This is unheard of for other opportunistic infections, even TB."

Knox told Ostrom, "We just completed a study that we have submitted in which we examined 22 HIV-positive and AIDS patients. Every one of them has active replication of HHV-6A and it doesn't matter what stage of disease they're in, from frank AIDS, to autopsies, all the way up to people with CD4 cell counts of over 700. We believe there is a special interaction between HIV and HHV-6."

Ostrom asked Knox the politically and scientifically touchy question of whether HHV-6A can do everything HIV can do, and she replied, "As far as immunologic damage? Oh, HHV-6A does it more efficiently than HIV. . . . When we have seen HHV-6A in tissue, we see dead tissue. And where you see HIV—you know, you can have HIV alone, and you may see some reactive changes, like the immune system reacting to a viral infection as if you have flu or something like that. But you don't see dead tissue. You don't see destroyed organ and scar formation, and that's what you see when you see HHV-6A. We find replacement of the lymph nodes with scar tissue. HHV-6A kills it. It kills the lymph node tissue."

Knox also said, "If I were to place my bets—I do think the viruses HIV and HHV-6A are interactive. I think one of the reasons why you almost always find both of them is that there are viral products, some of the gene products that they make, they enhance each other's replication. I think they're a team. And when the two of them are present, they induce the production of more of each other. It's a mutually enhancing relationship. It's our feeling that if you could interrupt or limit or suppress the HHV-6A infection, the levels of HIV would go down tremendously and HIV would become just a chronic viral infection. And, potentially, the antiviral agents that are out there would be able to manage that."

And then Knox issued a challenge to the epidemic's conventional wisdom: "We don't have any evidence, looking in the tissue, that HIV is responsible for any of the destruction. And, if you think about it, HIV infects patients for years—a decade or more—without progressing to AIDS. When you look in their tissues, you have to ask how you can have such a long-term viral infection and have no damage. Then something seems to happen in their course of disease. In some people, it happens earlier; in some people it happens later; and there's that small percentage of people in whom it never seems to happen at all. Our hypothesis would be that, if we were to look in the lymph nodes of the long-term non-progressors, we would not find HHV-6A."

When Ostrom asked why there was not more funding for HHV-6 research, Knox replied, "Well, I don't know if you've been tracking the kinds of exposés that *Science* magazine and others have published, that 80 percent of AIDS research monies are retained within the federal government programs on AIDS research. And I think there's been a real resistance to entertaining hypotheses or directions of AIDS research that aren't looking specifically at HIV, and that is the basic problem. Our studies themselves have been enthusiastically received, but the funding hasn't followed. And that is funding through the federal agencies—like the NIH—and I think one of the things that has stopped that has been the confusion with HHV-6B. People think, well, if everybody's infected with HHV-6, why doesn't everyone have AIDS? Well, we're all infected with HHV-6B, but there's probably only a very small percentage of people infected with HHV-6A. And there's a very unique relationship between A and HIV—when we examine HHV-6B and HIV together, we don't see the same effects. They don't have the same interaction. So we're talking about two different viruses, essentially, A and B. And people have merged the two into just HHV-6 and have not appreciated the biologic difference between the two viruses. And actually, in our own research, this has only been clarified in the last year. In our earlier studies, we only had reagents to look at HHV-6. We did not have the specific reagents to separate the two when we look in the tissue; we could not tell if it was A or B. It's only been in the past year that we have developed the technologies to be able to distinguish between the two."

Near the end of the interview, Knox told Ostrom, "We believe that actually what destroys the immune organs, the lymph nodes, is HHV-6A. It is not HIV."

Such words, of course, did not endear her to the AIDS establishment. Even her attempt to show HIV respect by promoting an image of an HIV-HHV-6 pas de deux was too threatening to the prevailing AIDS paradigm.

In the May 6 issue, Neenyah Ostrom wrote a piece about one of the great moments of betrayal in the history of CFS: "The largest chronic fatigue syndrome patient advocate group in the United States has, for all intents and purposes, declared war on the epidemic's most prominent author over the subject that seems to draw the line in the sand between those who are willing to tell the whole truth about CFS and those who are not: contagion. In its most recently-published *CFIDS Chronicle* (Spring 1996), the CFIDS Association of America (in Charlotte, North Carolina) has mounted a merciless attack upon Hillary Johnson's new book, *Osler's Web: Inside the Labyrinth of the Chronic Fatigue Syndrome Epidemic*. Instead of celebrating the publication by a major publishing house of an important book describing in the minutest detail the history of the disease that the CFIDS Association has been attempting to publicize for nearly a decade, the organization has marshalled all its experts to attack Johnson because she writes that there is evidence to prove that CFS is contagious. In the spring issue of the *CFIDS Chronicle*, the Association consulted numerous physicians and researchers—most of whom are either government employees or receive government funding for their 'AIDS' or CFS research—and asked if they considered CFS to be contagious. Only one was brave enough to answer in the affirmative. Never mind that the CFIDS Association has distributed tens of thousands of dollars—collected from sick people, their families, and concerned individuals—for research to identify a causative agent of CFS. Much of this money has been spent investigating various viruses; considerable amounts were invested over the past few years to investigate a retrovirus as a possible cause of CFS."

The twisted logic, of the epidemic's opposite world, was all too clear in a May 1 page-one exposé in the *Wall Street Journal*, which revealed that the top scientists at the Centers for Disease Control admitted lying to the public about the 'AIDS' epidemic during the 1980s. In our May 13 issue, Neenyah Ostrom reported, "Amanda Bennett and Anita Sharpe are the staff reporters who broke the story, 'Health Hazard: AIDS Fight is Skewed by Federal Campaign Exaggerating Risks.' When 'AIDS' prevented programs and anti-'AIDS' education campaigns were blocked by the Reagan White House, the media, and public indifference, the CDC officials in 1987 made a fateful decision: They decided to lie. Although originally prompted by public health concerns, according to the *Wall Street Journal*, the untruths propagated by the CDC became the foundation for attempts to restructure society to fit a generally right-wing, 'pro-family' morality. In fact, as Bennett and Sharpe reveal, controlling people's sexual behavior—among heterosexuals as well as gay men—was and is still used as a justification for the lies told about the epidemic by CDC scientists."

Ostrom wrote, "According to *Journal* reporters Bennett and Sharpe, a decision was made by federal health officials in summer 1987 to 'bombard the public' with what they characterized as a 'terrifying' message: 'Anyone could get AIDS.' Calling the message 'technically true,' Bennett and Sharpe point out that it was also misleading. By the government's own reckoning, heterosexuals faced a far smaller risk of contracting 'AIDS' from a 'single act of sex' than did gays and IV drug users, their sexual partners, and their babies. Public health authorities, however, thought that 'lifting' the 'AIDS' epidemic 'from a homosexual concern to a national obsession' was necessary in mid-1987. 'But nine years after the America Responds to AIDS campaign first hit the airwaves, many scientists and doctors are raising new questions,' according to Bennett and Sharpe. 'Increasingly, they worry that the everyone-gets-AIDS message—still trumpeted not only by government agencies but by celebrities and the media—is more than just dishonest: It is also having a perverse, potentially deadly effect on funding for AIDS. prevention.' In other words, not only celebrities, but the media—who are supposed to serve, at least in part, as government watchdogs—were *and still are being* suckered by federal health officials who decided to lie about the 'AIDS' epidemic. And allocated monies, according to the paper, are being improperly used."

Ostrom noted, "Bennett and Sharpe argue that 'AIDS prevention' dollars need to be targeted primarily to gay men and intravenous drug users, citing a 1987 study that established the 'average risk' from a single heterosexual sexual encounter is one in five million if no condom is used and one in 50 million if one is. . . . A 1987 Gallup Poll apparently tipped the balance [at the CDC] against the truth. It showed that 25 percent of the public thought that employers should be able to fire people with 'AIDS'; 43 percent 'felt that AIDS was a punishment for moral decline,' Bennett and Sharpe report. Those working on 'AIDS' within the CDC became even more discouraged and upset. 'It was in this environment that the idea of presenting AIDS as an equal opportunity scourge began to form,' according to Bennett and Sharpe. 'As long as this was seen as a gay disease or even worse, a disease of drug abusers, that pushed the disease way down the ladder' of most people's concerns, [Walter Dowdle, one of the top scientists in the CDC's early prevention efforts], told the *Wall Street Journal*. . . . The misleading CDC campaign began to air in October 1987, and focused on the 'universality' of the disease. It was effective. By the end of 1989, a poll showed that 80 percent of Americans had seen one of the 'AIDS' propaganda pieces on television. 'Millions of people were thus sold and resold on the message: Though AIDS started in the homosexual population, it was inexorably spreading, stalking high school students, middle-class husbands, suburban housewives, doctor, dentists, and even their unwitting patients,' write Bennett and Sharpe. By 1991, even scientists within the CDC were uncomfortable with spreading a message their statistics showed to be untrue. 'Meanwhile, the CDC itself was producing research that made clear that heterosexual fears were exaggerated,' according to the *Wall Street Journal*."

Ostrom also noted, "CDC scientists were not only interested in legislating morality through untruthfully-induced fear, they were interested in interfering with peoples' private lives. John Ward, who is chief of the CDC division that counts 'AIDS' cases, told the *Wall Street Journal*, 'I don't see that much downside in slightly exaggerating [the AIDS risk]. Maybe they'll wear a condom. Maybe they won't sleep with someone they don't know.' Bennett and Sharpe conclude by questioning the morality of government health authorities lying to the public no matter how noble they believe the end result will be. 'Then there is the separate issue of honesty in government: Shouldn't the public hear the truth, even if there might be adverse consequences?' the *Wall Street Journal* reporters ask. Boston University ethicist George Annas commented, 'When the public starts mistrusting its public health officials, it takes a long time before they believe them again.' "

Ostrom pointed out, "The irony in all this, of course, is that the CDC's lie contains a deadly kernel of truth. Everyone is at risk of contracting 'AIDS,' because the chronic fatigue syndrome epidemic is an unacknowledged part of the 'AIDS' epidemic. . . . When the public discovers the magnitude of the lies the CDC has told about the 'AIDS' epidemic—as important as it is, Bennett and Sharpe's story is but a beginning—the credibility of the U.S. Public Health Service, as the lingering adverse effects of the Tuskegee syphilis study have demonstrated, may be damaged for decades."

In a sidebar for the piece about the *Wall Street Journal* article, Ostrom discussed another important episode in the history of the CDC's mendacity: "In 1987, when CDC officials were deciding to lie to the public about the 'AIDS' epidemic, one of the discoverers of the chronic fatigue syndrome epidemic was accusing yet another CDC official of lying about data. At issue was the number of patients involved in the 1984-85 Lake Tahoe outbreak of chronic fatigue syndrome and the severity of the illness they experienced. Dr. Paul Cheney, who along with Dr. Daniel Peterson identified the Lake Tahoe outbreak, was furious when he received the manuscript describing the outbreak, submitted for publication to the *Journal of the American Medical Association* (*JAMA*) by CDC field investigator Dr. Gary Holmes. Cheney was so upset, in fact, that he wrote a strongly-worded letter of protest to *JAMA* senior editor Dr. Bruce Dan."

Ostrom reported that, "In a letter dated February 23, 1987, Cheney

444

contended that, according to the raw data previously supplied to him by Holmes, 70 percent of the patients involved in the Lake Tahoe outbreak (93 of 134) were ill for more than one month (the cut-off point for being considered a 'case' in the CDC's examination). But when Holmes massaged the data for publication, he concluded that only 15 of the 134 patients were 'cases.' Cheney supplied Dan with the original data and noted, 'Thus Dr. Holmes's report is inconsistent . . . with *his* own data." Clearly, the real goal of all this shenanigans was to debunk the whole idea of a CFS epidemic in Lake Tahoe.

Ostrom noted that Cheney, who refused to be a co-author on the paper, wrote to Dan, "I cannot help but conclude that Dr. Holmes et al. have altered their own data to suit their particular purposes. . . . I can promise you that if this article is published in the *Journal of American Medical Association*, I will do everything in my power to bring this fact to light."

Ostrom reported, "Cheney received a reply not from *JAMA* editor Dan, but from Holmes, who, after offering to correct an obvious error in the paper that Cheney had noted, concluded rather insultingly, 'I have discussed your letter with Dr. Dan, who feels, as I do, that if you still wish to comment on the article once it is published, it would be appropriate to write a letter to the editor, as do other readers who wish to respond to articles in the *Journal.*' "

In light of the *Wall Street Journal* report on the 'AIDS' events of 1987, Ostrom asked, "As CDC officials were deciding to lie to the public, exaggerating the danger and importance of one epidemic, 'AIDS,' had they also decided to lie to the public about a second epidemic, 'chronic fatigue syndrome,' attempting to convince physicians and patients that it didn't even exist?"

In our June 10 issue, Neenyah Ostrom reported, "Representatives from the Government Accounting Office (GAO) have agreed to meet with New York Rep. Jerrold Nadler (D-8ᵗʰ District) . . . to discuss his request for an investigation into charges made by journalist Hillary Johnson. She alleges that the true nature and scope of the chronic fatigue syndrome epidemic have been misrepresented and possibly covered up by the Centers for Disease Control. . . . On April 16, Nadler read a statement on the floor of the House of Representatives detailing Johnson's allegations and requesting a GAO investigation into how the CDC has handled the CFS epidemic. Nadler pointed out in his statement, read into the *Congressional Record*, that Johnson's book 'asserts that CFS is an immunological disease with many of the same characteristics as AIDS.' In his April 16 statement, Nadler noted that he had also written a letter to Health and Human Services Secretary Donna Shalala requesting a reply to Johnson's 'disturbing allegations.' "

Ostrom reported, "Nadler's letter to Shalala points out that Johnson, in addition to presenting considerable evidence contradicting government scientists' conclusions about CFS, also 'alleges that CFS is a major, debilitating illness with enormous public health consequences,' but that 'CDC refuses to draw the obvious conclusion from this evidence because a handful of long-time CDC senior scientists and administrators have invested their reputations in the hypothesis that CFS is not a real illness.' "

In our June 17 issue, we published the text of an April 12, 1996, letter from Nadler to Charles A. Bowsher, the Comptroller General of the General Accounting Office: "A very serious charge has been made by author Hillary Johnson that the Centers for Disease Control (CDC) have covered up the existence of a significant public health issue: chronic fatigue syndrome (CFS). Ms. Johnson has asserted in her recent book, *Osler's Web*, as well as in interviews and in public appearances on *Good Morning America* and other major venues, that CFS is a real disease caused by a real pathogen, but that the CDC has attempted to portray CFS as a psychosomatic illness instead. She alleges that CFS is a major, debilitating illness with enormous public health consequences. In over 720 pages, based on [10] years of investigation, she sets out to prove that CFS is an infectious disease that attacks the brain and leaves its victims devastated. Ms. Johnson asserts that there already exists ample clinical and epidemiological evidence to support her conclusion, but CDC is hidebound in its determination to ignore this evidence—at the public's peril. She believes that CDC refuses to draw the obvious conclusion from this evidence because a handful of long-time CDC senior scientists and administrators have invested their reputations in the hypothesis that CFS is not a real illness. She charges that CDC scientists and other scientists who have attempted to draw the same conclusion that she has drawn have been ostracized and denied federal funding."

Nadler also wrote, "This matter was initially brought to my attention because of Ms. Johnson's assertion that there is evidence that CFS is an autoimmune disease with many of the same characteristics

446

as AIDS—except that HHV-6, rather than HIV, is present in the blood and tissue of CFS sufferers. In fact, in chapter 33 of her book, she calls CFS 'HIV-negative AIDS.' Ms. Johnson reports in that chapter that others have speculated that the virus HHV-6 may be involved as a precipitating factor or as a cofactor in other autoimmune illnesses, including AIDS. Because of the implications for public health and national health care costs, if Ms. Johnson's assertions prove to be true, and because of their serious impact upon the public's confidence in the CDC, Ms. Johnson's allegations deserve the most immediate and serious attention."

In the June 24 issue, we published an interview conducted by Ostrom with Representative Nadler who was "pursuing several lines of inquiry into the possibility that chronic fatigue syndrome research has not been conducted properly by the National Institutes of Health and the Centers for Disease Control." Ostrom wrote, "Nadler is concerned not only about CFS's potential threat to the public health, but also about evidence suggesting the misuse of Congressional funds intended for CFS research."

Ostrom reported, "On June 10, Rep. Nadler and his chief of staff Neil Goldstein met with the *Native* to discuss the outcome of the GAO meeting, as well as the next steps to be taken (i.e. other possible investigations) in pursuing the truth about how CFS research is conducted by federal health agencies."

Nadler told Ostrom, "Because GAO investigates only misuse of money, we tried to frame our information as much as possible in terms of misuse of money. But the programmatic question is basically, is the NIH systematically not looking at what it should look at? And is that because there is a clique of people who have their reputations invested in the proposition that CFS is psychosomatic, not a viral disease, therefore they are systematically not funding any research to answer the questions of viral etiology—GAO says they can't get into that. That's just not their bureaucratic niche—although they did recommend that we take some of those questions to the Inspector General at the Department of Health and Human Services, which we're going to do."

Ostrom asked Nadler what Congress could do to mandate CFS research and he replied, "Congress can mandate research into CFS as a viral disease. Maybe it will turn out that HHV-6A is the cause of CFS; maybe it will turn out that other viruses are involved. But Congress can mandate research into CFS as a contagious, viral disease. I will certainly try to get Congress to do that as soon as possible."

Ostrom asked how the rest of Congress "could be educated about the fact that this dangerous viral disease is loose in the population, possibly threatening public health and Goldstein said, 'The only way Congress will respond is if a constituency is developed. If there is a network of CFS sufferers out there who are willing to say to Congress, you should be studying the fact that this is a contagious disease, Congress will. If, on the other hand, the CFS network wants to hide the fact it is a contagious disease, then other members of Congress are going to come to Congressman Nadler and say, we won't support your bill; we're going to get roasted on this.' "

In the concluding section of the interview, Nadler said, "CFS is a tremendous public health menace which has not received the attention it deserves. Hillary Johnson has elucidated some of the reasons that it has not received some of the attention it deserves—some very deliberate reasons—and we have to break this open and make sure that it's recognized for what it is, a major communicable disease. We have to make sure we fund research into it, and we have to understand how the virus is transmitted and how to protect the public from it."

In the July 15 issue, Neenyah Ostrom covered the questionable nature of what was considered a major breakthrough in AIDS treatment: "The big news about to emerge from the international 'AIDS' Conference in Vancouver July 7-12 is, according to press reports, the too-good-to-be-true ability of a new class of anti-'AIDS' drug 'cocktails' to rid the bloodstream of all traces of HIV and to cause, in some individuals, remarkable clinical improvement. The 'cocktails' are composed of combinations of a new class of toxic drugs, called protease inhibitors, with older toxic drugs like AZT, DTC and DDC. There are, however, very serious caveats to this 'miracle cure' story. The extraordinary toxicity of protease inhibitors is one. Another is the fact that no one has any idea what the long-term effects of either protease inhibitors or the three drug 'cocktails' might be—despite suggestions that people with 'AIDS' might have to take these drugs for the rest of their lives."

Ostrom noted, "There is also an ominously dark, political side to this story. Protease inhibitors act by cutting an enzyme link in the reproduction of HIV; that is, they change the virus's composition as new generations are produced. Because of the mode of action, researchers who believe HIV alone causes 'AIDS' fear that discontinuation of the drugs could result in the evolution of new types of HIV that could, potentially, be more easily transmitted. In other words, patients who begin taking the drug cocktails and then stop *become threats to the public health*. Following their logic, some experts are suggesting that 'AIDS' patients who begin taking the drugs might have to take them forever, *to avoid becoming public health threats*. It will, therefore, be necessary to *mandate* that treatment continue without interruption once it has begun. To that end, some clinicians are now openly suggesting using the tuberculosis 'direct observation' treatment method as a model for treating 'AIDS' patients with protease inhibitor 'cocktails.' In the TB 'direct observation' treatment model, patients are required to attend a designated clinic when a public health worker watches him or her swallow the required number of pills—like the 'AIDS' drug cocktail, it is usually a combination of three different drugs—on an established schedule."

Ostrom pointed out, "If the TB patient doesn't comply with 'direct observation'—doesn't show up at the clinic, or refuses to take the drugs—the patient is put in jail and forced to take the treatment until he or she is declared cured. This is legal; TB patients who refuse to comply with treatment are considered to be public health threats. A physician who runs Harlem Hospital's infectious disease department (including the 'AIDS' clinic) and was responsible for the development of the 'direct observation' model for TB treatment, Dr. Wataa El-Sadr, told the *Wall Street Journal* July 2 that the TB 'direct observation' model is exactly what's needed to use the new anti-'AIDS' drug cocktails properly."

While ACT UP essentially assisted the government in the maintenance of the HIV/AIDS paradigm, a splinter group of ACT UP in San Francisco began to cut itself off from the mother group's agenda. In our July 29 issue, Neenyah Ostrom reported, "On July 10, in what was described as a 'bloodbath in Vancouver,' a drug company-sponsored seminar on toxic combination therapies was disrupted by ACT UP San Francisco members who dumped fake blood on leading AZT researchers Margaret Fischl (University of Miami) and Paul Volberding (San Francisco General Hospital), as well as prominent government 'AIDS' researchers. The seminar was part of the XI International Conference on AIDS that took place in Vancouver, British Columbia, July 7-12. The disruption of the meeting for more than an hour, according to ACT UP/SF, and the dumping of fake blood on the panel of 'AIDS' researchers, received no known media coverage in the United States, even though two members of the U.S.-based group were expelled from Canada."

Ostrom also reported, "The activists who disrupted the meeting demanded that Glaxo Wellcome, the manufacturer of AZT (one of the toxic drugs being used in the new combination therapies), immediately stop producing the drug. They also demanded that 'AIDS' researchers change the focus of their efforts from killing HIV to strengthening the immune system. The panel, 'Guidelines for Antiretroviral Therapy: Bringing the State-of-the-Art to Clinical Practice,' was disrupted by 20 protestors chanting, 'Margaret Fischl: You're a Fraud! You gave AZT the Nod!' and 'Volberding: Your Lies Kill! AZT's a Toxic Pill.' "

Ostrom noted, "The panel was convened to announce recommendations for the administration of combination antiretroviral therapy as outlined in the July 10 article in the *Journal of the American Medical Association*, 'Antiretroviral Therapy for HIV Infection in 1996: Recommendations of the International Panel.' The panel was sponsored by an alliance of drug companies, including Glaxo Wellcome, Bristol-Meyers Squibb, Hoffman-LaRoche, Roxanne Laboratories, Chiron Corporation, Agouron, Merck Laboratories, according to ACT UP/SF."

The official statement released by ACT UP/SF indicated that, "Over 2,000 stunned conference attendees, packed into two grand ballrooms, looked on in silence as ACT UP members threw real dollar bills labeled 'Glaxo Blood Money,' unfurled a banner, and splattered dazed and speechless panelists with liters of fake blood. AIDS activists charged panel members Margaret Fischl and Paul Volberding with murder for instituting and maintaining a scientifically flawed, yet highly profitable, AIDS treatment approach that urges people with HIV infection to combat the disease with potent regimens of immune suppressive agents."

Ostrom reported that, "According to the protesters, they kicked over chairs, threw microphones, smashed glasses, and overturned conference tables while demanding that the 'AIDS' research establishment stop advocating the treatment of patients with toxic, chemotherapeutic agents. The activists claim that the symposium was delayed for over an hour as panel members changed clothes and attempted to clean up the mess."

One of the protesters, Todd Swindell, told Ostrom, "The entire

AIDS conference was bought and paid for by the pharmaceutical industry as a way to hype their deadly drugs. These companies concoct expensive products. They then fund and execute tests of them on humans to generate fraudulent data supporting their supposed efficacy. Finally, they buy off mainstream AIDS organizations and conferences to push these unproven compounds down the throats of people with AIDS. The entire AIDS treatment approach is murderously misdirected and must change now."

In the August 12 issue, John Hammond reported on another draconian and punitive moment in the epidemic: "Rep. Tom Coburn (R-Ok) introduced legislation August 1 that, according to him, 'attempts to prevent more Americans from contracting HIV and to improve the quality of life of those who are infected.' Coburn is a conservative member of Congress and a medical doctor by profession. In a statement announcing the bill, Coburn charged, 'The federal government and the public health community have been AWOL in the battle against HIV. Sound medical practices have been abandoned and replaced with political correctness. HIV has been treated as a civil rights issue instead of the public health crisis that it is.' Citing assertions that the success of newly available drug therapies is dependent on 'getting treatment early,' he said, 'This bill aims at protecting the uninfected and at helping those who are infected to discover their status as early as possible to maximize the opportunities now available.' "

Hammond reported, "Rep. Susan Molinari, the Republican Congresswoman from Staten Island, signed on as an original co-sponsor of the measure and issued a strong endorsement of the bill, calling it 'a blueprint to coordinate our efforts to prevent further transmission of this deadly disease.' Entitled The HIV Prevention Act of 1996, the bill revives certain proposals for dealing with the epidemic—notably maintaining lists of those who test positive for HIV antibodies, and a system of aggressive contact tracing and partner notification—that were proposed by right-wing politicians early in the epidemic and long ago dismissed as counterproductive. Aggressive reporting and listing of HIV-positive individuals inevitably raises questions about confidentiality, potential abuses such as discrimination, and the ultimate specter of quarantine. Even most advocates of extensive HIV testing agree that such a reporting system would discourage people from being tested or from seeking treatment. 'In general, the coercive

451

measures included here have been repeatedly demonstrated to discourage individuals at risk for HIV infection from seeking appropriate counseling and testing and push the epidemic even further underground,' said Jay Coburn, legislative representative of the AIDS Action Council (AAC), a lobbying organization supported by 1,400 community-based AIDS service organizations throughout the United States."

The abject and self-defeating opposite-world-collaboration of the AIDS activists, was reflected in Jay Coburn's statement to John Hammond that, "None of these proposals do anything to further the community-based prevention efforts that have been highly effective in changing risk behaviors and significantly reducing the transmission of HIV in a cost-effective manner."

More evidence that no scientific anomaly could dislodge the totalitarian foundation of the HIV/AIDS paradigm emerged in the evolving story of Kaposi's sarcoma and the virus (HHV-8) that supposedly caused it. In our August 19 issue, Neenyah Ostrom wrote, "New articles claiming to provide definitive evidence that Kaposi's sarcoma (KS) is caused by a newly-discovered herpesvirus have just appeared in the July 25, 1996, issue of *New England Journal of Medicine* and the August, 1996, issue of *Nature Medicine*. Among the collaborators in some of this work are the two most prominent members of the team that discovered the new virus, Kaposi's Sarcoma Associated Herpes Virus (KSHV, or human herpesvirus-8, HHV-8), husband-and-wife team Drs. Patrick Moore and Yuan Chang of New York City's Columbia-Presbyterian Medical Center."

Ostrom reported that none of the papers "really addresses the oddity of the conventional wisdom that KS occurs overwhelmingly in gay men: Why is this single human herpesvirus restricted to infecting one category of individuals, when all other human herpesviruses are thought to be ubiquitous in the population? That question leads to others that the *Native* has been unsuccessful in convincing numerous physicians and researchers specializing in Kaposi's sarcoma, 'AIDS,' and chronic fatigue syndrome to attempt to answer: What proportion of 'AIDS' patients *really* has KS? How much internal KS goes undetected because virtually no autopsies are now performed on 'AIDS' patients? And are the 'crimson crescents,' frequent lung ailments, and gastrointestinal problems experienced by CFS patients (as well as those seen in 'AIDS' patients) due to undiagnosed, internal

452

KS? And is the seeming unwillingness to investigate these intriguing questions a sign of being afraid to answer them—a sign, in fact, of scientists *not acting* in order to conceal the truth?"

Ostrom noted that, "Even *Science* magazine's Jon Cohen questions that aspect of these and other recent reports on KSHV in *Science*'s August 2 issue. While he accepts unquestioningly that these studies strengthen the case for a non-HIV viral cause of 'AIDS,' most likely KSHV, he notes that it is strange that human herpesvirus should be confined to *any* group of people. 'The new studies don't explain one intriguing question facing the researchers: Why do other human herpesviruses appear widely throughout the population, while KS in AIDS patients is almost exclusively confined to gay men?' Cohen asks. 'Chang and Moore don't address why the virus has established itself in the gay population, but they believe their work shows it is not ubiquitous. . . .' For once Cohen [a loyal friend of the AIDS establishment] seems to be correct: KSHV or HHV-8 or whatever the virus is, is probably not confined to gay men—and neither is KS."

Ostrom noted, "In CFS patients, for instance, there are lesions—pink to red to purple in color, seen in the back of the throat—delicately referred to as 'crimson crescents.' In February 1992, Long Island CFS researcher Burke A. Cunha published a description of the crescents, which he wrote that he identified in 80 percent of his CFS patients in the *Annals of Internal Medicine*. Patients seen in Winthrop University Hospital's CFS Center, Cunha wrote, 'have a peculiar purplish discoloration of both anterior pharyngeal pillars [the back of both sides of the throat]. The crescents are an intense crimson color. . . . This appearance is most closely associated with elevated HHV-6 titers in our patients. . . .' "

Ostrom also reported, "In an article about the Cunha finding in a physicians' newsletter, *Infectious Disease News* (November, 1992), Cunha went even further, suggesting that the presence of the 'crimson crescents' alone was enough to diagnose CFS. Staff writer Robert B. Marchesani reported that 'After the word got out, Cunha received calls from other parts of the country. Physicians began telling him that they were also finding the crimson crescents in their patients once they looked for them.' . . . Cunha told Marchesani that he believes HHV-6 plays a role in causing not only the crimson crescents, but also CFS itself."

In our September 9 issue, Neenyah Ostrom reported on the latest development in the HIV/AIDS juggernaut: "In San Francisco, the City's Health Department Director Sandra Hernandez is advocating not only 'Directly Observed Therapy' (DOT) for individuals taking protease inhibiters but also *identification of every HIV-positive individual and mandatory reporting of cases* to facilitate the implementation of DOT. While advocating widespread (and potentially coercive) administration of the new 'cocktails' (which include protease inhibitors and AZT or one of its analogs), San Francisco's Health Department Director appears to be disregarding the numerous deleterious effects of these drugs, including episodes of hemorrhaging in hemophiliacs; increased peripheral neuropathy (pain in the limbs, usually the legs); development of incredibly painful kidney stones; potentially deadly interactions with common drugs such as antihistamines, and many others."

Ostrom also reported, "ACT UP/San Francisco has strenuously protested Hernandez's support of these coercive policies. On Tuesday, August 20, ACT UP/SF protestors invaded the monthly meeting of the City's health commission to challenge Hernandez's 'AIDS prevention proposal' that would force San Francisco's HIV-infected individuals to take the experimental drug cocktails."

The possibility that the so-called Gulf War Syndrome would bring the CFS and HHV-6 epidemic out of the political and epidemiological closet, was too much to expect from a government so deeply mired in deceit and self-deceit. But we were still hopeful when Neenyah Ostrom covered the story in our September 23 issue. Ostrom reported, "It was front-page news in the *New York Times* on August 22 when it was first revealed that the Pentagon 'acknowledged' that U.S. soldiers had, indeed, been exposed to chemical weapons agents during the 1991 Persian Gulf War. And it was front-page news in the *Times* again on August 28 when Philip Shenon, author of both reports, revealed the extent of the cover-up that had continued for five years: 'A long-classified intelligence report shows that the Pentagon, the White House, the Central Intelligence Agency, and State Department were alerted in November 1991 that chemical weapons had been stored in an Iraqi ammunition depot that was blown up earlier that year by a group of American troops.'"

This finding seemed to satisfy the liberal penchant for always blaming medical problems on toxic environmental factors that are supposedly being covered up—especially when the military is involved. Ostrom asked, "While this appears to prove that the U.S. government lied to its own soldiers about their exposure, however slight, to chemical weapons agents, does that mean that the whole truth about Gulf War Syndrome will now be revealed? Or is it one lie—about soldiers' exposure to chemical agents—simply hiding another bigger, even more frightening lie? What could that lie be? All the facts suggest that, as with chronic fatigue syndrome, the issue that government researchers are most reluctant to tackle in examining Gulf War Syndrome is transmissibility. If GWS is contagious, that means it is caused by a transmissible agent—probably a virus or bacterium. And if GWS is caused by a transmissible agent, that means government scientists should be doing something to protect the public health—i.e. to identify and limit the spread of the GWS agent. Currently, experts are vying to prove or disprove the hypothesis that low-level exposure to chemical agents could cause the symptoms of Gulf War Syndrome. No matter how convincingly the proponents of the chemical weapons exposure theory argue that such exposure could cause GWS, it doesn't answer another nagging question: Why are the spouses of and the children born to Gulf War veterans also getting sick and being born with sometimes catastrophic birth defects?"

In the October 7 issue, Neenyah Ostrom critiqued another piece by *Village Voice* writer Nat Hentoff which once again seemed to have captured the evil of the epidemic exactly backwards: "Currently, Hentoff has summoned the specter of [the Tuskegee Syphilis Experiment] to argue in favor of denying civil rights to HIV-positive, pregnant women, the overwhelming majority of whom are black and/or Hispanic. His column, in the October 1 *Village Voice*, argues the merits of a just-passed law requiring that new mothers be told the results of their newborns' state-mandated HIV antibody tests. He calls the years-long struggle of the sponsor of this bill, Assemblywoman Nettie Mayersohn, to repeal the civil rights of some pregnant women 'an inspiring profile in courage.' "

Neeenyah Ostrom wrote, "In support of his position, Hentoff cites another columnist, *New York Newsday*'s Jim Dwyer, who harkened back to Tuskegee in a series of articles arguing in favor of the newly-passed law. In the course of this series on the subject, Dwyer interviewed a pediatrician at the University of California, Dr. Arthur Ammann. Referring to the anonymous testing of newborns then taking place in

New York, Ammann said, 'The maintenance of anonymous test results at a time when treatment and prevention are readily available will be recorded in history is analogous to the Tuskegee experiment.' "

Ostrom pointed out, "Hentoff, Dwyer, and other journalists and lawmakers who argue all HIV-positive pregnant women should be identified and then given AZT and all HIV-positive babies should be identified so they, too, can be given AZT or other toxic chemicals immediately after birth, are, no doubt, doing so from the best possible motivation. (A single truncated government study, which has never been replicated and contains no data about long-term effects on children born to mothers given AZT, claims to show the drug stops transmission of HIV from mother to fetus in some instances.) Even these journalists' references to Tuskegee make superficial sense— except that, while they may think they understand Tuskegee, *they don't have a clue what is going on with AIDS*. And they don't really get Tuskegee, either."

Ostrom notes, "The parallel Hentoff draws between Tuskegee and the need for a law mandating reporting of infants' HIV antibody test results is that, in both cases, information is withheld from the patients. Unfortunately, that comparison is so oversimplified, it's useless. There are two true parallels between Tuskegee and 'AIDS': The first is the fact that patients are being told that they are being treated appropriately when the 'treatments' are actually harmful, and sometimes fatal; the second is the continuation of racism in medicine. At the time the Tuskegee experiment was begun, syphilis was believed to be a different illness in blacks than it was in whites; 'AIDS' in Africa and in African-Americans has always been portrayed as a different kind of illness than 'AIDS' in whites. In the Tuskegee experiment the government doctors lied to the all-black patients about the outcome of the 'treatment' they were receiving for their disease. The men in Tuskegee were told that the aspirin and sugar pills they were given would cure their 'bad blood'; they were never told that their disease could enfeeble their minds and bodies and kill them."

Ostrom concluded that there was a disturbing parallel: "The mostly black pregnant women and infants being given AZT are not being told the truth about the outcome of the 'treatment' they are receiving for their disease: Pregnant women aren't informed about the infants who received AZT in utero who've been born with heart defects, holes in their chests, misshapen heads, blindness, and other distressing, life-threatening birth defects."

456

In the October 21 issue, Ostrom wrote another piece about the *New York Times*'s ridiculous coverage of chronic fatigue syndrome: "The *New York Times*, the 'paper of record' that attempted to pretend the 'AIDS' epidemic wasn't occurring in the early 1980s, has now turned back the clock almost a decade on chronic fatigue syndrome. In the October 9 'Personal Health' column, Jane E. Brody characterizes CFS as a primarily psychoneurotic disease, relying upon an unpublished position statement from a group of British physicians and citing National Institutes of Allergy and Infectious Disease researcher Stephen E. Straus as her only named source. Straus is infamous among CFS patients for his efforts over the last decade to prove, contrary to all available facts and even his own research, that CFS is primarily a psychiatric disease. Brody's column lauds the British physicians' suggestion that psychotherapy be used to treat CFS patients [in order] to remove their delusions about their medical condition. Straus concurs with this suggestion, according to the *Times*."

Ostrom noted, "Although Brody writes as if Straus's characterization of CFS is widely accepted—certainly among government scientists—that is not at all the case: neither researchers at the Centers for Disease Control nor the Department of Health and Human Services Assistant Secretary for Health, Dr. Phillip R. Lee, so characterize CFS. . . . By promoting [Straus's] wrong-headed, faulty definition of CFS, Jane Brody and the *New York Times* have caused possibly irreparable harm to millions of very sick people."

In our December 9 issue, Neenyah Ostrom again took up the relationship between CFS and Gulf War Syndrome: "The Centers for Disease Control and Prevention will publish a study early next year linking Gulf War Syndrome to chronic fatigue syndrome, according to a page-one story by Philip Shenon in the *New York Times* on November 26. The *New York Native* has been suggesting that evidence pointed to a link between the two syndromes since August 1992. A second study, conducted by Navy researchers, will also be published in early 1997, according to Shenon. Both of these studies will 'show for the first time that veterans of the 1991 Persian Gulf War are far more likely to suffer from a variety of serious health problems than troops who did not serve in the war, a finding that appears to vindicate ailing veterans who have said that their service in the gulf has cost them their health,' Shenon reported. . . . The CDC results, which describe a study performed on 4,000 military personnel, show that 'troops deployed to

457

the gulf were more than three times as likely as troops who were elsewhere to suffer from chronic diarrhea, joint pain, skin rashes, fatigue, depression, and memory loss,' Shenon reported in the *Times*. 'They have also reported far higher rates of headaches, sinus problems, and sleep disturbances.' Shenon added, 'The CDC study is expected to link some of the Veterans' health problem to chronic fatigue syndrome and the physical aftereffects of battlefield stress.' "

A piece by John Lauritsen, titled "Tragedy by the Sea," which we published in the same issue, captured the way entire gay communities were absorbing the propaganda and indoctrination of the epidemic without having a clue about what was really going on. Lauritsen wrote, "The 'magic of Provincetown' has become a magnet for gay men with diagnoses of 'AIDS' or 'HIV-positive.' For a decade now they have been arriving in Provincetown—their medical records in hand, their various welfare benefits established, and their life insurance policies (if any) cashed in—to spend their final days here. All over the world gay men whose happiest memories are of vacations in Provincetown, which for most of the twentieth century has been the premiere gay resort. During the summer all of Commercial Street, from Town Hall west, is a promenade: drag queens mingling with grizzled old men in leather (even in August), bodybuilders strutting their stuff, local residents walking their mutts, and hundreds of all kinds of very nice guys who can relax and be themselves in the fellowship of their own kind. There are middle-aged and elderly couples who have been coming to Provincetown ever since they were young."

But Provincetown did not escape the totalitarian world of the HIV/AIDS paradigm. Lauritsen reported that, "Now Provincetown has its AIDS enclave, a full-fledged outpost of the AIDS industry. In addition to the AIDS support groups, the Unitarian Universalist Church has established an AIDS ministry and its own minister. One private clinic alone has 250 AIDS patients, and for those who need or prefer big city doctors, a van makes regular trips between Provincetown and Boston. Drug manufacturers come to town, offering free dinners along with 'treatment information' to those who are 'HIV positive.' On the average there is an AIDS obituary every week or two in the local paper."

In the December 23 issue, Neenyah Ostrom celebrated the courage of a journalist who dared to challenge the AIDS establishment: "Author, columnist, and host of talk shows on both radio and television, Tony Brown, is one of the very, very few individuals in the black community who has questioned the government's assertion that all HIV-positive people should take AZT and other, even more toxic drugs. Brown also questioned whether HIV is the cause of 'AIDS'; in his writings and on his talk show, Brown has urged people to think for themselves, wrench control of their health back from the bureaucracy that is attempting to mandate health care and, above all, to question, question, question."

Ostrom reported, "As a result of his refusal to urge African-Americans to be tested for the 'AIDS virus' and to take toxic chemicals if they test positive, Brown has been, according to our sources, identified as a major problem in controlling the behavior of black Americans. The *Native* has learned, in fact, that at the 'AIDS' policy meeting held by black leaders at Harvard in October, Brown was singled out as an impediment to educating African-Americans about 'AIDS' and convincing them to take AZT and future generations of toxic drugs."

Ostrom noted, "Brown is not a physician. He does not advise people on how to manage their health, or what drugs to take or avoid taking. The message that he broadcasts over and over again is: Think for yourself. Make your own informed decision regarding your own health. That Brown would be considered a 'problem' by other black leaders, as sources have alleged, appears to be yet another indication that, [where AIDS is concerned] there is no free speech."

1997: The End

Whatever free speech the *New York Native* was allowed—in the face of a boycott and increasing hostility from the AIDS activists and the AIDS establishment—was about to come to an end. The paper lost its financial struggle to stay alive and the January 19, 1997, issue was our final one. Donna Shalala, the Secretary of Health and Human Services, was featured on the cover with the headline, "The Cover-up Queen: Why is Donna Shalala Lying about 'AIDS,' CFS, and Gulf War Syndrome?"

Neenyah Ostrom wrote, "When a Democratic President was elected in 1992, there was hope among some investigators who had been attempting to expose the government's lie about the 'AIDS' and chronic fatigue syndrome (CFS) epidemics that the truth would finally be revealed—or at least sought. Then Donna Shalala was appointed Secretary of Health and Human Services. . . . Since her appointment . . . Shalala has appeared to shelter government scientists accused of scientific fraud—most prominently, former National Cancer Institute researcher Robert C. Gallo."

Ostrom argued, "Shalala has personally helped to perpetuate the cover-up of the connection between 'AIDS' and CFS, as correspondence between her and New York Rep. Jerrold Nadler (D-8th District) demonstrates. Nadler wrote to Shalala in early 1996 to ask for her help in investigating charges made by author Hillary Johnson in her book *Osler's Web* that 'CFS is a real disease caused by a real pathogen . . . but that the CDC has attempted to portray CFS as a psychosomatic illness instead.' Additionally, Nadler informed Shalala that Johnson's book uncovers evidence that CFS is a contagious illness."

Ostrom reported, "In June 1996, Shalala responded to Nadler's inquiries by defending the shoddy work performed on CFS by CDC and other government agencies: 'CFS is a debilitating disorder characterized by profound tiredness or fatigue. Federal government scientists have been involved in CFS research since 1979. CDC's program, which began in 1985, collaborates with other Federal and State government agencies, scientific researchers, health care providers, and patient support groups. . . . Well-designed case-control studies involving rigorously classified CFS patients and appropriate controls have found no association between CFS and infection with a wide range of microorganisms. . . . In addition, a large number of peer-

460

reviewed published studies have failed to detect any evidence that infection with human or animal retroviruses is associated with CFS. Furthermore, case-control studies have failed to document behavioral or other characteristics (e.g. IV drug use, exposure to animals, occupational or travel history) of CFS patients that would point to an infectious cause for the disease. The current body of scientific evidence argues against the possibility that CFS is caused by an infectious agent. Similarly, there is no epidemiological evidence to support the view that CFS is a contagious disease. CDC has been unable to confirm the occurrence of a cluster of CFS cases. . . . CDC has conducted large population-based surveys that found no increased risk for CFS among members of households in which a person with CFS resides. . . .' "

And so, as the *New York Native* faded into history, the government was standing its ground. The pandemic of AIDS, "chronic fatigue syndrome," and other HHV-6–related multisystemic illnesses would have to find new whistleblowers and independent journalists. The "Poison Kitchen" of the epidemic was permanently silenced. The hopes of the AIDS activists and the AIDS establishment had finally been fulfilled.

The *New York Native* may have left the scene, but subsequently, the intertwined biomedical and political events it had been reporting on became even uglier and more consequential. The surprising developments that occurred during the two decades following the demise of the *New York Native* (including the nation-destroying epidemic of HHV-6-related autism), are stories for another day.

Notes

Introduction

p. 7.   "woodenheadedness." Barbara Tuchman, *The March of Folly* (New York: Random House Publishing Group, 1984) p. 7.

p. 7.   "self-deception." Ibid.

p. 7.   "fixed belief." Ibid.

p. 7.   "evidence to the contrary." Ibid.

p. 7.   "a policy . . . hindsight." Ibid., p. 5.

p. 7.   "a feasible . . . available." Ibid.

p. 7.   "that the policy . . . individual ruler." Ibid.

p. 8.   "Poison Kitchen." Ron Rosenbaum, *Explaining Hitler: The Search for the Origins of His Evil* (New York: Random House, 1998) p. 37.

p. 8.   "nemesis." Ibid.

p. 8.   "the persistent . . . in his side." Ibid.

p. 8.   "The Munich Post . . . toward Berlin." Ibid.

p. 8.   "a dozen years." Ibid., p. 38.

p. 9.   "they knew . . . his skin." Ibid.

p. 9.   "It was . . . life miserable." Ibid., p. 40.

p. 9.   "the Hitler Party." Ibid.

p. 9.   "Their repeated . . . criminal pathology." Ibid.

p. 9.   "men such as . . . its limits." Ibid., p.42.

p. 9.   "even glimpsed . . . in the Third Reich." Ibid.

p. 9.   "as a homicidal . . . political party." Ibid., p. 52.

p. 9.   "the shocking . . . horrifically true." Ibid., p. 53.

p. 9.   "According to Rosenbaum . . . bitter end." Ibid., p. 53

p. 9.   "to restore . . . combat with [Hitler]." Ibid., p. 59.

1981-1984: The Fog of Epidemiology

p. 11.   I had asked Dr. Lawrence Mass, in May of 1981, to look into rumors of a rare form of cancer striking men and in the May 18, 1981, issue of the *New York Native* we ran a story with the headline "Disease Rumor Largely Unfounded." Dr. Mass wrote, "Last week there were rumors that an exotic new disease had hit the gay community in New York. Here are the facts. From the New York City Department of Health, Dr. Steve Phillips explained that the rumors are for the most part unfounded. Each year, approximately 12 to 14 cases of infection with a protozoa-like organism, Pneumocystis carinii, are reported in the New York City area. The organism is not exotic, in fact, it's ubiquitous. But most of us have natural or easily acquired immunity."

p. 16.   Jane Teas has a Ph.D. from Johns Hopkins University.

p. 18.   Arnoux, Emmanuel, JeanMichel Guerin, Rodolphe Malebranche, Robert Elie, A.Claude Laroche, Gerard Pierre et al.; "AIDS and African Swine Fever" ; *The Lancet*, July 9, 1983, p. 110.

1985: Throwing Down the Gauntlet

p. 35.   Ann Giudici Fettner and William A. Check wrote *The Truth About AIDS: Evolution of an Epidemic* (New York: Henry Holt & Co., 1984).

p. 38.   Nick Wade and William Broad wrote *Betrayers of the Truth: Fraud and Deceit in the Halls of Science* (New York: Simon and Schuster, 1983).

p. 64.   "The first . . . all conditions." Hess, William, "African swine fever: a Reassessment"; *Advances in Veterinary Science and Comparative Medicine,* Volume 25, 1981, pages 36-39.

p. 76.   "The purely . . . were doing." Young-Bruehl, Elisabeth, *Hannah Arendt: For Love of the World* (New Haven, Yale University Press, 1977), p. xiv.

1986: A New Virus or a Renamed Old One?

p. 84.   One of the people who accompanied American officials to Haiti in order to help eradicate ASFV by killing the entire the pig population came back with a mysterious chronic illness. I lost touch with her and don't know if she got better.

p. 87.   The misuse of funds at the CDC may be a chronic problem. Hillary Johnson details the misuse of CDC funds in their mishandling of research into chronic fatigue syndrome in her book, *Osler's Web: Inside the Labyrinth of the Chronic Fatigue Syndrome Epidemic* (New York, Crown Publishers Inc., 1996

p. 88.   Hannah Arendt discusses the nature of governmental image-making and propaganda in her essay, "Truth and Politics," in *Between Past and Future: Eight Exercises in Political Thought* (New York, Viking Press, 1961).

p. 93.   We portrayed Robert Gallo on the cover of *New York Native* as Carmen Miranda.

p. 93.   To really get a sense of Gallo's shocking antics and habit of threatening people, read John Crewdson's *Science Fictions: A Scientific Mystery, A Massive Cover-Up and the Dark Legacy of Robert Gallo* (Boston, New York and London: Little Brown and Company, 2002).

p. 97.   Statements like those of Dr. Peter Skrabanek inspired me to start doing some serious critical thinking about the political nature of epidemiology. Before long I was thinking of it as the used car salesman area of "science."

p. 99.   If the kind of sabotage that seemed to be going on at the CDC had been occurring in any other area of the government, the media would have assigned its best investigative reporters to cover it.

p. 103.   "It was an act . . . was Lysenko." Nicholas Wade and William Broad, *Betrayers of the Truth: Fraud and Deceit in the Halls of Science* (New York: Simon and Schuster, 1986), pp. 187-188.

p. 104.   " . . . Himmler was not . . . theoreticians as well." Richard Plant, *The Pink Triangle: The Nazi War Against Homosexuals* (New York: Henry Holt and co. and New Republic Books, 1986), pp. 88-91.

1987: An Epic Epidemiological Battle

p. 111.   James H. Jones, *Bad Blood : The Tuskegee Syphilis Experiment: A Tragedy of Race and Medicine* (New York, The Free Press, 1982).

p. 112.   John Lauritsen's books on AIDS are *Poison by Prescription: The AZT Story* (New York: Asklepios, 1990), *The AIDS War: Profiteering, and Genocide from the Medical Industrial Complex* (New York: Asklepios, 1993) and with Ian Young, *The AIDS Cult: Essays on the Gay Health Crisis* (New York: Pagan Press, 1997).

p. 115.   Darrell Yates Rist co-founded the Gay and Lesbian Alliance Against Defamation. He is the author of *Heartlands: A Gay Man's Odyssey Across America* (New York: Dutton, 1992).

p. 123.   I was very disappointed that Vidal never really took his usual cold hard look at AIDS and never helped raise the public profile of the epidemic's critics and skeptics.

p. 127.   That wasn't my only contact with the White House. During the Bush Sr. administration I reached Bush's personal physician in the White House and talked to him about the chronic fatigue syndrome epidemic. He was polite and seemed interested, but I got nowhere.

1988: The Public Relations of the Epidemic

p. 131.   Harvey Bialy is the author of *Oncogenes, Aneuploidy, and AIDS: A Scientific Life & Times of Peter H. Duesberg* (Berkeley: North Atlantic Books, 2004).

p. 137.   "vital lie." Daniel Goleman quoting Henrick Ibsen, *Vital Lies, Simple Truths: The Psychology of Self-Deception* (New York: Simon and Schuster, 1985) p. 16.

p. 137.   "a family myth . . . comfortable truth." Ibid., p. 16.

p. 137.   "We are piloted . . . psychological life." Ibid., p. 241.

p. 138.   "acceptable dissent." Ibid., p. 248.

p. 140. The three books we published by Neenyah Ostrom are *What Really Killed Gilda Radner?: Frontline Reports on the Chronic Fatigue Syndrome Epidemic* (New York: That New Magazine, Inc. 1991), *50 Things You Should Know About the Chronic Fatigue Syndrome Epidemic* (New York: That New Magazine, 1990) which was republished as a mass market paperback (New York: St. Martin's Press, 1993), and *America's Biggest Cover-Up: 50 More Things Everyone Should Know About the Chronic Fatigue Syndrome Epidemic And Its Link to AIDS* (New York: That New Magazine, Inc., 1993).

p. 143. My favorite fact about Mathilde Krim comes courtesy of her Wikipedia entry: "Krim then moved to New York and joined the research staff of Cornell University Medical School following her 1958 marriage to Arthur B. Krim—a New York attorney, head of United Artists, founder of Orion Pictures, and advisor to Lyndon Johnson. It was at Krim's NYC home on May 19, 1962 that the famous 45th birthday party for President John F. Kennedy was held, with many famous persons in attendance (Robert Kennedy, Marilyn Monroe, Maria Callas, Jack Benny, Harry Belafonte)."

p. 148. "The ability . . . of domestic pigs." Yechiel Becker, *African Swine Fever* (Boston: Martinus Nijhoff Publishing, 1987) p. IX.

p. 150. Michael Specter eventually became a writer for *The New Yorker* where he continued to enforce the AIDS establishment's dogma. In the March 12, 2007 issue of *The New Yorker* he wrote a piece titled "The Denialists: the dangerous attacks on the consensus about H.I.V. and AIDS."

1989: A Strategy Emerges

p. 155. We'll never know how many people died of heart attacks which were complications of so-called "chronic fatigue syndrome."

p. 156. Laura Pinsky and Paul Harding Davis wrote *The Essential AIDS Fact Book: Newly Revised and Updated* (New York: Pocket, 1996).

p. 157. Ironically, Stephen Straus died of brain cancer on May 14, 2007. The virus HHV-6, which has been linked to CFS and AIDS is also known to be involved in brain cancer. While the CFS patients often portrayed Straus as the central villain in the CFS cover-up, they seemed to be giving a free ride to his boss at NIAID, Anthony Fauci.

p. 161. If medical workers with CFS had formed their own organization to publicize the CFS epidemic, it could have had a huge impact. Unfortunately, most remained in the closet. It is kind of an open secret in the CFS community that many of the people treating or researching CFS themselves have CFS. The whole issue of CFS being transmitted from health care workers to patients (and vice versa) is one of the many taboo subjects in the CFS community.

p. 166. Paul Cheney eventually opened a clinic devoted to treating chronic fatigue syndrome in North Carolina. Patients have described seeing Cheney as a fairly expensive proposition. On the Cheney Clinic's website there is a relatively benign—almost watered down—description of the disorder: "Chronic Fatigue Syndrome is a disorder of unknown cause characterized by significant functional disability associated with fatigue, pain and neuropsychological complaints."

p. 167. Dennis King, *Lyndon Larouche and the New American Fascism* (New York: Doubleday, 1989).

p. 169. Project Inform was started in 1984 by Martin Delaney and Joseph Brewer. Delaney died in 2009. From a National Institute of Allergy and Infectious Diseases press release issued on January 22, 2009: " 'Millions of people are now receiving life-saving antiretroviral medications from a treatment pipeline that Marty Delaney played a key role in opening and expanding,' says NIAID Director Anthony S. Fauci, M.D. 'Without his tireless work and vision, many more people would have perished from HIV/AIDS. He is a formidable activist and a dear friend. It is without hyperbole that I call Marty Delaney a public health hero.' "

p. 175. "Tall sails . . . to New York." Randy Shilts, *And the Band Played On: Politics, People and the AIDS Epidemic* (New York: St. Martin's Press, 1987) p. 3.

p. 178. It became clearer throughout the epidemic of AIDS/CFS that one of the most important political aspects of epidemiology is the power to name diseases. It is not a science but rather a social act of demarcation that always has the unrecognized potential to stigmatize while appearing to being doing something utterly objective and humane. Epidemiology has all the public health propaganda tools it needs to create what Noam Chomsky calls "manufactured consensus."

1990: Creepier Events

p. 183. Michael Fumento, *The Myth of Heterosexual AIDS: How a Tragedy Has Been Distorted by the Media and Partisan Politics* (New York: Harper Collins, 1990).

p. 187. In the Feb. 12, 1990 issue of *New York Native*, Neenyah Ostrom reported, " 'Kaposi's Sarcoma Among Persons With AIDS: A Sexually Transmitted Infection?' is the lead article in the January 20 issue of *The Lancet*. Dr. Valerie Beral at the Imperial Cancer Research Fund in Oxford, England collaborated with Center for Disease Control (CDC scientists Thomas A. Peterman, Ruth L. Berkelman, and Harold W. Jaffe) on the research. A shorter 'Letter' by Alvin E. Friedman Kien (New York University Medical Center) and co-workers entitled "Kaposi's Sarcoma in HIV-Negative Homosexual Men" appears in the same issue."

p. 191.   Nicholas Regush is the author of *The Virus Within: A Coming Epidemic* (New York: Dutton Adult, 2000).

p. 192.   In 2014 the CFS community was still trying desperately to get the FDA to approve Ampligen.

p. 198.   Neenyah Ostrom also reported that "Ruth and her husband also had another pet, a cat. The cat developed cancer—not the fairly common feline leukemia—but a malignancy of the immune system, lymphatic cancer."

p. 198.   John Crewdson never noted or credited *New York Native* for its numerous articles (included several cover stories and major editorials) on the questionable science of Robert Gallo even though he was aware of what we were doing. I called him frequently during the period he was reporting on Gallo and his line was always "You may be 'righter' than you realize."

p. 200.   Neenyah Ostrom also reported, in the April 9 issue of *New York Native*, "Overall, 12 percent of the symphony orchestra were diagnosed as having chronic fatigue syndrome, mostly women. And four of the 68 people studied, or six percent, developed cancers. Herberman pointed out that this percentage of people developing cancers is 'remarkably high for a group of essentially young adults. What one would expect in the general population for individuals during this period of follow-up would be about .1 cases. This gives an odds ratio of about 27 times over the expected number of cases, a highly significant result. This is rather intriguing, and at least raises the question that there may be . . . more serious problems that might be occurring in these individuals . . . .' "

p. 202.   Neenyah Ostrom also reported, in the April 30 *New York Native*, "After 'being laughed out of' several prestigious infectious disease clinics, and even being threatened with commitment to a psychiatric institution, Shirley became a patient of Peterson's."

p. 203.   Dr. Carl Sandman presented his talk, "Is There a CFS Dementia," at the First International Conference on Chronic Fatigue Syndrome and Fibromyalgia held in Los Angeles February 16-18, 1990.

p. 203.   Neenyah Ostrom's report on Dr. David Bell, in the May 21, 1990, *New York Native,* was based on his presentation of "an overview of the immunologic abnormalities found in patients involved in the outbreak, at the First International Conference on Chronic Fatigue Syndrome and Fibromyalgia (Los Angeles, February 16-18, 1990)."

p. 204.   Levy, Jay A., Deborah Greenspan, Frank Ferro, and Evelyn. T. Lennette; "Frequent Isolation of HHV-6 From Saliva and High Seroprevalence of the Virus in the Population"; *The Lancet*, May 5, 1990, p. 1047.

p. 211.   Li-Min Huang, Chin-Yun Lee, Kai-Hsin Lin, Wen-Min Chuu, Ping-Ing Lee, Rong-Long Chen, Jong-Ming Chen, Dong-Tsamn Lin; "Human herpesvirus-6 associated with fatal haemophagocytic syndrome"; *The Lancet*, June 7, 1990, p. 60.

p. 214. "CFS is a form of acquired immunodeficiency." Klimas, Nancy G., Fernando R. Salvato, Robert Morgan, and Mary Ann Fletcher; "Immunologic Abnormalities in Chronic Fatigue Syndrome"; *Journal of Clinical Microbiology*, June, 1990.

p. 221. " 'CFS results . . . effector systems.' " Patricia Bradshaw; "What Has the NIH Done for You Lately?"; *CFIDS Chronicle*, January/ February 1989.

p. 222. Elinor Burkett is the author of *The Gravest Show on Earth: America in the Age of AIDS*, (New York: Houghton Mifflin, 1995).

p. 224. "transient blindness." Kamaroff, Anthony et al.; "A Chronic 'Post-Viral' Fatigue Syndrome with Neurologic Features: Association with Human Herpesvirus-6"; Abstract submitted to the Society of General Internal Medicine, Washington D.C. April 27-29, 1988.

p. 225. Helena Strandstrom, Joanne R. Higgins, Kevin Mossie, and Gordon H. Theilan: "Studies With Canine Sera That Contain Antibodies Which Recognize Human Immunodeficiency Virus Structural Proteins"; *Cancer Research*, September 1, 1990.

1991: Conspiracy of Dunces

p. 230. Neenyah Ostrom was supposed to appear on *Larry King Live* to discuss her book, but the appearance was canceled at the last moment because of some breaking news and was never rescheduled.

p. 236. Peter Duesberg's article, "AIDS Epidemiology: Inconsistencies with Human Immunodeficiency Virus and With Infectious Disease," was published in the February 1991 issue of the *Proceedings of The National Academy of Sciences* (Volume 88).

p. 238. "Using reagents . . . variant of ASFV." Beldekas, John, Jane Teas, and James Hebert, "African Swine Fever and AIDS"; *The Lancet*, March 8, 1986.

p. 239. Josephs, S.F., L Schler, D.V. Ablashi, W.C. Saxinger, H.Z. Streicher, and S.Z. Salahuddin; "HBLV Is Not ASFV"; *AIDS Research and Human Retroviruses* 4:317, 1988.

p. 239. Robert Gallo, *Virus Hunting: AIDS, Cancer, & The Human Retrovirus: A Story Of Scientific Discovery*, (New York: Basic Books, 1991).

p. 240. Paul Lavinger eventually died of cancer, a not uncommon outcome of so-called chronic fatigue syndrome.

p. 241. Neenyah Ostrom also reported in the July 1, 1991 issue of *New York Native*, " . . . Cheney and his colleague, Dr. Charles W. Lapp, are so concerned about the transmissibility of CFIDS that they have printed guidelines for their patients to follow ("Self-Care Manual, February, 1991," published in the March, 1991 *CFIDS Chronicle* Physicians' Forum).
    Those guidelines include:

—Do not allow others to eat after you eat or share food, glasses, cups, or utensils;

—Do not kiss others on the mouth;

—Do not feed table scraps to pets;

—Remind lab personnel to use 'precautions' when drawing your blood or handling body fluids; and

—Consider using a condom during sexual intercourse."

p. 242. Lifson, Alan, R., Susan P. Buchbinder, Haynes W Sheppard, Alison C. Mawle, Judith C. Wilber, Mark Stanley, Clyde E. Hart, Nancy Hessol, and Scott D. Holmberg; "Long-Term Human Immunodeficiency Virus Infection in Asymptomatic Homosexual and Bisexual Men with Normal CD4+ Lymphocyte Counts: Immunologic and Virologic Characteristics"; *Journal of Infectious Diseases* 163(5):959 May 1991.

p. 250. Morin published a paper on the respiratory syndrome in pigs: Morin M, Robinson Y. Porcine reproductive and respiratory syndrome in Quebec. *Vet Rec.* 1991 Oct 19;129(16).

p. 251. "The ability of ASF . . . domestic pigs." Yechiel Becker, *African Swine Fever* (Boston: Martinus Nijhoff Publishing, 1987)

p. 253. In the September, 9, 1991 issue of *New York Native*, Ostrom wrote, "Scholastic Aptitude Test (SAT) scores have fallen nationwide among teenagers planning to attend college, the College Board revealed on August 26. Average math scores fell for the first time to 11 years, and verbal scores were the worst ever," according to the *New York Post*, which headlined an August 27 article, 'SAT Scores: Kids Dumber Than Ever.' "

p. 256. Neenyah Ostrom wrote in the October 14, 1991, *New York Native*, "The two pieces of research come from separate research groups. The first is from Tracy A. Kion and Geoffrey W. Hoffman from the University of British Columbia and was published in the Sept. 6 issue of *Science*. . . . The second piece of evidence (which Maddox says will be published in the following issue of *Nature*) was produced by E.J. Stott and colleagues at the British National Institute for Biological Standards and Control."

p. 259. "that both . . . hypoanergy." Wakefield, Denis; "Immunological Markers in CFS"; *CFIDS Chronicle*, Spring 1991 Conference Issue.

1992: HIV-negative AIDS

p. 262. "It may take . . . the AIDS crisis." Larry Kramer interviewed by Helen Eisenbach, "Kramer Defies Convention," *QW*, no 37, July 19, 1992, p. 24.

p. 267. " . . . Herpes simplex . . . in thin sections." Hess, W.R. "Classification and Nomenclature"; in *African Swine Fever Virus* (Austria: Springer-Verlag, 1971).

p. 268.   In the April 27, 1992, *New York Native*, Neenyah Ostrom wrote, "A March 25, 1992, press release from the National Institute of Allergy and Infectious Diseases stated that, 'Approximately 15 million Americans suffer from asthma.' The cost of treating those 15 million asthmatic Americans was found to be $6.2 billion in 1990 alone."

p. 268.   The "1991 publication" Neenyah Ostrom refers to: Bell, Karen et al.; "Risk Factor Associated with Chronic Fatigue Syndrome in a Cluster of Pediatric Cases"; *Reviews of Infectious Diseases*, Volume 13, Supplement 1, January-February 1991.

p. 268.   The Ampligen research Ostrom refers to in the May 4, 1992, New York Native: Suhadolnik, R.J., N.L. Relchenbach, P.M Hitzges, D.H Gillespie, D.R. Strayer, and W.A. Carter; "Biochemical Defect in the 2-5A Synthetase/RNase L Antiviral Pathway in Chronic Fatigue Syndrome (CFS)"; submitted to the International Society for Antiviral Research, Fifth International Conference, Vancouver, B.C. Canada, March 8-13, 1992.

p. 269.   The source of William Carter's remarks: "Experimental Drug Held Effective for Chronic Fatigue Immune Dysfunction"; *Conference Journal, September 29-October 2, 1991*; published by the American Society for Microbiology.

p. 272.   Simms, R.W. et al.; "Fibromyalgia Syndrome in Patients Infected with Human Immunodeficiency Virus"; *American Journal of Medicine*, April 1992, 92(4):368-374.

p. 284.   The Kaposi's sarcoma research from the Florida scientists: Moskowitz, Lee B., George T. Hensley, Edwin W. Gould, and Steven D. Weiss; "Frequency and Anatomic Distribution of Lymphadenopathic Kaposi's Sarcoma in the Acquired Immunodeficiency Syndrome: An Autopsy Series"; *Human Pathology*, Volume 16, No 5, May 1985.

p. 285.   "Almost all patients . . . this room together." Jessop, Carol; "Clinical Features and Possible Etiology of CFIDS"; *CFIDS Chronicle*, Spring 1991 Conference Issue.

p. 285.   "The most common HIV-related causes of gastric symptoms . . . .": Roland, Michelle; Gastrointestinal Manifestations of HIV: Diagnosis and Treatment"; *AIDS Treatment News,* August 23, 1991.

p. 290.   In the August 10, 1992 issue of the *New York Native*, Neenyah Ostrom wrote, "A report about a cluster of a mysterious illness among Gulf War veterans was released by the Army's Office of the Surgeon General on June 25."

p. 291.   Jad Adams, *AIDS: The HIV Myth* (New York: St. Martin's Press, 1989). p. 172.

1993: The AIDS Thought Police

p. 310.   Neenyah Ostrom wrote in the February 22, 1993 issue of *New York Native*, "The report of the Phase I safety trial, "PASSHIV Treatment of Patients With HIV-1 Infection, A Preliminary Report of a Phase I Trial of Hyperimmune Porcine Immunoglobulin to HIV-1," was published in the December 1992 issue of the journal *AIDS*. The study included Verigen Inc. founder Dr. Kurt Osther and colleagues from the universities of Aarhus and Copenhagen in Denmark, and the University of Pennsylvania School of Medicine and the Children's Hospital of Philadelphia in the U.S."

p. 317.   The University of Rochester study: Dewhurst, S, K. McIntyre, K. Schnabel, and C.B. Hall: "Human Herpesvirus 6 (HHV-6) Variant B Accounts for the Majority of Symptomatic Primary HHV-6 Infections in a population of U.S. Infants"; *Journal of Clinical Microbiology*, February 1993.

p. 318.   The research Neenyah Ostrom's statement that the type of cell any one strain of HHV-6 "[is able to] infect can change after it has been grown in tissue culture for a length of time" is based on: Stewart, John A.; "Human Herpesvirus 6: Basic Biology and Clinical Associations"; in *Medical Virology 9* (L.M. de la Maza and E.M. Petersen, Eds.), Plenum Press, New York, 1990.

p. 319.   The Gallo research on HHV-6: Lusso, P., Malnati, M., Garzino-Demo, A., Crowley, R., Long, E., Gallo, R.; "Infection of Natural Killer Cells by Human Herpesvirus-6"; *Nature*, April 1, 1993.

p. 319.   The AZT study was known as "The Concorde Study." Aboulker, JP, Swart, AM.; "Preliminary analysis of the Concorde trial. Concorde Coordinating Committee"; *The Lancet*, 1993 April 3;341(8849):889-90.

p. 322.   The research Neenyah Ostrom's statement about asthma in children with CFS is based on: Bell, Karen et al.; "Risk Factors Associated with Chronic Fatigue Syndrome in a Cluster of Pediatric Cases"; *Review of Infectious Diseases*, Vol 13, Supplement 1, January-February 1991.

p. 322.   The research Neenyah Ostroms statement about anti-ulcer drugs and natural killer cells is based on: Nielson, Hans Jorgen et al., "Ranitidine Improves Certain Cellular Immune Responses in Asymptomatic HIV-Infected Individuals"; *Journal of Acquired Immune Deficiency Syndromes*, 46):577, June 1991.

p. 323.   Steere, Allen C., Elise Taylor, Gail L. McHugh, and Eric Logigan; "The Overdiagnosis of Lyme Disease"; *Journal of the American Medical Association*, April 14, 1993.

p. 325.   Burd, Eileen M. et al.; "HHV-6 May Block Differentiation of Macrophages From Marrow Precursors"; *Blood*, 81(6)1645, 1993.

p. 330.   Vito Russo died in 1990. According to Wikipedia, he was "was an American LGBT activist, film historian and author who is best remembered as the author of the book *The Celluloid Closet*" (New York, Joanna Cotler Books, 1981).

p. 331. Hyde, Byron, Sheila Bastien, and Anil Jain; "General Information: Post-Infectious, Acute Onset M.E./CFS"; *The Clinical and Scientific Basis of Myalgic Encephalomyelitis/Chronic Fatigue Syndrome*; The Nightingale Research Foundation, Ottawa, Ontario, Canada, 1992. Byron M. Hyde. Jay Goldstein, Paul Levine, Editors.

p. 331. Bovenzi, Pasqualina et al., "Human Herpesvirus 6 (Variant A) in Kaposi's Sarcoma"; *The Lancet*, May 15, 1993.

p. 332. Papadopulos-Eleopulos, E., Turner, V. F. & Papadimitriou, J. M., "Is a Positive Western Blot Proof of HIV Infection?" *Bio/Technology 11*, 696-707 (1993).

p. 337. Bruce Bawer, *Place at the Table: The Gay Individual in American Society* (New York: Simon and Schuster, 1993).

p. 343. Corbellino, Mario, Paolo Lusso, Robert C Gallo, Carlo Parravicini, Massimo Galli, and Mauro Moroni; "Disseminated Human Herpesvirus 6 Infection in AIDS"; *The Lancet*, November 13, 1993.

1994: Is HHV-6 the Real Virus?

p. 358. Knox, Konstance Kehl and Donald R. Carrigan; "Disseminated Active HHV-6 Infections in Patients with AIDS"; *The Lancet*, 343:577, March 5, 1994.

p. 359. Lusso, Paolo and Robert C. Gallo; "Human Herpesvirus 6 Infection in AIDS"; *The Lancet*, 343:555, March 5, 1994.

p. 362. Kashala, Oscar, Richard Arlink, Mbayo Ilunga Diese, Bobby Gormus, Keyu Xu, Pruence Mukela, Kabascle Kasongo, and Max Essex; "Infection with Human Immunodeficiency Virus Type 1 (HIV-1) and Human T Cell Lymphotropic Viruses Among Leprosy Patients and Contacts: Correlation between HIV-1 Cross-Reactivity and Antibodies to Lipoarabinomannan"; *Journal of Infectious Diseases* 169-296, February 1994.

p. 362. Papadopulos-Eleopulos, E., Turner, V.F. & Papadimitriou, J. M., "Is a Positive Western Blot Proof of HIV Infection?"; *Bio/Technology 11*, 696-707 (1993).

p. 369. "Reports on deaths from 'AIDS'-associated heart attacks." Cruickshank, Anne M., K.G. Oldroyd, and S.M Cobbe; "Serum Interleukin-6 in Suspected Myocardial Infarction"; *The Lancet* 343:974, April 16, 1994.

p. 369. "How does chronic fatigue syndrome affect the brain?" Schwartz, Richard B., Anthony L. Komaroff, Basem M. Garada, Marcy Gieit, Teresa H. Doolittle, David W. Bates, Russell G. Vasile, and B. Leonard Holman; "SPECT Imaging of the Brain: Comparison of Findings in Patients With Chronic Fatigue Syndrome, AIDS Dementia Complex, and Major Unipolar Depression"; *American Journal of Radiology* 152:943, April 1994.

<p. 371. Stephen C. Joseph, *Dragon Within the Gates: The Once and Future AIDS Epidemic*, (New York: Carroll Publishing, 1992).

p. 380. Dolcetti, Riccardo et al.; "Frequent Detection of Human Herpesvirus 6 DNA in HIV-Associated Lymphadenpathy"; *The Lancet*, 344:543, August 20, 1994.

p. 381. Michel, Detlef et al.; "Human Herpesvirus 6 DNA in Exanthematous Skin in BMT patient"; *The Lancet* 344:686, September 3, 1994.

p. 381. Yamanishi, Koichi et al..; "Identification of Human Herpesvirus 6 as a Causal Agent for Exanthem Subitum"; *The Lancet*, May 14, 1988, p. 1065.

p. 382. Kitamura K. et al.; "Idiopathic Thrombocytopenic Purpura after Human Herpesvirus 6 Infection"; *The Lancet*, 344:830, September 17, 1994.

p. 382. Jason, Leonard, et al.; "The Prevalence of Chronic Fatigue Syndrome: A Review of Efforts—Past and Present"; *The CFIDS Chronicle*, Summer 1993, p. 24.

p. 383. Wilburn F., Schmidt C. A., Zimmermann R., Brinkmann V., Neipel F., Siegert W.; "Detection of Herpesvirus Type 6 by Polymerase Chain Reaction in Blood Donors: Random Tests and Prospective Longitudinal Studies"; *British Journal of Haematology*, (88:187–192, 1994).

p. 385. Schwartz, Richard B. et at.; "SPECT Imaging of the Brain: Comparison of Findings in Patients with Chronic Fatigue Syndrome, AIDS Dementia Complex, and Major Unipolar Depression"; *American Journal of Radiology* 162:943, April 1994.

p. 388. Quint, Michael; "Bane of Insurers: New Ailments"; *New York Times*, November 28, 1994, page D1.

p. 389. Chang, Yuan et al.; "Identification of Herpes-Like DNA Sequences in AIDS-Associated Kaposi's Sarcoma"; *Science* 266:1885, December 16, 1994.

1995: Self-fulfilling Political Prophecies

<p. 391. Campbell, Maude; "Physician Commitment Essential to CFIDS Success"; *Medical Tribune,* October 20, 1994.

p. 392. Ho, David D. et al.; "Rapid Turnover of Plasma Virions and CD4 Lymphocytes in HIV-1 Infection"; *Nature* 373:113, January 12, 1995.

p. 395. Sternberg, Steve; "The Emerging Fungal Threat"; *Science* 266:1632, December 9, 1994.

p. 395. Report on Candida infections in CFS: Jessop, Carol; "Clinical Features and Possible Etiology of CFIDS"; *CFIDS Chronicle*, Spring, 1991, Conference Issue.

p. 395. Neubauer, Mary; "Senate Approves Criminal Penalties for Transmitting HIV"; Associated Press, February 5, 1995.

p. 396. Lusso, Paolo and Robert C. Gallo; "Human Herpesvirus 6 in AIDS"; *Immunology Today* 16(2):67, February 1995.

p. 398.   Knox, Konstance Kehl, Daniel P. Harrington and Donald R. Carrigan; "Fulminant Human Herpesvirus Six Encephalitis in a Human Immunodeficiency Virus-Infected Infant"; *Journal of Medical Virology* 45:288, March 1995.

p. 399.   Knox, Konstance Kehl and Donald R. Carrigan; "Active Human Herpesvirus (HHV-6) Infection of the Central Nervous System in Patients with AIDS; *Journal of Acquired Immune Deficiency Syndromes and Human Retrovirology* 9(1):69, April 25, 1995.

p. 410.   Kumar, Rachana M., Phillip F. Hughes, and Ashok Khurranna; "Zidovudine Use in Pregnancy and the Occurrence of Birth Defects"; *Journal of Acquired Immune Deficiency Syndromes* 7:1034, July 1994.

p. 414.   Bou-Holaigah, Issam, et al.; "The Relationship Between Neurally Mediated Hypotension and the Chronic Fatigue Syndrome"; *Journal of the American Medical Association*, September 27, 1995, Vol. 274, No. 12.

p. 415.   Qavi, Hamida B., M.T. Green, D.E. Lewis, F.B Hollinger, G Pearson, and D.V. Ablashi; "HIV-1 and HHV-6 Antigens and Transcripts in Retinas of Patients With AIDS in The Absence of Human Cytomegalovirus"; *Invest. Opthamal. Vis. Sci.* 36:2040, 1995.

1996: Enormous Public Health Consequences

p. 420.   Ablashi, D.V. et al.; "Ampligen Inhibits Human Herpesvirus-6 in Vitro"; *in vivo* 8:587, 1994.

p. 420.   Strayer, David R. et al.; "Long Term Improvements in Patients with Chronic Fatigue Syndrome Treated With Ampligen"; *Journal of Chronic Fatigue Syndrome* 1(1):35, 1995.

p. 421.   Ablashi, D.V. et al.; "Antiviral Activity in Vitro of Kutapressin against Human Herpesvirus-6"; *in vivo* 8:581-586, 1994.

p. 422.   Campbell. M; "Physician Commitment essential to CFIDS success"; *Medical Tribune*, October 20, 1994, p. 7.

p. 425.   Johnson, Hillary, "Journey into Fear," *Rolling Stone*, July 16 and August 13, 1987.

p. 425.   Johnson, Hillary, *Osler's Web: Inside the Labyrinth of the Chronic Fatigue Syndrome Epidemic* (New York, Crown Publishers Inc., 1996).

p. 439.   Waldholz, Michael; "Precious Pills: New AIDS Treatment Raises Tough Questions of Who Will Get It"; *Wall Street Journal*, July 2, 1996.

p. 442.   Shou-Jiang Gao et al.; "Seroconversion to Antibodies Against Kaposi's Sarcoma-Associated Herpesvirus-Related Latent Nuclear Antigens Before the Development of Kaposi's Sarcoma"; *New England Journal of Medicine* 335(4):233, July 25, 1996.

p. 442.   Kedes, Dean H. et al.; "The Seroepidemiology of Human Herpesvirus 8 (Kaposi's Sarcoma-Associated Herpesvirus): Distribution of Infection in

KS Risk Groups and Evidence for Sexual Transmission"; *Nature Medicine* (2)8:918, August 1996.

p. 442.   Cohen, Jon; "Reports Bolster Viral Cause of KS"; *Science* 273:573, August 2, 1996.

p. 442.   Cunha, Burke A; "Crimson Crescents—A Possible Association with the Chronic Fatigue Syndrome"; *Annals of Internal Medicine* 116(4), February 1992.

p. 445.   Kumar, Rachana M., Phillip F. Hughes, and Ashok Khurranna; "Zidovudine Use in Pregnancy and the Occurrence of Birth Defects"; *Journal of Acquired Immune Deficiency Syndromes* 7:1034, July 1994.

p. 448.   In her piece on Tony Brown, Ostrom wrote, "In his highly successful book, *Black Lies, White Lies* (William Morrow and Company, Inc., 1995), Brown addresses many controversial areas in race relations in the United States, including affirmative action, the impact of the black vote on national elections, how American can achieve financial independence, how fear between black and white people can be fought, and many others. Among the most controversial topics Brown discusses, however, is 'AIDS,' both with respect to how it is affecting African Americans, and how he fears it will affect the world population in the near future because of lies that have been told about it."

The Chronic Fatigue Syndrome Epidemic Cover-up

Volume Two

The Origins of Totalitarianism in Science and Medicine

Charles Ortleb

Contents

The Architects

How Three American Scientists Helped Create the
Nazi Science of Holocaust II

Introduction

If justice and truth prevail in the world, one day what has been called "AIDS" will be renamed "Holocaust II." While gay people were secondary victims of what is referred to as "The Holocaust," or "Holocaust I," they were the main attraction in "Holocaust II." The heterosexist motivation of their stigmatization and persecution in both holocausts were similar even if the manner in which they were harmed was different. I have coined the term "Iatrogenocide" to describe what happened to gay men (and others) during Holocaust II.

I was a witness to the AIDS epidemic from the very beginning. As the publisher and editor-in-chief of *New York Native,* I inadvertently oversaw the reporting of the very first story about the epidemic. After hearing about a strange pneumonia occurring in gay men in New York City, I asked a physician to make inquiries with the public health authorities. In a story headlined "Disease Rumors Largely Unfounded" published in our May 18, 1981 issue, Dr. Lawrence Mass wrote, "Last week there were rumors that an exotic new disease had hit the gay community in New York. Here are the facts. From the New York City Department of Health, Dr. Steve Phillips explained that the rumors are for the most part unfounded. Each year, approximately 12 to 24 cases of infection with a protozoa-like organism, Pneumocystis carinii, are reported in New York City area. The organism is not exotic; in fact, it's ubiquitous. But most of us have a natural or easily acquired immunity."

Six weeks later it turned out that the rumors were true when the CDC reported on the first cases of what would be called AIDS. It is hard to overstate the shock and terror that gripped the gay community in New York City and eventually around the world. People dreaded waking up each morning as bad news just got worse and worse. Given that my paper seemed to be at the ground zero of the event, I made the conscious decision to devote *New York Native* to covering every detail of the story. For the first two years our coverage was so thorough that some people started referring to my newspaper as "The New York Native Journal of Medicine." Many of our readers and advertisers resented our coverage and wanted us to focus on positive stories. But I felt that we had a responsibility get to the bottom of what was going on.

As the cases mounted and the gay community began to accept the reality of the epidemic, our coverage began to be appreciated and *New York Native* became a trusted source for the latest news about AIDS. In the April 25, 1985 issue of *Rolling Stone*, David Black said that *New York Native* deserved a Pulitzer Prize for our reporting. In his bestselling book, *And the Band Played On*, Randy Shilts wrote, "Because of the extraordinary reporting of the *New*

York Native, the city's gay community had been exposed to far more information about AIDS than San Francisco in 1981 and 1982." And in the March 23, 1989 *Rolling Stone*, Katie Leishman wrote, "It is undeniable that many major AIDS stories were Ortleb's months and sometimes years before mainstream journalists too them up." But that love affair with *New York Native* was about to end abruptly.

As I have detailed in my history of *New York Native*, *The Chronic Fatigue Syndrome Epidemic Cover-up*, as the epidemic went on and our reporting became more investigative, I began to notice serious credibility gaps in what the Centers for Disease Control was telling the public about the AIDS epidemic. AIDS increasingly reminded me of the period of egregious government mendacity that occurred during the Vietnam era. As the government began to build a paradigm around the notion that AIDS was caused by a retrovirus ultimately labelled "HIV," I watched as credible critics of the retroviral theory were silenced and vilified. I discuss the heroic voices that spoke out in *The Duesbergians*.

My newspaper became even more controversial when we began reporting on another epidemic called chronic fatigue syndrome. From our extensive reporting, it was hard not to conclude that chronic fatigue syndrome is part of the AIDS epidemic and was linked to AIDS by a virus called HHV-6 which government scientists refused to take seriously.

As AIDS activists increasing lined up behind the government's HIV/AIDS paradigm and draconian public health agenda, the inconvenient truths my newspaper was reporting about HHV-6 and chronic fatigue syndrome became increasingly unpopular. Nobody wanted to believe that the elite AIDS doctors and scientists might have gotten AIDS totally wrong. Act Up, New York's powerful AIDS activist group, voted to boycott *New York Native* and the did anything they could to put us out of business. Finally, in January 1997, we published our final issue.

In the last twenty years, I have given a great deal of thought to the nature of what happened to my newspaper and to the integrity of AIDS science and medicine. A number of my thoughts on the subject are collected in *Iatrogenocide: Notes for a Political Philosophy of Epidemiology and Science*. I have also written a play about the politics of the epidemic called *The Black Party*. My thoughts about the racial politics of AIDS can be found in a novella, *The Closing Argument*.

I have come to the conclusion that the similarities between AIDS science and Nazi science are too obvious for people of conscience to ignore. In his groundbreaking book about Nazi treatment of Jews, *"Life Unworthy of Life": Racial Phobia and Mass Murder in Hitler's Germany*, James M. Glass writes, "It was not cultural propagandists who organized the infamous 'special treatment' of the Jews; it was the public health officials, the scientific journals, the physicians, the administrators, and the lawyers, who feared the very presence of the Jews would endanger their families, their bodies, and ultimately their lives. To think of the Jew in such terms is insane from our perspective, but it was held to be sane in the culture caught up in the phobic projection of infection onto the Jews and the scientific authority legitimizing such beliefs." In many ways AIDS, or what I call "Holocaust II," involved what could be called "special epidemiological treatment" of the gays which was created and supported by health officials, scientific journals, physicians, administrators, lawyers, activists, celebrities, and many others. While the manner in which AIDS is understood by public health authorities and the general public is assumed to be sane, a closer look reveals that a genocidal insanity lurks beneath the surface. In the case of AIDS, a fraudulent and phobic epidemiology has been used to scapegoat and biomedically persecute the gay community. And many others.

In this book, I discuss three scientists who I consider to be among the important "architects" of Holocaust II. Each of them played an important role in creating the kind of science which I describe in *Iatrogenocide* as being abnormal, totalitarian, and sociopathic.

Also in *Iatrogenoicde*, I coined the term "homodemiology" to describe the kind of epidemiology that scapegoats gay people for epidemics. I describe the homodemiological politics of the Centers for Disease Control in *The Four Doctors of the Apocalypse*. While the CDC got the ball rolling, I don't think the homodemiological dystopia of Holocaust II would have happened with the contributions of Myron Essex, Anthony Fauci, and Robert Gallo.

Anyone who is reading this book may be tempted to think I am writing about a problem that only affects gay people. That is far from the truth. The frauds of these three scientists have helped conceal an epidemic of a virus called HHV-6 which threatens everyone. Since 2005, at HHV-6 University, I have been covering the biomedical damage that HHV-6 is doing to people all over the world. I have called HHV-6 "The AIDSdromeda Strain" and "The Fifty Shades of AIDS Virus." HHV-6 is a pandemic threatening everyone which has been hidden behind the political mask of HIV/AIDS fraud.

While the first Holocaust may have been focused on Jews, the whole world paid a terrible price for the anti-Semitism that fueled it. In *The Jew as Pariah,* Hannah Arendt wrote, "The comity of European peoples went to pieces when, and because, it allowed its weakest member to be excluded and persecuted." I hope Arendt will forgive me for arguing that the comity and health of the whole world is going to pieces because it is allowing its weakest member (the gay community) to be epidemiologically excluded, scapegoated, and persecuted.

How Harvard's Myron Essex Laid the Groundwork for the Pseudoscience of Holocaust II

FOCMA happened in the decade before the beginning of what could be called "Holocaust II" and the HHV-6 catastrophe, but it was a scientific omen of things to come. One could say that the decline and fall of American biomedical science had a dry run in the FOCMA episode at Harvard. In many ways Harvard was the ground zero for the pseudoscience and retroviral fraud of "Holocaust II."

FOCMA stands for "feline oncornavirus-associated cell-membrane antigen," and it was supposedly discovered in 1977 and named by Myron T. "Max" Essex, a Harvard School of Public Health researcher. According to *Chicago Tribune* reporter John Crewdson, Essex, when he was a post doc, came up with the idea that 'white blood cells from cats infected with the feline leukemia virus also exhibited a unique protein on their surface, "and Essex dubbed that protein 'FOCMA.'" (*Science Fictions* p. 40)

In *Science Fictions*, Crewdson's book on the questionable AIDS research of Robert Gallo, he notes that the importance of Essex's putative discovery was that "If FOCMA were a by-product of the cell's infection with feline leukemia virus, it might represent confirmation of a cellular defense against cancer, at least in cats. . ." (*SF* p. 40) This would have been a major scientific breakthrough, *if* true.

Unfortunately for a junior researcher who decided to devote the early part of his career to the study of FOCMA, it turned out *not* to be what Essex thought it was. The researcher, Wolf Prensky, discovered—to the great detriment of his budding career—that FOCMA "was just a viral protein and not a cellular antigen." (*SF* p.41) According to Crewdson, Prensky, with two other scientists, published a paper "that was a definitive demonstration that the FOCMA protein was encoded by the feline leukemia virus itself, not a cellular by-product of infection." (*SF* p.41) Crewdson notes that "The idea that cat blood cells had some built-in defense against cancer evaporated overnight." (*SF* p.41)

While this matter might seem like an esoteric issue only of concern to the priesthood of science, what happened next was a foreshadowing of the totalitarian culture of abnormal science that would happen throughout the three decades of the scientific shenanigans known as HIV/AIDS. And it would involve some of the same characters. The head of the National Cancer

Institute, Vincent DeVita, "selected [Robert] Gallo, despite his co-authorship of a FOCMA article with Essex two years before, to head an investigation of Prensky's claims." (*SF* p.41) This is the kind of little game that would be known throughout "Holocaust II" as "Henhouse, meet Fox."

While the committee came to the conclusion that neither undermined Essex or vindicated him, because, according to Crewdson, *Gallo claimed he didn't understand FOCMA—something he had co-authored a paper about,* a pattern was set of old boys performing due diligence on their own old boy networks. If this was the musical overture for three decades of AIDS science, one could call the melody "sham peer review" and "egregious conflict of interest."

Prensky's career was viciously sidetracked for many years for daring to challenge Essex, and perhaps most importantly, for getting anywhere near what some people eventually considered one of the most dangerous black holes in science: Robert Gallo.

Crewdson, who paradoxically supported the Gallo HIV theory of AIDS despite writing an epic exposé of Gallo that makes Gallo look like the greatest pathological liar in the history of science, doesn't dwell on the FOCMA matter much or with any great outrage, perhaps because Essex's subsequent career would eventually have what Crewdson considered a happy scientific ending due to his peripheral early involvement with HTLV-III, the virus that was officially declared by the government and the AIDS establishment to be the real cause of AIDS in 1984. Crewdson writes that "rather than withdrawing or correcting his FOCMA articles, Essex simply stopped referring to them in his subsequent publications." (*SF* p. 41) He *disappeared* the episode. Crewdson doesn't write a single word about the tremendous damage done to Prensky's career which was the price he paid for telling the truth about one of Essex's discoveries. Prensky's fate foreshadowed the fate of Peter Duesberg, the scientist who would eventually be severely punished for basically saying that HIV was about as much the cause of AIDS as FOCMA was a cellular protection against cancer.

Insofar as Essex just left his "discovery" floating like the undead in the scientific literature without ever retracting it, this little incident of uncorrected science was akin to the broken window theory of crime, in that it may have led to bigger evasions of the truth with far greater implications for mankind. And it also foreshadowed the degree to which both Essex and Gallo would have amazing political and "scientific" power that would allow them to survive and even thrive financially during "Holocaust II." FOCMA was the grain of sand in which one could see the whole universe of HIV/AIDS fraud.

Journalist Barry Werth wrote about FOCMA in an article called "The AIDS Windfall" in *New England Monthly* in June, 1988. He writes that "Dozens of scientists went off in pursuit of FOCMA. But no one could prove that FOCMA existed. Essex abandoned the subject, and he refused to pursue the criticism of those following it up, or to retract it. He simply let FOCMA hang, and other scientists were understandably incensed. 'We'd have figured it out ten years earlier if Essex had only done his homework,' complains one researcher."

Essex was able to move on without ever having to admit he had made a mistake. Werth notes that Essex was able to conveniently change the subject from FOCMA to HTLV: "Essex's work connecting HTLV with AIDS was published in the spring of 1983." The actual so-called AIDS retrovirus, HTLV-III, was a year away from being declared the official cause of AIDS, but Essex had helped pave the way to, depending on your point of view, the Nobel-worthy notion or "Big Mistake" that AIDS was caused by a retrovirus. Werth writes that "the AIDS virus was a retrovirus, just as Essex had said. He's been wrong in all the particulars, but right in general, and being half right secured him the undisputed mantle as the prophet of AIDS." Or as the perpetually witty HIV critic Peter Duesberg might say, the prophet of the most tragic scientific boondoggle in history.

Given Essex's financial and career interest in maintaining the legitimacy of the notion that a retrovirus was the cause of AIDS, it shouldn't surprise anyone that he played an intense enforcement role during the next three decades by helping to elbow out anyone or any that threatened the hegemony of the HIV theory of AIDS. His willingness to play power politics would be dramatically in evidence at the 1992 International AIDS Conference in Amsterdam at which several scientists announced that they had discovered cases of AIDS in which there was *no evidence of HIV*. It didn't take long for the HIV establishment to realize that such cases could turn their retroviral empire into a falling house of cards overnight. In what could be called one of the greatest games of scientific three-card monte, and in the true spirit of abnormal, totalitarian science, the Centers for Disease Control and the powerful HIV establishment effectively swept the paradigm-challenging anomalies under the rug by giving the HIV-negative AIDS cases a new category and a brand new complicated name, idiopathic CD4 T-lymphocytopenia (ICL)."

Because the very embarrassing HIV-negative cases were found *outside* the so-called risk groups, they just couldn't be AIDS. It was a classic instance of circular homodemiological groupthink. *If it wasn't gay, it wasn't AIDS*. Case closed. When researcher Subhir Gupta reported at the 1992 conference that he had found evidence of a retrovirus other than HIV in a sixty-six-year-old woman who had AIDS-like symptoms, but was negative for HIV, Essex stepped right up to the plate. Gupta had published his findings in the *Proceedings of the National Academy of Science*. The findings should have inspired an emergency rethinking of AIDS epidemiology and virology. In *Osler's Web*, Hillary Johnson described the whole incident: "Max Essex, a Harvard AIDS researcher, expressed skepticism bordering on ennui. 'I'm not overwhelmed by it,' he commented after reading the paper. 'I'd place the odds at five to ten percent that this might lead to something.'" (*OW* p.601) (The odds, of course, were nearly 100 percent that Essex would do what he could so that such an outcome was not achieved.) According to Johnson, "Both [David] Ho and Essex raised the specter of laboratory contamination in the matter of Gupta's findings. Microbes such as Gupta described, they said, were notorious laboratory contaminants and could easily have come from an animal cell line." (*OW*. p.601) The AIDS establishment's findings always tended to be scientifically unquestionable (and miraculously contaminant-free) but any findings that challenged the HIV paradigm tended to be contaminants, artifacts, irrelevant correlations. Only the inner circle's labs were pristine and above suspicion.

The very threatened CDC stepped in and quickly reassured the shocked world that there was *not* a new virus causing *another* AIDS epidemic. (This was also at the same time they were—by ignoring it—indirectly assuring the public that there wasn't a contagious immune-system compromising chronic fatigue syndrome epidemic in the general population. In retrospect, and full of the irony that "Holocaust II" is replete with, they were right. It wasn't a new AIDS epidemic, it was part and parcel of the old one, *the one they had gotten the epidemiology and virology wrong on*.) When the CDC's director of AIDS Research, James Curran, told the press that the cases of HIV-negative AIDS like illness were not "AIDS caused by something else," he was just whistling in the dark while HHV-6 spectrum pandemic was having its insidious way with the world and creating a disaster that could not be seen by the abnormal and totalitarian science that was generated by the CDC's homodemiological vision of the epidemic.

From his position on the Mt. Olympus of AIDS, Essex had done his part at that Amsterdam AIDS Conference to help the HIV establishment avoid a crisis of confidence and keep a lid on the horrifying truth about *the real epidemic*. He saved his reputation as the prophet who knew what kind of virus caused AIDS. The coming decades would be a professional dream come true for the man who discovered the nonexistent FOCMA. "Holocaust II" and The Age of Totalitarian, Abnormal and Sociopathic Science could not have existed without Harvard's Myron Essex. He has secured Harvard's place in the history of AIDS fraud.

Anthony Fauci, the Bernie Madoff of Holocaust II

November 2, 1984 was an especially tragic day in the Chronic Fatigue Syndrome/AIDS epidemic. That was the day Anthony Fauci became the Director of the National Institutes of Allergy and Infectious Diseases. (NIAID). (*Good Intentions* p.128) It was the day a thin-skinned, physically ultra-diminutive man with a legendary Napoleonic attitude was positioned by destiny to become the de facto AIDS Czar. In the fog of culpability that constitutes what could be called "Holocaust II" one thing is clear: the buck, on its way to the very top of the government, at least pauses at the megalomaniac desk of Anthony Fauci.

In his book, *Good Intentions*, Bruce Nussbaum writes, "Fauci looked as if he had just stepped out of a limousine. Trim and athletic, Fauci's tailored suits, cuff-linked shirts, and aviator glasses set him far apart from the rest of the scientists and administrators at the NIH." (*GI* p.128) Fauci had risen quickly at NIH. According to Nussbaum, he began work at NIH in 1968 after his residency and "by 1977 he was deputy clinical director of NIAID." (*GI* p.128) Nussbaum describes Fauci as "an aggressive administrator," not a "details man," "a big picture kind of guy." (GI p.128) Nussbaum reports that "Fauci saw AIDS as a dreadful disease—and an opportunity for NIAID to grow into a much bigger, more powerful institute. AIDS was his big chance. He wasn't known as a brilliant scientist, and he had little background in managing a big bureaucracy; but Fauci did have ambition and drive to spare. This lackluster scientist was about to find his true vocation—empire building." (*GI* p.128) Unfortunately, the empire his extreme ambition would build was "Holocaust II." If the mantra during Watergate was "follow the money," the mantra for uncovering the crimes of "Holocaust II" (other than "follow the heterosexism") could be "follow the empire building." And one of the morals of the story is that "lackluster" can have extreme consequences.

According to Nussbaum, in order to make his dreams come true, Fauci had to fight "for a bigger piece of the AIDS research pie" which he succeeded at by getting a sizable amount of the funds that Congress appropriated for AIDS research. (*GI* p.129) Fauci also had to fight to get AIDS out of the claws of the National Cancer Institute where the virus that was believed to be the cause of AIDS had been discovered (or, more accurately, stolen). Fauci argued that it was his institute's right to take on the lion's share of the research because, although AIDS did involve cancer (Kaposi's sarcoma), it was, after all, an infectious disease. Fauci got his way and his success is reflected in the evolving financial numbers Nussbaum provides: "A growing budget for AIDS research, like a rising tide, lifted Tony Fauci's profile considerably on

490

the NIH campus. In 1982, NIAID received $297,000 in AIDS funding. In 1986 it received $63 million. In 1987, the sum reached $146 million. By 1990, NIAID's annual AIDS funding was pushing half a billion dollars. Tony Fauci's ship had come in." (*GI* p.132)

Fauci's ship coming in meant the gay community's would be sinking fast. It would fall to Anthony Fauci to be the Enforcer-in-Chief of the "homodemiological" HIV/AIDS and "chronic fatigue syndrome is not AIDS" paradigms of "Holocaust II." No one can argue that he didn't do a spectacular job of paradigm enforcement for three dreadful decades.

Starting in the mid-1980s, an organization called the American Foundation for AIDS Research (amfAR) played a multifaceted role of raising money for HIV research and enlisting celebrities in a glamorous and ultimately shameful HIV propaganda campaign that made the putatively private organization essentially a de facto arm of the government's HIV/AIDS establishment. If one considers the HIV theory of AIDS a Potemkin biomedical village that gays were forced to live in, then amfAR as one of its leading real estate agents. John Lauritsen, in his book, *The AIDS War*, writes that "[amfAR] was founded as an alternative to the AIDS establishment, to provide funding for research that was *not* predicated on the 'AIDS virus' hypothesis. It didn't last long. . . . I am not aware that even a penny has ever been given to a researcher who publicly expressed doubts as to the etiological role of HIV or the benefits of the nucleoside analogues." (*AW* p.437)

In addition to becoming one of the leading private promoters of the government's HIV/AIDS paradigm propaganda, amfAR played a disturbing role in squelching serious scientific criticism of the HIV hypothesis and in helping turn the entire field of AIDS into a world of heterosexist, totalitarian, and abnormal science. Lauritsen describes an historically important amfAR moment in the AIDS disaster in his first book *Poison by Prescription*: "A 'Scientific Forum on the Etiology of AIDS,' sponsored by the American Foundation for AIDS Research (amfAR), was held on 9 April 1988 at the George Washington University in Washington, D.C. In the words of the amfAR 'fact sheet', the forum was convened to critically examine the evidence that human immunodeficiency virus (HIV) or other agents give rise to the disease complex known as AIDS." (*PBP* p.143)

According to Lauritsen, it was supposedly an opportunity for Peter Duesberg, the University of California at Berkeley retrovirologist who first challenged the HIV theory of AIDS "to confront members of the 'AIDS Establishment' over their hypothesis." (*PBP* p.143) He reports, however, that "Despite these praiseworthy intentions, the forum appears to have had a hidden agenda; to discredit Duesberg." (*PBP* p.143) Lauritsen characterized the forum as a "Kangaroo Court." The forum would make great scene in a play about the nasty, zany world of AIDS and HIV pseudoscience. It was anything but an honest, open collegial discussion about the nature of AIDS.

491

Scientific philosopher Thomas Kuhn would roll over in his grave if anyone called it genuinely scientific. By Kuhn's standards, some of the leading voices at the forum may have even demonstrated that they should not even have been considered real scientists. Politicians, yes, scientists not so much. Even the HIV theory's ardent acolyte, Michael Specter, the reporter from *The Washington Post* (and future *New Yorker* writer) who was among the 17 journalists at the Forum, saw through the charade, noting that the meeting "was billed as a scientific forum on the cause of AIDS but was really an attempt to put Duesberg's theories to rest." (*PBP* p.144) It was more like they wanted to put Duesberg himself permanently to rest.

The meeting had the tone and style that was endemic to HIV/AIDS research and characteristic of abnormal and totalitarian science. Lauritsen reported, "While no blows were struck, some of the HIV protagonists fell below the standards of civility that are expected in scholarly debate. At all times Duesberg retained good manners and a sense of humor, in the face of invective, insults, and clowning from his opponents." (*PBP* p.144)

One of the signs that AIDS in general was being conducted in the opposite world of what could be called abnormal, totalitarian science was the uncanny willingness of the scientists to abandon the traditional rules of evidence known as Koch's postulates. Instead, AIDS researchers, including the ones at the amfAR forum, were willing to "revise Koch's in a more permissive direction: it would no longer be necessary to find the microbe in all cases of the disease. Mere correlations between microbial *antibodies* and the progression of the disease would be sufficient. HIV could be proved 'epidemiologically' to be the cause of AIDS." (*PBP* p.145) Given the unrecognized sexual politics of the science that was operative among this crowd, they were basically saying, without realizing it, that causation could be established *"homodemiologically."* The presumptions of heterosexist and political epidemiology would trump the traditional rules of evidence. And those rules could basically be summed up as "Heads I win and tails you lose." "You" basically being gays and eventually blacks.

Lauritsen caught the powerful HIV advocates in the act of doublespeak that is common to abnormal, totalitarian science: "Actually, the HIV advocates talked out of both sides of their mouths with regard to Koch's postulates. On the one hand, they disparaged them as in need of 'modification' (read abandonment); on the other hand, they were doing their best to come up with data that would satisfy at least the first postulate." (*PBP* p.145)

Duesberg's opponents at the forum included a living, breathing example of scientific conflict of interest, William Haseltine, a scientist who was in the process of making a lot of money from HIV testing, and Anthony Fauci, the empire-building Director of NIAID.

At the amfAR Forum, Fauci and others played a curious unfair game with Duesberg. Hypocritically they accused Duesberg of citing research that was out of date even though it was basically *the same research quoted at that time* by the AIDS establishment. On the other hand, when Duesberg would ask Fauci and others for actual references to support *their* statements at the amfAR forum, he was "rudely rebuffed," and according to Lauritsen, they tried to shore up their viewpoint about HIV with unpublished data, or "their own private facts." (*PBP* p.147) "Private facts" not on the public record are another sure sign that AIDS was a manifestation of the opposite world of abnormal, totalitarian and sociopathic science. Unfortunately, their private facts about AIDS were also connected to each other by a private scientific logic.

The 800-pound gorilla at the amfAR forum was the fact that evidence of HIV could *not be found in all AIDS patients*, which should have been strong—damning even—evidence that HIV couldn't possibly be the cause of AIDS, that is, if Kuhnian normal science was being practiced. As scientist Marcel Beluda pointed out at the meeting, "sometimes even a single exception is sufficient to disprove a theory. . . . This is the crux of the matter. The virus cannot be found in all cases of AIDS." (*PBP* p.151) One could say that still believing that HIV is the cause of AIDS in the face of evidence that it could not be found in all patients is Exhibit A that delusion and denial were running the show.

Fauci's answer belongs in a beginner's textbook on the card tricks of abnormal science: "Fauci responded to Beluda by saying that a good lab was able to isolate the virus in 90-100% of the cases, that there was 'no question about it.' Fauci did not provide a reference to published data, nor did he indicate what the 'good labs' were, or how exactly they differed from the not-so-good labs." (*PBP* p.151) References belong to the abandoned Kuhnian world of normal science.

Duesberg made a number of arguments, based on his years as one of the celebrated deans of retroviral research, about why HIV could not possibly be the cause of AIDS.

Lauritsen wrote that Fauci's presentation "while aspiring to be a point-by-point rebuttal to Duesberg, consisted mainly of disconnected assertions, delivered in a tone of petulant indignation. Epidemiological studies conducted in San Francisco and unpublished laboratory reports seemed to be the basis of most of his statements. So far as I could tell, he understood none of Duesberg's arguments . . . ." (*PBP* p.155)

The role of the AIDS politics of epidemiology in AIDS research showed itself dramatically at the forum. According to Lauritsen, "In the question period, Beluda asked if the evidence were sufficient that HIV is necessary for the development of AIDS, Fauci replied that he hoped the epidemiologists would answer that question." (*PBP* p.157) (Given the political and heterosexist nature of AIDS epidemiology, one could guess how *that* was going to turn out.)

The most shocking and downright hilarious episode at the forum occurred when Harvard Medical School's William Haseltine spoke. Lauritsen reported that "His presentation was devoted largely to personal attacks on Duesberg." (*PBP* p.157) Ironically, *he* accused Duesberg of resorting to personal attacks. In another telltale moment of abnormal and totalitarian science, Lauritsen caught Haseltine trying to explain away the anomalies about the evidence of AIDS in men and women in America: "He attacked Duesberg's 'paradox,' that the AIDS virus seemed to be able to discriminate between boys and girls, by saying that this was not true outside the U.S.—in Africa, about equal numbers of men and women develop AIDS. (He seemed oblivious to the paradox that a microbe should be able to discriminate in one country, but not in another.)" (*PBP* p.158) In a memorable moment that perfectly captured the essence of the past and future of AIDS research, Haseltine showed the audience a slide of a graph that was meant to absolutely demolish Duesberg's argument. The slide was supposed to show a correlation between the rise in HIV titers with the decline of T cells in the progression of AIDS. There was just one small problem: Duesberg quickly noticed that *there were no units on the vertical axis of the slide*. Haseltine was angry and flustered by the charge and had to ask Dr. Robert Redfield, an AIDS researcher from the military, how the slide was prepared. At the forum Redfield said, "different measurements were used," but later that night at a post-forum party, according to Lauritsen's report, Redfield told Duesberg and other people at the gathering that "the graph had been prepared to illustrate a theoretical possibility. It had no units on it for the simple reason that *it was not based on any data at all*. In other words, the slide was a fake." (*PBP* p.161) That's the kind of ideology-based data that was used to back up the HIV theory of AIDS which changed the course of millions of lives and fostered the HHV-6 catastrophe.

In terms of the habitual use of political epidemiology (or "homo-demiology") rather than real science to deal with AIDS during "Holocaust II," the most disturbing talk was given by Warren Winkelstein, Professor of Biomedical Environmental Health Sciences at U.C. Berkeley. Essentially, he too suggested that AIDS would require *a new kind of science*. According to Lauritsen, "the point of Winkelstein's presentation is that Koch's postulates should be superseded by new standards for establishing the causal relationship between microbes and disease, and that these standards should be based upon 'epidemiology' or, as it were, correlations of various kinds." (*PBP* p.162) If this crowd had superseded traditional science any more than they did, we all would probably be dead. (But wait. There is still time.)

Most of the scientific world was not aware of the degree to which this zany cast of characters was improvising a questionable newfangled science as they went along. And it was being done in a Fauci-style of "petulant indignation," to reprise Lauritsen's very apt phrase. That it was all dependent on a loosey-goosey, all too subjective political "discipline" like epidemiology

494

should have disturbed Lauritsen's sixteen journalistic colleagues who were at the amfAR affair. But there was already a tragically cozy relationship between the media and the abnormal, totalitarian and sociopathic scientists of "Holocaust II." For three decades as the HIV/AIDS paradigm held sway, most of the reporters who covered AIDS were a self-satisfied, inattentive, group-thinking, intellectually slothful bunch who wouldn't know independent, journalistic due diligence if it bit them. A corrupt scientific community could totally depend on them.

Lauritsen's eyewitness record of the forum (originally published in _New York Native_) was an important contribution to the history of the flakey beginnings of the science and totalitarian politics of AIDS. His diligent and critical reporting is proof that _not every journalist_ was hoodwinked by these charlatans. He didn't buy into this new improvised epidemiological science that the AIDS establishment was dumping on the public: "I do not accept the proposition that Koch's postulates should be abandoned in favor of epidemiological correlations. This would be a step backward, a step away from scientific rigor, a step towards impressionism and confusion." (_PBP_ p.162) Lauritsen didn't acknowledge it, but it was also a big heterosexist (and ultimately racist) step backwards.

Like many others, Lauritsen came face to face with totalitarian, abnormal, and sociopathic science. Unfortunately, even though he was openly gay himself, he didn't grasp the manner in which the infernal game was being played—or what the game was actually concealing. He didn't fully perceive the homodemiological underpinnings of what was happening before his very eyes. But he definitely grasped the fact that the science of the budding AIDS Establishment was utterly bogus. He concluded his report by writing, "I am more convinced than ever that HIV is not the cause of AIDS. If the HIV advocates were sure of their hypothesis, they would want to enlighten Duesberg and the rest of us; they would want to publish their arguments in a proper scientific journal complete with references. They would not need to resort to stonewalling, deception, and personal abuse." (_PBP_ p.168) Science had been supplanted by totalitarian petulance.

The 1988 amfAR Forum was another one of the tragic "What if?" moments in the dark history of AIDS. What if the reporters had looked closer at Haseltine's fake slide and realized that it was the tip of the iceberg, a little like the scientific version of the Watergate break-in that would have led them to a much bigger crime if they only followed the lies? What if they had reported that AIDS science, as practiced by Anthony Fauci, was simply out-to-lunch? What if they had been independent enough to notice that epidemiology was overplaying its arrogant, biased hand and that, in reality, it is actually a soft, subjective enterprise vulnerable to political manipulation? Why was it beyond the pale to wonder if this defensive and cranky gathering was actually the expression of some rather unsavory feelings and hostilities directed at the so-called beneficiaries of this new kind of "science," namely the gay community? Maybe someone should have asked if there was something funky about a group of hostile, arrogant, white heterosexual mostly-male scientists performing their jerry-built kind of seat-of-the-pants epidemiological science on gays. Wasn't that a formula for all kinds of prurient, heterosexist pseudoscientific mischief if ever there was one? In terms of majorities doing their science on minorities, hadn't anyone ever heard of Nazi science or the Tuskegee Syphilis Experiment? God only knows what personal sexual issues were being acted out by this elite motley crew under the cover of what has turned out to be highfalutin retroviral claptrap. Why didn't anyone other than Lauritsen notice the peculiar, unscientific defensiveness of the whole affair, i.e. that the ladies had protested too much? And most importantly for the main event, why was HHV-6, which had been discovered in AIDS patients two years before that curious amfAR forum, not put on the table for discussion?

Fauci believed in the kind of transparency and communications with the public that are typical of abnormal science. He laid out the draconian media policy that he would maintain for the nearly thirty years he ran the totalitarian HIV/AIDS empire in a brief piece he wrote for the AAAS Observer on September 1, 1989.

Fauci wrote, "When I first got involved in AIDS research, I was reluctant to deal with the press. I thought it was not dignified. But there was a lot of distortion by those who were speaking to the press so I changed my mind." The "distortion" was, of course, coming from those who didn't agree with the very dignified Fauci about the etiology of AIDS. Fauci had his own idea of what the media's responsibility is. He notes that his interpretation of what the media is supposed to do "doesn't even jibe with what competent journalists think." He asserts that the big dilemma for journalists is between what is "important" and what is "newsworthy" and he notes that they sometimes "are not the same." He whines about the fact that journalists are more interested in the latest story of a cure than the "magnificent science" involving the regulatory genes of HIV.

Fauci describes what he thinks is the hierarchy of media. It ranges from *The New York Times* and *The Washington Post* all the way down to publications that "care only about sales or have axes to grind." (He had yet to face the unwashed barbarians of the blogs and the commenters of the online forums.) One can safely assume that the publications with axes to grind were the ones who didn't agree with the axe that the petulant Fauci himself was grinding. It is amusing that Fauci pontificated in 1989 that "the media are no place for amateurs, particularly when talking about a public health problem of the magnitude of AIDS." Especially when one considers the magnitude of the HHV-6 public health problem that this very self-reverential scientist (that Bruce Nussbaum described as "lackluster") himself helped create for the whole human race. While Fauci would make one think that the real problem in AIDS journalism was the clownish journalist who can't spell "retrovirus" or one who didn't listen carefully after asking questions, his real quarry in this peevish little piece is something far more serious. Fauci's real problem was journalists who not only *could* spell "retrovirus" but could also actually hear what he was saying *all too well.* The kind of journalists who also knew things about retroviruses and listened to what he was saying so closely and critically that they could make life unpleasant for Fauci and his powerful AIDS cronies by asking inconvenient questions.

Fauci's nose should have grown several feet when he wrote, "We know that reporters must consult more than a single source and make room for dissenting opinions." What was yet to come in the AAAS piece made that one of the biggest fibs in the history of American science. Under the pretense of giving us a little lesson in the relationship between science and the media and warning that people too often believe what they read in the papers, Fauci reveals his real agenda: "One striking example is Peter Duesberg's theory that HIV is not the cause of AIDS. I laughed at that for a while, but it led to a lot of public concern that HIV was a hoax. The theory had a great deal of credibility just on the basis of news coverage." This was Fauci being intellectually dishonest on a couple of counts. Duesberg never said it was a *hoax.* He said it was a *mistake.* A hoax is a whole other ball of wax, and it is an example of using language politically to deliberately misrepresent the opposition. Duesberg wasn't saying something similar to those who say that the landing on the moon was just staged with props and a camera. He was a Nobel-caliber expert on retroviruses pointing out the deficiencies of the HIV theory in AIDS using basic logic and analyzing the available evidence. And blaming the media for the credibility given to Duesberg's ideas ignored all the scientists, (eventually including two Nobel Prize winners), who publicly supported Duesberg's skepticism. Fauci was Trumpian in that he was essentially accusing those who spotted his fake science as being purveyors of fake news.

Fauci then introduces us to the smarter member of his family, his sister: "My barometer of what the general public is thinking is my sister Denise. My sister Denise is an intelligent woman who reads avidly, listens to the radio, and watches television, but she is not a scientist. When she calls me and questions my integrity as a scientist, there really is a problem. Denise has called me at least ten times about Peter Duesberg. She says, 'Anthony'—she is the only one who calls me Anthony, 'are you sure he's wrong?' That's the power of putting someone on television or in the press, although there is virtually nothing in his argument that makes any scientific sense." This captures how touchy Fauci was. No one was questioning his "integrity as a scientist." His sister was simply asking him if it was *possible* that he was wrong, and the answer that would have shown some scientific integrity would have been, "Yes, my dear Denise, it is always possible that I'm wrong, although I think the evidence suggests I'm right." The fact that Fauci took this *sooooo* personally speaks volumes about the petulant chip-on-the-shoulder attitude problems of those in charge of AIDS. Fauci put it all on the line. Questioning his so-called science was a threat to his very being. It shouldn't surprise anyone that he was willing to viciously fight for so long during "Holocaust II" to keep everyone from seeing what a house of cards he had helped build. The funny thing is that in a number of ways this scientific masterpiece suggests he *did* have serious problems in the integrity department. (Between the lines of the piece Freudian historians may one day even find the glimmer of a guilty conscience.)

Fauci, like most of the crowd that gave us "Holocaust II," knew only too well what normal, nontotalitarian science is supposed to look like: "People are especially confused when they see divergent viewpoints about the same thing. They do not understand that the beauty of science is that it is self-corroborating and self-correcting, that it is important for scientists to be wrong." (If that's really the case, Fauci *was* indeed doing something incredibly important with HIV.) It was actually Fauci who didn't understand that the whole process of self-corroboration and self-correction was being short-circuited by the totalitarian hijinks of the touchy HIV/AIDS establishment that was growing more dominant by the day. The very tone of Fauci's piece, its extraordinary imperiousness and presumptuousness about the stupidity of the public, points to the fundamental problem for a society in which arrogant and dishonest elite scientific communities have more and more power. Fauci would not only be the judge and jury of what was true in science, but he also wanted to decide *who* deserved to write about it and *what* they should write. He clearly left no room for the possibility that the really good journalists would be the kind that questioned what *he* had to say.

Fauci also made it pretty clear in the piece that, try as they might, AIDS critics and dissidents would get absolutely nowhere because he was permanently stacking the deck against them: "The lack of clear-cut black-or-white answers plagues the biomedical sciences compared with the physical sciences. Stanley Pons and Martin Fleishmann said they had achieved nuclear fusion at room temperature. Other scientists tried, but they could not reproduce it. Bingo it's over. But because we cannot ethically do clinical trials to establish that he is wrong, I am probably going to be answering Peter Duesberg for the rest of my life." Someone near him should have tried to convince Fauci that it wasn't all about *him*. One also loves the presumption that he was going to control the official etiology of AIDS *for the rest of his life.* Unfortunately, *he almost has.* Beyond the breathtaking megalomania of the statement is the stupidity that the only way to show HIV wasn't the cause of AIDS was to do clinical trials with patients. All it would have taken would have been a few patients with AIDS *who had no evidence of HIV*. The only people that would be hurt by the implications of that finding would be the dishonest and incompetent scientists, like Fauci, whose undeserved reputations and incomes had depended upon the HIV theory. Those HIV-negative patients would be forthcoming—in spades. In fact those patients were basically the very immune-compromised chronic fatigue syndrome patients a doctor named Richard DuBois had seen in his Atlanta practice *before* the socio-epidemiological construction of the heterosexist and racist HIV/AIDS paradigm.

Hillary Johnson reported on the DuBois Atlanta cases in *Osler's Web: Inside the Labyrinth of Chronic Fatigue Syndrome Epidemic*, her epic work of journalism detailing the CDC's failure to acknowledge the true nature of the chronic fatigue syndrome epidemic. It is now all too painfully obvious that the DuBois cases—with the telltale signs of hypergamma-globulinemia, t-cell perturbations and persistent reactivated EBV and CMV infections—were the beginning of the real AIDS/CFS/HHV-6 disaster. According to Johnson, in 1980 Richard DuBois "saw a thirteen-year old girl who suffered from a seemingly endless case of mono. As the months passed, he identified several more cases of the curious syndrome in his practice." (*OW* p.7) He wasn't alone. Johnson reported that he was in touch with other clinicians who had seen similar cases and he and his colleagues eventually had a research article published about it in the *Southern Medical Journal* in 1984, the same year the big consequential government mistake of certifying HIV as the official AIDS virus occurred. According to Johnson, "they [DuBois and his colleagues] had believed that they were describing a new syndrome, one that would have increasing importance and was worthy of national attention." (*OW* p.7) The DuBois patients morphed into the millions of chronic fatigue syndrome and HHV-6 patients that Fauci and his organization (which was supposed to handle infectious diseases) were willfully ignoring while building their Potemkin HIV/AIDS empire.

At the end of Fauci's little *AAAS* piece comes the shot across the media's bow from the tiny AIDS czar: "Scientists need to get more sophisticated about expressing themselves. But the media have to do their homework. They have got to learn the issues and the background. And they should realize that their accuracy is noted by the scientific community. Journalists who make too many mistakes, who are sloppy, are going to find that their access to scientists may diminish." In other words, the scientists that journalists reported on were going to be the high-handed and underhanded final arbiters of what the public knows about science. They could decide to cut off journalists *they* defined as making mistakes and being sloppy, and one would assume that one of those sloppy mistakes would probably entail giving any coverage to scientists like Peter Duesberg, who raised serious questions about what was being called good science by Fauci and the rest of the HIV/AIDS establishment. Fauci was basically saying that he and his cronies would only be accountable to themselves which is the hermetically-sealed, closed-community essence of should be called totalitarian, abnormal, and ultimately sociopathic science.

If anyone ever makes a serious film about "Holocaust II" it will have to include the shocking revelation (already referred to above) that came to light during the Eighth International Conference on AIDS in Amsterdam during July of 1992. Its historic importance rivals that of the Wannsee conference during World War II or the Gulf of Tonkin incident. It was *the moment of no turning back*, the moment a fateful line was crossed, a life of virtual pseudoscientific crime against humanity was virtually signed onto and those responsible for "Holocaust II" lost all forms of plausible deniability. AIDS almost overnight became AIDSgate and a very unique Nazi-like biomedical and epidemiological assault against humanity. And, ultimately, the man who stood at the center of the developments that came out of Amsterdam was Anthony Fauci. Before Amsterdam one might be able to say that Fauci wasn't exactly the Bernie Madoff of the biomedical Ponzi Scheme that maintained AIDS, chronic fatigue syndrome and the HHV-6 spectrum catastrophe. *But not after Amsterdam.*

Hillary Johnson provided a detailed account of what happened at that Amsterdam conference in her book. She recounts how the conference was electrified by news from a small press conference that was held in California at which a scientist named "Subhir Gupta, a University of California immunologist, reported he had isolated particles of a previously unknown retrovirus from an HIV-negative, ailing sixty-six-year-old woman, her symptomless daughter and six other patients." (*OW* p.600) According to Johnson, "Investigators and the lay press gathered in Holland were riveted by Gupta's announcement that the older woman suffered from an 'AIDS-like' condition wherein a component of her immune system, a subset of T-cells called CD4 cells, were severely depleted. In addition, she had suffered a bout of *Pneumocystis carinii* pneumonia, a so-called opportunistic infection that afflicted many AIDS patients whose CD4 cells were depleted." (*OW* p.600)

That announcement was soon outdone by a flurry of shocking revelations from additional scientists at the Amsterdam conference who had "findings of retrovirus particles in HIV-negative patients with AIDS-like symptoms." (*OW* p.601) A near panic was almost set off internationally by the possibility that there was a second previously unrecognized AIDS epidemic on the horizon that was caused by a non-HIV agent. (*OW* p.601)

According to Johnson, it turned out that the Centers for Disease Control *was already aware* of such HIV-negative cases of an AIDS-like illness. (*OW* p.601) Johnson reported that months before Gupta's press conference two CDC scientists had reported on "six cases of non-HIV positive AIDS." (*OW* p.601) Their conclusion was that "HIV may not be the only infectious cause of immune deficiency." (*OW* p.601) Two AIDS viruses? A gay one and a straight one? OMG!

The HIV-negative cases of AIDS-like illness set off an explosion in the press, most notably from Lawrence Altman, the reporter who guided *The New York Times* dreadful, sycophantic reporting on AIDS throughout "Holocaust II." In the *Times* Altman wrote that the CDC's embarrassment was "huge because the agency had lost control over the dissemination of new

500

information in the field of AIDS." (*OW* p.602) (That anyone at the *Times* could stress the importance of a government agency *controlling information* with a straight face is pretty amazing and revealing.)

According to Johnson, the CFS research community was especially fascinated by the fact that the Gupta HIV-negative AIDS-like cases were chronic fatigue syndrome sufferers. (*OW* p.604) And for anyone following the bizarre scientific politics of AIDS, it was interesting that Gupta's colleague, the man who supposedly isolated the new retrovirus was none other than Zaki Salahuddin, the scientist who had worked for Robert Gallo and had faced criminal charges for creating a company that garnered illegal self-dealt income from his position at the National Cancer Institute. Johnson reported that when Salahuddin was asked whether HIV-negative AIDS might be chronic fatigue syndrome, he said, "It's a fair statement. But I'm not a prophet. Time and money [are] required for this." (*OW* p.604) Johnson also reported, "Salahuddin confirmed that he and Gupta, who had a cohort of CFS patients in his clinical practice and who had presented papers on the immunology of CFS at medical conferences on the disease, had discussed the possibility that CFS and non-HIV positive AIDS were the same disease." (*OW* p.604) Also, according to Johnson, the non-HIV positive AIDS cases caught the attention of Paul Cheney, one of the two pioneering Lake Tahoe chronic fatigue syndrome researchers. Johnson wrote, "For years he had observed that some CFS patients met the government's defining criteria for AIDS on every count except infection with human immunodeficiency virus." (*OW* p.604) He also told Johnson that "It was hardly unheard of . . . to diagnose the kinds of opportunistic infections that torment AIDS victims— maladies like thrush, candida and pneumonia—in CFS." (*OW* p.604) In the world of normal science this would have been called "the smoking gun."

The AIDS conference in 1992 should have been one of those great moments in normal science as described by Thomas Kuhn. It could have been a moment when disturbing "anomalies" should have attracted the "attention of a scientific community." (*The Structure of Scientific Revolutions* p.ix) But this would not be a moment for AIDS research that "the profession can no longer evade anomalies that subvert the existing tradition of scientific practice" which would "begin the extraordinary investigations that lead the profession at last to a new set of commitments, a new basis for the practice of science." (*SSR* p.6) This would *not* be one of those eureka moments in science characterized by "the community's rejection of one time-honored scientific theory in favor of another incompatible with it." (*SSR* p.6) There would be no "transformation of the world within which science was done." (*SSR* p.6) There would be no "change in the rules governing the prior practice." (*SSR* p.7) As a result of what happened in Amsterdam, scientists would *not* alter their "conception of entities with which [they] had long been familiar." (*SSR* p.7) Amsterdam would *not* cause the AIDS researchers' worlds to be "qualitatively transformed as well as quantitatively enriched by fundamental novelties of either fact or theory." (*SSR* p.7) After the revelations of HIV-negative AIDS cases, the researchers would still *not* give up their "shared paradigm." (*SSR* p.11) No new AIDS (or chronic fatigue syndrome = AIDS) paradigm was allowed to reveal itself in Amsterdam and subsequently be fairly examined and debated. The HIV-negative cases of AIDS would *not* be recognized as an important scientific surprise that would lead scientists "to see nature in a different way." (*SSR* p.53) The scientific world of AIDS researchers did not change "in an instant" (*SSR* p.56) the way it might have if AIDS research was taking place in the world of normal science. (And consequently, immune-system-destroying HHV-6 would remain locked in the basement of "science.")

Tragically, the HIV-negative AIDS cases were not a wake-up call for the scientists that "something had gone wrong" and hence the anomalous cases were not "a prelude to discovery." (*SSR* p.57) Even though the HIV-negative AIDS cases "violated deeply entrenched expectations," (*SSR* p.59) they were not allowed to change *anything* about the AIDS paradigm. In Kuhn's world of normal science, the "traditional pursuit prepares the way for its own change.' (*SSR* p.65) Amsterdam showed that AIDS research was being conducted in normal science's cockamamie opposite world, one that should be called "abnormal, totalitarian and sociopathic science." Even if the HIV-negative AIDS cases could have ultimately led to a new paradigm that was "able to account for wider range of natural phenomena," (*SSR* p.66) they were dead on arrival. No "novel theory" about AIDS which was a "direct response to crisis" (*SSR* p.75) was allowed to emerge because the abnormal, totalitarian, and sociopathic science of AIDS was *politically invulnerable* to crisis. At that historic conference there was never any chance that the HIV/AIDS theory would be "declared invalid" even though a new "CFS is a form of AIDS" paradigm was staring out at the conference from the new anomalous data and was a perfectly credible "alternate candidate." (*SSR* p.77) Kuhn wrote that the decision to reject one paradigm is always simultaneously the decision to accept another, and the judgment leading to that decision involves the comparison of both paradigms with nature and with each other." (*SSR* p.77) The HIV-negative AIDS cases were *not allowed* to catalyze that kind of fertile intellectual process in Amsterdam. Kuhn would probably argue that absent a new paradigm to examine and accept in Amsterdam, there was no exit from the HIV/AIDS paradigm because "To reject one paradigm without simultaneously substituting another is to reject science itself." (*SSR* p.79) In a way, much of what happened at the AIDS conference was based on appeals to something quite characteristic of the AIDS establishment and abnormal science: *authority*. The petulant HIV/AIDS authorities basically said, "Nothing here, folks. Please move along." And unfortunately, the scientific community and the media (with a few notable exceptions) did exactly that. Kuhnian *anomaly* didn't turn into Kuhnian *crisis* and that in turn did not explode into Kuhnian *scientific revolution* as it should have. The HIV-negative

502

cases in Amsterdam should have led to a period of what Kuhn called "extraordinary science" (*SSR* p.82) in which "the rules of normal science become increasingly blurred." (*SSR* p.83) (Although one could argue that the rules of AIDS research already actually were a shocking chocolate mess.) Amsterdam would not be the transformative moment when "formerly standard solutions of solved problems are called into question." (*SSR* p.83) The conference should have been a fruitful time when scientists were "terribly confused." (*SSR* p.84) If things had gone the way they should have at that conference, the assembled AIDS researchers would have ultimately changed their view of "the field, its methods, and its goals." (*SSR* p.85) HHV-6 might have been allowed to reveal itself in all its pathological glory. And the scientists who had given us the HIV paradigm would have been revealed in all their vainglory.

Had the science of Amsterdam been *normal*, both AIDS research and chronic fatigue syndrome research might have morphed into one unified discipline. The dismantling of the "chronic fatigue syndrome isn't AIDS" paradigm should have begun in earnest. HHV-6 (and its spectrum or family) might have emerged quickly as the unifying viral agent(s) of those two epidemics which should have always been considered one in the first place. And those two epidemics were just the tip of the HHV-6 iceberg. What happened in Amsterdam was a virtual nosological and epi-demiological crime. It was the deliberate attempt to use *sheer political force* to make a legitimate scientific crisis disappear. As a result, scientists would not turn to what Kuhn describes as a "philosophical analysis as a device for unlocking the riddles of their field." (*SSR* p.88) "Philosophical analysis" was Greek to this confederacy of dunces. The crisis was not allowed to play itself out and would not loosen what Kuhn calls the "stereotypes" and provide "the incremental data necessary for a fundamental paradigm shift." (*SSR* p.89) There would be no Kuhnian "transition from normal to extraordinary research." (*SSR* p.91) It should have been painfully clear in Amsterdam "that an existing paradigm [had] ceased to function adequately in the exploration of an aspect of nature to which that paradigm itself had previously led the way." (*SSR* p.92)

A potentially life-saving scientific revolution in AIDS and CFS research was politically nipped in the bud in Amsterdam and in the months that followed. No "new theory" was allowed to surface that would "permit predictions that are different from those derived from its predecessor" (*SSR* p.97) Kuhn asserted that "the price of significant scientific advance is a commitment that runs the risk of being wrong."(*SSR* p.101) Those in control of the abnormal science of AIDS had no interest in engaging in *any* kind of science that would prove *them* wrong. "Wrong" was not in their cultish vocabulary. They had bet their white heterosexual male professional reputations and the credibility of American science on their ridiculous and dangerous HIV/AIDS and "chronic fatigue syndrome is not AIDS"

503

paradigms. Fake dividends of their scientific Ponzi Scheme would be paid out for decades.

What happened in Amsterdam was the opening and almost simultaneously closing of a Pandora's Box of incredibly important scientific questions and implications. The person most responsible for keeping that box closed then and for the next two decades was the de facto AIDS Czar, the tantrum-prone Anthony Fauci. This may have been the last chance for Fauci and the HIV/AIDS establishment to turn back from the precipice of the HHV-6 spectrum catastrophe. But even his sister Denise could not save him from securing this dark place in history.

According to Hillary Johnson, "On August 15, federal scientists convened a meeting in Atlanta to discuss the emerging health threat of non-HIV positive AIDS. In the three weeks since Sudhir Gupta's paper on his isolation of a new intracisternal retrovirus in a handful of cases, the number of reported cases had risen from approximately thirty to fifty. Nobel prize winners, members of the National Academy of Sciences, CDC's AIDS administrators, and Anthony Fauci, head of the National Institute of Allergy and Infectious Diseases, formed a panel to query scientists Gupta, David Ho of the Aaron Diamond AIDS Center in New York and Jeffrey Laurence, a Cornell Medical College cancer and AIDS specialist and associate professor of medicine, each of whom had been studying cases of the syndrome and discovered evidence of retroviral infection in patients." (*OW* p.606) It didn't matter how many brilliant scientists from different institutions were queried at the meeting, because their mindsets about HIV were all the same. It was like a mini-Woodstock of groupthink. There was no turning back from the HIV/AIDS and "chronic fatigue syndrome *is not* AIDS" paradigm. The carved-in-stone paradigm was eight years old at that point and the nation's heterosexist and racist AIDS propaganda and public health policies had been built on its assumptions. The gay and black communities had been herded into it like cattle into a train. It was another moment in abnormal science in which the privileged and paranoid foxes had formed a panel to investigate the henhouse.

The manner in which Fauci and his colleagues basically covered up the shocking anomalies of HIV-negative AIDS was relatively simple and Orwellian: as previously noted, they disingenuously gave the HIV-negative cases an obfuscational new name (Idiopathic CD4 T lymphocytopenia or ICL) and they insisted by fiat that they were not really AIDS cases. The HIV/AIDS elite insisted that because there was no unifying geographic or chronological "risk factor" (OW P.603) to be found in these ordinary Americans and they shared no official AIDS risk factors, there was no HIV-negative AIDS or AIDS-like epidemic covertly occurring in the general population. Fauci's concerned sister Denise would not have to lose sleep at night.

504

Because the "chronic fatigue syndrome *is not* AIDS" paradigm was not challenged by what happened at the Amsterdam Conference in 1992, for at least another two more decades, the chronic fatigue syndrome patients were locked into their pathetic heterosexist wild goose chase to find a cause while constantly avoiding the obvious links between their medical issues and AIDS. They had Tony Fauci's blessing for that fool's errand. His basic attitude toward CFS was that people shouldn't be ashamed of being told that their problem was psychiatric, (*OW* p.334) which was how the disease was deceptively framed by the government for nearly three decades. And of course, they were just the canaries in the HHV-6 mine. Everyone suffering from multi-systemic problems of the HHV-6 spectrum (like multiple sclerosis, fibromyalgia, autism, and even Morgellons) would ultimately pay a heavy price for the intellectual dishonesty and legerdemain of the 1992 AIDS conference.

Fauci and his colleagues told the public that the HIV-negative cases of AIDS-like illness were rare, but of course it all depended on disease definitions and *who* was doing the defining and counting. Fauci disingenuously sent out a call that summer asking that all HIV-negative cases be reported immediately *to him*. An editorial in *New York Native* heeded his call: "Last week Anthony Fauci of the National Institute of Allergy and Infectious Diseases asked that all cases of HIV-negative AIDS be reported to him. We reported thirteen million American cases. That's the estimate of the number of cases of chronic fatigue and immune dysfunction, a condition that research (if anyone bothers to read it) suggests is essentially HIV-negative AIDS." (*OW* p.605)

The editorial had no impact on Anthony Fauci and it would not be the only time he would ignore the *New York Native* during "Holocaust II."

One could ultimately say that Denise Fauci's petulant brother himself represented one of the most significant scientific paradigm shifts, one that moved the whole world from normal to abnormal, totalitarian, and sociopathic science. During the Fauci years, The Age of Scientific Racketeering began in earnest. Bernie Madoff has a twin in science whose Ponzi Scheme is a gift that keeps on giving.

The Pulitzer Prize Winner and Robert Gallo's Little Lab of Horrors

What the world didn't know, of course, is how much Gallo had done to create the image of an obsessed [*Chicago Tribune* reporter—and chronicler of Robert Gallo's misdeeds—John] Crewdson. Only Crewdson, who recorded the defamation of his character with the same diligence and care that he recorded everything else, knew. He knew it from having to answer when his sons asked why the police were coming to the door at dinner time [after Gallo suggested to police that Crewdson might have broken into his house]. And he knew it from the rumors he kept catalogued in a file at home. Only one of those, he says, truly bothered him, because it reflected on his family. It was that Crewdson had divorced his wife to join a gay commune in San Francisco and had then "set up housekeeping with his boyfriends" in Bethesda. Though it was unclear if this tale, like the others, had originated with Gallo, Gallo had often tried to label his critics in AIDS as being gay; the story seemed to bear his stamp.

"I've caused problems for other people in my career," says Crewdson, understating the damage he helped unleash upon the Nixon White House, the FBI and the CIA, all of which were known to retaliate against journalists for less. "But I don't ever remember a government official engaging in a sustained personal attack on me or any other reporter." That Gallo is a physician, sworn to compassion, seems to make the situation all the more unusual.
                    —Barry Werth, "By AIDS Obsessed," *GQ*, August, 1991

"Gallo was certainly committing open and blatant scientific fraud," Sonnabend says. "But the point is not to focus on Gallo. It's us—all of us in the scientific community, we let him get away with it. None of this was hidden. It was all out in the open but nobody would say a word against Gallo. It had a lot to do with patriotism—the idea that this great discovery was made by an American."
                    —Celia Farber, "Fatal Distraction," *Spin*, June 1992

Robert Gallo was a sine qua non of what should be called "Holocaust II." It is unimaginable without him at the very core of its deadly insanity. He wasn't just a run-of-the-mill scientific villain. He was larger than life, someone you would expect to see in a Batman movie. One where Batman dies. The world owes a great debt of gratitude to John Crewdson, the Pulitzer Prize winning *Chicago Tribune* journalist who mastered the irritating minutiae of retrovirology (and pseudoretrovirology) in order to capture Gallo in all of his exasperating and pathological glory.

In *Science Fictions*, the underappreciated book of microscopic reporting, John Crewdson piles up detail after detail of Gallo's career like a skilled novelist, determined to sear Gallo's essence into our consciousness and to leave us in a state of shock about what actually took place behind trusted laboratory doors while people were dying horrific deaths from AIDS all over the world. When Crewdson is done with his awesome dissection of Gallo, and we have seen the innards of the world's most amazing pathological liar laid out on the autopsy table, no reasonable observer should take *anything* Gallo said about AIDS seriously. Yet Crewdson himself seems to have ultimately had no qualms about leaving Gallo's theory that HIV causes AIDS standing totally hegemonic and unchallenged amid all the shocking evidence of Gallo's chronic incompetence and perfidiousness. It's a real puzzlement.

According to Crewdson, the early career of Robert C. Gallo, the world's most famous AIDS researcher at the National Cancer Institute, got off to a precocious start as a lab chief at the age of twenty-seven. But it was subsequently unsuccessful and frustrated until Gallo accomplished what appeared to some scientists at the time to have been his first viral theft. That may have involved stealing credit from the Japanese who discovered a virus named ATLV by renaming the same virus HTLV. Regardless of whether Gallo did steal credit for *that* virus, the questionable fog of its discovery certainly fit the funky pattern of what occurred in his lab during the 1980s when Gallo sank his teeth into the search for the cause of AIDS. And even beyond that. Crewdson establishes early in his lengthy book that Gallo is a man of great manipulative shtick. Gallo's mythological song and dance about himself and his origins is a somewhat revealing Dickensian story about the source of his professional drive and his great destiny: Crewdson writes, "In newspaper and magazine articles, Gallo's single-mindedness was frequently attributed to the death of his five-year old sister, Judith from childhood leukemia, an event Gallo recalled as the most traumatic of his young life, and which had transformed the Gallo household into a grim and joyless place without music or laughter where Thanksgiving and Christmas was no longer observed." (*SF* p.15) How could anyone question a man of such noble motives? (Actually, how could anyone *not*?)

In *Science Fictions*, Crewdson presents a Gallo who is a loud, crass braggart who people either loved in a toadying manner or, if they were streetwise, considered him to be what one scientist once described as a "black hole" that destroyed everything in its vicinity. Crewdson describes a period of early disgrace at the NCI during which Gallo had supposedly discovered the first evidence of reverse transcriptase "in human leukemia cells" which subsequently turned out to be irreproducible when another scientist tried to replicate the finding. (*SF* p.14) Bad luck struck again when Gallo was celebrated on the front page of *The Washington Post* only to have his discovery, a virus called HL23, undermined by one of his enemies who proved that what Gallo had was not a human retrovirus "but a melange of three animal viruses—a woolly monkey virus, a gibbon ape virus and a baboon virus— jumbled together in a retroviral cocktail." (*SF* p.19) A humiliating retraction was made subsequently in *Nature*. Unfortunately, this kind of failure in the life of a character like Gallo only made the man *more* determined to vindicate himself at all costs as a great scientist. The whole world would pay a terrible price for his extraordinary determination.

507

There is something about Robert Gallo—if you've ever met him in person or seen him on television or talked to him on the phone—that makes you wonder what planet or species he is from. Crewdson captures his uncanny strangeness when he notes, "Gallo's conversations often sounded as though a tape recording were being played back at faster than normal speed, and his syntax frequently lent the impression of someone whose first language was not English." (*SF* p.19) By the time Crewdson is done with him 600 pages later, one is convinced that Gallo's first language is falsehood.

Crewdson presents Gallo's lab in its early days as a place where things were *always mysteriously going wrong*. It wasn't just that the scientific findings the lab produced couldn't be replicated, but there were also odd break-ins and very peculiar acts of sabotage. But the best was yet to come.

Unfortunately, as Gallo's desperation for a big discovery grew, so had the budget of the National Cancer Institute as the nation committed itself to the desperate hunt for the viral origins of cancer. Richard Nixon cancer initiative was the wind beneath Gallo's wings. However, things got off to a disappointing start for many years and, in a moment of political bad timing, Gallo's HL23 scientific embarrassment happened shortly after there had already been numerous viral dead ends at NCI and the whole program was losing its luster and in real jeopardy of being cut back.

That the HL23 virus turned out to be a laboratory contaminant rather than a new virus *after it had been touted in the press,* even before its publication in a scientific journal became a familiar pattern in Gallo's scientific lifestyle (and may have been adopted by some of his underlings). Also to be repeated throughout his career was his inability to admit he was wrong about this HL23 until it couldn't seriously be denied. (*SF* p.19) The fact that the contaminant looked like it had to have been a deliberate act of sabotage by somebody suggested that even darker things were going on at the National Cancer Institute around Gallo, things that even ubersleuth John Crewdson may have been unable to nail down. This dark possibility of an *even bigger missed story* is a cloud that hovers over all the events in Crewdson's narrative.

According to Crewdson, the only reason that Gallo's career didn't go down the tubes over the HL23 debacle was because he had a protector at NCI, his boss Vincent DeVita, someone who would come to Gallo's rescue more than once during his troubled tenure at the Institute. (*SF* p.20) Crewdson writes that DeVita was one of a number of people who held the opinion that Gallo was basically a genius who was also a handful. This was a tragic flaw in DeVita's judgment that would have terrible consequences for the legacy of American biomedical science and the health of every person on this planet.

Crewdson portrays Gallo as a man rabidly obsessed with winning a Nobel Prize (*SF* p.20) He was ready to do whatever needed to be done and to elbow out everyone who got in his way. He had no qualms about cheating his subordinates out of appropriate credit for their (sometimes questionable) discoveries. He was also happy to reward achievement of subordinates by unceremoniously getting rid of them when they threatened to outshine him. (*SF* p.23) Gallo's bizarre, paranoid laboratory was the object of suspicion from other scientific quarters. When his lab supposedly discovered HTLV, Gallo refused to let samples of that virus leave his lab and Crewdson quotes a colleague of Gallo's as saying there was "a feeling around the N.I.H. that there was something, ah, wrong with HTLV." (*SF* p.31) Gallo may have realized early in his career that if you didn't want people to find anything wrong with your work the best thing to do is to *not share your viruses—or anything else—with them*.

The funny thing about Gallo, surely one of the most paranoid people to ever call himself a scientist, is that he was always accusing *others* of paranoia and baseless suspicion—toward him and his eminently questionable motives. When it seemed to some scientists that Gallo's lab had switched the Japanese virus, ATLV, with the Gallo lab's supposed version of the same virus (the soon-to-be celebrated HTLV), he argued that it was paranoid for anyone to even dare to think that way. (*SF* p.32) For Gallo, there was always something structurally wrong with the brains of the people who witnessed his crimes. They were always crazy, and he was always sane. You could say that Gallo was from the blame-the-victim-school of scientific fraud.

Adding insult to injury, after what looked like a viral theft of ATLV from the Japanese, he barely gave them any credit at all for their research into the very virus his lab seems to have taken advantage of. And he mocked the work of the Japanese on ATLV several times (*SF* p.36) The Crewdson picture of Gallo throughout the book is of a man with absolutely no shame.

Two of Gallo's subordinates, the so-called hands-on discoverers of the suspiciously discovered HTLV, Bernard Poiesz and Francis Ruscetti, got the usual treatment that putatively successful people (or co-virus-lifters) got in Gallo's lab. Ruscetti went on "the endangered list" and was never cited in the award Gallo was given for the discovery of HTLV. Poiesz was betrayed by Gallo in the form of receiving a lukewarm endorsement from Gallo when he applied for a grant. Crewdson quotes Poiesz as saying about Gallo's credit-grab for the discovery of HTLV that it was "like saying that Queen Isabella discovered America after Columbus came home told her about it." (*SF* p.37)

Unfortunately, in terms of the world's biomedical safety, Gallo was in the wrong place at the wrong time when AIDS occurred and initially he had the wrong virus at the ready: HTLV, of course, because that's what he happened to be working on. Just the adoption of the idea that HTLV might be the cause of AIDS (an idea supposedly given to Gallo by others) was patently absurd and raises questions about Gallo's scientific judgment. It may have been purely driven by the prurient fact that the Japanese, according to Crewdson, "had shown that HTLV was transmitted by sexual intercourse." (*SF* p.39) The fact that the CDC had given him a gay-obsessed and sexual epidemiological paradigm to work with didn't help matters. One feels a sense

509

of dread at the prospect of Gallo getting involved in anything with a sexual angle when Crewdson quotes the CDC's Cy Cabradillo talking about Gallo: "He [Gallo] didn't seem that interested. . . . I don't think he wanted to get involved with a gay disease. What turned him around was Max [Essex]." (*SF* p. 41) One almost wishes that Gallo's homophobia or gay-antipathy had been even more pronounced and that Essex had weaker powers of persuasion and that Gallo had blown off requests to get involved in AIDS. It would have saved the gay community and the rest of the world from decades of grief.

What was so intellectually challenged about Gallo's notion that HTLV could even remotely be the cause of AIDS was the fact that, as most retrovirologists knew, "quite apart from killing T-cells," HTLV "transformed them into leukemic cells." (*SF* p.44) But that didn't stop Gallo once it became his idée fixe. Gallo was always light-years ahead of his data—imaginary and real.

While Gallo was promoting the silly notion that HTLV was the cause of AIDS, French researchers at the Pasteur Institute in Paris discovered a retrovirus they called "LAV" in the lymph nodes of AIDS patients. Gallo pulled off one of his many fast ones when he offered to submit Pasteur's LAV paper on the discovery to *Science*. When they took him up on the offer, he noticed the Pasteur scientists had failed to write an abstract, in a moment of fake generosity he called Luc Montagnier and said he would be willing to write the abstract (*SF* p.56) One should always beware of Gallos bearing gifts. According to Crewdson, "To his everlasting regret, Montagnier agreed." (*SF* p.56) What Crewdson described at this early point in his account of Gallo is so egregiously crooked that it boggles the mind that anyone subsequently ever took at face value *any of the science* that came out of that NCI den of biomedical iniquity. Gallo completely distorted the meaning of the Pasteur paper in the abstract he concocted, an intellectual act of dishonesty so in-your-face that it takes one's breath away. In the true spirit of the opposite world of abnormal science, Gallo twisted the whole meaning of the Pasteur paper to point towards his own birdbrained notion that *their AIDS related virus was actually HTLV*. According to Crewdson, "As summarized by Gallo . . . the French manuscript appeared to be reporting, if not the isolation of HTLV itself, then a very closely related virus." (*SF* p.56) And to add humor to injury, Gallo ran the abstract by the French on the phone, reading it so quickly that, according to Crewdson, they didn't even understand it. It didn't stop there. Robert Gallo also altered some of the text of the French paper, again in the direction of making it sound like the French retrovirus was from the same viral family as his own misguided HTLV. Montagnier had deliberately called it a "*lymphotropic virus*" to make sure it was *not* confused with the members of the HTLV family. Montagnier criticized Gallo's obsession with HTLV, insisting "Gallo didn't believe there could be more than one kind of human retrovirus. He was fully convinced that HTLV was the right one, that there was only one human retrovirus involved in AIDS." (*SF* p.57) As was typical

510

in the self-dealing abnormal, totalitarian science of AIDS, the reviewer for the paper turned out to be the paper's re-writer himself, Robert Gallo. Not surprisingly, he gave the French paper that he himself altered "his enthusiastic endorsement." (*SF* p.57) And for good measure he basically misled again in his letter to *Science* with the paper, telling the editor that Montagnier agreed with it all. (*SF* p.57)

Curiously, in terms of the role of HHV-6 in AIDS, Crewdson notes the fact that at that point Gallo's boss, Vince DeVita, thought that HTLV, the virus Gallo was pushing, was actually *a passenger virus*. De Vita may have been a true visionary.

Gallo's HTLV baloney gained credibility when his Harvard pal, Myron Essex, published a very questionable report that "between a quarter and a third of the AIDS patients he tested had antibodies to HTLV." (*SF* p.58) The publication made Essex an instant millionaire the day after its publication because Essex owned stock in a company that manufactured tests for HTLV, the virus that ultimately would turn out to have nothing to do with AIDS. (*SF* p.58) He wasn't the only one to get rich peddling bogus science during "Holocaust II."

What could have been a cautionary note about the herd-of-sheep psyche of the abnormal, totalitarian world of AIDS research in general can be found in Crewdson's amusing passage about other scientists' ostrich-like inattention to the total lack of logic in blaming a leukemia causing virus for a disease that involved the killing of t-cells. Instead of questioning Gallo and Essex's bizarre HTLV logic, according to Crewdson, potential critics and people who should have known better *doubted themselves*. They had been successfully gaslighted. He quotes one of the deferential self-doubters: "'I didn't consider myself capable of questioning Max Essex,' one researcher recalled. 'Max Essex was a person at Harvard. That meant that Max Essex would probably be right. The likelihood that he needed me to re-evaluate his data was zero.'" (*SF* p.59) This was Myron "FOCMA" Essex he was talking about. In the abnormal scientific community of AIDS research your data wasn't the issue. The school you were associated with was all that mattered. (If historians ever wake up and there is any justice in the world, one day, thanks to Essex, the word "Harvard" will be a synonymous with scientific fraud. Maybe one day it will be even used as a verb, as in "to Harvard the data" or "to Harvard the books.")

Much like Gallo, Essex usually had a reason why he was always right and others were always wrong. According to Crewdson, "asked why *if* [HTLV] was the cause of AIDS, he had only found antibodies in fewer than half the AIDS patients he tested, Essex replied that his test probably wasn't sensitive enough." (*SF* p.59) When Gallo was asked the same question about his own study that found HTLV in only four of three dozen AIDS patients Crewdson notes, "Gallo suggested that the virus was difficult to find when the number of remaining T-cells was small." (*SF* p.59) And Crewdson reports that Gallo even had a Galloesque answer for why there was virtually no AIDS in Japan where there was a great deal of HTLV: "Gallo replied that AIDS simply hadn't been noticed in Japan or maybe the Japanese responded differently to HTLV than Africans or Americans." (*SF* p.59)

Gallo's prestidigitations were very successful at making the media and the public think the French researchers were barking up the same HTLV retroviral tree he was. He highhandedly went so far as to suggest the French should actually *stop working* on their virus if it wasn't the same as HTLV. And Gallo did everything he could do to encourage other scientists not to take the French discovery seriously. Crewdson artfully captures Gallo constantly talking out of both sides of mouth about the relationship—or lack of one—between the French virus and his beloved HTLV. Crewdson reports that Gallo's own staff *had in fact* done the necessary research to determine that they were different viruses and according to Crewdson, "Whatever Gallo was saying in public, in private he agreed with his staff." (*SF* p.63) One could always count on there being two sets of books in the abnormal science of AIDS, especially in Gallo's laboratory.

The French were in a vulnerable position where Gallo was concerned because, according to Crewdson, they were afraid that he might cut off their access to scientific publication. (*SF* p.71) Gallo was a serious power broker in the world of science and that certainly should have been more of a warning sign to the scientific community that the very essence of AIDS science was mired in questionable hardball politics. Gallo even had enough power to be able to threaten the Centers for Disease Control. When the CDC dared to complain that Gallo was not sharing his HTLV probes, according to Crewdson, Gallo sniffily threatened to not cooperate with the organization. (*SF* p.74) "There was a fight," one scientist told Crewdson, "between the CDC and Gallo over who was supposed to be gathering data from research. Gallo felt they should be gathering data, and he should be doing the science." (*SF* p.74) Whatever that means. Gallo didn't realize what a perfect match his kind of virology actually made for the CDC's kind of epidemiology. Scientifically speaking, it was like the mafia families of two major cities joining forces.

One crossed Gallo at one's great peril. According to Crewdson, when a scientist named David Purtillo began to find serious evidence that *not a single AIDS patient in his study was positive for HTLV*, he found that *Science* magazine "wasn't interested in undercutting its high-visibility articles." (*SF* p.75) When Joseph Sonnabend, a New York AIDS doctor who was the first editor of *AIDS Research*, a small journal, dared to publish the Gallo-challenging Purtillo findings, according to Crewdson, "the publisher of *AIDS Research* replaced Sonnabend with [Gallo crony] Dani Bolognesi, who promptly installed Gallo on the journal's editorial board." (*SF* p.75) That's how scientific publishing worked during "Holocaust II." You scratch *my* back and I'll destroy *your* enemies.

As evidence piled up showing that the French had found the so-called AIDS retrovirus, Gallo imperiously dug in his heels for his HTLV. So did his Harvard pal Myron Essex who had spent his formative years with his buddy Gallo just trying to convince the scientific community that retroviruses *do* really cause cancer. Together they did their best to dampen the world's enthusiasm for the French virus as the probable cause of AIDS. It was one of the great examples of teamwork in science.

Gallo saw his HTLV dream start to fade when Montagnier showed up at a scientific meeting that was focused on Gallo's own candidate for AIDS virus. Montagnier presented evidence that patients who were positive for the French retrovirus were *not* positive for Gallo's HTLV. (*SF* p.81) And even worse, according to Crewdson, he "pointed out the similarities between LAV and the Equine Infectious Anemia Virus rather than HTLV." (*SF* p.81) And most threatening of all to Gallo's dreams of a Nobel Prize was the fact that Montagnier had found LAV in "63 percent of pre-AIDS patients and 20 percent of those with AIDS but less than 2 percent of the general population." (*SF* p.81) At the meeting at which Montagnier made his dramatic presentation, Crewdson wrote that Gallo did his best to cast aspersions on the research, bizarrely "questioning the reality of the reverse transcriptase activity." (*SF* p.81) According to one scientist at the meeting who is quoted by Crewdson, "[Gallo] insulted Montagnier. It was a disgusting display, absolutely disgusting. He told him it was terrible science, that there was no way it could be true. He ranted and raved for eight or ten minutes." (*SF* p.81) And of course, while Gallo was publicly humiliating Montagnier, *privately* he was asking for more samples of the French virus. (*SF* p.81)

The French discovery made it clear that Gallo had led the whole scientific community into a retroviral cul-de-sac, but at a later conference in Paris, he was at it again, playing the same tiresome duplicitous game, pushing bogus HTLV while evidence was clearly accumulating against it. Gallo could feign and bully like nobody else in the history of science. One scientist described to Crewdson a fight Gallo had with Montagnier: "During that fight one had the impression Montagnier was a little boy and Gallo was a genius. Because Montagnier didn't argue well." (*SF* p.87) Gallo wore his opposition down with over-the-top verbal displays. The word "bully" comes to mind.

Gallo changed gears from the deadender HTLV to a virus that he could get away with calling the cause of AIDS the old-fashioned way: he stole it. The complicated manner in which that was obfuscated and outrageously covered up makes up the main investigative feast in Crewdson's book. Gallo's decade of gymnastic AIDS mendacities might have been lost to history without the laser vision and crystal clear exposition of John Crewdson. If not for *New York Native* and John "Javert" Crewdson, Gallo would have gotten away with murder. Make that "genocide."

Even when Gallo's lab was pursuing a new virus like the one the French had, Gallo kept up the public pretense that HTLV was the very best candidate for the cause of AIDS. His laboratory was secretly and frantically playing a game of catch-up with the French. They had received samples of the French virus and were not honest about what they were doing with them. Gallo's subordinates privately confirmed that the French virus could be found in AIDS patients, but it would never be admitted publicly. Adding insult to deception, because Gallo had so polluted the scientific community with his stubborn, delusional notion that HTLV had to be the only possible cause, the French had trouble getting their growing body of research on LAV published. *Science* turned down an important paper that made it clear once and for all that the French LAV was not the Gallo HTLV. (*SF* p. 98) Gallo was dismissing their discovery with one hand and appropriating it with the other.

At a conference in Park City, Utah in late 1983, Gallo played his familiar game of asking disingenuous and disparaging questions publicly after a Pasteur presentation on LAV. Meanwhile, Gallo ignored doubts about his own HTLV by scientists like Jay Levy, "who wanted to know why, if HTLV caused AIDS, AIDS patients didn't have T-cell leukemia." (*SF* p.99) According to Crewdson, the obdurate Dr. Gallo insisted to Levy that "HTLV itself . . . *could* still cause AIDS." (*SF* p.99)

Luckily for the French, scientists at the CDC, home of the "impeccable" original AIDS nosology and epidemiology, had growing doubts themselves about HTLV, and even Myron Essex's old protégé, AIDS researcher and retrovirus aficionado, Donald Francis, was ready to jump ship. Crewdson captures one of many ironic moments in "Holocaust II" when he quotes Don Francis as saying, "It had become clear . . . that we had made a very big mistake." (*SF* p.100) Unfortunately, Francis didn't have a clue that he and his associates at the CDC and NIH were about to make an *exponentially even bigger virological mistake* that would threaten the whole world's health.

Thanks to the fact that his staff was working with the retrovirus foolishly supplied by the gullible French scientists, Gallo was finally seeing some interesting numbers of AIDS patients testing positive—and given what he was working with why wouldn't he? After he developed his own blood test for his purloined retrovirus, the CDC tried to determine if the French or Gallo had the best test for detecting an AIDS case. The Pasteur test did slightly better in a competition between the two country's tests and lest things be done on the up and up, according to Crewdson, Gallo wanted the CDC to *alter the results* so as to reflect a better score for Gallo's version of the test— another typical moment in the abnormal, totalitarian, and sociopathic science of "Holocaust II." To his eternal discredit, Jim Curran, the top AIDS researcher at the CDC, *actually agreed to Gallo's ridiculous request to alter the results*. To do otherwise would have been to commit normal science. Giving Gallo that unholy advantage was just one more enabling act that helped Gallo become the top spokesman for the infernal HIV/AIDS paradigm throughout "Holocaust II."

The minute that the CDC gave Gallo the word that his test for the so-called AIDS retrovirus was as good as the Pasteur one (or *sort of* as good), Gallo went into extreme Gallo mode, crowing to the world about his supposed achievement, and even more charmingly, according to Crewdson, he began "denigrating the work in Paris." (*SF* p.109) He told people he was "far ahead of the French." (*SF* p.109)

Gallo subsequently submitted data on his retroviral "discovery" in four papers to *Science*. The papers never said where the virus actually came from because they didn't dare. Mika Popovic, the unlucky scientist in Gallo's lab who did most of the bench work on the virus Gallo stole, watched as his manuscripts about the so-called discovery of the AIDS virus were methodically altered by Gallo. According to Crewdson, "entire sentences, even whole paragraphs had been excised, replaced with Gallo's scrawled additions. Crossed out altogether was the paragraph in which Popovic acknowledged the Pasteur's discovery of LAV and explained here that the French virus was 'described here' as HTLV-3." (*SF* p.111) From the scientific documents that would change the world forever, Gallo had taken out any acknowledgement of the Pasteur discovery. (*SF* p.111) In one of the most notorious notations of Gallo's whole wackadoodle career, next to a passage in which Popovic wrote something about LAV, Gallo scribbled, "Mika, are you crazy?" (*SF* p.111) Screamed the pot to the kettle.

One of the most important of the four seminal *Science* papers contained the egregious falsehood that Gallo's virus, which he called HTLV-3, had been isolated from 48 patients. Gallo also made sure, according to Crewdson, that the only reference to the French virus in the paper "sounded as though the French had the wrong virus." (*SF* p.111) Even though Gallo had basically used LAV to "discover" HTLV-3, he kept disingenuously insisting that LAV and HTLV-3 were different viruses. And even though the French had provided Gallo with LAV, and Gallo's staff knew all too well that they were not different in the least, Gallo lied to the French when they asked why he had not compared HTLV-3 to LAV and reported on it in the seminal science papers. One of Gallo's biggest lies to the French was "that Popovic hadn't been able to grow enough LAV to make comparisons." (*SF* p.118)

As Gallo was preparing to present the world premiere of the so-called virus that causes AIDS, he at first offered to include the French in the announcement to the world about the "discovery" of the virus and to cut the CDC—which had also played a role in the process—out of the deal. He then turned around and offered to make the announcement with the CDC and cut the French out of the deal. (*SF* p.119) Polyamory in the Gallo universe consisted of everyone having a chance to screw other people with Gallo before they themselves got screwed.

A sign of Gallo's enormous power in the intellectually challenged world of abnormal, totalitarian and sociopathic AIDS science was the fact that his "manuscripts were accepted by *Science* nineteen days after their submission."

(*SF* p.123) A suggestion from *Science* that four papers were too many got the immediate Gallo threat that he could easily take his papers elsewhere. (*SF* p.123) The original papers had needed pictures of the virus that Gallo had supposedly discovered, and Gallo had them: they were pictures of the French virus relabeled as Gallo's HTLV-3. At least Gallo was consistent.

Crewdson's book doesn't just focus on the fact that Gallo's historic AIDS papers in *Science* were full of purloined credit he didn't deserve. In terms of the thesis that much of AIDS science was the work of pseudoscientific sloppiness, it is important to point out that Crewdson also wrote, "An astute reader might have noticed that Gallo's condition for labeling a virus HTLV-3 were so ambiguous that nearly any retrovirus, animal, or human, would have qualified." (*SF* p.124) In the opposite world of abnormal science here are no rules to keep science from becoming a big Alice-in-Wonderland mess. About the original papers Crewdson said something that only increased the irony and tragedy of Crewdson ultimately himself accepting the HIV/AIDS paradigm: ". . . a perceptive reviewer might even have questioned Gallo's claim to have found the presumptive cause of AIDS." (*SF* p.124) (If only Crewdson had jumped in for the sake of the whole world and done with his acute journalistic skills what a perceptive reviewer *should* have done. Tragically, two frauds were passing in the night.)

A strange incident occurred just prior to the publication of the big four papers in *Science*, one that captures Gallo in all his zany treacherousness. Gallo had voluntarily given a European reporter copies of his forthcoming *Science* papers, and when the reporter published a story about them—under the reasonable impression that he wasn't breaking any embargo—Gallo accused the reporter "of having stolen the four *Science* manuscripts from his office while Gallo's back was turned." (*SF* p.126)

The theft of the French virus was not just a theft of credit from the French. It was also a theft of money in the form of lost royalties for the tests that would be developed from the purloined virus thought to be the cause of AIDS. Gallo's lab had essentially pulled off an unarmed scientific robbery; the French were destined by Gallo's shenanigans to lose millions of dollars. The matter was made even ethically worse (if the virus actually was the true cause of AIDS) by the fact that the test Gallo's people developed using the stolen virus was inferior to the test developed by the Pasteur Institute. (*SF* p.128)

Some in the American government knew from the start that Gallo was pulling off a scientific heist. On the eve of the announcement by HHS Secretary Margaret Heckler, NIH Director Ed Brant received a phone call from James Curran and Donald Francis of the CDC warning him "that Heckler was about to make a huge mistake: the French, not Gallo, had been the first to find the cause of AIDS." (*SF* p.130) Unfortunately, the duplicitous train had left the station and the American government's scientific establishment was about to apply several layers of egg to its face. (And that didn't even involve the fact that the stolen, supposedly exogenous, retrovirus wasn't even the cause of AIDS.) During the April 23, 1984 announcement debacle, Gallo even went out of his way to make sure that absolutely *no credit* was given to the French for their role in the discovery. As if it wasn't absurd enough that the Secretary of HHS was celebrating a stolen discovery, she also confidently announced, "We hope to have . . . a vaccine ready for testing in about two years." (*SF* p. 135) She seems to have been off by, well, like forever.

The credulous media fell for the Gallo scam, generally downplaying the French contribution and the Pasteur scientists were appropriately apoplectic. Predictably, Gallo, according to Crewdson, "set about expunging the evidence that he had spent two years chasing the wrong virus. (*SF* p.144). Not only could Gallo do viral theft, but he was also one of science's greatest expungers and time travelers. He rewrote the remarks he had given at past scientific conferences to make it look like he was on the trail of the AIDS virus (which he called HTLV-3) all along when in actuality he had aggressively been pushing the lost cause, HTLV. In abnormal, totalitarian and sociopathic science the past is carved in sand.

After Gallo's big splash in *Science*, he often bragged about things that were not even in the papers, findings that had actually never even been accomplished in his lab. He also violated one of the collegial rules of science by refusing to share his viruses or cell lines with other scientists unless they agreed to certain bizarre and highly suspect preconditions. (*SF* p.149) According to Crewdson, for some scientists "Gallo tried to impose conditions on which experiments they could perform and which they could not." (*SF* p.149) Gallo forced one scientist to sign an agreement not to compare Gallo's virus to other viruses. (*SF* p.150) One either played by the rules of abnormal, totalitarian, and sociopathic science or one did not play at all. Gallo wanted to control what people said about his virus and who they shared it with. He knew what was at stake if the truth ever came out.

Even the powerful Centers for Disease Control could not get Gallo to cooperate by sharing his cell lines. When noises started to be made in Paris and down in Atlanta at the CDC that Gallo had not really discovered the "AIDS retrovirus," Gallo went grandiosely ballistic, saying strange things like "We started the field. We predicted AIDS." (*SF* p.153) Like a Donald Trump of science, he accused anyone who tried to tell the truth about the matter of spreading "plot and innuendo." (*SF* p.156) The husband of Flossie Wong-Stahl, a woman who worked closely (actually, more than closely) with Gallo in his lab astutely described Gallo and his milieu to Crewdson: "The whole business has the ethics of a used-car lot. It's what you can get away with. The older-style scientists are falling by the wayside. To be a success in science these days, you need a big operation. . . . It's become an entrepreneurial business and Gallo's good at that . . . He was one of the first big-time laboratory operators." (*SF* p.158) One could say that "Holocaust II" was partly born in a used-car lot in which nobody was allowed to kick the tires.

The world fell easily for Robert Gallo, his stolen virus, and his very questionable science. According to Crewdson, Gallo received a major honor from "the Italian-American Foundation . . . that compared Gallo to Galileo." (*SF* p.158) Lysenko would have been a more appropriate comparison. If that wasn't enough, both his boss and the future Director of the NIH would compare him to Mozart. To the rest of the world he would be the great man who had discovered the cause of AIDS. You could say it was the triumph of Salieri.

When his luck did start to change and people spoke more openly and brazenly about Gallo's virus-lifting, Gallo predictably tried to turn the tables and actually suggested that the French had made the mistake as a result of a contamination by *his* virus, which was patently ridiculous, as Crewdson shows in his book with detailed chronology of the actual events. All the evidence pointed to a contamination in Gallo's lab—at best. (*SF* p.162)

Unfortunately for the future scientific credibility of the American government, Crewdson points out, "The National Cancer Institute preferred Gallo's version of events." (*SF* p.162) It's interesting that the NIH uncharacteristically tried to silence Gallo when he actually may have been inadvertently trying to tell the truth about the nature of *the real epidemic.* Crewdson writes that the Director of NIH "tried to muzzle [Gallo]" when he "speculated publicly on the risk of transmitting AIDS to women via heterosexual contact." (*SF* p.163) But, Crewdson notes, "Gallo wouldn't stay quiet. After Jerry Groopman and Zaki Salahuddin reported detecting the AIDS virus in the saliva of nearly half of pre-AIDS patients, Gallo warned the American people that direct contact with saliva 'should be avoided,' setting off alarms about the safety of oral sex, water fountains, restaurant cutlery, and cardiopulmonary resuscitation." (*SF* p.163) That wasn't exactly how the government wanted to frame and promote the epidemiological image of the AIDS epidemic. Very interesting, in retrospect. Propaganda was about to control everything the world knew about AIDS.

Even after it was clear that HTLV-3 (as Gallo renamed LAV) was not a member of the HTLV family of retroviruses, Gallo stubbornly and perversely continued to aggressively promote the bogus notion. He even published data trying to fudge the issue. (*SF* p.163) And as could be expected, according to Crewdson, he continued his two-faced act: "Whatever Gallo was saying in print, in private he was far from certain that the AIDS virus had anything in common with the HTLVs." (*SF* p.163)

One of the more bizarre things about the so-called discovery of the AIDS virus in Gallo's lab was the fact that early on, according to Crewdson, "Gallo hadn't said a word about the patient in whom Popovic had found it." (*SF* p.164) It turned out that it hadn't even been found in an individual patient but it had "been isolated from the T-cells of several AIDS patients, whose cultured cells Popovic had pooled together." (*SF* p.164) As some scientists would say, WTF? As was typical of the kind of science and reporting that underlay the HIV/AIDS paradigm, this Frankenstein of a "patient pool" was not mentioned in the seminal, history-changing paper published in *Science*, the cornerstone of the HIV/AIDS paradigm. According to Crewdson, Donald Francis of the CDC "thought it odd still that Popovic had pooled patient material in the first place, something Francis viewed as a certain way not to know which patient was the source." (*SF* p.164) Not really knowing where a virus had come from was the characteristic way science was done in the opposite world of AIDS research. Assuming where things came from characterized the nosology, epidemiology and virology of AIDS.

Like many of Gallo's lies, the LAV lie was not without its dark humor. Not only was the virus Gallo worked with the same virus that the French had discovered, but most damning, *it even turned out originally to be from the exact same patient.* (*SF* p.165) A scientist named Murray Gardner confronted Gallo about this malarkey and according to Crewdson, Gardner said, "Bob browbeat me, in his way, for about an hour. . . . He questioned my patriotism, He asked me, 'Are you French or are you American? Aren't you an American?'" (*SF* p.167) If nothing else, the pseudoscience was patriotic.

At a time when Gallo should have been bathing in the glow of being the discoverer of the so-called AIDS virus, according to Crewdson, "Most of his energy was being devoted to fending off suspicions that his discovery was really somebody else's discovery." (*SF* p.177) It was becoming clearer to the world that "the virus discovered in Paris in 1983 was the same virus Gallo claimed to have discovered in 1984." (*SF* p.178)

Even after the discovery issue was on its way to being resolved in the favor of the French scientists, Gallo, without a single qualm, bizarrely insisted in retaining his HTLV-3 name for the virus. It mattered not to Gallo that the virus was obviously *not* a member of the HTLV family. And just as absurdly, he performed all kinds of silly mental acrobatics to try and explain why his virus was exactly like the French virus, suggesting that his virus came from someone who must have gotten infected at the same place and the same time as the French AIDS victim from whom the French had isolated their virus. You could call the mythic person Gallo's own "Patient Zero." According to Crewdson, "The French dismissed Gallo's explanation as balderdash. (*SF* p. 180)

What was it like to be a part of the Gallo team during those heady days when the French virus was stolen and the pseudoscientific foundation of "Holocaust II" was laid down? Omar Sattaur, a journalist who covered Gallo for the publication *New Scientist*, recounted to Crewdson that one of Gallo's subordinates told him "that everybody in Gallo's lab felt paranoid in some way and that it was quite an awful place to work. Because it was very high-pressure and he ran it like an autocrat. They were his minions." (*SF* p.183) Anybody who messed with Captain Hook walked the plank.

519

The *New Scientist* reporter was one of the first people to nail the details of the Gallo theft in print. The piece resulted in one of Gallo's biggest critics, Oxford scientist Abraham Karpas referring to the affair as "Gallogate." (*SF* p.184) Karpas was on the money in more ways than he ever realized. But the real "Gallogate" went way beyond the stealing of a retrovirus. Unbeknownst to Karpas and Sattaur, it was ultimately about something that would cause biomedical consequences for every member of the human race. Gallo's world class narcissism manifest itself in the fact that he told Sattaur that he was of a mind to have the government start a libel action against him. What is even more absurd is that given the government's bizarre (and not fully-fathomed in Crewdson's book) relationship with Gallo, one could almost imagine that actually happening. Omar Sattaur astutely captured the Gallo psyche when he said to Crewdson, "Gallo has this ability to just absorb everything . . . He's wonderful at it. He's so good at manipulating things that I'm pretty sure that unconsciously he's doing it most of the time. If you talk to him about other people's work, he'll say, 'Well, he worked in my lab for six weeks. I taught him everything he knew.' He's a real megalomaniac." (*SF* p.185) There was something uncanny about Gallo that, unfortunately, seemed to bemuse people at the same time that it disturbed them, so that even some of the most sober minds that came into his outrageous orbit somehow missed that fact that they were in the presence of a very unique kind of monster, a human whose actions and statements, from his victim's and history's point of view, heralded from a psychic netherworld located somewhere in the vortex of clownishness, sociopathology and downright evil. One can't help but speculate that because the marginalized people whose lives hung in the balance were "gay,"—or "very gay," as the CDC's James Curran would say— that extreme moral outrage on the part of most heterosexual scientists (and some gay ones too, unfortunately) often took a vacation in Gallo's presence. Gallo wasn't playing his infernal games with breast cancer, prostate cancer, or heart disease. No matter what lip service people gave to broaden the perceived social spectrum of this particular disease, from the extant scientific community's perspective (and the public's) *it was gay through and through.*

As previously pointed out, Gallo's crime against the French was not just the intangible one of falsely claiming primacy of discovery. The theft was also a major financial crime in that he was also stealing the Pasteur's rightful royalties from the test for the so-called AIDS retrovirus. The American government's patents had all been hurriedly filed under the false pretenses that Gallo had created them with a virus that he had actually discovered. And to make matters even crazier, in terms of testing for the retrovirus virus that was now considered to be the cause of AIDS, his fraud-based test *didn't even work as well as the French test*. (*SF*. p.188) Gallo's rushed filing for the AIDS test patent, according to Crewdson, "had been approved in near-record time," (*SF* p.191) another dramatic indication that the government was in bed with

Gallo. Crewdson reported, "The French application had fallen between the cracks, and nobody at the patent office seemed to have noticed." (*SF* p.192)

One of the zanier details of the Gallo biography is the fact that he had a baby with one of the married scientists who worked with him, Flossie-Wong Stahl, which was awkward for the rest of his staff—and for Wong-Stahl's husband. According to Crewdson, the messy affair resulted in Gallo "being put in the hands of a psychiatrist for a while." (*SF* p.194) In terms of Gallo's impact on the world, it may be a shame that it was only for "a while." (The catastrophic HHV-6 pandemic might have been nipped in the bud if the whole Gallo lab had been put in the hands of a psychiatrist.)

When journalists all over the world started to wake up to the fact that Gallo had stolen credit for discovering the AIDS virus, Gallo became a whirling dervish. One science reporter told Crewdson, "Bob Gallo would write to every journalist in the world who would publish an article that wouldn't be completely in favor with his point of view. He would explode. He would immediately conclude that the journalist who had written the article that was not in favor of his genius was prejudiced, was poorly informed, was a friend of Pasteur or something like that." (*SF* p.196) He could have taught Donald Trump a trick or two.

Ever proactive, Gallo went to Paris and got Jean Claude Chermann, (one of the members of the Pasteur's LAV team) drunk and had him sign a phony, Gallo-friendly rewrite of the history of the discovery of the so-called AIDS virus. (*SF* p.198) According to Crewdson, "Gallo promised the document would never see the light of the day. Back in the United States, however, Gallo sent a copy to Jim Weingarten [the Director of NIH]." (*SF* p.198) And when the incorrigible Gallo sent documents to a French journalist in order to bolster his claims that he had not stolen the virus from the French, he included an old letter from Chermann which had been doctored in classic Gallo style. Chermann happened to see the doctored letter and according to Crewdson, "When Chermann compared the letter sent by Gallo to the original in his files, he saw that someone had cut out his signature and posted it at the end of the third paragraph, transforming what had been a scathing two-page critique of Gallo's behavior into a one-page testimonial. (*SF* p.199) This is not exactly what Thomas Kuhn would call "normal science."

It will forever be a dark blemish on the integrity of the top people in the American government's scientific establishment that the Health and Human Services elite went to bat for this scientific shyster. The Pasteur Institute could not believe the institutional support that the Gallo was getting, but now they were not about to be intimidated. They were ready to sue their way to the truth about the discovery in the American courts and to secure their just rewards from the AIDS test patent. What is really disturbing in the Crewdson account of the affair is that the government gradually *did* start to realize that Gallo's discovery claim was bogus, but the authorities shamefully continued to bolster Gallo's defense. And, in keeping with the Gallo habit of leaving no supportive deed unpunished, he turned around and blamed the American government itself for filing the patent that had enriched him and had enhanced his reputation. Even more outrageous was the fact that he was telling people that he made no money from the patent, about which one government official said to Crewdson, "Well I didn't see him turn his checks down when they came to him." (*SF* p.204) According to Crewdson, " . . . with the AIDS test earning millions—both Gallo and Popovic qualified for the maximum payment—$100,000 a year during the lifetime of the patent, a total of $1.5 million apiece over fifteen years. The AIDS test had made them millionaires."(*SF* p.278) Some of the biggest beneficiaries of AIDS fraud would be Gallo's favorite restaurants.

One of the most stunning revelations in Crewdson's book, as we have already pointed out, is that Gallo's lab wasn't just mendacious, but at the same time it also seems to have been surprisingly sloppy and disorganized which is exactly what one wants to hear about the place that helped lay down the foundation of the AIDS paradigm. The Pasteur Institute, on the other hand, (at least on the surface) seems to have been a model of fastidiousness. Crewdson describes their record keeping: "Pasteur scientists kept the records of their experiments in the European style, in sequential hardbound volumes that made it impossible to insert or remove pages of what had transpired in their labs." (*SF* p.206) In the opposite world of Gallo's lab, Mika Popovic, who did much of the work on the discovery or rediscovery of the AIDS virus "didn't have any notebooks." (*SF* p.206) Gallo is quoted as saying, about Popovic's record keeping, "We were finding stuff in drawers, pieces of paper . . . I mean we pulled out stuff that Mika didn't even know he had. And there it was. You know, old stuff, old archaic papers with scribbles on them." (*SF* p.206) Crewdson reported that "the scraps proved to be the only records Popovic could produce of what the government now counted a landmark achievement." (*SF* p.206) Given what the landmark "achievement" would actually turn out to be, it shouldn't surprise anyone that it was arrived at in such a ramshackle "scientific" style. Popovic was quite generous with his scraps of paper once under investigation. According to Crewdson, when investigators came to look at his records he said, "Take whatever I have. I don't want to go to jail." (*SF* p.207)

It was convenient for Popovic's records to be that sloppy because the Humpty-Dumpty pieces of evidence almost made it impossible to reconstruct a credible narrative of exactly how Gallo had succeeded in using the French virus to pretend he had discovered his own. (Lesson to fraudulent scientists everywhere: sloppiness creates fabulous plausible deniability.) But Crewdson, the master detective, worked his way patiently though the devious trails of disorganized paper to make Gallo's theft of credit for the discovery painfully obvious. In the process, Crewdson found evidence that Gallo altered memos to reflect fraudulent dates for when important experiments were done. (*SF* p.208)

Gallo stonewalled when Health and Human Services tried to find out what happened in his laboratory in order to put together a defense for Gallo's claims in court. As Gallo tried to rewrite the past, Crewdson reports that all kinds of discrepancies emerged. There was a clear record that he had been pursuing HTLV-1 as the cause in the period that he now was disingenuously trying to convince the world that he was actually pursuing HTLV-3, which of course turned out to be the LAV which the French had provided his lab with.

The Perry Mason smoking gun moment that destroyed Gallo's credibility for all eternity came when it was discovered that the so-called AIDS virus was incredibly *changeable* and every isolate was dramatically different from every other isolate. When it was discovered that there was virtually *no difference* between Gallo's isolate of HTLV-3 and the French isolate of LAV, it was obvious that Gallo had indeed been working with the Pasteur's isolate, not an isolate that he had discovered.

As Gallo's luck would have it, his test for the AIDS virus, which was based on the stolen French virus, was not very reliable. The French test was supposedly much better but the Gallo test had won the licensing race politically and was often failing to detect blood that was supposedly infected. Gallo's test not only had a high rate of false negatives, but it also had false positives. Gallo's incompetent test ended up ruining a number of people's lives. (*SF* p. 228) (Of course the real problem with the testing for the retrovirus by either the French or American test was that it begged the larger theoretical question of whether either test was really the test for the true cause of so-called AIDS.)

Gallo exceeded his usual standard for craziness in the fight over the name of the virus he had stolen from the French. How dare the French want to name the virus they discovered! According to Crewdson, "When Gallo discovered the French were using the term LAV alone, he sent Montagnier a peevish letter." (*SF* p. 235) In the end the French were only half-screwed when the Gallo name of HTLV-3 did not prevail and the virus was labeled "Human immunodeficiency virus or HIV." (*SF* p.236) The fact that the new name was a kind of Orwellian way of disingenuously establishing that the virus was the cause of AIDS without the inconvenience of further debate was lost on most people. The lesson of this episode of abnormal, totalitarian, and sociopathic science is that if you want to prove that a virus is the cause of a disease, just *give it a name that implies that it is the cause*. With "Human immunodeficiency virus or HIV" that mission was brilliantly accomplished. A fun bit of trivia about the voting on the name change is that the only person to support Gallo's preference of HTLV-3 was—guess who?—Myron Essex. (*SF*. p.236) (The name of the virus was "Harvarded" into history.)

One of the most embarrassing moments in the Gallo affair was the point at which it was discovered that the photographs that Gallo's lab had submitted to *Science* which were identified as photos of *their* virus turned out to actually be photos of the French virus. According to Crewdson, "the revelation dealt a major blow to the [National Cancer Institute's] credibility. (*SF* p.240) Gallo himself had a copy of the photo of the purloined virus in a framed collage on his office wall and Crewdson reports, "When Gallo found out the virus in the collage was LAV, Salahuddin [his subordinate] recalled 'he took it down from the wall and threw it on the floor, smashing glass everywhere.'" (*SF* p.241) One can only assume that like every other Gallo mess, someone else in his lab cleaned it up. The fake photo caper was one of the things that, according to Crewdson, helped turn Gallo's NCI boss, Vince DeVita, against him. Crewdson wrote, "DeVita was determined that Gallo would correct the record." (*SF* p.241)

What is mind-boggling about Gallo is that even while under investigation for the LAV fraud, he and his staff still continued to churn out *more* fraud. A letter from the Gallo folks published in *Nature* in May of 1986, meant to exonerate Gallo, contained brand new fibs. Gallo claimed to have isolated HTLV-3 from a patient he hadn't even been looking for the virus in at the time that was clearly impossible because it was the same period in which all the evidence showed he was still obsessed with HTLV-1. Gallo reconstructed a fictional past in the letter and included a picture that had just happened to have both HTLV-1 and LAV/HTLV-3 in it. According to Crewdson, he pretended to have discovered HTLV-3 earlier than he really did just by the happenstance of it being in the same photo. (*SF* p.244) One could call it a classic Gallo scientific discovery. Once again it was as if Gallo had a time machine that allowed him to go back into the past and fashion history more to his liking. Crewdson describes NCI scientist Berge Hampar's reaction to the new photo caper that appeared in *Nature*: "'When we saw *Nature*, we laughed,' Hampar said. 'We said, "Is this the only photograph they got? They're staking all their claims on one photograph with two particles in it." That's when I said to myself, 'These people are crazy.'" (*SF* p.245) It's too bad that the NCI scientist didn't do more than just say truthful things to himself because these crazy people helped give us "Holocaust II."

Gallo still wouldn't back down in the spring of 1986 when, at an AIDS conference, according to Crewdson, he referred to "the Pasteur's contribution to the search for the cause of AIDS as inconsequential." (*SF* p.246) The Pasteur scientists gave as good as the got. One of their lawyers, Jim Swire, according to Crewdson, "upped the ante by accusing someone in Gallo's lab of having stolen LAV. 'They simply studied it,' Swire said, 'concluded we were correct, renamed it, and claimed it as their own.'" (*SF* p.247) Otherwise known as the classic Gallo Three-card Monte.

The person in Gallo's lab who would ultimately get hung out to dry for the handling of the fake discovery of HTLV-3, Mika Popovic, was eager to give investigators the impression that if anything untoward had happened, it was just an innocent mix-up. But according to Crewdson, the French were just not having any of that. (*SF* p.248) The bottom line for the French was that they wanted their "share of the patent royalties."(*SF* p.249) After all, Gallo had used *their* supposedly exogenous retrovirus to make his lousy test.

Things got even more sinister in this story when the lawyer for the Pasteur Institute used the Freedom of Information Act to try and obtain documents from Gallo's lab that would support the French case against Gallo's claims. According to Crewdson, "the memos that would have been most helpful to the Pasteur's case—and most detrimental to the government's—were withheld, in some cases without any indication that they even existed." (*SF* p.259) One of the withheld documents which Crewdson ultimately obtained, made it clear that Gallo had lied about *when* he had isolates of his so-called AIDS virus. (*SF* p.260) According to Crewdson, the most damning document that was withheld was a memo from Gallo about growing the French virus *at a time that he later insisted he had not been growing it.* (*SF* p.260) The only documents that seem to have been withheld were ones that supported the unavoidable conclusion, that Gallo was one of science's greatest pathological liars.

Joanne Belk, the government's person in charge of providing the documents requested under the Freedom of Information Act, described her interaction with Gallo to Crewdson: "I didn't know how rude he was . . . . This man called me and started blasting me on the phone. 'Who the hell do you think you are?' He was terribly profane. Nobody ever talked to me like that. That was my introduction to this so-called eminent scientist." (*SF* p.260) Gallo was totally uncooperative. Interestingly, in terms of the basic quality of Gallo's science, Belk's overall impression of his lab from a visit was that it was "impressively messy." (*SF* p.261) When Gallo finally did comply with the F.O.I.A. request, Belk got a call that she could pick them up at "Biotech Research laboratories in Rockville which Beck thought surpassingly odd." (*SF* p.262) One wonders, like so many other parts of this sometimes mysterious story, what was *that* about?

The documents that were turned over to Belk were very much in the Gallo lab's signature style. According to Crewdson, ". . . none of Popovic's pages was signed. Neither were any of the pages evidently kept by others in Gallo's lab.' (*SF* p.262) Most shockingly, considering his pivotal role in creating the scientific paradigm at the heart of "Holocaust II," "Popovic's notes, written in an unmistakable middle-European hand, resembled a diary or a journal, filled with retrospective observations and abbreviated descriptions of each day's work, but scarcely any experimental protocols or new data." (*SF* p.262) The lawyer for the Pasteur Institute is quoted by Crewdson as saying that the notes looked like they had been "shuffled like a deck of cards," and when he "tried to assemble the notes in chronological order, he found that the follow-up results for one experiment were dated three weeks before the experiment." (*SF* p.262) This was the orderliness of the abnormal, totalitarian, and sociopathic science of HIV/AIDS at its very best. According to Crewdson, one Popovic page "dated Jan 19, 1984 was continued on a page

Nov 7, 1983." (*SF* p.262) The Mad Hatter would have been at home in a white coat at a workbench in Gallo's laboratory. Best of all, according to Crewdson, "Several of Popovic's pages weren't dated at all." (*SF* p.262) As was typical for a laboratory skilled at rewriting the past, Crewdson reports that several of the Popovic pages "were whited out" and "In a sequential log of laboratory specimens, the year '84' had been crossed out and replaced by '83.'" (*SF* p.262) That describes what they found, but according to Crewdson, once again the scarier thing was what the lawyers *did not find*: "In the notes that did exist, Swire and Weinberg could find no support for many of the experiments described in Popovic's *Science* article." (*SF* p.262) Swire could find no evidence of the isolation of the so-called virus from patients that Gallo had written about in his letter to *Nature* which was meant to exculpate him. (*SF* p.262) Most importantly, in terms of the French lawsuit, important documents reflecting the Gallo lab's work with the French retrovirus were missing, and one of Gallo's subordinates told Crewdson that the staff *had been told to leave them out*. Crewdson wrote, "to Swire, it looked as if somebody had systematically tried to replace the evidence of Popovic's work with LAV [the French virus] with something that would appear innocuous to the Pasteur's lawyers." (*SF* p.265) There was also evidence that the French virus had gone through a process of renaming in the documents *in order to obscure the origin of the virus the Gallo lab worked with.* (*SF* p.265) In many ways, disingenuous wordplay is at the heart of the deceptions of "Holocaust II."

None of this came as a surprise to Gallo's close observer and arch enemy in England, scientist Abraham Karpas, who watched all of this unfold in an "I told you so" mode. He told Crewdson, "Dr. Gallo still believes that in this age of communication and science he can get away with not only saying, but even writing, that black is white and vice versa." (*SF* p.269) If only people like Karpas, who seemed to astutely recognize that Gallo lived psychologically in some kind of sociopathic opposite world, had gone a step or two further and realized that when Gallo often said that HIV was the indisputable cause of AIDS that "killed like a truck," he was also saying something akin to "black is white and vice versa." But that was a bridge too far.

As the noose tightened, Gallo went into advanced paranoia, suggesting that the lawyer for the French was "hiring people to come to restaurants to sit where I go to eat, to try and hear what I say." (*SF* p.271) Crewdson quotes one rant that makes Gallo sound like he had completely lost it: "I look at the French capitalizing on their food industry from some places where my ancestors came from . . . I think they do great in getting credit for nothing half the time, more than any people I've ever seen. That's the bias I would have against France . . . They helped us get into Vietnam." (*SF* p.273) Sound like anyone you know with weird hair?

One of the more revealing moments of Freudian projection in Crewdson's portrait occurs when he quotes Gallo telling the editors of *Nature* in an unpublished interview that Montagnier "hasn't a single collaborator left, because no one trusts him. I find him extremely political, always not sure what he believes. People who are full of distrust and see the world scheming to screw them. That's the way I look at the guy . . . Montagnier's an example of a small guy who stumbled into shit. And he got famous. More than he deserves. He can't handle it, sees everybody as plotting against him." (*SF* p.273) This from the most flamboyantly paranoid man in science, the man who was always accusing everyone of being out to get *him*. The real tragedy of "Holocaust II" was that the world was not and is not out to get *him*. At least not yet.

In the unpublished *Nature* interview, Gallo contradicted things that had been published in that very publication. According to Crewdson, "*Nature* had previously assured its readers that Gallo had grown LAV for one week only and in small quantity. Now Gallo admitted that LAV had grown for at least three months and there had been plenty of virus." (*SF* p.275) The fact that this vital information was never published is consistent with what we have said about the manner in which information is managed in the world of abnormal, totalitarian, and sociopathic science. Crewdson writes, "Had the Gallo interview been reported, it would have dramatically changed the face of the dispute with Pasteur. But *Nature* never published a word of what Gallo had said—or anything else about its investigation." (*SF* p.275) Gallo could even count on international protection for his sociopathic kind of science.

As the Gallo dispute with the Pasteur Institute got more cantankerous, the scientific community began to fear the collateral damage it was doing to the image of science itself. Legendary scientist Jonas Salk sought to lower the temperature of the conflict and according to Crewdson, he "spent the end of 1986 and the beginning of 1987 shuttling between Robert Gallo and Luc Montagnier in search of a shared version of history." (*SF* p.293) These scientists seem to have had a very abnormal idea of what history actually is. It is not the difference you split between two warring scientists, especially when one of the scientists is a world-class pathological liar. Eventually, according to Crewdson, "Jonas Salk had nearly given up hope of working out a history acceptable to both Gallo and Montagnier. 'Insanity afloat,' was the way Salk described the process to Don Francis." (*SF* p.295) "Insanity afloat," unbeknownst to Jonas Salk, was the best way to describe the all of the science and epidemiology of "Holocaust II." And it is still afloat.

Eventually, worn down, Montagnier stupidly agreed to a publication of a joint chronology of the discovery of the so-called AIDS virus with Gallo in *Nature*. As is typical of abnormal, totalitarian, and sociopathic science, it was published without any peer review which, according to Crewdson, "may explain why it contains a number of factual mistakes, why several names were misspelled and why portions of the text read as if they had been translated from Chinese." (*SF* p.296) And Crewdson notes that the chronology's preamble began with a real mutually-agreed-upon whopper: "Both sides wish it known that from the beginning there has been a spirit of scientific cooperation and a free exchange of ideas, biological materials and personnel between Dr. Gallo's and Dr. Montagnier's laboratories. The spirit has never ceased despite the legal problems and will be the basis of a renewed mutual cooperation in the future." (*SF* p.296) Beyond enjoying the hilarious absurdity of this big lie, one also starts wondering about the integrity of the French discoverers of the so-called AIDS virus. Note to future historians: Gallo apparently wasn't the only one willing to cut corners. The French may have also had something to hide.

Crewdson reports that despite whatever peace Gallo got from the pile of loopy revisionist lies published in *Nature*, he was soon disturbed by a new investigative piece in *New Scientist* written by Steve Conner. The article began, "In the war against AIDS scientific truth was among the first casualties. No one listened when Luc Montagnier at the Pasteur Institute in Paris said that he had found the virus that causes AIDS. Scientific journals and scientists preferred to hear what Gallo was saying from The National Cancer Institute in the U.S." (*SF* p.298) The article included Gallo's photos which had been misrepresented as HTLV-3 as well as the accusation that Gallo's outrageously dishonest behavior had cost many lives. Gallo's protectors didn't waste time coming to his rescue. Crewdson reported that one of Gallo's cronies, Dani Bolognesi, wrote a letter to his colleagues urging them to respond to the article. (*SF* p.299) And even the Reagan administration got involved in trying to get the French AIDS officials to join Health and Human Services in condemning the article, even though, as Crewdson points out, "no one could say what inaccuracies Connor's article contained." (*SF* p.299) Such awesome power can only make one wonder what Gallo had on the government that made the authorities so ready and willing to always come to his rescue. Was there a cat in the bag called "AIDS" that Gallo could always have let out? (See my book, *The Chronic Fatigue Syndrome Epidemic Cover-up*, if you want to hear that cat meow.)

When a settlement agreement was finally signed by the French—so that they could at least get their royalties for the AIDS test—they had to agree to renounce "any statements, press releases, charges, allegations or other published or unpublished utterances that overtly or by influence indicated any improper, illegal, unethical or other such conduct or practice by any scientists employed by HHS, NIH, or NCI." (*SF* p.299) The royalties the French would receive had officially become hush money. Crewdson notes, "With the stroke of a pen, the accusations and contentions of the past two years had been erased." (*SF* p.299) More importantly for the larger issue and the real history of "Holocaust II," the French *agreed not to tell the whole truth* about the history of AIDS, again making them in some ways not all that different from their American counterpart.

In the Gallo tradition of biting the hand that had saved him, Gallo, according to Crewdson, threatened the White House if they dared to try and take any credit for the mendacious agreement. (*SF* p.300) Who the hell did the American government think it was? After the bizarre, outrageously dishonest agreement with the French was signed, in a statement that should have made everyone who died of AIDS roll over in their graves, Gallo said, according to Crewdson, "Now, instead of being distracted by all the legal business, I'll be able to return full time to trying to do something about this disease." (*SF* p.301) In other words, the bad luck of the gay community (and the black community) was about to get much worse.

The agreement rankled the Pasteur team who felt that French politicians like President Chirac, who had put pressure on Pasteur to sign the agreement, had betrayed them. According to Crewdson, "Jean-Claude Chermann couldn't comprehend why someone who had chased the wrong virus for so many months was now being anointed in the press as the co-discoverer of the right virus." (*SF* p.302) Of course the whole situation was even wackier than Monsieur Chermann realized. His awesome date with destiny is still to come.

One of the absolute worst things that happened to the world as a result of the Gallo crime was that Gallo became the go-to spokesperson for AIDS science. According to Crewdson, "The settlement notwithstanding, the newspapers and magazines continued to laud Gallo as the discoverer of the AIDS virus while rarely mentioning Montagnier" and "whatever Gallo said was likely to make news." (*SF* p.310) He had become the Pope of AIDS under false pretenses. Even David Remnick, *The Washington Post* reporter who would years later become the ubiquitous editor of *The New Yorker*, had a warm shoulder for Gallo to whine on: Gallo complained to him that the settlement with the French had failed to end the "accusations" and "hatred" from some of his scientific colleagues. (*SF* p.310) In a hyper-ironic candid confession, Gallo said to Remnick, "I'm telling you, there are days when I wake up in the morning and feel like the Archangel Gabriel. By the time I go to bed at night, I feel like Lucifer. What's going on? Please tell me why they do this to me. Why do they say these terrible things about me? Do you know? Do you?" (*SF* p.310) Is it possible that deep down Gallo may have known himself that the questionable science of the HIV/AIDS paradigm was crafted in part by a Dr. Jekyll and Mr. Hyde?

Gallo's propensity for boilerplate homophobia kicked in a bit when Randy Shilts's book, *And the Band Played On* came out. Crewdson quotes Robert Gallo as saying, "It never ceases to me to be a source of great wonder . . . how people such as a gay young man on the West Coast think they know more when they're stimulated [sic] by the same two people over and over again. Namely Don Francis and what I would regard as a psychotic who lives in Cambridge." (*SF* p.311) In the heterosexist world of abnormal, totalitarian, "homodemiological" science that characterized AIDS, there was nothing more threatening than a "stimulated" gay reporter, especially one who had been "stimulated" by a psychotic. As for Gallo's ludicrous charge of psychosis clearly directed at his critic Abraham Karpas who was at Oxford, well, let's just say that science's largest glass house had rocks flying in every direction.

Gallo was so angry at the things that Randy Shilts quoted the CDC's Donald Francis saying about him that he penned a letter of retraction and he demanded Francis sign it. He told Francis that if he didn't (according to Crewdson), he had a "plan of action against Don Francis, which included evidence like letters and tape recordings, that would show financial impropriety in Francis's relationship with Randy Shilts." (*SF* p.313) One wonders: What, no gay sex? But wait. According to Crewdson, he also threatened to expose things from Don Francis's personal life. (*SF* p.313) Gallo was the J. Edgar Hoover of science with a real or imagined dossier on everyone. The long arms of this vindictive scientist are reflected in the fact that, according to Crewdson, "When it became clear Francis had no intention of signing Gallo's letter, word reached Berkeley [where he was happily working] that he was being transferred back to CDC headquarters in Atlanta—to work not on AIDS, but on tuberculosis." (*SF* p.313) It was the career equivalent of sleeping with the fishes.

Eventually, even Gallo's boss, Vince DeVita, tired of his antics. He told Crewdson, "there was always some crisis with Bob Gallo . . . He has an arrogance about him, that he felt he could talk to you and persuade you to his way of thinking. And he almost always failed." (*SF* p.314) Crewdson reports that Gallo, as per usual, refused to share his "AIDS" viruses and his cell lines which prompted people like Nobel Laureate David Baltimore to join another scientist, Howard Temin, "in worrying that Bob's way of handling himself does significant harm to both himself and to the national AIDS effort." (*SF* p.310) Baltimore and Temin were only aware of the tip of the iceberg. (Of course, Baltimore himself wasn't exactly the Mother Teresa of science.)

Gallo exhibited the censorious style typical of abnormal, totalitarian, and sociopathic science when a book which was critical of him by Michael Koch was published in Europe. Koch's book contained entertaining sentences about Gallo like, "He was so fond of his own ideas that he saw evidence where there was no evidence." (*SF* p.320) Koch in due course got the Gallo treatment. According to Crewdson, when Koch ran into Gallo at a scientific conference, Gallo told him, "Here is a five-step program to destroy you. You, your job, your position, your damned Carnegie Institute in Stockholm." (*SF* p.320) One thing you could say about Gallo is that even his rants had power points. (*SF* 320) One thing Gallo said about Koch underlines the danger of ceding absolute power to scientific elites. According to Crewdson, Gallo insisted, "I do not feel he was qualified to write such a book. Moreover, Koch has no experience in retrovirology . . ." (*SF* p.321) Perhaps the only person qualified to write about Robert Gallo was Myron Essex, Anthony Fauci, or Gallo himself. Or <u>Professor Irwin Corey</u>.

530

After Gallo's administrative assistant, Howard Streicher, wrote a threatening letter to Cambridge University Press, the firm that was going to publish the English language edition of the Koch book which had been first published in Germany, the book was cancelled. Streicher wrote in his letter that the book was "both maliciously damaging and likely to be scientifically, historically and medically unsound." (*SF* p.322) Translation: the book told the truth.

On the heels of the settlement with the French, a new Gallo scandal emerged. It turned out that the cell line Gallo's lab had supposedly created to grow the stolen French AIDS virus was also basically, well, stolen. Gallo had used his familiar modus operandi; he just changed the name of the cell line which had actually been created by a scientist named Adi Gardner and— Presto! Chango!—it was Gallo's. According to Crewdson, "When Gazdar told a Public Health Service lawyer he thought Gallo and Popovic had appropriated his discovery, he was advised not to pursue the matter. (*SF* p.333) Some scientists are said to have green thumbs because they are so good at growing things like viruses and creating cell lines. Gallo didn't need a green thumb. He had sticky fingers.

The idea that this character seriously thought he would win a Nobel Prize by operating in the manner he did challenges all definitions of sanity. Scientist Sam Waksal (who went to jail for the insider trading financial scandal that involved Martha Stewart) described a special night with Gallo in which "Gallo was drunk, and he had a tear in his eye, and he said, 'You know, I would do anything—anything—to win the Nobel Prize.' I always thought it was the most telling thing about him. Because in the world of science the goal is the pleasantry of the discovery and he could never find as much satisfaction in the discovery as he could in the limelight." (*SF* p.336)

There was still more public humiliation in store for Gallo when sophisticated genetic analysis of Gallo's so-called HTLV-3 made it painfully, embarrassingly clear that it was LAV and that whatever happened in terms of contamination or theft, *it had definitely all happened in Gallo's lab.* (*SF* p.341) And then the darkest moment of Gallo's travails happened on November 19, 1989 when John Crewdson's 55,000 word piece with all the details of his pseudo-discovery of the AIDS virus was published in *The Chicago Tribune.* The piece's conclusion was that "What happened in Robert Gallo's lab during the winter of 1983-84 is a mystery that may never be solved. But the evidence is compelling that it was either an accident or a theft." (*SF* p.343) Crewdson was being kind. Or the newspaper's lawyers were. The *Chicago Tribune* piece aired all of Gallo's dirty laundry, exposing him making bogus claim after bogus claim; it showed him perpetually rewriting history, and the article displayed his stealing-and-renaming habit as well as his penchant for deliberately altering scientific documents. As was typical of this master double-talker, according to Crewdson, in an interview about *The Chicago Tribune* piece, "Though [Gallo] claimed not to have read the *Tribune,* Gallo nonetheless took umbrage at a number of the quotes it contained." (*SF* p.344) What Crewdson had done in his amazing *Tribune* piece (and subsequently in his book) was to show the dark side of science: "The reality that scientists often engaged in the same kind of back stabbing and throat-cutting as politicians and businessmen had remained behind laboratory doors."(*SF* p.347)

As Congress began to slowly wake up to the general issue of fraud in science, the NIH had been guilt-tripped into creating "a new agency, the Office of Scientific Integrity" which was responsible for "investigating and deciding cases of suspected plagiarism, falsification, or other scientific misconduct." (*SF* p.349) In other words, all the dishes that could be found at the Gallo buffet table. After reading the Crewdson article on Gallo, the acting director of the new Office of Scientific Integrity decided that the Gallo affair deserved to be investigated." (*SF* p.351)

Even as the Gallo investigation was getting underway, he was out in the public serving up more scientific baloney. According to Crewdson, he "was at Fordham University in the Bronx where he announced a breakthrough discovery—a cure for Kaposi's sarcoma, the malignant lesions that account for about one in five deaths among AIDS patients." (*SF* p.354) The only problem, according to Crewdson, was that "Gallo hadn't published any such results, and he hadn't presented any data at Fordham to back up his claims." (*SF* p.354) In other words, for Gallo it was business as usual. When a desperate AIDS patient contacted one of the scientists in Gallo's lab he was treated badly. The man subsequently wrote a letter to the scientist and Crewdson quotes it: "You have probably forgotten our conversation . . . But I have not and I will not forget it in a long time. I have never in my life been talked to in such a demeaning, condescending, rude and abrupt manner by anyone let alone an alleged health care professional on the public payroll. I am dying from AIDS and in particular Kaposi's sarcoma . . . Which is what motivated me to call Dr. Gallo's office in the first place . . . How cruel it is to publicly talk about a cure and then refuse the information to the public." (*SF* p.354) Demeaning? Condescending? Rude? Cruel? When Gallo's boss heard about the exchange, he ordered Gallo to apologize to the man, and, according to Crewdson, "to explain that he didn't have a cure for Kaposi's sarcoma after all." (*SF* p.354) It was one of the few times that being Robert Gallo *didn't* mean never having to say you're sorry.

As the full-scale investigation of the Gallo affair by the Office of Science Integrity got under way, Gallo was fully cooperative. Not. Crewdson reports, "It had been early January of 1990 when Suzanne Hadley requested the originals of the Gallo lab's notebooks, but by mid-March she still didn't have them." (*SF* p.355)

Because of both Crewdson's *Tribune* piece and the OSI investigation, Monagnier felt emboldened to ignore the agreement to "ferme le bouche" and he admitted to *Le Monde* that there was a real possibility that Gallo had stolen LAV. (*SF* p.356) Gallo was furious and once again ran to the sympathetic *Washington Post* with his bogus version of the story. (*SF* p.357) (This was clearly *not* the same paper it had been during the Woodward and Bernstein era.) Gallo also hired a P.R. firm and a lawyer but, according to Crewdson, told his staff, "It should not be obvious that we are using a P.R. firm or a lawyer." (*SF* p.358) Abnormal, totalitarian, and sociopathic science cannot be conducted without a P.R. firm and a lawyer that agree to keep a low profile.

The list of property crimes committed by Gallo's gang expanded while he was under investigation by OSI when it was discovered that Zaki Salahuddin, the Gallo subordinate who was supposedly the co-discoverer of HBLV (eventually called HHV-6) had set up a company called PanData in order to funnel money into his own bank account by selling medical supplies to the National Cancer Institute—supplies which he himself ordered. (*SF* p.322) (At least he wasn't out stealing viruses, although, when the whole story of HHV-6 is told, that might not exactly be the case.) According to Crewdson, Congress got wind of the scam and John Dingell eventually called it "'a gross conflict of interest . . . on the part of a prominent AIDS researcher at the National Institutes of Health' who had hidden his 'improper financial interest in a biomedical firm doing substantial business with his own laboratory at NIH.'" (*SF* p.362) According to Crewdson, Gallo told the General Accounting Office that he knew about the Salahuddin company only three months before the investigation, but he told *The Washington Post* he had known about it for a year. (*SF* p.362) Crewdson reports that Salahuddin was also selling viruses and cell lines derived from Gallo's lab. One could say that abnormal science and abnormal commerce are bosom buddies.

Salahuddin was ultimately investigated by a Grand Jury. During his tribulations, Salahuddin said an all too true and disturbing thing about Gallo: "Here's Gallo, they provide him double coverage, internal investigation and so forth, all this moral turpitude he is accused for such a long period of time. No one ever talks of suspending him. In my case they go immediately for the knife and throw me to the wolves." (*SF* p.363) Salahuddin was eventually "formally accused of violating conflict-of-interest statues and accepting illegal gratuities in the PanData case." (*SF* p.375) As part of his punishment the was supposed to perform community service by researching HHV-6, the virus he purportedly discovered, which was a little like sentencing Bernie Madoff to selling stocks and bonds.

During the OSI investigation, more mind-blowing information surfaced. Mika Popovic provided a shocking description of his period in Gallo's lab: "When I came here nobody gave me whatsoever any instructions how we should write out notes or anything else. And when the litigation started, suddenly I was asked for notes." (*SF* p.364) That anyone in any way trusted the basic science that came out of this scientific pig pen is unbelievable. The OSI investigation identified new misrepresentations that Popovic had made in the *Science* papers that had supposedly nailed HIV down as the cause of AIDS. According to Crewdson, Popovic didn't have data to back up statements in the signature AIDS papers about patients he had described as showing evidence of reverse transcriptase. (*SF* p.364) (And the scientists who questioned the HIV theory were the really crazy ones. Go figure.)

According to Crewdson, in the course of the OSI investigation, Gallo's testimony basically revealed that he had misrepresented the truth during the period in which the government was aggressively and groundlessly defending him against the French lawsuit. (*SF* p.371) He admitted he had no AIDS virus before his lab got its hands on the French virus. (*SF* p.371) He also confessed he didn't have the isolates of the AIDS virus that he had bragged about at the time of his *Science* paper appeared. (*SF* p.371) It had all been just the usual Gallo malarkey. According to Crewdson, Gallo told the OSI that he had made the false claim about the isolates because "to be quite frank, I was nervous." (*SF* p.371) Crewdson points out that if Gallo had been as honest during the French lawsuit, Pasteur would have walked away with *complete ownership* of the patent of the so-called AIDS blood test. (*SF* p.372) And reporters might not have been calling up Gallo and hanging on to his every word of wisdom about AIDS.

A panel drawn from the Academy of Science that was called in to oversee the OSI investigation voted to move the OSI investigation from an inquiry to "a formal misconduct investigation of Gallo and Mika Popovic." (*SF* p.373) They were shocked by "the apparent lack of supporting data for Popovic's key experiments." (*SF* p.373) The Academy of Science panel didn't realize that they were conducting an investigation in the opposite world of abnormal, totalitarian, and sociopathic science. One of the panelists noted—about the basic work on the AIDS virus done in Gallo's lab—that "It may not be that you will be able to find a written record of all the data that are in print." (*SF* p.374) One could say that the data that helped build the HIV/AIDS paradigm of "Holocaust II" wasn't worth the paper it was *not* written on.

Gallo kicked and screamed when OSI went so far as to requisition materials that had been used in the original AIDS experiments. When Suzanne Hadley arrived to collect those materials, according to Crewdson, she "felt like the vampire surrounded by angry villagers." (*SF* p.375) She told Crewdson, "His whole lab, they just worship Gallo and will not challenge him. Anybody who gets a bunch of people around him who gets a mindset that he can do no wrong and that everybody else is wrong and wants to get him, you know that's a prescription for disaster. Because nobody is asking the tough questions on the inside." (*SF* p.375) Gallo's own description of his gang in Crewdson's book is quite revealing: "About seventy-five percent of the people with me are from foreign countries, their salaries are twenty to thirty thousand dollars, they're M.D.-Ph.D.s, they work day and night, they work seven days a week." (*SF* p.385) It would appear that the virological fraud that helped create "Holocaust II" may have been crafted in what could be deemed a scientific sweatshop. What Zaki Salahuddin said about Gallo's rosy prospects during the investigation deserves close scrutiny by anyone trying to understand the nature of Gallo's political power: "Nothing will come out of it. No one wants America to go down. They just rally around the flag. NIH and Gallo are inseparable right now. If he goes down, NIH goes down." (*SF* p.376)

One of the more amusing moments in the Crewdson book concerns an NPR radio show on which *Business Week* reporter and author Bruce Nussbaum was being interviewed during the promotion for his book on AIDS, which according to Crewdson, purported "to show that Wall Street and NIH had conspired to slow the approval of potential AIDS drugs." (*SF* p.384) One of the people calling into the radio show attacked Gallo by name, saying that he had "'done a disservice to research in general.'" (*SF* p.384) Gallo just happened to be listening to the radio and he angrily called the show. When Gallo started going on and on about how he and his associates had risked their lives doing AIDS research and basically suggested that Nussbaum didn't have "a depth of understanding of science," (*SF* p.385) Nussbaum responded, "I think you're expressing the type of attitude which is part of the problem. . . . You simply dismiss anyone who is criticizing NIH in any way." (*SF* p.385) He also said, "Your attitude is one of incredible arrogance . . . . I think you're really expressing the type of attitude that is really at the core of the problem of the NIH. And you're not open to criticism . . . . Even if that criticism is valid. You simply dismiss all criticism as invalid." (*SF* p.386)

Popovic's defense of himself during the OSI investigation continued to provide evidence that Gallo's lab had the rigorous organization of a town dump. According to Crewdson, he told investigators that he had been "working under a great deal of pressure, under very difficult conditions, and without technical support," and he complained that the equipment was of "poor quality." (*SF* p.387) Unfortunately, we now know that the science that came out of that equipment was of the same quality. He complained that the seminal AIDS virus articles in *Science* had been written in his bad English very quickly because of intense pressure from Gallo. (*SF* p.387) And the world would live with the tragic effects of that bad English and that rush job for many decades.

The Office of Scientific Integrity wasn't buying anything Popovic was selling. The committee was especially concerned about a key falsehood in the original *Science* papers which was that the French virus LAV hadn't been growing in the Gallo lab at the time the so-called Gallo virus, HTLV-3, had been discovered. Popovic betrayed the boss by saying that *he* wasn't the one who wrote the offending sentence in the *Science* paper and according to Crewdson, that basically left Gallo as the chief suspect. (*SF* p.389) Popovic had dared to be honest about the matter. He is quoted by Crewdson as telling

OSI, "I am sure that originally I had referenced the LAV in my very rough draft. Even I think I insisted on it. I thought that we should include the LAV data in the paper . . . . Then it was changed in the editing . . . LAV was put to the end of the manuscript, in the end, and I think it was Dr. Gallo's decision not to include LAV." (*SF* p.389)

While this investigation was underway, another scandal broke out in the Gallo lab. Gallo's deputy lab chief, Prem Sarin, had taken money under false pretenses from a company that wanted Gallo's lab to test a potential AIDS drug called AL-721. (*SF* p.390) Sarin, according to Crewdson, was convicted "of embezzlement and making false statements to the NIH" and he "got two months in a halfway house in Baltimore." (*SF* p.391) While he had been under investigation, his fellow financial felon in the Gallo lab, Zaki Salahuddin, had urged Sarin to avoid going to jail by spilling some beans on Gallo, but given Gallo's psychological and professional iron grip on his staff *that* would never happen. (*SF* p.391) It will fall to future historians to determine the nature of the beans that were never spilled and what bearing they might have on the true and complete narrative of the AIDS era.

Peter Stockton, an aide to Congressman John Dingell, was amazed to see Gallo get off while his subordinate was nailed. (*SF* p.399) When Dingell's committee staff interviewed Gallo about his responsibility for all the financial misbehavior in his lab, Stockton, according to Crewdson, said that Gallo excused himself by saying, "'Hey, come on, it's not my job to be doing that kind of thing. I'm a scientist and I'm trying to cure AIDS, and I can't be bothered with this kind of crap.'" (*SF* p.392) And Stockton's committee basically said back to Gallo, according to Crewdson, "Somebody's got to be concerned about this. You just don't turn laboratories over to felons to run wild. You've got to keep some control over what's going on." (*SF* p.392) What Stockton didn't realize was that AIDS research in general had been turned "over to felons to run wild." Gallo was an iconic role model for everyone in that field. He was their Fagin.

The Pasteur Institute eventually published a paper in *Science* that settled the matter genetically and established conclusively that LAV and Gallo's supposed discovery were the same virus and that everything Gallo had said about the matter was a crock. It was the beginning of the end of Gallo at N.C.I. He had embarrassed the whole NIH. (*SF* p.402-403) But with Gallo there was always time for one more scandal and the next one may have been his ugliest one yet because it involved the deaths of human guinea pigs. Gallo had gotten involved with French researcher named Daniel Zagury in a research project that involved testing experimental vaccines on Africans. And not just any Africans—the test subjects were children. In the course on testing the vaccine, there were three deaths. Gallo and "Zagury had failed to mention that in the report on the vaccine." (*SF* p.406)

One of the most fascinating revelations in Crewdson's book is the fact that while using LAV in his experiments, Popovic was so afraid that Gallo might screw the French that he had given his sister in Czechoslovakia "the early drafts of the *Science* article for safe keeping" because, according to Popovic, "I believed that sometimes in the future I might need them as evidence to prove that I gave fair credit to Dr. Montagnier's group." (*SF* p.411) According to Crewdson, "the hidden manuscripts suggest that Gallo was guilty for his rewriting of Popovic's paper." (*SF* p.411) Popovic clearly knew all too well what Gallo was capable of.

The OSI report which was drafted by Suzanne Hadley stated that both Gallo and Popovic were guilty of scientific misconduct. (*SF* p.414) But when the higher ups saw it, they balked and *wanted the guilty verdict against Gallo erased.* (*SF* p.414) Gallo once again ducked the bullet. But Gallo didn't go completely unscathed. According to Crewdson, the OSI report "said that Gallo's behavior 'had fallen well short of the conduct required by a responsible senior scientist and laboratory chief.' Gallo had 'acquiesced in Dr. Popovic's wrong doing.' He 'may even have tacitly encouraged, and at a minimum, he did not discourage, the conditions that fostered the misconduct.'" (*SF* p.418) What was actually fostered in those conditions was far worse than anyone could have imagined.

Suzanne Hadley, according to Crewdson, felt that the conclusions of OSI supported the perception that Gallo had lied under oath during the dispute with the French over the AIDS virus patent. (*SF* p.419) She was upset when her superior, NIH Director Bernadine Healy, wanted her to rewrite her report. (*SF* p.420) She asked Healy to make the request for a change in writing and warned that it would compromise "the OSI independence from NIH." (*SF* p.420) Healy then backed down. But Hadley would pay a price for standing up to her boss. She was told she was being "reined in" and would make no more "decisions in the Gallo case." (*SF* p.421) Crewdson notes that previous to her involvement with the Gallo case, Hadley "had been one of the NIH's rising stars." (*SF* p.420) But given her perception of Healy's power and temperament, Hadley completely withdrew from OSI's Gallo case, saying, according to Crewdson, "The hell with it, I just want to get rid of it. I don't need this shit anymore. . . . I never wanted anything out of this . . . except to do it right. But I certainly never wanted to get just absolutely destroyed. I would have been demolished by Bernadine. She absolutely would have destroyed me." (*SF* p.422) That's what happens in abnormal, totalitarian, and sociopathic science in general when one tries to tell the truth or do the right thing.

When the OSI report was released, Gallo got the kind of cover he often received from an uncritical press. According to Crewdson, "The Associated Press declared Gallo's vindication," and said nothing about the Popovic misconduct verdict. (*SF* p.422) Crewdson reports that all that Healy did to Gallo was issue a directive ordering him to "'familiarize himself with all HHS and NIH regulations relevant to his job, including standards of conduct for federal employees and the rules governing medical experiments on human subjects.'"(*SF* p.423) Gallo was also, according to Crewdson, ordered "to review 'all primary data' produced by any scientist under his supervision before the data was submitted for publication, and to ensure that his assistants maintained 'written laboratory notebooks and records sufficient to permit scientific peers and supervisors to adequately interpret and duplicate the work.'" (*SF* p.424) If such rules had been in place for Gallo—and followed—*before* he got his mitts on AIDS research, HIV may never have become the central fraud of "Holocaust II."

Gallo decided to set the record "straight" in his inimitable style by writing a book called *Virus Hunting*, which was as flattering to himself as one would expect, and according to Crewdson, was a project in which he didn't even get Montagnier's first name correct. (*SF* p.429) According to Crewdson, "Buttressed by scant documentation, Gallo's book was drawn mainly from his own recollections and those of his staff. Perhaps for that reason, it frequently left the impression that some insight or discovery occurred sooner than it did." (*SF* p.429) It was interesting that according to Crewdson's account at least one member of the French team seemed to also be capable of playing the kind of games that Gallo played. Crewdson writes that "a preface by Jean-Claude Chermann recounting the discovery of LAV . . . read as though Chermann had done it single-handedly." (*SF* p.430) One begins to wonder if any leading scientist during the AIDS era got enough love and attention as a child.

According to Crewdson, when the OSI report came out, the "publicity in Paris" inspired the Pasteur Institute to consider "the possibility that the 1987 agreement [with Gallo] would have to be renegotiated." (*SF* p.430)

Looking back on her work on the Gallo OSI investigation, Suzanne Hadley, according to Crewdson, was most "dismayed" by her failure "to get an early handle on the full compass of the case—to see how some of the entries in Mika Popovic's notes, or some of the phrases in his *Science* article, while seemingly disconnected might have implications in a larger context for the patent, the blood test, the veracity of the Reagan administration, and the settlement with the French." (*SF* p.434) Crewdson reports that she said, "It was so much bigger than we imagined. Once I began to get my wits together, it was too late." (*SF* p.434) Crewdson summed up the dilemma: "So broad was the scope of the Gallo case that it seemed ludicrous in retrospect, to have attempted to fit it into the narrow framework of a scientific investigation, which typically focused on the misreporting of an experiment in a published article. Even more than whatever had happened in Gallo's lab, Hadley was appalled by the government's behavior, in and out of court." (*SF* p.434) Hadley told Crewdson, "Whatever one thinks about Gallo . . . he had support all the way up the line. They had data back in 1984 showing they were the same virus . . . There never was an iota of a chance that HHS would do an honest thing. Before anything had even happened, the die was cast, the decision was made. After that it was simply a matter of crafting a litigation strategy." (*SF* p.434) Hadley deserves great honor for doing the right thing but even her intense epiphany about Gallo and the outrageous fraud she was staring at was just scratching the surface. Beneath the mendacities by Gallo and the Reagan administration concerning *who* discovered the so-called AIDS retrovirus lay far more catastrophic secrets and lies that would ultimately blossom into a world of HHV-6-related immune dysfunction.

When the scientific community saw the watered down OSI report—which Crewdson described as almost completely changed from the Suzanne Hadley version (*SF* p.436)—with its main misconduct charge focused on Popovic, and Gallo once again ducking the main bullet—many were horrified. But *The Washington Post*, once again played the role of Gallo enabler and declared Gallo vindicated. (*SF* p.436) One scientist, Gene Myers, when he heard Gallo was still not willing to admit that his discovery was actually the French retrovirus, is quoted by Crewdson as comparing Gallo to Dostoyevsky's Karamazov. (*SF* p.436)

When Bernadine Healy met with the panel that was overseeing the final watered-down OSI report, one of the members described what she said to them and it was chilling and ironic. Crewdson quotes Alfred Gillman's account of Healy's remarks: "What she wanted to know . . . is does Gallo have no redeeming qualities at all? Is this guy the scum of the earth? Or is there a spark of genius there that ought to be nourished? Or is he mentally ill?" (*SF* p.438) One can reasonably guess that the victims of "Holocaust II," voting from their graves, would probably vote "no" on redeeming qualities, "yes" on scum of the earth, "not so much" on spark of genius and "absolutely yes" on mentally ill.

While *The Washington Post* bent over backwards to help Gallo, ABC's Sam Donaldson went in the other direction when he took up the story. Donaldson's TV report began, "It may be the greatest scientific fraud of the twentieth century." He also warned that "important elements of the United States government seem reluctant to have all the facts revealed." (*SF* p.442) If he only knew. Donaldson was just one more reporter who didn't see the even more important issue lurking beneath the surface of the LAV story.

One of the most disturbing moments in the government's peculiar protection of Gallo, and one that should be pondered and investigated by historians of "Holocaust II" for many decades to come happened when Congressman John Dingell's office began their investigation of the Gallo affair. Dingell brought the beleaguered Suzanne Hadley into his congressional investigation of Gallo because she knew where all the Gallo bodies were buried. But when the committee requested the files from the preceding OSI investigation she herself had conducted, it turned out that notebooks from the investigation *had been shredded by Hadley's replacement at OSI*. (*SF* p.461) Gallo was a cat with more than nine lives. Abnormal and totalitarian science had abnormal and totalitarian oversight.

For anyone who believes that some kind of bizarre group psychosis characterized the whole enterprise of AIDS research, it is of interest that when Peter Stockton talked to famous Nobel Prize winning scientist James Watson during this period about Gallo, according to his account in Crewdson's book, Watson's "big point was that Gallo is a manic depressive. He thinks the subcommittee should back down because Gallo's crazy. He thinks we should talk to Gallo's shrink." (*SF* p.473) One could say that to comprehend all the pseudoscientific underpinnings of AIDS or "Holocaust II" one must talk to Gallo's shrink.

As could be expected in the arbitrary and opposite world of AIDS science, OSI itself was changed into the Office of Research Integrity and the rules were changed even while the Gallo investigation was ongoing—just like the rules of science were altered by bogus AIDS research. Instead of simply finding scientists guilty of publishing fabricated scientific results, under the new rules the committee had to show that the scientists who was charged *had intended to do so*. (*SF* p.466-475) That ridiculous new standard made it nearly impossible to find any scientist guilty because, according to Crewdson, the scientist "could simply claim he hadn't intended to deceive anybody." (*SF* p.454) Gallo's most powerful Guardian Angel had arrived on the scene in the form of this crazy new rule. Another dark legacy of AIDS and "Holocaust II" would be that the government's process of trying to defend Gallo would make it easier for *all* American scientists to commit fraud and get away with it. Gallo was truly an historic figure in that he paved the way for many more years of plausibly deniable scientific fraud. It is a breathtaking legacy.

Even with the rules of evidence loosened in Gallo's favor, he continued to behave like a cornered Mafioso as he told scientists who were expected to testify before the new committee that if they testified it might not turn out too well for them. (*SF* p.499) He told one scientist that he might "spill the beans on him." (*SF* p.480) Gallo was a virtual Boston of spillable beans.

The final OSI report on the Gallo affair was basically a whitewash, a true-blue cover-up. Suzanne Hadley described it as a "version of history" that "parroted the government's arguments years before in defense of the blood-test patent." (*SF* p.503) She told Crewdson, "There's too much pseudoscience in the opinion. They got it from somewhere." (*SF* p.503) Again, what Hadley didn't grasp was how catastrophically deep the pseudoscience laid out before her was.

When an appeals board reversed the verdict of the ORI, Gallo was elated. According to Crewdson, Gallo said, "I will now be able to redouble efforts in the fight against AIDS and cancers. There are several hopeful new avenues of AIDS research that my laboratory is pursuing." (*SF* p.505) The business of "Holocaust II" could continue in earnest. *The New York Times* reporter, Nicholas Wade, one of the AIDS paradigm's truest believers, wrote that Gallo was "the one scientific hero who has yet emerged in the fight against

AIDS." (*SF* p.505) With heroes like that, gays, blacks and anyone suffering on the HHV-6 spectrum illnesses didn't need enemies.

But John Dingell wasn't done with Gallo. His staff attempted to get prosecutors to charge Gallo and Popovic with making false statements under oath, but between complications involving the statute of limitations for the crime and problems of involving the jurisdiction the crimes took place in, that never happened. (*SF* p.510) Bullet ducked again.

All of this mishegas took its toll on Gallo's new boss, Sam Broder, who had succeeded Vincent DeVita. According to Crewdson, "Since replacing Vince DeVita, Sam Broder had defended and protected Gallo. Now there were indications Broder, like DeVita before him, was growing disillusioned. Reportedly, horrified by Daniel Zagury's use of Zairian children in his AIDS vaccine research, Broder had ordered Gallo's name removed from the pending HHS patent on Zagury's vaccine. When Suzanne Hadley showed Broder Gallo's outrageous statement that the patent had been initiated by Broder himself, Broder exploded, He said, 'That's bullshit!' Hadley recalled." As if that wasn't enough, according to Crewdson, Hadley used the same meeting with Broder to tell him that her investigation "had turned up evidence that several of Gallo's subsequent articles also contained false statements." (*SF* p.514) Hadley told Broder about a paper Gallo published in 1985 which contained false statements about the AIDS virus isolates he had in 1982. According to Crewdson, "The paper was a political exercise, a pollution of the scientific literature intended to help lay the groundwork for a defense against the French." (*SF* p.515) Crewdson reports that Sam Broder told Gallo that if he didn't retire he would order a new NCI investigation of him. (*SF* p.515) Suzanne Hadley is quoted by Crewdson as remembering that Broder said to her, "I told Bob, 'You've degraded the institute, you've degraded the public and you've degraded reporters by lying to them. . . .We owe things to the people of another time. They need to know what things were really like during the era of AIDS research.' One of Bob's biggest sins is his overdriven compulsion to claim all the credit and to trace it all to his great intellect." (*SF* p.515) As true as Broder's words were, he was still missing the sin beneath the sin, not the sin of stealing credit, but the sin of egotistically leading the world down a deadly misbegotten path, manipulating science and the public into thinking he had delivered the truth about AIDS to the world. And as far as *that* sin was concerned, Broder himself was joined at the hip with Gallo.

As quoted by Crewdson, something else Hadley remembered Broder saying sizzles with irony: "He was confused out of his mind. Bob was so thoroughly wrong. The AIDS virus had to fit the retroviruses as he knew them, and he was wrong. He needed to listen to his data, and he did not want to do that . . . Bob writes all these historical things that have no relationship to the way it really was. I told Bob, 'I have not forgiven you for this. People are dying of real diseases, and this is not a game.' . . . Frankly Suzanne, it was

541

a Nobel Prize run. You guys don't talk about that, but I was there, and I know. And frankly he almost got it. And if he had gotten it, he would have been truly invincible." (*SF* p.516) Where to begin? Well, first of all, Gallo's word of choice for the people this science involved, at least on occasion (as reported by *New York Native*), was "fag" which may have had a little something to do with the level of moral seriousness with which Gallo dealt with the AIDS issue. Second of all, who is Broder to talk? He was the scientific genius behind the aggressive pushing of AZT into the bodies of AIDS patients, something akin to pouring gasoline on a fire.

In 1994 there was a revised settlement with the French which Crewdson described as "a clear victory for the French." (*SF* p.585) Suzanne Hadley, working for the Dingell Committee, wrote a 267-page account of the whole matter that according to Crewdson "spared no one" in assigning culpability "starting with the Department of Health and Human Services." (*SF* p.526) Crewdson writes that the report said that "HHS did its best to cover up the wrongdoing" and "meanwhile the failure of the entire scientific establishment to take any meaningful action left the disposition of scientific truth to bureaucrats and lawyers, with neither the expertise nor the will essential to the task. Because of the continuing HHS cover-up it was not until the Subcommittee investigation that the true facts were known, and the breadth and depth of the cover-up was revealed. . . . One of the most remarkable and regrettable aspects of the institutional response to the defense of *Gallo et. al.* is how readily public service and science apparently were subverted into defending the indefensible." (*SF* p.527) As profound and disturbing as the report was, it was naively focused on only the tail of a far bigger unseen monster, namely the "HIV-is-the-cause-of-AIDS" mistake itself and the entrenched world of abnormal, totalitarian, and sociopathic science that it represented. The report was clueless about the psychotic and deeply biased paradigm at the very center of "Holocaust II." It was commendable for Dingell, Hadley, and Stockton to nail Gallo on the viral theft from the French, but relatively speaking, it was, in essence, a successful prosecution of a misdemeanor that missed the exponentially more important underlying medical and scientific crime against mankind.

To say that Gallo landed on his feet after this disgrace is an understatement. When he left NCI, he had to rough it at the brand new, built-just-for-him, multi-million-dollar research Institute of Human Virology in Baltimore financed by the state of Maryland. And as one could expect in the opposite world of Robert Gallo, one of the people he invited to come work for him at the spiffy new institute was the paragon of great science, Mika Popovic, a man who will probably take some of Gallo's juiciest secrets to the grave with him. Gallo's ability to either discover things or steal them, depending upon how you looked at his career, seems to have diminished in Baltimore. According to Crewdson, "During its first five years of life the Institute for Human Virology hadn't come up with any marketable discoveries." (*SF* p.537) AIDS patients were clearly safer with Gallo out of NCI and eating crab cakes in Baltimore.

Near the end of his account of the Gallo affair, Crewdson writes his most chilling sentence: "The Popovic-Gallo Science paper, among the most-cited scientific articles of all time, is laden with untruths that have never been retracted or corrected." (*SF* p.539) In other words, the very foundation of "Holocaust II" is laden with untruths that "have never been retracted or corrected." Every living scientist and doctor should hang their head in shame. They are the apathetic, compliant "ordinary Germans" of this period in history. And anyone who describes *Science* as a prestigious publication worthy of any kind of reverence at all should put on a pair of clown shoes.

Crewdson closes his awesome dissection of Gallo's misdeeds and character on a philosophical note: "Being wrong in science is hardly a sin. Scientists are wrong every day, and their mistakes are what pushes science forward. What set Gallo apart, was his profound disinclination to acknowledge his mistakes, preferring instead to ignore them, insist they hadn't occurred, blame someone else, or propagate outlandish explanations and outright fictions that only confused science further and slowed its forward march . . . . In the end, the most compelling question was one only Gallo could answer: Had he somehow convinced himself that all the lies were true? Or had he known better all along?" (*SF* p.540) Actually, a more fundamental and philosophical questions would be whether Gallo was capable of honestly answering that question or even understanding it. Was Gallo a true sociopath? And that leads to the larger historical question about the degree to which a kind of enabling group psychosis and sociopathology went way beyond Gallo and underwrote all of "Holocaust II." It may have taken a whole psychotic village to empower a Gallo.

While the world owes journalistic genius John Crewdson a debt of gratitude for laying bare the mind-numbing complexities of Gallo's scientific fraud regarding the discovery of the so-called AIDS virus, the larger story that Crewdson missed, the one he failed to see beneath all the masks that he successfully did rip off, was the game-changing story that the so-called stolen AIDS virus *wasn't even the cause of AIDS*. While Crewdson was writing his masterpiece, which was ultimately published in 2002, evidence was accumulating that the other virus that Gallo claimed to have discovered, HHV-6, actually *did play a major role in AIDS*. In fact, *the* major role. The virus was not an unimportant pathogen as portrayed by Crewdson in *Science Fictions*.

The *New York Native,* the little gay newspaper that pioneered the Gallo story even before Crewdson got to it, followed the HHV-6 trail that led to a far bigger and more disturbing story about AIDS than just Gallo's appropriation of LAV. While covering HHV-6, the *New York Native* broke one of the biggest AIDS stories of all, the breakout of acquired immune deficiency in the general population which the CDC and the NIH hid behind the ridiculous euphemism of "chronic fatigue syndrome." The *New York*

543

Native's reporter, Neenyah Ostrom covered chronic fatigue syndrome, AIDS and their relationship to HHV-6 from 1988 until the paper went out of business at the beginning of 1997.

The parent company of *New York Native* published three books on Ostrom's reporting about the relationship between HHV-6, AIDS and chronic fatigue syndrome. The first book, *What Really Killed Gilda Radner? Frontline Reports on the Chronic Fatigue Syndrome Epidemic*, was published in 1991. In the book's introduction, Ostrom wrote "For whatever reasons—like reluctance to admit the presence of another AIDS-like epidemic sweeping the nation in the shadow of (and linked to) the official AIDS epidemic, simple incompetence, or more sinister reasons—health authorities have tried to deny the very existence of the chronic fatigue syndrome epidemic in the U.S., have tried to prove that the illness of immune dysfunction is caused by 'psychoneurosis,' [and] have delayed for years determining how many cases actually exist in the country . . . ." (*WRKGR* p. 10) The next Ostrom book, *50 Things You Should Know About the Chronic Fatigue Syndrome Epidemic* was published in 1992. In its introduction, she wrote, "America is facing a health crisis of unprecedented proportions, a crisis that has been misleadingly labeled chronic fatigue syndrome. This health crisis has been bungled by government health officials from the very beginning: It has been ignored, misrepresented, and investigated ineptly until, as I write this in January, 1992, untold millions of Americans already have contracted this potentially disabling, AIDS-like illness. . . . CFS is clearly an AIDS-related illness that puts the entire population at risk." (p.13-14) The final Ostrom book, *America's Biggest Cover-up*, which was published in 1994, was even more uncompromising in its conclusions. Ostrom attempted to explain why officials refused to admit a link between AIDS and chronic fatigue syndrome: "AIDS patients, and people who test HIV-positive (whatever that actually turns out to mean), have been so badly treated, so discriminated against, so scapegoated and demonized that it is not surprising that there is an almost reflexive recoiling from the possibility that AIDS is not the narrowly-defined illness that it has been portrayed as being." (*ABC* xvi) She asserted that "Until the denial among medical professionals about the relationship between the AIDS and chronic fatigue syndrome epidemics is overcome, however, it is difficult to imagine how either epidemic can be ended." (*ABC* xvi) Had John Crewdson not just taken the lead on Gallos's theft of HIV from *New York Native*, but also followed the trail of Ostrom's reporting on chronic fatigue syndrome and HHV-6, he might have broken a bigger and far more important story.

Two years before Crewdson's book on Gallo hit the bookstores, Nicholas Regush's book on HHV-6, *The Virus Within: A Coming Epidemic* was published. Regush had been a reporter for the *Montreal Gazette* as well as an award-winning and Emmy-nominated medical and science journalist at ABC News, where he produced segments for World News Tonight with Peter

Jennings. Regush's book covers the history of HHV-6 from its discovery through a succession of shocking discoveries made by two researchers at the University of Wisconsin, Konnie Knox and Donald Carrigan. Regush's picture of HHV-6 bears little resemblance to the failed Gallo co-factor of Crewdson's book.

The HHV-6 story that emerges from Regush's book should have made the scientific community's collective head spin. In a series of experiments on a variety of patients, the two relatively young Wisconsin researchers showed, without even fully admitting it or shouting it out to the world, that *HHV-6 was the real villain in AIDS*. They showed that HHV-6 is capable of wreaking havoc in both the central nervous system (*TVW* p.9) and the immune system itself. Prior research by R.G. Downing had shown that HHV-6 was capable of destroying T-cells (curiously, the only so-called herpes virus to do so) which was something that the AIDS establishment insisted on blaming HIV alone for doing indirectly even though HHV-6 destroyed the cells dramatically, directly and unambiguously. As Regush pointed out, "Here was a herpes virus that could destroy T-4 lymphocytes at least in the test tube more powerfully than HIV." (*TVW* p.54) Had Crewdson dug deeper on the HHV-6 story, he would have learned that there are supposedly two strains of HHV-6, an A and a B strain. And he would have found out that HHV-6A was indeed starting to look more and more like the significant co-factor in AIDS or even more surprisingly, like *the chief viral culprit itself*. Gallo wasn't lying about the power of HHV-6. According to Regush, "In November 1993, Robert Gallo's lab published data gleaned from autopsies of five people who had died of AIDS, demonstrating an abundance of HHV-6 infection. Footprints of the virus were found in areas such as the cerebral cortex, brain stem, cerebellum, spinal cord, tonsils, lymph nodes, spleen, bone marrow, salivary glands, esophagus, bronchial tree, lung, skeletal muscle, myocardium, aorta, liver, kidney, adrenal glands, pancreas and thyroid." (*TVW* p.84) If anything, Gallo was underestimating the power of HHV-6 in order to keep his beloved stolen virus HIV alive. Ironically, one of the reasons Gallo didn't do more work on HHV-6 during the 80s was because he was busy fending off investigations from Congress and journalists like Crewdson (and pesky newspapers like *New York Native*.)

One of the early HHV-6 research projects conducted by the Wisconsin researchers showed that HHV-6 is a major lung pathogen in AIDS, a fact that tragically had been largely ignored in the treatment of AIDS. And one of the most important findings on HHV-6 that could have an impact on everyone's health was Carrigan and Knox's determination that "Direct infection of the [bone] marrow by HHV-6" was possible (*TVW* p.62) According to Regush, their research showed "that HHV-6 could infect—and suppress—bone-marrow cells." (*TVW* p.64)

While Konnie Knox was focusing on HHV-6's relationship to HIV, her research actually began the shocking process of pulling the rug out from under HIV itself. Her work with Carrigan showed that HHV-6 could also seriously dysregulate monocytes and macrophages, making it a very creative and dangerous *AIDSish* pathogen. (*TVW* p.68) She made HHV-6 the subject of her doctoral thesis and Regush reports that she wondered if she was "throwing herself into the hurly burly of Big Science politics." (*TVW* p.69) Actually, she was throwing herself into the hurly burly of Big Abnormal, Totalitarian, and Sociopathic Science politics.

Knox started sealing the deal for HHV-6's role in AIDS when she studied tissue samples of a group of people who had died of AIDS. According to Regush, "The results of her experiments gave her a jolt: all 34 tissue samples of lung, lymph node, liver kidney and spleen revealed that at the time of death there was active HHV-6 infection as opposed to merely a biological sign that the virus was 'latent' (embedded in tissue)." (*TVW* p.83) Her experiment also showed that one of the big AIDS showstoppers, CMV, wasn't even as important because she found it active in only nine of the 34 tissue samples. (*TVW* p.84) Most alarmingly in terms of the way lung issues had been treated in AIDS was the fact that she found evidence in some of the patients that HHV-6 was probably responsible for the destruction of the lungs. (*TVW* p.84)

Knox, not knowing the real nature of AIDS politics, told Regush that she was "amazed that so little HHV-6 research had actually been done on AIDS patients . . . . It didn't make much sense." (*TVW* p.85) She was another scientist who had found her way into HIV/AIDS Wonderland. She didn't have the right compass for the science of opposite world or the nasty retroviral and heterosexist (and racist) politics that had laid its foundation.

The profile of HHV-6 as a virus capable of destroying the immune system was dramatically increased when, according to Regush, "various labs exposed HHV-6 as" capable of targeting T-8 cells and when scientists at the National Cancer Institute showed that "HHV-6 infects and kills natural-killer cells. These are the immune cells that destroy abnormal cells in the body, particularly those that are infected by viruses. HHV-6 is the first virus known to be capable of targeting and seriously damaging such a vital element of the immune system's antiviral defenses." (*TVW* p. 87) (The fact HHV-6 was capable of killing natural-killer cells should have alerted the whole scientific community to the link between AIDS and chronic fatigue syndrome which are both low natural-killer cell syndromes. It should have also raised the question of whether HHV-6 should be in a different viral category. It increasingly seemed *sui generis*.)

Knox found that HHV-6 "could cause major damage during the early development of AIDS," (*TVW* p.89) *and didn't need HIV to do it*. According to Regush, "Her autopsy-tissue study had already shown that macrophages were often depleted in the lungs of HIV-infected AIDS patients," and she was determined "to know how HHV-6 was capable of knocking out those cells . . . . Her tests showed that, besides destroying macrophages, HHV-6 interfered with the normal functioning of the scavenger cells by blocking the release of a type of oxidant, a substance that cells normally generate to attack microbes. Knox noted that HIV was not known to be capable of this specific type of action." (*TVW* p.95) She concluded that HHV-6 had the potential to destroy the macrophages in the lungs *without HIV*, a totally sacrilegious idea in the abnormal science of AIDS. According to Regush, she dared to wonder heretically if HIV was "doing any killing in the body, or was HHV-6 the lone assassin?" (*TVW* p.96)

Knox also found that HHV-6 was capable of causing brain infection or encephalitis without any signs that HIV was involved. (*TVW* p.97) And the same no-show behavior on the part of HIV occurred in the case of the bone marrow in AIDS: "Knox's lab studies demonstrated that HHV-6-infected marrow cells—not the HIV infected ones—blocked the ability of the marrow to produce mature, differentiated cells." (*TVW* p.97) The same scenario was manifest when she looked at the brain damage in AIDS patients. Regush writes, "When Knox studied the brains of six people who died of AIDS and found extensive damage in four to their nerve fiber sheathes she also detected active HHV-6 infection. The infected cells were only in areas where the damage had occurred and never unhealthy tissue. The damaged tissue tested negative for signs of HIV, CMV, and other microbes. Again, there was only HHV-6." (*TVW* p.101) According to Regush, all of this inspired the very dangerous doubt in Carrigan and Knox about whether "HIV was even necessary for AIDS to occur." (*TVW* p.101)

The pièce de résistance of the Knox and Carrigan research involved the lymph nodes of AIDS patients. According to Regush, "the development of AIDS has largely been viewed as a progressive destruction of the networks of lymphocytes and fibers known as the lymphoid tissue. AIDS scientists, however, have been unable to associate the presence of HIV in the lymph nodes with any damage to the tissue." (*TVW* p.98) While the conventional wisdom was that HIV was hiding in the lymph nodes and destroying them, what Knox and Carrigan found turned the conventional wisdom upside down. In perhaps their most important study they found that "16 lymph-node biopsies from HIV-positive patients all contained cells actively infected with HHV-6A. Twelve of 16 patients who had been diagnosed with progressive disease had more dense infection that the four patients who had been diagnosed as having a stable condition. Knox and Carrigan also found more dense infection in areas where the lymph nodes were losing lymphocytes than in areas free of destructive change or where normal tissue in the nodes was already being replaced by the formation of scar tissue. HHV-6 was the apparent cause of the destruction of lymphoid tissue that occurred in these HIV positive people." (*TVW* p.114) Regush didn't mince words about the implications: "HHV-6 was not only at the scene of the crime, but it appears to have committed the crime as well." (*TVW* p.114) Regush describes Knox and Carrigan as wondering if they had found a "smoking

547

gun" because "there were no convincing studies demonstrating that HIV could cause similar pathology." (*TVW* p.114) They submitted their research to *The Lancet*, but as could be expected, it was not accepted. It was ever thus during "Holocaust II."

In the world of Kuhnian normal science Carrigan and Knox would have had their Nobel Prizes by now for showing that HHV-6 was the real AIDS virus and was even more important than just that as other research began to connect it to many other diseases that would turn out to be part of an HHV-6 spectrum of disorders. But not in the opposite world of abnormal, totalitarian, and sociopathic science that was dominated by the heterosexist and racist HIV/AIDS paradigm. HHV-6 threatened the whole epidemiological house of cards the CDC and the NIH had presented to the world. Good luck to future HHV-6 scientists and historians all over the world when they try to put Humpty Dumpty back together again.

In an interview with Robert Gallo, Regush asked him about Knox and Carrigan. Regush reported, "Gallo spoke very generously about what Knox and Carrigan had accomplished, but he also emphasized that they work in too much obscurity to obtain any funding. 'They have clearly shown that HHV-6 is a powerful pathogen,' Gallo said. 'If they were headliners at a major university, it would make a huge difference.'" (*TVW* p.223) How two scientists who were essentially doing a controlled demolition on the HIV/AIDS paradigm could ever even hope to be allowed positions of prominence in a scientific world dominated by disingenuous scoundrels like Gallo requires a huge stretch of the imagination. As Regush concluded, their research "suggests that HIV may not always be necessary as a companion to HHV-6 when the herpes virus is destroying tissue. But even suggesting that in writing would raise the hackles of HIV researchers. In fact, some AIDS scientists compare any questioning of the HIV hypothesis as it currently stands, to denial of the Holocaust. With such emotions running strong in AIDS science, why take a chance of boldly presenting alternative hypotheses?" (*TVW* p.224) Unfortunately for the world, Regush reported that Knox and Carrigan didn't have the stomach to go more public with their story or to join forces with the AIDS critics and dissidents: "Knox and Carrigan, while aware of the issues, want no active part of this often hostile debate." (TVW p.224)

It was very unfortunate that the brilliant, tireless John Crewdson never found his way into this shocking HHV-6 part of the AIDS story. His exposé of Gallo and the purloined retrovirus had caught the eye of the NIH's investigative body and Congress itself. Had Crewdson found his way to the Knox and Carrigan laboratory at the University of Wisconsin and done the same kind of Pit Bull due diligence on the primary role of HHV-6 in AIDS, he might have helped bring "Holocaust II" to an early end and everything would have been different for people on the HHV-6 spectrum. And knowing how Gallo had stolen HIV, Crewdson might have eventually looked into the allegations that he also stole credit for discovering HHV-6, which is another story. And just as creepy.

The Four Doctors of the Chronic Fatigue Syndrome Apocalypse

How the Bigotry and Incompetence of Four Scientists at the Centers for Disease Control Helped Create the Chronic Fatigue Syndrome Disaster

Introduction

During the last several decades, I have known four remarkable women with a serious illness that has been given the extremely deceptive diagnostic label of "Chronic Fatigue Syndrome." Three of the women are still "living" with the illness. "Living" with Chronic Fatigue Syndrome generally means facing a cascade of disturbing medical events that leave them in a constant state of dread about what will happen next. One of the women was so incapacitated that she had to travel around on a motorized scooter and she was killed when she was hit by a truck on her way back from the grocery store. Chronic Fatigue Syndrome is such a hellish disease that there are those with the illness who would sardonically say that she is one of the lucky ones. All four of the women had very promising futures ahead of them. They outclass me in so many ways that they probably would not even give me the time of the day had they not been stricken with Chronic Fatigue Syndrome and met me because of my interest in the subject.

I was the publisher of a newspaper that is credited with doing the first major reporting on the AIDS epidemic. My newspaper, *New York Native*, was a relatively new gay publication in New York City when I got a phone call about a strange pneumonia affecting gay men in New York City. I asked a doctor to investigate and he wrote a story in which the New York City health authorities said that the rumors were unfounded. Several weeks later, that all changed when a *New York Times* story appeared in which the CDC confirmed that indeed, a strange illness seemed to have broken out in the gay community. I detail my newspaper's coverage of the emerging epidemic in my book *The Chronic Fatigue Syndrome Epidemic Cover-up.*

The early reporting in my newspaper is almost universally praised. In *Rolling Stone*, David Black said that the paper deserved a Pulitzer prize. Also in *Rolling Stone*, Katie Leishman wrote, "It is undeniable that many major stories were Ortleb's months and sometimes years before mainstream journalists took them up." In his bestseller, *And the Band Played On*, Randy Shilts wrote, "Because of the extraordinary reporting of the *New York Native*, the city's gay community had been exposed to far more information about AIDS than San Francisco in 1981and 1982."

But the love affair with *New York Native* quickly fizzled out as my newspaper dug deeper into the story. Our early reporting was fairly straightforward and, in retrospect, typical of most medical and scientific reporting then and now. It basically translated semi-arcane information provided by government and establishment officials for a lay public. It was not particularly skeptical. As time went on, our reporting became more investigative and we began to notice serious problems with the competence and honesty of scientists at the Centers for Disease Control and the National Institutes of Health. It didn't help when I learned that one of the top AIDS researchers referred to gays as "faggots." When I learned that particular scientist and his close colleague at Harvard were both considered to be crooks by serious scientists in Europe, all bets were off.

One of the transformative moments for me and *New York Native* occurred when one of my readers sent me a clipping of a curious article in the March 25, 1986 issue of the *Los Angeles Examiner* by Ben Stein. In *Truth to Power*, I reported, "Stein wrote that it seemed to him that everyone in Los Angeles seemed to be sick at the time. People would develop a flu which lasted two weeks and then they would recover. But then a few weeks later they would get sick again. He described 'a vague, spaced-out feeling, chronic fatigue just over your shoulder, always breathing down on you, a susceptibility to wild upsets of the bowels all became part of daily life.' Stein complained that even though an incurable flu seemed to be spreading throughout Los Angeles, no one was doing anything about it. Public health officials were silent. Stein also wrote, 'Already my friends in the East tell me the non-stop flu has hit Washington and New York in a big way. This nation can be genuinely disabled by these incurable diseases. The individuals who have them are severely pained, physically and psychically. Having the flu half your life hurts, take it from me. Can anyone help? Isn't this worthy of national attention? Are we just going to have the stock market go up forever while everyone gets incurable viruses? I'm scared.'"

That mysterious flu, of course, turned out to be Chronic Fatigue Syndrome. It gradually became clear as day to me that this was the part of the AIDS epidemic that the Centers for Disease Control did not want the general public to know about because it would suggest that the CDC did not know what it was doing and the real epidemic could cause mass panic. (It has become evident over the last four decades that controlling panic is part of what most top public health officials would describe as a major part of their job description.) The idea that Chronic Fatigue Syndrome was another face of the AIDS epidemic became solidified when Hillary Johnson penned a two-part series on what would turn out to be Chronic Fatigue Syndrome in *Rolling Stone* in the summer of 1987. I had a total sense of "Eureka" when I read her articles and didn't rest until I tracked her down and shared idea that AIDS and Chronic Fatigue Syndrome were Tweedledum and Tweedledee, linked together not by HIV, but rather by a virus called HHV-6 which had the misfortune of being discovered in AIDS and Chronic Fatigue Syndrome patients after the book had been closed on the HIV theory of AIDS.

One of the most controversial series of stories that my newspaper broke involved our coverage of a distinguished scientist, Peter Duesberg, who raised serious questions about the HIV theory of AIDS. I ran stories about Duesberg numerous times on the cover of *New York Native*. You could say that Duesberg was the kid who said the Emperor had no clothes on, but this kid had a "genius grant" from the National Institutes of Health and was considered to be doing Nobel caliber work. As I watched Duesberg's critique suffer the slings and arrows of the powerful and corrupt scientific establishment, I began to fully understand how political science is in general, and how sinister the politics of AIDS are in particular. While I don't agree with everything Duesberg has to say about AIDS, I try to give his critique of HIV the respect it deserves in my book, *The Duesbergians*. And the political attacks on Duesberg are part of the inspiration for my book *Iatrogenocide: Notes for a Political Philosophy of Science and Epidemiology*.

The more my newspaper covered the connection between AIDS and Chronic Fatigue Syndrome and the HHV-6 challenge to the HIV theory of AIDS, the more controversial it became. One Nobel Laureate let me know what the scientific community thought of *New York Native* when he said to me on the phone, "If it's in your newspaper I know it's not true." And it wasn't just the AIDS medical and scientific establishment that wanted us to shut up. The AIDS activist group, Act Up, which posed as a revolutionary group demanding more funding for AIDS research, turned out to be just a de facto street mob arm of the AIDS establishment. Their supposed activism and angry performance art were essentially premised on the government's AIDS paradigm. I got a taste of what they were really up to when Peter Duesberg was about to share his ideas about with a Presidential committee in the 80s and Act Up members stood up to boo him. They were not only out to silence Duesberg. Eventually they voted to boycott my newspaper and they played no small role in the eventual demise of *New York Native*. I refer to the AIDS activists as "the Blackshirts" in my play about the AIDS epidemic, *The Black Party*.

I always held out hope that my newspaper would receive support from the Chronic Fatigue Syndrome community. We made a mark on journalistic history by assigning a writer, Neenyah Ostrom, to cover Chronic Fatigue Syndrome in virtually every issue of my paper starting in 1988. Article after article showed the connections between Chronic Fatigue Syndrome and AIDS. We also published three books by Ostrom, *What Really Killed Gilda Radner?, 50 Things You Should Know about the Chronic Fatigue Syndrome Epidemic,* and *America's Biggest Cover-up*. While we were doing that, the Centers for Disease Control and the so-called AIDS Czar, Anthony Fauci, the Director of the National Institutes of Allergy and Infection Diseases, were refusing to even admit that CFS was a real medical condition, let alone another face of AIDS. With a few notable exceptions, the Chronic Fatigue Syndrome community was not happy about our reporting on the links between AIDS and Chronic Fatigue Syndrome.

In a way, the fact that AIDS has never ceased to be a "gay disease" in the public mind is confirmed by the resistance of the Chronic Fatigue Syndrome community to even discuss the obvious AIDS and CFS connections. I've said on numerous occasions that members of the CFS community would rather die that admit they are in anyway linked to the AIDS epidemic. And, unfortunately, more than a few have. I think I have learned more about the degree to which heterosexism and homophobia are hardwired into our science and culture from the CFS community than I have from any other stories about homophobia that my gay newspaper covered in its fifteen years of publication.

In some ways, because my gay newspaper paper did the world's most extensive coverage of HHV-6, you could say that it became an honorary "gay virus" in the minds of many members of the CFS community. Even if it was destroying every cell in their body (and it clearly was multisystemic) many wanted no part of it. When an intellectual and CFS activist reported that her Ampligen (a CFS drug) treatments seemed to make her better when they were controlling her HHV-6 infection, she was basically ignored by the community. I should point out that many in the community have also evolved into believers that they are not carriers of a contagious *anything*, so that also prevents HHV-6 from being taken seriously. A contagious "gay virus" associated with gay AIDS? OMG! Better to come up with theories of spontaneous CFS combustion than that!

While the CFS community refuses to deal with the evidence-based connection between CFS and AIDS and the reality of highly pathogenic HHV-6 in their beleaguered bodies, a virtual clown car of opportunistic scientists has arrived on the scene. Every few months it seems like some new scientist announces that *he or she alone* is taking CFS seriously and all the previous work is strictly amateur hour. An adult has finally entered the room! The newbie scientist then focuses on some small part of what is clearly a multisystemic disease and seduces the patients into thinking that he or she is on the path to "the truth." One prominent geneticist who entered the field tried to raise awareness about Chronic Fatigue Syndrome by wearing his underwear outside of his clothes. And after two eminent scientists at Columbia University, Mady Hornig and Ian Lipkin, made a dramatic entrance into the field, they helped garner more attention for CFS when according to *The New York Post*, Dr. Hornig alleged that Dr. Lipkin "repeatedly dropped his drawers and demanded she diagnose a lesion on his butt" and "kicked her under the table at meetings to keep her from speaking; presented her work as his own, and kept her from getting tenure."

And, of course, every colorful new Pied Piper leads the patients further and further away from the AIDS and CFS connection and the role of HHV-6, "the gay virus." A kind of medical AIDS/CFS apartheid is maintained that is a fool's paradise full of CFS corpses. And while everyone is not looking, the HHV-6 epidemic gets bigger and bigger and manifests itself in new ways. Just look at autism. (But that is another long story.)

One of the big problems for the CFS issue is that a big streak of authoritarianism runs through the community. There is a great deal of abject bowing and scraping to the government's medical authorities. The constant cry for more research money begs the question of the legitimacy of the recipients of all the research gold. I've often said that CFS needs less money and *more* honesty and forthrightness. The CFS community does not realize that they are victims of a major cover-up which is a biomedical *crime involving deceit*. This is a job for whistleblowers, not hapless activists who think at worse this is a crime of neglect that only requires more money and attention.

And so, we continue to find ourselves in very dark times that are perilous for truth and truthtellers. The real nature of the HHV-6, AIDS, and Chronic Fatigue Syndrome catastrophe is an inconvenient truth. We are now in the third generation of people who are affected by HHV-6. I have written this book in hopes that some members of the new generation will not be blinded by the prejudices that have prevented their parents and grandparents from seeing what is before their very eyes. If scientific clarity and moral courage can't be found, a new generation of HHV-6 and CFS victims will be condemned to a perpetual wild goose chase in a biomedical Tower of Babel.

This little book is a work of reverse-engineering. It takes the reader back to the beginning of the AIDS epidemic to show all the formative parts of the infernal machine that Chronic Fatigue Syndrome patients are trapped in. It all begins with a handful of scientists at the CDC whose incompetence and prejudices built the unmovable AIDS paradigm that now threatens everyone's health. My reverse-engineering of this mess shows that the inexorable Chronic Fatigue Syndrome train wreck originates in the misjudgments involved in the nosology, epidemiology and virology of AIDS.

And it didn't have to happen. In Hillary Johnson's masterful book about Chronic Fatigue Syndrome, *Osler's Web*, there is a discussion of an Atlanta doctor I actually think I may have talked to back in the 80s. In 1984, Richard Dubois reported in a medical journal on cases of what turned out to be Chronic Fatigue Syndrome. According to Johnson, "DuBois had first observed the phenomenon in 1980." (*Osler's Web*, p. 6) An important year for anyone who knows the history of the AIDS epidemic. And he didn't keep it a secret from the Centers for Disease Control. Johnson notes, "Richard DuBois had made a presentation to agency staff on the malady early in 1983, even proposing that the new mono-like syndrome might be a second epidemic of immune dysfunction rising concurrently with AIDS." (*Osler Web*, p. 31)

"Concurrently" is what this writer calls whistling in the dark. Why didn't anyone at the CDC (which is also in Atlanta) consider the real possibility that this other AIDS-like epidemic wasn't just "concurrent" but was yet another presentation of AIDS? Hopefully, by the time the reader finishes this book, the "why" will be painfully obvious.

*

A few definitions and elaborations are in order.

I coined the term "homodemiology" to describe epidemiology that is inherently homophobic and heterosexist. It is epidemiology that is always poised to blame epidemics on gay people. This book does not deal with the racist aspects of the AIDS paradigm. I use the term "Afrodemiology" for that. I have tried to capture the racism of AIDS in my novella, *The Closing Argument.*

To describe the nature of AIDS science, I use the words, abnormal, totalitarian, and sociopathic interchangeably. I use abnormal to capture the dark side of what Thomas Kuhn refers to as "normal" science. Kuhn has played a major role in my thinking about science and it is my little homage to him. "Sociopathic science" is fraudulent, conscienceless science. I explain my concept of "sociopathic science" more fully in my book, *Iatrogenocide: Notes for a Political Philosophy of Science and Epidemiology.*

I often refer to the AIDS epidemic as Holocaust II. While gays were not the primary target in "The Holocaust," they have that dubious honor in Holocaust II.

For more background on HHV-6 go to my site, HHV-6 University.

For more information on the *New York Native* visit New York Native University.

Randy Shilts and the Keystone Kops of AIDS

"Human destiny involves no greater misfortune than for the most powerful men on earth to be less than first-rate. Then everything becomes false, distorted and monstrous.
—Nietzsche

"And it is much easier for the aristocrat to be ruthless if he imagines that the serf is different from himself in blood and bone."
—George Orwell

" . . . society has discovered discrimination as the great social weapon by which one may kill even without bloodshed.
—Hannah Arendt

At the center of the unfortunate mythology of the early part of the AIDS epidemic stands Randy Shilts, the gay reporter from the *San Francisco Chronicle* and the author of a highly successful book that some people, mistakenly, think is the definitive history of the early history of "AIDS." *And the Band Played On,* was for many years considered the rock solid account of the first four years of the "AIDS" epidemic. Wikipedia summarizes Shilts's biography: "Shilts graduated near the top of his class in 1975, but as an openly gay man, he struggled to find full-time employment in what he characterized as the homophobic environment of newspapers and television stations at that time. After several years of freelance journalism, he was finally hired as a national correspondent by the San Francisco Chronicle in 1981, becoming 'the first openly gay reporter with a gay "beat" in the American mainstream press.' Coincidentally, AIDS, the disease that would take his life, first came to nationwide attention that same year, and soon Shilts devoted himself to covering the unfolding story of the disease and its medical, social, and political ramifications." *And the Band Played On* is described in Wikipedia: as "a best-selling work of nonfiction written by San Francisco Chronicle journalist Randy Shilts published in 1987. It chronicles the discovery and spread of HIV and AIDS with a special emphasis on government indifference and political infighting to what was initially perceived as a gay disease that has impacted the United States and the world for decades after."

Insofar as the history of the science and politics associated with the first years of the epidemic were filtered through the journalistic judgment of Randy Shilts, one could say that epidemiological folly was compounded by journalistic folly. But to be absolutely fair, one can not underestimate the importance and usefulness of the basic raw facts reported in Shilts's book, even if they are naively framed and misunderstood by their author. Amid the wooden-headed (and unintentionally hilarious) credulousness of Shilts's conclusions throughout *And the Band Played On*, are reliable historical bits and pieces necessary for future historians who try and reconstruct an accurate myth-busting history of the epidemic and Holocaust II. A corrective forest needs to be put together from Shilts's credible trees.

When "AIDS" came to the medical community's attention in 1981, it was as though a small car called the Centers for Disease Control pulled up to the curb of the American public's consciousness and a gaggle of heterosexist clowns emerged who would craft the government's response to the epidemic and inadvertently lay the groundwork for Holocaust II, the HHV-6 catastrophe and the devastating age of autism. Randy Shilts's book is an important guide to *who* those biased clowns were and what they were thinking or perhaps more importantly, *what they were not thinking.*

Donald Francis: Scientist Zero

In many ways, Donald Francis, the epidemiological superstar of Shilts's book is also the star of the titanic HIV mistake that led to the HHV-6 spectrum catastrophe. Shilts's unfortunate hero worship begins with this description of the man: "Although he was only thirty-eight, Dr. Don Francis was one of the most eminent experts on epidemics at the CDC, having been among the handful of epidemiologists who literally wiped smallpox off the face of the earth in the 1970s." (*ATBPO* p.73) Harvard retrovirologist Myron Essex thought Francis "had gained an international reputation for singular brilliance." (*ATBPO* p.73) The colorful crew that crafted the official AIDS paradigm in the early 80s was off to a great start as a rather grandiose mutual admiration society. That might have been an early telltale sign of a groupthink catastrophe in the making.

Donald Francis had worked with Essex at Harvard on feline leukemia. No more precise nucleus of the tragic HIV mistake can be found than the moment when Francis (according to Shilts) *decided* that Gay Related Immunodeficiency (GRID, as it was known early on) was feline leukemia in people because both diseases were marked by weakened immune systems and opportunistic infections. Feline leukemia is *not the only animal disease to behave that way*, but Francis's myopic familiarity with feline leukemia would tragically keep all other more likely possibilities at bay while he pursued his pet theory under the guidance of his Harvard mentor and future Harvard AIDS millionaire.

A sure recipe for hubristic mischief could be found in the fact that Francis seemed so *very* sure of himself and his intuitions. He was also very sure that other people with their competing ideas for the aetiology of the mysterious epidemic were dead wrong. According to Shilts, "Francis didn't think the gay health problems were being caused by cytomegalovirus or the other familiar viruses under discussion. They had been around for years and hadn't killed anybody. It was something new; it could even be a retrovirus, Francis said." (*ATBPO* p.73) Saying it "could be a retrovirus" was disingenuous because other possible causes that were not retroviral were not welcome at the table. Ironically and tragically, Shilts foolishly celebrates this determined rush to judgment: "Francis was already convinced. He quickly became the leading CDC proponent of the notion that a new virus that could be spread sexually was causing immune deficiencies in gay men." (*ATBPO* p.74) Both epidemiology and virology were rather quickly being carved into stone with horrific consequences. One can now see the seeds of the Chronic Fatigue Syndrome epidemic and the HHV-6 pandemic in this misjudgment.

Donald Francis was the human embodiment of a stern, uncompromising public health message that can be heard constantly playing over the P.A. system throughout *And the Band Played On*. The questionable behavior of all other scientists at the time and what Shilts perceives as the self-destructive dithering of gay leaders is judged harshly against what Shilts considers the courageous, take-no-prisoners approach of Francis during epidemics he had previously worked on: "Years of stamping out epidemics in the Third World had also instructed Francis on how to stop a new disease. You find the source of contagion, surround it, and make sure it doesn't spread." (*ATBPO* p.107) Couldn't be any simpler than that. But nobody, Shilts included, was stopping to ask if Francis was fighting the last epidemiological war rather than the new one.

The Don Francis no-nonsense approach, a manly approach, was one Shilts clearly admires. While Francis will be the voice of moral testosterone throughout *Band*, according to Shilts's black and white schema, it falls to the gay community to play the role of denial-ridden, weak-kneed, self-destructive imbeciles. In the dark days of the early epidemic only the wise-beyond-his-years Francis *sees the light* and knows what to do. The Francis buzz word is "control." Dr. Donald Francis knew how to "control" epidemics. If only the dopes at the top of the nation's AIDS effort (and the epidemics uncooperative gay victims) had let him take control.

Francis's African experiences were epidemiologically formative. He had worked on Ebola Fever in Africa in 1976 and he will now look at this new disease through Ebola-colored glasses: " . . . the disease [Ebola] was a bloodborne virus, wickedly spreading both through sexual intercourse, because infected lymphocytes were in victims' semen, and through the sharing of needles in local bush hospitals." (*ATBPO p.118*) Shilts also looks at "AIDS" and public health itself through Francis's Ebola glasses: "When it became obvious that the disease was spreading through autopsies and ritual contact with corpses during the funerary process, Dr. Don Francis, on loan to the World Health Organization from the CDC, had simply banned local rituals and unceremoniously buried the corpses. Infected survivors were removed from the community and quarantined until it was clear that they could no longer spread the fever. Within weeks, the disease disappeared as mysteriously as it had come. The tribespeople were furious that their millennia-old rituals had been forbidden by these arrogant young doctors from other continents. The wounded anger twisted their faces." (*ATBPO p.118*) This passage is a key to understanding the moral of *And the Band Played On*, and the theme Shilts also promulgated in his publicity campaign for his bestselling book. It becomes the schtick he will hector his own community with. For "tribespeople" fill in the word "gays." If only the government had acted, had done something, anything, sooner. But what? Clearly Shilts wanted the country, under Dr. Francis—as a kind of extra-political AIDS Czar—to go into the same emergency mode reflected in the kind of ritual-banning measures he took toward the benighted tribespeople in Africa. In a manner of speaking, in a perfect Donald Francis public health universe, gay rituals (i.e. sex) would be banned, infected people would be removed from the community and quarantined. Whenever anyone will talk about the government not doing enough after *Band*, what will always be disingenuously unsaid is *what a heavy-handed government could have done if it had wanted to*. In the name of doing something—anything—involving a not much loved minority, things could have gotten extremely dicey in the inconvenient Bill of Rights sense, and there is nothing about what one detects in the character of either Francis or Shilts in the book to suggest that they would have done anything other than cheer such a development on. Gay men performed many foolish, politically self-defeating acts throughout the epidemic, but applauding Shilt's silly message about the heterosexist government of a heterosexist country *not doing enough*, with all its dark unconsidered implications of what draconian things might have been done in the name of dealing with a public health emergency, is surely one of the most foolish. Anything done under the biased auspices of Don Francis during the early days of the epidemic, can now be appreciated as an example of an incompetent government with questionable motives *doing too much too fast and using poor judgment*.

The impatient Dr. Francis considered the ideas of those at the National Institutes of Health who were looking at alternative theories like amyl nitrite or sperm as the cause of AIDS to be "ludicrous." (*ATBPO* p.119) Instead of suffering these fools, Francis set up his own laboratories and went to work to lay down the foundation for what would turn out to be the CDC's greatest epidemiological and virological mistake in its history. As for gay people, like the indigenous people of Francis's African epidemics, "Customs and rituals would have to be dramatically changed, and he knew from his hepatitis work in the gay community that customs involving sex were the most implacable behaviors to try to alter." (*ATBPO* p.119) Yeah, changing gay customs is like herding LGBT cats.

Shilts portrays Francis as a man of destiny: "Don Francis viewed his life as an accumulation of chance decision that had put him in the right place at the right time." (*ATBPO* p. 128) In retrospect, perhaps destiny had brought together exactly the wrong man, the wrong institution, the wrong epidemic at the wrong time to create the most perfect coalescence of misbegotten epidemiology and virology in history. Shilts swoons over the synchronicities of the Donald Francis life journey thus far: "By chance after chance, Don Francis felt he had been delivered to this moment in early March 1982, when it all fit together. The retrovirology, the cat leukemia, the experience with African epidemics, and the long work with the gay community—it all let him see something very clearly." (*ATBPO* p.128) Oy vey.

Francis looked through the world through the cockamamie *retroviral* lenses of Myron Essex. Francis had completed his doctorate on retroviruses and he was like the hammer that sees the world in terms of nails. It is a curious factoid of history that originally Francis thought that AIDS was co-factorial: Shilts reports he said, "Combine these two diseases—feline leukemia and hepatitis—and you have the immune deficiency." (*ATBPO* p.129) If Francis had only kept his co-factorial notion alive, there would have at least been a small chance that the HIV mistake might have corrected itself quickly rather than rolling out thirty years of hell on earth. Co-factors might have kept the great minds of epidemiology from closing.

To Francis, the conclusions were painfully obvious, and it was also clear what needed to be done. The Center for Disease Control needed "to launch some educational campaigns among gays to prevent the disease." (*ATBPO* p.129) The Great White Doctor had arrived among the ignorant, indigenous gays of America. The gay "implacable" behaviors had to change. Cut to the gay versions of "twisted faces" and "wounded anger" Shilts described in Africa. The CDC's age of epidemiological brainwashing had begun.

Often when a detective makes a major wrong turn, the suspect is right there in front of him. In Francis's attempts to fulfill the destiny of his retroviral dissertation, he overlooked the most obvious viral suspect of all, the one the size of a barn that was just staring at the CDC researchers, begging to be discovered. Francis memorialized this Missed Opportunity when he himself wrote in one of the very first books on the epidemic (a collection of essays on AIDS edited by Kevin Cahill), "Blood sampling of the intravenous drug users also revealed that although many were infected with cytomegalovirus, the viral strains were different. This was strong evidence that this herpes virus, which many scientists considered a strong candidate for a causative agent, had not developed some new virulent strain." (*The AIDS Epidemic, Edited by Kevin Cahill, St. Martins Press, 1983 p.*) No single strain emerged, lending further weight to Don Francis's hypothesis that a new virus, not CMV was at work. If only he had wondered if there was some new *DNA virus* that resembled CMV in some way that was hidden in the mix, the retroviral obsession might not have ultimately ruled the day. We know now that they were staring at HHV-6 and not seeing it. It would have been recognized as a new virus and probably declared the leading suspect. And then of course the HHV-6 spectrum pandemic and Holocaust II might never have happened. But it did.

Anyone who disagreed with Francis during this early period of the epidemic was considered stupid or stubborn. (This is how eras of abnormal and totalitarian science get their start in putative democracies.) We're constantly told throughout Shilts's book that Francis hoped "somebody would see how catastrophic the epidemic *would* become." (*ATBPO* p.147) Ironic, when you consider that indeed an apocalyptic catastrophe was coming and Francis himself was inadvertently taking a leadership role in making the key mistakes that would help to make it happen.

An amusing note is struck when Shilts points out that Francis wanted more labs to work on "AIDS" research because "they might get off on a bum lead and retard research at a time when people were dying." (*ATBPO* p.151) Francis, as it turns out, might live to see his name become synonymous with bum leads, and as far as dying is concerned, the show had only just begun.

There is no place that Shiltsian worship of Francis wouldn't go. He even followed Francis to bed: "The dream came to Don Francis often during those long, frustrating nights in the gathering darkness of 1982. Just beyond his reach, a faint orange light was suspended, shimmering with promise. It was The Answer, the solution to the puzzle. He reached for it, stretching so he could draw the light toward him. But it drifted farther and farther out. The answer was always there before him, tantalizingly close, and still beyond his grasp. Don's wife usually awoke him at that point. His mournful groaning would disturb the kids." (*ATBPO* p.159) Or, perhaps, in retrospect, it was just indigestion.

Our dreamer-scientist is portrayed as the solitary man of reason in an obstinate, irrational world: "The logical science of GRID (gay-related immunodeficiency) demanded that logical steps be taken . . . or people would die needlessly. However, as would be the case with just about every policy aspect of the epidemic, logic would not be the prevailing modus operandi." (*ATBPO* p.170) "The logical science of GRID" is perhaps the most oxymoronic phrase in the history of phrases. In what sounds now like ironic chutzpah, Shilts had the nerve to write, "Science was not working at its best, accepting new information with an unbiased eye and beginning appropriate investigations." (*ATBPO* p.*171*) From a Kuhnian promontory, one must ask, *whose* unbiased eye it is, *who* decides what is appropriate? But why even bother accepting new or contradictory information if you're being beamed up to "the Answer" by an orange light?

By January 1983, Don Francis is pounding his fists on tables. He is enraged at the blood banks. No one was doing enough to "control" the disease. There were fools full of denial everywhere and people shortsighted enough to express concerns about trifles like civil liberties in the face of the mounting death toll. Shilts, as usual, opined that the "problem, of course, was that such considerations constantly overshadowed concerns of medicine and public health." (*ATBPO* p.224) Public health logic is inexorable and very useful for those in the emotional blackmail game. Only Francis knew exactly what needed to be done: "In his windowless office in Phoenix, he began laying out his own long-range plans for getting ahead of the epidemic." (*ATBPO* p.232) He wanted an outside advisory group of immunologists and retrovirologists to guide the CDC. New-fangled retrovirologists — not old-fashioned virologists.

With his retroviral thinking cap on, Francis wanted to hone in on implacable retrovirus-spreading sexual behaviors of the gays: One of his almost salivating tough love memo's said, "I feel that to control AIDS we are obligated to try and do something to modify sexual activity. No doubt neither the fear of gonorrhea nor syphilis nor hepatitis B has decreased the number of sexual partners among homosexual men. *But fear of AIDS might.* [Emphasis mine] It seems mandatory for CDC to spread word of AIDS to all areas of the country. We have the network of VD clinics by which this word can be spread. Why not try?"(*ATBPO* p.233) Word certainly had no trouble spreading—and turning everything in its path into what I call Holocaust II. Thus, a biased, gay-obsessed presumption about the nature of AIDS was seamlessly stitched into the thinking and public health message right from the get-go. Every time the nature of the epidemic would be discussed, it would send a clear anti-gay message. Every time a public health warning about the epidemic would be given, it would repeat what I call the biased conventional "homodemiological" wisdom. If it was not consciously a big lie, it was a Big Mistake being promoted with the same effective propagandistic techniques. And over time the Big Mistake would evolve smoothly and inexorably into the Big Self-deception and the Big Lie.

Francis was so committed to his retroviral explanation of AIDS that he could not let any anomalous or contradictory data get in the way of his retroviral, venereal, and gay paradigm. He had created what Hannah Arendt might have called an "epidemiological image." He began to build an empire around his AIDS paradigm, firing off memos insisting that "as part of CDC's continuing pursuit of the cause of AIDS, a laboratory with retrovirus capabilities is necessary at CDC." (*ATBPO* p.266) He moved to Atlanta and assumed the title of "Lab Director for the AIDS Activities Office." A great time was about to be had by all.

The CDC bureaucracy that Francis had to deal with is portrayed in the Shilts book as unenlightened and slow to respond to the AIDS mensch. Historians will have to do some homework here and figure out if maybe there were some unsung heroes of insurgency at the CDC who actually took the correct measure of Francis and acted appropriately. Sabotage of the Francis agenda might in retrospect have been the work of unrecognized saints. Shilts portrays Francis as someone who was heroically willing to go outside legal channels to achieve his worthy (in his own visionary mind) goals. Francis was willing to spend money without congressional authorization. (Yes, AIDS now had its own Oliver North.) Francis was often so busy with his "AIDS activities" that he didn't have time to write up findings for publications. Why write up findings for publications when people were dying? This was an implacable gay behavior emergency. Not bothering to write things up is a chronically disturbing meme in the abnormal science of AIDS.

Francis is characterized as the voice of sanity compared to Shilts's portrayal of Robert Gallo, the scientist who will claim—with guns blazing— to have discovered the true AIDS retrovirus. There was a curious meeting in July, 1983 (two years after the first formal newspaper reporting of the sighting of the epidemic) at the CDC which "had been called to try to coordinate the search for the retrovirus responsible for Acquired Immune Deficiency Syndrome." (*ATBPO* p.349) Historians who like to know what people knew and when they knew it will chomp at the bit to figure out the prescience of *knowing* it was a retrovirus before they had found it. There will always be the whiff of phoniness about the search for a predetermined cause and that phoniness will certainly give birth to all kinds of conspiracy theories as historians excavate this somewhat hazy period at the CDC. God only knows what they will find.

Shilts's depiction of Gallo's vainglory and hair-trigger temper serve only to increase the number of halos floating above Don Francis's head. When Francis tries to recruit one of Gallo's assistants (also known as "flunkies"), Gallo goes ballistic, which is not surprising as the story about what really goes on in Gallo's lab will reveal later in the decade. The skeletons in *that* scientific closet are a Halloween unto themselves. The Gallo assistant who jumps ship receives the usual Gallo going-away gift for such an occasion: "I will destroy you," Gallo says to the man, according to Shilts. (*ATBPO* p.368)

Without understanding the disturbing implications, Shilts haplessly does a decent job of providing a snapshot of the political pressure that the CDC was under to name something (perhaps anything—and this retrovirus fit *that* bill) as the cause of AIDS: "James Mason, the CDC director, had a blunt directive for Don Francis on March 21 [1984] 'Get it done,' he instructed. In his scientific notebook, Don Francis wrote PRESSURE and underlined the word twice. The heat was on to resolve the 'AIDS' mystery, and Francis didn't have any doubts that the proximity of the presidential election motivated the unusual administrative concern." (*ATBPO* p.434)

Historians will have to ask themselves if the roots of the titanic mistake made on HIV, AIDS and HHV-6 was actually just driven by the politics of a presidential election year. Was it just that tragically simple? Did the dynamics of one presidential race give birth to the era of mistaken, sociopathic science that will refuse to correct itself for three decades? Did "Get it done!" lead, as night follows day, to Holocaust II?

Francis played pivotal role in the CDC's ultimately disastrous judgment that LAV, the retrovirus discovered by the French in AIDS patients, was the cause of AIDS. The bums-rush speed with which Francis moved from deciding it was the cause to creating inexorable public health policies based on his theory was stunning. Within a very short time frame there was an action agenda from Francis, and according to Shilts, "With the cause of AIDS found, scientists could now get on with the business of controlling the spread of the epidemic and finding a vaccine." (*ATBPO* p.409) Indeed. Given that the CDC could control *the information* about the spread of the epidemic (the manufactured Arendtian image, so to speak), they could certainly give the appearance of controlling the actual epidemic. That's how abnormal, totalitarian and ultimately sociopathic science, works.

Ironically, maybe one of the most important inadvertent contributions that Don Francis made to ultimately undermining the HIV/AIDS paradigm was his *inability* to create a model for "AIDS" by infecting monkeys with the retrovirus supposedly discovered by the French and Robert Gallo. This helped give birth to the first whistleblower of AIDS, retrovirologist Peter Duesberg, who used the failure to create an animal model as one of the arguments bolstering his growing doubts that the retrovirus was the real cause of AIDS. The health of those monkeys may have serendipitously saved all the people who heeded Duesberg's warnings about the questionable science of HIV.

Shilts portrays Francis as an earnest man committed only to furthering the interests of public health, the perfect foil to Robert Gallo. As Gallo appeared at a press conference with Secretary of Health and Human Services, Margaret Heckler, to claim that the cause of AIDS had been found, Saint Francis watched in horror: "After years of frustration, the announcement of the HTLV-III discovery deserved elation, Don Francis thought as he watched the live Cable News Network coverage of the Heckler press conference in the CDC's television studio with other members of the AIDS Activities Office. Instead, he felt burdened by the conflicts he saw ahead. The French were being cheated of their recognition and the U.S. government had taken a sleazy path, claiming credit for something that had been done by others a year before. Francis was embarrassed by a government more concerned with election-year politics than with honesty. Moreover, he could see that suspicion would play greater, not a lesser role in the coming 'AIDS' research. Competition often made for good science, Francis knew, lending an edge of excitement to research. Dishonesty, however, muddied the field, taking the fun out of science and retarding future cooperation." (*ATBPO* p.451) Sleazy paths? Dishonesty? Suspicion? The world hadn't seen anything yet.

Luckily for the health and civil liberties of the American people, Donald Francis, sooner rather than later "was beginning to feel beaten down." (*ATBPO* p.462) While others focused on a search for a treatment for "AIDS," Francis was itching to take it to the gay tribespeople and to "implement widespread voluntary testing for gay men."(*ATBPO* p.*469*) And gay men just couldn't wait until he got his hands on them. The "voluntary testing," of course, was based on his heterosexist notions of the epidemiology and virology of the disease. Francis penned a visionary nine-page program called "Operation AIDS Control" and his plan "employed the only two weapons with which health authorities could find the epidemic—blood testing and education." (*ATBPO* p.*524*) Luckily for the gay community, he never completely succeeded in getting the CDC into the full monty "control modality." But the early work of Francis succeeded in creating a paradigm that would help steer the AIDS agenda for three sociopathic decades, one that implied that the only way to control the epidemic was to find ways to intervene medically and social-engineeringly in the lives of gay people. If civil rights, demedicalization, and privacy had been spoils of gay liberation, they were now under direct threat from the public health vision presented by Francis and his colleagues. According to Shilts, "Francis drew his two circles.

One circle represented men infected with the AIDS virus; the other men who weren't. The point of AIDS control efforts, he said should be to make sure that everybody knows into which circle they fit." (*ATBPO* p.549) Dante couldn't have drawn better circles for the gay community. You could also say it was the epidemiological equivalent of dividing and conquering.

To their credit, not all gay men were eager to split their community up into Don Francis's two vicious circles. For the majority of the gay community, who began to live their lives in the shadow of the two fraudulent circles, trusting in Francis's vision proved a huge mistake. By 2010, one study of gay men showed that the big circle had not been protected from the real epidemic by avoiding contact with the smaller circle. One study showed that 60% of all gay men were testing positive for HHV-8 the so-called Kaposi's sarcoma virus, originally a marker for AIDS. In terms of the AIDS-like illnesses not related to HIV, that would turn out to be the tip of the iceberg. Trusting white knights like Don Francis and believing in HIV did not save the gay community from the real epidemic. In fact, for many, that made it worse.

Even his boss, James Curran, was not quite willing to turn over the epidemic to the gung-ho Donald Francis. A disgruntled Francis eventually left the CDC to go work in the San Francisco Health Department. Shilts leaves us with the impression that the proactive Don Francis could have saved the world if only the system hadn't gotten in his way. Francis had warned the world but he "had only been beaten by the system, and because of that the disease had won." (*ATBPO* p.600)

A disease had definitely won, but not the one Francis thought he had been fighting while wearing his venereal and retroviral glasses—the ones with the heterosexist frames. That disease, of course was the HHV-6 pandemic which includes Chronic Fatigue Syndrome, autism, cancer, etc. The list goes on and on.

James Curran and the Really Identifiable Gays

"What a man sees depends on what he looks at and also upon what his previous visual-conceptual experience has taught him to see."
—Thomas Kuhn *(SSR p.113)*

The Centers for Disease Control's James Curran was one of the chief architects of the original AIDS paradigm. Curran had the perfect medical background for laying down the formative heterosexually-biased interpretations of the early data that epidemiologists gathered about the sick gay men who were thought to be the patients zero of a new supposedly gay epidemic. Jacob Levenson described Curran in *The Secret Epidemic: The Story of AIDS and Black America*: " . . . Jim Curran, the Chief of the CDC's Venereal Disease Control Division was tapped to head up a Kaposi's Sarcoma and Opportunistic Infection Task Force. Despite being short staffed and underfunded, the Task Force managed to bring together experts from diverse fields like virology, cancer, and parasitic diseases in addition to a small team of epidemiological intelligence officers, who were the agency's foot soldiers for disease prevention. . . . He had done quite a bit of work on hepatitis B with gay men in the 1970s, and he almost immediately suspected that he had a similar sexually transmitted and blood borne disease on their hands." (*The Secret Epidemic: The Story of AIDS and Black America*) And that suspicion paved the way for one of the biggest conceptual mistakes in the history of epidemiology.

According to Shilts's *Band*, when Curran saw the first reports on PCP in gay men, he wrote an odd note to one of his colleagues saying, "Hot stuff. Hot stuff." (*ATBPO* p.67) Shilts also described a rather revealing meeting at a subsequent CDC conference at which Curran was briefed on the sexual behavior of gay men by a chatty gay physician named David Ostrow. According to Shilts, "Ostrow mused on the years he had spent getting Curran and Dr. Jaffe [Curran's CDC colleague] acculturated to the gritty details of gay sexual habits. . . . Curran had seemed uptight at the start, Ostrow thought, but he buckled down to his work. Both Jaffe and Curran were unusual in that federal officials rarely had any kind of contact with gays, and the few who did rarely wanted to hear detailed gymnastics of gay sex." (*ATBPO* p. 68) They clearly buckled down to their work a little *too* well. With their heterosexual sense of noblesse oblige (venereal division), these high-level clap doctors gone wild, set out to understand what the mysterious new gay epidemic was all about. Gay men would have run for the hills or hidden in basements if they had known what would result from the efforts of these two quick learners about "the gymnastics of gay sex" who were headed their way loaded for bear. The CDC's new experts in the joy of gay sex were now about to destroy the joy of gay sex.

Curran was married and the father of two children. Three days into what he thought was the sexually transmitted epidemic, he was examining gay patients and, already, according to Shilts, he "was struck by how identifiably gay all the patients seemed to be (*ATBPO* p.70) These gays were apparently *really gay*, not the plainclothes kind who could pass. According to Shilts, these gays "hadn't just peeked out of the closet yesterday." (*ATBPO* p.71) It may have been the perceived intense gayness of the first patients—the really gay ones—that resulted in Curran's huge, consequential mistake of erecting a mostly gay venereal epidemiological paradigm that would become the virtual thirty year hate crime against all gays, both the ones who could pass and the ones who were *really* gay. It wasn't just the patients who were strange. The strangeness of the people who had the disease would inspire a strange new kind of science, epidemiology and virology that was in essence "homodemiology." It was destined to make everything worse for gays and everyone else who had the bad luck of getting caught up in the CDC's paradigm. And that would ultimately even include members of the heterosexual general population. Otherwise known as epidemiological collateral damage.

Shilts tried to capture Curran's thought process when he wrote, "It was strange because diseases tended not to strike people on the basis of social group." (*ATBPO* p.71) He added, "To Curran's recollection . . . No epidemic had chosen victims on the basis of how they identified themselves in social terms, much less on the basis of sexual lifestyle. Yet, this identification and a propensity for venereal diseases were the only things the patients from three cities—New York, Los Angeles, and San Francisco—appeared to share. There had to be something within this milieu that was hazardous to these people's health. (ATBPO p. 71) Well, there certainly was something about to enter this "milieu" that would be extremely hazardous to these people's health, and that was Curran himself and his merry band of gay-sex-obsessed groupthinking epidemiologists who were about to hang the albatross of the venereal AIDS paradigm around the neck of the entire gay community.

When Shilts discussed Curran confronting "sociological issues" that were involved in the mysterious illness, it escaped Shilts that Curran and his associates *were themselves sociological (and political) issues* as they plopped themselves in the middle of the gay community (at a time when the community was most vulnerable and nearly hysterical) with all of their own peculiar heterosexual and heterosexist baggage. According to Shilts, "About a dozen staffers from all the disciplines potentially involved with the diseases volunteered for the working group. They included specialists in immunology, venereology, virology, cancer epidemiology, toxicology and sociology. Because the outbreak might be linked to the Gay Bowel Syndrome, parasitologists were called in. (*ATBPO* p. 71) The fact that any illness was labeled "Gay" should probably have been a red flag for the kind of heterosexist thinking that would soon be rolling across the gay community like a tsunami.

Once the guiding gay-obsessed premise was set, it was a matter of gay epidemiological garbage in and gay epidemiological garbage out. Questions with mistaken premises were about to lead the researchers and their medical victims down a deadly primrose path. Shilts summed up the basic direction of the inquiry: "Researchers also sought to determine whether the disease was indeed geographically isolated in the three gay urban centers. Did the detection of cases in the three centers make the patients appear to be only fast-lane gays because gay life tended toward the fast track in those cities? Was the disease all over gay America but in such low numbers that it had not been detected?" (*ATBPO* p. 81) Now we know, of course that there *was* indeed something else out there, but not just "all over gay America." Something wasn't playing by the rules of the CDC's gay-obsessed epidemiology. And that something was the very epidemiologically inconvenient Chronic Fatigue Syndrome epidemic

There is something almost laughable about the notion of Curran's CDC working group going out into the gay world and asking themselves what "new element might have sparked this catastrophe." (*ATBPO* p.82) One brand new element in the gay community that actually was the most significant spark for the coming catastrophe that was about to unfold was the CDC's own incompetence and heterosexist epidemiology.

Given the way AIDS would evolve into the kind of abnormal and sociopathic science that doesn't even require the usual rules of evidence, common sense, or logic, it is interesting that Curran *did* apply those old-fashioned rules early on when they were needed to build the venereal AIDS paradigm. Shilts wrote, "To prove an infectious disease, Curran knew, one had to establish Koch's postulate. According to this century-old paradigm, you must take an infectious agent from one animal, put it into another, who becomes ill, and then take the infectious agent from the second and inject it into still a third subject, who becomes ill with the same disease." (*ATBPO* p.105) Curran certainly tried to apply some semblance of the paradigm—or the logic of it anyway—when, by finding people who had AIDS often had slept with people who also had the disorder, he saw the links as a kind of epidemiological proof of transmission even though they weren't strictly speaking the fulfillment of the animal experimentation inherent in Koch's postulate. At least Curran knew the basic rules of science. Unfortunately, these very same rules would subsequently be thrown out the window to maintain the belief that the retrovirus eventually linked to AIDS was the one true cause of AIDS. Had those Koch's postulates been adhered to faithfully throughout the epidemic, we might be calling HHV-6 the virus of acquired immunodeficiency today and there might have been no Holocaust II or mysterious Chronic Fatigue Syndrome epidemic to write about.

The CDC, in an evolving and de facto manner, conducted something that could be called "the Atlanta AIDS/CFS public relations experiment" at the expense of everyone's health. What I mean by that coinage is a kind of postmodern public health political experiment in which rather than truly controlling an epidemic by being truthful and effective and scientific, the public health institutions of the CDC and the NIH tried to control and manipulate everything the public *knew* (and didn't know) about the epidemic of AIDS and CFS. It may have been quasi-innocent and simply the product of unrecognized sexual bias and old-fashioned self-deception when it started, but it evolved into something far more sinister and destructive. In the early days of AIDS, as described by Shilts, Curran was seemingly the embodiment of good-egg innocence when it came to the realization that it would be necessary for him to figure out some way to get the media's attention in order to increase public pressure for providing the funding the CDC needed for AIDS research. Unfortunately, the manipulation of the media by scientists or public health officials can—and did—have grave consequences for scientific, medical and epidemiological truth. In AIDS it became a kind of cancer that spread to the farthest reaches of public health.

In 1982 Curran appeared before a group of gay physicians in New York and told them "It's likely we'll be working on this most of our lives." (*ATBPO* p. 134) Historians one day will want to probe deeply into whether he knew anything that everyone else didn't know at that point. At the very least, it was as though he was an inadvertent prophet. He and his colleagues were indeed in the process of screwing things up for many generations to come. Curran's mistakes assured that his grandchildren's grandchildren will probably still be working on this problem. If they're not suffering from the myriad consequences of HHV-6 infections.

Shilts, in another moment of ironic journalistic naiveté, wrote this about Curran: "As a federal employee Curran had a thin line to walk between honesty and loyalty" (*ATBPO* p. 144) when he was describing the AIDS situation to Congress. Shilts notes that Curran could not ask Congress for money when he testified, "but he could nudge facts toward logical conclusions." (*ATBPO* p. 144) The nudging of facts would become an art form at the CDC over the next three decades and sometimes the facts that had to be nudged were so large they virtually had to be moved with bulldozers and the conclusions they were nudged towards were always more political than logical. One could almost faint from the irony of Curran telling Congress in 1982, "The epidemic may extend much further than currently described and may include other cancers as well as thousands of persons with immune defects." (*ATBPO* p. 144) Had he or his colleagues at the CDC recognized that cases of AIDS-like Chronic Fatigue Syndrome were simultaneously occurring all over the country, he would have been talking about millions (if not billions) of cases and he would not have had to play games with words to get Congress and the White House to do the right thing financially. One disturbing aspect of his manner of thinking was reflected in how Shilts summed up his testimony: "With death rates soaring to 75 percent among people diagnosed with GRID for two years, the specter of 100 percent fatality from the syndrome loomed ahead, he added." (*ATBPO* p.144) It would be nearly impossible to dial back on the distorted image of the epidemic he was presenting and frankly, dialing back on anything was something that the CDC (like the NIH) would turn out to be constitutionally unable to do. That, as we have said, is another sign that we are living in a period of totalitarian, abnormal, and sociopathic science.

Curran's peculiar attitude towards gays surfaced revealingly again when Shilts described his refusal to meet Gaetan Dugas, the unfortunate gay man who would be eternally scapegoated in the echo chambers of the media as the "Patient Zero" of the AIDS epidemic because he had supposedly slept with a number of the original AIDS cases: "Jim Curran passed up the opportunity to meet Gaetan, the Quebecois version of Typhoid Mary. Curran had heard about the flamboyant [flight] attendant and frankly found every story about his sexual braggadocio to be offensive. Stereotypical gays irritated Curran in much the same way that he was uncomfortable watching Amos n' Andy movies." (*ATBPO* p.158) One doesn't know quite where to begin on this one, except to note that Curran would be able to use his clap-doctor and gay-obsessed epidemiology to act on his feelings and beliefs about both stereotypical and non-stereotypical gays, and every other kind of gay in between. The way that Shilts described Gaetan Dugas should have been a warning to the whole gay community of what kind of medical and social treatment was in store for them: "Gaetan Dugas later complained to friends that the CDC had treated him like a laboratory rat during his stay in Atlanta, with little groups of doctors going in and out of his hospital room. He'd had his skin cancer for two years now, he said, and he was sick of being a guinea pig for doctors who didn't have the slightest idea what they were doing." (*ATBPO* p.158) Of course when those doctors eventually thought they *had* figured out what they were doing—that was precisely when they really didn't really have a clue about what they were doing. The Holocaust II era of the gay guinea pig had only just begun. The CDC's epidemiology would create a whole new gay stereotype. Curran's difficulty in getting researchers to come into the field was the fallout of the gay and sexual way the frightening disease had been framed for the public—something that might never have happened if the heterosexual Chronic Fatigue Syndrome cases had been included in the epidemiological and virological template for the epidemic.

It's amazing how many people seem to have been assigned credit (by different sources) for bringing (dragging?) Robert Gallo into AIDS research. Shilts has Curran on that Washington-slept-here list too, noting that he said to Gallo when he was receiving an award at a medical conference in 1982, "You've won one award. You should come back when you win another award for working on AIDS." (*ATBPO* p. 201) Bringing Gallo into the field was like putting a pair of retrovirus-obsessed eyeglasses over a pair of gay VD-obsessed eyeglasses and expecting to see the epidemic for what it was. Otherwise known as the blind recruiting the blind.

One of the more grimly amusing passages in Shilts's book concerns Curran's thought about the fears in the gay community that AIDS would result in gays being put into concentration camps: "Curran thought the train of thought was curious. After all, nobody had suggested or even hinted that gays should be in any way quarantined for AIDS. The right-wing loonies who might propose such a 'final solution' were not paying enough attention to the disease to construct the Dachau scenario. Still, it was virtually an article of faith among homosexuals that they should end up in concentration camps." (*ATBPO* p. 228) Silly gays. Frankly, who needed concentration camps or "the Dachau scenario" when you had CDC epidemiology. CDC epidemiology saved the country a load of money on barbed wire. And Holocaust I, where gays actually were made to wear pink triangles in real concentration camps— that was so 1940s.

One of the most unfortunate and tragically wrongheaded things about Curran is that, according to Shilts, he held his colleague Donald Francis "in awe, given Francis's international reputation for smallpox control." (*ATBPO* p.262) As one looks back at the circle jerk that also got Germany's Holocaust I going, one might hypothesize that all holocausts begin in passionate mutual admirations societies.

Something began to surface during James Curran's reign over AIDS at the CDC that bears close scrutiny by any enterprising historian interested in identifying the institutional roots of Holocaust II. In 1983, when Susan Steinmetz, an aide to Congressman Ted Weiss, visited the CDC in an oversight capacity, she was prevented from seeing files she automatically should have been able to audit as a representative of a Congressional Committee that had oversight responsibilities on health and the environment. According to Shilts, she was told by the then CDC Director William Foege, "she would not have access to any CDC files, and she could not talk to any CDC researchers without having management personnel in the room to monitor the conversations. The agency also needed a written, detailed list of specific documents and files Steinmetz wanted to see." (*ATBPO* p.292) Shilts reported that "Steinmetz was flabbergasted. What did they think oversight committees did? Their work routinely involved poring through government files to determine the truth of what the high-muck-a-mucks denied, and then privately talking to employees who, without the prying eyes of their bosses, could tell the truth. This was understood, she thought." (*ATBPO* p.292) What she didn't realize was that the CDC's de facto counterrevolution against science and the ideal of transparency in democratic processes had begun before her unassuming eyes and this would become business as usual at the clandestine CDC for the next three decades. The iron curtain of secrecy (de rigueur in all abnormal and sociopathic science) that would enable Holocaust II and the cover-up of the CFS and HHV-6 epidemic had descended.

While Steinmetz was just trying to find memos that would contradict the CDC's public posture that it had enough money to research the emerging epidemic of AIDS, without realizing it, she had stumbled onto the fact that the CDC had begun acting more like a government intelligence agency with vital national secrets—possibly even embarrassing ones—to keep, than a public health organization that was committed to truthful science and was accountable to the American people. In essence the CDC was showing that it wasn't above any of the legerdemain that any other part of the government was capable of. It was showing us that it was very much cut from the same cloth as the government gremlins that gave us Watergate and Vietnam. You could say that the CDC was perhaps the deepest part of the putative Deep State.

Steinmetz wanted to see files that pertained to budgets and planning, but she was bizarrely told that she couldn't see the files because they had patients' names in them and that violated patient confidentiality. It strained credulity to argue that patients' names were involved in organization budgets and planning. and in retrospect, it was a very lame excuse. This wouldn't be the first time in Holocaust II that a dishonest explanation with a fake concern and compassion for patients' welfare would be used by those in authority to stonewall the very people who were actually trying to *do* something about the welfare of patients. The CDC was already in a paranoid circle-the-wagons mode that characterizes abnormal and totalitarian science. According to Shilts, "The CDC personnel, who struck Steinmetz as peculiarly contentious, wanted to conduct their own review of the files before letting Steinmetz see them." (*ATBPO* p. 292) And "as another demand, the CDC insisted that before any interviews with CDC staff took place, the agency would screen questions that Susan Steinmetz put to scientists." (*ATBPO* p.292) On the eve of the HHV-6 catastrophe and Holocaust II, government science was going into the lockdown of abnormal, sociopathic science. Shilts wrote, "This is getting pretty strange, Steinmetz thought." (*ATBPO* p.292) Strangeness was but a puppy at that point.

This new emerging opposite world of public health and scientific duplicity and defensiveness didn't make sense to Steinmetz's colleagues back in D.C.: "On the phone, other oversight committee staffers in Washington confided that they had never heard of an agency so recalcitrant to Congress . . ." (*ATBPO* p.292) It got even worse for Steinmetz at the CDC in Atlanta when, on the second day of her oversight visit, she was told by the CDC manager who was handling her visit that her "presence would no longer be permitted in the CDC building and that no agency personnel would be allowed to speak to her." (*ATBPO* p. 293) The stonewalling and the lockdown were not confined to the CDC in Atlanta. Shilts reported that Steinmetz also faced new obstacles in her path when "The National Cancer Institute officials issued a memo demanding that all interviews with researchers be monitored by the agency's congressional liaison. At first the National Institutes for Allergy and Infectious Disease was cooperative, but then, in an apparent NIH-wide clampdown, information became difficult to excavate there as well." (*ATBPO* p.293) Science and public health in America were about to play the same kinds of political games that are played in totalitarian countries. Public health information was about to be totally controlled by the government.

Curran can himself take a great deal of personal credit for the HIV mistake. Shilts writes that "During the summer of 1983, Dr. James Curran had grown fond of citing the 'Willie Sutton Law' as evidence that AIDS was caused by a retrovirus. The notorious bank bandit Willie Sutton was asked once why he robbed banks, to which he replied, "Because that's where the money is." Curran, according to Shilts, would ask "'Where should we [at the CDC] put our money? . . . 'Where would Willie Sutton go? He would go with retroviruses, I think right now."' (*ATBPO* p. 331) There is a revealing amount of cockiness and arrogance in Curran that remind one that pride goeth before a fall. But one Willie Suttonish thing was certainly true: retroviruses turned out to be exactly where the big money was for a number of dishonest and incompetent retrovirologists. And there would be serious consequences for anyone who noticed the AIDS had turned into an enormous confidence game.

It is fascinating to see Shilts catching Curran red-handed as he lies about the inadequate funding for AIDS. Publicly, Curran would say "we have everything we need," (*ARBPO* p.331) but Shilts was able to use the Freedom of Information Act to locate documents that "revealed that things were not so rosy at the CDC, and Curran knew it. Even while he reassured gay doctors in San Francisco, he was writing memos to his superiors begging for more money." (*ATBPO* p. 331) For anymore cognizant of the overwhelming mendacity that characterized just about everything concerning Holocaust II, it is especially disturbing to read Shilts's account of Curran's excuse: "'It's hard to explain to people outside the system,' he said. 'It's two different things to work within the system for a goal and talking to the people outside the system for that goal,' he said." (*ATBPO* p. 332) Curran was basically making the anti-transparency excuses people inside of the government always make for talking out of both sides of their mouths. It's too bad Shilts didn't consider the possibility *that this character trait was also reflected in the basic science and epidemiology of AIDS* that was being churned out by the CDC.

Curran got the venereal HIV/AIDS paradigm he and his colleagues wanted, the one that could be expected to materialize given his background. It wasn't surprising then, that he said in 1984, according to Shilts, "Gay men need to know that if they're going to have promiscuous sex, they'll have the life expectancies of people in the developing world." (*ATBPO* p.416) Actually, given the crazy toxic fraud-based treatments some gay men were going to be medically assaulted with, he was a true visionary.

As could be predicted, according to Shilts, "Jim Curran also viewed testing as essential to any long-term strategy in fighting AIDS." And so, the Pink Triangle medical apartheid agenda of testing and stigmatizing gays as HIV positive (or as an HIV risk group) began in earnest. And the gay community got specially tailored forms of communication from Curran. According to Shilts, "Curran was always cautious when he talked to newspaper reporters, fearful that his observations on the future of the AIDS epidemic might be fashioned into the stuff of sensational headlines, but he felt no inhibition with the gay community. Instead he felt his mission was to constantly stress the gravity of the unfolding epidemic." (*ATBPO* p.483) Of course, while he was giving the gay community the tough love, behind his epidemiological back was the looming HHV-6 spectrum and Chronic Fatigue Syndrome catastrophe, a biomedical event which was exponentially worse than anything his little team of jiggy clap doctors and pseudo-epidemiologists could possibly have imagined. Given that it was the CDC's AIDS paradigm that in essence scapegoated the gay community for what would turn out to be everyone's HHV-6 problem, it is the epitome of irony that according to Shilts, Curran thought that "the question was not if there would be a backlash against gays, but when. It might come soon. 'You should get ready for it,' he said." (*ATBPO* p.484) How does one prepare for a backlash against gays? Buy extra canned goods? Bake an extra quiche? It was certainly nice of him to give the gay community a heads up, but in truth, the pseudoscience, the incompetent fact-gathering implicit in ignoring the Chronic Fatigue syndrome cases that were occurring simultaneously, and the hard-wired homodemiology of the CDC, constituted a kind of epidemiological backlash *before* the backlash. Curran and his team needed only look in the mirror to see the kind of anti-gay values that could do far more mischief to the gay community than an army of right wing loons.

Journalist David Black caught some of the underlying psychological problems at the CDC in his book *The Plague Years*. He wrote, "In fact the CDC, like many physicians and scientists, seemed embarrassed by the gayness of the disease." (*TPY* p.57) We now know only too well in retrospect is that the best science and epidemiology cannot be conducted in an atmosphere of gay-sex-related embarrassment. Black quoted one CDC researcher as saying to a visiting gay activist, "This never would have happened if you guys had gotten married." (*TPY* p.57) When the activist asked if the researcher meant to each other, the researcher said, "To women." (*TPY* p.58) The CDC researchers conducted their epidemiology and science in an awkward atmosphere of antipathy to gays, surely not a fertile field for scientific objectivity. According to Black, when he asked Curran to explain exactly what he means by "'intimate contact' [between men] the phrase researchers kept using to describe the conditions under which the syndrome spread, he seemed uncomfortable, squeamish. He stammered and glanced anxiously around the room." (*TPY* p.58) If some of Jim Curran's best friends were gay, they had clearly done very little to make him comfortable with their sex lives. One suspects that most of Jim Curran's best friends were not gay.

One absolutely show-stopping moment in Black's rich little book is a criticism that was leveled at Curran: "He started making up these 'facts' from the data as he interpreted it,' said one unnamed gay critic of Curran." Who was that astute gay critic? Please stand up now, take your bow.

Mary Guinan's Missed Opportunity

Historians who want to trace the series of missteps that led to the HHV-6 pandemic and Holocaust II may benefit from taking a close look at a little known researcher at the CDC who played a curious role in both of the supposedly separate AIDS and Chronic Fatigue Syndrome epidemics. Her surprising inability to see an obvious link between the two syndromes may be one of the important seeds of the whole HHV-6 disaster. She is mentioned in both the Shilts history of the early AIDS epidemic and Hillary Johnson's *Osler's Web*, the definitive journalistic account of the CDC's bungling of the epidemic of facetiously-labeled Chronic Fatigue Syndrome.

According to Shilts, Mary Guinan worked for James Curran in the CDC's venereal disease division. She was the person who sent James Curran the first ill-fated report on the first cases of what would eventually be called "AIDS" in "homosexuals." With fellow VD chasers Harrold Jaffee and Curran, she shared the CDC AIDS Task Force's hoochie-coochie preoccupation with venereal diseases epidemiology. She helped impose the CDC heterosexist venereal groupthink on the emerging data of what would eventually be *gayified* epidemiologically into "Gay Related Immunodeficiency (GRID)."

Ironically, considering what turned out to be the role of HHV-6 in AIDS, Shilts reported that in 1981, "on a hunch, Guinan called a drug company that manufactured medicine for severe herpes infections. They told her about a New York City doctor who had been seeing . . . dreadful herpes infections in gay men." (*ATBPO* p.72) Shilts wrote that "Guinan was shaken by her investigation. She was accustomed to dealing with venereal diseases, ailments for which you receive an injection and are cured. This was different. She couldn't get the idea out of her head: There's something out there that's killing people. That was when Mary Guinan hoped against hope that they would find something environmental to link these cases together. God help us, she thought, if there's a new contagion spreading such death." (*ATBPO* p.72) One way that God certainly wasn't helping was by having a VD-obsessed doctor and her colleagues trying to comprehend a pandemic that wasn't, strictly speaking, venereal.

In Shilts's account of Guinan, seeing the epidemic through gay-obsessed lenses was a given. He wrote about one of her days in 1981: "It had been another typical day of gay cancer studies for Mary Guinan. She had wakened at 6 a.m to breakfast with gay doctors and community leaders and asked again and again, 'What's new in the community?' What new element might have sparked this catastrophe." (*ATBPO* p.82) It was just gay, gay, gay—24/7—for the AIDS Task Force. They simply couldn't wash the gay out of their hair. It was one of those times when every gay person should have checked to see whether they still had their wallets. Someone was about to sell them a gay epidemiological bridge.

As Shilts sympathetically presents Guinan, he inadvertently nails the whole CDC psychological and sociological bias problem: "Guinan felt helpless and frightened. This was the meanest disease she had ever encountered. She strained to consider every possible nuance of these peoples' lives." (*ATBPO* p.83) What she really meant was gay nuances of gay lives. It is supremely ironic that Shilts wrote, "The CDC, she knew, needed to work every hypothesis imaginable into the case-control study." (*ATBPO* p.83) *Every* hypothesis imaginable? Really? Not by a long shot. How about the hypothesis that these cases were just extreme versions of the Chronic Fatigue Syndrome cases that the CDC had been informed about? The un-gay cases.

The process of identifying the emergence of the epidemic in nongay drug users, as described in Shilts's book, makes it clear how gaycentric the thinking of the pioneers of the AIDS epidemiological paradigm was: "At the CDC there was a reluctance to believe that intravenous drug users might be wrapped into the epidemic, and the New York physicians also seemed obsessed with the gay angle, Guinan thought. 'He's said he's not homosexual but he must be,' doctors would confide in her." (*ATBPO* p.83) Everybody was becoming an expert on gayness in those days. Given the reluctance to even see connections in those cases of nongay drug-using outcasts, it should come as no surprise when years later anyone who saw the obvious connections between the epidemics of AIDS and Chronic Fatigue Syndrome was treated like they were strictly out to lunch. The AIDS paradigm was fatefully and messily intertwined with all the psychological baggage of sexual titillation and repulsion. (Hannah Arendt describes a similar phenomenon in the psychology of antisemitism.) If the CDC was unprepared psychologically to see drug users "wrapped into the epidemic," how about all the good clean living white heterosexuals with the AIDS-like permutations of the immune system that characterize Chronic Fatigue Syndrome? Can't go there.

Guinan's San Francisco trip with Harold Jaffe to interview AIDS patients and heterosexual controls also revealed the CDC mindset: "The CDC staffers could tell gay from straight controls by the way they reacted to the questions about every aspect of their intimate sexual lives. Heterosexuals seemed offended at queries about the preferred sexual techniques, while gay interviewees chatted endlessly about them." (*ATBPO* p.96) Oh those gays! A herd of chatty Cathies if ever there was one. Given the bias-laden epidemiology that this chattiness was about to imprison the gay community in, one is tempted to say that loose gay lips sank a proverbial legion of gay ships. If one were watching this on a screen in a movie theater, one would want to scream out to the clueless gay interviewees for their own sake, "For Heaven's sake, shut up!"

Guinan was one of the CDC researchers credited by Shilts with recognizing that hemophiliacs and blood transfusion recipients might ultimately also become victims of "gay pneumonia." She also was one of the first to worry about the AIDS infection possibilities of "semen depositors." (*ATBPO* p.132) Guinan cast a wide net: "No sooner had she convinced the CDC that intravenous drug users were indeed a category of GRID cases separate from gay men, then her field of investigations discovered the first reported GRID cases among prisoners and prostitutes." (*ATBPO* p.132) Unfortunately epidemiological net wasn't wide enough to catch the concurrent cases of AIDS-like Chronic Fatigue Syndrome. Also, unfortunately for her, she helped create the very consequential epidemiological urban myth of Patient Zero. She was the first person to come in contact with Gaetan Dugas the so-called gay Typhoid Mary who the CDC would turn into the "Patient Zero" or more appropriately, "Scapegoat Zero," of the epidemic depending on your point of view. He would become an icon for all the venereal *gaycentric* thinking down at the CDC.

In one of those amazing moments in Holocaust II in which a scientist comes so face-to-face with the truth but fails to see what is right before their eyes, Shilts reports that when Guinan was studying drug users, "blood sampling of the intravenous drug users also revealed that, although many were infected with cytomegalovirus, the viral strains were all different. This was strong evidence that the herpes virus had not developed some new virulent strain. No single strain emerged, lending further weight to Don Francis's hypothesis that a new virus, not CMV was at work." (*ATBPO* p.133) The CDC, in retrospect, was most likely eyeballing strains of an undiscovered virus that would be called HBLV when Gallo's scientists supposedly "discovered" it in 1986. It was subsequently named HHV-6. In retrospect it is pretty obvious that the CDC was looking at HHV-6 but thinking it was only CMV. (And those who *wanted to see a retrovirus* would have been especially predisposed *not* to see a new DNA virus like HBLV/HHV-6.)

It is interesting and perhaps revealing that Guinan and her colleagues could deal with the fact that the disease or syndrome *manifested itself differently* in gay men and drug users—presumably for reasons that would ultimately be figured out. But God forbid that anyone would subsequently suggest that even though there were differences in the manifestations of Chronic Fatigue Syndrome and AIDS that they were essentially manifestations of the same agent and the same pandemic. Distinctions were not turned into differences where drug users and gays were concerned, but where the gays with AIDS and the middle-class straights with Chronic Fatigue Syndrome were concerned, every distinction,—even the teeny-tiniest or most irrelevant kind—was immediately considered a dramatic how-dare-you-compare-these-apples-and-oranges difference. Such bogus thinking would be at the heart of the "Chronic Fatigue Syndrome is not AIDS" paradigm which would guide public health through the next three decades.

For all her good work Guinan was eventually rewarded with the position of assistant CDC director. Unfortunately for all the victims of HHV-6, what she did do at the CDC didn't have as much impact on the well being of the world as *what she did not do*. It was Guinan in 1985 who got a call from Dan Peterson, a former colleague and one of the two doctors who are credited with recognizing an outbreak of the absurdly named "chronic fatigue syndrome" in their Lake Tahoe practice. According to Hillary Johnson, "The two had become friends during a shared stint at the at the University of Utah hospital in Salt lake City in 1976." (*OW* p.31) Also, according to Johnson, "Peterson had frequently sought her counsel on different infectious disease cases; he had also struck her as a gifted diagnostician.' (*OW*. P.31)

Johnson reported that "Guinan listened as her former colleague described his Tahoe patients, her curiosity aroused by the possibility that this ailment, which three recent medical papers had described, was occurring in epidemic form. Previously, researchers had described it as a sporadic illness. She remembered too, that Atlanta clinician Richard DuBois [mentioned in my introduction] had made a presentation to agency staff on the malady early in 1983, even proposing that the new mono-like syndrome might be a second epidemic of immune dysfunction rising concurrently with AIDS." (*OW* p.31)

Did this lead Guinan serendipitously into a more complicated epidemiological vision of a variable epidemic that included both what was called "AIDS" and "Chronic Fatigue Syndrome"? Not on your life. These first CFS patients were not gay and not drug users. They were from medical practices that could be described as being devoted to folks who ride in the middle and front section of society's bus. Such stark social differences would make it of no consequence or interest that study after study would show one immunological and neurological similarity after another between AIDS and Chronic Fatigue Syndrome. Guinan had helped build a paradigm that was so gay, gay, gay and so socially radioactive that the links between AIDS and CFS would be willfully ignored, buried alive by denial, and through a kind of determined public health radio silence, for all intents and purposes, be covered-up big time.

Ignoring the obvious, Guinan sent the future "CFS" patients of America on one of the greatest medical wild goose chases in history. According to Johnson, she passed the Peterson cases on to Larry Schonberger, chief of the CDC's epidemiology within the Division of Viral and Ricketsial Diseases. Not surprisingly, Johnson reports that "Schonberger and his staff of epidemiologists had a mandate to monitor and occasionally investigate outbreaks of viral diseases, with the exception of AIDS, which by 1985 had been awarded a separate division and staff and more than half of the federal agency's entire annual research budget." (*OW* p.32) And so, because of Guinan's phone call and her very questionable judgment, CFS research headed down exactly the wrong road. Or, I should say, rabbit hole.

Had Guinan wisely directed the Lake Tahoe cases in the direction of the CDC's AIDS division back in 1985, there was still a chance that the political and medical apartheid of the "Chronic Fatigue Syndrome is not AIDS' paradigm and Holocaust II might not have been able to fully materialize. But AIDS had been so *gayified* and turned into such a sexual bogeyman and scarlet letter syndrome, that Guinan and everyone else at the CDC couldn't for the life of them admit that average (i.e. white heterosexual) Americans were coming down with any similar or related form of acquired immunodeficiency. Instead, those people were given the whitewash of a diagnosis of Chronic Fatigue Syndrome. Those good country people, to borrow a term from Flannery O'Connor, couldn't in a million years be suffering from something that had at one time or another been called Gay Cancer, Gay Plague, Gay Pneumonia, and Gay Related Immunodeficiency. After all, they weren't gay.

James Mason "Gets it Done"

"The sexual transmission of this illness, considered by most people as a calamity one brings on oneself, is judged more harshly than other means—especially since AIDS is understood as a disease not only of sexual excess but of perversity."

—Susan Sontag, *AIDS as Metaphor*

In its dark hours of 1983, the gay community needed nothing more than to have added to its tribulations the appointment of Dr. James Mason, a devout Mormon, to the office of Director of the Centers for Disease Control. They probably should have just counted their lucky stars that a member of the John Birch Society or Lyndon LaRouche himself wasn't appointed. According to Randy Shilts, "Until recently, he had served as state public health director for Utah. It was his friendship with conservative Utah Senator Orrin Hatch, the Chair of the Senate committee in charge of HHS, that had netted him the job as CDC director." (*ATBPO* p.399)

As we have already noted, James Mason uttered the fateful words ("Get it done!") that captured the whole pressure cooker environment that everyone working on AIDS operated in the first few years of the epidemic—both in and out of the government.

One useful thing that Mason *did do* was create an "AIDS Review Committee" to determine whether there were adequate resources for AIDS. According to Shilts, what the group discovered was that resources were being directed from other programs for AIDS: "Some 70 percent of the CDC's AIDS staffers were people diverted from other programs and not funded by federal AIDS appropriations." (*ATBPO* p.444) While the study ostensibly pointed to the need for more money for AIDS research, it also inadvertently showed *how easily the CDC could override the will of Congress* in terms of what actually got funded and therefore what actually got done. It was another disquieting bit of evidence that suggested something about the rogueish way the CDC did its own clandestine thing throughout the epidemic. What happened during Holocaust II shows that in some ways the CDC operates in some weird extralegal zone outside of the United States government and abides by its own rules. If nothing else, AIDS has taught us that public health can operate as a shadow government.

Mason seems to have been prone to the same kind of squeamishness toward all things gay as James Curran. Shilts reported that "Even Dr. James Mason was heard complaining that since he had become CDC director, he found himself talking to complete strangers about sexual acts he would not discuss with his wife even in the privacy of his own home." (*ATBPO* p.586) Time didn't seem to mellow or loosen up the good doctor because in 2009, according to a report by writer Jake Crosby on the Age of Autism website, James Mason was a member of the board of trustees for Evergreen International. According to Crosby, "Its mission is to help homosexuals 'diminish same-sex attractions and overcome homosexual behavior,' by the faith of Jesus." That a person with those kinds of beliefs played a key role in the development and implementation of the HIV/AIDS paradigm which launched and maintained Holocaust II should come as no surprise to anyone.

*

Everyone at the CDC must have been relieved and proud that sensational day in April of 1984 when Margaret Heckler took the stage wearing a very funky looking wig in Washington with Robert Gallo to announce that the virus that he basically had stolen from the French was the cause of AIDS and that treatments and vaccines would follow in short order. All the CDC's scapegoating and running around in obsessive gay circles for three years had paid off handsomely. It was one more successful chapter in the history of one of the greatest public health operations in the world. The problem, of course was, that their hard work and gay-obsessed heterosexist medical sleuthing had resulted in the biggest medical and scientific mistake in history. And there would be an inexorable price that we the people—gay and nongay—would all have to pay for that egregious error for many decades to come. I am, of course talking about the tragic multisystemic HHV-6 epidemic which I have continued to cover for more than a decade at HHV-6 University.

The Duesbergians

How a Brave and Brilliant Group of Scientists
Challenged the AIDS Establishment and Why
They Failed

Introduction

According to the *Holocaust Encyclopedia*, "The Nazis believed that male homosexuals were weak, effeminate men who could not fight for the German nation. They saw homosexuals as unlikely to produce children and increase the German birthrate. . . . Because some Nazis believed homosexuality was a sickness that could be cured, they designed policies to 'cure' homosexuals of their 'disease' through humiliation and hard work." The Nazis who were "interested in finding a 'cure' for homosexuality" developed a "program to include medical experimentation on homosexual inmates of concentration camps. These experiments caused illness, mutilation and yielded no scientific knowledge."

I refer to what happened to gays during this period as "Holocaust I." According to the United States Holocaust Memorial Museum website, "The severity of the persecution of homosexuals increased after the war's outbreak. In July 1940, Himmler directed that any convicted homosexual who 'seduced more than one partner' be sent to a concentration camp after completing his prison sentence to prevent the homosexual 'contagion' from spreading. After 1942, the SS embarked on an explicit program of 'extermination through work' to destroy Germany's 'habitual criminals.' Some 15,000 prisoners, including homosexuals, were sent from prisons to concentration camps, where nearly all perished within months."

It is also noted on the website that in the camps prisoners were forced to wear "marks of various colors and shapes which allowed guards and camp functionaries to identify them by category. The uniforms of those sentenced as homosexuals bore various identifying marks, including a large black dot" and later a "pink triangle."

The Holocaust Museum also notes, "After the war, homosexual concentration camp prisoners were not acknowledged as victims of Nazi persecutions and reparations were refused."

What I refer to as Holocaust I for gays was a part of what is traditionally referred to as "the Holocaust" or "the Shoah" which was a genocide in which six million Jews were killed. In the Holocaust the homosexuals were not the primary target. Their "crime" was not one of "racial inferiority" but rather for "behavioral inferiority." In Holocaust II they are the primary target.

In his book, *Life Unworthy of Life*, James M. Glass writes about the overlap of the medicalization of the Jews and the gays in Nazi Germany:
"It is critical not to underestimate the power of phobia in driving the perception of the Jew as bacillus translated into the public policy of sanitation and infection. Certain stories filtering back to Germany about the condition of the ghettos—the extent of disease, the deadly environment—added to the prevailing view of the Jew as bad blood. A similar attitude prevailed regarding homosexuality. In 1938, Reich Legal Director Hans Frank, who later became head of the General Government in occupied Poland, wrote that

589

homosexuality 'is clearly expressive of a disposition opposed to the normal national community. Homosexual activity means the negation of the community as it must be constituted if the race is not to perish. That is why homosexual behavior in particular, merits no mercy.' In his diary Goebbels called homosexuality a 'cancerous disease.'"

What I call "Holocaust II" is the event that began in 1981, thirty-six years after the German forces surrendered to the Allies: the so-called "AIDS epidemic." As the publisher and editor-in-chief of a gay New York City newspaper called *New York Native*, I was destined to have a front row seat on the tragedy of Holocaust II as it unfolded. In the early years of the epidemic I focused my newspaper continuously on the epidemic and earned nearly universal praise for doing so when most of the media preferred to look the other way. In *Rolling Stone*, David Black said that we deserved a Pulitzer for our early coverage and Randy Shilts also gave it high marks in his bestseller, *And the Band Played On*. I have detailed that coverage and the entire history of my newspaper in my book, *The Chronic Fatigue Syndrome Epidemic Cover-up*.

While my newspaper's early coverage of the epidemic from 1981 to 1983 has been widely celebrated, our commitment to independent investigative and critical reporting about the epidemic eventually earned us the enmity of the government's medical and scientific establishment as well as the AIDS activist community. Things began to sour for us when we introduced our readers to the thinking of a molecular biologist named Peter Duesberg. Penned mostly by a writer named John Lauritsen, we gave extensive coverage to Duesberg's doubts about the HIV theory of AIDS. At first Duesberg was not sure what the cause of AIDS was, but he was certain it was not caused by a transmissible agent. As time went on, he began to promote a lifestyle theory of AIDS causation, pointing mainly to the use of recreational drugs.

Even though the scientific establishment did everything it could to debunk and silence Duesberg, he stood his ground and gained the support of a number of respected scientists and intellectuals who were also pilloried in one way or another for questioning the official AIDS dogma. I refer to his supporters and intellectuals who were inspired by him as "the Duesbergians." Even though there was a small army of Duesbergians, I have chosen to focus this book on four of the most prominent ones. Many of them had their own public and private theories about the causation of AIDS, but they generally had the same doubts about HIV as Duesberg. As the American government's official AIDS paradigm was increasingly carved into stone, Duesberg and the Duesbergians found themselves being called "AIDS denialists" who were a threat to public health. Some of the most powerful publications in the world mocked them, including *Science*, *Nature*, *The New York Times*, *The New York Review of Books*, and *The New Yorker*.

In addition to detailing Duesberg's critical thinking about the AIDS paradigm, John Lauritsen also reported on Duesberg's opposition to the use of some very toxic treatments for AIDS, most prominently, the drug called

AZT which was being given to people who were diagnosed with AIDS or who had tested positive for HIV. Lauritsen's reporting on these matters are gathered in two important books, *The AIDS War*, and *Poison by Prescription*.

The *New York Native* became even more controversial in 1988 when I asked a writer, Neenyah Ostrom, to begin covering the relationship of AIDS to the mysterious emerging epidemic of what almost jokingly was called "chronic fatigue syndrome (CFS)." The obviously AIDS-like CFS epidemic had broken out concurrently with AIDS and seemed at first to mostly affect white heterosexual women. Ultimately, it was Ostrom's reporting in *New York Native* that was the biggest challenge to America's biomedical establishment, for it threatened to reveal that the entire AIDS paradigm was a house of cards and that the Centers for Disease Control was totally incompetent. Unfortunately for Duesberg and the Duesbegians, it also threatened to undermine the lifestyle paradigm of AIDS many of them were married to. Ostrom's reporting suggested that AIDS and chronic fatigue syndrome were actually two faces of a large pandemic caused not by the retrovirus HIV but by HHV-6, a DNA virus that was able to infect and harm many systems in the body and seemed to cause variable illnesses. Her reporting supported the notion that the Centers for Disease Control had defined the AIDS epidemic *too narrowly*, and as a result they had made one of the biggest errors in the history of science and medicine. The HHV-6 theory of AIDS challenged everything about the epidemic: the nosology, the virology, the mode of transmission, and the epidemiology. It meant that at best HIV was an exponentially stupid mistake or, at worst, a nefarious cover-up.

The picture of an HHV-6 epidemic that could endanger the health of the entire public in a variety of ways was terrifying. Given that it is no secret that public health officials seem to consider "panic control" part of their job description, it really is not shocking that the Centers for Disease Control has foolishly tried to keep a lid on information about the HHV-6 pandemic for more than three decades.

I have been studying this cockamamie political and medical event for more than half of my 67 years on this planet. It has been the center of my adult life. I sometimes think of it as an existential Rubik's Cube that I needed to be able to figure out as completely as possible. I think Hannah Arendt felt the same way about the Holocaust and Nazi Germany and it inspired her to write *The Origins of Totalitarianism*. You could say that much of what I have been writing about the AIDS epidemic constitutes my attempt to come to grips with the origins of what I call "totalitarian science," "sociopathic science," or "abnormal science." Thomas Kuhn's discussion of "normal science" in *The Structure of Scientific Revolutions* inspired my opposite-world label "abnormal science" for the pseudoscience of AIDS and its related biomedical issues. Both Kuhn and Arendt have been for me what Arendt refers to as "bannisters" in my attempt to think my way through the moral, political, and scientific disaster that is Holocaust II.

Much of my thinking about Holocaust II is contained in my book, *Iatrogenocide: Notes for a Political Philosophy of Epidemiology and Science*. In the introduction to that book I write, "I have concluded that what we think of as the epidemiology and science of AIDS are essentially a corrupted hard drive. Virtually all science and epidemiology conducted on that hard drive is false even though it has the appearance of being rational, progressive, and normal."

I have also come to the conclusion that science is inherently political and the politics of AIDS science are both antigay and racist. Antigayness and racism are hardwired into the epidemiology and pseudoscience of AIDS in the same way that antisemitism was hardwired into Nazi science. I came up with the term "homodemiology" to describe the kind of antigay epidemiology and science that blames diseases and epidemics on gays and cherry-picks or distorts data to support unwarranted and bigoted conclusions. ("Afrodemiology" is my word for the racist version of the same concept.) In the so-called AIDS epidemic, "public health" is the mask that homodemiology and Afrodemiology wear.

In many ways, my journey to these conclusions began with Peter Duesberg and the Duesbergians. Peter Duesberg and his courageous colleagues spoke out when the science of AIDS contained elements that just didn't make sense. They all took great risks in speaking out and they inspired people like me to think critically about every element of the AIDS epidemic. Ironically, the more critically I thought about the epidemic the more I saw that the members of the AIDS establishment were not the only ones who were getting the epidemic wrong. As right as they were about some things, I came to the conclusion that Duesberg and the Duesbergians did not fully grasp the mistaken nosology and epidemiology or antigay politics of the epidemic. Furthermore, they did not see the massive epidemic of HHV-6 that was driving an apocalyptic and variable epidemic in plain sight—one that included chronic fatigue syndrome, autism, multiple sclerosis, and many other "mysterious" illnesses.

For the last three decades, Duesberg and Duesbergians have been sucking up all the oxygen in the AIDS debate. Their arguments about HIV not being the cause of AIDS are cogent and it has been frustrating for them to watch the conventional wisdom triumph over truth. I think many of them are puzzled about their inability to wake up the intellectual community, the media, and the general public. I imagine many of them must lie in bed at night thinking "How can people be so stupid?"

I have written this book to celebrate their brilliance and bravery and to point out *what they got right*. I also discuss *what they got wrong* and explain why their mistakes prevented them from undermining a very corrupt AIDS establishment and thereby ending Holocaust II.

I hope they will accept my critique in the spirit of friendship and believe me when I say that, no matter what, I can never thank them enough for what they did.

Peter Duesberg

Half a Hero is Better than None

"As Max Weber put it, 'An exhaustive causal investigation of any concrete phenomenon in its full reality is not only impossible, it is simply nonsense.' Epidemiologists know this and do not attempt to include all causal factors in their analyses. They select some causes and omit others. Since the epidemiologist must, however, employ some criteria in the selection process, whether consciously or not, the final roundup of causes is never neutral. It necessarily reflects both the (human-made) rules of epidemiology and the values and assumptions of the person selecting the cause. The list probably reproduces many elements of the dominant political ideology as well, if only because the language we use to describe reality is so heavily influenced by the interests of powerful groups."
—Sylvia Noble Tesh, *Hidden Arguments: Political Ideology and Disease Prevention Policy* (Page 68)

To say that the achievement of Peter Duesberg is a glass half-full should never be seen as damning with faint praise. Unflappable, imperfect Peter Duesberg heroically changed the course of the AIDS epidemic and history itself by his actions and part of his personal tragedy is that he could have changed it even more if he had looked deeper and been more critically attentive to the politics of the Centers for Disease Control's heterosexist epidemiology.

In the introduction to his 1987 interview with Duesberg, John Lauritsen wrote, "Peter Duesberg came to the United States about 20 years ago from Germany. He is professor of Molecular Biology at the University of California in Berkeley. It is because of his interest in retroviruses, on which he is an authority, that he became involved in questioning the 'AIDS virus etiology.'" (*The Aids War* p.47)

In that interview Duesberg argued that HIV could not be the cause of AIDS because of "the consistent biochemical inactivity of the virus." (*AW* p.47) He told Lauritsen that "Even in patients who were dying from disease, the virus is almost undetectable, while RNA synthesis is essentially not detectable, (*AW* p.47) Duesberg also said, "So that is one of the key arguments, and there is no exception to the rule that pathogens in order to be pathogenic have to be active." (*AW* p.48) He insisted, "very few potentially susceptible cells are ever infected, and those that are infected don't do anything. The virus just sits here." (*AW* p.48)

Duesberg also argued that the long latency period of the disease was "a very suspicious signal that the virus is unlikely to be solely the direct cause as they claim." (AW p.48) He pointed out that retroviruses "are the most benign viruses that we know" and "they can remain in the cell in latent form." (*AW* p.49) And most damning of all to the HIV hypothesis, according to Duesberg, was the fact that "When AIDS is diagnosed, they say that now it's possible for the disease—but the virus is not doing any more than it had done before when there were no symptoms of the disease." (*AW* p.49) Duesberg concluded that the presence of antibodies to HIV was proof that the virus had been neutralized and asserted that it was "a gross injustice to discriminate against anyone on the basis of having antibodies." (*AW* p.50)

One of the most noble aspects of Duesberg's AIDS criticism and whistleblowing on the HIV mistake (or fraud) issue was his extraordinary— almost visionary—sensitivity to the damage it was going to do to the health and liberties of those who were victimized by it. In general, the people he argued with, those who benefited financially and professionally from the HIV hypothesis, had a rather cold and cavalier attitude toward the effect their brilliant ideas often had on the minorities who were affected. (They certainly never seemed to ask themselves what the consequences would be if *they* were wrong.)

Duesberg deserves credit for being one of the first people to realize (without saying as much) that the HIV/AIDS theory was an instance of what I've called "abnormal science." One of the wittiest men engaged in the AIDS issue, he could often find the humorous absurdities implicit in the HIV theory. When HIV was called a "slow virus," he said, "There are no slow viruses, only slow scientists." In public forums, he always presented his opinions in a collegial manner, but he was also always capable of leaving his opponents hemorrhaging from a cutting sarcasm presented with deadly charm. It may have been the fact that he verbally earned the role of the alpha intellect in any professional gathering that inspired both envy and vengeance from his powerful HIV establishment opponents. They were often simply intellectually outclassed, even if they held all the money and the political cards. Nothing rattles totalitarian science more than a clever and steadfast nontotalitarian scientist.

If Duesberg suffered from any deficits in the area of judgment, it may have been an inability to imagine a different AIDS epidemic caused by a dynamic, multisystemic virus like HHV-6 (and its family) which could manifest itself in a variety of surprising ways (like AIDS, chronic fatigue syndrome and autism) depending on other factors. Duesberg told Lauritsen, "AIDS is a condition which includes so many parameters that it's almost inconceivable to define a simple pathogen as the cause, considering the diverse patterns of the disease." (*AW* p.52) Duesberg didn't think outside the box of the CDC's nosology or epidemiology. He never considered the possibility that the CDC had missed a whole world of undetected nosological and epidemiological data (like the data from the chronic fatigue syndrome epidemic) that would have completely changed the picture of the disease's patterns. And the idea that there might be something in the world that could be called a multisystemic virus like HHV-6 which *could* cause many different patterns of disease, was simply not on his radar.

At the time that Lauritsen first interviewed Duesberg—in 1987—Duesberg remained a bit of an agnostic on what was actually causing AIDS, saying, "We haven't excluded anything" and "I really wonder what it could be." (*AIW* p.53) Compared to where he would end up, he was a demure etiological virgin at that point. He was only beginning to consider the role of recreational drugs as a possible cause saying, "I'm really just guessing here, but I think this is where more research should be done." (*AIW* p.53)

Unfortunately, as time went on Duesberg seems to have been encouraged or even pressured by some of his colleagues to take a stronger public stand on what he thought actually *was* the cause of AIDS and he became far less tentative and open-minded, passionately adding to his anti-HIV gospel a seemingly unshakable conviction that recreational drugs explained AIDS in gay men. Regardless of its merits, such a position immediately lost him the readymade constituency of the gay community who seemed to have been invited by Duesberg and his followers to be exonerated for a transmissible infection only to be convicted as a group in an alternative fashion for having a unique gay (and—let's not forget— criminal) drug-taking lifestyle. With some notable exceptions, Duesberg walked into a big gay "thanks but no thanks." He had jumped the gay shark. It was a tragic development for both parties, because politically, Duesberg really needed gay supporters to help him challenge the mistaken HIV hypothesis, which he felt was unfairly threatening their liberties and health of the gay community. He was the enemy of the gay community's determined CDC/NIH enemy, but he wasn't perceived as its friend. By rejecting Duesberg's half-a-glass of truth about the virus, the gay community ended up in the open arms of the AIDS establishment and crusading public health authorities complete with all the goodies they had in store for their willing, eager and all too compliant patient population.

Peter Duesberg detailed his argument about the nature of the AIDS epidemic and his struggle with the AIDS establishment in his book, *Inventing the AIDS Virus*, which was published by Regnery Publishing in 1998. In the publisher's preface, Alfred Regnery notes, "AIDS is the first political disease." In his acknowledgments, Duesberg wrote, "I extend my gratitude to my most critical opponents in the AIDS debate, who have unwittingly provided me the great volume of evidence by which I have disproved the virus-AIDS hypothesis and exposed the political maneuverings behind the war on AIDS." (*IAV* p.x)

Duesberg's book could be used as a primary text if college courses are ever given on the politics, sociology, and psychology of what I call "abnormal science." He fleshes out many parts of his argument against the HIV theory of AIDS causation already mentioned in his 1987 interview with Lauritsen.

While Duesberg is often thought to be someone who encouraged the rethinking of the AIDS issue, the book supports the notion already mentioned that, in reality, he actually *never went far enough*, never really did a true radical rethinking of AIDS because he works with a tacit acceptance of the basic epidemiological premises and "facts" provided by the CDC and the HIV/AIDS establishment. By leaving their paradigm's "factual" assumptions standing, he ultimately jeopardized his own analysis. Duesberg's critical tact was to take the "facts" as they were provided by the CDC and to try and poke holes in their etiological logic by showing how they failed to successfully make predictions about the course of the epidemic or by arguing that the facts as given by the CDC contradicted other formally known (hence, published) facts. The problem was that AIDS involved ground zero nosological and epidemiological definitions of what an AIDS case actually was, and *if* that definition had, at the very beginning of the epidemic, been distorted by evidence that had been cherry-picked, or had been ignored because of political blinders, then there was a good chance that Duesberg— even with his superb skills of logic and reason—was trapped in an pseudoscientific funhouse of "garbage in garbage out." Saying the CDC mistakenly linked the wrong virus to cases of AIDS begs a question: And what if the CDC completely got the definition of AIDS cases wrong to begin with? Or, more troubling, that what the CDC thought were epidemiological apples and oranges were really all apples or all oranges. Duesberg never illuminated *all* of the fundamental possibilities of what could have gone wrong nosologically and epidemiologically. Duesberg was in a Donald Rumsfeld situation where he didn't know what he didn't know.

Duesberg worked with the epidemiological predictions the AIDS authorities were giving him and tried to show that when the predictions based on them did not work out, they reflected poorly on the credibility of the HIV theory. He argued, "Officials have continually predicted the explosion of AIDS into the general population through sexual transmission of HIV, striking males and females equally, as well as homosexuals and heterosexuals, to be followed by a corresponding increase in the rate of death. . . . In short, the alleged viral disease does not seem to be spreading from the 1 million HIV-positive Americans to the remaining 250 million." (*IAV* p.5)

Duesberg's logic brilliantly skewered the CDC's notion that AIDS was an equal opportunity disease. But again, one has to note that the one caveat he didn't acknowledge was that if the CDC's definition of what an AIDS case was *turned out to be dead wrong*, then all bets were off about correlated and potentially causative factors. Just debunking the logic behind the weak correlation of putative AIDS cases with HIV was not the same as debunking the notion of *some fundamentally different kind of AIDS epidemic* still occurring, not only in the gay community, but also in some form in the general population. If, at the very basic level of defining what a case is and what a case isn't, profound mistakes had been made, then one couldn't really know where the disease was and where it wasn't. And then the issue of HIV not being the cause of what was being called AIDS would, in that case, be *totally beside the point*. If anything, the HIV mistake should have made people wonder if those in charge at the CDC had gotten something even more profoundly wrong in the initial working definition of AIDS which subsequently was carved in stone thanks to the totalitarian scientific culture that protected it.

Insofar as Duesberg recognized that it all just didn't add up, he graciously performed a great humanitarian service over and over again by telling the world that as long as the HIV establishment was in charge of AIDS we were essentially trapped in a realm of unreliable and untrustworthy pseudoscience where people were going to get hurt. And luckily, for three decades, at great personal expense, Duesberg valiantly refused to shut up. Perplexed, Duesberg wrote, "Something is wrong with this picture. How could the largest and most sophisticated scientific establishment in history have failed so miserably in saving lives and even in forecasting the epidemic's toll?" (*IAV* p.5) Ironically, given that Duesberg himself was blind to what turned out to be the CFS epidemic and HHV-6 spectrum catastrophe, the premise of his rhetorical question turned out to be a tragic understatement.

Duesberg's suggestion about what should be done reinforces the notion that his call to a reassessment of AIDS and HIV just wasn't intellectually radical or fundamental enough. Duesberg's prescription for the problem was that "Faced with this medical debacle, scientists should re-open a simple but most essential question: What causes AIDS?" (*IAV* p.6) Again, it was not really a radical return to epidemiological ground zero. A return to ground zero would have involved asking if the epidemiological common immunological denominator that determined what a case actually was itself needed to be audited by looking closely—and in an immunologically sophisticated manner—*at the entire population*. Duesberg was like an accountant who looks at the books for discrepancies, but never goes into the warehouse to see if what's there matches the inventory numbers. His due diligence only went so far. The definition of AIDS was on the books and unfortunately, taken at face value by Duesberg. It didn't necessarily match what was actually going on in doctor's offices all over America and it didn't necessarily reflect the actual disaster that was occurring in the immune systems of the entire American population. There was a whole immunologically-challenged world beyond the CDC's published data and the peer-reviewed papers Duesberg used to play "gotcha" with the CDC's facts, logic, and conclusions.

There was an interesting groupthink bias in Duesberg and many of his followers, most of whom were heterosexual—some emphatically so. Not surprisingly, their notion about what was wrong with AIDS etiology *was always biased in the direction of heterosexuals being less (or not at all) at risk for AIDS* as a result of the CDC's scientific errors. Sometimes one got the uncanny notion that Duesberg and his followers were whistling heterosexually in the dark, engaged in trying to convince themselves that *they as a group* were safe from the "gay lifestyle" epidemic. Ironically, considering their apparent need for personal immunological safety, though, is the fact that *if* the CDC was wrong then all bets about their safety could have been off and the actual level of risk could have gone the other way. *They could have been in more, not less danger.* But that possibility never seemed to consciously dawn on them, and their AIDS dissident movement, in all its forms, seemed bent on making sure that it never did. They created a kind of dissident groupthink that made them odd bedfellows with the mostly white male heterosexual HIV establishment who also could absolutely not let themselves see the connection between AIDS, chronic fatigue syndrome, HHV-6, and ultimately the simmering HHV-6-related autism disaster.

Duesberg got a lot of things right and a lot of things sort of right. He was right when he wrote, "Without going back to check its underlying assumptions, the AIDS establishment will never make sense of its mountain of data." (*IAV* p.6) He didn't quite get it right when he concluded, "The single flaw that determined the destiny of AIDS research since 1984 was the assumption that AIDS is infectious. After taking this wrong turn scientists had to make bad assumptions upon which they have built a huge artifice of mistaken ideas." (*IAV* p.6) Duesberg very simply failed to notice the fundamental wrong turn that was made before *that* wrong turn. He never considered the possibility that if the definition of AIDS itself was wrong, the corrected definition just might support the notion of an infectious epidemic and a virus-AIDS hypothesis, *just not the mistaken HIV one.*

The great thing about Duesberg—for students of what I've called homodemiology or heterosexist epidemiology—is that he criticized the logical absurdity of what I call GRID-think, (Gay-related immune deficiency) which is in part the rather superstitious and bigoted notion implicit in HIV epidemiology that *viruses know intuitively who gays are* so they can choose to infect them and only them. Unfortunately, Duesberg built his own quasi-GRID-think drug-and-lifestyle-paradigm on a similar reality-challenged premise by saying that something non-infectious must explain an epidemic confining itself mainly to a risk group. By pointing out the logical absurdity of a virus limiting itself to one group of people, he opened the way for a more radical critical political rethinking about what was going on in the CDC's epidemiology that he seemed unprepared to do himself. He started the job, but homodemiological and sociological analysis had to finish it. Blaming lifestyle factors of gays was just another not-very-great correlation fingered as causation, generating an alternative scapegoating epidemiology of blaming the victims for what turned out to be the HHV-6 spectrum catastrophe. Unfortunately, Duesberg exposed one wild goose chase and started another one when he wrote, "The only solution is to rethink the basic assumption that AIDS is infectious and is caused by HIV." (*IAV* p.7) The only solution? Well, not exactly.

Duesberg's book will always be an important source for anyone who wants to understand the evolution of the AIDS mistake, even if Duesberg's own theory turned out to be wrong. Most importantly, Duesberg details just how abnormal and nearly psychotic the whole scientific process of AIDS was and his work supports the argument that something with a totalitarian *je ne sais quoi* was unfolding in the name of AIDS science.

The very manner in which HIV was announced in 1984 as the probable cause of AIDS, according to Duesberg's account, was scientifically deviant: "This announcement was made prior to the publication of any scientific evidence confirming the virus theory. With this unprecedented maneuver, Gallo's discovery bypassed review by the scientific community. Science by press conference was substituted for the unconventional process of scientific validation, which is based on publications in the professional literature. The 'AIDS virus' became instant national dogma, and the tremendous weight of federal resources were diverted into just one race—the race to study the AIDS virus . . . . The only questions to be studied from 1984 on were how HIV causes AIDS and what could be done about it." (*IAV* p.8)

At that point in time, Duesberg noted that "serious doubts are now surfacing about HIV, the so-called AIDS virus . . . . The consensus on the virus hypothesis of AIDS is falling apart, as its opponents grow in number." (*IAV* p.8) At that moment Duesberg still seemed optimistic, as AIDS seemed to be taking place in the good faith universe of normal science which was open to change and paradigm shift. Unfortunately, because he was blind to the heterosexist sociological issues underpinning AIDS, he was incapable of perceiving the unmovable backstage anti-gay epidemiological values that were controlling the public health agenda and polluting the science. He couldn't see that it wasn't just a matter of the practitioners of this deviant science were digging in professionally; the whole homodemiological culture was dug in, which was far more formidable than anything Duesberg could have imagined. The political consensus about the etiological nature of "AIDS" was not a just stone in the road of scientific process. Peter Duesberg had found his way into abnormal science's opposite world.

As a paradigm that was supposed to capture people's imagination and cause a major shift or Kuhnian conversion—or visual gestalt-shift—from one consensus to another, Duesberg's paradigm was nearly dead on arrival. If he had simply taken his stand as a dean of retrovirology and just left the cause of AIDS up in the air and concentrated on demolishing the HIV theory once and for all, the HHV-6 catastrophe and what I call "Holocaust II" might have been stopped in their tracks.

Duesberg charged that the CDC's paradigm was "ineffective" and that "public fear was being exploited." (*IAV* p. 9) From his perspective, the public was being told the problem was bigger than it actually was. True, public fear was being shamelessly exploited, but *not in the way Duesberg thought*. By framing the epidemic in an anti-gay manner, public fear of gays, society's

601

sexual outsiders, *was* being manipulated to hide the painful truth about the public's risk of developing a complex form of immunodeficiency or dysfunction. The public was being provided with what Daniel Goleman called "a vital lie." A terrified public, to the great detriment of its future health was getting the reassuring heterosexist pseudo-facts about "AIDS" it wanted to hear with the gay community losing what I call its *epidemiological human rights* in the process. And again, ironically, Duesberg and the Duesbergians had their own set of heterosexist concoctions that were *even more reassuring* to the heterosexual general population. And wrong. Both the CDC paradigm and the Duesberg paradigm misled a clueless and anxious public.

Duesberg's shock at the nature of what was going on is exactly why a formal theory of abnormal or totalitarian science is required to comprehend and illuminate the AIDS era, just as the concept of totalitarianism was required to understand the Hitler and Stalin eras. Duesberg asks a big, ugly, rhetorical question: "How could a whole new generation of more than a hundred thousand AIDS experts, including medical doctors, virologists, immunologists, cancer researchers, pharmacologists, and epidemiologists— including more than half a dozen Nobel Laureates—be wrong? How could a scientific world that so freely exchanged all information from every corner of this planet have missed an alternative explanation for AIDS?" (*IAV* p.9) Too bad he didn't ask how the exact same crowd could not see the chronic fatigue syndrome epidemic for what it was. Ditto for HHV-6 and its insidious spectrum.

Again, Duesberg's answer to his own question was that AIDS had been misclassified as an infectious illness and his theory rested on the notion that "the premature assumption of contagiousness has many times in the past obstructed free investigation for the treatment and prevention of a non-infectious disease—sometimes for years, at the cost of many thousands of lives." (*IAV* p.10) Duesberg was setting the terms of the twenty-five-year debate between the mainstream AIDS establishment and what became popularly known as the AIDS dissidents, or the Duesbergians. This unfortunate dichotomy set the course for the wrong kind of debate, a contest between HIV and Duesberg's non-infectious drug lifestyle hypothesis, leaving out the possibility that there might be a dynamic infectious agent *other than HIV* that did indeed fit the causation criteria of a redefined AIDS epidemic. No space was left in the debate for something like a new multisystemic virus such as HHV-6, which was capable of causing an epidemic of a more broadly defined variable illness. Duesberg asserted HIV "could be the most harmful of . . . fatal errors in the history of medicine if AIDS proves to be not infectious." (*IAV* p.10) Of course, if AIDS was incorrectly defined and a dynamic viral agent other than HIV was spreading *silently and exponentially* while the false Duesbergian debate sucked up all of intellectual and scientific oxygen in the debate on AIDS, the harm could have been exponentially worse. And it was.

602

In order for abnormal or totalitarian science to hold sway over a society for a long period of time, it must have ample cooperation from both the scientific and media communities and the Duesberg story provides evidence that such was the case in AIDS. To explain how the media was continuously kept in its subservient place during the AIDS debacle, he quotes reporter Elinor Burkett of *The Miami Herald*: "If you have an AIDS beat, you're a beat reporter, your job is every day to go out there, fill your newspaper with what's new about AIDS. You write a story that questions the truth of the central AIDS hypothesis and what happened to me will happen to you. Nobody's going to talk to you. Now if nobody will talk to you, if nobody at the CDC will ever return your phone call, you lose your competitive edge as an AIDS reporter. So it always keeps you in the mainstream, because you need those guys to be your buddies . . . ." (*IAV* p.388)

Duesberg insists that the very defensive and insular AIDS scientific establishment was determined to "confine the debate to scientific circles." (*IAV* p.389) He quotes a rather shocking threat from the de facto AIDS Czar, Anthony Fauci, who said, "Journalists who make too many mistakes, or who are sloppy are going to find that their access to scientists may diminish."(*IAV* p.384) In a totalitarian world of homodemiology and abnormal science the definition of "sloppy" will be that which contradicts the powers that be. Question AIDS and you will need to look for a new career. (Given the degree to which AIDS science often looks like a big unmade bed, it's amusing to hear Fauci say the word "sloppy" with a straight face.)

Duesberg also quotes two of the powerful, public-relations-savvy virologists who suggested another tactic for dealing with Duesberg and the critics of the HIV establishment: "One approach would be to refuse television confrontations with Duesberg, as Tony Fauci and one of us managed to do at the opening of the VIIth International Conference on AIDS in Florence. One can't spread misinformation without an audience." (*IAV* p.39) There's nothing in Thomas Kuhn's theories about the process of normal science about deliberately denying one's critics an audience, or denying the public exposure to scientific second and third opinions.

One of the more outrageous moments in his book occurs when Duesberg writes, "Based on an anonymous source, key officials of the United States government specifically engineered a strategy for suppressing the HIV debate in 1987 while Duesberg was still on leave at the N.I.H. The operation began on April 28, less than a month after Duesberg's first paper on the HIV question appeared in *Cancer Research*, apparently because several journalists and homosexual activists began raising questions." (*IAV* p.32) A memo about Duesberg's critique of the HIV theory was sent out from a staffer in the Office of the Secretary of Health and Human Services: "This obviously has the potential to raise a lot of controversy (If this isn't the virus, how do we know the blood supply is safe? How do we know anything about transmission? How could you all be so stupid, and why should we ever believe you again?) And we need to be prepared to respond. I have already asked N.I.H. public affairs to start digging into this." (*LAV* p.390) This is an extremely important memo from the point of view of future what-did-they-know-and-when-did-they-know-it histories that try to fathom all the government's motivations throughout this scientific and political disaster. It shows how clearly at least one person in the government could see the potential dire consequences for the government of being wrong about HIV. Somebody knew *exactly* what was at stake.

In his book, Duesberg gives a number of examples of the media seeming to have been pressured by the HIV establishment *not to cover the story of the controversy*. According to Duesberg, "The MacNeil Lehrer News hour sent camera crews to do a major segment on the controversy. But when the . . . broadcast date arrived, the feature had been pulled. Apparently AIDS officials had heard of its imminent airing and had intercepted it." (*LAV* p.392) Television shows on Duesberg involving Good Morning America on ABC, CNN, Italian television, and Larry King Live met with a similar fate.

According to Duesberg's book, he "appeared on major national television only twice. The first time was on March 28, 1993 on the ABC magazine program *Day One*. Even in this case, according to the producer, Fauci tried to get the show canceled days before broadcast.' (*LAV* p.393) When Duesberg was interviewed for *Nightline*, he ended up only being given a small amount of air time and Fauci showed up and was given the lion's share of the show to make the HIV establishment's case. And Duesberg fared no better overseas. The British medical and public health establishment greeted a pro-Duesberg program with "stern condemnations" and subsequently the British press "turned around and began criticizing the program." (*LAV* p.323)

One of the most interesting moments of censorship occurred at the highest level of government when "Jim Warner, a Reagan White House advisor critical of AIDS alarmism, heard about Duesberg and arranged a White House debate in January 1988." (*LAV* p.394) Duesberg writes, "This would have forced the HIV issue into the public spotlight, but it was abruptly canceled days ahead of time, on orders from above." (*LAV* p.394)

Duesberg didn't fare much better with the print media. He notes that *The New York Times* had written about him only three times in the first seven years of the controversy and all of it was negative. The same kind of treatment was doled out by *The Washington Post* and "the *San Francisco Chronicle* intended to cover the story, until it encountered opposition from scientists in the local AIDS establishment." (*LAV* p.394) Even the countercultural or alternative press could not be counted on to give the controversy balanced or independent-minded coverage. Duesberg reports, "In 1989 *Rolling Stone* had commissioned a freelance writer from New York to write a Duesberg article, but then canceled it during the interview with Duesberg in his lab." (*LAV* p.395) Both *Harper's* and *Esquire* killed articles that had been commissioned on Duesberg during the same period. The media was essentially acting as an enabler of the culture of abnormal or totalitarian science.

Even more evidence that AIDS was a manifestation of abnormal science can be found in the way that Duesberg experienced censorship from formerly adoring scientific circles and experienced roadblocks to having his ideas and criticisms presented in the professional scientific literature. Duesberg writes, "Robert Gallo and some other scientists began refusing . . . to attend scientific conferences if Duesberg would be allowed to make a presentation." (*IAV* p.396) During the same period Duesberg rarely was "invited to retrovirus meetings and virtually never to AIDS conferences, despite seminal contributions to the field, including the isolation of the retroviral genome, the first analysis of the order of retroviral genes, and the discovery of the first retroviral cancer gene." (*IAV* p.396)

Duesberg reports that his scientific papers on AIDS "would constantly run into obstacles at every turn, from hostile peer reviews to reluctant editors."(*IAV* p.393) The rules mysteriously changed for "the *Proceedings of the National Academy of Sciences*, where Academy members such as Duesberg have an automatic right to publish papers without standard peer review." (*IAV* p.397) An editor rejected Duesberg's unique and provocative submission by bizarrely saying that it was not "original." And, supporting the case for the arbitrary make-it-up-as-you-go-along nature of abnormal AIDS science, a subsequent replacement editor decided tradition had to be completely ignored for this special case and the Duesberg paper had to be peer-reviewed *because it was "controversial."* (*IAV* p.397) It took several months of hostile reviewers negotiating with Duesberg before the paper was finally published. According to Duesberg, "Robert Gallo was asked to write a rebuttal, but never did." (*IAV* p.357) Strategic silent treatment is part of the arsenal of abnormal science.

The punishments for anyone standing up to totalitarian, abnormal science can be severe. Duesberg reports that "the AIDS establishment made its most effective counterattack by going after Duesberg's funding, the lifeblood of any scientist's laboratory. After coming out against the HIV theory, Duesberg was denied continuation of an N.I.H. Outstanding Grant by a group of scientists which included two who were proponents of the HIV paradigm and three scientists who never even reviewed the grant. When a review committee considered Duesberg's grant proposal a few months later, "they did . . . complain about Duesberg's questioning attitude as the major obstacle to funding him and singled out AIDS." (*IAV* p.402) Subsequently, "every one of his seventeen peer-reviewed grant applications to other federal state or private agencies—whether for AIDS research, on AZT and other drugs, or for cancer research—has been turned down." (*IAV* p.403) Thus did Duesberg come face to face with one of the telltale signs of abnormal and totalitarian science: blacklisting. The long arms of HIV/AIDS politics reached into his life at his university where "Several fellow professors" maneuvered "against Duesberg in various ways." His promotions in pay were "blocked" and he was denied "coveted graduate lecture courses." (*IAV* p.404)

One of the most dramatic and creepiest abnormal science moments in the Duesberg saga occurred in 1994 when a high-ranking geneticist from the N.I.H. flew to California to present Duesberg with an unpublished paper titled "HIV Causes AIDS: Koch's Postulates Fulfilled." Duesberg was asked to be a third author on a paper *he hadn't even collaborated on*. The paper had been commissioned by *Nature* editor and HIV theory proponent, John Maddox. Duesberg was warned by his high-ranking visitor that by continuing his opposition to the HIV theory he "would even risk his credentials for having discovered cancer genes." (*IAV* p.406) (The willingness to "disappear" the past is another one of the telltale signs of totalitarian science.) The geneticist told Duesberg that if he agreed to be an author on the paper it would "open the doors for Duesberg's reentry into the establishment." (*IAV* p 406) Duesberg said thanks but no thanks in the form of offering to write something for *Nature* that said the direct opposite of what that proposed unsigned paper posited.

A very thoughtful and philosophical man in many ways, Duesberg sought to understand the recalcitrant system that was making it so difficult for his ideas to be heard and tested, let alone prevail. He blamed it on "command science" which by his analysis, derived its power from three sources in the medical establishment: "(1) enforced consensus through peer review, (2) enforced consensus through commercialization and (3) the fear of disease, particularly infectious disease." (*IAV* p.452)

Because all serious medical scientists in America need grants from the NIH to survive, they often need to conform to the establishment viewpoint. While the "peer-review system" is supposed to be like an independent jury system, in reality, according to Duesberg, "a truly independent jury system would be fatal to the establishment." (*IAV* p.452) The result is "the peers serve the orthodoxy by serving their own vested interests." (*IAV* p.452) Duesberg warned that "as long as a scientist's work is reviewed only by competitors within his own field, peer review will crush genuine science." (*IAV* p.454)

Ominously for AIDS patients and the myriad victims of the real AIDS epidemic, Duesberg concluded that "Through peer review the federal government has attained a near-monopoly on science." (*IAV* p.454) Abnormal science loves the absolute power of monopolies. HIV became hegemonic because "a handful of federal agencies, primarily the NIH, dominate research policies and effectively dictate the official dogma . . . . By declaring the virus the cause of AIDS at a press conference sponsored by the Department of Health and Human Services, NIH researcher Robert Gallo swung the entire medical establishment and even the rest of the world, behind his hypothesis. Once such a definitive statement is made, the difficulty of retracting it only increases with time."(*IAV* p.454)

Duesberg criticized the huge conflict of interest in science that is caused by its commercialization. He argued that the FDA, by essentially banning competing therapies, often helps the pharmaceutical industry develop monopolies. Profits from products approved by the FDA often find their way back to scientists who sat in judgment on fellow scientists "in the form of patent royalties, consultantships, paid board positions, and stock ownership." (*IAV* p.455) In addition, "in order for a research product to find a market, the underlying hypothesis for the product must be accepted by a majority of the practitioners in the field." (*IAV* p.455) In the case of AIDS "commercial success can be achieved only by consensus. For example, an AIDS hypothesis would not be approved unless it miraculously cured AIDS overnight." (*IAV* p.455) Thus Gallo's royalties from an HIV patent as well as those with financial interest in HIV tests (Like William Haseltine and Max Essex) indicate that they may not be the most disinterested parties to make important decisions about the direction of AIDS research. And yet they were among the powerful inner circle of AIDS research. No wonder Duesberg often experienced forms of petulance and hostility from such characters rather than open-minded collegiality. In essence, by telling an inconvenient truth he was a threat to their lifestyles and reputations.

The third arm of the "command science" which Duesberg discusses goes in the opposite direction of the overriding conclusion of my newspaper's reporting about the real AIDS epidemic. Duesberg writes, "Traditionally, the power of medical science has been based on the fear of disease, particularly infectious disease. The HIV-AIDS establishment has exploited this instrument of power to its limit." (*IAV* p.456) Duesberg assumes that an infectious epidemic has essentially been invented out of whole cloth by incompetent epidemiology. His book would have been more accurately titled "Inventing the AIDS Epidemic." Duesberg accuses the CDC of delusional epidemiology driven by opportunism and hysteria. The manipulated paradigm of an infectious AIDS epidemic was used to create a "stampede," to create "irrational" fear in the public, to cynically manipulate, to mislead. And most importantly, from the Duesberg perspective, to build a lucrative new empire for the CDC.

While most of my work which began at *New York Native* supports the notion of a reign of intellectual dishonesty at the CDC, my conclusions about AIDS turn this part of the Duesbergian thesis on its head. Duesberg sees a devastating, apocalyptic epidemic being cynically and opportunistically *imagined*, and my reporting sees it as *existing—big time—and being concealed*. Other than HIV not being the cause of AIDS, the only thing Duesberg and I fundamentally agree on (in addition to the questionable behavior of many powerful individuals) is that the AIDS establishment was not really doing science as we expect it to be done. Duesberg might even agree with the premise that the science of AIDS was abnormal, totalitarian and even psychotic.

There is one other thing that Duesberg got right that deserves special mention. Duesberg performed an heroic whistle-blowing act during dark hours of the epidemic: his fearless adoption of a principled stand against the administration of AZT to AIDS patients. In a chapter of his book aptly titled, "With Therapies Like this, Who Needs Disease?", he discussed Azidothymidine, or AZT. About this very toxic drug that was being given to AIDS patients, Duesberg writes, "AZT kills dividing cells anywhere in the body—causing ulcerations and hemorrhaging; damage to hair follicles and skin; killing mitochondria, the energy cells of the brain; wasting away of muscles; and the destruction of the immune system and other cells. . . . Amazingly, AZT was first approved for treatment of AIDS in 1987 and then for prevention of AIDS in 1990." (*IAV* p.301) Duesberg didn't say it, but he didn't have to: AZT was more of a cruel, sadistic, toxic punishment than a medical treatment for AIDS patients.

AZT beautifully expressed the AIDS zeitgeist. AZT was invented in 1964 to kill cancer tumors, but the drug also effectively killed healthy growing tissues and was shelved without a patent because it was too toxic. Twenty years later scientists reported that it was capable of stopping HIV from replicating. Duesberg had serious doubts about even the basic AIDS research that was done with AZT which suggested that it could be given in small enough doses so that it would kill the virus without also killing the t-cells and other cells in the body. Not surprisingly, given the nature of AIDS science, the research that supported the safety of using AZT could not be subsequently replicated and showed that "the same low concentration [of AZT] that stops HIV also kills cells." (*IAV* p.313) Like much of the abnormal science of AIDS, if you looked diligently beneath one fraud, you could find yet another.

The person most responsible for foisting this quasi-genocidal toxic drug on AIDS patients was Sam Broder, the man who was Gallo's boss at the National Cancer Institute. He was the man responsible for the original questionable research suggesting that AZT could be given in doses that wouldn't harm patients. AIDS patients would pay a horrifying price for his scientific slovenliness. Duesberg notes, "Broder and his collaborators have never corrected their original reports, nor have they explained the huge discrepancies between their data and other reports." (*IAV* p.313)

Duesberg's critique of AZT gets even more devastating when he points out that the virus is dormant and therefore the virus "can only attack growing cells" and "like all other chemotherapeutic drugs, is unable to distinguish an HIV-infected cell from one that is uninfected. This has disastrous consequences on AZT-treated people; since only 1 in about 500 t-cells of HIV anti-body positive persons is ever infected, AZT must kill 499 good t-cells to kill just one that is infected by the hypothetical AIDS virus." (*IAV* p.313) In a sardonic understatement, Duesberg concluded, "It is a tragedy for people who already suffer from a t-cell deficiency." (*IAV* p.314) Needless to say, as time passes, giving people AZT sounds more and more unquestionably like a form of genocidal insanity or what I call "iatrogenocide." For a few who watched in horror as this transpired, it did *then*, too. Duesberg wrote "A toxic chemotherapy was about to be unleashed on AIDS victims, but no one had the time to think twice about its potential to destroy the immune systems of people who might otherwise survive." (*IAV* p.314) AZT belonged more in a court room as Exhibit A of a crimes against humanity trial than in the bodies of AIDS patients.

Unfortunately, given the all the surreal terror and hysteria of the time and the prevalent abject mentality of the patients, the gay community and its doctors wanted something—virtually anything—that could (or seemed to) address the problem. But make no mistake about it. There were also financial considerations that helped create the AZT disaster. Burroughs Welcome, the company that owned the patent on the drug, was eager to win approval for the treatment of AIDS by the FDA. Unfortunately for the AIDS patients, Burroughs Welcome's head researcher worked closely and effectively with Sam Broder to get FDA approval.

The process of testing the effectiveness of the drug was also highly questionable. The double blind, placebo-controlled studies of AZT on AIDS patients were not exactly double blind and placebo controlled. They were as abnormal as just about everything else in the Kafkaesque world of AIDS science. The list of things that went off the rails in the study was long. The study was stopped prematurely because the positive "results seemed stupendous." (*IAV* p.316) But as scientists looked more closely at the details of the study it turned out that the AZT trial was just as unreliable as much of the basic laboratory science that had launched AZT in the first place. More placebo patients had died than seemed reasonable. A close look at the study revealed that many of the AZT users had suffered horrific side effects which were downplayed even though they "more than abolished its presumed benefit." (*IAV* p.317)

When more information surfaced about the AZT trial, it turned out that the controls for the study were a complete mess. It was virtually impossible to conceal which patients were on AZT because in patients on AZT the drug killed bone marrow cells so quickly, that patients would come down with aplastic anemia, a not-hard-to-detect dreadful disease. According to Duesberg, "the patients, needless to say, often found out what they were taking" from clues like throwing up blood or changes in their blood counts. (*IAV* p.318) That had a grimly ironic effect on the study because those who discovered they were on the placebo, by comparing the tastes of their pills with the pills of those who were actually taking AZT, *wanted to take what they had been told was the life saving AZT*. It was a heartbreaking sign of the desperation and helplessness of their situation. According to Duesberg, "the patients had bought the early rumors of AZT's incredible healing powers, and they really did not want to take a placebo. Some of the placebo group secretly did use AZT, explaining the presence of its toxic side effects among those patients." (*IAV* p.318)

Because doctors easily noticed in the so-called "blinded" study that the AZT patients *seemed* to be doing better than the non-AZT patients, the study was ended early. The study's credibility was in shambles when it turned out that some of the patients on AZT had to be taken off of it because it was so toxic. According to Duesberg, "many of the patients simply could not tolerate AZT, and the physicians had to do something to save their lives." (*IAV* p.319) And "15 percent of the AZT group disappeared, possibly including patients with the most severe side effects." (*IAV* p.319) An inspection of documents pertaining to the study obtained under the Freedom of Information Act revealed a wide array of abnormalities in the study that suggested the study was one of the more notable frauds of the AIDS Era and Holocaust II.

While the initial results of the AZT study indicated an improvement of t-cells, it turned out that a temporary increase of t-cells did not really indicate that the patients were getting better. And there might have been some improvement of the patients from a broad spectrum antibiotic effect. The only problem was that *the drug was also toxically undermining the immune system*. It was opposite world science at its best. AZT was in essence becoming another cause of AIDS.

Tragically, even though the study was a scientific train wreck, the FDA approved AZT. The FDA panel that approved AZT included two paid consultants from Burroughs Wellcome. Duesberg notes, "the FDA endorsement could seem a cruel joke perpetrated by heartless AIDS scientists. Patients on AZT receive little more than white capsules surrounded by a blue band. But every time lab researchers order another batch for experimentation they receive a special label . . . A skull-and-crossbones symbol appears on background of bright orange, signifying an unusual chemical hazard." (*IAV* p.324)

Kary Mullis

The Nobelist with a Conscience

Kary Mullis is a biochemist who won the 1993 Nobel Prize for the Polymerase Chain Reaction. He, like Duesberg, was eventually troubled by the lack of evidence that HIV is the cause of AIDS. In the foreword he wrote for Duesberg's *Inventing the AIDS Virus*, he reported on the events that led to his criticism and ultimate confrontation with the AIDS establishment. Mullis had been hired by a firm called Specialty Labs to set up "analytic routines" for HIV. In the process of writing a report on the progress of his project, he went in search of support for this statement that was going to appear in the report: "HIV is the probable cause of AIDS." (*IAV* p.xi) He was puzzled that there was no paper to be found containing definitive proof of the statement and one that was "continually referenced in the scientific papers" about the epidemic. (*IAV* p.xi) He was puzzled that such a large enterprise involving so many scientists and growing numbers of sick and dying people did not rest on a solid foundation of a published paper that established with great certainty that HIV was the probable cause. A computer search came up with nothing. He started asking for the definitive reference at scientific meetings, but after attending ten or fifteen meetings over a period of a couple of years he "was getting pretty upset when no one could cite the reference." (*IAV* p.xi)

Mullis, without realizing it, had stumbled into the world of the abnormal totalitarian science of AIDS. He wrote, "I didn't like the ugly conclusion that was forming in my mind. The entire campaign against a disease increasingly regarded as a twentieth century Black Plague was based on a hypothesis whose origins no one could recall. That defied scientific and common sense." (*IAV* p.xii) It did however, make the opposite world kind of sense that is associated with abnormal science. Like the protagonist in Kafka's novel, Mullis had arrived at the Castle of HIV research. Science, logic, and common sense would be utterly beside the point. And pungent homodemiology (antigay epidemiology) was in the air, but Mullis, famous for his flamboyant, unapologetic heterosexuality, couldn't smell it.

When Mullis approached one of the founding fathers of the HIV/AIDS paradigm, the French discoverer of HIV himself, Luc Montagnier, he got the pass-the-buck, run-and-hide treatment that characterized the behavior of many of the top HIV authorities. When Mullis approached Montagnier at a San Diego scientific conference with his question Montagnier said, condescendingly, "Why don't you quote the report from the Centers for Disease Control?" (*IAV* p.xii) This from the future winner of a Nobel Prize

611

for the discovery of HIV and one of the two people most responsible for an empire of HIV testing, stigmatization and toxic treatments that has entrapped millions of trusting people in its draconian public health agenda. When Mullis pointed out the weakness of the answer, that it didn't address the question, Montagnier suggested that Mullis look at the work on Simian Immunodeficiency Virus. Mullis responded that the research on that virus *didn't* remind him of AIDS at all, and didn't answer the more basic question about the whereabouts of "the original paper where somebody showed that HIV caused AIDS." (*IAV* p. xiii) At that point, Montagnier just abruptly walked away from Mullis. One could say that it was a typical interaction between the two different cultures of normal and abnormal science.

Mullis finally got his answer to the question when he happened to be listening to the radio in his car and heard an interview with Peter Duesberg. Mullis writes that Duesberg "explained exactly why I was having so much trouble finding the references that linked HIV to AIDS. *There weren't any*. No one had proved that HIV causes AIDS." (*IAV* p.xiii)

Interestingly, although Mullis is often considered a "Duesbergian," in the foreword to the Duesberg book, he writes, "I like and respect Peter Duesberg. I don't think he knows necessarily what causes AIDS; we have disagreements about that. But we're both certain about what *doesn't* cause AIDS." (*IAV* p.xiii)

Mullis also acknowledged in the foreword the outrageous iatrogenic tragedy that was occurring in the name of the HIV theory: "We have also not been able to discover why doctors prescribe a toxic drug called AZT (Zidovudine) to people who have no other complaint than the presence of antibodies to HIV in their blood. In fact, we cannot understand why humans would take that drug for any reason.' (*IAV* p.xiv)

Without formally calling HIV science anything like a totalitarian opposite world of abnormal science, he came very close when he wrote, "We cannot understand how all this madness came about, and having lived in Berkley, we've seen some strange things indeed. We know that to err is human, but the HIV/AIDS hypothesis is one hell of a mistake." (*IAV* p.xiv) It's fair to say that he seemed to sense that we were in a period of scientific psychosis.

When reporter Celia Farber asked Mullis about "the guardians of the HIV establishment, such as Gallo and [Anthony] Fauci," in a July, 1994 interview in *Spin* in July, 1994, Mullis said "I feel sorry for 'em" and "I want to have the story unveiled, but you know what? I'm just not the kick-'em-in-the-balls kind of guy. I'm a moral person, but I'm not a crusader. I think it's a terrible tragedy that it's happened. There are some terrible motivations of humans involved in this, and Gallo and Fauci have got to be some of the worst. . . . Personally, I want to see those fuckers pay for it a little bit. I want to see them lose their position. I want to see their goddamn children have to go to junior college. I mean who do we care about? Do we care about those people who are HIV-positive whose lives have been ruined? Those are the people I'm the most concerned about. Every night I think about this. I think, what is my interest in this? Why do I care? I don't know anybody dying of it. They're right about that, well except one of my girlfriend's brothers died of it, and I think he died of AZT."

In a chapter on AIDS in his own book, *Dancing Naked in the Mind Field*, Mullis angrily described the world of AIDS research: "In 1634 Galileo was sentenced to house arrest for the last eight years of his life for writing that the Earth is not the center of the universe but rather moves around the sun. Because he insisted that scientific statements should not be a matter of religious faith, he was accused of heresy. Years from now, people looking back at us will find our acceptance of the HIV theory of AIDS as silly as we find the leaders who excommunicated Galileo. Science as it is practiced today in the world is largely not science at all. What people call science is probably very similar to what was called science in 1634. Galileo was told to recant his beliefs or be excommunicated. People who refuse to accept the commandments of the AIDS establishment are basically told the same thing. 'If you don't accept what we say, you're out.'" (*DNITMF* p.180)

Mullis got the same kind of hostile and dismissive treatment from the scientific profession that Duesberg did: "The responses I received from my colleagues ranged from moderate acceptance to outright venom. When I was invited to speak about P.C.R. at the European Federation of Clinical Investigation in Toledo, Spain, I told them that I would like to speak about HIV and AIDS instead. I don't think they understood exactly what they were getting into when they agreed. Halfway through my speech, the president of the society cut me off. He suggested I answer some questions from the audience." (*DNITMF* p.181) Playing the all too predictable emotional blackmail card of AIDS orthodoxy, the president of the society then asked the first question himself—whether Mullis was being irresponsible and possibly causing people to not use condoms. The same game of AIDS emotional blackmail was played by virtually every institution of public health and science for three decades.

Unfortunately, in his book Mullis joined in the same kind of speculative, homodemiological free-for-all that many of the Duesbergians succumbed to, in which they concocted their own, usually heterosexist-flavored paradigms. Mullis's seat-of-the-pants paradigm was based on "highly mobile, promiscuous men sharing bodily fluids and fast lifestyles and drugs." (*DNITMF* p.182) Mullis accepted the basics of the CDC's deficient epidemiology without asking whether that too was more like the science of 1634. His encounter with abnormal science never got him close to lifting the veil on Holocaust II and the HHV-6 spectrum catastrophe and the viral and epidemiological passageways between AIDS, CFS, autism etc. But his challenge to the orthodoxy was certainly better than nothing and his notoriety got his views broadcast widely. Even *The New York Times* was forced to deal with Mullis, which they did in the characteristic arrogant and dismissive way that they dealt with all important challenges to the HIV hegemony. History will hopefully honor Mullis for using the leverage of his Nobel Prize for a humanitarian purpose.

Without trying to be, Mullis was briefly one of the more articulate voices of what could be called "the sorrow and the pity of Holocaust II." In his book, like Duesberg, he protested the use of AZT on AIDS patients. Mullis wrote, "About half a million people went for it. No one has been cured. Most of them are dead." (*DNITMF* p.185) And ne notes, "I was thinking that this technique of killing people with a drug that was going to kill them in a way hardly distinguishable from the disease they were dying from, just faster, was really out there on the edge of the frontier of medicine. (*DNITMF* p.186) It was also, unbeknownst to Mullis, on the frontier of homodemiological (and ultimately racist) medicine.

Robert Root-Bernstein

The Critical Genius

One of the most celebrated intellectuals who joined Duesberg and Mullis in their skepticism about the HIV theory of AIDS was Robert Root-Bernstein. Duesberg described him in *Inventing the AIDS Virus*: "Barely out of graduate school with a degree in the history of science, Root-Bernstein was awarded the MacArthur Prize fellowship—a five-year "genius grant—in 1981. This afforded him the opportunity to work alongside polio vaccine pioneer Jonas Salk, followed by a professorship at Michigan State University in physiology." (IAV p.245) Because of his background in the history of science, Root-Bernstein brought an academically analytical and philosophical perspective to the problems with the HIV theory. His book outlining his doubts about HIV, *Rethinking AIDS*, was published in 1993.

According to Duesberg, sometime in "early 1989 he had begun corresponding with Duesberg and other critics of the HIV hypothesis. Scouring the scientific literature, Root-Bernstein found hundreds of cases of AIDS-like diseases dating back throughout the twentieth century. These data he extracted into a letter published in *The Lancet* in April 1990, showing that Kaposi's sarcoma had not been as rare as supposed before the 1980s. The next month he fired off in rapid succession several more papers on the history of other AIDS diseases, all of which the same journal now rejected." (IAV p. 246) (*The Lancet*, especially under the guidance of Richard Horton, would play a major role in the maintenance of the HIV/AIDS paradigm throughout Holocaust II.)

In what Duesberg calls Root-Bernstein's major 1990 paper, "Do We Know the Cause(s) of AIDS?" he posited that "It is worth taking a skeptical look at the HIV theory. We cannot afford—literally, in terms of human lives, research dollars, and manpower investment—to be wrong. The premature closure leaves us open to the risk of making a colossal blunder." (IAV p. 246) Oh, yes we could.

Root-Bernstein's own book was not as Duesbergian as Duesberg probably would have liked because *he found a place for HIV in AIDS* by theorizing that it might be a part of some sort of multifactorial assault on the immune system that resulted in an autoimmune process. Duesberg had no patience with the autoimmune theories of AIDS for a number of reasons, including that fact that "if AIDS did result from autoimmunity, it would have spread out in its original risk group into the general population years ago, rather than striking men nine times out of ten. (*IAV* p.248)

Regardless of the fact that, like Duesberg, Root-Bernstein seems blissfully unaware of the presence of the heterosexism in the manner in which the ground-zero definition of AIDS was cooked up and despite his blind spot towards the existence of the chronic fatigue syndrome epidemic which resulted from the CDC habit of cherry-picking data, Root-Bernstein's book was a strong scientific wake-up call that urged a greater due diligence about the logic of AIDS and the emerging anomalous data that contradicted and challenged the prevailing paradigm. Root-Bernstein brought a distinctly Kuhnian sense of the nature of scientific process to his critique of HIV/AIDS and he seemed to be very aware (without exactly naming it) that it was engendering a culture of abnormal or totalitarian science. The epigrams in his books are like shots across the bow of the conventional view of AIDS. He quotes John Stuart Mill: "The fatal tendency of mankind to leave off thinking about a thing which is no longer doubtful is the cause of half their error." And Rollo May: "People who claim to be *absolutely* convinced that their stand is the only right one are dangerous. Such conviction is the essence not only of dogmatism but of its most destructive cousin, fanaticism. It blocks off the user from learning new truth and it is a dead giveaway of unconscious doubt." His quote from William Trotter M.D. may be been even more appropriate for a book on AIDS than even Root-Bernstein realized: "When we find ourselves entertaining an opinion about which there is a feeling that even to enquire into it would be absurd, unnecessary, undesirable, or wicked—we may know that the opinion is a nonrational one." (All quotes are from the frontispiece of *Rethinking AIDS*)

Root-Bernstein subsequently backed away from his position challenging HIV, but his book is so powerfully written that the damage it did to the credibility of the HIV paradigm could not be undone. Without flinching, in the preface he seems to have detected the bizarre nature of AIDS research: "I have read the medical literature assiduously, looking for studies that test our current theory of AIDS. I have analyzed and synthesized this information and found that our theory of AIDS is full of glaring holes, confusing contradictions, and outright discrepancies. I am saying nothing more than what the medical literature itself says about AIDS. The only difference is that I am willing to say this in public, whereas most practitioners are not. (*RA* p.xiii) (The bit about the practitioners deserves a little attention from future historians of the epidemic. What does that tell us about the character and ethics of the people who did the hands-on management of AIDS patients?)

Root-Bernstein says that he wants to identify "the extent and nature of our ignorance" and that by doing so "we will be able to do something about it. In science, to define the problem correctly takes one more than halfway to its solution." (*RA* p.xiii) Very Kuhnian of him, but Root-Bernstein's biggest mistake may be that he was prepared to take the research he was studying at face value. With overabundance of optimism about science and scientists, he writes, "my critique of AIDS theory assumes that most of the published experiments and clinical observations are accurate" having been conducted by "many dedicated and hard-working scientists." (RA p.xii) That generous trust kind of contradicts the radical statement he makes near the end of the book: "I have put my scientific reputation on the line in this book in order to make certain that we accept nothing about AIDS uncritically." (RA p.373) Well, not exactly "nothing," if one assumes all "the published experiments and clinical observations are accurate." Therein lies the rub.

Root-Bernstein is basically saying that, *even giving* the basic researchers and their "facts" the benefit of the doubt, the interpretations and theories about the facts just don't compute. He begins his critical journey by pointing out that facts require theories and are not facts until they are "interpreted in light of a theory." (RA p.xiv) Where the "facts" about AIDS are concerned he notes that "the data are all easily validated by repeated observations and measurements, and yet may still be misunderstood. A great deal of evidence suggests, for example that we have attributed much too much to HIV . . . and too little to other causative agents." (RA p.xiv) He concluded that "it is imperative to rethink and research AIDS." (RA p.xv)

Like Thomas Kuhn, Root-Bernstein seems inadvertently to be conveying an image of science with more of a sinister potential than he realizes. He points out that "Most scientists believe that we understand AIDS and have trumpeted their belief to each other and the public as well . . . . This is the public face of AIDS—the face that is meant to exude confidence, to reassure." (RA p.1) But if this public face was false it makes one wonder to what degree the whole AIDS effort was an episode of misbegotten groupthink from the very beginning. He points out, "Scientists are much more reticent about revealing their other face—the one that displays their ignorance, confusion, and puzzlement over the aspects of the disease that they do not understand. The best kept secrets about AIDS are the questions unanswered, the puzzles unsolved, the contradictions unrecognized, and the paradoxes unformulated." (RA p.1) One doesn't know whether to laugh or cry over the casual way Root-Bernstein is basically telling us that the powerful AIDS establishment, almost a decade into the epidemic, was keeping two sets of books—an essential ingredient of abnormal science and homodemiology. Once again, like Kuhn, he may have been telling us far more about the real nature of science than he realized.

By calling his first chapter, "Anomalies," Root-Bernstein is signaling a belief in the power of unexpected findings and contradictions to force a critical reconsideration of paradigms, a distinctly Kuhnian notion of the way the process of normal science and scientific revolutions work, or are supposed to work. By doing so he is also in a way reassuring us that he was operating in a world of normal science which turned out—without him recognizing it—not to be the case at all. He asserts, "the existence of significant anomalies or departures from the regular expectations of the current theory must raise a red flag warning that our understanding of AIDS is not as profound as we might wish." (RA. p.1) Like any scientist in the collegial, reasonable world of normal science, he thought that the anomalies "are important enough to warrant serious rethinking of the causes and nature of AIDS." (RA p.2) We should note that, like Duesberg and many of the Duesbergians, he was not going all the way and calling for a rethinking of the ground zero epidemiology and nosology of AIDS.

The first anomaly he deals with is the fact that "there were a large number of pre-1979 AIDS-like cases that have not been accounted for in our current theories of AIDS." (RA p.21) He asks, "If HIV is a new and necessary cause of AIDS, as most AIDS researchers argue, what was the cause of these pre-1979 AIDS-like cases? Are there causes of acquired immune suppression other than HIV that may explain AIDS?" (RA p.21)

Root-Bernstein's second major anomaly focused on his contention that "HIV is neither necessary nor sufficient to cause AIDS." (RA p.21) He notes that the prevailing notion was that "infection with HIV is supposed to cause destruction of a specific type of immune system cell known as the t-helper or T4 cell." (RA p.22) Like more than a few others he noted the odd manner in which the government stepped in and basically established by fiat that the retrovirus HIV (or HTLV-III as it was then called) was the cause of AIDS. He also notes the troubling fact that the government announcement about the retrovirus happened "even before Gallo's paper [on HTLV-III] had undergone peer review and publication." (RA p.24) He also points out that the announcement was followed by a commitment to HIV research that made AIDS research "virtually synonymous with HIV research." (RA p.24) In effect, *all other avenues of research were closed off* from financial assistance or intellectual support from the HIV-obsessed AIDS establishment.

One curious and important point that Root-Bernstein acknowledges and historians won't want to let go of in reconstructions of that period is the fact that subsequently Gallo's so-called French co-discoverer, Luc Montagnier, had surprisingly indicated that HIV was actually *not sufficient* to cause AIDS. Montagnier had uncovered evidence that bacteria called mycoplasmas are necessary to stimulate HIV, making mycoplasmas at least a co-factor of AIDS, and possibly even more important than HIV, raising *the scandalous question of whether HIV was even the cause of AIDS*. Root-Bernstein also notes that, ironically, Gallo eventually also discovered his own co-factor, Human Herpes Virus Six (HHV-6) in AIDS patients, also potentially pulling the rug out from under Gallo's own HIV-alone-causes-AIDS theory. (RA p.26) The two so-called discoverers of the cause of AIDS laid the groundwork for their own eventual scientific fall from grace.

It's a tragedy for all the ultimate victims of HHV-6 and its family of viruses that Root-Bernstein didn't look harder at the virus. He might have helped make the public aware of the blossoming HHV-6 pandemic. He did recognize the chicken-or-egg threat that cofactors posed to the credibility of the HIV theory: "The only problem with the scenario is that it raises the question of which came first—the HIV or the cofactor." (*RA* p.26) Like a number of HIV critics, Root-Bernstein recounts the shocking paradigm-challenging moment at the 1992 International AIDS Conference at which it was announced that *there were AIDS patients without detectable HIV*: "Suddenly AIDS without HIV became big news because too many cases had surfaced to be ignored. There is no longer any doubt that HIV is not necessary to cause acquired immunodeficiency." (*RA*. p.29) Although at the time there were those who argued that there were not a large number of such cases, Root-Bernstein stood his ground, noting that "The actual number of HIV-negative AIDS cases is irrelevant. The existence of even a handful of HIV-negative AIDS cases is sufficient logically to raise doubts concerning the necessity of HIV as a cause of AIDS." (*RA* p.30)

Root-Bernstein came as close as he could to stumbling into the raw truth about the pandemic of HHV-6 when he hypothesized that one possibility implied by the HIV-negative cases was "that there is a second epidemic masquerading under the guises of AIDS, which has yet to have been detected and separated out from AIDS." (*RA* p.30) We now know that there *was* that other HIV-negative AIDS epidemic and it was, to the detriment of the health and human rights of all the patients involved, separated politically from the so-called AIDS epidemic. He was a witness to a growing state of medical apartheid that was concealing the HHV-6 catastrophe without realizing it.

His third anomaly focused on the mystery of where HIV was in the body and how it was transmitted. He pointed out that HIV was "anything but typical of sexually transmitted diseases. It can take hundreds of exposures for HIV for transmission to occur at all." (*RA* p. 31) It was rare to find HIV in semen. The way that HIV actually was transmitted was complex and didn't fit the STD picture the AIDS public health establishment was promoting—another strike against the consistency and trustworthiness of those guiding the AIDS effort. The data about HIV suggested "it is probable that those who become infected must be exposed repeatedly to many HIV carriers or have some unusual susceptibility for the virus." (*RA* p.38)

His fourth anomaly focused on the fact that people could be exposed to HIV without seroconverting. Given the numbers of sexual partners of HIV positives who did not seroconvert and oddities like the fact that prostitutes who did not use intravenous drugs rarely became HIV positive, he concluded, "HIV cannot be a sexually transmitted disease, in the usual sense of the term." (*RA* p.41) Other studies suggested that people had to be immune suppressed *before* they became HIV positive. He asserted, "Individuals with normal immune function should therefore be resistant to HIV." (*RA* p.42) And that comes very close to saying flat out that HIV is an effect rather than a cause.

As we have said, like most (but not all) of the heterosexuals in the Duesberg camp, he concluded that "one clear implication of these studies is that the non-drug abusing heterosexual community should have little or no risk of HIV or AIDS." (*RA* p.43) Root-Bernstein was blissfully unaware, like all the rest of the Duesbergians, that a highly variable epidemic of HHV-6 was raging all around him while being hidden epidemiologically behind the euphemism such as "chronic fatigue syndrome." Like most Duesbergians, his main agenda often appears to be debunking the myth of heterosexual AIDS.

Given that HHV-6 would ultimately be seen as a trigger for some cases of multiple sclerosis, it is interesting to note in passing that Root-Bernstein writes about one unlucky heterosexual woman who did seroconvert to HIV "suffered from multiple sclerosis, which had been repeatedly treated with immunosuppressive drugs." (*RA* p.44) Again in a French Farce moment of the tragic AIDS story, he may have been an unopened door away from the smoking gun.

The entire Duesberg camp seemed determined to provide themselves a margin of safety that separated them and their fellow heterosexuals from the possibility of the scarlet letter diagnosis of AIDS. Root-Bernstein gave his fellow heterosexual Duesbergians the ultimate reassurance when he wrote that "the transmission of HIV through heterosexual intercourse is so rare that two heterosexuals without identified risks for AIDS have an equal probability of being struck by lightning, dying in a commercial airplane crash, or developing AIDS." (*RA* p.44) Unfortunately, he could not provide the same reassurance for the heterosexual Duesbergians about chronic fatigue syndrome, autism or any of the other medical problems related to the unrecognized immune-system-challenging epidemic of HHV-6. The one that was hiding in plain sight.

One of the most damaging facts for the credibility of the HIV theory was the matter of transmission (or non-transmission) to health care workers. He writes that "there have however, been more than 6,000 verified cases of health care workers reporting subcutaneous exposure to HIV-infected blood or tissue as a result of needle-stick injuries, surgical cuts, broken glass and so forth. . . . And yet only a few dozen health care workers are known to have become HIV seropositive during the entire decade of the 1980s in the United States. (*RA* p.44) He was all too unaware that health care workers were, however, coming down with illnesses associated with the so-called AIDS cofactor, HHV-6, and being diagnosed with chronic fatigue syndrome and other diagnoses on the HHV-6 spectrum. Being in the health care field actually was one of the biggest risks for developing chronic fatigue syndrome. Root-Bernstein, again relying on the CDC's questionable ground zero epidemiology, notes that AIDS was not being transmitted to patients by health care workers. (The same could not necessarily be said for HHV-6 and chronic fatigue syndrome.) He accuses the HIV establishment of not being sufficiently skeptical but the truth is that his own skepticism never really went deep enough. But in his favor there is the undeniable fact that he did ask the kind of provocative questions that *should* have helped alert the scientific profession that something *was* terribly amiss in the world of AIDS research. The fact that most of his colleagues, throughout the three decades of Holocaust II, didn't listen to warnings like his and put their heads in the sand will be puzzled over by historians for a long time to come.

Root-Bernstein, on some level, was not-so-quietly outraged by what he was seeing and brought a much-needed dose of sarcasm to the field when he asked if "HIV is so radically different from all other viruses that we cannot compare it to them?" (*RA* p.42) Actually, he should have asked if there was something so radically different about the science and epidemiology of AIDS that no educated and decent person in their right mind could possibly understand it. He certainly seemed to be onto the fact that whatever the cause of AIDS was, *if it was a virus, it had to be unique.* Which is exactly what the multi-systemic virus HHV-6 turned out to be. If there is a virus more unique than HHV-6 I would like to know what it is.

Root-Bernstein's fifth anomaly concerned the ability of some people to fight off an infection of HIV. Some people never even developed antibodies to the retrovirus. Some tested negative for the virus years after testing positive. Some tested positive and remained perfectly healthy with intact immune systems. He caught a whiff of the Kafkaesque politics that controlled the developing AIDS empire (and its homodemiological reign of abnormal science) when he wrote, "Oddly, the ability of adults and infants to control or eliminate HIV infection in the absence of medical treatment is not seen by researchers as a source of hope for those at risk for AIDS but rather as a new public health threat." (*RA* p.54) In that lucid statement he inadvertently comes face to face with the looniness of HIV/AIDS "science" and kind of shrugs his shoulders in puzzlement.

Because Root-Bernstein, like nearly all the Duesbergians, didn't seem to grasp the sexual (and ultimately racist) politics driving the psychology of the establishment he was challenging, he didn't understand why his statement "that even people in high risk groups who may have initially had multiple contacts with HIV may successfully combat the viral infection" (*RA* p.54) would not comfort a heterosexist scientific establishment that was determined not to look back at its possible epidemiological and virological mistakes. No "source of hope" that didn't involve social control, stigmatization and the administration of toxic drugs could be given to gays (or blacks) in AIDS epidemiology and virology. The AIDS agenda was inexorable and unforgiving. Public health had adopted a scorched earth policy against those it was supposedly helping.

When Root-Bernstein brings up the evolving latency period of AIDS, he may have touched on the most important anomaly of all. He writes that "one of the oddest observations that strikes a historian of the epidemic is that the latency period—the estimated time lag between HIV infection and the development of clinical AIDS—has expanded almost yearly. In 1986, the figure was less than two years; in 1987, it was raised to three; in 1988, it became five; in 1989, ten; and as of the beginning of 1992, the latency period was calculated to be between ten and fifteen years (*RA* p.55) He wondered whether it was because the virus had become less virulent, or had killed people with the highest risk lifestyles—in terms of drugs and multiple sex partners—first. He concluded that "attributing AIDS to nothing more than an infection by HIV is too simplistic. It leaves too much unexplained and creates too many anomalies to be a satisfying scientific explanation. HIV is not sufficient to explain the anomalies of AIDS. These anomalies represent the challenge of understanding AIDS. A more thorough and skeptical analysis of the data is needed." (*RA* p.56) Blind to the heterosexism hardwired into the "science" and epidemiology he was confronting, he didn't understand that an anomaly-riddled HIV theory was a very adequate and politically useful scientific explanation in the opposite world of totalitarian, abnormal science that AIDS represented. Something far more politically and emotionally satisfying than reason and logic was at work here.

A rather democratic, collegial attitude about science and scientists comes across in Root-Bernstein's book. He was not one to put people he disagreed with on the rack. (One doubts that the HIVists would ever return the compliment.) He asserted optimistically, "anomalies, problems, paradoxes, and contradictions are only the incentives for research. If no one pays attention to them, they are fruitless. Even when they are identified and scrutinized, they are only a beginning; they define the areas of our ignorance." (*RA*. p.57) Unbeknownst to him, the gang he was dealing with was not interested in "our ignorance." They had a commitment to not paying attention to "anomalies, problems, paradoxes, and contradictions."

Having initially accepted the basic ground zero definition of AIDS with its subsequent ground zero epidemiology—a big mistake with horrific consequences—he is left praising HIV with faint damning: "The upshot of the discussion will be that HIV has not satisfied any established criteria for demonstrating disease causation. Thus, although, there is no doubt that HIV is an integral player in the drama of AIDS, we cannot say, for certain that it is beyond a doubt, a solo actor doing a monologue." (*RA* p.58)

Like others who concocted their own theories of AIDS causation before him, Root-Bernstein heads off into the wild goose chase of multifactorial causation where HIV has "a whole cast of supporting characters that foster its villainous work." (*RA* p.58)

Root-Bernstein does at least give *some* lip service to the importance of digging under the surface of the early epidemiology of AIDS in his chapter on the role of HIV in AIDS. He notes the disturbing history of the unstable definition of AIDS that always seemed to be changing. He was troubled by the notion that there were people in the high-risk group with AIDS indicator diseases like Kaposi's sarcoma *who were HIV-negative*. He noted that "AIDS, in short, has become a schizophrenic disease . . . Some people are AIDS patients if they develop opportunistic infections even in the absence of evidence of HIV, and in the presence of HIV, almost any rare disease is diagnostic for AIDS regardless of whether the person has other, more fundamental causes of immune suppression." (*RA* p.63) And, at the time his book was written in the early 90s, the CDC was proposing a change in the definition of AIDS that meant "People may be diagnosed as having AIDS even if they have no infections typical of AIDS, as long as they have a significantly low number of T-helper cells and antibody to HIV." (*RA* p.63) What Root-Bernstein had to say about the proposed change came into close proximity of *this book's thesis*: "The reason for this latest definitional alteration is social and economic, not scientific. AIDS activists are now dictating how AIDS is to be diagnosed and who is to be included in the count. For them, the issue is not one of correct diagnosis or elucidating the cause of AIDS; it is the understandable desire to increase access to health care." (*RA* p.64) And what great humanitarians those activists were, and what wonderful health care AZT and its toxic siblings turned out to be! What Root-Bernstein failed to perceive was that the definition of AIDS, drawn from the wrong first impressions of the real HHV-6 pandemic, was a groupthink-biased epidemiological product developed by scientists who looked at the epidemic through heterosexist and retroviral glasses.

Those who define the terms of an epidemic can control how large or small it appears at any point, which gives them de facto political power not only over the epidemic but potentially—with the broad and invasive powers of public health sanctions—a whole country. The chief definers would also be the chief deciders of the AIDS public health agenda. One of the great ironies of Root-Bernstein's often cogent criticisms of AIDS is that he understands the political nature of this phenomena but comes to a conclusion about the politics of the AIDS epidemic which is actually the direct opposite of the inconvenient truth. And it is tragically typical of most of the Duesbergians. Root-Bernstein points out that the CDC could say that AIDS cases doubled by just changing the definition, or what he called "definitional fiat." (*RA* p.64) He is on the money that the epidemiological appearance of AIDS was controlled by "definitional fiat" but not in the statistically upward direction he and the Duesbergians imagined. In truth, it was the CDC's heterosexist and ultimately racist "definitional fiat" that was keeping the public from seeing the connection of AIDS and CFS (and ultimately autism) in an exponentially larger unified multisystemic epidemic via the pathogen HHV-6. The difference between Root-Bernstein vision of the epidemic and the truth was the difference between using public relations to overstate an epidemic and using public relations to conceal one

Like the point in a movie when the audience sees a protagonist come within inches of a culprit without the protagonist realizing it, Root-Bernstein came tantalizingly close to the truth about the HHV-6 catastrophe when he notes, "We must be absolutely certain that HIV is not an epiphenomenon of AIDS before we assert that it is a primary cause. The fact that it is an extremely frequent finding in AIDS patients is not logically compelling. It is only suggestive. Other active infections, such as cytomegalovirus, are nearly universal among AIDS patients. If both are correlated with AIDS, which is the cause?" (RA p.66) He was *so very close* to the real issue of HHV-6 at that point and yet ultimately so far away.

He zeroed in on the tragic truth about HIV when he wrote, "HIV may be an epiphenomenon of immune suppression rather than a necessary cause."(RA p.66) This very bright history-aware thinker was also on the money when he wrote "one gaping lacuna in the AIDS definition" was that "There are no criteria listed in any definition of AIDS that allowed for a person to fight off AIDS or to be cured of it." (RA p.67) He noted that such a definition was "a medical novelty." (RA p.67) Actually, the whole field of AIDS research was one big cockamamie medical novelty. He thoughtfully notes that "this makes AIDS the first disease that no one can survive, by definition. Not only is this description of AIDS logically bankrupt, it sends the demoralizing and inaccurate message to people with HIV or AIDS that they have a disease that is not worth fighting." (RA p.68) Such a logically bankrupt demoralizing definition is of course, the work of the abnormal science of homodemiology on a productive day. But how could Root-Bernstein know that something like homodemiology was in play if it was a construct completely absent from his conceptual universe?

Like Thomas Kuhn, Root-Bernstein seems keenly aware that the psychology of scientists affects the decision-making process. In frustration, he asks questions like "Why is it so difficult for them to admit . . . that AIDS may have more than one cause?" (RA p.84) He knows he is dealing with "dogma" but he doesn't consider the possibility that the confounding issues like the threat to institutional pride and credibility as well as serious potential financial losses would follow upon the admission that HIV was not the one and only cause of AIDS. Those pedestrian kinds of conflict of interest could have done the trick even if the more esoteric underlying issues of heterosexism and racism were not involved. But, unfortunately, *they were*.

Again, Root-Bernstein asserted the point that most of the other Duesbergians believed as an article of faith about the risk of AIDS to heterosexuals: "If AIDS is a simple, sexually transmitted virus then it should be running rampant in the heterosexual community by now." (RA. p.87) Cut to the real epidemic: HIV may have not been running rampant in the heterosexual community, but HHV-6 (and its spectrum of related viruses) certainly was and if the Duesbergians could have just looked behind the euphemism of "chronic fatigue syndrome," they would have had a ring side seat from which to watch the real heterosexual epidemic of variable immune dysfunction unfold all around them.

Root-Bernstein insists, "Evidence of the necessity of co-factors for HIV was found at the outset. (RA p.92). What he didn't realize is that co-factors were a political and economic threat to those seeking Nobel prizes for HIV and those members of the public health (and pharmaceutical) establishment who were rolling out a draconian heterosexist (and eventually racist) toxic agenda around the seeming inexorable public health logic of HIV control. One can't assign medical Pink Triangles based on a salad bar of co-factors.

Like the brightest Duesbergians, Root-Bernstein notes that an unprecedented scientific logic was afoot, one that cavalierly discarded Koch's postulates. He describes the issue succinctly when he writes "The logic of Koch's postulates is straight forward: Demonstrate that one, and only one, organism is associated both with the occurrence of a specific disease and with its onset by isolating and controlling its transmission independent of other factors." (RA p.95) He emphasizes that "Every controllable infectious disease known to medical science . . . has been solved by following Koch's postulates." (RA p.95) The totalitarian, Kafkaesque quality of AIDS research is inadvertently but beautifully captured in Root-Bernstein's statement that "the fact that HIV does not satisfy Koch's postulates does not convince HIV proponents that it is not the cause of AIDS. On the contrary, 'knowing' that HIV causes AIDS most researchers reject Koch's postulates." (RA p.99) The mad hatters of AIDS research generally hated to be confused by the facts or standards of proof and logic. Root-Bernstein underlines the outrageousness of this new form of "scientific reasoning" when he writes, "AIDS researchers have ignored previous criteria for establishing disease causation in favor of ad hoc inventions of their own." (RA p.100) Ad hoc inventions by AIDS researchers? Hello!

Root-Bernstein points out how flimsy the original evidence for HIV was: "What is somewhat astonishing is that in 1984, when Gallo first championed HIV as the cause of AIDS, the correlation between HIV and AIDS was not even particularly convincing." (RA p.101) (It was somewhat astonishing *if* you didn't know how HIV charlatan Robert Gallo and his homies rolled.)

Gymnastic attempts were made by scientists to concoct criteria to replace Koch's postulates in such a way that they could be conveniently used to prove HIV was the cause of AIDS. You could say that gays were such very special people that the HIV/AIDS scientists wanted to come up with very special rules that a proved that this very special virus was infecting *them* in a very special way, and mostly *only them*. In a Procrustean manner, the rules would be shaped in a heterosexist, racist, and illogical manner to fit the evidence and support a pre-ordained biased conclusion. This is how abnormal science and homodemiology seized the day.

Root-Bernstein sums up the infernal game being played in this scientific madhouse: "In short, HIV does not satisfy any of the etiological criteria that existed prior to its discovery, and the etiological criteria that have been developed since are all logically flawed." (RA p.103) Calling this kind of science abnormal or psychotic almost seems like an understatement.

In a rather gentlemanly tone Root-Bernstein *does indict* a whole generation of doctors and scientists who stood by as collaborators, enablers and useful idiots of this scientific debacle when he writes, "Given this state of affairs, attempts to modify Koch's postulates after the assertion that the causative agent has been identified smack of a posteriori reasoning. Such reasoning is always suspect to logicians and should be equally suspect to physicians and scientists as well." (RA p.104). In the world of normal science maybe, but not in the heterosexist world of abnormal science and homodemiology.

Knowing that scientific change only occurs when a new paradigm is offered that is more logical and attractive than the prevailing one, Root-Bernstein takes his own out for a spin. He plays around with the notion that AIDS may be "a synergistic or stepwise multifactor disease." (RA p.108) He tosses into his speculative multifactor salad of immunosuppressive elements: things like semen and addictive or recreational drugs. He spends much of the rest of his book backing up his contention that "there is a well-established set of diseases that have many of the characteristics of AIDS—multiple disease causing-agents—that may provide an as yet untested model for AIDS." (RA p.109) One thing that strikes one as refreshing about Root-Bernstein throughout his book is that, unlike many of the people in the Duesberg camp, he doesn't seem to be faithfully married to his own dogma. In the spirit of keeping an open mind, he asserted, "The case that HIV causes AIDS is still open, and surprises are still possible." (RA p.109) By exploring a number of possible non-infectious causes of immunosuppression like semen, recreational drugs, anesthesia, surgery, pharmaceutical agents like antibiotics, blood transfusions, clotting factors, and aging itself, he tries to build a case that any combination of these factors might lead to immunosuppression and that the assumption that HIV "is the only immunosuppressive agent in those at risk for AIDS and the only agent necessary to explain the immune suppression that characterizes the syndrome." (RA p.111) He was saying that many different combinations of elements might be creating a perfect immunological storm.

He also explored the possibility that AIDS was the result of multiple, concurrent infections, arguing, with a somewhat overzealous heterosexist bias, that "Perhaps no other group in history has ever sustained anything like the disease overload experienced by highly promiscuous homosexual men and intravenous drug abusers, with the sole exception of people who live in Third World nations. . ." (RA p.149) While he explores a laundry list of infections that he thinks may synergize into AIDS (CMV, EBV, HBV, mycoplasma and others), he once again comes painfully close to the smoking gun of the HHV-6 catastrophe at the core of Holocaust II when he writes about HHV-6 that it "may be of particular importance in AIDS because Robert Gallo's laboratory has demonstrated that it is common among people at risk for AIDS and acts as a cofactor to increase infectivity and cell-killing by HIV under test tube conditions." (RA p.152) (Not to mention that it was also found in HIV-negative patients with the heterosexual not-so-distant cousin of AIDS—chronic fatigue syndrome—but that was something he seemed destined to not know *anything* about.)

Root-Bernstein devotes an interesting chapter to the notion that AIDS may be a disease of autoimmunity noting, "autoimmunity has a wide range of manifestations in AIDS patients and people at risk for AIDS." (*RA* p.185) He argued that "autoimmunity directed at lymphocytes is only one of the many forms of autoimmunity that manifest themselves during the process of AIDS." (*RA* p.190) He certainly had a much more complex vision of what was going on in AIDS than the rather simplistic (and manufactured) HIV-infecting T-4 cell disease image that the patients and the public were indoctrinated with. When historians go back and try to determine why scientists and epidemiologists didn't recognize that AIDS and chronic fatigue syndrome actually were part of the same variable but unified epidemic, they will wonder why Root-Bernstein's description of the complexities of AIDS didn't have an eye-opening impact on anyone who was watching the emergence of chronic fatigue syndrome in the general population at that point in the late 80s and early 90s. The honest, open-minded critics of the HIV theory of AIDS and those concerned about CFS were just ships passing in the night. (And the passengers on those ships were replete with white heterosexual privilege.)

Root-Bernstein wrote, "Many AIDS patients develop an autoimmune form of arthritis; autoantibodies directed at muscle proteins; and symptoms similar to both Sjögren's syndrome and systemic lupus erythematosus, including skin rashes, kidney damage, and antibodies against DNA, thyroglobulin, and adrenocorticosteroids." (*RA* p.191) He was not ready to just glibly attribute all these complications to HIV. The patients back then would have probably been better served if the people attending to their health hadn't been forced by the establishment to adopt the simplistic "HIV-only" and "T-4 cells-mainly" way of looking at the disease

Root-Bernstein was concerned that "HIV is only one of a multitudinous cast that cooperate to produce autoimmunity." (*RA* p.203) He felt that scientists were making a major mistake in ignoring "the huge number of other infectious agents that are also present in AIDS patients, often concurrently." (*RA* p.203) Among those concurrent infections was of course, one very special one, the star of the multisystemic biomedical catastrophe, being mostly ignored and hiding behind the alibi that it was just another not-so-interesting infection that AIDS patients supposedly got secondarily: HHV-6.

Root-Bernstein was particularly interested in CMV which was a major viral problem in AIDS and which he thought could cause autoimmunity when it combined with other infections. He was especially intrigued by the possibility that CMV or some other herpes virus (he didn't bring up the then recently discovered HHV-6 here) was causing encephalitis or demyelization in a significant number of AIDS patients. The AIDS establishment of course, was determined to blame this, like everything else in AIDS, on HIV alone, to

627

which he replied, "My opinion is that we have asked HIV to be responsible for too much of AIDS." (*RA* p.209) This statement from Root- Bernstein captures how potentially damaging this over-simplification of AIDS into "HIV T-4 cell disease" was: ". . . autoimmunity has many manifestations in AIDS besides that directed at lymphocytes. The causes of lymphocyte depletion may be entirely unrelated to causes of specific autoimmune symptoms, such as demyelization and thrombocytopenia, that are frequent concomitants of AIDS. It is possible that HIV may play the major role in one form of autoimmunity, and none in others. A concerted effort is needed to disentangle the many different forms of autoimmunity. As these various manifestations become distinct, they will inevitably call for new treatments unrelated to retroviruses." (*RA* p.218) Unfortunately, Root-Bernstein didn't realize just how much control the HIV mafia would continue to have for decades over the AIDS public health agenda—control that AIDS patients would pay an unprecedented medical and social price for. And they would hardly be alone.

Root-Bernstein seems to have been operating under the belief that the genteel Thomas Kuhn universe of normal science was the one he was living in when he wrote, "The purpose of theorizing is to cause us to rethink things we thought we understood in order to go out and ask new questions." (*RA* p.219) To which the AIDS establishment snarkily could probably have replied, "And who said anything about asking questions?" Given the relationship of AIDS to chronic fatigue syndrome and all the other manifestations of HHV-6 it is quite ironic to hear Root-Bernstein state ever so innocently and plaintively, "There may be major discoveries still left to be made not only concerning AIDS but the entire field of immunology— discoveries that may illuminate many diseases besides AIDS. With these discoveries will come new possibilities for treatment." (*RA* p.219) Unfortunately, in the nasty Realpolitik of Holocaust II, it was simply not meant to be.

As we have pointed out, the whole Duesbergian critical-thinking and re-thinking movement seemed to revolve around attempts to prove that heterosexuals were essentially *not at risk* for what the CDC called AIDS. They were on thin ice because they depended upon the CDC's ground zero epidemiological judgment calls. In a chapter titled "Who is at Risk for AIDS and Why," Root-Bernstein throws down the gauntlet: "If exposure to HIV is sufficient to cause AIDS, then everyone should be at equal risk, and AIDS should develop at an equal rate among different risk groups once infection has become established. Clearly that is not the case." (*RA* p.220) Earth to Root-Bernstein: HHV-6 and chronic fatigue syndrome. For starters.

Root-Bernstein, like all the rest of the Duesbergians, confused the threat of AIDS with the threat of being diagnosed HIV positive. Just because heterosexuals were not being labeled as HIV-positive or as having AIDS, didn't mean that a large number of heterosexual Americans were not starting to develop a broad range of immunological dysfunctions and other problems that resembled the AIDS spectrum of pathologies. The Duesbergians, keenly unaware of the wildfire of HHV-6 and CFS, loved to make statements similar to Root-Bernstein's that "Some calculations place the figure of contracting AIDS from a heterosexual without risk factors as low as 2 in 1 million or the same risk as being struck by lightning." (RA p.220) About as close to never as you can get.

Working with the CDC's flawed, heterosexist data on what was AIDS and what wasn't, Root-Bernstein goes to town on the gay community and writes, "Until we understand exactly what these predisposing factors are for each separate risk group, we will not be able to identify, treat, control, or eliminate the risks of AIDS." (RA p.222) Never in the history of mankind has there been such a showboating of intense benevolent interest in understanding the gay community, and with understanding like this the gay community didn't need enemies. As could be predicted by this heterosexual noblesse-oblige-driven journey into the sex and drug habits of the gay community, the blame for AIDS is laid (more or less) on "promiscuous, drug-abusing, multiple-infected gay men." (RA p.232) You know, people who like to party. Coincidentally, since the general heterosexual population was not "promiscuous, drug-abusing, multiple-infected," they had no worry about contracting what the CDC had branded as "AIDS." Unless, of course—and this was not on Root-Bernstein's radar—they came in contact with the immune-system-compromising buzz-killer of a casually transmitted virus, HHV-6.

While Root-Bernstein also points to the multiple-infection lifestyle of drug users and the multiple-immunosuppressive risks of transfusion patients and hemophiliacs—and some infants born to parents with immunosuppressive drug-using lifestyles—they do little to take away from the notion that the driving force of his theorizing about AIDS was the same kind of GRID-think, or Got-AIDS-Yet?-think, that dominated the AIDS establishment's ground zero epidemiology. GRID-think was the heterosexist gift that just kept on giving for three decades. Root-Bernstein looked at AIDS as the inexorable price that some gays paid for an overindulgent lifestyle. That kind of thinking, which made heterosexuals feel comfy-cozy inside the Schadenfreude of their invulnerable biomedical cocoon, blinded society to the catastrophe of CFS, autism and everything else on the HHV-6 spectrum.

While the critical mission in his chapter on immunosuppression in AIDS was to expose the power of co-factors in the so-called AIDS risk groups, he may have inadvertently discovered that a broader definition of AIDS that focused on a wide range of indicators of immunosuppression (or more appropriately, immune dysfunction) would have shown that there was a far bigger and more variable AIDS or AIDS-like epidemic happening *even in the gay community itself*. In his chapter on the matter he promises to "show . . . that significant immune suppression is present in large numbers of people in high-risk groups for AIDS in the *absence* of HIV infections. Sometimes the degree of immune suppression is equal to, or even greater than, that experienced by HIV-positive, matched patients." (*RA* p.259) In the world of normal science this should have been all you needed to know to have an anomaly-driven epiphany that HIV was probably *not* the cause of AIDS. But not in the opposite world of abnormal science that Root-Bernstein was unknowingly adrift in. If that wasn't enough, he points out that "many people in the high-risk groups for AIDS have significant immune impairment prior to contracting an HIV infection and are thus susceptible to both infection and the effects of infection than are immunologically healthy individuals." (*RA.* p.259) It's almost like he's saying that people have HIV-negative AIDS (something CFS turned out to be) before they have HIV-positive AIDS. He strengthened his case by noting that "it is clear that acquired immune deficiencies do not require the presence of HIV infection." (*RA.* p.259) The chronic fatigue syndrome epidemic that he, for whatever reason, didn't know about was certainly a neon sign for *that* notion.

Rather than suggest that there may be some other agent responsible for both HIV-positive AIDS and what looked like HIV-negative AIDS in the gay community, (while also not considering that there might be an unseen HIV-negative immunological event going on in the general population—which there was), he instead went on a fishing expedition for *infections associated with gays* that could support a multi-factorial HIV-plus-something-else theory of AIDS. It's a shame that he didn't take the HIV-negative AIDS issue and run with it, launching an all-out assault on the HIV theory. As they say, he who would wound the lion must kill him. He was merely wounding the paradigm. If HIV-negative AIDS was nature's way of saying flat out that HIV couldn't be the cause of AIDS, then Root-Bernstein wasn't listening closely enough. It's amazing that Root-Bernstein didn't see more red flags considering that he wrote, "In fact, a large body of evidence demonstrates that significant immune suppression occurs in the absence of HIV infection in groups at high risk for AIDS but not among low-risk groups. HIV seropositive individuals within each identified risk group are no more immune suppressed than those who are HIV seronegative, as long as they do not contract other active infections." (*RA* p.261) He also reports that "the laboratories of Jerome Groopman and Robert Gallo [of all people] found that as many as 50 to 80 percent of HIV-seronegative homosexual men and hemophiliacs had significantly reduced T-helper/T-suppressor ratios during 1984." (*RA* p.262) Again, it was as though they had found a big gay HIV-negative epidemic of immunosuppression that might have pulled the rug out from under the HIV-positive paradigm that was about to trap the gay community in the draconian and toxic public health agenda I call Holocaust II.

While Root-Bernstein points to studies that suggest that Cytomegalovirus (CMV), the under-appreciated virus that the CDC initially suspected was the

630

cause of AIDS, was responsible for the immunosuppression in HIV-negative men who were immune-suppressed, it was the HIV-negativity itself rather than the CMV that should have sent everyone back to the nosological and epidemiological drawing board to see if they had overlooked some other new infection—like the recently (at that point) discovered HHV-6. It was a huge missed opportunity, to say the least.

One of the most damning studies for the HIV theory of AIDS "consisted of an immunological and infectious disease evaluation of 100 'healthy' homosexual men in Trinidad in 1987 carried out by Robert Gallo, William Blattner, and their colleagues. Nearly all the men in the study, whether they were HIV seropositive or not, had a significant depletion of T-helper cells." (RA p.265) On top of that they also discovered "that some HIV-infected men had normal T-helper cells. Thus, HIV alone did not uniquely signify concomitant immune suppression." (RA p.265) Once again, that might have finished HIV off if research was occurring in the world of normal science rather than in one guided by homodemiology.

Given the confusion between CMV and HHV-6 in AIDS, Root-Bernstein again came close to peering into the HHV-6 catastrophe when he wrote, "In fact, although very few studies have been performed, cytomegalovirus appears to be as good a marker for increasing immune incompetence as HIV. R.J. Biggar and his colleagues reported in 1983 (prior to the isolation of HIV) that a very good correlation existed between the excretion of CMV in the semen of homosexual men and the degree of the immune suppression." (RA. p.279) CMV was good. But the HHV-6 family, as it turns out, was better.

And similarly, given the role of EBV in CFS (sometimes considered to be HIV-negative AIDS), which some people had called "chronic mono" because of the EBV reactivation or infection that it was associated with, Root-Bernstein also came tantalizingly close to inadvertently letting the cat out of the bag about the link between AIDS and CFS when he noted, "In 1986, Charles R. Rinaldo, Jr., and his co-workers demonstrated that homosexual men who seroconvert to HIV simultaneously experienced a fourfold increase in antibody titers to EBV VCA antigen (virus capsid antigen). Furthermore, they documented a direct correlation between HIV antibody titer and EBV antibody titer. The higher the one, the higher the other." (RA p.280) Again, inadvertently, Root-Bernstein may have uncovered the fact that AIDS was just a serious development in gay men who essentially had all the signs of "chronic mono" or "chronic fatigue syndrome." Root-Bernstein appropriately chided his fellow scientists: "Whether other viruses associated with AIDS . . . are similarly predictive of disease progression remains to be seen, since no one, as far as I can tell, has even bothered to look. This failure to look has left us in the position of assuming that HIV is the only valid measure of disease progression in AIDS, without the scientific benefit of having checked the assumption." (RA p.280) Checking assumptions was something that was only done on the alien non-homodemiological world of normal science.

In his chapter, "Why AIDS is Epidemic Now," Root-Bernstein may have jumped the heterosexist shark as he entered the dangerous area of speculation about the sociological underpinnings of AIDS, asserting, "To understand AIDS, we must document and understand the sociological changes in homosexuality, drug use and medical practice that have created the conditions that allowed the syndrome to explode into prominence during the past decade." (RA p.282) The chapter gets everything backwards. It's not that anything he says is flat out factually wrong. It's just that he misses the heterosexist context in which everything he asserts actually takes place. Every negative statement he makes about gays could be matched with a critical or negative statement about a biased heterosexual white-privileged society and the scientists who eventually entrapped gays in the bogus HIV/AIDS and "chronic fatigue syndrome is not AIDS" paradigms. Changes in homosexuality were not the only thing that needed to be discussed in order to understand the true nature of the epidemic. Changes—not good ones—in the application of society and science's white heterosexism kept up with them.

Root-Bernstein confidently notes that the "sociological manifestations of homosexuality have changed in the recent past. . . . New expressions of homosexuality concomitant with the gay liberation movement have created an unusual and new disease profile for gay men." (RA p.282) Root-Bernstein was clearly not applying for the position of Grand Marshal of any Gay Pride parade. While he notes, "The medical literature is quite explicit about some of these new manifestations of gay male life" (RA p.282)—promiscuity-related infections—he again misses the sociological fact that for every gay action there can be a heterosexist reaction and in this case "new manifestations of gay male life" were accompanied by new manifestations of heterosexist bias in science, medicine and epidemiology. Root-Bernstein certainly had a "Got-AIDS-Yet" eye for the gay guy, that focused on various aspects of gay sex that he thought were potentially linked to "AIDS." He found his smoking gun in the studies that showed "an increase in risky behavior among gay men immediately preceding the exploding in AIDS." (RA p.286) He also pointed to the enablers of the new "way of sex as recreation and pleasure," (RA p.286) namely "bath houses, backroom bars and public cruising areas." (RA p.286)

AIDS was—in his own epidemiological vision—the result of the sexual and recreational drug revolution. Whether it was the increase of CMV or amebiasis in gay men, *the tipping point for AIDS was gay liberation*: "AIDS became a problem for homosexual men only when rampant promiscuity, frequent anal forms of intercourse, new and sometimes physically traumatic forms of sex, and the frequent concomitants of drug use and multiple concurrent infections paved the way. As Mirko Grmek has concluded, 'American

632

homosexuals created the conditions which, by exceeding a critical threshold, made the epidemic possible.'" (*RA* p.292) Basically this was as good as homodemiology gets. AIDS was a gay disease, so its cause ipso facto had to be intimately related to gay behavior and gay culture. It was this kind of tragic myopic epidemiological obsession that would allow the HHV-6 catastrophe to quietly simmer all over the world in all kinds of people who had never marched in a single gay liberation parade or enjoyed the diverse hedonistic pleasures that Root-Bernstein saw as the sine qua non of AIDS. Root-Bernstein doesn't say it, but it's hard not to connect the dots and conclude that the implications of his sociologically biased epidemiology that AIDS could only be stopped with a political or sociological intervention. One can only assume that in one form or another such an intervention might mean rescinding the whole gay liberation movement—or at least its sexual side.

What would never occur to Root-Bernstein was the possibility that the uneven distribution of AIDS and the apparent total safety of the heterosexual general population was a actually a mirage of groupthink, a byproduct of the political use of a heterosexist definition of AIDS that the CDC had put into play. A far more radical political and sociological analysis actually needed to be conducted *on the epidemiologists themselves* who were blind to the emerging CFS form of AIDS and the pandemic of HHV-6 that was all around while they were doing their thinking in heterosexist boxes.

Given Root-Bernstein's homodemiological approach to AIDS and his acceptance of the CDC's ground zero epidemiology, it is not surprising that he took issue with Stephen Jay Gould who wrote an alarming piece in 1987 in *The New York Times Magazine* "proclaiming heterosexual AIDS a 'natural' and therefore inevitable phenomenon." (*RA* p.299) This was like waving a red flag at everyone in the Duesbergian heterosexual-AIDS-is-a-myth camp. Root-Bernstein disapprovingly quotes Gould proclaiming that "the AIDS pandemic . . . may rank with nuclear weaponry as the greatest danger of our era. . . . Eventually, given the power and lability of human sexuality, it spreads outside the initial group into the general population, and now AIDS has begun its march through our own heterosexual community." (*RA* p.299) Gould went on to say that those infected would be "our neighbors, our lovers, our children and ourselves. AIDS is both a natural phenomenon and potentially, the greatest natural tragedy in human history." (*RA* p.299) Inadvertently sounding like "The Great Prophet of the chronic fatigue syndrome and Autism Epidemic," Gould was uncannily and inadvertently prescient about what was actually going on behind the CDC's biased epidemiological concoctions and sexual balkanization. He would have been spectacularly on the money if he had been referring to the HHV-6 pandemic. But HIV—not exactly.

Root-Bernstein took issue with Gould and others who in any way tried to extrapolate a picture of the future of the AIDS epidemic from what was going on in Africa. He insisted "AIDS in Africa cannot used as a model for AIDS in Western nationals because typical sub-Saharan Africans are not comparable to Western heterosexuals in their disease load, their nutritional status, or their immunological functions." (RA p.301) This was an example of heterosexist presumptions morphing into racist presumptions. Homodemiology was becoming what I call Afrodemiology. Just as he blamed the gay revolution for AIDS in America, he noted that "Social and political revolutions are also taking their tolls on African health." (RA p.308) He pointed to Daniel B. Hrdy's notion that population movements and what Hrdy called the "sexual mixing" "of various African groups may be related to the spread of AIDS." (RA p.308) He also blamed wars in Africa which could lead to the kind of breakdown of public health infrastructure as a possible foundation for AIDS. He insisted that as far as heterosexual AIDS was concerned, "Europe and America were not Africa," (RA p.310) and "Far from presenting us with a look at the future of AIDS in North America and Europe, African heterosexuals simply confirm the fact that AIDS is a problem only for individuals who have multiple causes of immune suppression prior to, concomitant with, or independent of HIV exposure. AIDS will never become a major health threat to Americans and Western Europeans that it has become for Africans. AIDS will be a continuing problem only for individuals whose life-style, medical histories, or socioeconomic conditions predispose them to immune suppression in general." (RA p.311) This Root-Bernstein conclusion was on target only because he was blissfully unaware that whenever his fellow white American heterosexuals saw their immune systems go either south or haywire, it would be deceptively called chronic fatigue syndrome. And those unfortunate white American heterosexuals would be called crazy if they happened to notice in any way that their illness, which would be trivialized as "Yuppie Flu," was even real, significant or transmissible.

As already pointed out, like most of the Duesberg camp, Root-Bernstein was incredulous about the notion that healthy heterosexuals could ever in a million years get AIDS: "In fact, the chances that a healthy, drug free heterosexual will contract AIDS from another heterosexual are so small they were hardly worth worrying about." (RA p.313) One gets the feeling that he actually thinks it was almost literally impossible. He even doubted that cases of heterosexual cases of AIDS (as identified by the CDC) were really what they were cracked up to be. He went so far as to question the credibility of the world's most famous case of heterosexual AIDS, basketball player Magic Johnson: " . . . no one knows what risk factors Johnson did or did not have for contracting HIV other than extraordinary promiscuity. We have only his world that he contracted HIV from a woman. He has never directly stated that he never engaged in homosexual activity or used intravenous drugs." (RA p.313) In other words, he had never gotten the homodemiological third degree or the Got-AIDS-Yet? enhanced interrogation. Root-Bernstein was skeptical and asserted that "a variety of other cases touted by the government and media as heterosexually acquired AIDS cases are similarly suspect." (*RA* p.314)

Root-Bernstein applies the homodemiological way of sorting things out by also bringing up the possibility that the unmentionable practice of heterosexual anal sex may be a stealth factor for heterosexual AIDS in America. He argues that the female inhibition towards discussing anal sex was concealing the real reason for any supposed heterosexual AIDS. He also points out that many woman "are reticent to discuss the sharing of sexual toys such as dildos and butt plugs that may also represent modes of transmitting sexual diseases." (*RA* p.322) In an uncanny way, it is not too much of a stretch to suggest he was coming very close to saying that heterosexuals contracted AIDS because, although they were straight, *they had done something gay.*

One doesn't want to go too negative on Root-Bernstein, however, even if his thinking did somewhat reflect the hegemonic heterosexist culture he was part of, because at a critical time during Holocaust II, along with several others, he did play a significant part in keeping minds open enough to prevent the HIV/AIDS research elite from going completely unchallenged. He put his own reputation on the line in doing so. He also kept the door open for additional critical scientific thinking that could pick up where he left off. For those bravely standing up to a very hostile and powerful HIV/AIDS empire, his call for better science and creative scientific thinking was manna from heaven: "We must elaborate possibilities. In science, as in theater or fiction, the tension of the plot is produced by the alternative resolutions we can imagine. A plot that unfolds without suspense is boring. Similarly, in science research that can only reach one conclusion is hardly worth performing; it has no potential to yield discoveries. We want a plot that proffers alternatives. HIV has been set up as the villain of this piece, but it is still possible that we have been led [on] a merry chase away from the real culprits?" (*RA* p.327) He didn't realize the degree to which he was trapped in an opposite world of abnormal, totalitarian science that was driven by an agenda and a mindset that had no real interest in surprises and plot twists, discoveries and anomalies. Channeling Thomas Kuhn, he wrote, "I have previously defined scientific discovering as a process of elaborating all imaginable explanations for a phenomenon, constrained by an ever-increasing body of observation and experiment. The resulting recursive interplay of imagination and reality assures us that we have reached the correct answer." (*RA* p.328) That kind of Arendtian freedom-to-imagine was not permissible in a totalitarian world in which scientists were expected to follow HIV dogma.

When historians try to assign culpability to all the scientists who stood passively and silently on the sidelines while the medical and scientific atrocities of Holocaust II occurred, they will want to investigate the trails suggested by this statement by Root-Bernstein: "Thus, despite repeated statements by government officials that the cause of AIDS is known and that it is HIV, I can no longer find any major investigators in the field of AIDS who will defend the proposition that HIV is the only immunosuppressive agent involved in AIDS." (*RA* p.330) Whoever these scientists were, they will have to face the judgment of history when it asks why they sat on their hands and allowed the HIV mafia of Holocaust II to build a monolithic and hellish public health empire for AIDS patients and the gay community around the notion that "HIV is the only suppressive agent involved in AIDS."

It is only fair to pay special tribute to the fact that Root-Bernstein gave some rather astute, prescient attention to HHV-6 in his penultimate chapter. In discussing co-factors, he notes that even Robert Gallo had one, namely HHV-6. He quotes Gallo himself saying, "Another candidate [for an AIDS cofactor] is human herpes virus 6 (HHV-6, originally designated human B-lymphotropic virus), which has not only been identified in most patients AIDS by virus isolation, DNA amplification techniques and serological analysis, but is also predominantly tropic and cytopathic *in vitro* for CD4+ T lymphocytes . . . These observations indicate that HHV-6 might contribute directly or indirectly to the depletion of CD4+ cells in AIDS." (RA p.330) Root-Bernstein was far too optimistic about the flexibility and good faith of the AIDS establishment in general and Gallo in particular when he concludes, "Statements such as this one [about HHV-6] suggest that even mainstream HIV researchers are beginning to consider the possibility that HIV may not be sufficient to cause AIDS. They do not doubt that it is necessary." (*RA* p.330) To Gallo, HIV never really stopped being the "truck" that killed patients. The Nobel Prize which he felt he deserved (and still hasn't gotten) was totally dependent on that theory.

History might have been different if at this point in his rethinking Root-Bernstein had looked more critically at the psychology, sociology and politics of the world of AIDS science and epidemiology. Absent an ability to detect the presence of heterosexism and the negative effects of its cognitive bias, he was left clueless—a little like Kafka's K trying to understand what was going on in the Castle. He was sensitive to the bullheadedness of those in power but couldn't peer into the twisted souls of those in charge. He quotes the imperious Anthony Fauci, the Director of NIAID, as saying that "critiquing a dubious theory would take time away from more productive efforts." (*RA* p.331) And he quotes James Curran as stating unequivocally at the Amsterdam AIDS Conference in 1992 (at which it was announced that there were cases of HIV-negative AIDS), "There is not AIDS without HIV." (*RA* p.331) What Curran was really stubbornly saying was, "We're the Centers for Disease Control. We have the power to define disease and epidemics, and if there is HIV then we say *there has to be AIDS*, and if there is no HIV *we won't call it AIDS*. Period. End of discussion. And if you call that circular reasoning, you can just suck it up." Fauci and Curran weren't exactly stupid. They must have known where the cofactor argument might lead—to the conclusion that they had both made major contributions to the biggest scientific mistake in history. That they themselves were the final arbiters of the legitimacy of their own work is just one more factor that made AIDS a period of accountability-free abnormal and totalitarian science.

Again, Root-Bernstein seemed like he was making his own pact with the devil in giving HIV too much credibility by shaping his critique around finding cofactors for HIV rather than going all the way and asking a far more radical question of whether HIV was a total disaster-inducing red herring, the biggest scientific mistake in history. In a way, he was inadvertently helping to keep the HIV agenda alive through faint (sometimes slightly fawning) criticism. He goes out of his way to give HIV sufficient deference: "There is no doubt that HIV is highly correlated with AIDS. Correlation is not, however, proof of causation." (RA p.329) He chose to enter his own dog in the race in the form of an "HIV-plus-cofactors theory." (RA p.337) But even his theory that AIDS might be "a multifactorial, synergistic disease" kept a place for HIV as an important but not necessary opportunistic part of the disease process. He didn't fully seem to grasp that it would be *game over* for the HIV establishment if it became known that they had built their scapegoating, dystopian antigay empire around a virus that was not even necessary for AIDS. People were not jumping out of skyscrapers because they tested positive for an AIDS cofactor. People were not be arrested for transmitting an AIDS cofactor to others. People were not being turned into toxic dumps filled with AZT (and its toxic siblings) because they were infected with an AIDS cofactor.

Root-Bernstein tries to have his cake and eat it too by sticking it to Duesberg: "I believe that Duesberg is wrong in ignoring the role of HIV in AIDS. It is certainly highly correlated with the syndrome (even given the methodological sleight of hand involved in defining the syndrome by the presence of the putative causative agent prior to definitive demonstration of causation) . . . . It is just as big a mistake to ignore the potential role of HIV in AIDS as it is to ignore the roles of all other immunosuppressive agents that affect AIDS patients." (RA p.343) The AIDS establishment was not shaking in its boots about the latter charge. The AIDS empire was not being built on the premise that HIV *contributed* to AIDS like a wide array of other immunosuppressive agents. HIV was being packaged as the Gay Andromeda Strain. It was an evil and inexorable agent. Those infected with it carried an evil germ and were capable of doing a great deal of damage to society with the venereally-transmitted agent, meaning that those people's very sexual identities were being permanently tied to the single evil virus.

In many ways, the notions that Peter Duesberg proffered about AIDS were not any less heterosexist than Root-Bernstein's, but with far more political sensitivity than Root-Bernstein, Duesberg grasped the personal implications for anyone who got caught in the labyrinth of epidemiological fraud and ended up labeled HIV positive, the virtual medical Yellow Star (or more accurately, a Pink Triangle) with all the perks that went with it. They weren't just being labeled "cofactor positive." Peter Duesberg had the kind of empathetic x-ray vision that could see the human toll the scientific mistake (or fraud) of HIV was taking.

For all we know, Root-Bernstein may have thought that his was a kind of big tent compromise position that could bring the anti-HIV camp back to the scientific table with the growing HIV establishment so as to develop a new synthesis of both positions, but it was all for naught regardless of his good intentions. The AIDS establishment had bet their professional and financial lives on HIV and Duesberg thought HIV was a non-negotiable crock and that was that. And while all of these scientists fiddled with arguments about HIV, Rome was burning with HHV-6 and its family of viruses.

Root-Bernstein ends his important book by asking how so many scientists could be so wrong about something and reminds his readers that "Science, despite its elusive goal of objective truth, is just as human and just as fallible as any other human activity." (RA p.350) It is his belief that oversimplification and gullibility have contributed to the mistake of thinking HIV is the cause of AIDS. He asserts, "authority—even wishful thinking— is just as powerful and prevalent in science and medicine as it is in any other sphere of human endeavor." (RA p.353) He also points out the scandalous and unbelievable fact that studies have shown that "physicians are perhaps the most authority oriented of all professionals. They are evaluated in medical school not on the basis of their critical thinking skills, their creativity, or their independence but their ability to learn quickly, to memorize well, to act prudently, and to be able to quote authority extensively." (RA p.353) They would clearly also make good priests—which is what some of them seemed like during Holocaust II. He goes to the tragic heart of the matter when he writes, "There can be no breakthroughs without research, but breakthrough research is not possible when conformity is rewarded and skeptical inquiry punished. AIDS may continue to plague modern society, just as other preventable infections such a puerperal fever plagued our forebears, because of the closemindedness of the very physicians whose job it is to diagnose, treat, and prevent these diseases." (RA p.354) He didn't know the half of it. In the solace of his certainty that these mistakes didn't put the heterosexual general population at risk, he thought he was throwing life rafts at pathetic, drowning risk groups from a boat that couldn't sink. He didn't know he was standing on the white heterosexual Titanic.

As with Duesberg and Kary Mullis, one must express gratitude that he joined those who spoke out against AZT and similar treatments: "One caveat concerning long-term prophylaxis for AIDS is in order. As I have pointed out repeatedly, chronic use of antibiotics can lead to immune suppression. . . . There are, however, almost no long-term studies of the effects of chronic exposure to the vast majority of drugs that might be used prophylactically in AIDS. . . . We do not want to be in the position of saying that we cured the patient but the treatment killed him." (*RA* p.337) We don't? We didn't? Could have fooled us. He caught the real tragedy of blaming the wrong agent for AIDS when he pointed out that "It may prove easier to stop a mycoplasmal or cytomegalovirus infection [or any infection that be part of the mutifactorial mix in AIDS] than to stop HIV." (*RA* p.357)

It is once again disquieting to note how close to the truth of the HHV-6 catastrophe Root-Bernstein actually got and how much help he could have been if he had stayed with the issue—as focused and critical as he was in his book—for another decade. Thinking way outside the AIDS box, he even theorized that scientists could have gotten the whole orthodox paradigm of immunosuppression in AIDS *backwards* when he speculated that "One very odd possibility is also raised by alternative theories of AIDS, particularly by the theories that incorporate autoimmunity as a major event in the prognosis of the disease. Immunosuppressive drugs may actually benefit AIDS patients." (*RA* p.358) Such a radical change in the AIDS paradigm would have caused what Kuhn refers to as a "visual gestalt shift," but that was simply not allowed in the totalitarian, abnormal, paralyzed world of AIDS science. Without fully realizing it, Root-Bernstein was tilting at political windmills when he wrote, "In the meantime, various aspects of medical practice must change to accommodate the possibility that HIV is not the sole agent responsible for AIDS." (*RA* p.358) To which one could hear every member of the HIV establishment thinking, "Over our dead bodies." There would absolutely be no dialing back on the AIDS paradigm or agenda. Rethinking was for "denialists." HIV would never ever be considered "no more than a serious warning that a patient has multiple risks that need to be ferreted out and controlled and corrected." (*RA* p.358.) He might just as well have proposed that homeopathy be applied to AIDS. There was no way that the crown jewel of homodemiology (and Afrodemiology) was going to be abandoned. Its totalitarian power to stigmatize, control and for some to make a lot of money and advance careers was not something to be given up without a vicious fight to the death.

Like a good Kuhnian, Root-Bernstein thought that the answers to AIDS might come from unexpected sources, from people not at the center of the reigning establishment that controlled the shape of the official paradigm: "I would not be surprised if the most important innovators in AIDS research and treatment turn out to be peripheral members of the research and treatment communities." (*RA* p.363) Following the rules of abnormal science, AIDS research was the enemy of true innovation. AIDS was dogmatic and innovation was heresy and worthy of inquisition. To cross the AIDS leadership was to become a peripheral member of the research and treatment communities.

Near the end of his book the very earnest Root-Bernstein makes a statement full of laugh-out-loud irony for any student of Holocaust II: "We need to solve the social, economic, health education, and medical care problems that create the conditions that permit AIDS to develop in the first place." (*RA* p.368) Fair enough, but the number one problem hidden in that politically correct smorgasbord is something that Root-Bernstein was himself an (albeit relatively decent) ambassador of: white heterosexism. White heterosexism may have had social and economic cofactors in the creation of Holocaust II, but it still was the sine qua non. White heterosexism is what held the AIDS quilt—so to speak—together. And ultimately it would also blindly hold the CFS and autism quilts together.

Root-Bernstein closes his book by asserting that "The only path to the truth is to continue questioning—even things that are taken to be undeniable facts." (*RA* p.373) Given that we are now in the middle of an HHV-6 spectrum catastrophe which is potentially affecting everyone immunologically, neurologically and in a variety of other ways and manifesting itself as an alphabet soup of AIDS, CFS, MS, autism, cancer, Morgellons and God knows what else, he may want to question some of the ground zero data and epidemiology that led to his belief that *the general population had nothing to worry about* where the virtually impossible lightning strike of AIDS was concerned. One day he just might want to write a sequel to *Rethinking AIDS* called "Rethinking My Rethinking of AIDS."

Serge Lang

The Righteous Mathematician

Serge Lang (1927-2005) was one of the most distinguished elder academic statesman in the group intellectuals and scientists that challenged the science of HIV. A mathematician known for his accomplishments in number theory and as the author of numerous graduate level mathematics text books, he taught at the University of Chicago and Columbia University. He was Professor Emeritus at Yale University at the time of his death. He was very active in the Vietnam anti-war movement and spent a great deal of time challenging the misuse of science and mathematics and identifying the spread of misinformation on a number of issues. Lang was rewarded for his interest in the Duesbergian criticism of HIV and for speaking out on the questionable scientific procedures of the HIV establishment, by having his distinguished career in mathematics framed by the same dirty little Orwellian trick used on other HIV critics: he was labeled an "AIDS denialist," by that paragon of sober objectivity, Wikipedia.

As Lang surveyed the manner in which AIDS research was being conducted and the outrageous way that Duesberg was being treated, he was appalled and feared for the integrity of science itself. In 1984, his long critique of the HIV/AIDS theory was published in the Fall issue of *Yale Scientific*. He opened his piece by pointing out the sleight of hand involved in the naming of the virus *only associated* with AIDS which was called "Human Immunodeficiency Virus" before adequate evidence had been gathered to show that it actually deserved that title. Which, of course it didn't. Lang's critical vision of what was transpiring in AIDS was quite damming: " . . . to an extent that undermines classical standards of science, some purported scientific results concerning 'HIV' and 'AIDS' have been handled by press releases, by misinformation, manipulating the media and people at large." Much of Lang's analysis of AIDS science supports the contention that AIDS could best be described as science at its most abnormal. But he stayed away from the matter of the motivation behind the breakdown of science, asserting, "I am not here concerned with intent but with scientific standards, especially the ability to tell the difference between a fact, an opinion, a hypothesis, and a hole in the ground." Even though Lang steered clear of digging into the bigotry that motivated and unified the whole pseudoscientific enterprise, he did make it abundantly clear that there was something *not kosher* about the field of HIV/AIDS research. He argued that there wasn't even a proper definition of "AIDS" and "thus a morass about HIV and AIDS has been created." Lang called the established view of AIDS "dogma" and he was horrified by the way people who dared to challenge the "dogma" were being treated, noting that critics were unfairly being maligned by being called "flatearthers" or told that by just asking questions or being skeptical they were themselves threats to the public health. He was very sensitive to the emotional blackmail that was a staple in the AIDS establishment's psychological armamentarium.

In the *Yale Scientific* piece, Lang argued that "the public at large are not properly informed" and in order for them to know what was really happening, people had to turn to sources outside of the official scientific media. He thought that the way AIDS misinformation was being spread was itself an important issue that needed a focused study. He charged that the official scientific press had failed miserably by obstructing legitimate dissent and that not only would the public lose "trust in the scientific establishment," but people would not be "warned of practices which may be dangerous to their health." As we now know, he was only seeing the tip of the pseudoscientific iceberg.

Lang reiterated the Mullis contention that there were no papers that provided proof that HIV is the cause of AIDS, and no serious HIV animal model for the disease. He was very concerned about the unreliable tests for HIV: "The blood test for HIV does not determine directly the presence of the virus." The test cross-reacted with numerous other diseases. He argued that the AIDS numbers coming out of Africa were based on faulty testing. In terms of the HHV-6 catastrophe that everyone was willfully blind to at the time, it is interesting to note Lang's argument that "there exist thousands of Americans who have AIDS-defining diseases but are HIV negative." Had he said millions, we might be calling him a prophet of the HHV-6 spectrum catastrophe. The argument for HIV was made even worse by the fact that there were "hundreds of thousands who test HIV positive but have not developed AIDS-defining diseases." He accused the CDC of playing games with numbers to support their official image of the epidemic. He was also critical of the CDC's circular definition of AIDS that made it look like there was a 100% correlation between HIV and AIDS in the public's mind. He argued that HIV positivity might "be merely a marker rather than a cause for whatever disease is involved." He was intrigued by the Duesbergian recreational drug hypothesis, but remained open-minded. He wrote, "I have no definitive answer. I merely question the line upheld up to now by the biomedical establishment, and repeated uncritically in the press, that 'HIV is the virus that causes AIDS.'" He felt that because most scientists treated HIV=AIDS as a given, "some scientists try to fit experimental data into this postulate, actually without success." They succeed even when they fail: when the so-called AIDS virus doesn't meet expectations, Lang notes that it is then called "enigmatic" without anyone going back to basics and questioning the science and logic that form the foundation upon which it stands.

Lang was troubled by the unwillingness of the establishment to fund research into alternative hypotheses about AIDS causation—particularly Duesberg's recreational drug hypothesis. He felt that the evidence that the recreational inhalant, "poppers" (amyl nitrite), played a role in AIDS via the development of Kaposi's sarcoma, was compelling enough that it didn't deserve the cold financial shoulder it was consistently getting from those in charge of the governmental funding of AIDS research

In the *Yale Scientific* piece, Lang also criticized "establishment scientists who have tried, so far mostly successfully, to keep reports questioning the establishment dogma about HIV out of the mainstream press." The Pacific Division of the American Association for the Advancement of Science organized a symposium for June 21, 1994 called "The Role of HIV in AIDS: Why There is Still a Controversy." Lang reported that the AAAS "has come under fire from U.S. AIDS researchers and public health officials" and the symposium was almost cancelled. An article about the symposium in the journal, *Nature,* quoted a professor from Harvard as saying that the people involved were "fringe" people. David Baltimore was quoted as saying, "This is a group of people who have denied the scientific facts. There is no question at all that HIV is the cause of AIDS. Anyone who gets up publicly and says the opposite is encouraging people to risk their lives." Again, the emotional blackmail of what today would be called the "concern trolls of HIV/AIDS."

Lang reported that while the symposium was finally held, *Nature* made a point of *not* covering it. Lang sharply noted, "*Nature*'s readers are not given evidence on which to base an informed or independent judgment. Thus does *Nature* manipulate its readers." And thus did that esteemed journal help enable the abnormal science of Holocaust II.

Lang captures the manner in which the media was manipulated during the AIDS era in his description of a study meant to demolish Duesberg's drug hypothesis: "A piece, 'Does drug use cause AIDS?' by M.S. Ascher, H.W. Shepherd., W. Winkelstein Jr. and E. Vittinghoff was published in the *Nature* issue of 11 March 1993. This piece was published as a 'Commentary.' About a week before publication, nature issued a press release concerning this piece headlined: 'DRUG USE DOES NOT CAUSE AIDS.' The press release concluded: 'These findings seriously undermine the argument put forward by Dr. Peter Duesberg, of the University of California at Berkley, that drug consumption causes AIDS.'" Lang noted that Duesberg was blind-sided because the press was notified and was asking him for a response *even before* he had even had a chance to see the forthcoming piece. Lang wrote bitterly, "Thus *Nature* and the authors of the article use the media to manipulate public opinion before their article had been submitted to scientific scrutiny by other scientists (other than possible referees), and especially by Duesberg who is principally concerned."

Lang attacked the press release, writing that it made several misrepresentations including the manner in which the sample of men studied was gathered: " . . . the press release suppressed the additional information that the sampling came from a definite segment of San Francisco households." Lang's analysis of what the Ascher group called "a rigorously controlled epidemiological model for the evaluation of aetiological hypotheses" pointed to numerous flaws that made the study look like a bad joke—which was par for the course in the world of AIDS science. He notes that predictably, *The New York Times* which, with the help of Lawrence Altman, a reporter who was a former CDC employee, was the world's most prestigious echo chamber for the government's AIDS research, ran with the ball. An article by Gina Kolata called "Debunking doubts that H.I.V. causes AIDS," propagated "the misinformation of the [*Nature*] press release and of the 'Commentary.'"

Lang's sense of scientific standards was offended by the whole picture of AIDS science that he saw: "I take no position here on the relative merits of the AIDS virus hypothesis or the AIDS drug hypothesis (in whatever form they may be formulated). I do take a position against the announcement of purported scientific results via superficial and defective press releases, and before scientists at large have had a chance to evaluate the scientific merits of such results are purportedly based." What Lang didn't fully understand was that this kind of propagandistic manipulation of truth was actually business as usual in the totalitarian abnormal science of Holocaust II.

One of the more amusingly outrageous aspects of Ascher's 'Commentary' in *Nature,* appears at the end of the piece: "The energies of Duesberg and his followers could be better applied to unraveling the enigmatic mechanism of the HIV pathogenesis of AIDS." To this patronizing bums rush Lang responded, "I find it presumptuous and objectionable for scientists to tell others where energies 'could better be applied.' Scientific standards as I have known them since I was a freshman at Caltech require that some energies be applied to scrutinize data on which experiments are based, in documenting the accuracy of the data, its significance, its completeness, and to determine whether conclusions allegedly based on these data are legitimate or not." Lang didn't realize that Ascher was part of a political bandwagon driven by social forces which Lang, as brilliant as he was, was not interested in or perhaps even capable of fully fathoming.

In his piece in *Yale Scientific*, Lang also raised the issue of the role of other viruses in AIDS, stating, "No hypothesis can be dismissed a priori. It is still a possibility that some viruses other than HIV sometimes cause some of the diseases listed under the "AIDS" umbrella by the CDC." One of those he mentions in the piece is HHV-6. He clearly was intrigued by the paradox of a supposedly ubiquitous and usually (or also supposedly) harmless virus also being associated with pneumonitis in compromised hosts. He inadvertently went right to the heart of the political and scientific problems that HHV-6 would be entangled with in the years ahead when he wrote, "Here we meet typical examples of rising questions: whether there is merely an 'association' between a virus and some disease, or whether a virus is a cause, and if so how. It is then a problem to make experiments to determine whether a given virus is merely a passenger virus, whether it lies dormant, and if it is awakened (how?). Whether it merely shows its presence by testing positive in various ways (antibodies?), or whether it is or becomes harmful (how?), under certain circumstances (which?)." He had unknowingly stumbled into the tragic intellectual fog of the HHV-6 catastrophe, the biomedical tragedy that the Orwellian propaganda about HIV was obscuring.

One of the more curious episodes in the struggles of the Duesbergian camp concerns Serge Lang's encounter with Richard Horton, the then youngish editor of *The Lancet* who was pretty much in the bag for the HIV establishment. It is described in *Challenges*, Lang's book of essays. It is a must-read for anyone interested in the slovenliness of the intellectual community during Holocaust II. Horton had written a 9,000 word review article, "Truth and Heresy about AIDS" which was critical of Duesberg and published in the *New York Review of Books* (May 23, 1996). In response, Lang submitted a letter as long as Horton's book review itself to *NYBR* but it was rejected. Lang's unpublished letter charged that Horton's review gave "a false impression of scientific scholarship" and did not convey to the readers the complexity of the debate about HIV and AIDS. Horton had reviewed two books by Duesberg and one book which was a collection of 27 articles called *AIDS: Virus—or Drug Induced?*, which included two articles by Lang. Horton completely ignored the more important of Lang's two articles—the one we just discussed that was reprinted from *Yale Scientific*. Not only did Horton ignore Lang's detailed critique of HIV, but he also ignored everyone published in the collection *except* Duesberg, contributing to the image of Duesberg that the HIV establishment had cleverly manufactured and marketed, namely the fringy lone gunman: Lang wrote, "Horton mentioned Duesberg repeatedly as a critic of the established view, but by not referring to the multiple articles in the . . . collection he made it appear as if Duesberg is more isolated than he actually is in raising objections." In addition to criticizing Horton for personalizing the issue rather than engaging in scientific discussion, Lang criticized Horton for not informing his readers about misinformation the government had put out about AIDS and for ignoring legitimate questions about the reliability or credibility of the HIV test. He suggested that Horton had fudged "the issue about relationships between AIDS (whatever it is), HIV and other viruses such as a persistent herpes virus." (The truth about the looming HHV-6 catastrophe was so close to Lang that it could have bitten him.)

Lang pointed out that Duesberg was getting the silent treatment from Horton's own publication, *The Lancet*, where he "has not been allowed to publish longer pieces, [other than letters] either as a scientific article, or as a 'Viewpoint.'" Lang also attacked Horton for resorting to what could be called "emotional public health blackmail" when he pointed to the fact that Horton wrote in his review, "Duesberg's arguments take him into dangerous territory. For if HIV is not the cause of AIDS, then every public health injunction about the need for safe sex becomes meaningless." Dangerous territory? (Certainly dangerous territory for those behind the Potemkin HIV paradigm that hid the truth about Holocaust II.) Lang held that Horton's warning "bypasses the specific objections and questions, and draws an invalid extreme conclusion." As was typical throughout Holocaust II, every time anyone asked a critical question about HIV it was as though they had taken a bullhorn and were shouting out encouragements to the public to run wild and naked in the street without condoms. It often came across as a veiled, patronizing, heterosexist assault against the dignity and intelligence of the gay community. Remarks like those made AIDS look like a public health campaign that was more concerned about behavioral control than truth—which in many ways it was.

New York Review of Books published an exchange of letters between Duesberg and Horton on August 8, 1996. Among a number of things Lang was critical of in Horton's letter, he was especially incensed by Horton's challenge that "If Duesberg seriously believes there is nothing to fear from HIV, he can easily prove it. If Duesberg seriously believes that HIV is harmless, let him inject himself with a suspension of the virus." Lang asserted, "Horton's logic is deficient on several counts. First, self-experimentation by Duesberg would not 'prove' (let alone 'easily prove') anything about a virus which is supposed to take ten years to achieve is pathogenic effects. Second, the negation of one extreme is not the extreme of opposite type. Here may be something to fear from poppers (amyl nitrites) or AZT, as well as HIV." Serge Lang perceptively honed in on the very peculiar debating style that characterized Holocaust II when he wrote, "Horton's reply with the above challenge to Duesberg pushed the discussion to extremes in an unscientific and ad hominem manner. He turns the discussion to considerations of beliefs, rather than facts ('If Duesberg seriously believes . . .'). But it is not a question what 'Duesberg believes.' What's involved scientifically are, among other things: the possibility of making certain experiments (some of them on animals); whether certain data (epidemiological or laboratory) are valid (e.g. properly gathered and reported); whether interpretations of the data are valid; the extent to which certain hypotheses are compatible with the data; and whether scientific objections to specific scientific articles are legitimately or substantially answered, if answered at all."

There was a second exchange between Horton and Duesberg in *NYRB*. According to Lang, "Horton devoted the greater part of his second reply to the ad hominem challenge, and some history of self-experimentation. Thus Horton compounded the problems raised by his ad hominem attack. Self-experimentation is something which a scientist may offer unprompted, as has sometimes been done in the past. Whether to do so or not is for each scientist to decide individually. I object to other scientists putting pressure for self-experimentation especially in a journalistic context." On 2 August 1996, Lang submitted a letter to the editors of the *New York Review* which was about 500 words long. The letter was rejected. Lang was so disturbed by Horton's unprofessional suggestion of self-experimentation that he submitted his rejected letter as a half-page advertisement to *New York Review* with a check for $3,500 to cover the cost. The editor returned the check and agreed to publish the letter.

Lang was incensed that *NYRB* had not published several other letters from scientists defending Duesberg. The *New York Review's* behavior shocked Lang who had been both a contributor and an admirer of the publication's integrity and intellectual legacy. He summarized its importance: "With its world-wide circulation of 120,000, it is very influential in the academic and intellectual community. Members of these communities rely on the *New York Review* for information they cannot get easily elsewhere. Flaws in the *New York Review* editorial judgment are therefore very serious." (Lang would live to see the *New York Review* betray its ideal even more egregiously years later when they attacked South Africa's brave HIV critic, Thabo Mbeki.)

Lang wrote about the pseudoscience of HIV/AIDS like someone whose scientific heart was breaking. In the Horton/*NYRB* piece he wistfully quotes Richard Feynman who called for scientists to have "a kind of scientific integrity, a principle of scientific thought that corresponds to a kind of utter honesty—a kind of leaning over backwards. For example, it you're doing an experiment, you should report everything that you think might make it invalid—not only what you think is right about it: other causes that could possibly explain your results; and things you thought of that you've eliminated by some other experiment, and how they worked—to make sure the other fellow can tell they have been eliminated. Details that could throw doubt on your interpretation must be given, if you know anything at all wrong, or possibly wrong—to explain it. If you make a theory, for example, and advertise it, or put it out, then you must also put down all the facts that disagree with it, as well as those that agree with it. In summary, the idea is to try to give all the information to help others to judge the value of your contribution; not just the information that leads to judgment in one particular direction or another."

Feynman's good faith vision of science operating at its best was like the opposite world of AIDS and Holocaust II. Richard Horton was one of the powerful little princes of that opposite world and the very principled Serge Lang's unflappable, stubborn and inspiring confrontation with Horton on the intellectual world stage during the depressing days of Holocaust II reminds one of what Hannah Arendt wrote about Karl Jaspers in *Men in Dark Times*: "It was self-evident that he would remain firm in the midst of catastrophe. . . . There is something fascinating about a man's being inviolable, untemptable, unswayable." (*Men in Dark Times* p.76) But even the inviolable, untemptable, and unswayable Serge Lang could not stop the catastrophe of Holocaust II.

Rebecca Culshaw

The Whistleblower Who Almost Nailed It

Hopefully, when filmmakers finally start to realize how many rich narrative possibilities there are in the real history of Holocaust II, Rebecca's Culshaw's dramatic awakening to the dark nature of HIV/AIDS science or pseudoscience will be recognized as a compelling story that deserves to be a movie by itself. Culshaw received her Ph.D. in 2002 for work constructing mathematical models of HIV infection, a field of study she had entered in 1996. In an essay, "Why I Quite HIV," (available online) she said that her entire adolescence and adult life "has been overshadowed by the belief in a deadly, sexually transmittable pathogen and the attendant fear of intimacy and lack of trust that belief engenders." During her work on AIDS she came to realize "that there is good evidence that the entire basis for this theory is wrong. AIDS, it seems is not a disease so much as a sociopolitical construct that few people understand and even fewer question."

At one point earlier in her life, she was led to believe that she had contracted "AIDS" and she took an HIV test. She spent two weeks waiting for the results, convinced she was going to die and blaming herself for whatever she might have done to cause the development. She tested negative and "vowed not to take more risks."

Ten years later when she was a graduate student analyzing models of HIV and the immune system, she was surprised to discover that virtually every mathematical model of HIV infection she studied was unrealistic. She concluded that the "biological assumptions on which the models were based varied from author to author." She was also puzzled by the stories of long-term survivors of AIDS and the fact that all of them seemed to have one thing in common—very healthy lifestyles. It made her suspect that "being HIV-positive didn't necessarily mean you would ever get AIDS."

When she ran across the writing of one of Peter Duesberg's supporters, David Rasnick, it all began to make more sense to her. Rasnick had written an article on AIDS and the corruption of modern science which resonated with her own troubling academic experience. She found an intellectual soulmate when she read Rasnick's assertion that the more he "examined HIV, the less it made sense that this largely inactive, barely detectable virus could cause such devastation." Culshaw continued to work on HIV, however, and published four papers on HIV from a mathematical modeling perspective. She wrote, "I justified my contributions to a theory I wasn't convinced of by telling myself these were purely theoretical, mathematical constructs, never to be applied to the real world. I supposed, in some sense also, I wanted to keep an open mind." But eventually she reached a breaking point on HIV.

She had been taught early in her career that clear definitions were important and as far as she could tell, the definition of AIDS was anything but. AIDS was not "even a consistent entity." She was concerned that the definition of AIDS in the early 1980s was a surveillance tool that bore no resemblance to the AIDS of the current time. She was troubled by the fact that *the CDC constantly changed the definition*, that people could be diagnosed when there was no evidence of clinical disease and the fact that the leading cause of death of HIV positives was from liver failure caused by the AIDS treatments (protease inhibitors) themselves.

The epidemiology completely puzzled her. The fact that the number of HIV positives in the U.S. "has remained constant at one million" seemed to make no sense. She wrote, "It is deeply confusing that a virus thought to have been brought to the AIDS epicenters of New York, San Francisco and Los Angeles in the early 1970s could possibly have spread so rapidly at first, yet have stopped spreading as soon as testing began." She had entered the gates of the opposite world of totalitarian, Orwellian, abnormal science where the numbers of positives could remain constant because their origins were political and not based on factuality.

She also thought that the theories about how HIV destroyed t-cells didn't add up and was disturbed that after so many years of study there was still no "biological consensus" about the manner in which HIV did its dirty work. Culshaw was frustrated by the fact that "there are no data to support the hypothesis that HIV kills cells. It doesn't in the test tube. It mostly just sits there, as it does in people—if it can be found at all." The shocking fact that Gallo had originally *only found the virus in 26 of 72 AIDS patients* was also a dramatic strike against the notion that it was the cause of AIDS.

Culshaw found further support for her growing skepticism in the testing for HIV which relies on antibody tests rather than searching for the virus itself because "there exists no test for the actual virus." The fact that so-called viral load tests relied on sophisticated PCR techniques that had never actually been tested against a gold standard of HIV itself made the whole enterprise of HIV testing look like a cruel and dangerous farce. The fact that the criteria for a positive result for the antibody varied from country to country also undermined the credibility of the HIV tests. Culshaw concluded, "I have come to sincerely believe that the HIV tests do immeasurably more harm than good, due to their astounding lack of specificity and standardization. . . . A negative test may not be accurate (whatever that means), but a positive one can create utter havoc and destruction in a person's life—all for a virus that most likely does absolutely nothing. I do not feel it is going too far to say that these tests ought to be banned for diagnostic purposes."

She indicted thousands of her intellectual and professional colleagues when she wrote, "After ten years involved in the academic side of HIV research, as well as in the academic world at large, I truly believe that the blame for the universal, unconditional, faith-based acceptance of such a flawed theory fall on those among us who have actively endorsed a completely unproven hypothesis in the interests of furthering our careers."

Culshaw summed up her thoughts on AIDS in a brief but brilliant book, *Science Sold Out*, which was published two years later by North Atlantic Books. The book is so tautly written and sizzles with so much moral outrage that one could say that she was the Thomas Paine (or one of them) of Holocaust II. She opens the book with an anecdotal challenge to HIV from her personal life: "The boyfriend of a woman I work with died suddenly this year from a raging infection. He became very ill, and his immune system collapsed, unable to handle the infection, and he died. He was not HIV-positive, but if he had been he would have been an AIDS case." (SSO p.viii) While most of the Duesbergians focused mainly on what *was* diagnosed mistakenly as AIDS— diagnoses they disagreed with—it is interesting that she begins her little masterpiece with a case that might inadvertently have pointed to a far darker implication of the CDC and the AIDS establishment's misguided epidemiology: *that they were missing the real epidemic and as a result an unknown number of people were dying mysteriously.*

None of the arguments in her book were completely new, but her presentation was a tour de force. It was full of the most righteous indignation of any of the critical books on HIV and AIDS, with the possible exception of the work of John Lauritsen, who I have discussed at length in my book, *The Chronic Fatigue Syndrome Epidemic Cover-up*. She also brought an astute political and sociological analysis to the table that helped make what we've called Holocaust II more understandable as a historic event: "AIDS has become so mired in emotion, hysteria and politics that it is no longer primarily a health issue. AIDS has been transported out of the realm of public and personal health and into a strange new world in which pronouncements by powerful governmental officials are taken as gospel, and no one remembers when, a few years later, these pronouncements turn out to be false." (*SSO* p.4) That the scientific establishment had been so quick to accept the HIV theory was shocking. The willingness of the public to trust proclamations from the government on the issue was also unsettling. She made it her job to try and sort out the sociological reasons for the rush to judgment and the bizarre and stubborn anti-scientific refusal to entertain second and third opinions on the matter.

As Culshaw looked back at the history of AIDS, she saw a disturbing pattern that made it appear as if scientists were making everything up haphazardly and illogically as they went along: "Science, of course, is meant to be self-correcting, but it seems to be endemic in HIV research that, rather than continuously building an accumulating body of secure knowledge with only occasional missteps, the bulk of the structure gets knocked down every three to four years, replaced by yet another hypothesis, standard of care, or

651

definition of what exactly, AIDS really is. This new structure eventually gets knocked down in the same fashion." (*SSO* p.11) Inadvertently, she was actually sensing the totalitarian, abnormal, deviant, ad hoc, a posteriori nature of criminal, scientific opposite world she had stumbled into. She could grasp the hypocritical and dishonest nature of the infernal game that was being played in the name of science when she wrote, "Even more disturbing is the fact that HIV researchers continuously claim that certain papers' results are out of date, yet have absolutely no hesitation in citing the entire body of scientific research on HIV as massive overwhelming evidence in favor of HIV. They can't have it both ways, yet this is what they try to do." (*SSO* p.12) In the opposite world of AIDS science meant having everything every-which-way all of the time.

As Culshaw wrestles with the question of why so many scientists could be so wrong for so long, she points out that, contrary to the HIV establishment's propaganda, a significant number of scientists actually did join Duesberg in his skepticism and dissent. One of the more interesting scientists she mentions is Rodney Richards, "a chemist who worked for the company Amgen developing the first HIV antibody tests [who] contends that the antibody tests are at best measuring a condition called hypergammaglobulinemia . . . a word that simply means too many antibodies to too many things." (*SSO* p.13) (This—unknown to Culshaw—may have been the major clue that CFS and AIDS were manifestations of the same hypergammaglobulinemia epidemic, and explain why both groups, in addition to testing positive for HHV-6 also tested positive for retroviral activity due to the hypergamma-globulinemia.)

Culshaw agreed with the HIV/AIDS critic David Rasnick, that a contributing factor in the reign of scientific error was an "epidemic of low standards that is infecting all of academic scientific research." (*SSO* p.13) She argued that "it was almost inevitable that a very significant scientific mistake was going to be made." (*SSO* p.15) Culshaw was very critical of the AIDS establishment's refusal to publicly discuss and defend its science: "If the AIDS establishment is so convinced of the validity of what they say, they should have no fear of a public, adjudicated debate between the major orthodox and dissenting scientists, and the scrutiny of such a debate by the scientific community." (*SSO* p.17) Scrutiny to AIDS researchers was like sunlight to vampires.

Culshaw was just as flabbergasted at the very strange moment that HTLV-III was transformed politically into the "AIDS virus" as the rest of the Duesbergians: "It was sometime in 1985 that HIV conspicuously went from 'the virus associated with AIDS' to the 'virus that causes AIDS,' squelching debate in the scientific arena. What changed? What happened to make scientists come to such certainty? If you look at the actual papers you'll see quite clearly that the answer is nothing." (*SSO* p.19) In other words, this life-and-death matter was settled by politics and public relations rather than anything resembling Kuhnian normal science. HIV/AIDS, according to Culshaw, then became a "machine" that kept moving despite all efforts at dissent. It had an evil life of its own.

Culshaw focuses on the protease inhibitor part of the tragedy of Holocaust II by walking her readers through the chronology of the questionable science that the so-called "cocktails" were based on. Papers by David Ho (*Time*'s Man of the Year) and Xiping Wei that were published in *Nature* inspired an approach to treating AIDS of "Hit hard, hit early," that was to turn the hoodwinked and cheering gay community into one big deadly .iatrogenic AIDS cocktail party. The only problem with the cocktails, according to Culshaw, was that "few people are aware that the conclusions" that supported the approach "were based on very poorly constructed mathematical models," and "to make matters worse, the statistical analysis were poorly done and the graphs were presented in such a way as to lead the reader to believe something different from what the data supported." (SSO p.20) Deceptive, abnormal science was alive and well during the David Ho HIV/AIDS cocktail era. Ho's slovenly work was called "ground breaking" by Sir John Maddox of *Nature* who said that it provided a compelling reason that the critics of HIV (especially Peter Duesberg) should "recant." (*SSO* p.20) A perfect word for the AIDS Inquisition.

Culshaw saw the circular logic game of molding data to fit the theory being played out in AIDS in the mathematics-based papers that were used to justify the protease inhibitor era, noting that "such tactics by definition, are excellent at maintaining a façade of near-perfect correlation between HIV and AIDS and of providing seeming convincing explanations of HIV pathogenesis." (*SSO* p.21) Once again the public relations requirements of the HIV/AIDS paradigm were being serviced by the fancy footwork of abnormal science. The inexorable nature of Holocaust II is captured in the fact that even though "the Ho/Wei papers have been debunked by both establishment and dissenting researchers on biological as well as mathematical grounds," the therapies that were concoctions based on *that* discredited science "are used to this day." (*SSO* p.21) The reader stares in helpless horror at the atrocities of the HIV/AIDS era as Culshaw reiterates that " . . . a large population of people have been, and continue to be, treated on the basis of a theory that is unsupportable." (*SSO* p.21) Culshaw's moral outrage is riveting: "You might imagine that people might feel an urge to discuss the manner in which the papers got published and whether other such mistakes have happened since that time. You might imagine that the failure of the peer-review process to detect such patently inept research would send off alarm bells within the HIV-research community. You would be wrong." (*SSO* p.21) Standard operating procedure in Holocaust II.

Without calling it virtual iatrogenic genocide, she indicts a whole generation of clinicians who continued to base their treatment of patients on Ho and Wei: "HIV researchers know the Ho/Wei papers are wrong, yet they

653

continue along the clinical path charted by the papers. They know that the quantitative use of PCR has never been validated, yet they continue to use viral load to make clinical decisions." (*SSO* p.21) As we have said, it took a village of professionals to create Holocaust II.

One thinks about the proverbial story of the drunk looking for his car keys in the parking lot under a light far from his actual car because that's the only place there is light—when one reads this analysis from Culshaw about a scientist's discovery in the first so-called AIDS patients: "Upon measuring their t-cells, a subset of the immune system, he found that in all five men they were depleted. What is quite curious about this discovery is that the technology to count t-cells had only just been perfected."*(SSO* p.23) This is yet another way of saying that epidemics never get a second chance to make a first impression. Shiny new toys can create erroneous new paradigms in science.

Culshaw gets to the crux of the AIDS establishment's mistake by noting that they rushed to judgment on HIV and *then were then trapped* and had to trim data and cook the books (like the frantic maintainers of a threatened Ponzi scheme) in order to fit their stubborn theories to match disparities in the growing number of people they were designating as having AIDS: "As the definition expanded and as it became more and more clear that HIV did not do at all what it was purported to do—that is, kill CD4 t-cells by any detectable method—researchers began to invent more and more convoluted explanations for why their theory was correct." (*SSO* p.24) Good money was constantly thrown after bad. Of course, from this writer's perspective, had they also expanded the definition so much as to include the chronic fatigue syndrome epidemic, things might have miraculously straightened themselves out and HHV-6's role in the hypergammaglobulinemia epidemic might have become painfully obvious.

Channeling Thomas Kuhn, Culshaw is all too old fashioned and normal-science-ish when she so reasonably writes, "The logical scientific thing to have done would have been to notice their original disease designation did not accurately identify the causative agent or agents, rather than changing the syndrome, throw out the supposed causative agents and find one that explained the observations better. As we know, this has not happened." (*SSO* p.24)

Culshaw decried the bogus logic behind the universal celebration of protease inhibitors, noting that " . . . the proportion of AIDS cases that resulted in death experienced a large drop in 1993-1994, which orthodoxy and the mass media were more than happy to portray as decreased mortality thanks to protease inhibitors. However, protease inhibitors were not even generally available to AIDS patients until 1996, over two years after the decline in the death rate began." (*SSO* p.27) She challenged the notion that they had been proved to extend life and argued that one only had to look at the packet inserts to see that they could "cause debilitating side effects, some of which are indistinguishable from the symptoms of AIDS itself." (*SSO* p.27)

She was horrified by the insane logic of HIV drug manufacturers who would insist "that since someone who was healthy when they started therapy happened to stay healthy for some time on the drugs, that is some sort of credit to the medications." (*SSO* p.28) She warned that "there is no evidence to say that they would not have remained healthy even if they never took any medication at all." (*SSO* p.28) She noted that the HIV establishment had basically gamed the system by never using placebo-controls so that it could not be determined *if nothing was actually better* than the AIDS drugs. "Do no harm" was a quaint joke from the distant past. As far as the reports of the supposedly positive effects upon very sick people who took the drugs, she pointed out, as others had, that reverse transcriptase inhibitors are non-specific cell-killers an in addition to harming healthy cells, could be attacking "those cells that are dividing fastest," (*SSO* p.28) such as the opportunistic bacteria and fungi that were the cause of acute illnesses in AIDS patients. In other words, their reputation was based on the mistaken impression that it was *their effect on HIV rather than the other infections* involved in the syndrome. She noted that protease inhibitors had been shown to control two of the more important infections associated with AIDS: candida and pneumocystis. (*SSO* p.28)

Culshaw came down hard on the absurd Orwellian invention of the term "Immune Recon stitution Syndrome" which was used to explain away the development of opportunistic infections that occurred *when people were taking the miraculous protease inhibitors*. The convenient ad hoc explanation was that the immune system of AIDS patients was getting "confused" as it was getting stronger. She slapped that one down, writing that "In reality, it seems to be just another attempt to explain away the fact that clearly the medications are nor working as they were intended. . . ." (*SSO* p.29) She zeroed in on one of the disturbing consequences of all this, one that supports our notion that the whole era should be called Holocaust II: "Consider also that the leading cause of death among medicated HIV-positives is no longer even an AIDS-defining disease at all, but liver failure, a well-documented effect of protease inhibitors." (*SSO* p.30)

Throughout Holocaust II, where there was AIDS there was also state coercion (the social and political face of totalitarian science) sponsored by the inexorable public health logic of the HIV/AIDS establishment. Culshaw noted, "Infants born to HIV-positive mothers are in many states forced to undergo anti-retroviral therapy and since only a few drugs have been approved for children, the drugs administered are the most toxic, AZT and nevirapine being foremost. Oftentimes this drug regimen begins before the baby is born, in certain cases against the wishes of the mother, and continues throughout childhood." (*SSO* p.30) And the tragedy was cruelly compounded by the fact that half of HIV-positive babies revert to negative *in any case*.

Unforgivable iatrogenic scars from this age of medical atrocities were everywhere. (Hopefully, historians will do a good job one day of documenting them all for posterity.)

In terms of the real underlying pandemic of HHV-6, it is interesting that Culshaw zeroed in on the politically motivated nature of concocting a definition of AIDS as a disease characterized mainly by the decline in CD4+ cells: "But what was known from the beginning of AIDS—though bizarrely, not investigated to nearly the extent that CD4+ cells have been investigated—was that *AIDS patients suffered disruptions in many subsets of their blood cells.* [emphasis mine]. Virtually all of these patients had elevated levels of many different types of antibodies, indicating that something had gone wrong with the "antibody-arm of the immune system." (*SSO* p.33) (God forbid that they had looked at what was going on in the "antibody arm of the immune system" of the CFS patients and the rest of the general population.)

In her book, as she had done in her previous essay, she emphasized that the HIV tests themselves were an unreliable technical mess and was horrified at how diagnostics that were "some of the worst tests ever manufactured in terms of standardization, specificity, and reproducibility" (*SSO* p.35) were being used "as a weapon of discrimination ever since testing began." (*SSO* p.35) Everything about the way viral proteins were identified as belonging to HIV she found questionable. She described one of the common tests (the ELISA): " . . . the proteins are present in a mixture and the serum reacts with the proteins in such a way as to cause a color change. The color change is not discrete—meaning that everyone has varying degrees of reaction." (*SSO* p.39) It gets totally Alice-in-Wonderlandish as she notes that "there are varying degrees of the color change, and a cutoff value has been established, above which the sample is considered reactive or 'positive' and below which it is considered 'negative.' Clearly, this language is absurd, since *positive* and *negative* are polarities and not positions on a sliding scale." (*SSO* p.39) Such was the crazy way medical tests were conducted in the reign of abnormal science that was Holocaust II.

Culshaw also noted that *everyone could test positive for HIV*, depending on how the serum was diluted when the tests were run. She was inadvertently saying more about the catastrophic effects of HHV-6 on the body when she pointed out that the tests were actually detecting the previously mentioned condition of hypergammaglobinemia, or "having too many antibodies to too many things." (*SSO* p.44) Again it must be pointed out that, unknown to her and her colleagues in AIDS dissent, the biomedical face of the complex HHV-6 catastrophe was simultaneously revealing itself in the widespread chronic fatigue syndrome epidemic in the form of people "having too many antibodies to too many things."

The other thing which she pointed out which connected with the oft-detected evidence of retroviral activity in CFS was the possibility that the HIV test was simply detecting *endogenous retroviral activity*, hence just an artifact (or epiphenomenon) of the biological chaos that was going on in the bodies of AIDS patients. The retroviral activity could be "Simply a marker for cell decay and/or division." (*SSO* p.44) (And, in the case of HHV-6's devastation, we know there was and is a lot of *that* going on.) And, again, the fact that the HIV tests had never been "validated against the gold standard of HIV isolation" (*SSO* p.45) decimated their credibility. Or should have

Culshaw could see that the slovenly and shady science of HIV had led America and the rest of the world into an ethical quagmire: "Since the diagnosis HIV-positive carries with it such a stigma and the potential for outrageous denial of human rights, it is only humane that doctors, AIDS researchers, and test manufacturers would want to make absolutely certain that the tests they are promoting are completely verifiable in the best possible way. This is not happening." (*SSO* p.45) Like some of the other HIV critics, she pointed out that the retrovirus *had never been unquestionably isolated in an irrefutable way* in the first place—and still hadn't been, potentially making AIDS one of the biggest scientific mistakes and scandals in history. She reinforced the point, writing, "You might think that with hundreds of billions of dollars spent so far on HIV, there would have been by now a scientific attempt to demonstrate HIV isolation by publication of proper electron micrographs. The fact that there has not indicates quite strongly that no one has been able to do it." (*SSO* p.46)

In addition to the HIV test not working reliably, she also questioned the viral load test, which is used "to estimate the health status of those already diagnosed HIV-positive" because "there is good reason to believe it does not work at all." (*SSO* p.46) She pointed to a paper that indicated "fully one-half of . . . patients with detectable viral loads had no evidence of virus by culture." (*SSO* p.47) It was as if the Three Stooges were in charge of every aspect of HIV testing. Culshaw was uniquely sensitive to the ugly political nature of all this and perceptively saw how the HIV tests "are used essentially as weapons of terror." (*SSO* p.48) She writes, "This medical terrorism reached new heights in June, 2006 with the CDC's new HIV testing guidelines, which recommended that everyone between the ages of thirteen and sixty-five be tested for antibodies to HIV." (*SSO* p.48)

Culshaw was outraged that the faulty test for a virus not proven to cause AIDS could force perfectly healthy people "into undergoing a regimen that will inevitably cause long-term toxic effects (and even death), a more sinister complication is the violation in human rights that occurs following a positive HIV test. Every state in the U.S. and every province in Canada maintain a list of 'HIV carriers' in that region."(*SSO* p.49) That was just one more aspect of Holocaust II that made it seem very much like Holocaust I.

Culshaw could see the heavy political hands that were keeping the hellish paradigm and draconian public health agenda in place. When they were confronted by criticism grounded in logic and reason, "The AIDS orthodoxy's only counters to the points made and the questions raised consist of ad hominem attacks including use of the term 'denialist' as well as stating that dissenting views have 'long since been discredited' without any reference to exactly *where* these views have been discredited. Unfortunately, words are powerful and personal attacks are very effective at silencing people." (*SSO* p.60) She felt that it was a campaign of "fear, discrimination, and terror that has been waged aggressively by a powerful group of people whose sole motivation was and is behavior control." (*SSO* p.60) Of course, those would be the lucky ones. The dead ones would have no behavioral issues.

More than any other AIDS critic, she came the closest to seeing the heterosexist and racist underpinnings of the whole creepy game: "To understand the sociological motivations behind the HIV/AIDS paradigm, one must understand the racism and homophobia that has persisted in society for centuries. It is only very recently in the timeline of history that gays and blacks have been accorded equal rights under the law. . . ." (*SSO* p.61) Her thinking supported my contention that what the law can give gays and blacks with one hand, epidemiology in the form of homodemiology and Afrodemiology *can take away with the other*.

Culshaw came breathtakingly close to seeing both the forest and the trees insofar as she called it a rush to judgment at the beginning of the epidemic when the first cases of AIDS were assumed to be sexually transmitted even though *the original gay men with it had no contact with each other*. She was onto the heterosexist or homodemiological lenses through which the original ground zero data was being observed by the VD- and gay-obsessed pioneers of the HIV/AIDS paradigm. And she recognized that the assumption of sexual transmission was not easily dialed back or reconsidered. In terms of the HHV-6 catastrophe it is of interest that she recognized that "Despite the fact the other viruses (cytomegalovirus and herpes virus, to give two examples) were far more prevalent in AIDS patients than HIV ever was, the HIV train started rolling and hasn't lost momentum since. Would this have happened if the first AIDS patients had been heterosexuals in the prime of their lives?" (*SSO* p.62)

One of the most admirable things about Rebecca Culshaw is the fact that she was not afraid to use the fierce polemical language of moral indignation when confronting the reign of pseudoscientific evil: "Many of the biggest crimes committed by the AIDS orthodoxy are psychosocial and not medical at all." (*SSO* p.62) What the charlatans of AIDS in their white coats were doing to humanity was not something she—unlike most of her fellow scientists and intellectuals—could look away from: "The discrimination leveled against those given the HIV-positive diagnosis has reached a level not seen since leprosy was common . . . HIV-positives are the modern equivalent of lepers (and in Cuba, where they are quarantined, are even treated as such) . . ." (*SSO* p.63) The enforcers of the paradigm were "vultures who will stop at nothing to prop up their paradigm." (*SSO* p.65) While Culshaw, unfortunately, didn't see the full nature of Holocaust II as clearly as she might have, she came closer than many, and what she did see she translated into an historically important outcry: "The HIV theory has never been about science but rather about behavioral modification primarily, and to a lesser extent, about money, power and prestige. Language surrounding HIV and AIDS is infected with a sort of pious moralism that is completely inappropriate in science. . . ."(SSO p.69) Maybe inappropriate for normal science, but it is the theme song constantly playing in the background of the abnormal science of Holocaust II.

Culshaw could see that, tragically, there was no turning back, because "First of all, there are tremendous financial and social interests involved. Billions of dollars in research funding, stock options, and activist budgets are predicated on the assumptions that HIV causes AIDS. Entire industries of pharmaceutical drugs, diagnostic testing and activist causes would have no reason to exist." (SSO p.70) If that doesn't sound like an empire of evil worthy of being called Holocaust II, I don't know what does.

Few saw the costs and consequences of the HIV theory being wrong and articulated them as dramatically as Culshaw. It wasn't a small inconsequential scientific matter, a minor wrong turn that could be easily forgiven or forgotten: ". . . the scientific and medical communities have a great deal of face to lose. It is not much of an exaggeration to state that when the HIV/AIDS hypothesis is finally recognized as wrong, the entire institution of science will lose the public's trust, and science itself will experience fundamental, profound and long-lasting changes. The 'scientific community' has risked its credibility by standing by the HIV theory so long. This is why doubting the HIV hypothesis is now tantamount to doubting science itself, and this is why dissidents face excommunication." (SSO p.70) And she wasn't even aware that the fiasco included among its consequences, chronic fatigue syndrome, autism and many other "mysterious" epidemics that are being caused by HHV-6.

Culshaw is fairly unique among the Duesbergians and other HIV critics, dissidents, resistance intellectuals, whatever one wants to call them. Not only was she patently *not* heterosexist, not only did she *not* spin her own alternative "Got-AIDS-Yet, GRID-think" alternative lifestyle theory of AIDS, but she actually went in the opposite direction and argued that heterosexism, side-by-side with racism, was the driving force for the biomedical dystopia that was created by the pseudoscientific HIV/AIDS paradigm. And, in a near miss, Rebecca Culshaw almost got it right when she wrote that "powerful psychological forces are at work. It is simply easier for most people to project our neglect of disenfranchised groups—gay men, drug users, blacks, the poor and so on—onto a virus and accept those "infected" as sacrificial victims, than to recognize *that there is no bug*. For society, the latter would require acceptance of those disenfranchised groups as equal participants in mainstream society and culture." (SSO p.70) She would have won the "understanding Holocaust II lottery" if only she had written, "It is simply easier for most people to project our neglect of disenfranchised groups—gay men, drugs users, blacks, the poor and so on (and ignore the threat to our own health)—onto *the wrong, politically and fraudulently framed* virus and accept those labeled and scapegoated as "AIDS infected" and as sacrificial victims, *than to recognize that we are all at risk* for the real cause of this epidemic." But it was not to be. She certainly got the business about the bigoted politics right, but *there was a virus*, a very serious and deadly virus, but not a retrovirus. It was a DNA virus, one that was, even as she wrote her wonderful book, having its pathological way with both franchised and disenfranchised groups all over the world.

If one were to ask all the Duesbergians—including Culshaw—if the egregious errors of the AIDS medical establishment had put the heterosexual general population in *more danger* of becoming immune-compromised, they all would probably have said a resounding "No!" The fact that they would have been absolutely wrong (considering the HHV-6 spectrum catastrophe in the general population that was masked by the HIV "mistake") shows that their critical brilliance and their unique ethical bravery went only so far in the search for the ultimate truth about the epidemic. They failed to stop the forces of heterosexism and racism that crystallized into Holocaust II, but without all of them, our very dark time would be even darker.

Made in United States
Orlando, FL
07 December 2022

25760902R00395